RECENT PHILOSOPHY

RECENT PHILOSOPHY

Volume One: *From Hegel to Sartre*

Étienne Gilson *and* Thomas Langan

CLUNY
Providence, Rhode Island

CLUNY EDITION, 2023

This Cluny edition is a republication, in part, of *Recent Philosophy: Hegel to the Present* (forematter and Parts One and Two), originally published by Random House Inc., in 1966.
....
For this Cluny edition, citation and reference styles have been updated and developed, as needed, for the purposes of clarity and accessibility.

For more information regarding this title or any other Cluny Media publication, please write to info@clunymedia.com, or to Cluny Media, P.O. Box 1664, Providence, RI 02901

❖ VISIT US ONLINE AT WWW.CLUNYMEDIA.COM ❖

Recent Philosophy: Hegel to the Present copyright © 1966 by Pontifical Institute of Mediaeval Studies, Toronto.

All rights reserved.

ISBN (paperback) | 978-1685952075
ISBN (hardcover) | 978-1685952143

Nihil obstat: Eduardus A. Synan, *censor librorum deputatus*
Imprimatur: Philippus F. Pocock, *archiepiscopus coadiutor torontinus*

Cover design by Clarke & Clarke
Cover image: Giorgio de Chirico, *La matinée angoissante*, 1912, oil on canvas
Courtesy of MART, Italy

CONTENTS

INTRODUCTION to A HISTORY OF PHILOSOPHY   i

PREFACE to RECENT PHILOSOPHY   v

PART ONE: *German Philosophy* (Thomas Langan)

INTRODUCTION   2

I. *Post-Kantian Background*   5
    JOHANN GOTTLIEB FICHTE   9
    FRIEDRICH WILHELM JOSEPH VON SCHELLING   18
    GEORG WILHELM FRIEDRICH HEGEL   26
    MARXISM-LENINISM   49
    ARTHUR SCHOPENHAUER   64

II. *The Original Existentialist Revolt*   75
    SØREN KIERKEGAARD   77
    FRIEDRICH NIETZSCHE   87

III. *Beyond Positivism and Psychologism*   105
    WILHELM DILTHEY   105
    THE PHENOMENOLOGICAL MOVEMENT   113
    EDMUND HUSSERL   118
    MAX SCHELER   134
    NICOLAI HARTMANN   146

IV. *Two German Existentialists*   164
    MARTIN HEIDEGGER   164
    KARL JASPERS   173

PART TWO: *French and Italian Philosophy* (Étienne Gilson)

INTRODUCTION   192

V. *Ideology in France* 193
    CABANIS 193
    DESTUTT DE TRACY 196
    MAINE DE BIRAN 202

VI. *Ideology in Italy* 216
    FRANCESCO SOAVE 216
    MELCHIORRE GIOIA 220
    GIANDOMENICO ROMAGNOSI 224
    MELCHIORRE DELFICO 230

VII. *The Christian Reaction* 234
    LOUIS DE BONALD 235
    JOSEPH DE MAISTRE 241
    FÉLICITÉ DE LAMENNAIS 244
    LOUIS BAUTAIN 249
    FROM TRADITIONALISM TO CHRISTIAN PHILOSOPHY 254

VIII. *The Philosophical Reaction in France and Italy* 261
    FRENCH SPIRITUALISM: VICTOR COUSIN 261
    THE ITALIAN METAPHYSICAL REVIVAL: ANTONIO ROSMINI
        AND VINCENZO GIOBERTI 267
    THE SPREADING OF ONTOLOGISM 293

IX. *French Positivism* 299
    AUGUSTE COMTE 300
    POSITIVE PSYCHOLOGY 312
    POSITIVE SOCIOLOGY 318
    PHILOSOPHICAL REFLECTION ON SCIENCE 322

X. *Maine de Biran's French Posterity* 326
    FÉLIX RAVAISSON 327
    JULES LACHELIER 333
    EMILE BOUTROUX 338
    HENRI BERGSON 344

XI. *In the Spirit of Criticism* 357
    RENOUVIER'S NEOCRITICISM 357

OCTAVE HAMELIN	360
LÉON BRUNSCHVICG	366

XII. *In the Spirit of Scholasticism* — 370
- THE ORIGINS OF THE MOVEMENT — 371
- LEO XIII — 379
- NEOSCHOLASTICISM — 387

XIII. *In the Spirit of Augustinianism* — 398
- ALPHONSE GRATRY — 398
- LÉON OLLÉ-LAPRUNE — 401
- MAURICE BLONDEL — 404

XIV. *Early Twentieth-Century Philosophy in Italy* — 407
- BENEDETTO CROCE — 408
- GIOVANNI GENTILE — 410
- CRITICAL IDEALISM — 413

XV. *Existentialism and Phenomenology in France* (Thomas Langan) — 419
- GABRIEL MARCEL — 419
- JEAN-PAUL SARTRE — 426
- MAURICE MERLEAU-PONTY — 433
- MIKEL DUFRENNE — 443
- PAUL RICOEUR — 450

❖ ❖ ❖

Notes — 459

INTRODUCTION TO
A History of Philosophy

THIS *History of Philosophy* is intended as an introduction to philosophy itself. The approaches to philosophy are many, but if one aims to give the reader, beyond mere factual information, a genuine philosophical formation, the historical approach becomes a necessity. Much more important than knowledge about philosophy is a true notion of what it is to philosophize. And what better way is there to learn to philosophize than to observe the great philosophers of the past? If one has the understanding and the patience to follow the discussions of Plato, Aristotle, Thomas Aquinas, or Kant, he cannot fail to appreciate what it means to philosophize. And, equally important, he will have a standard of philosophical excellence that will deter him from confusing a shabby piece of philosophy with one that is first-rate.

Those who take philosophy seriously must have some knowledge of its history, because philosophy is a collective enterprise in which no one can pretend to take part unless he is first properly introduced. Before playing a game, one must learn its rules, must even practice for a long time under the coaching of some expert. The same can be said of the future philosopher, or of any educated man who wishes to share in a philosophical discussion without incurring ridicule. In our own day, philosophy is to be found everywhere; it is hardly an exaggeration to say that it dominates our political life, since Hegel, Marx, and materialistic scientism provide some of our greatest political powers with the ideology they need to justify their actions. At the very least, an equally well-thought-out ideology is necessary to meet this challenge and, if possible, submit it to a rational critique.

Why is its history a necessary introduction to philosophy? Because philosophy is actually a continuous chain of philosophers who have conducted in the West, for twenty-five centuries, a sort of conversation on the ultimate problems the human mind can ask. What stuff is reality made of? How did it come to be? What is the place of man in the universe? How is knowledge possible? Can we form a sensible opinion concerning our future destiny? Whatever our answer to such questions, it is bound to be a philosophical one. Even to say that they should not be asked and that, anyway, they cannot be answered, is to take a big philosophical chance. These questions, and others like them, have been discussed by countless philosophers, among whom there is at least one point of agreement: that a definite technique be adhered to by all those who want to share in this collective inquiry. First defined by Socrates, followed by Plato and Aristotle, this technique can be found at work in all philosophical doctrines. Two faults will at once disqualify any newcomer to the inquiry: one is not to have learned the technique of philosophical discussion; the other is to want to share in the dialogue without adequate knowledge of the history of philosophy. In the words of the French critic Albert Thibaudet: "Experience shows that during these twenty-five centuries, no self-taught man, no mind uninformed about the work of its predecessors, has been able to make any valuable contribution to philosophy."

A history that aims to make readers feel at home in the great family of philosophers should be neither an accumulation of proper names and dates, which would be better provided by dictionaries and encyclopedias, nor a mere juxtaposition of philosophical doctrines, which would amount to a succession of unrelated monographs. To avoid the first defect, we had to decide which philosophers would be singled out for detailed examination and, within each particular philosophy, what parts of it should be presented. Choice entails arbitrariness; in some cases, other choices could have been made with equal justification. The only rules we have tried to observe were not to omit any really great doctrine and never to mention one of which not enough could be said to relate it to some definite philosophical position. The second defect has been avoided, we hope, by our effort to relate every great doctrine to those with which it was vitally linked. Here, again, enough had to be said to achieve philosophical intelligibility without burdening our history with purely dogmatic considerations.

The last remark leads us to a further question. How should this *History* be used? The answer cannot be the same for all classes of readers. Students will have their teachers to help them make their own selection according to the various kinds of philosophical studies they are engaged in. The only general hypothesis we can visualize is that of the reader who is free to make whatever

Introduction to A History of Philosophy

use of the book he thinks best. To him our advice would be, first, to read the *History* in a rather cursory way so as to gather a general picture of the growth of philosophical doctrines within any one of the four main periods into which it has been divided. A second reading should be both selective and exacting, with the reservation, however, that after making his own choice of the particular philosophy he intends to study more precisely, the reader will not submit it to a hasty criticism. As a rule it takes much more cleverness to understand a philosophy than to refute it. Moreover, no doctrine should be discussed on the basis of its interpretation by any historian, whose role is merely to introduce the reader to the study of the writings of the philosophers themselves. Last, not least, one should always keep in mind that, since philosophy is about ultimate problems, each particular doctrine is determined by its particular way of approaching such problems.

The slightest deviation in the understanding of philosophical principles brings about important differences in the conclusions. In critically assessing a philosophy, therefore, the greatest attention should be paid to its initial data. To discuss a philosopher's conclusion without understanding his principles is a waste of time. However, one will never regret the time and care devoted to a detailed examination of what a philosopher calls philosophy, of the method he advocates and uses in discussing its problems, and, more important still, of his own personal way of understanding these principles. If as much time were spent meditating on our own philosophical ideas as is devoted to refuting those of other philosophers, we would probably realize how much more important it is to set forth truth than to fight error. Hopefully, this *History* will convey to its readers a positive notion of philosophical wisdom, conceived as a never-ceasing effort to deepen the understanding of the first principles of human knowledge. We have planned the *History* as a guide for those who need an introduction to a very wide field of historical information and philosophical speculation. If, as we would like to think, the readers of this *History* want to continue beyond it to some exploring of their own, we trust that they will find themselves at least proceeding in the right direction.

The present general history of philosophical doctrines in the Western world falls naturally into four Parts, and therefore into four volumes: I. *Ancient Philosophy*; II. *Medieval Philosophy*; III. *Modern Philosophy: Descartes to Kant*; IV. *Recent Philosophy: Hegel to Dewey*. The distribution of the materials within each Part is dictated by the variations in philosophical thinking itself during the course of centuries, in its way of approaching problems as well as in its mode of expressing them. Even so, the emphasis is always on the doctrinal content of each particular philosophy. Biographical and bibliographical information is limited to what is needed to embark on a personal study of any one of the philosophers, schools, or periods represented. For indeed the very substance of a history of philosophy is philosophy itself. That is why, so far as possible, everything in these four volumes is made to serve this truth.

Étienne Gilson

PREFACE TO
Recent Philosophy

THE philosophical unity so visible in Europe at the time of the Reformation and still perceptible during the seventeenth and eighteenth centuries began to disintegrate in the early years of the nineteenth century. The accession of new languages to the status of scientific languages, the rise of nationalistically minded generations of philosophers, the progressive multiplication of the professors of philosophy, many of whom became philosophical writers, created a new historical situation. Descartes wrote his *Meditations* in Latin, so they were read at once in the whole of civilized Europe; one hundred years later, Condillac could not read Locke in the original, and when Kant published his masterwork in German, it remained for many years a sort of mystery philosophy chiefly known from summaries, interpretations, and even criticisms. It is therefore almost unavoidable to take into account the nationalities of the philosophers in the nineteenth century and, up to a point at least, to order their doctrines accordingly.

The method followed in the preceding sections of this history has not been modified. We wanted to avoid the danger of turning a history of philosophy into an encyclopedia of proper names and dates. It was therefore necessary to eliminate many philosophers for the sole reason that too little would have been said about them for it to make philosophical sense. In such cases, arbitrariness is unavoidable; we can only apologize for it.

Similarly, the temporal limit assigned to this history deserves comment. In principle, it was intended to cover the philosophy of the nineteenth century and of the first third of the twentieth. A few exceptions were made in order to include two or three contemporaries whose doctrines have assumed a recognized importance in the Western philosophical world. It was felt that their places should at least be marked, pending the time when an objective assessment of their work becomes possible. Specialized histories of today's philosophy in some particular countries will direct the readers to appropriate sources of information.[1]

PART ONE

GERMAN PHILOSOPHY

by Thomas Langan

INTRODUCTION

IN Volume III of our *History*, we found it advisable, even at the risk of making the development of philosophical inquiry from the Renaissance to Kant appear more unilinear than it in fact was, to stress a single, main problem moving from Descartes' "Copernican revolution" to a climactic grasp of its implications in Kant's *Critiques*.

The German section of our *Recent Philosophy* begins where our *Modern Philosophy* ends; and with a persistence worthy of its subject, prolongs the exposition with basically the same focus. In this section, and in the section devoted to those French phenomenological-existentialist thinkers who depend on this same tradition, we shall not hesitate to stress the Kantian patronage of the whole affair—and ultimately, of course, the Cartesian. (Descartes, not Kant, is philosophy's Copernicus. We have summed up in Chapter I the essential outlines of this story needed for following the present exposition.) That this connection is not made arbitrarily in the case of the philosophers we have chosen to study here the text itself will show. We have been somewhat arbitrary, however, in the decision to concentrate on the major thinkers and the central current of the tradition. Even then, we are still pressed by the sheer bulk of the material. Although fully cognizant of the truth that history moves in the minute articulations provided by secondary thinkers oft forgot, and fully in agreement with Merleau-Ponty when he asserts, explicitly against the Marxists, implicitly against all philosophers of history, that "History does not have *a* sense but *many* senses," we have nevertheless thought it preferable to write about *a* main sense thoroughly enough for it really *to make sense* for the reader.

Glancing at the Table of Contents one might still, despite these remarks, be shocked by two apparent absences: Where is romanticism, and where are those German philosophies which draw their inspiration primarily from physical science? The answer to the first question is, "It is everywhere—and nowhere"; to the second, the answer is less puzzling—it is simply in another section of our book.

"Romanticism" is a rather vague term. If it is taken to mean the assertion that our cognitive powers cannot be limited to the descriptions of "reason" implicit in the empiricist philosophies of the seventeenth century, then there is a lot of romanticism in the philosophies we shall be studying. But if "romanticism" means a rejection of every form of reason as the ultimate court of appeal and a turning instead to an ultimately inexpressible, or only poetically expressible, *feeling*, then indeed we shall be guilty here of ignoring "romanticism." As historians of *philosophy* we are concerned with enterprises of reason, that is, with explanations of the world that manifest logical cogency and consistency, and require no ambiguity of expression. Hegel, for instance, enjoys a sweeping command over the romantic notions of his time; what makes him a philosopher, however, and therefore a most suitable subject for a work like ours, is his genius for stating precisely what the problem of feelings and intuitions *means*, thereby opening himself to genuinely philosophical criticism of the rational consistency and adequacy of his account. Kierkegaard is a more difficult case. His influence on a properly *philosophical* tradition is incontestable—as is the fact that the tradition is *philosophical*. But is *he*? To some extent he is; and it is to that extent, precisely, insofar as what he says can be reduced to consistent propositions, that we shall deal with him here.

The "romanticism" charge made against contemporary existentialism is confusing and confused. If one troubles to read the thinkers we shall present here, he will find that they are all making consistent, intelligible claims in their own technical language. Some people who are unfamiliar with that language save themselves a lot of trouble by dismissing it as "unclear"—the way some others will skip over all arguments couched in logical symbols, muttering "obscurantism," because they suspect beforehand that, once they have deciphered the symbols, they will not like what they will see anyway. Whether what some of the existentialists are arguing strikes us as an adequate account of our common experience and as offering sufficient direction for the human enterprise is another question. Some of them are really advocating an aestheticism; their appeal to human creativity as the ultimate "answer" is in one sense indeed "romantic": what reason has to work on, according to such thinkers, is a truth itself created by human energies and which reveals itself only to co-creators. Whether or not one is sympathetic to that position, its presentation must be recognized as *philosophical* because it offers itself to the bar of reason in the form of consistent, cogent claims. It is in that spirit that it will be presented.

It is obvious that the tragic political events of the Third Reich not only influenced the philosophical landscape, but that the events themselves grew out of it. Grave problems in the philosophical tradition undoubtedly contributed to making that situation as bad as it was. The attaching of political labels will not make those problems disappear. Only a careful and responsible exposition against a rich historical background can contribute something lasting in this regard. That should be the ambition of every historian of philosophy.

I. Post-Kantian Background

ONCE we have abandoned the only safe definition of *contemporary philosophy*—namely, that it is the philosophy being propounded by people still alive—it is hard not to push straight back to Thales. In any event, we do not consider ourselves forcing the term in the least when we apply it to Kant, and only very little when we apply it to Descartes. One simply does not know Husserl, Heidegger, Sartre, Merleau-Ponty, or Ricoeur if he does not know Descartes and Kant. The twist that Fichte, with whom we shall begin the present survey, gave to the Kantian problem is so contemporary that one must resist the temptation to interpret the living phenomenologists as so many commentators on the *Wissenschaftslehre*! Karl Jaspers makes no secret of his debt to Schelling. In fact, he has written a long study of Schelling's philosophy which makes the connections with his own existentialism clear to all. And we do not study Hegel today as background for contemporary Marxism and existentialism, but as a living Cronus threatening to eat up all his offspring.

Only a study the length of Nicolai Hartmann's two-volume *German Idealism*[1] could provide the background adequate for understanding all that is happening now in German philosophy and French existentialism. We shall be limited here to the barest outline of how the main influences are transmitted from Kant and the romantics and are transformed in the post-Kantians. To relieve the skeletal starkness of the present chapter a bit, however, let the reader repeatedly remind himself that most of what follows in the rest of our story is foreshadowed, even though we do not pause to mention it, in the works of the post-Kantians and in the essential original insights of Kierkegaard and Nietzsche.

Let us state as simply as possible the historical legacy upon which the philosophers treated in this section have drawn. Descartes, in searching reflectively within the experience of the consciousness for the certain foundation of all truth, reversed the movement of the realistic-common sense quest for being among things taken to be "in themselves" as they present themselves in sense experience. Here is roughly how Kant reinterprets what Descartes accomplished: Our knowledge reveals to us, not things as they somehow are independently of our experience, but things as experienced. Our ideas are the product of a co-operation between whatever is given and the formative activity of the consciousness which must make sense out of the infinite multiplicity of given data. The mind acts to structure experience, to render it intelligible, which means getting data to refer to one another within one grand interpretative scheme, whose forms are time and space. Descartes discovered this transcendental principle, that the sense of the world is founded in the activity of the *cogito*; he saw clearly that substance is an "intuition of the mind" (*Second Meditation*) and that it is grounded in the mind's grasp of its own cognitive unifying activity (implication in the *Third Meditation*).

The mind gives unity to the experimental world; so in grasping the unity of the world the mind is grasping the product of its own activity. Still he could not overlook the common sense conviction that the "world" of the experience thus formed is not *just* the product of one's individual cognitive organizing power. Rather, it presents itself as a *reality* existing independently of one's will and offering itself as the same to all finite minds, itself structured by absolute and eternal truths. That is why Descartes, when discovering the subjective ground of all experience, insisted that this ground is not accounted for by just *this* individual thinking substance. Rather, an infinite ground of all truth—God the Creator of all the particular minds and all the things represented by the truths discoverable in those minds—alone can account for its objectivity, its "Truth."

Kant was later to be very much impressed by Hume's "demystification" of all this. Hume had insisted that the habits of our finite minds quite adequately explain our readiness to accept as "necessary" the familiar scheme of things. Kant was not prepared, though, to embrace this empirical psychologism just as it stood. It is one thing for Hume to have brought out that the world of experience is really formed by the individual mind and thus is not dependent on the Cartesian God (which brings with it the advantage of scotching Spinoza's pantheism); it is quite another thing to go as far as Hume, to the point that the universal, rational moral order seems to rest only on the chance accumulation of fairly widespread habits.

I. *Post-Kantian Background*

Kant's compromise, though, is an uneasy one: As it is the mind which imposes an order on things, one cannot argue legitimately from the study of "phenomena"—what appears in experience, whether subjective or objective—to a "dogmatic" metaphysics, as Kant and Fichte say, pronouncing absolutely on the ultimate constitution of things as they really are "in themselves." Kant in this regard is much closer to Hume than will be his immediate successors. Still, Kant was convinced, as Hume seemed not to be, that the fact that the mind moves *inevitably* from its grasp of its own formation of a *necessary* world toward the positing of an absolute ground and an absolute unity for the world implies something definitively exceeding the merely psychological. Yet—and here we feel all the precariousness of the delicate Kantian balance—this impulse can be said to *incline* us only toward belief in God and not toward an adequate grounding of objective knowledge of Him. This inclination to believe is strongly reinforced by the realization that in the moral order we cannot get along practically without these postulates of unity: the oneness of the world of experience, its absolute ground in God, and the unity of one's experience in the soul. Unbending in its insistence on founding morality universally, Kantian formalism finds itself turning back *practically* toward the Absolute that it has had to refuse *theoretically*. In the last *Critique*, Kant displays great virtuosity in interweaving these practical and theoretical themes in a way that brings out implications of God more clearly than ever, while suggesting, intriguingly but obscurely, that *art* somehow enjoys a privileged position in the revelation of this ultimate unity.

Several aspects of this enterprise as Kant left it were to strike the post-Kantians as particularly underdeveloped. Despite Kant's stress on the mind's discovery, within itself, of its own unity, that of the world, and the unity of world and mind in experience, it still seemed as though Kant were moving from this personal experience to suggestions of its supposed universality (in the sense that truths known to Kant are known by him as valid for any mind whatever) without any adequate ontological grounds transcending the individual *psyche*. Fichte and Schelling would consider it necessary unabashedly to posit the Absolute as common ground of subject and object and unity of all subjectivities.

Secondly, in describing the unity of experience, Kant had attempted to analyze the essential relation between the organizing categories of the mind and had once, in a famous passage, tried to show how all the categories are reducible to functions of time—clearly a suggestion worth following up. But the whole matter needed reworking, with stronger emphasis on the unity of the ego and a more forceful temporal interpretation of the perceiver's organizing schemes. This effort culminates in Hegel's development of Schelling's insight: that the dynamic relationship between the categories is reflected in both the historical development of the individual and the historical self-discovery of mankind.

In the process of this reworking, a third problem area is restudied. By more consciously exploiting the "transcendental viewpoint" so as to show the *interpenetration* of subject and object, of mind and nature, of *noesis* (knowing act) and *noema* (that which is known, as Husserl will put it), Fichte is able to ground the theoretical order in the practical—mind in will. Thus he declares that consciousness, unfolding in time, is to be treated not as something that eternally just happens to be, but as a function of existence temporally working out in liberty the unfolding of the Absolute. The existentialists will be only too happy to avoid putting asunder what Fichte hath thus joined.

Other developments of the times helped the drive toward introducing an Absolute and toward achieving an increasing interpenetration of *theoria* and *praxis* which we feel already in Kant's *Third Critique*. The French Revolution intensified the feeling that a decisive hour had come upon mankind. Through a long and slow process of education man had become truly free to legislate creatively, poetically (so, anyway, Lessing sees it). And what is to be laid down by law is not mere arbitrary whim, nor the result of the contingencies of history, but an ultimate expression of *what is*. For the Absolute manifests itself through the finite spirit of man. Fichte would be ready to throw off Kant's hesitations about metaphysics precisely because he would feel that, by affirming that the Absolute was working through us, he could save what is legitimate in the Kantian discovery: to start with the critical point—the world should indeed be looked upon from the transcendental viewpoint; subject and object are to be recognized as "made for each other." Fichte interprets this in his own absolutistic way: finite consciousness needs an object so that in reflection from the object it can come to know itself; the reason its object is valid for it, is that the consciousness itself puts it out there; and the reason all the objects of all the different subjects have a *universal* validity for all egos is that this activity of the ego is not a phenomenon of one finite psyche but the manifestation of the Absolute itself.

I. *Post-Kantian Background*

The positing of the object is not an act of passive receptivity, but an act of the subject, a doing, a *praxis*. By grounding the order of knowledge in the productive-practical principle (that is, in creative freedom) Fichte paves the way for his philosophical interpretation of the romantics' main intuition. Goethe and Schiller had moved their contemporaries with poetic visions of life as a continual self-creation. Novalis summed up the thrust of this vision—destined to be transmitted to us today in a philosophical form by existentialism—that poetic creation is the mode of action proper to humankind. A century and a quarter later, Heidegger would rediscover in the romantic contemporary of Schelling and Hegel, Friedrich Hölderlin, the poet who had sung his own dark version of the human existent's struggle to create sense from the nothingness surrounding him through the word-creating activity of *poiein*.

Fichte puts all this poetic self-creation squarely under the patronage of the Absolute. That is why the beginning of our story uncovers themes that are at once strangely contemporary—we feel that Husserl, Sartre, and Merleau-Ponty are hiding behind every pillar of the edifice and still astonishingly metaphysical, in the sense (given the word by Heidegger) of the positing, beyond the totality of the experienced world (*phusis*), of an absolute ground which is intended, like the God of Descartes, to guarantee the reality of our truth productions.

Let us go on to Fichte now and see the turn he gives the themes of transcendental philosophy by molding the Kantian transcendental problematic philosophy into its contemporary form.

Johann Gottlieb Fichte

Kant had realized something of the tremendous potential of Descartes' Copernican revolution when, taking firm possession of the "transcendental viewpoint," he asserted that discovering the unity of wisdom means finding the ultimate principle within our knowledge upon which all the moments of that knowledge depend. But Kant's actual exploration of this transcendental unity of our knowledge proved only a partial success. He did indeed point the way through his revolutionary "deduction of the categories of the understanding," which sought not only to catalogue the organizing conceptions through which all experiences are rendered intelligible, but even to show their essential relationship to one another. But Kant, as J. G. Fichte[2] evaluates his achievement, was still too impressed by empiricism. The activity of knowledge remains for him merely formal, the matter which it organizes is somehow *given*, and so must be radically *other than the knower* (without adequate explanation offered why the form and the matter should turn out, in the instance of *a priori* synthetic judgments, to be "made for each other"). As a result Kant's "transcendental viewpoint" fails to englobe the "thing-in-itself." Because Kant hesitated to pursue Descartes' Copernican revolution to its logical end, because he refused to see that all there can *be* is what *we know*, or to affirm that the things known are somehow simply the creation of consciousness, he was unable to push to the point which Fichte himself would now reach: the deduction of *all reality* from a *single* principle, the Absolute, common source of both "subject and object," revealed in the practical-theoretical operations of the finite ego.

the unity of transcendental philosophy

Here is how Fichte achieves this deduction. The world is represented in all its aspects within the unity of each consciousness. It must therefore ultimately be reducible to a single principle, its ground in that consciousness. The quest for rigorous knowledge (*Wissenschaft*) has always implicitly been the effort to unify all that we know by bringing it under a single principle; not just *formally*, in the sense that everything be shown to be known by the same consciousness, but *materially*, in the sense that all the objects within that one conscious world be shown to have some relevance to one another. Fichte would show that from the pure subject, the *Ich*, a whole theory of knowledge can be suspended—a *Wissenschaftslehre*—in which every phenomenon, theoretical or practical, whether "form" or "matter," will find its explanation.

Suppose we look for the simplest, the most certain principle possible.[3] Is it not the simple statement of identity: A is A? No matter what "A" turns out to be, the statement will be true; for in the principle of identity, subject and object being one and therefore the need of a third thing as ground of their unity having been eliminated, the principle is absolutely unconditioned, both in form (what it says) and in matter (what it says it about).

However, "A is A" does not tell us whether anything really exists, but just that *were* it to exist it would have to be what it is. But there is one singularly significant instance in which a proposition of identity, in view of its matter, does manage to include existence, without losing for all that any of its certitude and

I. *Post-Kantian Background* 11

transcendentality. That is when *Ich bin*, "I am," is the matter of the statement. There is a subject and a predicate in the statement, but they are the same; I indeed have an object, as one must for knowledge, an object with a real content; but in this instance that object is the same as the subject. Here Fichte finds the model for all certitude in knowledge: All that is *other* becomes for me certain by being related to me, all "matter" loses its foreignness as soon as, and only when, its place in *my* world of consciousness is shown. What is so strange about that, once we suppress that hangover from empiricism, the *Ding an sich*, and recognize once and for all that what I know is my world of consciousness, that I am for my ideas and my ideas are for me?

We can then understand the next move Fichte makes. The ego is not alone, but knows, standing over against it, in op-position, ob-jects (*Gegen-stände*). The *ob-jectum* is *not-I*, says Fichte, in a declaration destined to draw Hegel's praise; for here we see that the object, though "of my consciousness," is yet other than the subject. The subject is not-object, the object not-subject. The subject discovers itself only as over-against this otherness, and this other can only be insofar as a subject makes it to be. The ego, then, as activity, poses, or rather op-poses to itself an *ob-jectum*, which is dependent for its reality as *objectum* upon the ego's activity of *cogitare*; yet the *objectum* determines the very ego upon which it depends. A curious situation! From one point of view, the subject is active producer of the object, itself passive, receiving its being from the subject; from another point of view, the object is active, producing the objective knowledge-determination in the subject. Fichte's hopes of advancing beyond Kant are inextricably linked to this paradox. In the first instance, he declares, we encounter ego as *will*, as producer, as *Vor-steller* of the *Vor-stellungen* (representations); in the second instance, we see the reflux of what the transcendental ego has produced back upon itself, accounting for the activity in the practical order and the passivity in the theoretical.

The young Hegel[4] complained that this effort to deduce speculatively an explanation of the unity of reality—of truth as the oneness of subject and object— fails because Fichte does not make comprehensible how the object can be the product of the subject and still be really other; that is, how it can, under those circumstances, be considered "real" at all. The problem can be put the other way around. How can the subject be considered a free creative source when its *need* (*Bedürfnis*) to establish an object for itself proves a lack on the subject's part, and when that object is seen to be a limit and a determination for the subject, whose freedom would at best seem to be, in the theoretical order, only a negative one—the subject is *not* the object—and in the practical order, a striving (*Du sollst eins mit dem Objekt werden*), the exact sense of which is not clear? Fichte's suggestion that both the subject, "self-limiting in order to be self-revealing," and the object which the subject establishes for itself are moments of one Absolute does not, Hegel points out, in any way attenuate the difficulty of understanding how the move is made from the self-establishing identity of the *Ich-Ich* to the relevance of an object which is *Nicht-Ich*. The *Ich*-subject and the *Ich*-object are not the same; therefore their reintegration into one philosophical explanation leads to the subordination of one principle to the other. What invites Schelling and Hegel to level the charge of "subjective idealism" against Fichte is that thinker's derivation of the object from the subject as the subject's own self-limitation. Schelling, we shall see, attempts to circumvent this difficulty by declaring the Absolute to be equally in both principles, so that in the object (i.e., in nature) there is idea, and in consciousness there is the given (i.e., nature).

Fichte was sensitive to the cogency of Schelling's and Hegel's indictment; in a later phase (incorrectly and misleadingly termed by some his "second philosophy"), spurred on by the accusation of atheism leveled against him at Jena,[5] he turned to probing the ultimate secrets of the Blessed Trinity, thinking that if he could explain why the Absolute manifests itself in creation, he could support the leap in his philosophy from logical principles to idealistic ontological declarations.

But without going so far, if we will once grant that everything flows from the absolute liberty in its act of discursive self-realization, Fichte's explanation of *how* to follow the descent from the *one* to the *many*, or the ascent from the *thing* to the *absolute principle*, will prove breathtaking and remarkably coherent. In both the theoretical and the practical orders, he shows the two movements to be facets of the same reality. We have followed one leg of the theoretical explanation in discussing the significance and interconnection of the principles of identity (I am I), contradiction (the not-I is not I), and relation (the final synthesis of I and not-I in the Absolute). A reflection of the same structure can be observed in the simplest experience of sensible knowledge[6]: In sensation, the impulse of consciousness encounters the opposition of the non-ego without

I. Post-Kantian Background

clear awareness of self, so that only the dynamism of the process is experienced, as a constant flight of conscious images succeeding one another in the stream of sensuous activity. But consciousness is able to struggle against this unclearly felt but nonetheless real opposition and rise to a higher level of activity and a more stable grasp on its ob-ject: this is the *understanding*. The *understanding* is thus explained by Fichte as a fixing or stabilizing of the fleeting image to bring it into rapport with other images, thus immobilizing them all into an enduring thing shaped out of the fleeting sands. (The German word *Verstand* expresses the idea perfectly, since it suggests a kind of fixing.) The activity of consciousness can rise to further heights in its struggle for self-realization against its opposition: In *judgment*, consciousness can voluntarily join and separate those things it had organized in the *Verstand*. And finally, *reason* (*Vernunft*), consciousness' highest flight of self-realization, confronts it with the fact that it is its own liberty which courses toward the non-ego in sensation, which organizes the thing in the *Verstand*, and joins and separates things in judgment. In grasping all its acts of consciousness as activities of liberty, the reason faces the primordial source of unity and activity, the Absolute as *act*.

Such an explanation of the theoretical reality of the human existence makes it remarkably easy for Fichte to root the most fundamental forms of sensibility in the *praxis* as act, i.e., in a kind of exteriorization of liberty through action. The way Fichte explains the origin of space and time as expressions of the absolute liberty in its act of self-realization is most astonishing. The Marxist epistemologists are here thoroughly outdistanced! Space becomes the very interval created by the ego's opposition of the object to itself, and must have, then, a meaning that is uniquely "practical" in the sense defined above, of freedom actualizing itself. Space is thus the form of sensibility, as the understanding is the fixing of the thing by the understanding corresponds to the spatialization and temporalization of the object by the liberty which opposes it to the consciousness. Time, which becomes in this explanation the very flow and self-discursion of the Absolute itself, is perfectly correlative to space, for both are the active manifestation of the same *praxis*. Fichte in this way offers an ultimate, metaphysical explanation for Kant's insights into the imagination's activity as link, through the forms of space and time, between the multiplicity of sensation and the unity of understanding. Kant's explanation remained fundamentally frustrated as long as he viewed a categorized understanding imposing itself on an objective reality which, as multiplicity, and as thing-in-itself, remained essentially foreign to the conditions of understanding. But Fichte would eliminate the problem of deriving understanding, sensibility, and the imagination from the same ultimate unifying source, correlating all these factors in a scheme of practical self-realization.

Fichte conceives the imagination, as Descartes and Kant had before him and as Heidegger, Sartre, and Merleau-Ponty would after him, to be the keystone to this structure of existence. Participating in both the indetermination of liberty and the determination of consciousness, an activity with limits, but limits which it seems able to roll farther and farther back, which furnishes objects, without being fixed to any one of them, capable of being both objective and spontaneous, the imagination is certainly the faculty capable of giving to the unbounded in itself, the infinite liberty, an always renewable determinate real form. Without the imagination, would the intelligence ever be able momentarily to surpass itself, as it were, toward other possible new conceptions and thus realize that these conceptions—its *fixings*—are limited? The imagination is the very center of the battle of the Infinite to concretize itself in finite forms, of the ego wishing "to unite that which cannot be united, trying to make the Infinite enter into the form of the finite, then pushing what was just settled beyond its form, while trying at the same time to make it enter into a form at all."[7]

practical consequences

A measure of the success of this derivation of the principles of knowledge from a single, dynamic source is to be found in Fichte's analysis of the concrete structure of human existence. Here again, as when he was suppressing the "thing-in-itself" and grounding *theoria* in *praxis*, we find this unabashedly idealistic philosopher developing, in the name of the Absolute, themes central to today's phenomenology. A good part of his analysis of law and morality,[8] far from reproducing the formalism of the *Critique of Practical Reason*, seeks to show the sense of concrete human encounter—taking as its for-granted starting point, of course, that *liberty* is the fundamental existential principle, and that everything in man exists, therefore, for the sake of the discursive self-expression of liberty. Existentialist philosophers like Sartre, Heidegger, and Merleau-Ponty also unite their analyses of existence around the principle of liberty; but, being post-Nietzschean, they no longer interpret these phenomena as in any way

I. *Post-Kantian Background*

manifestations of an Absolute. It will be one of the most interesting tasks of this study to find out whether any of the contemporary existentialist thinkers has really been able to offer an intellectually satisfying explanation of the phenomena of existence without having recourse, like Fichte, to a transcendent Absolute. This problem will become all the more interesting in the light of what Karl Jaspers has done: While insisting on the need to deidealize the very phenomena Fichte considers signs of the Absolute, Jaspers, in dramatic opposition to Heidegger, nevertheless insists upon reading the total situation as a sign of the transcendent.

Fichte's starting point seems teleological. The purpose of there being any object at all is the necessary contribution of the object to the ego's self-discovery. If the *Ich* wishes to think of itself as spirit through a self-realization made possible by self-encounter in an op-posing objectum, it must provide itself with the means of communication with this objectum, the necessary milieu of contact. Here lies the foundation of the juridical reality.[9] If the *Ich* is a kind of radiation of liberty encountering an opposition which causes the proper kind of recoil or reflection, the liberty must express itself as finite within suitable limits which make possible meaningful contact with the "other." This explains the role the body plays for the intelligence. Sensation permits my reaching out to contact that other which lies at my limit. The space I occupy, like the time I extend toward the future, marks the limits of this kind of radiation of my freedom. Thus, far from being a hindrance, an enigmatic burden borne by the soul (as it was construed by inadequate idealisms that never probed into the finality of intelligence), the body, as Fichte sees it, is the very concretization of the liberty in the world. The analysis of perception has already made it evident: The brute encounter with the flux of material reality would be one of sheer necessity were it not that the body in all its activities works with and for our freedom. Instead of simply inserting us into a flow of activity where the self would be swept along the current of sensations, caught up and lost in an overpowering "other," the body works with liberty through the *Verstand* to fix and organize impressions, eventually rising through reflection to a self-knowledge for which the perception of fleeting sensations has been made to act as a bridge. On the level of the simple "internal senses," this organization-for-liberty can already be seen at work as images are combined and as the imagination begins its task of fixing and organizing images into thoughts.

The body politic has the same role on a higher plane. Despite the clever use for self-discovery that liberty can make of the material object, would the subject ever discover itself in the fullness of its freedom if its encounter with the world were limited to grasping the purely determined other? Certainly not; full discovery of the deepest significance of personal liberty is made, not in the encounter with things, but in the encounter with other free subjects. Opposing free forces enter into a relation of mutual free limitation of liberty by liberties. Thus the *First Principle of Right* is "that each individual must restrict his freedom through the conception of the possibility of the freedom of others."[10] Here is the true foundation of law. The realm of law enjoys an intermediary reality, expressing as it does both the limitation of the ego in its op-position to the non-ego, and the *Aufhebung* of free reflection moving toward the highest flights of self-realization.[11] In less abstract terms, law is ideally dedicated to regulating the social intercourse of the many subjects in a way that will permit, not only survival of all, but *high self-realization* through reflective self-knowledge made possible by leisure time and education. The fruit of good law is thus the founding of a climate of morality, *morality* meaning the inner act of reflective self-realization achieving its highest grasp of the meaning of the free self.

The fact that, for Fichte, liberty can be exercised by the individual only through a community of free beings points up the big difference between the ethics he will found on this theory of law and the Kantian ethics, which was itself presented as the basis of law rather than vice versa. Kant's ethics is individualist, while Fichte's is an ethics of intersubjectivity. The fundamental reason for this difference lies in Kant's having conceived the human individual, the subject of liberty, as a self-sufficient absolute, while for Fichte the individual as liberty exists in the full sense of the word only in the community of finite reasonable beings. Fichte, having made sense of the body as translating spiritual liberty into practical action in the world, stresses community as intersubjective body in a way that anticipates (like Husserl) Merleau-Ponty. It becomes clearer and clearer that upon a philosopher's making sense of the role of the body will depend his accomplishing what Fichte set out to do, but only barely began—a reconciliation of realism and idealism.

Fichte's effort to unify the subjective and objective orders in the practically oriented operation of the free spirit achieved, as we have said, remarkable unity between the practical and intellectual orders; but the solution whose main lines

I. Post-Kantian Background

we have just sketched by no means resolves all problems. Schelling protests that the objective world ("nature") is in this scheme too subordinate to the ego, and the ideal order to the practical. Although both Schelling and Hegel accept as inevitable in the Kantian order of things Fichte's insistence that *spirit* discovers itself only in passing by way of *the other* (the object, "nature," or the other person), they hasten to point out that this need of the Absolute to exteriorize itself raises an ultimate teleological question: *Why* does the Absolute realize itself through the mediation of finite things and individual consciousness? Schelling, borrowing from Leibniz, puts the question[12] in perhaps its most unanswerable form: "Why is there anything at all, rather than nothing?" Hegel examines the whole historical process of the Absolute's self-realization in time in an effort to accumulate a kind of intelligibility *in extenso*. Schelling turns, in the last half of his career, to the concept that God, as creative impulse, acts through freedom to achieve a form of expression. Fichte himself was moving in a markedly similar direction when he was struck down in 1814 by a typhoid epidemic. In his so-called "last philosophy," which is in fact nothing more than a logical consequent of the whole development we have just been exposing, Fichte was seeking in the relations within the Blessed Trinity the key to all creative activity.

In this last phase Fichte was being pressed harder and harder by his enemies to respond satisfactorily to the charges of "atheism," i.e., of reducing God to an absolute *idea* immanent in the world of human existence, a charge that had already been formally leveled against him at Jena in 1799, bringing about his dismissal. Fichte's defense consisted in pointing out that, though he may have identified the world with reason and said that reason was the *idea* of God, or the Divine Word, reason can know God only "exteriorly," according to the idea that is one with the world, while God's absolute existence remains hidden from us. The *form* known to reason is, from an absolute point of view, enjoyed only by God; it is one with the divine existence; but from the human point of view, a separation is there which can be closed only non-cognitively through love, which, mystically considered, is the work of the spirit, a dynamic process bridging time and eternity. As we mentioned above, this was the direction Schelling would later pursue. Hegel was to prove more resistant than either Fichte or Schelling to the temptation of implying some sort of extra-rational contact with an Absolute somehow transcending the phenomenal order.

Friedrich Wilhelm Joseph von Schelling

Schelling's philosophical life is marked by an exceptionally restless evolution of thought.[13] His refusal to arrest the development of his conceptions at any one point in order to explore fully their systematic possibilities naturally made it impossible for him to develop his fertile intuitions completely; some claimed that he simply lacked powers of systematization. What is certain is that Schelling's failure to erect a single great system worked against his popularity. Hegel's powerful synthesis was destined to seduce young Schelling's public away.

the philosophical problem

Nevertheless, there is a unity of quest that gives a sense to Schelling's development. The seed is the problem posed in his first independent work, the *Letters on Dogmatism and Criticism* (1795–1796). What the youthful Schelling there declares to be the philosophical problem about which all the history of philosophy has turned[14] never ceases to be the central concern of his subsequent inquiries. The problem has two aspects, one subjective, one objective. The subjective problem: Why does phenomenal reality, as it appears to consciousness, have a meaning *for me* which is yet a meaning enjoying universal necessity? Viewed in terms of the objects themselves, the question can be put this way: Why are there many things, which are yet reducible to an intelligible, necessary unity? Kant's great merit consists in his having seen that this was *the* central problem when he posed, in the *Critique of Pure Reason*, the decisive question that was to divide the history of philosophy into two camps: Why is synthetic judgment *a priori* possible? For synthesis to take place with absolute necessity, there must be a multiplicity of things that yet presupposes the possibility of absolute unity. Kant's question, then, calls for an explanation of how it is that there was an original thesis, implying the unity of all things; how and why it came to be objectified into a reality of many things; and how these are destined to be reintegrated into the *identity* of an absolute consciousness. Kant had the merit, too, of seeing that neither of the opposed theoretical positions advanced by the great philosophers, *dogmatism* or *criticism*, is capable of resolving the problem theoretically, and that the resolution of the problem needs to be shifted, somehow, to practical grounds.

Dogmatism (which Schelling distinguishes from mere *dogmaticism*, i.e., running to a *deus ex machina* to solve philosophical problems), represented

I. *Post-Kantian Background*   19

most notably by Spinoza, attempts to solve the problem by absorbing the subject—the finite ego which I am—into an infinite object. The theoretical merit of this position (the mystical totality of which, with its call for losing oneself in the infinite substance, came to appeal to Schelling very strongly, just as it did to the whole circle of romantics—Goethe, the Schlegels, and others—who exercised a great influence on the young Schelling at Jena) lies in its unequivocal insistence upon the foundation of everything in the Absolute, and in its treatment of the finite subjective order of the ego and the objective order of nature as coequally derived therefrom.[15] Its failure as a theory, though, is its inability to explain the need for finite consciousness and nature, its denial of real process and struggle in nature, which renders all creativity, motion, and causality meaningless.[16]

    Criticism (which Schelling also calls "subjective idealism," in contrast with Spinoza's "objective realism") proves itself theoretically bankrupt in just the opposite way. The critical philosopher (Schelling is thinking, above all, of Fichte) reduces the object to the subject, the object's only role being that of an op-position projected by the subject—the transcendental understanding—as a means to its own self-discovery. The real core of Schelling's criticism, as the preoccupation of subsequent works so eloquently demonstrates, is that subjective idealism does not take into account that nature appears of equal importance with our consciousness, and that our consciousness actually seems more derived from nature than nature from consciousness. Criticism, in short, has failed to provide a satisfactory theoretical explanation for the appearance of the many, for our grasp of reality along with necessity and universality, or for the unity of ego and object in an absolute in which both are retained rather than nature's being suppressed. Yet criticism does provide an essential insight, a precious indication of the road around the impasse encountered in the theoretical bankruptcy of these two great systems. For criticism develops Kant's suggestion that the significance of the deduction of the many from the one reveals itself in the practical order.[17] In emphasizing the *opposition* of subject and object, criticism has suggested that an effort to grasp the relationship of infinite and finite, one and many, subject and object, in terms of goal and process, might lead to the answer to *the* central philosophical problem.

    The practical consequences of Spinoza's dogmatism reveal the system's failure to explain satisfactorily that union of finite consciousness and finite objective reality in the identity of the Absolute which it so grandly affirms. The ego is reduced to such insignificance that its only practical course is to seek absorption in the *all*; this has the gross inconvenience of eliminating the sense of the *infinite object*, once there is no longer a subject to contemplate it![18] Criticism, on the other hand, reduces the object to a mere thought, in turning it into a self-limitation of the Absolute subject, as a result of which, I, an activity knowing no limits really outside myself, should be unable to re-flect from a real other on myself, and, therefore, should just drift off into unconscious felicity![19]

In the last "Letter" Schelling points out very clearly the "practical" road his attack on the problem would pursue in subsequent works. The relationship of man as knowing subject and nature as his object will have to be understood in its ground—*the process of the Absolute*—and this in a way that accounts for the historical appearance of human freedom in the world, struggling for a more and more adequate conscious grasp of nature. The immediate problem, then, that has to be solved—that of deducing nature and consciousness from the Absolute—is a practical one, in this sense: It is a question of understanding the *how* of a process.

the deduction of nature and finite consciousness from the absolute

The following year (1797), in *Ideas for a Philosophy of Nature*, Schelling presented the key features of his solution to the problems of "Why there is something, rather than nothing at all" (as he later put it) and how and why we can know what is by necessity. Future developments of Schelling's thought will in large measure be efforts to defend this basic solution by digging deeper into its implications in answer to critics of its various features.

Schelling states the basic principle of his solution in these terms: "Nature must be visible Spirit, and Spirit invisible Nature. It is here, in the absolute identity of the Spirit *in us* and of Nature *outside of us*, that the solution of the problem of the possibility of nature outside of us will find resolution."[20] The absolute spirit is an eternal one, but a one in never-ending process; for the act of eternal consciousness eternally wills to exteriorize itself, "to come out from the night of its essence, to manifest itself in the full light of day," continuously, as essence, particularizing itself as *form*. The Absolute takes on finite form so that it will be able to recapture its own essence in an ideal, conscious way. The eternal one in process comprises necessarily these three eternal aspects: the *essence*, or the *di-*

I. *Post-Kantian Background*

vine idea as such; the *form*, or the externalized particularizations of the essence achieving its manifestation; and the *absolute identity of essence and form* (i.e., of *universal* and *particular*) in the depths of the unity of the Absolute. The three aspects are present in both nature and finite spirit. In nature, where they are so many steps toward the self-recovery of the Absolute, they take the form of three "potencies": (a) the impregnation of the finite by the infinite, represented by the relationship of the universal, general structure of the world to the various series of particular bodies; (b) the reabsorption of the particular by the universal, represented by "the universal mechanism," wherein the universal (i.e., the essence) exteriorizes itself as light, the particular as *body*; (c) the synthesis of universal and particular in the life of *organisms*, "the perfect image of the absolute in nature." Organism is the highest development of nature, the most perfect natural exteriorization the Absolute can achieve. To develop beyond this point, the Absolute must become reason, evolving to accord with organism, that most perfect symbol of the Absolute, a corresponding image of absolute ideality.[21]

The concordant appearance of the Absolute in both nature and reason requires the philosophy of the future, then, if it is to be adequate to the reality of the Absolute, to consist of two branches of equal stature: *the philosophy of nature*, which will seek to read in nature the signs of the Absolute manifesting itself; and *transcendental philosophy*, which will start with the phenomenon of finite consciousness and derive from it the natural objects of knowledge. The conscious grasp of the concordance and unity of the two by the mature absolute idealism would be "reason's ideal representation of the Absolute as indifferent identity," which achieves the Absolute's process toward consciousness.

Schelling's description of the preoccupations and method of *transcendental philosophy* provides us with another strong anticipation of Husserl's conception of phenomenology. After explaining that belief in the existence of independent objects must be suspended to focus attention on all perceptions and conceptions as subjective acts, Schelling goes into some detail concerning the effect of adopting "the transcendental attitude."

> In perception, only the object penetrates into consciousness, the perception losing itself in the object, while in the transcendental way of looking at things, it is *by way of* the act of perception that one becomes conscious of that which is perceived.... Transcendental thought breaks

through the mechanism (of conception) to grasp the consciousness of concept as act, raising itself to the concept of concept.[22]

Schelling's statement of what Husserl will later term "the reduction" shows the tradition moving toward an increasing realization of the implications involved in assuming the "transcendental viewpoint." Coupled with this is an awareness that as an act of the consciousness, theoretical knowledge is a genuine *doing* and therefore must ultimately be explained by a philosophy of *praxis*. Schelling brings this out clearly in his discussion of the divisions of transcendental philosophy.

Transcendental philosophy has three parts: the *theoretical*, which is concerned with discovering the subjective roots of our knowledge of objects, posing the question of how it is that we have knowledge that conforms to things; the *practical*, which seeks to discover in the subjective how it is that we can make the order of things conform to our conceptions; and the highest branch, the *aesthetic*, which seeks the unity of the preceding aspects and explores man's creative artistic powers as evidence of the unity of the theoretical and the practical. The philosophy of art, declares Schelling, "is the general organon of philosophy," for there philosophy unearths the reality of the "pre-established harmony" that makes real knowledge and real volition possible.

Transcendental philosophy is itself essentially an aesthetic act, accomplishing for the interior world what *poesie* (in the sense the Greeks meant by *poiein*, i.e., any aesthetic-creative act) accomplishes for the external world.[23] "In art, production is directed toward the outside, seeking to express the unconscious by means of art; philosophical production is directed toward the interior, in an effort to present the unconscious to intellectual intuition."[24] *Intellectual intuition* and *productive imagination* are really the same, with only this difference, that in intellectual intuition we come to be reflectively aware of the originative activity of the imagination as self-initiated, i.e., as an ultimate manifestation of the Absolute.

The difficulty with making intellectual intuition a principle of philosophy is its subjective character. It was precisely in order to minimize this inconvenience that Schelling gave such an important role to art—going beyond even Kant's *Third Critique* in this regard.[25] For a work of art, in objectifying what would otherwise remain interior and personal, suggests not only the reality

I. *Post-Kantian Background*

of what is interior as interior, but also its ability to impose itself on a world of nature that seems predisposed to accommodate its kind of existence. When arguing that both consciousness and nature are part of the same process—the self-exteriorization of the Absolute—Schelling can find no better support than this harmony achieved in art between things and the most secret inner life of the spirit.

the rational and the irrational: symbol and freedom

The times were ripe for a favorable reaction to this emphasis on the aesthetic element, but Schelling's basic conceptions were far from satisfying as explanations of the finite's relation to the infinite. One very basic principle remained exceptionally disturbing. Schelling's critics were not satisfied with his conception of the infinite as the *absolute indifference* in which all elements, the rational and irrational, nature and consciousness, meet in unity. Schelling was under pressure to elaborate further an explanation of how the rational and the natural elements emanate from God, and of how they are discoverable in our finite experience.

Schelling, writing in 1809 in the wake of Hegel's *Phenomenology of the Spirit*, is certain that the principles he has already laid down potentially contain the solution to these problems, if they can be properly developed. He has come to see ever more sharply that something of the clarity and unity of Spinoza's "dogmatism" should remain the ideal of philosophical explanation. But he is no more ready now than he was earlier (if anything, Hegel's over-explanation of the process of the world was driving him with new fervor along his own natural course) to minimize the irrationality of free process. Rather, what Schelling attempts at this period is to exploit his earlier general conception in the direction of a coherent rational explanation of how the irrational arises from the very nature of God.[26]

God is process and stands in relation to his creation as the subject to the predicates which depend on it, the connection between the two being a dynamic one. Returning to his old idea of aspects *within* the eternal God, Schelling modifies the doctrine to explain that in God is to be found: (1) the necessary fundamental ground (*Ur-grund*), or what God has to be because of his very nature; (2) the ground of existence (*Grund von Existenz*), or God as actual development; and (3) the actual existing being (*Das Existierende*), or God as manifest in the world. Out of the dark ground of God's necessity comes the yearning for personal existence, which develops as the personal, creative God of love or freedom that creates itself in exteriorizing itself in its own predicates, i.e., as the world of creatures. The ultimate ground of God's free act of creation is the necessity of his nature. In creating man free, he acts necessarily. However, man is not immediately determined by what is traditionally considered as "God." He is determined by God as eternal *ground*, not by God as a striving, living, personal emanation of the eternal ground. This gives man some freedom in relation to God as a person, enough anyway to have the freedom to love him. Man is also free from the world, since he can receive illumination from God, and, like nature itself, he comes from a higher principle. So man is free to dedicate the action of his particular will to God, that is, to the service of the *universal*; or he can oppose his particularity to the universal, use it to block the course of God's realization, and thus turn it into a positive force of destruction. Evil, according to this conception, is something positive, being the particular will in revolt against the universal.

Schelling's emphasis on the irrational—on the impenetrable *Ur-grund* prior to and source of God as will and intelligence—brings him to realize that it is not the same kind of encounter which reveals the *necessary ground* and the free God of love to us; that although we encounter the God of truth at the end of the path of scientific reasoning, we shall have to encounter the God of love concretely through another act—an act of *will*, at the very beginning of the road of freedom. Schelling came to conclude, as he expresses it in the late work, *The Philosophy of Mythology*, that philosophy, both historically and *de jure*, has two aspects, which he names *negative philosophy* and *positive philosophy*. In the beginning of human speculation, man encountered God negatively, as *force*, as *will*, as dynamic reality. In his efforts to codify his direct experience of the omnipresent reality of God's divinity, he was not always successful in reading God's symbols in the concrete. His efforts to understand the Divine Unity gave birth to systems of philosophical explanation which demanded purification by criticism. System called forth system, as one such effort sought to correct a preceding one. The age of mythology in religion gave way to the age of dogmatic religion; and as the spirit of criticism gradually developed, dogmatic religion, subordinate to the power of the organized church, was challenged by rational religion after the Reform. Concomitantly, rational philosophy reached its highest point when Spinoza discovered God as essence, God as the unity of the world, which is as far as reason can go in conceiving this unity as an idea.

Schelling views the whole development of philosophy to this summit as "negative," emphasizing the need for a "positive" act to propel man beyond the limited idea of God as essence. He declares that all philosophy—including his own speculation up to this point—has been dealing only with essence, form, idea, working basically to reduce all reality to the absolute unity of the *idea* of God. But reality is not only essence and formal intelligibility; it is existence and brute encounter with the factual *thatness* of things. At the culmination of negative philosophy stands the realization of the need for an act (existential, to use a term borrowed from a later day) to unite one with the dynamic principle in reality. Only a dynamic encounter of the will with God as Existent can reveal his reality as more than essence, as transcending all representation in a rational system of ideas. This step, which Schelling felt compelled to initiate, would carry man beyond speculation to action, beyond closed system to a complementary effort to read the world as symbol of the divine dynamic striving, as an "always more," unenclosable in clear and distinct ideas, reflecting its infinity. In short, Schelling proposed as *positive* philosophy the rebirth of mythology on a new, higher level of consciousness. Indeed Schelling's *positive philosophy* would be an *Aufhebung*, to borrow Hegel's term, synthesizing primitive man's awareness of God as *force*—as the immediate and the over-dark—with modern man's conception of God as light, end, idea. The unity of negative and positive philosophy in the new religion would actually accomplish the unification necessary for God's ultimate self-discovery.

Schelling's later lectures were rich in "existential" suggestions, in impulses toward that "breakthrough to actuality" of which he spoke; but they remained poor in systematic exploitation of these suggestions. Schelling, in the late autumn of Hegelian influence, could point to his invention of the primacy of struggle and movement, of the fundamental reality of history, of time as the battleground of the Absolute working out its self-realization—all this in writings that antedated Hegel's *Phenomenology of the Spirit* by five to ten years. He could continue to underscore the weaknesses of an effort to reduce history to too rational a principle of movement; but it remains a simple (and for him unhappy) fact that he could never match Hegel's ability to wring insights from such intuitions by his extraordinary systematic exploration of their possibilities. That is why later tradition will be more concerned with Hegel than with Schelling. Thinkers have only recently begun to realize that Schelling contributed more than precocious Hegelianism.

GEORG WILHELM FRIEDRICH HEGEL

the dialectic as intentional analysis
Hegel's[27] philosophy can be viewed in two ways: (1) phenomenologically (genetically); or, (2) systematically (ideally). From the first standpoint, *The Phenomenology of the Spirit* (Hegel's introduction to his philosophy, 1807), follows the process of the struggle of the spirit to achieve in *experience* (*Erfahrung*) that degree of self-awareness of *truth* in which the finite human consciousness recognizes in itself the work of the Absolute, knows itself as spirit. The second viewpoint is an achievement of the first. Once spirit has historically achieved the raising of itself to that self-awareness in which it knows itself as the Absolute, the *all of* which particular determinations, all essences, all forms (*Gestalten*) of becoming are but aspects (*Momente*), then the philosopher can proceed to a systematic laying-out of the interrelationship of all those aspects, a "demonstration," a manifestation of the *logos*, the truth of Being, the sense of all its moments, in which the implication of all the other moments is grasped from the point of view peculiar to each.

But, once the truth has been realized and Spirit has grasped itself as idea, will not the "phenomenology," the study of Spirit's long, painful work, its gradual "happening" (*Geschehen*), cease to be of capital importance? There can be no doubt that Hegel later came to look upon his work of 1807, *The Phenomenology of the Spirit*, as an "early" work, full of hesitations and obscurities about matters later more lucidly commanded in the "System." But his return to the study of history—the history of peoples, of the development of civil order and law, of religion and philosophy, and of science (or of the development of a philosophy of nature à la hauteur du système)—again and again, and never more than in the Berlin lectures, proves that he thought it is in history that we uncover all the "positive" (in the sense in which we speak of "positive science") determinations of the *idea*, the *essences* intricately interconnected in the time-spanning and space-englobing totality of Being-known, which compose the spirit's self-pos-

I. *Post-Kantian Background*

session in the "System." Nowhere is that "history" presented on so many levels of intentional reality as in the *Phenomenology*, which hence remains an indispensable instrument of propaedeutic.

The problem of evaluating the sense of the *Phenomenology* in relation to the works composing the "system" is but one form of the central difficulty facing the whole tradition of transcendental philosophy which is still so much the motor force of contemporary continental philosophy from Marxism to existentialist phenomenology. Once one adopts the position that what is known are not "things-in-themselves," but only "phenomena," the problem is to explain credibly the undeniable experience of the things as *other*, i.e., as passively perceived, as making demands on us, as enjoying some importance in their very difference.

Hegel began and ended as an idealist, convinced not only that *what is* is totally intelligible, but that the human spirit can and must come to know it in its "truth," that is, as the complete structure of an idea; philosophy is nothing other than that endeavor, and nothing less than such an absolute undertaking is worthy of the name "love of wisdom." The young Hegel energetically rejected every suggestion of the "romantics" that Being is in itself an incomprehensible *all* with which we can only mystically feel ourselves one; he considered this judgment characteristic of an earlier stage in Spirit's struggle to come to full self-realization and a block to it. However, after witnessing the efforts of Fichte and Schelling, he soon likewise became convinced of the perfect hopelessness of attempting a deduction of Being from an Absolute given *a priori*, which itself would be mere formal identity, "A is A." The Absolute is not an empty *nothing*, the contentless Infinite, "a dark night in which all cows are black," merely *für sich* (for-itself) but lacking the *an sich* (in-itself) content of reality. Rather, the Absolute is the positive *all*, both *"an und für sich,"* made up of the totality of the determinations, moments, essences, notions, individuals that have ever appeared in history or in nature; it is in them, in their interconnections, in their dynamic revelation of themselves in time that the Absolute has its matter and reveals to itself its form, which is *their* necessity. It was to establish this that *The Phenomenology of the Spirit* was written. It is a work of transcendental philosophy written against the "abstract" idealists with the intention of showing the indispensability of the content and the ultimate (the ideal) sense of the moments—of the "figures" (*Gestalten*)—of consciousness; consequently, the ineluctable irreducibility of the moment is perforce more persistently brought out in this than in the "systematic" works. It is from those elements of the *Phenomenology* which contrast most with the *Logic* that "the Hegelian Left" (Feurbach, Bauer, Rüge, Marx, Engels) and the existentialists (Heidegger, Sartre, Merleau-Ponty, Ricoeur) have drawn their inspiration, and they have used it precisely to oppose the idealism which often drove Hegel himself to complete schemes too facilely and to move the dialectic swiftly along its course rather than dwelling patiently with the *"Sachen selbst"* (the things themselves), the particular phenomena as they actually appear.

Yet, often the description of the *Sachen* within a given stage or figure of the "dialectic" will be so compelling, so insightful, that we are not only left with the conviction that every "figure" deserves to be studied for the light it can throw on reality, but wonder at the strange power this philosophy possesses for illuminating the things themselves. How can this gigantic construction accommodate so many and such varied phenomena—indeed, in one way or another, find a place for everything? Why are some relationships illumined by it better than ever before (and, often, ever since), while, on the other hand, the reduction of everything to ideal moment is itself painfully felt as unfaithful to the common conviction that some things manifest *in experience* their objective reality as things not dependent on that experience for their existence?

The answer lies in understanding what this "dialectic," operating from the "transcendental viewpoint," actually is. One must first realize that Hegel, from the initial figure of the *Phenomenology* to the last description of the *Encyclopedia*, is dealing with intentions, i.e., with phenomena; the point of view of the "observer" who is following the unfolding process described in the *Phenomenology* is explicitly post-Kantian; what Descartes sought to accomplish by "methodical doubt" is now already presupposed. The *Phenomenology* begins with a description of the object of sensible knowledge which, to the unreflecting man absorbed in his limited-range practical projects, seems at first glance to be a self-standing reality-in-itself. But at once the *Phenomenology* begins underlining the fact that the object is thing-perceived, a *"Vorstellung"* (representation) that requires the activity of the subject in order to be *vor-gestellte* (literally, "to be set out there," or thrown [*jacere*] *over* against [*ob*] the subject). This polar switch of attention from the phenomenon "out-there" to the intentional subject's *activity* as an indispensable condition for there being any object is the

I. *Post-Kantian Background*

very heart of the dialectic as it unfolds in the *Phenomenology*—"the perceptual thing" is seen to require "the perceiving consciousness"; "the master's domination of the slave" requires "the slave's acceptance of domination"; "the world of culture" can only be in virtue of "self-consciousness' alienation of itself in a culture"; and "God" himself can only be because of "the finite consciousness' awareness of Him." The object can only be object for a subject, just as, conversely, the subject cannot be without an object. The movement back to the next higher "objective" pole is assured by this fundamental principle of what Husserl will term "intentionality": he will point out that knowledge (whether perceptual, intellectual, affective, etc.) is always knowledge of. The "noetic activity" has as its correlate the "noematic object" in which the activity itself figures—a tree seen is not exactly the same as the identical tree remembered, poeticized about, absorbed into an economic plan, etc. In each step of the dialectic, Hegel equally emphasizes the other side of this reciprocal relationship—the fact that the existent is only his world, as the later existentialist might put it. This polarity of the *noesis* and the *noema* is the driving force of the dialectic; it is a tension (which is why it is a motor force), presenting the ultimately inseparable moments of a living process, because neither subject nor object *is* completely its other; however, each depends on the other in order even to be. The human existent's intentional encounter with the world is, then, an active grappling with the resisting "matter" known in an effort to take full conscious possession of it in bringing the light of rational necessity to shine where before there was only the darkness of the contingent and the accidental.

Now, as everything we encounter in the world is indeed an *intended phenomenon*, Hegel can find a place in his intentional analysis for everything: every aspect and sort of experience is accommodated, precisely *as experience*. And that explains why the *"logos"* sought by Hegel—and by the later phenomenologists—tends to be not the "essence" of things insofar as they are able to present themselves interior to intentional experience as transcending it in their substantial otherness, but rather the *Wesen* of the intentional processes—the work, the *Tun*—required to produce this or that kind of notion (*Begriff*).

This further explains why in Hegel's *Phenomenology*, as in all phenomenological descriptions, the status of the lower moments that have been synthesized ("*Aufgehoben*" lifted up and retained in a higher form, involving a clearer and deeper awareness of their intentional nature) is always difficult to determine. On the one hand, they present themselves with their characteristic objective determinations; on the other, these are looked at, from the transcendental viewpoint, as so many ideal differences, negations—as that which holds this determination separate from the *all*, so that it can be a particular form. When I realize this, however, in effect I negate the negation, linking the particular determination again to its encompassing ground, the *all*. But, as that all is not itself a mere formal *nothingness*, but would be construed by Hegel as the *totality* of the moments, then, somehow, the determinations must be retained as moments in the ideal synthesis. The tension between their original claim to apparent substantiality (*Selbstständigkeit*) and the synthesis of them into the total ideal structure by the intentional analysis is irresolvable, at least as long as the moments (all individual things, particular kinds of essences, all psychic moments, etc.) are *uniquely* accorded the intentional reality due a "phenomenon."

In the light of these remarks, we can better understand why some of the individual descriptions, some of the moments or figures along the way of Hegel's dialectic, satisfy the reader more than others, and tend to become rallying points for the later phenomenologists.[28]

the phenomenology of the spirit

The preceding section holds the key to understanding the struggles in the succeeding tradition of transcendental philosophy; what is more to the point here, they help us grasp the text of Hegel as no dry recitation of chapter headings could. And they suggest a solution to the problem of why the *Phenomenology* tended to strike later philosophers as a work somehow more in contact with reality than some parts of the "System."[29] The *Phenomenology*, we have seen, is particularly concerned with showing both the need for the moments through which Spirit passed—the ineluctability of the travail, as Hegel puts it[30]—and why and how they can ultimately be grasped by Spirit as moments of the Absolute structure. Instead of the abstract ideas with which the *Logic* begins (to the universal dissatisfaction of the greatest of the post-Hegelians), the *Phenomenology* deals exclusively with contentful notions in *most* of which the social struggles of an historically developing humanity are recognizable. The only exception is to be found in the first section, "Consciousness," where perception and the most elemental knowledge of nature are considered precisely as intentional processes—and these are among the most strained pages in the

I. *Post-Kantian Background* 31

entire work. Once the level of self-knowledge is achieved, however, the work moves along almost effortlessly under the impulsion of the authentic dialectic of moments in an essentially intentional process, each of which requires a polar opposite for its completion, and all of which (being, as we said, *essentially* intentional) actually reveal their inner nature in that "tending-toward" (*intendere*).

To sum up: There are in the *Phenomenology* a minimum of the two kinds of analyses, frequent in the works of the "System," which historically have tended to arouse the most anti-Hegelian dissatisfaction: (1) dialectics between mere concepts (legitimate in itself, but tending to be so abstract, i.e., far removed from the concrete things and real people of daily experience, that it becomes difficult to evaluate by "anchoring" it in reality; this is what gave rise to both the reaction of the Marxist materialization of the dialectic and the existentialist rehabilitation of the individual); and (2) explanations by dialectical-intentional analyses of phenomena which are not essentially intentional.

Let us now see something of how the dialectical-intentional analysis moves through this work of propaedeutic and how it introduces us to the point of view which will be that of the "System." The first thing to be underscored is that each *Gestalt* or moment is only an apparent stability; the endeavor of each *Gestalt* to achieve enduring stability leads either to death, skepticism, or the leap (*Sprung*) to the higher form in which it may be preserved, although transformed. From the superior vantage point from which the *Phenomenology* looks back on the process of the progressive unfolding of Being we can see what was not so visible from a standpoint that still was confined to a given stage of development. The master and the slave, for instance, at first (and surely to themselves) seemed bound up in a kind of eternal, static relationship of domination. The slave, because he fears death, accepts the master's command to work for him. What have we here but a simple relationship of force? The slave has only to "knuckle down" and get to work. But from our superior vantage point we know that an interior dynamism, born of a tension between its members, drove this form to open beyond itself. The master, in enslaving the other person, has put himself in an (intentionally grounded) relationship of dependence—he can *be* master only so long as the slave prefers working for him to dying—a relationship which for the master is itself a kind of dead end: all he can do is continue to dominate and to consume the products of the slave's work. The slave, meanwhile, likewise stands in an intentional relationship, but one that does not terminate in a dead end but rather opens a whole future. Through his work the slave learns that he is master over nature, as well as he upon whom the master must depend. Because he has experienced "anguish" before death, "The Absolute Master," which dissolves the hold of *things* on him, he knows himself then as superior to things—thus arises the moment of "self-consciousness" out of which the whole progressive Christian mentality will be born.

This brings us to the second point, the nature of the superiority of succeeding over preceding *Gestalten*. Each form in the *Phenomenology* involves a different degree of elaboration; each is more sophisticated than those which precede it. The earlier *Gestalten* presuppose the later ones as part of their ultimate explanation, and traces of what was accomplished through the earlier forms are retained as part of the very sense of the later. Thus, for instance, when the simple perceptual situation is shown to imply and require *understanding* (of a set of forces) for the full unfolding of its sense,[31] the explanation leans on the previous analysis of the perceptual matter (the "here" and the "now," and the "thing"); and when the description moves us further along to the realization that "things" and "forces" are not ultimately just contemplative objects for the Kantian kind of mind (which is everyone and no one), but are perceived by *persons*, and that these persons stand in relationships of practical tension to one another, it is then understood that there could be no such properly human relationship between individuals if they did not share the common perceptual-intellectual world described in the earlier chapters.[32] Conversely, the later forms often make explicit elements we are then able to recognize as having been implicitly operative in the earlier moments. When Hegel shows us that these human relationships are mediated through things (the "slave" works to transform things of nature to render them suitable for the "master's" consumption[33]), we realize that this discovery, like those of all the superior stages of the *Phenomenology*, is to be applied retroactively—at this point, for instance, we come to realize that the original perception itself was a *Tun*, a doing, a transformation of the world, bringing the thing "to stand" within the transcendental horizons of consciousness through an act of inner-possession (*Er-innerung*) through which spirit takes re-possession explicitly of its own substance, which it has experienced, objectified (*ent-äussert*).

It calls for a great effort on the reader's part to remember the presence of all the earlier moments in the later and to think the later moments back into the

I. Post-Kantian Background

more primitive stages; Hegel cannot possibly pause to spell them all out each time, lest the *Phenomenology*, instead of five hundred and sixty pages, were to become three thousand. Thus one might fail to realize, for instance, that the rather primitive relationships of human will to human will described early in the work as the "master-slave" structure is still the foundation for the extremely complex society we encounter later as the production of "the cultural world," described in the fourth chapter. There, using the society of the seventeenth and early eighteenth centuries as an illustration of the spirit "alienating itself," Hegel describes the production of a "world" characterized by a complex economic and monarchical system to which the person then has to conform in order to recover his own substance.[34] At first we wonder what the description of such a civilized complex society can have in common with that of the primitive master-slave relationship, and what either of them, seemingly so "psychological," can have to do with the apparently epistemological analysis with which the work began. But just as we earlier became aware that *perceiving* and *doing* are not alien to one another, and that even the simplest perceptual truth implies a community of reason through which individual wills accede to the truth of what is known, so now we realize that the primitive relationships all underlie the sophisticated ones described in "the cultural world." The economic considerations which tie the later world together are but a development of the fundamental discovery that men are mediated through things, and that in working to transform things for consumption by the master, the slave is carrying out an eternal act: the practical transformation of the "given" through work, relevant in every subsequent society.

Interior to each particular *Gestalt*, the "form" of the dialectic is adjusted to the "matter," that is, the "positive" content of the individual moments. This realization, coupled with a healthy reaction against Hegel's tendency at times, especially in the "System," to force the data to fit the stiff triadic schema, thesis-antithesis-synthesis, has led some recent commentators (e.g., Nicolai Hartmann) to assert that the dialectic, when best fulfilling its descriptive role, presents an infinity of forms, adjusting supplely to fit the matters described. We would caution, however, both in the interest of a correct interpretation of Hegel and as a warning not to fall into the "opportunist dialectic" of the authors of the official Soviet "Handbook" in materialist dialectic,[35] that the key to the sense of the dialectic and the explanation for its built-in, forward-moving, pole-reversing drive is to be sought *in every instance*, as we have contended, in the *noesis-noema* polarity inherent in intentionality and in increasing reflective awareness that the sense of the phenomenon lies in its "intentional constitution by the transcendental ego," as Husserl will put it, or in Hegel's own terms, that "substance is subject."

What distinguishes the later from the earlier figures (*Gestalten*) in the *Phenomenology*, then, is not only the progressive complexity but, above all, Spirit's increasing awareness of its involvement, its "remembering-interiorizing" (*Er-innerung*) of what it has exteriorized, objectivized of its own substance; in Hegel's terminology, what was simply "*an sich*"—*in*-itself—is moving toward the moment when it will be "*für sich*"—*for*-itself—which is manifest in the greater degree of "spirituality" apparent in the later, more complex situations. There is, for example, something immediate, unreflecting, "natural" about the master-slave relationship, compared with the more self-conscious (and more consciously cultivated) "being a bourgeois" or "being a noble" that might characterize a more advanced state. Or again, two individuals of different decrees of self-consciousness relate themselves differently to the *same* society. A little child and a mature dandy may be objectively in the same cultural world; but the child born and being raised in it is there, as Hegel would say, *an sich* but not yet *für sich*, which we can best paraphrase: He is in the society *in fact* without yet being himself aware very much of what this means. The violent split Marx saw as the prime mover of history in the nineteenth century—that between the bourgeoisie and the proletariat—derives much of its tension, according to him, from the fact that the two classes are "*an sich*" in the same society but in different stages of development, "mediated" to the whole differently, "aware" spiritually very unsimilarly.

To become aware (whether we are speaking of a child growing up in a particular moment of history, in a certain culture, or whether we are speaking of mankind becoming more aware of itself historically) involves more than just getting to know what is already there. The cognitive act, we saw above (and this is important), is always a *doing*, an intentional transforming; so every "becoming aware" adds to and transforms noematically "what is there"; the *Er-innerung* (recalling) is creative. The awakening of new consciousnesses to awareness of what is "going on" (for instance in eighteenth-century society the addition of a new "adherent" to the movement of the *Aufklärung*) is no historically neu-

I. Post-Kantian Background

tral fact; this *prise de conscience* (becoming aware) adds another element to the situation, advancing the day when the built-in tensions will grow so tight, the general awareness of its implications so clear, that a new stage will become necessary, perhaps even an explosive one (like the French Revolution), if only to keep what one has come to realize has been previously gained.

These last remarks help us to understand better the restlessness that characterizes the *Phenomenology*. From the introduction of naïve perception to the final revelation of the dynamic spirit that was there latent and now finally stands revealed in all its moments and their relationship, we are made to see that the human spirit is of its very nature swept along in pursuit of a destiny that will allow it no ultimately secure resting place.[36] There can be no final "figure." All figures, from the simplest sense intuition to the highest artistic production, are *acts* of Spirit; therefore transformations, creations, every form of cognition and action must be dynamic; the very process of knowing changes what *was* and calls for what shall then *have* to be; every act posits a possibility which needs further acts to fulfill its sense. New figures are, then, no utterly original beginnings, no creations from nothing, but the prolonging and expansion of what already is; their development is not arbitrary, goalless, but is teleologically oriented toward full self-consciousness—it is a *Wenden*, a restless seeking to fulfill the posited "need," the *Not* set by the earlier act in this process of necessity (*Not-wendigkeit*). Thus, not only does history enjoy a sense, a continuity, but the "tragedy" of the suppression of earlier forms[37] is much relieved; for, as we have seen, each new step forward, being built on all that preceded it, and serving to "realize" its potentialities, carries what was previously accomplished into a new synthesis in which the deeper sense of what was begins to appear. *Aufhebung*, Hegel's renowned term for this process of lifting up the old into a more adequate synthesis in which what was retains a place but in a new form, while untranslatable, clearly has no tragic, but rather victorious, overtones. As the "end" of the process is the realization of the deepest sense of each of the moments; these obviously "come into their own" with the development of the advanced stages of awareness. This also explains how, from within his own experience in the present time, the philosopher can set out to the rediscovery of all the moments that have gone into the patient realization of present forms, conquered through the travail of a long series of *auf bebenden* syntheses.

This also further explains the status of the often very oblique allusions to particular moments in history that illustrate the moments of the *Phenomenology*; the phenomenological stages are more ontological than (in any strict sense) historical. Because of this, the sense of the historical correspondence is different with each major division. The *Gestalten* unfolded in the first section, "Consciousness," enjoy a partial applicability to the fundamental cognitive situation at any time, anywhere; that is to say, much of what is there described can be taken as a dynamic psychology of basic epistemological processes discoverable in the development of any individual. The forms in the second section, "Self-Consciousness," are already a little more tied to an epoch, but by no means exclusively so—the master-slave relationship, Stoicism, and skepticism are not exclusively phenomena of the ancient world in which they make their first full-blown and perhaps purest appearance; they can reappear, in very different forms to be sure, but not so different that we cannot inform ourselves about them by studying the basic nature of this relationship in the classical situation Hegel has described in this section. To return to the same example: The discovery that human relationships are mediated through things, illustrated in its most primitive from by the slaves transformation of material reality through his work, retains its validity even though in the later *Gestalten* the mediating matter is spiritualized, taking, as it finally does, the subtle form of language, Spirit's ultimate form of incarnation. Moreover, even when the court's "language of flattery" provides the central form of social mediation, the bruter forms of material transformation, serving as mediation between selves, retain their place as substructures of the society. The structure of the state is intricately intertwined with a system of production and capital, or "wealth," as Hegel calls it, in eighteenth-century terms; and implicit in the economic structure is still the fundamental productive act, *work*—the transformation of brute nature. (Marx never hid his debt to Hegel for this discovery.) Similarly, "skepticism" is a recurring form, a moment of doubt destined to exercise its dissolving action against any form of flight from the real, from engagement in dialectic's work; such escapism is a recurrent possibility, not limited just to the appearance in classical times of the purest manifestation of Stoicism. Here, then, we see why the *Phenomenology*'s historical references are usually so oblique: the reader must be made to realize that all the *Gestalten*, while perhaps manifest in their purest form at a certain moment in history, are recurrent phenomenological structures limited essentially to none.

I. *Post-Kantian Background*

The *Phenomenology* is not, then, a history; rather it is itself a *becoming-aware* (a *prise de conscience*, as the French say so well) on the part of Spirit; instead of being about history, the *Phenomenology* is itself history in the making. What the individual philosopher expresses in his own peculiar creation is what Spirit has already prepared socially through the patient working-up of its "matter"—human nature as it is found in a people or tradition. It is understood by many because they are able to recognize in what he says the "truth" already incarnate in their own existences, their "experience." The philosopher's (or the novelist's) *prise de conscience*—his rendering explicit what before was only directly lived—is, however, a genuine victory of Spirit; for now an informed public can consciously will the kind of existence the book holds up to their contemplation, which brings the society closer to the moment when it realizes the implications of its situation, with the result, ironical and inevitable, of making its tensions so manifest that only a completely new ordering—the leap to a new form—can relieve them.[38] The *Phenomenology* is the latest and most aware in the long series of such expressive acts of becoming "conscious"—it is itself the *Gestalt* that will not pass away, for it has achieved *absolute knowledge*.

This brings us to an inevitable and very difficult question: How is one to envision the last stage depicted in this Odyssey of the human spirit? The problem has two sides: (1) How is the "final" stage, which receives its expression in the last pages on "Absolute Knowledge" and in the Foreword (*Einleitung*, finished on the eve of the Battle of Jena), related to the long course of preceding moments? (2) In what sense is the climactic *Gestalt* of the *Phenomenology* final—it may be the end of the *Phenomenology*; but then...?

It is difficult to answer the first question with assurance of speaking Hegel's mind correctly. Suppose we ask: Was the end predestined? There is one sense of predestination which can immediately be excluded. While there is some sense in which it may be said that Spirit has presided over the unfolding of this "destiny," it is clearly false to take this to mean that some sort of infinite, transcendent Absolute consciousness has somehow stood clear of the process of becoming described in the *Phenomenology* in order to direct it, making certain that it "comes out right." On the other hand, it is equally certain that when he tells us the whole phenomenology describes a necessary process of Spirit, Hegel means that Spirit is in some sense present as "end" in the very beginning, that is, in the most primitive human cognitive situation. As we suggested above, all the subsequent developments are consequent upon what is initially revealed, which earlier moment "needs" them to fulfill its latent, its "forgotten" sense as moment of Spirit's self-exteriorization (*Ent-äusserung*). From the first moment of that awareness which has perpetuated itself within the transcendental horizons of human historical consciousness (the forms of which can be rediscovered in our own experience, operative as the fundamental substructure of our present intentional relations with "the world"), there was manifest a certain necessity, posited first as the determinate structure of human consciousness; in other words, the dialectic is commanded by the givenness of *human nature*. Toward the end of the *Phenomenology*, in the section devoted to "The Moral View of the World," and with the *Critique of Practical Reason* obviously in mind, Hegel speaks of a "postulate of human nature" in the following terms: Nature is not only the independent, exterior world in which, as object, the consciousness will have to realize its goal, "but it [nature] exists again in the very core of consciousness as its nature. Man is a natural reality, he is directly linked to the exterior world by impulses and inclinations which influence his action."[39] This declaration that man is "an accidental and natural essence" (*ein Zufälliges und Natürliches Wesen*) must be interpreted, as usual, in accord with its position in the *Phenomenology*. It is a stepping stone to the full truth. The *auf gehobene* realization of this truth, its final and fullest form, would be as follows: There is a fundamental givenness, a structure operative from the beginning of this Odyssey, so that all the subsequent moments of its development *make a sense*. To be sure, there is real becoming; the very nature of this nature is to become—more precisely, to become free in becoming master of itself—freedom being immediate self-determination (*sich selbst setzen*) rather than dependence on another as ground. The becoming of Spirit "makes sense"—we can retrospectively see the end in the beginning—because the same *conditions* are present throughout the development. What it means for a transcendental ego to set over against itself its object and to conquer its own substance by reconquering what it has "alienated" in its object remains basically the same, from the primitive (or infantile) encounter with the object of sensible certitude (*sinnliche Gewissheit*) to the highest self-conquering which Spirit enjoys when its gaze ranges freely over the whole span of the *Phenomenology*; and the *Gestalten* involving highest self-awareness are but the realization of the ultimate implications of the most primitive; indeed, they are its sense.

I. Post-Kantian Background

Because this development has a sense, there is implicit in the *Phenomenology* (as there should be in any ontology) a general ethical vision—if we may so term the "sense of a sense"—where the role of free choice, however, is most obscure. Some development of this point will help us in our understanding of the accomplishment of the *Phenomenology* and its relationship to the remainder of Hegel's philosophy. First of all the *Phenomenology* is an ontology—or, better, introduces an ontology. The *Phenomenology* traces the progress of Spirit's self-awareness, from the positions of an "immediate certitude of Being" which serves without stabile content, to the realization that the substance is subject and that all existing determinations refer necessarily to one another as moments of the same all-englobing intentional subject-spirit.

The absolute knowledge (*das absolute Wissen*) is thus an onto-logy; the *logos* of the *on* is thought when Spirit fully recognizes its own transcendental reality, that *logos* being nothing other than the *idea*; and the idea, being nothing but the necessary structure revealed by the process of becoming what is now freely commanded because comprehended in its ultimate sense, is thus what was said above to have originally been given as *nature*. This "*Wissen*" is Absolute—is indeed the *realization* of the Absolute—because here what *ultimately is* knows itself most fully; thus is established the "free" reign of the true "concrete universal," that conscious adherence of all individual selves to a reasonable order which they recognize as their own reality.

From the superior vantage point of a moment when the fullness of this onto-logical vision has been realized we can now distinguish, back along the tortuous and arduous course of the spirit's Odyssey, those moments which reveal themselves to us as advancing the movement forward from those of stagnation and retrogression. The fruitful moments were those in which a people fulfilled themselves in their work, bringing mankind a step closer to that ultimate realization of all that has had to go into the construction of the reign of the spirit. Those actions which turn away from the mainstream, which assert mere givenness, mere particularity (Hegel would in such a context term them "abstract") rather than joining with the movement toward the general realization of spirit have proven to be destined to relative non-being. They have proven to be inauthentic.[40]

This "ethical" (or, anyway, *teleological*) note, while never explicitly spelled out in such a general fashion in the *Phenomenology*, is rather directly proclaimed in the Introduction to the lectures on *The Philosophy of History*. There Hegel contrasts merely particular aims, which often seem to come to tragic ends, with the positive nature of what is actually accomplished.[41] What (from the limited standpoint occupied at the moment of the event) can seem an insupportable evil may later reveal its extreme usefulness to the whole enterprise of the advance of the spirit. Hegel does not hesitate to term his *Philosophy of History* a *Theodicaea*, justifying the ways of God to man,[42] for in its pages one will find the sense of all the sacrifices of history, with the result "that the ill that is found in the World may be comprehended, and the thinking Spirit reconciled with the fact of the existence of evil." Jean Hyppolite has declared, "One could condense the whole problematic of Hegel's youthful writings into a single formula: What *value* should be attributed to *positivity*, that is to say to the historical, to *experience*?"[43]

We would extend the question to the whole tradition of transcendental philosophy from Kant to Heidegger and Merleau-Ponty. It is the same as asking: How does one account for all otherness, objective resistance, irreducible determination, once one has realized that all that appears is simply *idea*? Hegel refused the "easy" solution to the problem of knowledge, the reconciliation of the subject and its object by positing an Absolute in which the difference between "Being" and "truth," the "in-itself" and the "for-itself" is resolved *a priori* (along with it being *dissolved* all sense of concreteness, positivity, history!): but in so adjudging that the Absolute can realize itself only through the painful, patient command of a resisting particularity, Hegel decided not just to accept the fact of "nature," but to embrace it eagerly as the very "matter" Spirit must learn to work up with its own developing "form." In consequence, far from ignoring the problems posed by a resisting "nature" and the difficulties of "evil," "pain," "waste," the *Phenomenology* accepts the challenge of placing these negative phenomena in their whole positive complex.

This inevitably raises the correlative question, in what sense the Absolute is Absolute. Although Hegel terms the Absolute Spirit "God," it is evident that "God is only God in so far as He knows Himself," as Hegel puts it in a famous passage in the *Enzyklopädie*,[44] and that, as the same text goes on, "His knowledge of Himself is moreover the self-knowledge of man, and the knowledge that man has of God is continuous with the knowledge that he has of himself in God." But what precisely does this mean? What have we here, a renewal of the

I. *Post-Kantian Background*

mysticism of Jakob Böhme,[45] or the real origin of Feuerbach's humanism?[46] If more the latter, as now seems apparent, there remains the problem of explaining why Hegel uses such absolutistic language to describe the result: man becoming aware of himself as the bearer of light gradually illuminating the surrounding darkness and thereby giving natural being some human sense. In this regard, Feuerbach was surely right to underscore the significance of Hegel's unwillingness to strip away the equivocations arising from his talk about Spirit as God.

However, we must be careful to keep our historical perspective here. It is very difficult when confronted, as one inevitably is in reconstructing the history of philosophy, with the problem of determining what a great philosopher ultimately *really means* not to read subsequent history back into the texts. Knowing the development through Feuerbach to Marx, and seeing the dangers of voluntarism that arise, for instance, in the philosophy of Nietzsche, where all suggestion of an Absolute somehow transcending man is squarely eliminated, one might be tempted to say that Hegel retains the absolutistic language as a way of dramatizing that Spirit discovering in itself the unity of being and truth is not the product or the plaything of any concrete human will in its particularity; voluntarism is ruled out because the individual must still confront the reign of truth and law as (for him, *qua* individual) a destiny, yet a destiny the realization of which requires his co-operation, his co-creation.

It is not possible to understand Hegel, nor is the subsequent history we are to trace in this volume comprehensible, if one fails to face the fact that Hegel is struggling here with another side of the central problem which, we have suggested, is inevitably raised by transcendental philosophy. The nature of the difficulty has been hinted at several times since we began our discussion of the post-Kantians. Once the last bonds of common-sense realism imposed by custom and ratified by practicality are dissolved[47] and we finally realize what it really means to affirm that all experience is *our representation*, i.e., is *vor-gestellt* by the subject, the problem arises: Does the object have any reality in itself, independent of the subject? From the transcendental viewpoint, the question is almost meaningless. To have a reality beyond my consciousness would mean for the object to have a reality *unknown* to consciousness, enjoying no intentional relation to the subject at all, so that it would be something we could say nothing about and do nothing about; in short, an object which Hegel successfully dissipated in banishing the thing-in-itself.

Yet our experience presents the object as *other than* me, the concrete subject; and even when we recognize that the object, as object of consciousness, is necessarily the consciousness' representation, we are sure that it is not merely an arbitrary creation from nothing on the part of a particular will. Our representations make demands on us, we must respect them for the being and sense they have in themselves; consciousness' unfolding a truth in the presentation of representations involves an element of destiny. The ultimate transcendental subject is not "subjective"; the *Vorstellung* is not the creation of the individual ego out of nothing; on the contrary, as we have suggested before, the subject finds itself in its world—and *is* its world: the master is master, for instance, only because of the slave's acceptance of bondage rather than death; Spirit has exteriorized itself and now the individual subject must discover the ground of its being in the necessity of that objectivity which can only be through it. The problem in interpreting Hegel is that of understanding precisely the relationship of the individual ego to the necessary ground that is Spirit itself.

These considerations place the difficulties inherent in the *end* of the *Phenomenology* and in understanding the ontology of the *Logic* in the proper perspective. We may be able to see better now the relationship between the problem of the transcendence of the Absolute and the question of the exact here and now (at the end of the *Phenomenology*) status of the moments along Spirit's way. Looking back from a post-Marxist, indeed a post-existentialist perspective, one might be tempted to say that recourse to absolutistic expressions was Hegel's way of attempting to compensate for his failure to account adequately for the persisting otherness of the object, to protect "Being" from voluntarism. This is not to say in the least that the *Phenomenology* ignores the element of a resisting otherness of "nature," nor that in passing over into the *Logic* it is devoid of suggestions concerning the retention of this otherness in the *absolute Wissen*. The problem is that when a given resistance is *auf gehoben*, it no longer retains its "natural" otherness, its "negativity" is negated—and yet, we are assured that in some way it persists, adding to the structure of the final synthesis. This *somehow* is left vague in the *Phenomenology*, the work in which it should have been explained—if explicable it is. We are made aware that mankind is, in the described process, becoming educated; but in what sense the earlier moments of this education are retained in the end moment (for instance, to capitalize on a suggestion made rather in passing, are they retained as *habits*

I. *Post-Kantian Background*

in the individual and as institutions binding individuals together?) is left very implicit. The very notion of "sedimentation" will not be explicitly developed until Husserl. Looking on from our own de-Absolutized time one is tempted to add: Had Hegel been able to show *how* "Being" gets incarnated in the intersubjective world, how the accumulations of the past, now as realities, are here making demands on the individual, requiring his free co-operation, he might have felt easier, as the phenomenologists of our own time have been, about dispensing altogether with suggestions of a transcendent Absolute "exteriorizing" and "forgetting" itself.

But Hegel, after all, lived in the shadow of Fichte and Schelling, not of Feuerbach, Marx, and Nietzsche. His concern was to describe the Absolute correctly, not to suppress it as a concept somehow unworthy of modern times! Hegel never for a moment considered himself a mere pioneer in phenomenological psychology; he was convinced that through him the Absolute Spirit—reducible neither to himself, to any individual man, nor even to human logic as such, but embracing both "*Logos*" and "Nature"—was making its highest revelation. Consequently, what must concern us here is *Hegel's* conception of what the *Phenomenology* achieved and its relationship to the *Logic*, not what later thinkers in the tradition were to adjudge was "really" accomplished there.

from phenomenology to logic

The absolute, we have seen, not being empty identity, does not transcend its "moments" in the sense of being able to be without them, but only in the sense that consciousness is higher than that of which it is conscious, except when it is its own object. The major difference between the "standpoint" of the *Phenomenology* and that of works composing the "System," we have suggested, centers about a change in perspective regarding these "moments." The *Phenomenology* traced the process of Spirit's coming to know itself; until the end, when it has achieved full self-possession, reason finds the object "*an sich*"—in-itself—opposed to the understanding, so that a certain separation of Being and truth persists. But once it is realized that the object is for the subject ("*für sich*"), and that both understanding and that which is understood are, taken by themselves, but abstract moments within one Absolute Spirit and are just that—*moments* of its self-knowledge—the difference between being and truth dissolves, the *aufgehobenen* moments exist now "*an und für sich*"—in and for themselves.

> The element...of separation of knowledge and truth is surmounted. Being is absolutely mediate; it is substantial content which, just as immediately, is property of the "I"; it has the character of Self.... It is at this moment that the *Phenomenology of the Spirit* ends.... The moments no longer fall outside one another in the opposition of being and knowledge, but they remain in the simplicity of knowledge, they are the true in the form of the true (i.e., are "concept"), and their diversity is only a diversity of content. Their movement which develops itself as an organic Whole is the *Logic or Speculative Philosophy*.[48]

The moments, then, do not disappear in the *Logic*; there is never the slightest suggestion of the Schellingian Absolute of pure identity. But what offered itself in the *Phenomenology* as individual "figures of consciousness," distinguishable through their various degrees of self-awareness, is presented in the *Logic* under the aspect of determined *concepts*, or *Denkbestimmungen*, comprehended within a global structure, their relation to each other explicitly understood thus as absolute *idea*. In the *Phenomenology*, "experience" appears as an oscillation between a truth which begins as a contentless certitude, passes by way of a subjective certitude which is as yet without truth, and finally arrives at a subject which is substance; in the *Logic* "experience" as such is surpassed—it is truth itself which is seen developing in and for itself, and the "certitude of self" proper to "*Wissenschaft*" (science) is presupposed as "that unity which constitutes the concept." The form of the concept binds in an immediate unity the objective form of truth and that of the self who knows. That "scientific" self-awareness assumed by the *Logic* is the *result* achieved by the *Phenomenology*.[49] In it Infinite and finite are one, because in it the human self-consciousness existing in time recognizes the sense of the necessity of its thought and so transcends itself, becoming the self-consciousness of the Absolute Spirit, which thus knows itself too, and engenders itself through the finite consciousness. Religions (already criticized in the last part of the *Phenomenology*) conceive of the Absolute as essentially other than the finite consciousness. Religion in its fullest form (revealed Christianity) recognizes the supreme reality of Spirit, but only as it is "in-itself," not yet as it is "for-itself"; that is, it does not yet recognize that it is the finite self which "alone actualizes the life of the absolute Spirit."

I. Post-Kantian Background

divisions of the "system"

The absolute spirit first exists "alienated" from itself, exteriorized both in time (in "history") and in space (as "frozen" natural determinations, as "nature"). Hence the divisions of the "System": The *Logic* considers the Absolute as *concept*, the formal determinations of which are seen as moments in the very life of reason itself. *The Philosophy of Nature* (outlined in the last part of the *Encyclopedia of the Sciences* and augmented by lecture notes taken by students) is the study of rational concept as it exists outside its own sphere, that is, as negation of thought, as unrecuperated Spirit (Hegel would show the parallel between the developments in logic and the corresponding progress in Spirits ability to think nature, the more adequate categories developed in logic being reflected in a more complex and adequate philosophy of nature). Because the Absolute is destined to the high unity of perfect self-consciousness, logic and philosophy of nature must ultimately lead to a higher (because more self-aware) life of the spirit in which they are *aufgehoben*. This highest dialectic is the "philosophy of concrete spirit."

The triad in this highest of dialectical movements is: life of subjective spirit, objective spirit and absolute spirit respectively. The life of the spirit enters the first moment of this final dialectic with the birth of *subjective* spirit, when human nature first becomes aware of itself as soul; then is pure philosophy of nature surpassed, as nature reaches self-consciousness in the strict sense for the first time. In the first phase of this awareness, the problem of the relationship of body and soul dominates all other considerations. In the next higher phase, *phenomenology* develops, as mind moves from naïve consciousness to the full consciousness of itself as reason (which movement is exposed in the *Phenomenology of the Spirit* and first dealt with "truly," i.e., as "*Wissenschaft*" in the *Logik*).[50] The highest phase of subjective self-awareness is the development of "the free spirit," the human individual in the fullest sense.[51] Hegel terms this phase "psychology," because the psyche or *Geist* here develops as individual its highest subjective potentialities, which consist of on the one hand its theoretical qualities (intuition, imagination, remembrance and rational thinking), and on the other its practical ones (feeling, instincts, will), both of which (theoretical and practical qualities) unite in the life of the individual's reason. The rationally free will is not, of course, a disembodied spirit, but one that must work to achieve the fullest realization of its goals. Hence the development of the subjective spirit engenders the development of the objective spirit through the founding of human institutions.

In the first stage of objective spirit, dominated by the notion of *Recht* (right), freedom objectifies itself in the exterior world. The categories of Mind, which are the ultimate guide for freedom, are in this "alienated" form at first conceived as belonging primordially to the things themselves (they are *property* which I must and can own). Then, as it comes to be recognized that ownership depends on the free consent of other men, it is realized that right must be incarnate in the free consent of individuals. Finally it comes to be seen that freedom inevitably involves a conflict of the universal will with the interests of individual wills, and the categories of right become recast in terms of the possible "wrong" that can be done against the universal will.

In reaction against the abstractness of the various conceptions of right, emphasis switches to the individual responsibility exercised freely through morality. The history of morality is a long development toward the ultimate sublimation of abstract right and individual morality into the higher synthesis of ethical life (*Sittlichkeit*). The individual's free, conscious willing of the universal good realizes the "universal rational will," achieving the ethical counterpart of the "concrete universal." This high ethical synthesis is embodied in the three-fold social reality of family, intermediate social organizations, and the state. As is always the case within the highest synthesis, the Absolute moment, the state, unifies both the other poles, the family and the intermediate social organizations, and it itself without them would be an empty identity. The state suppresses neither the individual, nor right, nor property, nor contractual free consent, nor the "wrong," nor morality in any of its three stages, nor the family, nor the diversity of particular groups. Rather it subsumes (*aufhebt*) them into a higher unity, the total self-awareness of which purifies and gives direction to every level and aspect of existence, bringing them to participate in the absolute life of "objective spirit."

The state is the highest development of objective spirit; yet it has a purpose beyond itself which can only be realized in its synthesis with the highest development of subjective spirit, making possible the phases of *absolute spirit*: art, religion and philosophy.[52] Art seeks to render the Absolute visible; it is a way of intuiting the ultimate reality through concrete presentation of the Absolute, for in the artwork the external world is directly invaded by the world of

I. *Post-Kantian Background* 47

spirit. The spirit is still limited, however, in this sensuous presentation of the Absolute; for it cannot achieve a totally adequate representation of itself in an imagination that is still weighted more toward the concrete than toward the universal. In religion, this slight imbalance is redressed, for there is a feeling of greater unity with the universal divine principle. Yet the gap between the finite and the infinite, which remains in all religions, requires the spirit to move beyond representation in religious image to achieve perfect unity with itself. Hegel distinguishes three types of religion: the Oriental religions represent the divine too objectively, as nature; the Greeks turn to *art* to find an embodiment of their religious intuitions, emphasizing above all the human body as an expression of the ultimate principle assuming an objective form; *revealed religion* achieves the highest summit, for it realizes that the ultimate reality is spiritual, even though its imaginative representation of the presence of God in humanity, of the universal in the particular, namely the image of the one God-Man still fails to penetrate to the real unity of God and man in the whole course of history. Christianity too literally reduces history to a supreme moment. Only the philosophy of the Absolute Spirit enjoys the freedom to go beyond the God-Man to a grasp of the true presence of the Absolute Spirit in history as the "divine universal Man."

hegel's posterity

The preceding miniature survey of the topography of the Hegelian philosophy cannot begin to suggest the wealth of dialectical interweavings of positive matter it achieves. (It required twelve pages for Findlay to set down the topic headings of the main dialectical movements of Hegel's major works.) By concentrating our discussion on the problem of the "positivity" of the moments, best seen in the *Phenomenology*, and on a summary of the higher synthesis of the System, the realization of Concrete Spirit, where the sense in which Hegel conceives the anterior moments of spirit's development to be preserved is most clearly illustrated, we have admittedly been studying the problem of Hegel's philosophy as introduction to the viewpoint dominating the tradition of philosophy—which is the subject of this section. If we have neglected to enter into any detail concerning Hegel's philosophy of nature, or into the very abstract movement of the most idealistic moments of the *Logic*, it is not because we esteem them insignificant, but rather because we have had to limit ourselves to bringing out the central movement in a way which makes the actual posterior historical developments comprehensible.

In summary then let us sketch the sense of that movement again and then offer a schematic suggestion of how the most important later figures in this tradition will react to it. That will furnish our story its frame.

Because transcendental philosophy realizes that our experience is made up of representations (*Vorstellungen*), it is incumbent upon phenomenology to make clear the evidence, interior to that experience, for the "otherness" of the object, in the sense that it is not reducible to the finite consciousness knowing it but rather presents itself as in some way "thrown-over" against it, i.e., as *ob-jectum*. The Hegelian construing of the ultimate ground of experience as "*absolute Wissen*" had the merit, as we saw, of protecting "being" from dissolving in the voluntarism with which existentialist theories will flirt when they emphasize the creativity of human will as source of values and "sense" in experience. But it has the gross inconvenience of making it hard to understand why the "object" is not simply once and for all absorbed into the infinite absolute spirit. All of the idealist suggestions about spirit having to externalize itself in order "to recover itself" seem unconvincing, especially as long as it is not made clear how and why the moments retain some autonomy in the final synthesis, when spirit has already realized itself.

Faced with this problem, Feuerbach and then Marx dispel all hesitation; they suppress all suggestion of an ideal "absolute." In their systems, "being," i.e., given material nature, becomes the unequivocal source of all consciousness. The Marxists will then start with the objective givenness of the thing, "out there," and hence have no difficulty explaining why for us it is opaque, and why we have to struggle with it, work on it, transform it practically, in order to penetrate its mysteries. On the contrary, their problem will be to explain how a consciousness which is merely the "superstructure" of a material nature can assume initiative in guiding the transformations of that nature.

Nietzsche also eliminates the absolute, replacing it with the individual finite will as giver of value. But he does not, as Marx did, emphasize the material status of what men have wrought, that is, of the things, the institutions, the languages in their reality *en soi*. There are suggestions of this, of course, but they get drowned out by fervent hymns to creativity. For Nietzsche recognizes that the supreme problem of transcendental philosophy is accounting for the origin

I. *Post-Kantian Background* 49

of the originative element—what is really *new*—in each forward step within the transcendental horizons. Because the element of otherness—of a reality existing in itself upon which creativity can draw—is not emphasized, Nietzsche is finally led to absolutize the historical in the extraordinary doctrine of the "eternal return of the like."

In Heidegger's philosophy there is evident both an effort to underscore the recognition of a certain "otherness"—the element of what history has already accomplished, things already given a sense by human creativity—and an effort to acknowledge honestly the strangeness of the truly creative element. It comes, declares Heidegger, from nothing.

But ultimately, we shall be forced to ask, have any of these philosophers—including even the French phenomenologist, Maurice Merleau-Ponty, who tries hardest to emphasize Marx's discovery of the need to see being sedimented, materialized in an intersubjective reality enjoying some status *en soi*—succeeded essentially any better than Hegel in giving transcendental philosophy substance, in solving the dilemmas that arise when being is said to come out of spirit? Ultimately the student of contemporary European philosophy is led to inquire most profoundly into the basic sense of the transcendental viewpoint as such.

That is what makes Husserl so interesting: No one has explored so systematically, so radically, what it means to say there are "transcendental horizons of experience." Husserl and Hegel, then, are the pivotal *dramatis personae* of all post-Kantian philosophy; Hegel, because nothing approaches the *Phenomenology*'s rich vision of the intertwining existential themes as they appear to transcendental philosophy—here is truly the sourcebook par excellence of phenomenological materials; Husserl, because he has come closest to giving us a sense of what is necessary methodically to unravel them.[53]

Marxism-Leninism

dialectical materialism

From his studies of Hegel, Karl Marx[54] became convinced that in the dialectic, the law of the opposition of "contradictory" forces, Hegel had discovered the mainspring of history. Moreover, the relationship exemplified by the master-slave dialectic described in the *Phenomenology* struck Marx as holding the key to the very nature of human intercourse[55]: Men are not related immediately, the way two pure spirits would be, but mediately, through nature, of which the individuals and groups of individuals are themselves real moments. But what must be emphasized is the *reality* of that relationship: The individual's active confrontation of nature, his efforts to carve out of it for himself an *Umwelt*, is no mere ideal shuffling of concepts, but a real material struggle; *work* (already accorded a central role in the *Phenomenology*) is, after all, nothing more than the effort to form what is given in nature in order that it may conform to my interiorly felt and compelling needs. It was the effort to transform nature to conform to innate *natural* human impulses that brought men together in primitive societies. It is in the historical development of the forms of society, mediated by men's common transformation of nature, that we must seek to understand how men are today related, why groups of them are in conflict, and what form their struggle must take.

From the moment the young Marx conceived of the dialectical struggle between classes of men as a real struggle mediated through the material transformation of a nature unequivocally irreducible to idea, he was convinced that he had found the key to surpassing the problems and equivocations of Hegelian idealism; the dialectic could now be turned "right side up" and "put back on its feet"; dialectical *materialism* would derive idea from "being" (i.e., the givenness of nature) rather than "being" from "idea."[56] With "materialism" as his starting point, Marx could cut through all the equivocations surrounding the Hegelian notion of "nature"; exorcised once and for all, as Feuerbach suggested, is the slightest suggestion that some force above and beyond nature—be it God or be it simply "Idea"—is the source of the sense of nature. The very movement of the dialectic itself is now conceived "realistically" as the clash of forces incarnated in the extramental givenness of an objective social situation. Marx would then solve the central problem of Hegel's philosophy, that of securing some sort of convincing status for the "moments" in the dialectic by conceding to the basic ones a *material* reality: they are outside one another temporally and spatially, related as an opposition of real forces, negating one another in a struggle that has as its outcome a smelting in which limits are negated by being physically subsumed and really eradicated. The conflict in Hegel's *Phenomenology* is always more an ideal contradiction—for him, "alienation"—i.e., the fact that

I. Post-Kantian Background 51

the results of our nature-forming work are "out there" in the world and are no longer strictly mine is "*aufgehoben*" simply through recognition of the idea and its synthesis in a higher ideal unity; but Marx reminds us that exploited human beings will only cease seeing the results of their efforts taken away from them when they change the system, not ideally but materially, by themselves taking the means of production under control.

But what are these real material forces recognized by Marx? Why are they related as they are? What is the *sense* of their dialectical movement? Commentators are still struggling to define explicitly (from Marx's political-economic manuscripts, guided by a few suggestions in his early philosophical fragments) the underlying ontological-epistemological essence of the relationship between "forces of production" (*Produktionskräfte*) and "production relations" (*Produktionsverhältnisse*) (in conflicting disproportion in capitalist society) on the one hand, and the "superstructure" (Überbau) of juridical and ideological notions which crown a society and exercise a guiding influence on its development, on the other. Many of these discussions, however, fail to take Marx's "Hegelianism" seriously enough and thus miss the true center of the problems which Marx's "materialization" of the dialectic in its turn generates: that center is nothing less than the pivotal problem of recent German philosophy—the problem of the relationship between thing and idea as it is renewed through the transcendental version of "intentionality."

When he began his meditation by a "reversal" of the already existing Hegelian dialectic and with the social struggle clearly at the forefront of his attention, Marx was in fact concerned with relations between "practical" man and the nature he transforms and those between man and man through the mediation of that "worked" nature. In most of Marx's manuscripts, despite the heavy accent he lays on the *objective* aspect of the structures and forces he is describing, he keeps dealing in fact with social-economic relations that enjoy an overwhelming coefficient of intentionality. The "forces of production," for instance, are more than factories and machines taken as so many *things*. They are, rather, *ideas* of organization and "incarnations" of technical *ideas* in the machines themselves; the "production relations" are goals the "exploiting class" set for themselves and the servile acceptance by the "oppressed" class of the position they are being forced into (Hegel had already underscored the "fear of death" which makes the slave a slave); they are the cumulative results of past decisions which, once entered into, leave no issue precisely because the "exploiting class" will not give up what has become their vested interests.

As long as Marx was concerned with such *intentionally* explicable phenomena, the dialectic could continue to offer the spectacle of "*Wieder-spruche*" *contradictions* resolving themselves in a synthesis in which the *ideal proportion* of the moments of the dialectic is clearly manifest. We can see how central is the *intentionality* of the dialectic in the very objections Marx opposes to "the old materialism." Lenin, in a famous article on Marx, sums them up in three points: (1) The old materialism was "preponderately mechanical"; (2) it was "non-historical"; and (3) it had only an "abstract" notion of the human essence, failing to grasp it as "the ensemble of social relations."[57] The superiority of the dialectic in all three respects is ultimately explicable only in terms of the interpenetration of idea and thing, of the ability of a consciousness to grasp the sense of a real development. The culminating point in Marx's own construction of history is the revolutionary *class consciousness*. While this "*Bewusstsein*" is not merely ideal—not merely an ego's grasp of its own *Vorstellungen*, but its living, practical awareness of material limits and real opposing forces (whether natural or voluntary-social)—and hence has unequivocally broken with the tradition of German *idealism*, it is, nevertheless, a *consciousness of*; and what it is conscious of, in the class struggle, is no absolutely foreign thing but is rather the value of the subject's own work and the alienation of it because of his *acceptance* of certain historically developed social relations. The big difference from Hegel does not lie in the need merely to become aware of those social relations which in fact really limit the existent—that remains true for Marx as well as for Hegel—but rather in Marx's realization that that consciousness is not enough by itself to change them and thus to explain history's movement, for those relations themselves are *real*, not ideal. Hence only real, revolutionary action can suppress them; only in the order of *praxis* can man be led to the liberation of the classless society. The essence of Marx's notion of the "materialism" of the dialectic lies there.

Notwithstanding this reality, this *materiality*, the relations Marx had in mind when he combated materialist mechanism, when he emphasized the historical and the social nature of the class struggle, is the relationship between a knowing-willing subject and another knowing-willing subject mediated through their common interest in the objects transformed by their work and

I. Post-Kantian Background

expropriated by their conscious appropriating action. That Marx's insights in precisely this sphere—that of the social-historical relations of real incarnate existents whose intentions are, through their corporeal acts, out in things— were profound and original, the whole later development of phenomenological existentialism will prove. We shall consider the efforts of a Max Scheler and a Maurice Merleau-Ponty to save them from a materialism rendered narrow by Feuerbachian, anti-German idealism and antibourgeois religious prejudices.

"infrastructure" and "superstructure"

In the philosophical fragments of 1844,[58] in which the young Marx first formulated his objections to Hegelian idealism and his acceptance of the dialectic, it is striking how exclusively he is concerned with the problem of turning Hegel right side up. The result is that the intentional opposition of consciousness and object of consciousness there clearly commands, and with that reciprocal interpenetration characteristic of Hegel's intentional analyses; but the emphasis, of course, is now all on nature: Man is a natural essence; as such he has natural objects. That is to say that hunger, for instance, bestows interest in food, makes of food an ob-jectum, and thus brings things, *insofar as they are edible*, within the circle of the man's (or the animal's) interest. Marx *suggests*, by means of a fragment of description, that such a natural relationship need not even be conscious, indeed that it must presuppose nonconscious pairings-off on the lower levels of nature. "The sun is the *ob-ject* of the plant—to it indispensable, life-permitting object, as the plant is object for the sun, as exteriorization [Äusserung] of the life-awakening power of the sun, of the *objective* essential power of the sun."[59] This "Äusserung" is not incidental to the sun, but is the very essence of its "*Tätigkeit*," of its *objective* activity, just as man's "Äusserung" through his work is not incidental, but is his very reality as objective activity. However, man's, unlike other activity, is a *human praxis*. What is it that distinguishes human from all other activity? It is man's ability to reflect; for he is a *"für sich selbst seiendes Wesen, darum Gattungsavesen"*[60]—an essence existing *for* itself, and therefore an essence *aware* of its kind—a *social* essence, the properly human object of which is historical: what man has "exteriorized" is not immediately forgotten, is not *absolutely* other, but can be remembered and therefore can become the object of his desires in an effort to reappropriate to himself what has been perhaps not only "exteriorized" (*entäussert*) but *alienated* (*entfremdt*).

Marx largely leaves the matter at that. Friedrich Engels took it on himself (apparently, as he claims, with the complete approbation of his friend and collaborator) to develop some of the implications of the materialist dialectic. Unfortunately, neither of Engels' philosophical works addresses itself directly to the crucial, pivotal ontological-epistemological problem—the relationship of the "real" and the "ideal" poles in intentional "Being-in-the-world." However, in both the *Anti-Dühring* of 1873 and the unfinished *Dialektik der Natur* (on which Engels worked for ten years, until about 1883), what began as a suggestion of Marx's is now the central concern of Engels: to explain not only intentional relations, but all the relationships of nature, in terms of the dialectic—not just the relationship between the material conditions of a social class and its consciousness of those conditions, but the relations between a seed, the mature plant, and the next generation of seeds; or between earth strata and subsequent metamorphized formations; or between phenomena of electromagnetism; or between purely mathematical concepts. The matters considered burst all the bounds of the *intentional* dialectic.

When Lenin addresses himself in his unfinished work, *Materialism and Empirio-criticism*, to the task of working out some of the epistemological problems involved in the earlier suggestions that our ideas (from class awareness through philosophy to religion and art) are a mirroring (*Wie der Spiegelung*) of the real relationships of the natural and social-historical-material dialectics, there are already visible signs that the practical politician, who knows that ideas have to lead history, is concerned that theory be given its due, not as mere epiphenomenon, but as the very element of awareness in history, and hence as *guide*. This same advisability of avoiding "vulgar materialism's" notion of the ideal "mirroring" as merely a servile copy of sensed reality and of developing a theory of knowledge which can justify a leadership class's notion of "vision" has obviously made itself felt in the most sustained Marxist epistemological-ontological effort, that of the recent official Soviet ideological handbooks, *Principles of Marxist Philosophy* and *Principles of Marxism-Leninism*, written "socially" by a group of Soviet thinkers under the leadership of F. W. Konstantinow.[61] This realization, along with the need (incumbent neither on Marx, Engels, nor even on Lenin when, prior to becoming leader of a regime and hence official schoolmaster of a land, he wrote his principal philosophical works) to *systematize*, to develop the masters' suggestions and explanations, which were limited

I. *Post-Kantian Background*

to selected problems and areas, into a *Summa* capable of providing the principles of a complete intellectual life and a whole political-social program, has obliged the recent Marxist writers in the U.S.S.R. to explicitate implications and to take stands where their predecessors could leave matters on the level of suggestion—which helps us understand where finally the forces and the weaknesses of materialist dialectical realism lie.

The position taken in these official works rejects the "crude materialism" of some earlier Marxists in favor of a more complex stand capable of allowing in the end for some respect for national cultural differences and tending to maximize the role of the leadership group, whose ideas are needed in order to guide the revolutionary society in a development which can no longer, in the light of recent experience (especially Stalinism), be naïvely considered predetermined. In addressing ourselves to these recent handbooks we shall make little attempt to distinguish what is faithful to Marx, what is from Lenin, and what is mere recent innovation. The historical fact being that Marx left so much of the ontology-epistemology underlying his political-social-economic reflections only implicit, the recent efforts cannot be accused of being un-Marxist simply because they go considerably beyond what the founders themselves explicitly authorize. And indeed this systematization is revealing. Some see in it an effort to mold the tradition to fit the present aspirations of the ruling clique. This handling of philosophical problems which interest us, however, reveals a concern with the deep-lying difficulties of the Marxist materialization of the dialectic. The positions taken in the handbooks could be merely the result of an effort to make the most sense philosophically from the solution Marx suggested. It is in this spirit, and for the light they throw on the whole problematic of post-Hegelian philosophy, that we shall turn to these Marxist handbooks.

the origin, end, and freedom of ideas

"Vulgar materialism," which would make of consciousness but a slavish copy of Being, itself conceived of as a mechanism of one-way processes building from simpler to more complex unities without any distinct qualitative breaks between levels, is so mechanical, ahistorical, deterministic because it has not grasped the ground-principle of reality, its *dialectical* nature. Marxism-Leninism remains materialistic; idealism in every form is rejected, and the dependency of the higher forms of life on the lower as irreducible steps in their development is unequivocally affirmed; but because it is not only materialistic but also dialectical, it recognizes that matter of its very nature is not just in motion, but in motion dialectically, which is to recognize that every force is mirrored in a contrasting force, which relationship leads to their synthesis in a truly higher form; this qualitatively superior stage, while it could not come to be without the lower, enjoys, nevertheless, its own peculiar kind of mirroring. To limit our illustrations to the highest level of the dialectic, that of human consciousness, we see, for instance, that while the physiology of the human brain could not be without the complex chemical development of its cells and tissues, its peculiar operations are not describable uniquely in either chemical or electrical terms; and while human thought could not be without the prior development of the brain, and even now cannot survive its being damaged; and while certain very general correlations can be made between the topography of thought and that of the brain, "consciousness, thought, possesses no physical properties," it cannot be "seen, touched, or measured."[62] One may agree with Lenin that "consciousness is an inner condition of matter,"[63] but one must then see that it "is not something material" (*nicht Etwas materielles*).[64] To say otherwise would be to undermine the possibility of the existence of what we have called, in the language of the phenomenologists, the whole intentional order, and what the Marxists term "the relative independence of the superstructure"; it would render inexplicable the existence of the error of "idealism"; it would overlook the very central discovery of the Marxist "reversal" of Hegel: that reality does not pre-exist in idea, but rather that, through work, through *praxis*, we must bring our ideas to conform to over-new reality.

We shall better understand the nature of a truth relationship which conceives of idea at once as growing out of the material situation of men and yet as having to be brought through practice to conform to reality if we consider more systematically the development of the consciousness-reality relationship from the fundament—sense knowledge—up to the higher forms such as ideology, religion, art.

The simplest "reflexes" of the lowest organisms—to borrow from the terminology and experiences of the Soviet psychologist, I. P. Pavlov, as Soviet ideologists like to do—can be considered already a real mirror of the surrounding world, in the sense that they are reactions on the part of a natural structure to real influences of the surrounding reality. Now, either the organism's reactions are somehow in keeping with the influences, and thus permit it to win for itself a certain place over against those influences, or it is simply overrun by them, and thus ceases to enjoy an independent existence. "Conditioned reflexes" are a higher, more flexible development in which the reaction to the influence is that of a more developed structure, able to retain some results of an experience, and thus to take the present influence as a *sign* of something more than is actually present in this objective moment of influence. Thus, when the hen sees the light which before signaled the possibility of obtaining grain, she reacts to that renewed presence in view of obtaining the grain, which itself is not actually sensibly present. Such a higher sensing organism is able to extend its dialogue with the surrounding world beyond the strictest objective limits of the here and now given sensory stimulus. This wider range into time and space mirrors things more truly; that is to say, it permits a fuller reaction to a richer scope of reality.[65]

In the human consciousness we discover a still higher power, of decisive significance, that of *symbolization*, separating man forever from the animal once this qualitatively higher development had been achieved. Marxist speculation concerning how this came about, despite its extremely hypothetical (if not to say gratuitous) nature, is interesting for the light it throws on the Marxist interpretation of the central notion of *praxis*. It must have been that for climatic reasons a family of higher anthropoids was compelled to descend from their natural place of protection—the trees—and fend for themselves as a band, with only the meager natural protection provided by their agile fore-members and hands. The mobile, transforming power of these they learned to extend through the use of instruments, and, as they banded together for survival, they learned to coordinate with this new use of instruments a crude but already developing system of social communication. Senses, instrumentation, work, speech, social coexistence developed slowly together in a complex dialectic requiring that for every progress in each area—especially in those areas affecting the whole material situation of the proto-society, such as the discovery of new means of forming the *Umwelt* to fit a sense of developing needs—the others be brought up to the level of the new, real possibility this created, in order for progress to continue. The improvement of speech and the resultant improvement in social communication made possible the fuller exploitation of new tools and newly discovered means of production. These in turn brought men into richer contact with things on a broader scale, which opened the possibility for more adequate sensing, offered the challenge of more to talk about, and called for the development of more complex ideas, which in turn suggested further developments in the basic working contact with the world—that is, in new means of production.

From this description, it is clear that while the ultimate dependence of the ideal superstructures on the material, practical contact with the surrounding world is such that the superstructures cannot be expected to advance beyond it to such a point that they are no longer traceable in any way to the material situation, still, on the other hand, the ideal superstructures are not, to the Marxists, mere copies, without a life of their own, and hence without signification for the progress of the social-economic-political situation. Engels once protested vigorously:

> According to the materialist historical conception production and the reproduction of real life is *in the final analysis* [italics Engels'] the decisive moment. Marx never affirmed more than that. Now when one would twist that to mean that the economic factor is the *only* decisive one, he deforms the principle into a dumb, abstract, absurd phrase. The economic situation is the base, but the different moments of the superstructure—political forms of the class struggle and their results—constitutions established after victory by the winning class, etc.—forms of law and the reflections of all these real struggles in the heads of the participants, political, juristic, philosophical theories... [are in] interplay [with it], so that it is in the final analysis through the infinite manifold of accidents that finally the economic movement manifests itself as necessary.[66]

Later Marxist theorists explain the possibility of such a dialectical interplay between an ideal superstructure on the one hand and the practical-sensible-material dialectic between the active individual and his social situation on the other through recourse (as we have suggested) to a later Pavlovian conception, that of a level of consciousness, proper only to man, which we may designate the "signal of the signal."[67] This is a reference to the human symbolic power as the summit of abstraction—the ability to detach whole complex relationships from the limiting concrete circumstances of their first historical occurrence in order to apply them to other situations, different perhaps in every way

I. *Post-Kantian Background* 59

from the first, except in the one circumstance: that of the abstracted relation itself. The audacity of the abstraction makes it possible to push past the surface, more concrete, sensible manifestations of things to the deeper currents joining things—the more ultimate causes, the influence of which spreads through vaster spans of time and space[68]; but it also increases the possibility and the scope of error, for the wider the ideas range beyond the here-and-now givens of this concrete object, the freer they leave us to mold the future but also to *misapply* them again to the material situation, to "Being."

Praxis is, then, not only the concrete origin of the superstructures, it is the end to which they must be destined; what is most important, it is supplier of the criteria of their truth. Given that ideas, once born of a "material" situation, can lead something of a life of their own, surviving after the concrete situation which gave rise to them has ceased altogether to exist, interacting with other ideas and ideological systems originated in other moments of history or in other contemporary societies; and given that ideas penetrate more or less deeply into the natures of things and the realities of situations; it is evident that the only criterion, ultimately, for their validity will be their successful application through real *praxis*—work, experimentation, social change.

In this work of realization, the role of individuals is decisive but the individuals themselves are interchangeable. No individual can essentially affect the basic principles of social existence, nor even prove absolutely indispensable to a vast historical movement rooted in the basic givens of human nature and the deepest historical structures of a society; but even in the great historical social movements, the individual can contribute to speeding up the process or he can exercise a reactionary, retarding effect. Someone had to invent Pythagoras' theorem or geometry would have been stillborn; but had there never been a Pythagoras, eventually someone else would have discovered what he discovered; and had the greatest of the leaders of the workers' movement, Marx, Engels, Lenin, not appeared on the scene when they did, others would have unveiled the laws operative in the given social situation, if only later and perhaps less clearly. The fact of personal authority exists, but it should not be abused, as it was in the Stalinist cult of personality.[69] Great individuals, for all their importance, are expendable—at least replaceable; this strongly suggests that progress, though depending entirely on man's initiative, is ultimately inevitable. Can man then in any meaningful sense be said to be free?

The Marxist notion of freedom, which Engels had already formulated and which the authors of the official Handbooks strongly underscore, is not too far from Hegel's. The individual is not absolutely compelled by nature to bring his ideas into active contact with the real situation through work; but when he does not, he is indeed not free; rather he is darkly commanded, without his recognizing it, by the reality of *what is*. In contrast, he who strives to grasp the deeper laws so that he may co-operate with them and further their application everywhere and by all members of the great human society alone enjoys true freedom. Engels wrote:

> With the seizure of the means of production by society is the production of mere wares discontinued and therefore the domination of the product over the producer.... The objective, foreign powers, which until now have dominated history, come under the control of man himself. Only from that point on can men with full awareness take their history in hand, only from that point on will the social causes which he has set in motion start to have preponderantly, and to a steadily increasing degree, the effects he wanted them to have. That is the leap of mankind out of the kingdom of necessity into that of freedom.[70]

Freedom is thus no state of mind, the free man is not he who can escape into the realm of spirit. It serves no purpose to have *belles idées*, nor to direct social, even revolutionary movements, unless one can succeed in harnessing the actual material situation, allowing man to command the very productive processes he has earlier instituted instead of being commanded by them. The revolutionaries of 1848 had beautiful ideas of freedom, indeed they knew what they wanted and what they needed, but they did not scientifically command the laws of the situation and thus were not able to bring about freedom.

Here, then, is the key to the errors of "opportunism" and "revisionism": obtaining small alleviations of suffering and unhappiness often succeeds in merely shifting the suffering elsewhere—to a less privileged group of workers, or to colonialized workers whose conditions grow worse—thus tending to obscure, for those favored, the underlying economic laws and retarding the day when the necessary essential changes will permit a rational command of the basic forces which hold back the general development of all mankind.

I. *Post-Kantian Background*

All this should begin to suggest the major difficulty encountered by Marxist theory: the problem of ideas having to guide the development of the very material conditions from which these ideas alone can be born. This paradox confronts all realisms[71]; and the Marxist suggestion that this historical (and social) limitation of our ideas is fundamental evidence against idealism is also quite sound. But once it is put forward as explicitly as the Marxists have put it, the explicit affirmer assumes the burden of explaining not only the genesis of our ideas in a sensible experience of nature, but what it means to affirm that human social-political-economic relationships are "objective," that the results of human work are alienated in nature, and that these things should be taken back under our voluntary control. These problems—reducible essentially to one, that of understanding how intentional acts are incarnated (*"verkörpert"*)[72] in nature, whether as speech, as institutions, or as the products of work—rejoin us again to the whole tradition we are studying. Husserl's "idealism," like Hegel's, will struggle with the problem of explaining how intentionality can penetrate things and how ideas can have their origin in forms incarnated in matter without being reduced to a mere copying of them. Sartre will seek to avoid the problems posed by the materialist solution by making of the consciousness (the *"pour soi"*) an essentially negative creative principle which forms literally from *nothing* the negations separating things. Heidegger to this very moment continues to try to weave into one explanation the fact of the reality of the things that are (*die Seienden*) and the creative-interpretative, history-founding act of the existent. The Marxists enjoy much company in their embarrassments at this critical, pivotal point.

What is especially disturbing about Marxism in this regard, however, is that Marx, armed only with his not very highly developed suggestions about turning Hegel back on his feet, proceeded to develop a complex social-economic-political theory for which a precise ontological-epistemological justification was lacking. Efforts of subsequent generations of Marxists to build explicit philosophical foundations beneath the vast economic-political-social theory they inherited as a ready-made ideology have led to the sort of speculations we have been reading in the official handbooks. The inadequacies of these *Summae* are explicable on these two grounds: (1) The problems of class, institution, "social morphology"—in a word, the problems of our "Being-in-the-world," as the existentialist philosophers put it very well—being as they are at the very heart of much of recent philosophical speculation and forming the very subject matter of new and rapidly evolving disciplines, sociology and social psychology, are not ripe for "once and for all" solution.[73] Anyone obliged by circumstances at this point to write *Summae dialecticae* to justify a comprehensive political ideology is consequently bound to leave his gaps showing. (2) The last remark is not meant as an implied wholesale criticism of the philosophical endeavor to lay down, on the basis of insights into the fundamental relations between knower and known, between "truth" and "Being," the principal, indeed the transcendental guides for phenomenological and "scientific" investigation of the various, particular, "essential" relations interior to the discovered fundamental conditions of experience. But it has become apparent to all, in the course of the one hundred and fifty years of the transcendental philosophical tradition, that a flexible *va-et-vient* between philosophical theory and the results of detailed, indeed positive, investigations is necessary to the healthy progress of both. Uncritical neopositivist prejudices on the one side, and something like the Marxist (or, for that matter, the Fascist) Party vested interests on the other, harden the scientific arteries and complicate a living exchange between these interdependent *levels* of reflection. The difficult problems (revealingly investigated by the phenomenologists and by the neo-Thomists) of the relationship between *Glauben und Wissen*—to borrow Hegel's title—including the fact that no human existence is, or can be, carried out without some form of *belief*, if but philosophical,[74] are multiplied a hundredfold when a group of believers are in position to impose their ideology through the instruments of the modern technical-totalitarian state. It is this peculiar position of official Soviet Marxism which accounts for its present form and which makes dialogue with it humanly very difficult—just as it is difficult for a liberal Spanish intellectual to dialogue "scientifically" with Thomism in Madrid.

As we have confined our discussion of Marxism to the analysis of the ontological-epistemological background of the dialectic, with emphasis on its intentional origin, and to the later Marxist efforts to elaborate an epistemology which avoids the determinism of earlier materialisms (and of some earlier Marxists), instead of launching into a long inventory of the gaps between social-political-economic ideology and the philosophical justification thus far developed for it, or of the unanswered questions and hastily assembled explanations in the structure of that philosophical endeavor itself—a task that has already been

I. *Post-Kantian Background*

carried out patiently and thoroughly by others[75]—we shall content ourselves here with an indication of other developments given major Marxist ideas.

Max Scheler, for one, under the influence of Max Weber, conceded to Marxism that the real burden of historical ideas—their vital importance—can be understood only in terms of the whole social-economic situation with which they were interwoven. But, at the same time, he showed that this material relationship can exist and be important, without demanding that the question of the *truth* of the idea be reducible to it. Such a position evidently implies that the real structures grasped by our knowledge are involved in the historical movement, but does not imply that they be reducible to it. A good deal of the philosophical effort of the twentieth century, outside of neopositivist circles, will be devoted to developing the evidence for the existence of such structures, plagued neither with the immobilism and innatism of the Kantian categories nor the relativism of mere moments in a purely historical dialectic.[76] Scheler challenges the Marxist position to its roots with his further contention that no system of economic laws has ever itself been independent of ideas and valuations.[77] In place of Marx's and Engels' "in the final analysis the decisive factors in history are the economic relations," Scheler argues for a more complex dialectic of idea and objective relationship allowing no such decision "in the final analysis." He agrees with Marx that all "ideas" are derived from "being"—in this sense, that "all higher principles and forms of reason can be traced back to a functionalizing of already-grasped forms of being"[78]—but, unlike Marx, he would not reduce "being" to only *material* being, but would insist on a much more complex analysis of "the whole being of men." The details and justification of this more complex notion of Being will be discussed in the chapter on Scheler.

Perhaps the most penetrating criticism of the ambiguities of the Marxist position have been advanced by a French phenomenologist, Maurice Merleau-Ponty, who not only has never hidden his debt to Marx's inspiration, but has made meditation on incarnation—that is, how an intention can be "out there" in the world—the very center of his concern. Indeed, it is because he has succeeded with the help of Husserl and Heidegger in penetrating to the *fundamental* ontology underlying the whole discussion of the social psychologists and the Marxist dialecticians that Merleau-Ponty is able to expose the impossible problems raised by the objectivism of the Marxist theory, which sees in a social class the necessary bearer of historical destiny. The essence of Merleau-Ponty's criticism consists in showing that the historicity of human existence, represented by the march of the dialectic, is ontologically irreconcilable with the notion that the *negativity* of the dialectic be incarnated *objectively* in a social class. Analysis of the role of negativity in the human existent's Being-in-the-world is carried by Merleau-Ponty beyond Heidegger and beyond Sartre, and the possibility of the *incarnation* of negatively originated intentions is turned against not only the thing-like status Marx accords the proletariat but against all would-be unambiguous thing-like postulations.[79]

Marx's main effort was to counteract the ideal tendencies of the Hegelian viewpoint, but the materialism he opposed to it tends itself to remain an idea, indeed an ideology; the existentialists' suggestion is to oppose to Hegelian idealism the individual and his existential principle. Before we trace the origins of this endeavor to the extremely unsystematic philosophies of Kierkegaard and Nietzsche, we must consider one more system, in the strict sense of the term. Schopenhauer's philosophy provides the spectacle of a classical German system that would solve all the problems of Kant, Fichte, and Schelling through a methodical exploitation of, indeed virtually a deduction from, the *notion* of will. Nietzsche discovered the possibilities of voluntarism in Schopenhauer's philosophy. Through Nietzsche, this last of the great systematizers has come to influence recent German philosophy.

Arthur Schopenhauer

the world as will and presentation

Marx's dialectical-materialist realism was neither the only nor even the first effort to circumnavigate the idealism of the post-Kantian philosophical tradition. As a matter of fact, the primacy of reason had been challenged unceasingly since the heyday of the *Aufklärung* by the broad literary movement, the very varied creators of which one customarily gathers in the vague category of "romantics." Even Kant was deeply influenced by the greatest of the early "romantics," J.-J. Rousseau, and there is a very real sense in which Kant's efforts in the last *Critique* to ground the ultimate synthesis of pure and practical reason in aesthetic intuition is an *anti-Aufklärung*, antirationalist influence.[80]

I. *Post-Kantian Background*

Hegel, for his part, sought to cut the ground from under all the various efforts to substitute for philosophy some form of direct intuitive, *felt* relationship to a non-rational, indeed a *dark* absolute principle by showing that darkness is nothing, that the light of reason is one with Being's recuperation of itself, that intuition, precisely to the extent it is immediate, is incomplete in its self-possession, that subject and object must stand off from one another in order for re-flection to be possible in the first place, and that the whole struggle to bring the subject into an ever more adequate rational possession of an object that is at first simply given in its op-position is nothing more than the coming to be of the Absolute Ground itself. In analyzing Marx we saw what it was about Hegel's endeavor that failed to convince all his successors that the problem of the relationship between reason and that "other" which is the object—in Hegel's case, the *moments* through which reason passes—had been adequately dispatched: The status of those moments and of any otherness, once spirit has achieved full self-possession, is hopelessly ambiguous, as is the teleological role of Absolute Spirit in the historical-dialectical process prior to its final realization.

Arthur Schopenhauer[81] was convinced that the difficulty lay in Hegel's prejudice in favor of reason; despite his effort to make a large place for struggle, for opposition, for *temporary* darkness, one cannot escape the feeling that Hegel supposes reason somehow to know in advance where the process of its own self-discovery is going, and when it has realized itself, the reality of any opposition seems to lose all significance. Schopenhauer does not for an instant posit outside of experience a "real" or "material" principle, as Marx did (with what consequent problems, we have seen). Schopenhauer felt, rather that the solution lay in as systematic an interpretation of our experience as any the post-Kantian philosophers achieved, but one in which *will*, and not reason, is posited as the absolute principle, and "presentation" (*Vorstellung*) itself is shown to have its ground in the fundamental impulse which itself *is* reality.

In his key work, the title of which provides a neat summary of his major hypothesis, *The World as Will and Presentation*, Schopenhauer begins as a good Kantian who has grasped the superiority of the transcendental viewpoint should, by first considering the world just as it appears to us, that ob-jectum which Kant had the merit of showing to be the consciousness' *Vorstellung* (literally, what the consciousness has *placed* [*stellen*] before [*vor*] itself). The world considered *phenomenally* (that is, as it appears in my consciousness) is presentation (*Vorstellung*); considered noumenally (as thing-in-itself) it is will. The main point of Schopenhauer's reformulation of the Kantian phenomenal world is to show that it is neither the only reality nor the absolute reality. He first shows that every phenomenon is related to reason, meaning that each object can only take its place in the phenomenal world of our consciousness because of some connection with some other object, which connection provides the "sufficient reason" necessary to make the existence of the later object intelligible; he then shows the inability of "reason" to serve as its own ground. The only necessity the things of our experience enjoy, when they are viewed as *phenomena* in our presentified world, is that they make sense in some way, and they make sense because of their meaningful connections with other things. Schopenhauer very cleverly brings out the roles of the forms of space and time and of causality as providing the ultimate source of connection and organization of all the phenomenal objects into a single world. Such a world, Schopenhauer would then point out, cannot, if each thing depends on each other thing, be taken as a whole to be Absolute, nor does it in any way manifest a necessity that would seem to imply the existence of a God.

But even though the phenomenal world of theoretical reason can be shown to be something of an empty round-dance of presentifying consciousness, can we not yet agree with Kant that the *exigencies of practical reason*, that which sets the rules by which things make sense, might point to something of great ontological significance, might indeed hold the key to the reality of the thing-in-itself? Schopenhauer dismisses this possibility with an abrupt objection: There is no proof (nor indeed does Kant even try to offer any) that the ultimate ground of existence and action *is* rational and orderly. In fact, do not those realities of human existence which the idealists have sadly neglected—evil, suffering, death—suggest that whatever it is, the ultimate noumenal principle is other than the orderings of sweet practical reason?

Indeed, could it not be that we find access to the ultimate principle through wonder before the *tragedy* of life, which at times seems to throw into doubt the whole existence of the actual "order," and at the very least renders vain all the presumptuous positivist and naturalist efforts to make life intelligible without probing beyond appearances to find an explanation for the whole of experience? Metaphysics cannot go beyond experience; yet *in* experience it must find more than mere phenomenal appearances and search for the noumenal principle, which, although it cannot be grasped directly in itself, can be read implicated in the phenomena.[82] In a position that anticipates in a striking way Karl Jaspers' "reading of ciphers," Schopenhauer speaks of our discovery of this noumenal core lying behind appearances as the breaking of a code.[83] But where Jaspers will find signs of the transcendent in the insufficiency of the world of experience to account for itself, Schopenhauer searches for the key to his transcendent in a perfectly united account of things, synthesizing the most diverse phenomena, leaving nothing out, demonstrating a marvelous connection between all things. This comprehensiveness and integrity Schopenhauer claims for his own reading of the noumenal nature.

the noumenon as will

The key to the noumenal is man's ability to reflect on his own freedom. How can the way I grasp my own freedom illuminate the essential nature of all the other things that are? The very form of such a question implies that one has forgotten what constitutes a thing. The principle of individuation that permits a distinction of thing from thing is space-time, which grounds phenomenal form. But if space-time itself is purely phenomenal, the noumenal as such must not be differentiated; consequently, whatever can be discovered in our own experience to transcend the phenomenal categories must belong to noumenal being itself and is, therefore, a key to the nature of the thing-in-itself.

Our experience of human freedom is the primordial encounter with the noumenal reality; it is irreducible to and indeed somehow (this needs yet to be shown) supports consciousness. The first thing we notice about it is that its activity is centered in our bodies. Our bodies are both *phenomenal*, insofar as they can be objects for consciousness under the categories of time and space, and *noumenal*, insofar as they are *will* in the process of active objectification. The noumenal reality of my freedom and body reveal themselves as human will and bodily causality, the two forming the interior and exterior aspects of the same manifestation. Remembering our principle that the noumenal is undifferentiated, it must then be true of all things that they are fundamentally constituted of will and causality. Just as causal determinism can be discovered in the very heart of our own free activity, so we can presume that something of the creativity and spontaneity of freedom exists in the heartland of determinism, that is, in material things. The truth of this presumptive leap can be verified by no direct intuition of Being itself, but only by witnessing the extraordinary ability of this presumption, once made, to explain the most conflicting aspects of our experience.

If the world is *will* as well as *presentation*, if the whole world of phenomenality—my ego included as the subjective pole of that world—must be part of the noumenal Being, this rigorously excludes any possibility of reducing the thing-in-itself to a projection of my ego. The cosmic will is not in itself a knowing subject, the distinction between knowing and willing subject applying only to those special kinds of things which, like man, are perceptive; perception itself is only one particular embodiment of the unique fundamental force, the *will-to-live*, which manages various forms for itself within the phenomenal world of possible distinctions in space and time. It is the *will-to-live* which manifests itself in every force, tendency, appetite, attraction, and activity of whatever order, from gravitation to the loftiest reflective act of a human knower.[84]

Schopenhauer was faced with the problem which plagues any philosophy that posits for reality a dynamic first principle: the indisputable evidence of *structure* in the world. Whereas Hegel had found structure to be ultimately a property of the very process of Being itself (the way the motion of the dialectic unfolds being itself *the* law), Schopenhauer had to justify in terms of his own philosophy of will the perennial notion expressed by Plato in his doctrine of ideas, namely that there are objective structures according to which things manifest themselves. These *ideas*, explains Schopenhauer, are nothing but *will* cunningly developing forms of expression for itself which, because of their stability, appear to conquer the eternal flux of will. The victory, however, is only momentary and so not really a victory at all; for—and this Plato began to see by the time he wrote the *Parmenides*—no idea is lasting; on the contrary, each structure acquires its right to stand immobile simply by dominating the flux for a while. But the will-to-life will always burst its own temporary bonds, and newer structures will replace the old. In this way a higher form, the human will, has succeeded at a moment in time in subjugating certain chemical and physical forces to its purposes. Human will as it exists now shows how incomplete its victory is, though; for the lower forces manage to come back to plague the higher as pain, suffering, and finally death.

This inability of will to find a lasting stability in any form, even in the highest, the human will, reveals the deepest secret of noumenal will: it is, in itself, deficient; that, and that alone, is why it is of its very nature struggle. "The basis

I. *Post-Kantian Background*

of all willing is need, deficiency, and thus pain."[85] An important consequence for the ethical life can be drawn from this revelation. Since will comes closest to escaping from its deficiency in forming structure, man's greatest hope lies in contemplating those structures, the *ideas*, in their highest forms. If they can give us even the slightest glimpse of something *beyond will* toward which will may be striving, then "pessimism" may be not without issue.

aesthetic contemplation: negation of will

One of Schopenhauer's permanent contributions to philosophy is that he saw so clearly that a philosophy based on will must inevitably issue in a doctrine of aesthetic contemplation, a necessity which the contemporary existentialists do not always appear anxious to admit too frankly, but to which they are in the end obliged to submit by their very way of looking at things.

In the existentialist philosophies, the accent will be on the existent's aesthetic creation of a history-continuing sense for things in the world. For Schopenhauer the emphasis is rather on transcending the negativities of time and space. He is not yet resigned to seeing the ultimate sense of Being in the purely finite sense-giving of phenomenal will.

In the following passage Schopenhauer describes his notion of an aesthetic contemplation that lifts the knower beyond the immediate tyrannous grasp of the exigencies of the here and now to become the pure contemplating subject lost in the sempiternity of a pure object.

> The transition from the common knowledge of particular things to the knowledge of the Idea takes place suddenly; for knowledge breaks free from the service of the Will as the subject ceases to be merely individual, and thus becomes the pure Will-less subject of knowledge, which no longer traces relations in accordance with the principle of sufficient reason [i.e., according to causal and logical connections], but rests in fixed contemplation of the object presented to it, out of its connection with all others, and rises to it.[86]

Far from being a flight into the empty abstraction of reason, this act, in which subject and object become one concretely, is an intense presence so capable of dominating phenomenal will that it rejects its call to flow along with time, or to stay localized in space.[87] What really happens is that will (in the form of contemplating intelligence) comes to dominate will (in the lower form of particularizing phenomenal perception). Because such contemplation is really "Will knowing itself,"[88] it unfolds on a level superior to that of sufficient reason and needs none of its forms of particularization.

Schopenhauer's descriptions of how the various arts—music, painting, architecture, poetry—rise above the world in their contemplation of the idea provide some of the richest pages of modern aesthetic philosophy,[89] and influenced Nietzsche's youthful work on *The Birth of Tragedy*. Schopenhauer, however, does not hesitate to interpret all artistic phenomena one-sidely in order to favor the ruling idea of his exposition, that aesthetic contemplation provides a way of "negating the Will in its very nature," that is, of escaping from *need*, from the tyranny of the practical and the particular. It is easy to see that music would provide Schopenhauer with his best case, while architecture, subservient as it often is to practical needs, receives the most summary treatment. Schopenhauer, for example, finds the Greek temple a purer art form than the Gothic cathedral because it does not serve to shelter the congregation from the rains and snows of dark Northern skies.

Compelled to construct the peaked roof and the great vaulted spaces dictated by phenomenal will in the form of climate, the Gothic architect turned to useless, ornamental sculpture to fulfill his desire to break the bonds of the particular requirements imposed on him by time and space.[90] Rhythm and rhyme in poetry, being so evidently an expression of the essential temporality of the act of *poesis*, are typical of the phenomena which give Schopenhauer some difficulty.

> I can give no other explanation of their incredibly powerful effect than that our faculties of perception have received from time, to which they are essentially bound, some quality on account of which we inwardly follow, and, as it were, consent to each regularly recurring sound... [thus they] are partly means of holding our attention, and partly they produce in us a blind consent to what is read prior to any judgment....[91]

With this they are dismissed, evidently as having little right to consideration in the realm of ideas.

I. *Post-Kantian Background*

An important thing about this aesthetic doctrine, however, is Schopenhauer's thesis that such contemplation is not an adequate escape from life's realities. Aesthetic release is always temporary. What man needs is a way to neutralize permanently the tyranny of that phenomenal will which grips the world in its all-dominating causal chains, in other words *a way to permanent freedom*.

For the individual, phenomenal person is not naturally free. Only will as thing-in-itself is truly free. "The person is never free…for he is already the determined phenomenon of the free volition of this Will."[92] Man, caught in the chains of phenomenal existence, experiences a sense of choice which gives some illusion of freedom, but "freedom of choice is nothing but the possibility of a thoroughly fought out battle between several motives, the strongest of which then determines it with necessity."[93] Man is determined in many ways. But, if Schopenhauer's definition of acquired character acknowledges man's need to accept the rigid limits of his causally determined limits, it contains too a hidden promise of a sort of release. After explaining that man's *innate* character is the result of the meeting of chains of causality in one time and place, a meeting which provides a set of possibilities and limits for each individual, he goes on to explain that *acquired* character is "nothing but the most perfect knowledge of the unalterable qualities of our own empirical character, and of the measure and direction of our mental and physical powers and thus of the whole strength and weakness of our individuality."[94] This acceptance of my fate at the hands of phenomenal will is really the first step toward independence from its tyranny. Just as the Christians were told that the road to freedom lay in a sincere "Thy Will be done," so Schopenhauer, seeing what previous philosophies failed to see, realized that the road to the negation of the worst effects of will lies in accepting whatever vicissitudes life may have to offer. Declaring of his doctrine that it stands to previous ethical systems as the New Testament to the Old, he explains that previous ethics sought an earthly kingdom, and thus counseled pursuing the illusory hope of the good life, while the New Testament, in a spirit like his own philosophy, revealed the Cross as the way to solidarity with all men through acceptance of human suffering.

The first step toward negation of the will lies in recognizing that will flows through all men, just as it does in my own person, so that the distance separating us is phenomenal rather than an expression of will as ultimate thing-in-itself. Affirming my oneness with all men, I turn to seek justice for all, as well as for myself. As I thus grow to a full realization of conscious will expressing itself through me on an ultra-individual, prephenomenal level, I shall be led to suffer in common with all men the sorrows that arise in their lives from the circumstances in the phenomenal world. Sympathetically (*mit-leiden* means, literally, to suffer with) we comprehend, in an effective union with one another (this is *love*) the nothingness of the phenomenal life which we are all in together.[95] By taking on the sufferings of others, I am saved from being beguiled by the false hopes arising in moments of my own ephemeral pleasure; for if I love all men, I shall be bearing constantly the weight of someone's misery. Such common love and suffering will neutralize sin and malice within the bounds of the effectiveness of our personal responsibility; for these owe their source to the collision of cross-purposes arising from little lives all avid in the pursuit of happiness.[96]

But does not the ascetic renouncement of the pleasures, vain little hopes, and fleeting joys of this life bring the common-suffering denier of the individual will-to-life face to face with sheer nothingness? Indeed it does; the philosopher's vision may be heroic, but it seems also blackly nihilistic. Nowhere does the radical nature of Schopenhauer's pessimism make itself more apparent than in his response to the objection that ascetic withdrawal from life by all men would lead to elimination of man as a phenomenal appearance. He states:

> With the Will's highest manifestation (Man), the weaker reflection of it would also pass away, as the twilight vanishes along with the full light. With the entire abolition of knowledge the rest of the world would of itself vanish into nothing; for without a subject there is no object.... Sacrifice means resignation generally, and the rest of nature must look for its salvation to man who is at once the priest and sacrifice.[97]

Schopenhauer expresses at the very end of *The World as Will and Presentation* the severe shock such a nihilism is bound to produce in its followers. "When our investigation brings us to the point at which we have before our eyes perfect holiness, the denial and surrender of all volition, and thus the deliverance from a world whose whole existence we have discovered to be suffering, this will appear to us a passing away into empty nothingness."[98]

But is nothingness really Schopenhauer's final word? This great pioneer of modern nihilism, in the very last paragraph of his major work, deliberately

I. Post-Kantian Background 73

leaves the impression that the nothing is only philosophy's encounter at its own outer limits with an All lying beyond the nothingness of phenomenal life, and which cannot be named, since it is beyond the world as will or presentation. For not only does Schopenhauer speak of the elimination of the will-to-live as a *grace* and *rebirth*, he points explicitly to the undeniably *positive* character of the saint's mystical experience.[99] Since the denial of will is dependent on will's sudden knowledge of itself, and all knowledge, being determined, cannot simply be intended "but proceeds from the inmost relation of knowing and volition in man and therefore comes suddenly, as if spontaneously from without,"[100] such an event has a cosmic, fateful character pregnant with implications—for the deciphering of which Schopenhauer leaves us no indications. He does say that the state which follows the grace of such neutralization of will by will is so unlike the previous phenomenal life of will that it can only be called, as early Christianity understood, a complete *rebirth*.[101]

> Then, instead of the restless striving and effort, instead of the constant transition from wish to fruition, from joy to sorrow...we shall see that peace which is above all reason, that perfect calm of the spirit, that deep rest...only knowledge remains, the will has vanished.[102]

These obscure hints hardly offset the crushing effect of a systematically arrived-at nihilism. If we ignore the hints and look at the whole we see that the conclusion of Schopenhauer's vision is directly opposed to Hegel's notion that speculation must lead to the fruition of the world; instead, as Schopenhauer sees it, speculation leads us to the nothing and to the realization that philosophy cannot do anything to save the world, for man enjoys no truly free reign over his own destiny.[103] Schopenhauer's philosophy, indeed, is so much the negation of the Hegelian world that, like a photographic negative, it retains all its features transposed from white to black, which only serves to prove to the next generation of philosophers (although remaining in the same general lines of inquiry) the need to go beyond their common starting point. Schopenhauer's vision of the world as will is as *total* as Hegel's vision of Being as absolute idea; genuine freedom is as lost there, gobbled up in consequent necessity-become-antecedent, as it is in the dialectic's predisposing through the present event each subsequent historical step. Despite the inspiration of the notion that the ultimate real principle is will, Schopenhauer's dissolution of the absolute idea contributed nothing directly to the restoration of the lost reality of the individual, who requires a positive sense of his radical givenness and radical uniqueness. This is the task to which Kierkegaard and Nietzsche will turn. Their first step is a radical rejection of the systematization of the classical tradition, to which Schopenhauer too succumbed in making of will a notion from which he would spin out a consequent system for explaining phenomenon and noumenon. If will is indeed the first principle, should not a philosophy of will bear the signs not of the "undifferentiation of the noumenon," but of the dynamism and with it the multiplicity of a *real* voluntary force? We shall see that the existentialists' way is not an easy one, and that the slightest remains of Kantian presupposition will lay for them, too, some deadly traps of nihilism and skepticism.

II. *The Original Existentialist Revolt*

SUCH influential contemporary thinkers as Heidegger and Jaspers consider Kierkegaard and Nietzsche the center of a revolution in Western thought as fundamental as was the "Copernican reversal" which inaugurated the transcendental viewpoint. Because they agree in regarding the Hegelian "System" as ultimate fulfillment of what the *entire* "metaphysical tradition" had been aiming toward since the Greeks, they are bound to regard the existentialist revolt in its efforts to get away from an absolutizing which suspends everything in a system from an infinite ideal (or an absolute will), conceived itself as a super-thing, to be not merely a step beyond Hegel, but a breakthrough beyond the whole "metaphysical" tradition. With Nietzsche's declaration, "God is dead!" we have come, declares Heidegger, to the end of the West's quest *meta-ta-phusika* for an explanation of the Being of the things-that-are; Nietzsche's greatness lies in his discovery of the individual existent as the unequivocal "*lieu*" of historical Being's coming-to-be. His tragedy, according to Heidegger, is that he ultimately would reduce metaphysics to voluntaristic nihilism.

Jaspers also sees in Nietzsche's work, and in Kierkegaard's as well, a successful destruction of metaphysical pretense. Still, a leap with Kierkegaard beyond the suffocating circle of a self-justifying "ethical" philosophy into a *blind* faith in God appears to Jaspers too much like resigning from all traditional problems rather than making real sense of them. And succumbing to Nietzsche is the same as sinking into the "indeterminate, which does not seem to be a substance out of which we can live,"[1] a conclusion Jaspers comes to because he esteems Nietzsche's all-dissolving criticism of the old philosophies to be his main contribution, rather than the construction of the "eternal return" which Nietzsche (unfortunately) erected in their stead.

Even this summary estimate suffices to warn that the remark, "This is not philosophy!"—too often made about existentialist thinkers because they are anti-system—ignores the whole point of the existentialist critique. The sense of the movement lies in its efforts—sporadic and tentative in the two great pioneers—to establish a new kind of philosophizing.

Neither Kierkegaard nor Nietzsche intends to be a *rationalistic metaphysician*; they are indeed calling into question the presuppositions that have dominated the narrow, if not to say peculiar, conception of reason in metaphysics since Descartes. There is a fundamental relevance in their properly *philosophical* criticisms of the tacit presuppositions of such metaphysics, and indeed these criticisms stand as a permanent inheritance of our philosophical tradition, a definite contribution to the quest for being of this tradition. Instead of Schopenhauer's *notion* of will, they offer the *spectacle* of concrete wills seeking in real historical situations to achieve an individual authenticity, to make sense of their actual human lives. The dialectic here ceases to present itself as a general, abstract structure, or even as a conflict of classes; it now manifests itself as the struggle of the individual to impose sense on the opaque and resisting givens of the concrete situation in which, as he grows to self-awareness, he discovers himself already "thrown."

What makes Kierkegaard and Nietzsche the originators of a fresh element in the tradition of transcendental philosophy, rather than either the summit of the new development or the end of the kind of inquiry we have been witnessing in these pages, is precisely the shortcomings of their unmethodical explosions. It was left to a later generation of thinkers to show how the existentialist revaluation of the individual center of initiative offered possibilities for overcoming the *aporias* of traditional metaphysics. But that meant that the later philosophers would have to develop these implications in the light of the indisputable advantages of the transcendental viewpoint's discovery of intentionality. Only a methodically exploited phenomenology of our experience as voluntary-existents-in-a-situation will be able to bring together the insights of Kierkegaard and Nietzsche with the eternal acquisitions accumulated in Hegel's point of view on the "world." Heidegger's greatness is founded in his having seen this need clearly, historically, and in his ability to carry out the task fundamentally, methodically.

The two philosophies we are now going to study seem at first glance very different, Nietzsche's philosophy frankly rooted in the *nothing*, attenuated by the doctrine of the "eternal return of the like," while Kierkegaard frankly tries to move us to leap toward transcendence. Yet both grow out of the same effort to overcome Hegelian idealism, and both retain from the post-Kantian tradition (without perhaps realizing it) the difficulties which plague it and them in the effort, that is never conclusive, to escape totally from the clutches of nihilism. Both Heidegger and Jaspers, in declaring the need to "surpass" the positions of both Nietzsche and Kierkegaard, have in mind the dangers of nihilism inherent in their philosophies. Heidegger's pronouncements on the need to "protect" Being and Jasper's affirmation of the need to read signs of the transcendent in the wreck of finite reality should both be interpreted as positions directed against Nietzschean nihilism and Kierkegaard's irrational leap into religious faith.

Søren Kierkegaard

Probably nowhere is there a more powerful disruption of the tidy Hegelian ethical universe than in Kierkegaard's *Fear and Trembling*.[2] A meditation on the faith of Abraham in the light of his obedience to God's fantastic command to kill Isaac, the hope of all mankind, *Fear and Trembling* analyzes a case in which it is ridiculous to speak of an ego structuring the clear order of its own duty. Abraham's duty is not of his own rational discovering; in fact it is something that he is rigorously incapable of understanding, yet he is ready to do God's will though that which is commanded has no human meaning and calls for the sacrifice of what is more precious than life itself. Abraham's confidence that God will restore Isaac to him displays a humble, loving subordination that contrasts vividly with the vanity of the Hegelian pretension to make everything clear.

He who would *understand* the faith of Abraham must give up his enterprise in despair. Indeed, the very effort to conceive of such things smacks of the "System's" effort to conceive the world—which is itself an act of despair, for it is a refusal to seek salvation in a way consonant with what we really are. To grasp the conception of the human vocation that grounds such a criticism, we must first situate systematic philosophy in Kierkegaard's over-all scheme of existence; this will point out the road beyond the "System," namely the road of *faith*. Only then, from within the city of faith, can we understand the sense in which other forms of existence constitute a sin of despair against the authentic human vocation.

Man without faith, if he is not sunk in the mediocre morass that constitutes the almost subhuman existence of the mass of men, can attempt to build an existence either *aesthetically* or *ethically*. Each way has its attractions, but ultimately both are vain. Not only do the more attractive features of aesthetic existence collide with those of the ethic, both prove themselves internally self-destructive in the long run. Only in faith do these attractive features find an authentic sense; for that which the aesthete and the ethical man both sought in their own ways, the man of faith possesses whole and in a fullness that they have never dreamed of. Kierkegaard's meditations on the dialectic of aesthetics-ethics-faith functionally clarify the truth, "Faith alone can make man whole."

aesthetic man

"Aesthetics does not trouble itself greatly about time; whether in jest or in seriousness, time flies equally fast for it."[3] In *Either/Or*, Kierkegaard incarnates his conception of this kind of existence in the figures of Don Juan and Johannis the Seducer, and this so vividly—Mozart's music looms magically in the background, and there hangs about his hero, as about the diary of the seducer, an aura of fascination—that one feels the attraction, for that brilliant mind in an unattractive body, of just this form of inauthentic existence. Written to explain to Regina Olsen the deep reasons for his flight from their engagement, *Either/Or* speaks of the temptations of seduction with, something other than academic detachment.

Johannis the Seducer builds and schemes to enjoy the rapture of the instant; and when the instant comes, the fruit of his desire is destroyed, leaving nothing bur a memory. (Of course, before his conquest of the charming Cordelia was completed, the seducer had made mental note of the arrival of fresh material on the scene.) The only way he can mold disparate instances into the continuity of a life is to retain them in his diary. But this in itself is deadly:

> There is nothing more dangerous to me than remembering. The moment I have remembered some life-relationship, that moment it ceased to exist. People say that separation tends to revive love. Quite true, but it revives it in a purely poetic manner. The life that is lived wholly in memory is the most perfect conceivable, the satisfactions of memory are richer than any reality and have a security no reality possesses. A remembered life-relationship has already passed into eternity, and has no more temporal interest.[4]

II. *The Original Existentialist Revolt*   79

The eternity of memory is the graveyard of the instant—and the very antipode of that authentic eternal which gives sense and hope to temporal existence. Johannis the Seducer seeks being in the particular, in which respect he is closer to the truth than the "universal man" of the ethical sphere; but the way he seeks it is tragic, for he would seize it *immediately*, here and now and by his own power, as though it were some object under his control. But he discovers that he cannot possess the woman in her particularity for all time; he can only ravish her. He who would possess the present by his own power soon finds that his hope is in the past; it lies in memory. "I can describe hope," writes the poet-seducer, "so vividly that every hoping individual will acknowledge my description; and yet it is a deception, for while I picture hope, I think of memory."[5] And memory's ground is sterile, uncreative, past; it is that "ennui, that eternity without joy, that ever-hungry filling-up."[6]

Mozart's music is the only medium that ever succeeded perfectly in conveying the immediacy of that life of desire "which like a stone skipping across the waters, skims the surface of the abyss only to sink to the depths the moment it pauses in its flight." The rush of music has the ability to suggest an interpenetration of perfect moments, but within a course that must not stop (there is always the last scene, though, and the time must come, no matter how sufficient the music, when the musicians snuff out their candles and the theater grows dark and empty); the rush of sound provides the perfect evocation of the Don, who is far more immediate than the scheming Seducer: Johannis' *reflections* lack the immediacy of his actions and so are a potential chink in the armor of aesthetic life. Mozart succeeds in incarnating in the Don the coursing life of desire itself. Don Juan is not, as was Johannis the Seducer, obliged to promise marriage; nor does he ever pause long enough to need the solace of memory (the catalogue-keeping falls to Leporello, the unfortunate "secretary" who has been swept up by the dynamic rush of the Don's life). The very absurdity of the figure, "ed in Espagna mille e tre [1003]," conveys admirably, as does the very flight of Leporello's catalogue aria, the fantastic destiny of the Don. Nothing in this life can stop him; all find him irresistible; his immediacy is unrelieved. In the end, only a ghost (that of Don Juan's victim, the Commander, a spirit who proves that the past can live) can conquer Mozart's perfect incarnation of aesthetic existence. Yet even if for those captured within the music's immediacy this was soon lost in the gay mockery of Don Juan's irony, the fateful summons,

Don Giovanni! Don Giovanni! was already lurking in the first chord of the overture—for those who stand free of the course of Don Juan's life and thus can grasp the whole of time.

the ethical man
The ethical man, whose spokesman in the second part of *Either/Or* is the respectable Judge, William, abhors the poetic individual's life built on the fleeting sands of passion and lost in the blind current of irrational time. Judge William (in whom we recognize what Kierkegaard would consider a typical incarnation of rational Hegelian ethics) knows that a human life must be an ordered whole, constructed with unity and permanence according to a single *idea*, so that time is conquered in the consistent and rationally self-sufficient structure of a life I have "chosen for myself." This "ideal" state Kierkegaard symbolizes, in contrast with Johannis' seduction of one maiden after another, by presenting Judge William joined in faithful wedlock to the single woman he has chosen as the center of the ideal construction of his just life.

What Kierkegaard really wishes to illustrate through the example of Judge William is that mere duration, consistency, and unity of a life do not constitute an authentic "conquering of time," but rather banishment of the mystery of a real, rich temporal existence. He is warning us that in the Hegelian movement, for all its talk of time, history is not interested in the ineffable richness of the given, but prefers to embalm carefully selected material from the past in the arbitrary construction of a great scheme of life—whence an insensitivity to the real future that floods in on us beyond our making and beyond our comprehension. When the real future crowds in on the poor event uprooted by the constructing Hegelian from the true current of time, it is often embarrassingly different from what had been decreed. (The failure of Hegel's beloved Napoleonic revolution is a good example.) The constructed temporality of the ethical theory rejoins, for Kierkegaard, the "timelessness" of that *chef d'oeuvre* in the aesthetic order—the classic. The unity and the immediacy of the classic gives it a concrete greatness "for all times," which is really, as far as Kierkegaard's notion of authentic existence is concerned, for *no* time. You cannot build a life either on a perusal of the great classics or on the construction of a great ethical ideal, for the same reason: neither bears directly on the real *stuff* of selfhood, the authentic moment in the ineffable way it creates a past, a future, a present in their element of givenness, which transcends the ordered constructions of a rational ideal.

It is the banishment of the mystery of time that renders the ethical life insensitive to what Kierkegaard terms "the category of the individual"—sin. The ethical system talks incessantly of "the concrete universal." Yet when we meditate on the mystery surrounding the concrete exercise of our existence, we begin to realize how *abstract* the notion really is.

How can such a notion make anything out of transgression, original sin, the inclinations of the passions, indeed out of anything which bespeaks the *otherness* in the world? The exteriority to which we owe much can never be made to coincide with our notions of what we *are*; there is never to be found in real life that conformity of outside and inside which idealisms achieve in their-factitious concordance of "objectivity" and "subjectivity."

The writings of Kierkegaard as a whole are preoccupied with underscoring every aspect of the concrete mystery of existence, thereby enriching our notion of life lived in time, and in the process shaking any pretensions of idealistic conceptions to rational adequacy.

faith

Having turned the ethicist against the aesthete to show the fatal despair that underlies existence in the second sphere, and then having criticized the presumptuous self-sufficiency of Judge William's existence and of the rational totality of his "System," Kierkegaard has prepared his readers for his presentation of the saving sphere of faith. Since faith is not an idea but a state, it cannot basically be described, but only lived. Consequently, any literary effort to incite men to a realization of its importance is bound to be dominated by the negative mode. This points out that the fundamental, saving reality is situated where Hegel's rational categories cannot reach it; they cannot reach it precisely because the life of faith does bring with it salvation and opens for man the new dimension of the *future*.

Kierkegaard underscores the rational ineffability of the state in which infinite and finite meet concretely by characterizing it as the *absurd*. Johannis de Silentio describes in *Fear and Trembling* the impression faith makes on one who has come all the way that a man who would understand can come—even to the point of loving God—but who cannot achieve the final, all-important "embrace of the absurd."

> The dialectic of faith is the finest and most remarkable of all; it possesses an elevation, of which indeed I can form a conception but nothing more. I am able to make from the springboard the great leap whereby I pass into infinity.... I can walk about existence on my head; but the next thing I cannot do, for I cannot perform the miraculous, but can only be astonished by it.[7]

Some commentators have emphasized the element of leap without giving equal attention to Kierkegaard's counterbalance—the description of the calm, the solidity, the confidence, the simplicity of the man of faith who "looks disconcertingly like the tax-collector." These serene and sublime pages in *Fear and Trembling* convince us that from within the city of faith, the access of which to those without is redoubtable and severe, the concrete everyday world can begin to find its sense.[8] It is equally misleading to emphasize the paradox and the absurd without sufficiently recalling that Kierkegaard affirms reality itself to be intelligible—*to God*. "Existence forms a system for God, but not for man," for the finite existent cannot comprehend the Infinite, "certain philosophy professors" notwithstanding. Yet the finite existent *can* encounter the Infinite and embrace Him who is the fulfillment of time; but this embrace is existential, not theoretical; it is the embrace of His *will* by ours. To the man of faith has it been given to find the way toward the Infinite, a way that leads, not to the "System's" sacrifice of the concrete to the universal, but to Abraham's sacrifice, a movement toward God, done at His behest and in the confidence that He will restore the finite that He commands us to leave behind.

For that is the paradox of faith: the irruption of the veritable Infinite, into time, the fulfillment of time in an Infinite moment. The Incarnation made this possible; and it is realized again and again each time a finite liberty obeys the will of Him who knows where time is going. In this fashion, each moment is related to eternity in a way that guards and respects its uniqueness. Faith thus gives sense to futurity and meaning to hope, without requiring that either the particular moment or the whole course of time become, for the finite existent, translucently comprehensible.

It is clearer now why Kierkegaard emphasizes the inadequacy of reason. He gives two reasons why the encounter of the man of faith with the existential, temporal world proves it to be incomprehensible: first, since faith does not flee

II. *The Original Existentialist Revolt* 83

time but rather discovers here and now a way to its fulfillment, the individual mind remaining this side of the *not yet* can share in God's grasp of time's whole course only practically, by doing what God says to do. Abraham can never know why he is to sacrifice Isaac or how God is going to make it work out in the end. This, however, has the advantage of saving him from the dilemma of the aesthetic man who must dread "the last scene" which inevitably robs him of his time; rather the man of faith possesses a future which God in calling him gives him. At the same time, faith protects him from the dilemma of the ethical man, for he does not set up an inauthentic future before him, Hegelian-wise, attempting to comprehend it as though he were God. And so he is spared the frustration of the "System's" constructor who sees the French Revolution give way to the Prussian State, and this to something else, everlastingly, without ever coming closer to that instant in which everything becomes truly one in the eye of the Absolute. The man of faith does not grasp vainly toward the future from the present; without asking to know it all now, in his confidence he embraces the future that God holds out to him in a living way.

The second reason for the existential world's resistance to systematization by the finite mind lies in the density of the individual, concrete existent. (To encompass an individual object conceptually, one would have to envision at once, as Hegel said, its whole temporal course. The best the Hegelian has been able to do is to possess the object's past, and this viewed strictly from the "outside." If the finite individual proves too ineffable, how much more so THE individual, God Incarnate, the Infinite in time! The man of faith before the problem of naming the object of his faith can be true to his vision in only one way: by keeping silent. His task is not to name God, but to do His will; this vocation has been so fashioned for him that it can be carried out through the limited actions of his finite will, even if these should be such monstrous actions as wielding the knife against Isaac. What a contrast between this calm silence of the believer—the silence with which Abraham sets off for Mount Moriah—and the frenetic pretension of the ethical man to pronounce the last word on everything and to plan all according to the light of his reason! "In spite of the severity with which ethics requires revelation, it cannot be denied," says Johannis de Silentio, "that secrecy and silence really make a man great precisely because they are characteristics of inwardness.… If I go farther I stumble on the paradox, either the divine or the demoniac, for silence is both. Silence is the snare of the demon…but it is also the mutual understanding between the Deity and the individual."[9] The devil is in the secrecy of the scheming seducer; again, in a pure form of despair, the demoniac manifests itself in the isolation of the self who holds out against the true Infinite. But the authentic silence that enwraps the heart of the divine paradox is sign of the peace gained by the self who has accepted the Infinite existentially.

Thus it is that the ineffable character of the existential act of faith renders it difficult for Kierkegaard to talk positively about it. Indeed, it must be admitted that Kierkegaard's conviction that rational speculation is doomed to seek the universal (so that such speculation always blossoms in some form of "System") kept him from developing, a metaphysical foundation for the philosophy implied in his criticism of absolute idealism and in his advocacy of the priority of existence. As a result, his analyses tend to fly over-hastily into paradox, with too strong an accent on the crucifixion of reason. Kierkegaard was always worried lest he say too much about the properly unspeakable. So it is not surprising that his most detailed analysis of the self viewed through the eyes of faith is cast in very negative form: an exposition of the kinds of despair that keep the self from its authentic realization.

the sickness unto death

Despair is "the sickness unto death" precisely because it is that fatal failure of which we have just spoken, the failure to become a self. In *The Sickness unto Death* Kierkegaard takes only the first page to describe positively what the self is supposed to be. It is a description full of "leaps," in fact no justification at all is offered for any of the principal assertions. In this we recognize the authentic sign of Kierkegaardian faith; we are told simply and directly what the self *must* be if it is to be at all. "The Self is a relation which relates itself to its own self."[10] Man must relate in himself both "the infinite and the finite, the eternal and the temporal, freedom and necessity"; in short, "he is a synthesis." But the relation is "a derived, constituted relation," and man, to relate himself to himself, must relate himself to another, He who constituted that relation. Despair is "a disrelationship in a relation which relates itself to its own self and is constituted by another, so that the disrelationship in that self-relation reflects itself infinitely in the relation to the power which constituted it."[11]

Despair, consequently, is not just one of the many possible sins. It is rather *the* sickness unto death because it is the sin of failing to…become a self, of failing to relate oneself to God, of disjoining the finite and the Infinite, of not participating in the Incarnation. It is the sin without hope, because it is the sin which robs us of our authentic nature. All sin, actually, is a form of despair, for it is fundamentally a form of the sickness of the self that does not relate itself properly to God. Sin is more than a negation, a failure to live up to our vocation; it is a state of positive revolt. "The pagans within Christianity" reduce sin to acts, which, if not constantly becoming more heinous, tend to be looked upon as each not too important. The inauthentic Christian will even consider a week without an overt, sinful act a period of progress. To this Kierkegaard responds by pointing to the root of all our sins in a constant condition of "offense before God": the failure to relate ourselves authentically to God, so that the continuity of our temporal life, instead of finding its sense in Him, is turned constantly in another direction and thus away from Him. The individual sins I commit owe their profound gravity to their being moments in this continuous state of being "in offense before God." "Every unrepented sin is a new sin, and every moment it is unrepented is a new sin."[12]

Kierkegaard's description of the various ways one may fail to become oneself constitutes a pioneer effort at sustained psychological analysis. We shall discuss here only the three main categories.

1. *Despair by not being conscious of having a self.* This is the condition of the vast majority of men who simply do not realize that they have an obligation to become a self and therefore are incapable of motivating a conscious and consistent relation to God. This was the condition of the ancient pagan, as it is of those "modern pagans within Christianity" who never understand what it means to be a Christian. The fact that such people are so unconscious of being a self that they do not realize that their lives constitute in fact a sin of despair changes nothing in the reality of the situation; whether they know it or not, they are lost to the life of spirit and selfhood. Moreover, such a state is less involuntary than it seems, and always originates in a series of compromises. Such a person, living in "the sensuous categories agreeable/disagreeable, says goodbye to truth."[13]

2. *Despair by not willing to be oneself.* This is the case of the man who knows that he is supposed to be a self before the Eternal, but out of weakness despairs of realizing this self. This often happens from despair over some earthly thing; one may be too passively attached to the concrete "other" that one finds in this

world, "his self is something included along with 'the other' in the compass of the temporal and the worldly...wishing, desiring, enjoying, etc., but passively."[14] This would have been Abraham's despair had he found killing Isaac too unbearable. Such attachment to this world is really despair of the Eternal.[15] It is the sin of the aesthetic man who seeks satisfaction in the finite here and now because he despairs of the Infinite's ability to restore the finite in eternity.

3. *Despair by willing to be oneself despairingly.* The most rarely encountered case is that of the defiant self, "the despairing abuse of the Eternal to the point of being despairingly determined to be oneself."[16] This despair is "closest to the truth," since it does involve some sort of affirmation of the self; but by determining to be himself *his own way*, such a would-be self is really farthest from the truth. The defiant one occupies the exactly opposite pole from the man of faith, who has "the courage to lose himself to gain himself." The "infinite self" grasped by the noble despairer is "the abstractest form, the abstractest possibility of the Self, detaching the Self from every relation with the Power which posited it."[17] Leaving behind all the real necessities and concrete limitations of the individual self, the infinite negative self makes itself into the "free" empty universal. Kierkegaard distinguishes two forms of this eternal "Stoicism." The *active* Stoic is the kind of self that can become a Hegel, the typical ethical man. His way beyond the "Unhappy Consciousness" lies in the affirmation of the eternality and infinity of his own self. The *passive* form of "Stoicism" is a kind of reveling in the misery of man's fate, a perverse demoniac joy in embracing "the thorn in my side," because I not only have no real hope of God's removing it, but actually treasure it, for I can throw it in His face as grounds for my revolt before such an unjust Infinite Principle. (One thinks of Ivan Karamazov's turning in his ticket for life because of the "injustice" he could not bear—that little children should suffer. Nor is this attitude inapplicable to Schopenhauer.)

In whichever form, despair is an inordinance of either the finite or the infinite in the human synthesis. Defiance implies the affirmation of an infinitude to which we are not entitled; refusal to be oneself is a denial of the finitude to which we are legitimately to devote ourselves. The leap of faith alone can take us beyond Kierkegaard's fatal *Either/Or*: the finitude of the aesthetic life/the empty infinity of the ethical. Through faith in the paradox of the Incarnation of the Infinite in time (which shows us the possibility of the reconciliation of time

II. *The Original Existentialist Revolt*

and eternity in ourselves) we can escape the Scylla of aesthetic existence and the Charybdis of the ethical.

Such analyses as these are too negative to have invited the foundation of any "Kierkegaardian school" of philosophers, and, of course, Kierkegaard wanted none. He often spoke of himself as a lonely pine on the edge of the abyss (the same figure Nietzsche used to describe his solitary protests), and again as a sacrificed, unique experiment used by God as a warning to his generation. Yet, though there was to be no "Kierkegaardism," the message of his work and the lesson of his life were not to go unheeded. Just as Nietzsche's thrusts will give birth to the consciousness of a new era, so too will a later generation understand that underlying Kierkegaard's attack on Hegel, his call for the faith that can embrace paradox, his analyses of dread and despair, and, above all, his fear and trembling before the Transcendent, there runs the current of a new way of philosophizing. Jaspers will recognize signs of the new approach in both Nietzsche and Kierkegaard; but he will go further than either in developing the method of *Existenzphilosophie*, and will use it as a way of underscoring the evidences for the reality of a transcendence. But, ironically, although "faith" will be central to his doctrine, it will no longer be the Christian faith which, to Kierkegaard, was really all that mattered. Kierkegaard's unwillingness to develop positively a method to ground his theological positions has borne the strange fruit of a philosophical method substituting itself, in his name and in that of Nietzsche, for the faith in Christ "without which all else is vain."

Friedrich Nietzsche

Where would Kierkegaard's natural anti-totalistic tendencies have led him had God not moved him to believe? Henri de Lubac has suggested that Kierkegaard's philosophy, his paradoxical God once bracketed, would basically differ little from a Nietzschean nihilism. We have discovered that his work lacks even the positive methodic structure necessary to protect his faith logically against the nihilistic alternative. Still the whole sense of both his life and work lies in their sincere quest for God. If Kierkegaard's path skirts the abyss of nothingness, it is because he seeks not the God of the mathematician-philosopher, but the incomprehensible living Transcendent who commanded the sacrifice of Abraham. Anyone who queries finite being to its ultimate foundation will find there the most dangerous of alternatives: either abandon to the Transcendent or dissolution in nothingness.

Nietzsche[18] conducts the same radical quest, but opts instead for the self-sufficiency of finite existence, which he believes is nourished only on the wind of the night. For only the dark night, he is convinced, can let the finite stars shine in the brilliance of their eternally wheeling course. In the sincerity and the passion with which he seeks to bring to light the ultimate mysteries of an existence doomed to finitude, there shines a purity that sought to cleanse a whole society of the sham and the petty. Against "bourgeois" strains of nineteenth-century Christianity Nietzsche was a terrible enemy.

beyond good and evil, and the death of god

Zarathustra, returning from many years in the mountains, is amazed that the first person he meets should be a saint after the old manner. To the pious old hermit's query whether he brought any gifts, Zarathustra respectfully replies,

> "Let me rather hurry hence lest I take aught a way from thee!"—And thus they parted from one another, the old man and Zarathustra, laughing like schoolboys. When Zarathustra was alone, however, he said to his heart: "Could it be possible! This old saint in the forest has not yet heard of it, that *God is dead!*"[19]

Scattered throughout Nietzsche's works are pieces of the history, not only of how Christendom came to kill God, but of how "God" came to be in the first place. Gods are born of the genius of peoples. The wrathful, majestic Yaweh of the Hebrew tribesmen contrasts vividly with the frivolous and often charming divine population of the Greek Olympus. Although Christian writers chided them about the foibles, the play, the very multiplicity of their gods, the Greeks were content, as each people had always been, to divinize the qualities that made possible the development of their own greatness—their wiliness, a sense of the gratuitous, the struggle of Dionysiac creative power with Apollonian sense of clarity and balance. The God of the Jews on the other hand appointed for Himself the prerogatives of a desert chieftain—He ruled alone, pursuing with terrible justice anyone challenging His absolute position. When the Roman government brought unity to the Mediterranean world, the God of the

II. *The Original Existentialist Revolt*

desert, alas by then degraded and transformed, extended to the entire world His claim to rule alone. The Greek gods, confronted with the absurd claim of *one* God to rule alone, "simply laughed themselves to death."

The New Testament is an expression of "the Revolt of the Jewish slave mentality" against the Roman world of "good taste." It is the product of an era quite different from that of the Old Testament, the very grandeur of which gave a savor to the whole enterprise.[20] But Christianity is an ugly deformation of it; it is less a matter of fear and trembling than a cruel and narrow sacrifice of human nature,

> ...like the faith of Pascal, which resembles in a terrible manner a continuous suicide of reason...the Christian faith from the beginning is sacrifice: the sacrifice of all freedom, all pride, all self-confidence of spirit; it is at the same time subjection, self-derision and self-mutilation. There is cruelty and religious Phoenicianism in this faith, which is adapted to a tender, many-sided and fastidious conscience.[21]

Christian asceticism (which Nietzsche always misconstrues as a form of Puritanism) is a would-be purchase of holiness through the perversion of nature, rather than by its fulfillment. If there was real power in the lives of the greatest saints, it is because they strove to exercise *will* through their fanatical privations—that is why the great of this world have always feared them. But Christendom had few saints and many Christians. Incapable of sustaining any genuine religious instincts—for no crowd can—the Christians turned the God of justice into the God of mercy. The same God, who when he was young and harsh "built a hell for the delight of his favorites," became at last "old and soft and mellow and pitiful.... There did He sit shrivelled in his chimney-corner, fretting on account of his weak legs, world-weary, will-weary, and one day he suffocated of his all-too-great pity."[22] Even God has been democratized; and the crowd has traded in the saints' will-to-power for a more serene bourgeois *morality*.

A code of good and evil imposes on every people a constraint necessary to channel the public energy in some definite direction; for without it, the dumb energy of their wills would be dissipated to the winds.[23]

> In order to understand Stoicism, or Port Royal[24] or Puritanism, one should remember that constraint under which every language has attained to strength and freedom.... Everything of the nature of freedom, elegance, boldness, dance and masterly certainty, which exists or has existed...has only developed by means of the tyranny of arbitrary law.[25]

The "long obedience in the same direction" which the challenge of moral systems provides is indispensable; it is nevertheless fraught with danger. Although different spirits must discipline themselves for the flights of creation in different ways, the mass will always tend to impose its aspirations for "happiness" uniformly on everyone. Each folk's system in any era obtains obedience by presenting itself as absolute, as though dictated by the gods. In the hands of the crowd, systems that may once have been spurs to greatness become in time deformed into instruments of expediency, enemies of emotion rather than fruitful direction for their creative energy.[26] Bourgeois morality begets no saints; in its sterility it can only crush dissenters.

The situation of a people—especially their situation vis-à-vis a dangerous neighbor—determines what they will seize upon as the "Good." In the early days of a people the good is always whatever is difficult and yet must be accomplished if the society is to survive.[27] Later, when "certain strong and dangerous instincts, such as love of enterprise, foolhardiness, revengefulness, astuteness, rapacity and love of power, which had to be not only honored from the point of view of general utility—under other names of course—but had to be fostered and cultivated (because required in the common danger against the common enemy)" are no longer needed, "the contrary instincts now attain to moral honor; the gregarious instinct gradually draws its conclusions." As before, "fear is the mother of morals," but now it is the crowd's fear that the exceptional individual will break beyond "the low level of the gregarious consciousness, that the self-reliance of the community will be destroyed."[28]

When the "love-thy-neighbor" code of morality reigns, God, transformed into a deity of pity, ceases to be the focal point for uplifting religious instincts and becomes, instead, a crutch, a guarantee to the herd that they will attain their mediocre aspirations. Democracy arises when genuine aristocratic fervor cools; God dies trying to be a good sport.[29]

We, who hold a different belief—we, who regard the democratic movement, not only as a degenerating form of political organization, but as equivalent to a degenerating, a waning type of man, as involving his mediocrising and depreciation: where have we to fix our hopes? In *new philosophers*—there is no other alternative: in minds strong and original enough to initiate opposite estimates of value, to transvalue and invert "eternal valuations."[30]

the new philosophers

Who are these new philosophers? They are the "free spirits" of *Beyond Good and Evil*; they are the brothers of Zarathustra—and it is upon the person of Zarathustra that we must meditate if we are to comprehend positively in what their "freedom" consists. An easier way of access, though, lies in Nietzsche's conception of what they—the free spirits—are not. Critics of Nietzsche's philosophy would do well to concentrate on the philosopher's condemnations of the worst "isms" of the nineteenth century; not only do they help focus on the authentic sense of Nietzsche's own effort (which is always difficult to grasp because of the epigrammatic, ironic, paradoxical, and even dialectical way his thought unfolds), they contain highly perceptive criticisms of other philosophies. From what, then, should the new philosophers be distinguished?

They are not the "philosophic workers."—"The philosophic workers, after the excellent pattern of Kant and Hegel, have to fix and formulate some great existing body of evaluations—i.e., former *determinations* of value, creations of value which have become prevalent, and for a time are called 'truths.'"[31] The majority of so-called philosophers create no new horizons of human possibility; they only consolidate them. When, for example, one attacks Hegel, it is not his formulation of the "System" that one really opposes, but the evaluation of the world as natural, conquerable, and absolute.

They are not positivists, scientists, objectivists.—"In relation to the genius, a being who *engenders or produces*...the man of learning, the scientific average man, has always something of the old maid about him; for, like her, he is not conversant with the two principal functions of man."[32] The pretensions of men of science and the "learned ones" to be free of philosophy—and even to replace it with scientific dicta—issue from two phenomena: (1) The scientist himself having once fallen under the spell of one of the "philosophical workers" systems, and having mistaken these dead codifications for philosophical creation, has come to prefer his own form of activity, which in fact does offer more than any outworn philosophy.[33] (2) The rise of democracy—the triumph of the mediocre man—brought disbelief in the genuinely great, the authentically creative; the substitution of controlled progress for the reign of the giants creates a less dangerous atmosphere. The man of learning "lets himself go, but does not *flow*; and precisely before the man of the great current he stands all the colder and more reserved—his eye is then like a smooth and irresponsive lake, which is no longer moved by rapture or sympathy."[34] The decline of philosophy has seen the substitution of the instrument for the master—for that is all the "objective man" is, "an instrument, something of a slave…measuring instrument and mirroring apparatus, which is to be taken care of and respected; but he is no goal, no outgoing or upgoing, no complementary man in whom the *rest* of existence justifies itself…"[35]

They are not the aesthetes, nor are they subjectivists—as one might over-hastily conclude from a superficial reading of Nietzsche's attack on objectivism and his praise of originativeness and creativity. Subjectivism founders on the rocks of solipsism.[36] Its isolation of the self has nothing in common with Zarathustra's withdrawal to the mountains. Zarathustra withdraws for the sake of gathering up his "self" that he may love again on a deeper level; the subjective ego, on the other hand, is locked in shallow arbitrary will, a perversion of genuine creativeness. "Who has not been sick to death of all subjectivity and its confounded *ipsismosity!*"[37] Those who cry *l'art pour l'art!* are little better; for do they really believe in anything?

Unfortunately, Nietzsche's condemnation of aestheticism is made in passing and is not developed; from the context it is clear though that he condemns it as just another form of an arbitrary relativism which he despised above all other philosophical dangers. The violence of this distaste and the absence of an argument against it may in fact be signs that this perversion is too close for comfort to the greatest weakness of Nietzsche's own philosophy.

They are not nihilists, skeptics, cynics.—Cynicism is the closest a base soul can come to shaking off the shackles of the herd. The "Beat Generation" in any era protests and isolates and dissipates. But their "creations" are little more than negative discharges from the low-voltage currents generated by a dragging mass of mediocrity. Cynicism is nurtured on skepticism, the basic "nervous debility and sickliness." Skepticism is present under all the forms of anti-philoso-

II. *The Original Existentialist Revolt* 93

phy we have been considering, taking alternately the forms of "objectivism," the scientific spirit, *l'art pour l'art* and "pure voluntary knowledge." This "mild, lulling poppyseed" is simply paralysis of the will; it grows out of the rootlessness that follows the mixing of races and classes to the point that no one any longer knows what he stands for.[38] This disease of the will is most advanced where the degenerative forces of civilization have longest prevailed, where "the mixture of classes which is equivalent to mixture of races" is most advanced—in France and southern Germany more than in northern Germany and Russia. In Russia, in fact, "the power to will has long been stored-up and accumulated. There the will—uncertain whether to be negative or affirmative—waits threateningly to be discharged." Nietzsche indeed foresees "such an increase in the threatening attitude of Russia, that Europe would have to make up its mind to be equally threatening—namely *to acquire one will,* by means of a new caste to rule over the continent...."[39]

The most terrible form of skepticism (here it is as though he foresaw the mockery some of his future exponents would make of his philosophy) Nietzsche portrays in a "parable" on the personage of Frederick the Great—the "skepticism of daring manliness."

> This scepticism despises and nevertheless grasps; it undermines and takes possession; it does not believe, but it does not thereby lose itself; it gives the spirit a dangerous liberty, but it keeps strict guard over the heart. It is the *German* form of scepticism, which, as a continued Fredricanism, risen to the highest spirituality, has kept Europe for a considerable time under the dominion of the German spirit and its critical and historical distrust.[40]

Are the new philosophers *nihilists*? Not if nihilism means only destruction, and, as such, is a veiled form of skepticism. But a leveling blast, more thoroughgoing and more profound than ever was seen, is evidently needed to carry away every vestige of the civilization built by herd mentalities. It is the law of life that the new must grow out of the destruction of the old. If, because of its negative phase, the new philosophy, in its role of *Umwertung*, in its task of reversing the old values, must be called momentarily a nihilism, then, provided that the *Umwertung* leads indeed to the creation of new values, we must be nihilists! But the nihilist and the critic are once again instruments, needed at one moment in the cycle of rebirth, but valid only if brought to proper use by the new philosophers. They do not possess of themselves the creativity of those "free spirits" who are to usher in the era of the new philosophy.[41]

Nietzsche contrasts these *free spirits* with the unfortunate "free thinkers" of the eighteenth and nineteenth centuries, "almost the opposite of what our intentions and instincts prompt." The free thinkers are not really free because they are chained to what they are against and can therefore never create. They blame everything "on the old forms in which society has hitherto existed," and direct their leveling energies against all causes of suffering. But this attack on "form," "suffering," indeed on every manifestation and type of *necessity*, saps the very conditions that make all human greatness and philosophy itself possible.[42] Instead of taking to task form itself, this misdirected nihilism should concentrate its energies on attacking out-worn forms, which the "free thinkers" inadvertently perpetuate by the very nature of their attacks.

In a two-page description of the "free spirit" Nietzsche gathers the rich reality of Zarathustra. The passage is so ironic, paradoxical and many-leveled, so sweeping and masterful that it defies summarization. We shall retain for development just two points, advising the student to read the excerpt in full himself.[43] The "free spirit" (1) respects nuance, the unknown, the limit; (2) finds his freedom through will responding to the challenge of necessity.

1. Nietzsche's works, much like Kierkegaard's, are a lyric expression of the mysteries of the concrete, the ineffable, the growing and changing reality of Being in time. Although for Nietzsche mystery does not imply the existence of a world beyond, he is as much a protector of the ungraspable-uncomprehensible as Kierkegaard. The root of the reality of mystery for Kierkegaard is the Infinity of God as Creator of the world. For Nietzsche it is the finitude of man's will. The individual who, through acts of finite will, makes time come to be can never grasp the totality of the future that is in the process of creation. When he stands in awe before the mystery of Being becoming in time, it is his own *creation through necessity* that he is really honoring with his astonishment, for it is by human creative acts that the horizons of new possibility are extended and the future is made possible.

2. Notice that we spoke of creation *through necessity*; for the passage we are considering makes that point very clear: human creation is not a wild arbi-

II. *The Original Existentialist Revolt* 95

trariness, but a willingness to work for the fulfillment of structures that already exist in part.

> Artists have here perhaps the finer intuition; they who know only too well that precisely when they no longer do anything "arbitrarily," and everything of necessity, their feeling of freedom, of subtlety, of power, of creatively fixing, disposing and shaping, reaches its climax—in short that necessity and "freedom of will" are then the same thing with them.[44]

There is no more serious question that can be raised about Nietzsche's philosophy than to ask what the nature of this necessity can be; indeed the philosopher's way of working out the paradoxical notion of a "structured freedom" is central to this as it is to many philosophies. This must become our concern as soon as we have looked a bit closer at just what it is the new philosophers are supposed to create.

Of course, not another tired theory; rather, nothing less than *a new man*. In this new man, theory and practice will be fused in real virtue, returning us to a unity of *theoria* and *praxis* as it still existed in Plato's *Phaedo*, where "justice" is at once a supreme principle of intelligence and of life.

Nietzsche's way of presenting the new man is a result of this fusion of life and idea; instead of launching into long discourses on virtue considered abstractly, Nietzsche incarnates the qualities of the new man in Zarathustra; or, more exactly, since Zarathustra is a transitional figure, one who prepares the way for the *new man*, we are forced to infer something of what he would be like by contemplating concretely both what Zarathustra says and what he does. The qualities which dominate his thought and which he strives desperately (but not always successfully, as we shall see) to realize in his life are "purity," "honesty," "generosity," "gaiety," "solitude" and "love," each conceived in a way that bears the Nietzschean stamp, which is one of freshness, daring, and, almost always, sincerity. Zarathustra's diatribes against their opposite vices provide many an illuminating, though once again negative, insight into the sense of these key qualities.

We can gain some notion of the nature of "the new man," and at the same time suggest something of how Nietzsche reconceives otherwise tired ethical conceptions, by pausing to consider rapidly how he shows wiliness-solitude-love to form one pillar of the great man; then how purity-honesty-generosity-gaiety go together to complete the form of his existence.

"Stow up that you may bestow," Zarathustra warns those who would become forerunners of the Superman.[45] The individual is going to have to look out for himself if he is to succeed in becoming enough of a person ever to have anything worth giving. "In an age that makes a virtue of disinterestedness, I preach self-interest as the foundation of all life." *Wiliness* to survive in the world, *solitude* making it possible to withdraw from it when necessary—these are the inseparable defensive weapons of the individual against "the mediocre [who] seek to destroy anything that rises above them."[46] Nietzsche labels the virtue of wiliness "selfishness," both to underscore the basic principle that there is no life, no love, no creation without those deep engagements whose roots are self-love; and to contrast genuine self-love with the shrinking miserliness of self that characterizes the small-minded egoist. The universality of the truly great man has absolutely nothing in common with the "togetherness" of the herd; nor has his creative dangerous isolation anything to do with the hoarding, protective self-isolation of the egoist. Creativity which bursts all bonds and shatters the delicate structures the less-great have built to protect themselves, driving off those the great man loves and would have love him, is a sort of alienation and often requires a certain retirement in which the great man, uncertain whether he can stand up with his conceptions against other great men's conceptions, attempts to consolidate his forces. Such dangers accompany all human strivings for greatness. Nietzsche's own life was plagued with the collision with a giant like Wagner and with ruptures of all his friendships. The Superman, of course, should be above such struggles. But in the new philosophers who only prepare his coming, love will have to be strengthened gradually as greatness grows, sometimes in union with others, but sometimes also in solitude. When Zarathustra withdraws to the mountains it is to "stow that he may bestow."

Selfishness is certain to turn into desiccating egoism if it does not aim at furthering "purity," "honesty," "generosity," and "gaiety." "Purity" is an absolutely fundamental notion in Nietzsche's conception of the new man. The kind of fundamental purity Nietzsche is thinking of would have to be present in the soul as a necessary condition for the flowering of any individual virtue, including genuine sexual purity. Nietzsche in fact delights in explaining how many so-called virtues are really, when nourished in the rotted ground of an envious and small soul, practiced for evil reasons, like the sexual purity of the invidious old puritanical harpy. The really pure man must drink deeply of the clear water of truth.[47] Rigorous honesty is the very root of purity; generosity is its motive force. To be in unity with himself, a man must be prepared to see the world as it is. Sometimes this requires a generous acceptance of situations and people who are not what we want. Gaiety is purity's highest manifestation, the calm, confident gaiety that is a sign of an absence of heterogeneity, and of a soreness about one's direction that makes it possible to laugh at oneself. Nietzsche expresses the self-sufficiency of the truly great in terms of "dance" and "play" and "the wheel that turns on itself."

As the reinventor of such notions, Nietzsche considers himself the last of the Greeks. It is true that with this existentialist the Western world is well into the ultimate phase in that highly inventive recreation of antiquity that began with the *quattrocento*'s reinvention of Roman culture, continued with the reinvention of Hellenism about the court of the New Apollo, "Louis le Grand," and culminated in the romantic reinvention of the Homeric and pre-Socratic beginnings of classical civilization. It is no accident, then, if the wiliness of Zarathustra reproduces the spirit of Odysseus, and if his gaiety is akin to the spirit that gave birth to Greek dance and song.

why zarathustra laughs

As with all the new Romans and, later, the new Greeks in our civilization, I think we must ask how authentically ancient this Zarathustra really is. A moment's historical comparison of Nietzsche's hero with Homer's Odysseus brings out all too well in Zarathustra qualities of a suspiciously Christian tint altogether absent in the classical hero. Zarathustra is above all a teacher of men; Odysseus was not given to preaching to anyone. Zarathustra may thunder against the mediocre, but at the moment he has built the most terrible picture of his enemies he seems ready to show them the greatest compassion; Odysseus seems more inclined to handle his enemies with merciless sword. Zarathustra would certainly approve of Odysseus' ruthless determination and his capacity to lead his men without flinching at their recriminations; but when he himself is confronted by the hostile indifference of his first audience, he retires to the mountain for more years of self-examination. Zarathustra condemns nothing more vigorously than pity, for it implies condescension and softness; but in practice, Zarathustra feels some compassion, else why would he continue to preach to the "little ones," and "the hens in the barnyard"? Beyond a recognition of man's domination by fate, there is little pity in the *Odyssey*, and certainly no mercy and no "softness" toward those who have transgressed the laws of human conduct. There is a sensitivity, a solicitude, an instinctive outgoingness, a "bestowingness" in Zarathustra that is pure and good in a special way. In his greatness, in his mercy, he is more than Greek.

Nowhere is this more obvious than in his yearning for gaiety—is this really a Greek ideal? There is a calm, a commanding confidence about Odysseus that may seem to suggest he dominates each situation enough to be "above it all." In this sense, he possesses some of the characteristics included in Nietzsche's notion of "gaiety." But his confidence is not unbounded; in fact, the ancient world marvels that he is confident at all, given the powerful camp of deities lined up against him, from whose animosity he is saved only by the power of his divine protectors. Indeed, it was this very self-confidence, overstepping its rightful bounds, that incurred the wrath of Poseidon. Only the gods really have reason to be "gay," only on Olympus can there be a command of fate sufficient to justify a thoroughgoing confidence and laughter; only there does tragedy have no role. And even then, when is it that the gods do laugh? When Aphrodite is scratched by the lance of Ares in an unseemly exploit, and again at the thought of Hephaistos' being left by Zeus to dangle from heaven by a foot. This is more ridicule than light-hearted gaiety.

Is Zarathustra really gay? He laughs a great deal. He ridicules with high good humor and apparent confidence the "chickens in the strange farmyard." He laughs with the old hermit in the forest, "This crown of laughter, this rose-garland crown: I myself have put on this crown; I myself have consecrated my laughter."[48] But is this show of confidence sincere, or is it a way to keep going, used to cover a sadness of heart? In the very chapter consecrated to "the Higher Man" and which climaxes with the admonition, "Ye higher men, *learn*, I pray you, to laugh!" Zarathustra explains the condition which alone makes laughter possible.

> Tortuously do all good things come nigh to their goal.... They purr inwardly with their approaching happiness—all good things laugh. His

II. *The Original Existentialist Revolt*

> step betrays whether a person already walketh on *his* path: just see me walk! He, however, who cometh nigh to his goal, danceth.[49]

Laughter is a manifestation of happiness, and happiness lies in the fulfillment of our goal, or at least in being on the right path. Gaiety depends on having a real goal and being able to attain it. Truth may be in the service of life; life may be will to power; but the will to power needs direction and fulfillment; it needs structure expressive of that *necessity* which is the sustenance of all creativity. Nietzsche's entire teaching depends for its sense on finding a conception of Being that can give direction to becoming; a goal for the will, satisfying the need for endurance, totality, necessity in a way that is not only not inconsonant with liberty, but gives it meaning, making of it choice of a destiny.

Nietzsche recognized the critical importance of his finding a way to protect Being from the dissolution of pure becoming. That Being was indeed becoming, he never doubted, characterizing this principle as "true, but deadly."[50] The entire Western philosophical tradition, according to Nietzsche, had recourse to the same solution for saving Being from becoming: it degraded the world of time in contrast with the supposed infinite principle existing "beyond the world" and upon which the mere shadow-world of appearance depended for its all-too-meager substance. This is because "revenge against time" and its "it was" is the natural spite of a rational animal destined to be gobbled up in due course by time itself. Posit the existence of an eternal God and neither past nor future can have any real importance.

The salvation of time begins with Zarathustra's liberating pronouncement, "God is dead!" Now, instead of degrading time to a position of no importance, it is in time that man must seek *his* salvation; he finds it when he realizes that all futurity comes to be out of the reality of the past. The past, instead of being a cemetery of dead and vain dreams insignificant in the face of eternity, becomes the veritable reservoir of possibility on which we must draw in creating a future.

> I walk amongst men as amongst the fragments of the future: that future which I contemplate. And it is all my poetization and aspiration to compose and collect into unity what is fragment and riddle and dreadful chance…to redeem what is past, and to transform every "It was" into "thus would I have it"—that only do I call redemption.[51]

Redemption lies not in revenging oneself on the past, but in accepting it, which means acceding to its eternal presence. This is the necessity that alone can save man from the dissolution of unstructured becoming. Nietzsche considered the most important moment of his life to be the instant he saw for the first time as a whole the eternal structure of the world's becoming. "The idea of the eternal return is from August 1881.... I was strolling that day in the forests of Silvaplana, I stopped near an immense boulder in the form of a pyramid.... It is there that the thought came to me."[52] "The instant in which I gave birth to the return is immortal. Because of that instant I can support the return."[53]

It too is an insupportable idea, but at least it is less so than its alternative. "Against the paralyzing sentiment of the universal dissolution and of inachievement, I posit the eternal return."[54] Absurd, indeed, taken at face value; of a greatness that can only be termed "pure," both in Nietzsche's sense of the word and in the traditional sense of a "pure position," if only we take the trouble to understand Nietzsche on the level where true philosophy begins. It is not extravagant to say with Heidegger that this is the climax of the whole movement of Western philosophy. The great discovery of time is swallowed again in the eternal circle of Greek thought.

Three problems connected with becoming as such drove Nietzsche to hold that in the fullness of time all things endure because all are contained in a circle of movement which brings each thing back an infinite number of times. (1) "Infinite becoming is impossible, for it is a contradiction. It would suppose an infinitely increasing force, but by what means would it increase?"[55] (2) Since the force is limited, "the number of positions, variations, combinations and developments of that force is enormously great and practically immense, but in any event determined and not infinite." Since time is infinite, "it must be that all possible developments have already been produced. Consequently the present development must be a repetition and likewise that which produced it. Everything has already happened innumerable times."[56] (3) Given the infinity of time, the state of repose "would have already appeared if it had been possible."[57] "That a position of equilibrium has never been attained, proves that it is not possible."[58]

Time having had no beginning (and of course no end) and all things still going on, though the forces of this world offer no evidence of dependence on a transcendence situated in a world beyond, we *must* conclude to the doctrine

II. *The Original Existentialist Revolt* 101

of the eternal return. The eternal return not only provides protection against the nothingness of endless becoming but explains the possibility of becoming in the first place. For to the question, whence the newness in every becoming, Nietzsche can now answer: There is nothing new—it is only *what was* coming back again.

The doctrine of the eternal return is, of course, more than a cosmological hypothesis—it is a moral one as well. For Nietzsche sees in it the answer to the problem of the pettiness of man: "'Ah, man returneth eternally!' ... All too small, even the greatest man!—that was my disgust at man! and the eternal return also of the smallest man!—that was my disgust at all existence!"[59] The very horror of this prospect is Nietzsche's strongest argument for the necessity of striving for greatness in every human action.

> If that thought [the eternal return] acquires power over you, it will transform you into what you are, the question a propos of all and each one: Do you wish to live that again and an infinite number of times? would be as the greatest weight of your life![60]

The eternal return not only gives an everlasting value to every action but an eternal worth to everything as well. It expresses the unity of all things in the One, the great chain of becoming. "I feel everything necessarily joined to all, all essence is divine to me."[61] Acceptance of everything that there is in the world for its positive, eternally significant reality not only gives a richness to one's life in the present, it makes ultimate sense of it by joining it in perfect union to the eternal *what is*.

It is the love for everything made possible by realizing its value in the eternal return that is supposed to make it possible for Zarathustra to be gay. "All joy wanteth the eternity of all things!"[62] Opposing the infinitely sad notion that things die like autumn leaves, Nietzsche declares: "On the contrary, it seems to me that everything has too much value to have to be so fugitive; I seek an eternity for all. It is my consolation that all which has been is eternal—the sea throws it back."[63]

This is the highest expression of the "new philosophy"—by accepting that-which-is, I give unity and reality in the present to the past, truly saving it from the *Rache des Willens Widerwille gegen die Zeit,* revenge of the will's opposition to time and its "it was." "Everything that was is fragment, enigma, horrible chance until the creative will adds, but I wish it thus!"[64] The creative will builds the future on the acceptance of the entire past: "Zarathustra will abandon none of man's past, but will cast it in his mold."[65] The "necessity" binding all artistic creation, of which we earlier heard Nietzsche speak, is precisely this need for a unifying sense to destiny, demanding that one respect the tradition for what it is and complete it creatively. This *amor fati* of a new kind is the foundation of the calm and gaiety with which Zarathustra faces what is yet to come.

> Emblem of necessity
> Supreme constellation of Being
> —Touched by no wish
> Soiled by no negation,
> Eternal affirmation of Being,
> Eternally I am your affirmation:
> For I love you, O Eternity![66]

Participation in the eternal return—the acceptance of necessity—is the role of creative will functioning as will-to-power, creating a future out of the past in keeping with the structure of the eternal return—the structure of what has to be, because it is. But how can the will know what it is to create? In what sense are its creations free? What is there to guide the individual in his concrete acts of decision? *How* can I be sure to carry out my destiny? Is Zarathustra himself sure that he can and does?

In one of the most startling pages of *Thus Spake Zarathustra*, Nietzsche's hero seems to ask himself in his own heart something akin to these questions. Having just explained that the key to life lies in the "thus do I will it," he then asks:

> But did [the creating will] ever speak thus? And when does this take place? Hath the will been unharnessed from its own folly? Hath the will become its own deliverer and joy-bringer? Hath it unlearned the spirit of revenge and all teeth-gnashing?[67] And who hath taught reconciliation with time, and something higher than all reconciliation? Something higher than all reconciliation must the will will, which is

II. *The Original Existentialist Revolt*   103

the Will to Power. But how does that take place? Who hath taught it also to will backwards?[68]

At this point Zarathustra unexpectedly interrupts his discourse and appears to be in the greatest alarm. With terror in his eyes does he gaze on the cripples and beggars following him, whose secret thoughts he reads. Is it what they are thinking that terrifies Zarathustra? The old hunchback who was listening to the discourse asks Zarathustra why he speaks differently now than he does to his disciples. Evasively, Zarathustra answers that "to hunchbacks one may well speak in a hunchbacked way." To this vague reply, the hunchback poses another question, and with this the chapter ends. Was this the thought that filled Zarathustra with terror: "But why doth Zarathustra speak otherwise unto his pupils—than unto himself?"[69]

Can Zarathustra answer the questions he has posed concerning the origins of the will-to-power? He makes no effort here or anywhere else to do so; rather it is likely that this is one of those moments in the history of philosophy when, like Plato objecting in the *Parmenides* to the doctrine of ideas, a philosopher confronts the central difficulty of his own philosophy. If Zarathustra is unable to offer any explanation of how finite will can create for itself a free and meaningful future, if he cannot explain how "willing backwards"—accepting what is because it has to be—can be considered truly "free," if he cannot offer the secret to the exercise of the will-to-power, if he cannot reconcile freedom and necessity, then Zarathustra's gaiety is an expression of groundless aspiration rather than of genuine self-sufficiency. The terror of Zarathustra, and not his gaiety, is the sincerest note of this courageous philosophy—and the note on which Nietzsche ended his own last years.

The wreck of Nietzsche's philosophy in an irresolvable tension between freedom and necessity, becoming and eternity, is no cause for later philosophers to celebrate. True, there is perhaps some petty consolation for those in whose hearts God has not died to know that the elimination of God is not without terrible problems of its own. Nietzsche has said, "He who does not believe in the circular process of the universe, must believe in a God-judge."[70] Whether this either/or is all that implacable will remain a question to be thoroughly explored by two of the contemporary thinkers we will study, Karl Jaspers and Martin Heidegger. Jaspers will see in the very frustration of Zarathustra's doctrine (and all other "metaphysical" solutions to the problem it poses) a sign of the transcendent. Heidegger, on the other hand, will consider Nietzsche's frustration the final breakdown of the occidental metaphysical tradition and will try by a new kind of *Denken* to overcome the "error" that has plagued the entire tradition. To both, then, Nietzsche remains the greatest challenge.

III. Beyond Positivism and Psychologism

Wilhelm Dilthey

Dilthey's philosophy[1] forms a bridge over the chasm of positivism[2] and psychologism; it leads from the post-Kantian metaphysical era when men believed in reflecting on our properly human and properly spiritual acts but could not resist speculating wildly about them to the twentieth-century phenomenological and existentialist effort to restore the status of the acts of the spirit but in a non-metaphysical way. We can gather an idea of Dilthey's important role in keeping alive the "existential" themes—history, the concrete uniqueness of human creativity, the importance of the poetic act—at a time when the success of the physical, sociological, and mechanical psychological sciences was tending to engulf philosophy in unrelieved positivism by examining his own estimate, written in 1907 at the end of his life, of where philosophy then stood.[3]

the total human effort

The breakdown of *metaphysics* (which Dilthey simply accepts as a *fait accompli*), although destroying any hope of erecting an "objectively valid," absolutely universal explanation of Being as such, has nevertheless not left philosophy without a role. Even those most anti-metaphysical of all philosophers, the positivists, are ready to admit that philosophy has a right to exist as the "theory of theories," as a logic of the sciences, studying their role and interrelation; in short as a *"gnoseologie."* This much even the scientists have to grant (witness the great Helmholtz in the 1830s); for they see that no one natural science nor even their ensemble is qualified to pronounce on the right of the sciences to speak in the name of objective experience. However, the way positivism (see the chapter on Auguste Comte) has gone about the task of "critique" in this sense of elaborating the limits, methods, and subordination of the sciences one to another shows that the mere desire to reorganize the sciences in acknowledgment that metaphysics is to be banished is no sure protection against *speculation*, even if it need not take the form of a metaphysical construction. The positivistic conception of science as a system of mechanico-causal explanations grouped under the positive science of the most general human phenomenon, "sociology," is itself "a particular philosophical doctrine," the narrowness of which destroys sensitivity to all in man that its own categories cannot readily accommodate.

Yet positivism, despite its failure to be more than just another particular philosophical theory, has made a vital contribution to advancing the tradition toward its goal of a proper "critique": It suggested that all phenomena should be referred in a non-idealistic, non-absolutistic way to the human spirit, where they can all be examined by a general psychology of internal experience *as* phenomena of consciousness. The problem now is to develop a valid psychology that can examine the unified field of consciousness in all its implications without mechanico-causal prejudices derived from the sole area of the physical sciences; for such prejudices blind us to some of the most astonishing aspects of the life of the spirit that we are going to ask the spirit itself to examine.

As soon as we understand the new challenge of erecting a universal science of the phenomenon of consciousness grasping itself reflectively, the history of philosophy takes on an amazing new aspect. The various philosophical systems, stretching from the earliest philosophical tentatives to our own psychology of philosophy, are not isolated, contradictory, and (taken as an ensemble of positions) meaningless affirmations, but constitute a history of the spirit, meaningful *teleologically*. They are the struggle of the human spirit seeking to understand, within the limits of each particular epoch, the enigma of life and the ultimate significance of reality. As soon as the life of consciousness is viewed as such a continuing effort to understand, we also see that the historical philosophical systems have to be treated as only a part of the endeavor to understand. The development of religious world views and the efforts of the great poets have been intermingled with philosophy as part of the entire human effort that has continued, since the Greeks, to pose the questions with which we are still struggling today. By showing the close interrelation of religious and poetic world views with the development of philosophy, Dilthey demonstrates that the key to understanding the ultimate foundations of the human quest for wisdom does not lie in philosophy as it traditionally developed, but in the new philosophy he is proposing, the *science of the spirit*.

III. *Beyond Positivism and Psychologism*

Take for example the relationship between philosophy and poetry. The history of literature reveals the existence of a kind of "poet" whose writings form an almost systematic whole: we can easily disengage the "philosophy" of, for example, Lessing, because such a writer is in close contact with the flowering of a new philosophy in the formal sense. But many poets are in violent opposition to the philosophy of the day and strike out against it and beyond it with piercing blows and often little regard for system (which does not mean, however, that they are necessarily inconsistent). Seeking to reach deeper into the mysteries of life, writers like Montaigne, Carlyle, Nietzsche follow the intuitions of feeling wherever they may lead, "interpreting life with the aid of life itself." Because the impulses expressed by the poet lie at the outer fringes of discovery, because they are the originative beginnings of a new era of thought and are undigested by any system, they are naturally more dense, less comprehensible, and less concerned with total explanation than philosophical systems, but they reflect the "free play of the spirit."

The poet advances history through the originativeness of his insights, which are left to the philosopher to harvest. The poet advances history, but is by no means independent of it; he stands at the outer limits of his epoch and brings a new time into being—but a new time which is still *his* time; he reacts against the philosophy and science of his time, and his insights are never independent of that against which he is reacting.[4]

As it is linked with contemporary literature, the philosophy of an epoch is also linked to the contemporary religious world views. The religious world view is a generalization of personal religious experience. The deepest religious experience, like poetic inspiration, dwells in the depths of the spirit. It is "commerce with the invisible, rooted in man's grasp of the independence of his will from all of physical nature,"[5] and thus it is an outpouring of the ultimate in human experience, of the wellsprings of creativity itself. Like poetry, it can prepare the way for new philosophies; however, more than poetry, it will seek to extend a basically personal experience into a dogma demanding universal acceptance while never really reaching philosophical rationality. These aspirations bring it to clash with philosophy: religion pretending in the name of the Source of Life, philosophy in the name of logic and reason, to speak to all mankind of all things significant.

The war between philosophy and religious dogma that has marked our tradition up to now is not destined to continue; for once critical idealism at last realized that all philosophies and all religion—as well as all poetry and all art—are expressions of the one human spirit, it became possible for the new science of the spirit to bring all into the harmony of a single inquiry capable of understanding every kind of act of the spirit teleologically, in terms of the common quest to understand the world in which we exist. Physical science has helped develop our present awareness of the need to view things in terms of their end, the furtherance of life. We have only to go beyond Darwin's too biological conception of life and Comte's prejudice-ridden conception of the spirit's social nature to bring to fruition this way of regarding things.

To sum up: The life of the spirit is indeed social and historical, one of commerce and interaction with other beings in a common human quest for spiritual development. The spirit, therefore, can only be comprehended when viewed in the entire context of each epoch, which in turn is comprehensible only when viewed as a moment in the traditional quest for the common goal, "a general state of sensibility which will put to rest in some way the ensemble of our desires"[6] ("desires" being understood here in no restricted, base manner).

But does not such a view lead to an historical relativism? Dilthey considered historical relativism to be the most dangerous form of skepticism; in condemning it, he wished to point out that the very continuity of the historical effort of the human community to fulfill itself through poetry, art, philosophy, and religion attests to the reign of one truth which guides the entire effort as common goal. There is one physical reality which forms a common context for the whole history, and one human nature, without which there could be no common history. This one truth resides neither in abstract ideas nor in a transcendent Absolute; rather it is immanent to the course of development of the concrete individuals socially interlinked in the historical evolution from epoch to epoch. When searching for it, the science of the spirit, to achieve the universality indispensable to all science, and to philosophy especially, has to find a psychological method by which to seek in the concrete acts of particular individuals the signs of what is common to all men, that which gives unity to their quest for satisfaction.[7]

analytic psychology and the "hermeneutic" of the individual
The search for what is common to all men, says Dilthey, must take the form of an "analytic psychology," which is possible because the individual enjoys access

III. Beyond Positivism and Psychologism

in himself to the secrets of that common human nature which makes social union and history possible. Unfortunately this inner structure does not exist as a page waiting to be read. It is a dynamic structure essentially in communication with the world, and therefore it must be caught in action, in social and historical union with the other people and things. Since the operations of the spirit are the doings of concrete individuals, the basic method for revealing the never-ending, rich reality of spirit must be a *hermeneutic* of the individual.

In three essays included with "The Essence of Philosophy" in the collection, *The Spiritual World*, namely, "The Origin and Development of the Hermeneutic" (1900), "Contribution to the Study of Individuality" (1895–1896), and "Ideas for a Descriptive and Analytic Psychology" (1894), Dilthey develops in detail this new philosophical method which substantially prepares the way for the phenomenology of Husserl, Scheler, and Heideigger.

Only in recent times have men started to learn how to read in a work of art the signs of concrete, unique human existence that the artist incarnates in his work. Literary interpretation of the kind pioneered by the Schlegels—the reading of a text for what it can reveal of a particular human's way of living in the world—is the key to a new way of doing history, one that turns its back on constructed abstractions, preferring to go about the task of learning how to read, in whatever posterity has left us, the rich details of humanity's struggles to develop itself.[8] The essence of interpretation consists in "transporting, as it were experimentally, one's own living reality into an historical *milieu*" other than one's own. This implies "momentarily accentuating and reinforcing certain psychic phenomena" which one has to experience oneself to some degree,[9] but the intensity and balance of which is different in the individual one is trying to understand, pushing at the same time some others, which may dominate in oneself, into the background, thus managing to "reproduce in oneself the life of the other."[10] Such a process, insists Dilthey, is an essentially creative one. Really to understand the other requires a feat of imagination that is properly prodigious. I have practically to re-create him for myself out of the materials which I can draw from that most intimate experience of humanity I can possess—my knowledge of myself. But this creation is not an arbitrary one; it must model itself on whatever "signs" of the other I am fortunate enough to recognize. "We see that an ensemble is known in this way with the help of different signs, determined in a very relative fashion, and with the constant collaboration of all the grammatical, logical and historical knowledge one possesses."[11] On the basis of these "signs," "a faculty which, by creative action, homogenous and unconscious, receives and elaborates the first suggestions of a work," thus "responds to our individuality's insatiable need to complete itself by the intuition of that of the other."[12] "Receptivity and spontaneous creation are here indissolubly united."[13]

Such a "hermeneutic" is at the root of all the sciences of the spirit. The answer to why and how this can be is the corollary to the principle that the subjective individual can understand what is individual to another subjectivity because we each have in us something of what the other enjoys, due to our common human nature. Reciprocally, when the hermeneutic awakens us to an exciting human possibility in, for example, Shakespeare, we can turn inward and discover directly and intimately something of that reality in the very life of our own spirit, so that the hermeneutic advances the task of "descriptive psychology," helping it to avoid overlooking important spheres of the spirit and keeping it sensitive to the fact that the spirit is not an easily decipherable network of mechanical causes. And without "description" there can be no "analysis"—that "analysis" Dilthey would have replace the constructions of "explicative psychology." For the psychic life cannot be understood by such a method, imitative of the approach of the physical sciences: the unification of bits of data under a conceivable hypothesis. It must be grasped as a whole, for the ensemble—personal, social, historical—of a life is the "primitive and constant given"[14] we are searching for. "The lived ensemble is here the primitive thing, the distinction of the parts composing it coming only afterwards."[15] It is true that we only acquire little by little the empirical knowledge of the ensemble that forms our interior life; but we soon come to see that the same associations reconstruct themselves again and again around various experiences, that groups of those associations also form recurring ensembles, and finally that the whole soul collaborates in each experience.[16] "The particular fact is borne by the totality of the psychic life."[17]

Once the whole is grasped, the essential detaches itself from the inessential, yielding the basis for the logical operations of comparison, distinction, graduation, separation and association, abstraction, reunion of the parts in the whole, deduction of similarities between particular cases, analysis of diverse processes, classification, which Dilthey terms *analysis*. All these possibilities of analysis are implicitly included in the original observation that "the mental life is com-

III. Beyond Positivism and Psychologism 111

prised of a functional ensemble connecting different parts and composed in its turn of certain special ensembles each of which poses anew the problems of psychology."[18] It is obvious that access to this "primitive givenness" of the psychological life as a whole brings with it a great advantage not enjoyed by those sciences that must work laboriously with the parts before discerning (and often only indirectly) the profound structure of the whole.

> Psychological thought finds in the living totality of the consciousness, in its ensemble of functions and in the realization that abstraction gives the forms and general combinations of that ensemble, the background of all its operations. Each problem that it poses itself and each concept that it elaborates is determined by that ensemble and there receives its place. The analysis is effectuated then by relating to the totality of the psychic ensemble the analytic processes which are supposed to elucidate a particular term. It retains something of the living, artistic process of comprehension.[19]

Dilthey outlines what he calls "three important chapters" to be developed eventually by a truly analytic psychology. First will come the task of disengaging the structure of the evolved psychic life—that is the general architecture of the finished edifice; this general description of the whole psychic context depends on the discovery of the law by which the structure of the intelligence, the instinctive and affective life, and the volitions compose into the organized totality of the mental life. We shall see that the character of this *Strukturzusammenhang* is at once teleological and causal,[20] that the various moments are dedicated to the end of human development and once posed exert a real and necessary influence on what inserts itself later into the structure of the same life.

The second chapter follows from the basic discovery of the first, that the psychic ensemble is teleologically structured; it analyzes the evolutionary character of the *psyche* in its effort to reach higher forms of life: "In man, this evolution tends to establish a stable psychic ensemble in harmony with his conditions of life."[21] All the processes of the psychic life bend themselves creatively to this end; this is the motive force of history and society.

But history is real only because "the acquired psychic ensemble" influences every new act of consciousness. A third chapter, bringing to light "this great relation," will at the same time illumine the well-springs of the creativity of consciousness—that always active bundle of instincts and sentiments which, in rapport on the one hand with external excitations and on the other with volitions, conditions the distribution of the states of consciousness, the reproduction of representations, and the action of the ensemble of acquired representations on the conscious processes.[22] Nothing could be more poorly adapted to such a description than mechanistic hypotheses. Very careful description will reveal the interplay between the law governing psychic evolution and the creativity making sense of the jumps and inventions which seem little prepared by the structures already elaborated. Only such careful description can hope to clarify, little by little, the incredible complexity of human psychic development.

Already in the "Ideas for a Descriptive and Analytic Psychology," which we have just been considering, it is apparent that Dilthey has some doubts about the efficacy of pure introspection as a means for comprehending our psychic structure. He insists, in the context of the passage we have just quoted, on the need to look in language, myth, and social institutions for evidence of the social spirit incarnated in its works. In his last years he came to insist more and more on the need to examine these incarnations—and especially grammar—for signs of the tripartite nature of the psyche as cognition, feeling, and conation.

Dilthey, we have said, forms a bridge over the chasm of positivism, leading from absolute idealism to the phenomenology of our century. We can see clearly now the two dominant ways in which his thought is going to influence German philosophy:

1. Dilthey's writings promoted a climate of systematic research into the structure of the full range of human experience in order to uncover the ultimate principle of transcendental unity which gives the finite consciousness its ability to know truth with universal validity. Husserl, taking seriously Dilthey's dictum, *Hinter das Leben kann das Denken nicht zurückgehen* (Thought cannot get back behind life itself),[23] will seek to discover the ultimate ground of truth within the intentional life of consciousness itself, avoiding both metaphysical absolutization and psychological positivism, as Dilthey so strongly urged.

2. Having substituted for the traditional ontology a philosophy of man as historical, Dilthey invited a later generation to rethink the question of Being precisely in terms of the human existent's creation of a history for himself. Husserl saw the need to recognize that any such effort would have to become a

III. *Beyond Positivism and Psychologism*

metaphysical ontology. Heidegger, accepting the full Diltheian challenge concerning man's historicity, was to develop an ontology which viewed the coming to be of the human historical event as the advent of Being itself.

All of this development Dilthey, still in an insufficiently ontological manner, seems to have foreseen. He saw the need to discover the common source of acts of knowledge, will, and feeling, and he saw that this common source would have to be viewed in terms of an end for life that gives meaning to history. It is a tribute to Dilthey that his intuitions helped bring about the great development that followed. Nonetheless, it is a tribute to the phenomenologists that they have been able to move boldly beyond Dilthey's formal positions toward their ultimate ground in a fundamental ontology. In so doing they have made it clear that Dilthey can be considered only a transitional figure.

THE PHENOMENOLOGICAL MOVEMENT

The most important catchword in Continental philosophy of the present century is not "existentialism," as one might be popularly led to believe, but "phenomenology." The roots of the phenomenological movement[24] are implanted in the last decades of the old century, and the term itself becomes current in the first decades of the new.

As with the term, "existentialism," which, strictly defined, would apply only to Sartre's philosophy, the title "phenomenology" can be used either in a strict sense to designate the full methodic program laid down by Edmund Husserl, or it can be granted to all the thinkers who have claimed it for at least portions of their philosophical achievements; in the latter case the term becomes very broad, applying to a host of German and French philosophers occupying a considerable spread at the center of the epistemological spectrum between the extremes of unabashed idealism and Thomistic realism.

We shall leave it to the chapter on Husserl to outline the details of the strict program. In this introductory note we shall enumerate the principal characteristics of phenomenology in a broader sense, though not in such a vague one as would be necessary to embrace absolutely everyone who has laid claim to the term. The genuine phenomenologists, in the broader sense, share a community of interest, have much the same idea of the aims of philosophy, and agree on some points of method.

Philosophizing should begin with a concerted effort to describe phenomena. This basic claim appears trite until we consider the precise sense the phenomenologists have given all its terms. *An express effort* is necessary for adequate description. Clear and particular motivation, somehow transcending the everyday horizons of what is ordinarily "taken for granted," is the necessary starting point—the modern counterpart of Aristotle's *"Thaumatzein"* (astonishment). Husserl spent a good part of his life trying to show what has to be done just to get the phenomena *to stand there* before the contemplative eye. Max Scheler probably put the point better than anyone when he sought to show that the natural movement of our common knowledge is toward action, that everyday action is very narrow in its orientation, that only a high motivation could possibly free us from its egoistical impulses, that natural science, motivated by the desire to dominate nature, does *not* transcend it, and that indeed the development of certain moral virtues, such as patience and humility and the exercise of love, is necessary to proper philosophical contemplation! By *description* is not meant any rambling invocation of some facets of things. In their various ways, all the phenomenologists worthy of the name envision methods for putting order into descriptions and, above all, for making the *essential structures* of the phenomena described stand out. (Husserl describes a technique of "eidetic reduction" and Scheler speaks often of the need for a *Wesensschau*. We shall examine these different notions in due course.) But above all, it must be realized—as we have tried to bring out in the earlier chapters—that the term *phenomenon* means something special for the phenomenologists; although there is disagreement among them as to its status as *reality*, there is unanimity that Husserl's war cry, *zu dem Sachen selbst*, does not mean that phenomenology is a return to objective interrogation of the Aristotelian realists' "things." A good way to obtain a notion of this characteristically phenomenological concept is to see its formation in the proto-phenomenology of Brentano.

Franz Brentano (1838–1917) seemed in his early career destined simply to write another chapter in late nineteenth-century psychology of the kind practiced by J. S. Mill, Lotze, Wundt, Fechner, and most brilliantly by the William James of the *Principles of Psychology*. Brentano was in accord with the necessity for psychology to be *empirical*; but from the very start he was dissatisfied with the psychologists' failure to clarify the sense of their fundamental concepts. His desire to probe to properly philosophical depths manifests itself clearly in the

III. Beyond Positivism and Psychologism

opening lines of his influential work, *Psychology from the Empirical Standpoint* (1874), where it is made clear that he has no intention of adhering to the artificial limits placed on "the empirical" by those who are positivistically inclined: "My standpoint in psychology is empirical: Experience alone is my teacher. But I share with others the conviction that a certain ideal intuition can well be combined with such a standpoint." What is meant by "ideal intuition" (*ideale Anschauung*) becomes clear only as the book unfolds.

Psychology concerns itself, not with physical, but with psychic objects. What characterizes the psychic object is its *intentionality*. "We can define psychic phenomena by saying that they are such phenomena as contain objects in themselves by way of intention."[25] Now while Brentano explicitly refers to the scholastic origin of the term (he had studied scholastic philosophy while training for the priesthood), it is a great mistake (and one that is often made) to think the conceptions are just the same.[26] What Brentano means by the intentionality of psychic acts is that every psychic act of its very nature refers to a content; there is "no hearing without something heard, no believing without something believed, no hoping without something hoped, no joy without something we feel joyous about." In the very text in which he first introduces the term, he speaks of it as designating the psychic acts' *immanente Gegenständlichkeit*, their quality of always having an object immanent to them.[27] This does not simply echo St. Thomas' emphasis on the fact that a real perception puts us in direct contact with a real thing known as it is in itself. The point is rather that what the psychologist must study are *psychic acts* (hence the phrase "ideal intuition") and that psychic acts cannot be understood as they really are without reference to that with which they are concerned. Far from being an invitation to turn to the objective examination of things existing "outside," Brentano's whole orientation becomes an invitation to Husserl and the other phenomenologists to seek out the essential structures of the phenomenal order, that is of things as they appear (of *ideas*) within the intentional horizons of a knowing-willing-feeling existent. In other words, Brentano asserts that psychology is not concerned with the existence-in-itself of things, but only with the phenomena as they are lived and in *how* they are lived.

Is phenomenology, then, as this might seem to suggest, going to be a *critical* philosophy, in the sense that it will reduce the problem of Being to a question of knowing how the phenomenon is constituted by the transcendental ego? The most "idealistic" of the phenomenologists, Husserl, would not go so far as to say that; for, after all, we do live in a universe of which we are a part and which we do not create, and hence we are interested in knowing about things as they really are in themselves. But Husserl is an idealist to this extent: that he considers our constituting the objects of our intentions to hold an essential key to the true judgment of what these things signify; hence he is a strict transcendental critic who insists that getting at the fundamental structures of consciousness is the indispensable task of philosophy.

But, as we shall see when we turn to the philosophy of Max Scheler, there is an important movement of phenomenologists who reject any formulation which might be taken to mean that things somehow depend for their structure and being on the intentional acts which make possible their appearing within our consciousness. These philosophers are realists to the extent that they maintain that our intentional processes are made for presenting things as they really are in themselves, and if phenomenology does begin with a reversal of a common movement toward a certain kind of market-place concern with concrete things, this reversal is intended only to liberate our gaze from its over-absorption in practical affairs so that we might see more fully the essential structures objectively present in our experience. But suppose we let the two sides tell their particular story their own way.

Within the bounds of this general history we can only treat those phenomenologists (all are Germans and Frenchmen) whose impact on contemporary thought has been widest. All the remaining German thinkers, except Jaspers, have claimed some connection with the phenomenological movement, although every one of them has moved quite independently of Husserl and at least one, Nicolai Hartmann, can be said to be on the periphery of the movement at best. All the non-Thomist thinkers most prominent in France at this hour, with the exception of Gabriel Marcel, would lay some claim to being called phenomenologists; and even Marcel has on occasion entitled some of his descriptive pieces (with justification) phenomenological, in the broad sense we have just sketched. There have been and are other thinkers associated with phenomenology who deserve more than the bare mention we shall now give them and who would have to be (and, indeed, since the publication of Herbert Spiegelberg's important two-volume study, *The Phenomenological Movement*, have been) treated at length in a history devoted specifically to this main branch of recent Continental philosophy.

III. *Beyond Positivism and Psychologism*

Two thinkers should be mentioned here, for like Husserl they had been students of Brentano in Vienna and their later, independent developments paralleled in some very general ways the directions Husserl took.

Carl Stumpf (1848–1936), the first phenomenological psychologist, like Husserl, insisted on the need for the methodical study of phenomena not handled by either the psychological or physical sciences as a necessary prelude to sound science. He pointed out, for example, that the *content* of our judgments is neither a thing nor even a collection of parts of things, but rather that the judgment expresses "a state of affairs" (*Sachverhalt*). The later phenomenologists not only adopted the term, many recognized that Stumpf had helped bring out very well the "in between" status of intentional phenomena as neither "real" physical things nor "merely" psychic processes.

Alexus Meinong (1853–1920) stressed the need for fresh description of whole classes of objects, like the negative ones, to which neither the physical nor the psychological sciences were paying the least attention. While not laying any claim to being a phenomenologist, Meinong bathed in the atmosphere from which sprang proto-phenomenology and remained sympathetic with its ambition. Bertrand Russell, G. E. Moore, and C. D. Broad evinced an interest in his philosophy—one of the few contacts, however indirect, between early phenomenology and the Anglo-Saxon philosophical world.[28] When Husserl's history-making *Logische Untersuchungen* were translated into English, the translated manuscript was submitted for an opinion to a Harvard professor, who duly opined: "Nobody in America would be interested in a new and strange German work on Logic." The Professor was no less than William James. Needless to say, the translation was never published.[29]

Alexander Pfänder (1870–1941), the soul of the so-called Munich circle of phenomenologists, whose general tendency was to remain faithful to the ideal of careful description of phenomena viewed from the subject's angle and with special attention to the acts which present each kind of object, nevertheless refused to follow Husserl to the radical depths of the phenomenological reduction. More realistic in his inclinations, Pfänder emphasized the need to cut under presuppositions to a direct perception of realities as they are in themselves, but he did not feel that it is only in probing the depths of consciousness in search of its essence that this can be done, or that such a radical "criticism" necessarily had to precede valid phenomenological description.[30] We shall find in Max Scheler an exceptionally versatile thinker who carries out a brilliant program more in sympathy with Pfänder's kind of phenomenology than with Husserl's. Let us first turn to Husserl, however, for he, with his rigor and consistency, is indisputably *the* phenomenologist of them all. Then we shall proceed to consider, when we study Scheler (and, among the Frenchmen, Ricoeur), what sets off the less criticist sort of phenomenology from the philosophy of Husserl.

It should be pointed out that the Husserl Archives at the Institut Supérieur de Philosophie of the University of Louvain, Belgium, are in a sense the world capital of the phenomenological movement, not only because scholars are attracted from everywhere by the unpublished Husserl manuscripts, but because of the program of publication being directed by the philosophers there. Under the general guidance of Father Hermann Van Breda, O.F.M., who saved Husserl's papers from the Nazi regime, the phenomenologist's major works are gradually being edited and brought to publication. At the same time, both historical and original studies akin to phenomenology are being published in the series "Phaenomenologica."[31]

An important group of philosophers has grown up in the vicinity of the Archives. Alphonse de Waehlens (1911–1981), after devoting the earlier part of his career to a very excellent critical exposition (the major fruits of this being a book on Heidegger, another on Merleau-Ponty, and a third on the conception of truth in Husserl and Heidegger), now appears (to judge from the announcement of the imminent publication of his *La Philosophie et les experiences naturelles*) prepared to establish an independent position. Canon Albert Dondeyne (1901–1985), in several penetrating works, the principal one of which has been translated into English under the title *Contemporary European Thought and Christian Faith* (Duquesne University Press, 1958) has sought to situate phenomenology and existentialism in relationship to traditional Thomism and Catholic dogma.

Edmund Husserl

the critical need for phenomenology

Edmund Husserl[32] received his university training in mathematics, in an atmosphere dominated by relativistic positivism and a psychologism that tended to compromise the absolute character of truth by viewing it merely as a function

III. *Beyond Positivism and Psychologism*

of psychological processes. But Husserl saw that mathematical truth, while internal and graspable by a non-sensuous intuition, enjoys an objective validity essentially independent of the psychological act in which it is conceived; he concluded that methods and presuppositions of positivistic psychology do not equip it to attack the problem of the necessity and universality of apodictic truth. A method was needed that could get at the foundations of consciousness in a way capable of determining the ground of those *a priori* judgments without which science could not exist and of determining how they can be objective. Husserl was convinced that such a method of analysis would lead the way into the very ground of consciousness, to that "ultimate living source" of experience in which all science is founded and which constitutes the unity of the "world." Because science plunges ahead without waiting for reflective, critical validation of its principles, it can never become truly scientific, but must remain gratuitously founded in presuppositions about the validity of different kinds of experience.

Husserl was fifty-four years old before he could bring out of his preliminary explorations the first developed description of phenomenology as a possible method for achieving an absolute analysis of consciousness[33]; and he was almost seventy years old before he was able to apply the method to the ultimate critical research he deemed the necessary prolegomena to any truly fundamental grasp of knowledge in any of its forms. Along the course of this development, Husserl's interest centers in discovering, behind the infinity of conscious acts, the essential structure (*eidos*) of each kind or "region" of intentional act, and behind all the various kinds of *eidos*, the structures common to all of them, "the widest possible *a priori*," the "*a priori* of pure reason," as he terms it later[34]; this should reveal the hidden underlying presence of the founding activity of consciousness itself, according to the ultimate form of which all "rendering present an object" of whatever kind must take place and lead eventually to the very sense of the unity of experience, and the unity of "the world."

The long reflective analysis achieved in the *Logical Researches* convinced Husserl that it is singularly difficult to orient our reflection toward the basic structures of consciousness. Because these are "intentional" and thus of their very nature directed outward toward the grasp of their object, they fail to call attention to themselves and to their contribution to the formation of the experienced world. The presuppositions of naïve realism (which science, of course, borrows uncritically so that it can go on its unreflective way) attest to this. Realism simply assumes that truth is a reflection of some absolute something existing in itself toward which we have only to direct ourselves in order to grasp it "objectively" as it is in itself. Both psychologism and idealism have contributed to the attack against such an uncritical attitude. Psychologism has pointed out that the attaining of any absolute is conditioned by the subjective processes of my consciousness. This would seem to suggest the need to develop a method that could uncover those conditions and could grasp their sense. But psychologism has been hampered from sizable advance toward truth by its propensity to conceive the processes of consciousness as mechanisms more important in themselves than as related to the absolute grounds of truth. Idealism, on the other hand, while contributing the awareness that the secret of the appearance of being is to be searched in these very depths of subjectivity, has never questioned whether being need be considered an absolute reality-in-itself. Convinced that it is, the idealists, as offspring of the same metaphysical tradition, have constructed metaphysical fantasies to represent an objective being-in-itself that would correspond to their often sound insights into the subjective constitutions of consciousness.

Only a radical antidote for our habitual unreflective realism will ever make it possible to break loose of psychologism and idealism. Husserl proposes in *Ideen I*, as just such an antidote, an act of radical suspension of belief in the existence of the real world. The point is not, of course, to fall into a crude inverted realism by really doubting the things of our experience, nor are we to leave anything out of our consideration; the point is rather the positive one of becoming conscious of the fact that everything that our experience tells us "exists" must, in order to "be," exist for *me*, i.e., as a phenomenon appearing in consciousness. Such an attitude radically eliminates any possible opposition of "internal-external," or "subjective-objective," and prevents the degradation of one moment of experience in favor of another which some prejudice—particularly the practically oriented prejudices of common sense—would esteem metaphysically prior. Such "equality" dramatically undercuts all questions of whether this or that is "really real" or not, assuring that every object and every subjective form of whatever sort will be called upon to display its evidential credentials and that each will have a chance to show its importance in helping us understand the consciousness' constitution of an objective world.

III. Beyond Positivism and Psychologism

Now begins the quest among the infinity of knowledge acts for essential structures, for the *eidos* under which particular series of acts can be grouped, to make possible the ultimate discovery of those absolutely universal structures—the *a priori* of pure reason, as Husserl later calls them—common to all knowledge acts because they are the very fundamental act of consciousness itself. Explication of these ultimate "forms" is the necessary prerequisite to man's understanding himself, his relationship to the world, and the ultimate grounds of his own self-direction.[35]

The realist has a tendency to consider the only truth-relevant structures in knowledge to be the forms of the things themselves, forms which the knower has discovered directly in things and disengaged by abstraction from the limiting conditions of particularity. But once the phenomenologist begins viewing all "intentions"[36] precisely as acts of consciousness, he brings out very clearly the fact that some of the structures in knowledge reveal in some way the structures of the things known, while others have to do with the way consciousness renders present its objects. This first kind of structure—the kind with which the individual sciences are primarily concerned—Husserl will later term the "contingent *a priori*,"[37] contingent because always associated with the way a kind of thing "gives itself" to us in perceptual experience. The ultimate structures of consciousness itself, however, Husserl terms in contrast "*a priori* of pure reason." A moment's reflection will reveal the essential subordination of the "contingent *a priori*" to the "*a priori* of pure reason," in this sense: the object can only appear as this or that kind of a structure because the consciousness is able, according to the forms of its own dynamic activity, to constitute the presence of this kind of objective reality before itself. This does not mean, however, that consciousness forces experience into an indifferent mold; rather the forms are active manifestations of the ultimate functioning of a pure reason ordered to the constitution of an intelligible world and therefore structured so as to make present "valid" objects—objects meaningful for a conscious human life in the world. The great discovery of transcendental philosophy must be recalled: what we know are not indifferent things-in-themselves but phenomena, correlates of our noetic acts, moments in a world enjoying a "sense" because it is a universe of discourse organized by an experiencing ego. We see a reflection of this fundamental principle in the fact that every change in the noetic activity of the ego affects the presentation of the object. Thus the same "matter," for instance this apple tree, can enter now, as I look at it, into the noematic configuration, "perceived tree," then, as I recall my previous perception, "remembered tree," or it could become a merely "imagined tree." A perceived tree and an imagined tree are not the same sort of phenomena; they have a quite different sense.

As the attitude or activity of the intending agent enters into the very sense of what is intended, and as the very significance of the lived world of our experience is indissociable from the intentional *a priori* forms of its organization, the task of a phenomenology will be to seek methodically to bring those structures and the sense of their rational connection to light. That is the task of the phenomenological reduction, or to use Husserl's special term, *epoché*. The purpose of the phenomenological *epoché* is to get us to turn our gaze away from the finished results of the transcendental ego's constitutive activity—from the objects as already determined in a world of discourse—toward their "archaeological underpinnings" in the transcendental ego's deployment of its forms of data unification. The special purpose of the "eidetic reduction" is to bring these *a prioris* to light—and ultimately the transcendental "*a prioris* of pure reason." Once these have been brought to light, then it will be the immense task facing a future army of phenomenologists to explore exactly how the various particular ways of knowing each kind or "region" of object affect the content of what is known. This essentially critical investigation will make it possible to discover the exact ontic status of every sort of object in every "region" of being. This alone can establish the ultimate validity, the truth of what is known, in this way and that, by now one science, now another. Only such critique is adequate to the task of putting order among, and a sound critical base under, the various sciences.

in quest of the a priori of consciousness

In *Ideen I* Husserl furnishes enough analyses of the noetic-noematic correlations in basic experiences[38]—such as the presentation of the concrete material object, and the modifications of such presentation by memory, imagination, signification, etc.—to give the student of phenomenology some idea how such analyses are to be made. But the purpose of these exercises is really to prepare the way for disengaging the structures of consciousness in their work of making the basic object of perception present to consciousness. From this long and rich series of analyses let us call attention here to what seem the two essential points that come to the fore.

III. *Beyond Positivism and Psychologism*

1. When an object passes through a series of noetic modifications (first perceived, it then becomes a memory, then the memory of a memory, and it can be presented imaginatively, can be signified, etc.) it undergoes, in each step, a noematic transformation (which is to say that in each step *what* is known—the object that is presented—is modified when the mode of knowing is changed). Analyses of this process serve the obvious purpose of demonstrating that the object depends for its being on the forms of consciousness. Less obviously, but nonetheless explicitly, it brings out the fact that the sustaining of the object in consciousness is an essentially temporal process. Husserl does not make a great point of this in *Ideen I* where his thought still seems dominated by the logician's tendency to conceive the *a priori* more as a form than as a function. But, in the light of Husserl's last works, we can perceive many signs that *Ideen I* is already moving toward a conception of consciousness as a dynamic process, as a life sustaining its object through the flow of time.

2. The study of one particular series of modification potentially throws a great deal of light on the sense in which the consciousness' posing its object constitutes the "being" of what is posed. This series of modifications Husserl terms, in fact, "the characters of being."[39] The noematic characters, "veritable being, doubtful being, likely being, possible being," correspond to the various noetic "doxic[40] modes"—certitude, doubt, conjecture, supposition, etc. Underlying every act of consciousness, regardless of its noetic-noematic genus, be it simple perception, volition, enjoyment of something, explication, memory, there is always "an actual doxic position,"[41] so that its object is always subject to the question, is it real, possible, probable? This tells us two important things about the constitution of objectivity: (i) all intention as it originates in a consciousness interested in "living" is ultimately concerned with the reality of its object, so that all the genera of knowledge acts are basically oriented toward *real being* (hence the primordial importance of perception, which is the primordial source of "givenness"); (ii) since the positing of all reality is a doxic act of consciousness, and since such an act accompanies every intention, it is possible both to suspend (however arbitrary and artificial such suspension may be) all belief in the independent existence of things; and then, if sufficient motivation for such previously naïve belief can be found within the subjective content of consciousness, to reinstate the doxic act on these new, critical, and immanent grounds.

This kind of consideration serves to reinforce a fundamental contrast which *Ideen I* emphasizes to the profit of its basic argument. I refer to the contrast between the incompleteness with which the external object is always given and the perfect totality of the internal intuition of my own intentional acts. Although we can suspend "belief" in the existence of every external object, the phenomenological reduction leaves the whole world of my consciousness unaffected. The whole content of all my intentional acts remains accessible to my reflection even after I decide to suspend judgment concerning the external existence of their objects. The *epoché* is very different from Descartes' methodic doubt in this respect. It does not leave us with the *cogito* alone thinking its own existence; rather we are left with a *cogito* complete with its full range of *cogitationes*. Every act of consciousness that makes "present" an "object" remains accessible to reflection, as an act of my consciousness, fully, perfectly, and in the totality of its reality. This, to Husserl, is an important sign that the conscious act as act of the *cogito* is more fundamental than the objective correlate of that act, considered as existing in itself.

Husserl further heightens this contrast by underscoring the always partial and discursive way in which the thing itself appears to us in perception. The perceived thing is never given to me totally, but only aspect by aspect (in *Abschattungen*); the thing can only possess a continuous structure for me because consciousness is able to correlate perception to perception, retaining what has gone before in memory, anticipating the fulfillment of what is given me at present. The thing itself is given only as "regulative Idea in the Kantian sense," that is to say, as unity of all the partial aspects of it given in perception, which unity itself is not given but only presumed—although *belief* in that unity is motivated by the consistency that is manifested among the profiles of the object given successively in perception. To understand the objectivity of the thing, then, it is the constancy of this dynamic keeping-present of the thing which needs to be probed. And since that is precisely the act of consciousness that is available to reflection most directly and adequately, it is evident that it is there that a critical phenomenology must direct its gaze.

Husserl took almost fifteen years to prepare the ultimate critique, that exposition of "the widest subjective effectuation, thanks to which that which is constituted in an actual manner for the knowing subjects and is drawn from the source of their habitus is more than the momentary thematic of the actual present."⁴² With the publication in 1927 of *Formal and Transcendental Logic*, Husserl is at last at the heart of the matter; the very statement of the "widest subjective effectuation" we have just quoted shows this clearly. It suggests (1) that the presence of what is present is due to the habitus of the consciousness, which retains the past to unify it with the present in a way that anticipates the continuance into the future of the duration of the thing; and (2) that such constitution is able to take place in a way that yields more than a concrete perceptual grasp of this thing here and now; rather it is capable of constituting a "contingent *a priori* structure," having a validity for all consciousnesses at all times and in all places. This indicates that the constitution of objectivity by the consciousness structures the essences with which science is concerned, meaning that so-called "timeless" eidetic structures themselves come into being in time.

The notion that we "constitute" our objects clearly has an idealistic ring to it. Indeed, Husserl was not above speaking of his philosophy as a "transcendental idealism." The transcendental ego is essentially active—knowing, willing, feeling, indeed living, are, after all, activities; our "being-in-the-world" is a way of forming a human world. But Husserl never overlooked our essential finitude, the fact that we are only a part of the reality which, as object, we "constitute," but which we are "motivated" to constitute as real and as an essentially other we are ourselves dependent upon. Indeed, nowhere is the paradox inherent in the notion of a finite knower better brought out than in Husserl's philosophy. All his life Husserl explored the question of how it could be that an active knower, upon whose taking a stand depends the "giving of a sense" to data spread out in time, can make be for itself, as its phenomenon, a world, part of the very sense of which is its reality; the passivity of the ego in the reception of the data and in the constitution of "contingent *a prioris*" has to be explained. Indeed, the paradoxical notion of "active receptivity" developed in *Erfahrung und Urteil* can stand as a kind of symbol of the Husserlian quest. The constitution of idealities enjoying an "eternal" validity from out of the flux of an essentially temporal experience is another aspect of the central problem. Husserl's "quest for an absolute" is the antithesis of the construction of some "thing-in-itself" or of a Mind which would draw the substance of reality out of itself; Husserl was not for a second tempted to see time "wiped out" (*vertilgt*), as Hegel says in the chapter on "absolute knowledge" at the end of *The Phenomenology of the Spirit*. Rather time is the very form of the transcendental ego, the coming to be of its objects is a coming to be within the horizons of a temporal experience.

> We have absolutized the truth, but not falsely, we have rather absolutized it in its horizons—which we have not neglected nor allowed to rest hidden, but have explicated systematically. In other words we possess the truth in a living intentionality (which is then called its evidence) the very character of which makes it possible to make the crucial distinctions: between "given effectively itself" and anticipated, or as "still in hand" in a retentional fashion or "appresented as foreign to me," etc.; and we are thus led, through the laying-bare of intentional implications, to all the relativities in which being and value are intertwined.[43]

The meaning of this passage, which states succinctly the central concern of Husserl's mature philosophy, is that the only real absolute is the ultimate criterion of truth. Phenomenology has shown that the criterion of truth must be *functional*: it must enable one to determine what is true by discerning that which is "given effectively itself" from that which is only retained or anticipated, or remembered or imagined. Revealing the different sorts and various degrees of evidence, phenomenology examines critically the constitutive building of every sort of object; it warns of the necessity of comprehending horizons as part of the "sense" of all that presents itself, and that the different sorts of truth—from the apodictic ideal certainty of mathematical knowledge, to the always partial, always to be corrected experience of material things—all have their own modes of validity.

> *Every* real truth without exception (be it daily truth of the practical life, or truth of the sciences, no matter how highly developed) remains by essence in *relativities* which can be related normatively to *regulative ideas*. The merchant has his marketplace truth; is it not in its sphere a good truth and the most useful to the merchant?[44]

The ideal truth that can function as "regulative idea" through which we anticipate the fullness of truth despite the "one-sidedness" with which most of the

III. *Beyond Positivism and Psychologism*

things of our experience are given is, we now know, attainable only through an adequate phenomenological *prise de conscience* of itself by the consciousness. The standard of clarity, directness, totality, derived from this self-knowledge of consciousness-in-action helps us realize how far many of our scientific "truths" about objects in the external world will always be from realizing such a plenitude. Yet for all their lack of totality, the various kinds of truth we can know about things constitute worth-while knowledge, necessary and useful for human existence; such truths are by no means "mere appearances." Husserl is very insistent in his later works in pointing out the danger of applying too crudely a criterion of truth derived from the sphere of ideal knowledge to all those important regions of experience whose "givens" will never permit the kind of "clear and distinct" intuitions that idealizing critics demand. If we must never cease striving to realize the *ideal* of a knowledge that is total and clear, we must never forget that such an ideal can never be realized fully in most spheres of experience.[45]

The goal of phenomenology is to make us see all of what is given and only what is given. "The beginning of all wisdom," declares Husserl, is knowing how to go to school "naïvely" to the thing, just as it is given to us.

> Judging in a naïve evidence signifies judging on the basis of a giving of the thing "itself" and submitting oneself to the constant question, what must one "see" there effectively and how can one succeed in expressing it faithfully; it is then judging with the same method used by the knowledgeable practical man when it is important to him to "find out how things really are." That is the beginning of all wisdom although it is not the end, and it is a wisdom with which one can never dispense, no matter how profoundly one may be engaged in theoretization.[46]

Nothing is more difficult and more sophisticated than a "naïve" grasp of things on the level of full consciousness. Only adequate phenomenological criticism—a criticism that lays bare every sort of prejudice that would substitute the merely anticipated for the "given in itself"—can assure an untrammeled vision of that which is given. "The will to hold oneself purely to that which is really given" can only succeed if, in every experience, we return to the "ultimate transcendental essential liaisons," so that "the pure intuition is constantly in play in a methodic way." "In proceeding thus one has always anew *a living truth drawn from the living source of the absolute life* and a self-consciousness turned toward that absolute life in a constant sentiment of responsibility to self."[47]

the problem of the other

The attaining of an absolute criterion of truth has not solved all problems, however; in fact, the very nature of an ultimate criterion of truth that considers the horizons of consciousness an absolute poses two very severe problems (the form *the* problem of transcendental philosophy—what we have termed the problem of the reality status of the "moment" in intentional consciousness—takes in Husserl's formulation). One aspect of it is the plague of all anti-realistic philosophical positions, solipsism.[48] The other is the problem of any philosophy that emphasizes the temporal foundations of truth, namely that of relativism. In the *Cartesian Meditations*, a work contemporary with the *Formal and Transcendental Logic*, Husserl makes a serious effort to show how his philosophy is really not a victim of these problems.

The two difficulties reduce to one, namely finding evidence for a real Other that itself displays something of the same absolute quality enjoyed by my own consciousness, in other words, evidence for the coexistence in the world with me of other *cogitos*. The discovery of another "ego" would unlock the prison of my solipsism; and were we to share the *same* world, the basis of that mutual participation would have to be something other than an ever-shifting fantasy of my own fabrication. Since the problem arises precisely because of the *epoché*, I must seek for evidence of the other within the phenomenologically reduced horizons, that is, I seek to describe how he is constituted within "the transcendental facts of my phenomenological sphere."[49] What are in my phenomenal field the facts appertaining to the appearance of the Other?

Husserl goes about answering the question in what seems a paradoxical way: by proposing a "second *epoché*"[50] that will isolate the ego even more drastically, separating out every foreign element to leave "only that which is proper to me (*das Mir-Eigene*)."[51] The transcendental *epoché* had merely suspended the naïve belief in the independent existence of every object of consciousness, but, as we have seen, it left intact the onto-noematic content of consciousness, including the presence of the things themselves. However, if we are to discover not only what is properly *other* but how it can appear to *me*, we must dis-

III. *Beyond Positivism and Psychologism* 129

cern more rigorously what within the phenomenal field belongs properly to me; hence this new act of "abstraction."[52] When I eliminate all otherness, what remains to me?

> A coherent layer of the world, transcendental correlative of the experience of the world, which unfolds in a continuous and concordant manner. We can, *despite* the abstraction which eliminates from the phenomenal "world" all that is not my exclusive property, *advance in a continuous manner in intuitive experience*, holding ourselves exclusively to this layer of "belonging."[53]

While all other objective bodies are left behind by this radical abstraction, one remains integral to the "layer of belonging," namely my own organic body,

> ...the only body interior to the abstract layer which I have cut in the world, to which, in conformity with my experience, I coordinate the fields of sensation... I perceive *with* the hands, with my eyes, etc.... These kinesthetic phenomena of the organs form a flux of modes of action and arise from my "I can." By putting them into action I can crash into things, push, etc., and thus act through my body.... Moreover by my perceptive activity I have the experience (or can have the experience) of all "nature," including that of my own body which by a kind of "reflexion" can be related to itself...the same conditions hold for a possible original action, exercised by the body on nature, and on the body itself.[54]

Since my body constitutes, then, an inalienable part of my experience, and since it is essentially directed toward action on an exterior world, I myself, in the depths of my subjective consciousness, must be essentially a psycho-physical organism; the essence of my psychic life must be precisely that of an experience-of-an-objective-"world."[55] "The totality of the constitution of the world, existing for me, as well as its later division into a constitutive system of what belongs to me and what is foreign to me, is, then, inherent in my psychic being."[56] I now discover that if the ego *constitutes* the world, it also constitutes *me* as psycho-physical organic unity *in* the world.

The Husserlian critique, having completed its radical plunge into the subjective foundations of consciousness, has then rediscovered objectivity at the root of subjectivity, and is thus well along in its necessary follow-up of building back the real world, "belief" in which was suspended by the first phenomenological *epoché*.

> The fact that in general I can oppose that being which is proper to me to something other, the fact that I, who am I, can be conscious of that other that I am not (of something which is foreign to me) presupposes that the *modes of consciousness which belong to me* are not all simply *modes of consciousness of myself*.[57]

This clears the way for us to ask more precisely how the other appears as a phenomenon among the "modes of consciousness which belong to me."

> The "other" enters into the field of my perception. I—the psycho-physical primordial I—am constantly "distinguished" in the interior of the primordial field of my perceptions, independently of the attention I devote to myself, that is whether I turn "actively" toward myself or not. There is in particular my body which *is always there*, distinctly present *for my sensibility* and which, what is more, realizes in a primordial and original manner the specific "meaning" of an organism (*Leibhaftigkeit*). If in my primordial sphere of perception there appears as a distinct object a body which "resembles" mine, that is to say if it has a structure thanks to which it must submit to the phenomenon of association (accouplement) with mine, it *seems* immediately clear that it must at the same moment acquire the signification of organism which is transferred to it by mine.[58]

The essence of Husserl's solution to the problem of knowledge lies in the theory of "accoupling association." All objectivity is the result of the unification of distinct experiences. Accoupling association is the "motivation" (cause and justification) for linking two intentions. It is based on there being, interior to these intentions, some similarity of nature that justifies my associating them. In the case of my knowing another ego we see concretely how one kind of

III. *Beyond Positivism and Psychologism*

"accouplement" can function. In the experience I have of my body as a psycho-physical organism "in the world" I encounter, among the other aspects of that experience which is part and parcel of my body's worldly existence, other bodies which are just like my own. Such bodies which act on nature in a way similar to mine, must also be the seat of a psycho-physical experience of the same general sort as my own, they must also belong to similar egos. Husserl wishes us to see that is it no "supposition" or mere "argument by analogy" that persuades me to make this connection; it is more in the order of a direct intuition of a parallel of natures, if we may so express it. Husserl stresses this point to emphasize the fact that our knowledge of the other is no solipsistic projection of self.

We have now solved the problem of how I know that the other body is really the psycho-physical organism of an ego that, like myself, is an original center of truth and therefore copartner in the founding of the absolute. But the importance of this theory goes far beyond this; actually, Husserl uses it to explain the ultimate basis for all connections in knowledge. For example, it is a form of accoupling that makes possible my unifying a memory of yesterday's with today's perception of the same thing, and both of them with other knowledge of different specimens of the same kind of being. The phenomenon of appresentation is part and parcel of the same "accoupling." "The experience of the exterior world," Husserl says in the chapter we have just been considering, "presents itself in this manner.... For the side of an object truly 'seen'—the face turned toward us—always and necessarily appresents its 'other side'—hidden—and makes us foresee its more or less determined structure."[59] This anticipation is no wild guess; rather it is a completion of what is already seen, justified on the basis of the structure already known. Husserl explains this very well for the important case of my knowing the other ego.

> The foreign organism affirms itself as a true organism uniquely by its changing comportment in a series of experiences, changing but always concordant.... This comportment has a physical side which appresents the psychic as its index. The original experience bears on the comportment, which is verified and confirmed in the ordered succession of its phases.[60]

Husserl develops together his notion of the motivation of objective constitution by concordant associative coupling, and the problem of my knowing other egos, because in this way he can eliminate simultaneously the terrible related problems of solipsism and relativism of which we have spoken. The reality of accoupling association makes it possible for me to know that there is an "other"; in its turn, the existence of the Other contributes to the solution of the problem of relativism. If there are many egos co-existing in the world, all constituting a common "real" time, sharing in a community of action and, through language, in a community of ideas, then this adds great weight to my world, a world containing other egos who find it to be much the way I do.

> The justification of the world of objective experience implies a consequent justification of the existence of other monads (i.e., egos). Inversely, I could not imagine a plurality of monads in any other way than in communication, explicitly or implicitly, that is to say as a society which constitutes an objective world and spatializes itself, realizes itself in this world in the form of living beings, and in particular, human beings. The co-existence of monads, their simple simultaneity, signifies necessarily a *temporal* coexistence and a "temporalization" in the form of real time.[61]

But the problem of the internal concordance of the moments of my knowledge within the flux of experience retains logical priority. We must not be deceived by the way Husserl builds up together the two moments of his solution into thinking that they are neatly solved together. The whole solution to the problem of the other depends on our accepting as convincing the notion that any object of knowledge must be built up within the flux of my temporal consciousness by the concordance of moments different in time and different in noetic status (perceptions added to memories, anticipations to perceptions, significations built on all sorts of knowledge, etc.).

Unfortunately Husserl again and again dangerously weakens the foundations for any absolute certitude in the objective sphere by insisting repeatedly that, while every ulterior intention is ultimately based on the "original creation" of a perception, yet all perceptions are *always subject to possible correction* by succeeding perceptions. Part of the meaning of any perception, as we have seen,

III. *Beyond Positivism and Psychologism*

is an anticipation, both of the "unperceived side" of the thing seen, and of the continuation of its presence to me, in a way that concords perfectly with what I know of the thing up to now. Husserl insists that we can never be certain that subsequent perceptions will not correct our present perceptions. He is constrained to reject the notion that any perception at a moment in time can be absolute, lest he risk installing belief in a kind of "otherness" which inevitably leads to the realistic belief in our attaining directly a thing which exists in itself.

Husserl did not hesitate to speak of the "formal ontological" implications of his work, meaning that phenomenology, having dispelled the absolute being in itself of naïve realism and the idealist's construction of the ego into an absolute thing, has brought to light the real sense of *being*, namely the ego's temporal constitution of a world. Husserl's one-time assistant, Martin Heidegger, will probe into the essence of the human existence seeking an ultimate explanation of how human freedom can bring Being to be, trodding a "forest trail" toward conclusions about the sense of human existence that Husserl did not seem to want to follow, but for which it is difficult nonetheless not to hold him partly responsible. Heidegger will develop radically two other areas of implication, both owing their parentage to the analyses we have just been studying, and again, neither ever explored by the father of phenomenology. The one is the possibility of using the superior phenomenological viewpoint from which to criticize the entire philosophical tradition of the West, seeing in it the whole drama of how historically Western man has brought Being to be in time, and judging the sense of what has happened in terms of the possibilities it presents to the contemporary existent, i.e., what it reveals concerning how we in turn can make Being be.[62] The other amounts to an ultimate consolidation of all these gains—the phenomenological view of the constitution of being, the notion of how history enters into the very fiber of the Being that comes to be, and the realization that the entire structure of Being is rooted in the freedom of the existent who lets Being be (themes scarcely touched in Husserl's authorized publications)—into a complex view of how these elements go together concretely to form "the thing" as we experience it. It is a difficult task confronting today's critics to determine precisely the degree to which Heidegger's conclusions are legitimate extensions of the hidden implications latent in Husserl's own philosophy. It is true that Heidegger has not been faithful to Husserl's call for careful description in "regional eidetic analysis." But if Heidegger has preferred to hurry off in the direction of an ultimate phenomenological theory of being, is it not because his master, Husserl, has left major implications of that basic critical phenomenology unexplored, and has he not himself trained us to realize that all else depends on these questions being answered first?

MAX SCHELER

scheler's phenomenology

As we suggested above, Max Scheler,[63] while unquestionably a "phenomenologist," was no mere camp follower of Husserl, any more than Heidegger was to be. In fact, there was a time, from just after World War I when he returned to teaching until his premature death in 1928, when this broad and penetrating thinker's popularity threatened to eclipse Husserl's, just as Heidegger's was to threaten from about 1927 on. Furthermore, and in this regard he was the opposite of Husserl, Scheler anticipated the existentialists (without being one) in his conviction that philosophy is above all concerned with man's historical situation, and is a message for one's times. Lavishing great attention on the problems of man in the bourgeois, technological era, he strove to make his contemporaries see that there had indeed occurred, principally for social reasons, a pragmatic "inversion of values," and, as Nietzsche had claimed, that a reinversion was urgently needed—an important collection of his essays is in fact entitled *Vom Umsturz der Werte* (*On the Inversion of Values*). But for Scheler, in contrast to the existentialists, what man must go back to is something like the old Christian values, which he insists—unlike the positivists—are objective, i.e., universally valid, and—unlike the Kantians—are not merely formal, but rather are historically discovered. His effort to establish this resulted in phenomenology's greatest ethical endeavor, begun in the imposing work *Formalism in Ethics and the Material Ethics of Value*.

His concern for founding an objective, non-formal ethics affects Scheler's conception of a phenomenological method. While Scheler's phenomenology is unthinkable without Husserl's groundbreaking, he goes his own way in developing a methodological tool in keeping with his own ontological convictions. As several of the most important works of phenomenology written in the last twenty years are closer in inspiration to Scheler's conception of phenomenolo-

III. *Beyond Positivism and Psychologism*

gy than to Husserl's, (e.g., Ricoeur's and Dufrenne's) the careful distinguishing of these two interpretations is essential for an understanding of recent intellectual history.

It is with the middle Husserl who came to feel that the study of being means first and foremost laying bare the constitutive acts of the transcendental ego, the Husserl to whom *to be* came to mean *to be constituted as a phenomenon in my experience*, that Scheler would break. For Scheler (as later for Ricoeur), the taking up of the transcendental viewpoint is not necessarily one with asserting that the only sense the phenomena can have is to be appearances in consciousness; indeed, so to affirm is to prejudge the case in favor of a transcendental idealism. The phenomenologist need not abandon but rather must justify his common human conviction that he encounters in his experience beings enjoying an existence of their own.

Is the criticism implied here entirely fair to the Husserl of the Fifth *Cartesian Meditation*, which concludes, after an ultimate *epoché* reducing everything "to my transcendental sphere of peculiar ownness" that I can accede to the Other, and that the very sense of the flow of "my own" experience lies in its reference beyond the constitutive act of the ego to that which is constituted?

Yes, those in the Schelerian tradition might answer, for the effort to introduce the Other through *Empfühlung*—a kind of sympathetic feeling—is, to say the least, tenuous, and certainly out of all proportion to the overwhelming presence of the Other which I actually experience, a reality which should not be weakened because of idealist predispositions.[64] And the effort to account for all objectivity in terms of the retension and protension of *"Abschattungen"* (perceived profiles) leads inevitably to the inherent weakness of a "philosophy of perception," namely the tendency to overlook the objective reality of structures (forms, essences), and to make them relative to experience. "Socrates is always strong in the face of the Heracliteanism of Protagoras," asserts Paul Ricoeur, in the best Scheler tradition.[65]

Scheler would agree rather with the Husserl of the early *Logical Investigations* that bringing to light "the essences" is phenomenology's real job. He agrees that the essences are "objective," i.e., universally valid *a priori*. But Husserl tended to explain this necessity as a property of the intentional acts constituting a region of objects, so that the "essence" is ultimately considered merely ideal. Scheler however was convinced that not only does this theory fail to account for the *otherness* of the things experienced, but also assumes an idealist ontology rather than exploring the sense of our experience in order to discover what role our knowing plays in the global scheme of things.

The question remains, what is the status and significance of the objectivity in knowledge, how is synthetic *a priori* knowledge of real objects possible? Scheler, as willing as the most critical of transcendental philosophers to go to the "bottom of things," ultimately faces up to *the* fundamental gnosiological question: *What is knowing?*

the ends and means of knowing

One of the strengths the phenomenological philosophers derive as continuers of the "critical" tradition is their unfailing attention to adequate context. The meaning of something, the phenomenologist is convinced, can be understood philosophically only when one has comprehended the ultimate horizons of significance which constitute it. Hence the restless search backward to the beginnings of conscious history, in depth into the hidden layers of the psyche, in extent to the outermost present social horizons of the knower. In this spirit, when Max Scheler undertakes to explain what it is to know, and, negatively, to criticize the pretensions of a narrow scientism that would apparently overstep the bounds of its inherent limits of signification, he does so against the background of a "Sociology of Knowing,"[66] in which it is shown that while ultimately truth is not conditioned by social factors, the tendency in certain eras to favor different kinds of knowing, to select what in general is going to be attended to, is socially conditioned. Scheler employs this realization to create a shock, achieving a kind of phenomenological reduction, helping us stand off from the preferred forms of knowing in our own era, in order to inquire into the whole life-complexus in which they play their overpowering restrictive roles.

Then in the long and rich essay *Erkenntnis und Arbeit*—"Knowledge and Work, a Study of the Worth and Limits of the Pragmatic Motive in Knowledge of the World"—the *ultimate* question is raised in a way characteristic of the phenomenologists[67]: Why do we know at all? What end does knowing serve? It is only against such an ultimate background that an effective criticism of any actual form of knowledge can be critically judged.

Scheler rejects the notion of knowledge for knowledge's sake as totally unrealistic and incapable of throwing the least light on the reality of our actual

III. *Beyond Positivism and Psychologism*

knowing. In this he is in agreement with the pragmatists: We have got to have an end, toward which we are striving, in order to go about knowing. "Knowledge must, like everything we love and seek, have a value and a final ontic sense,"[68] situated in the global complex reality of a life that itself is a becoming.

In order to understand the proper achievement of knowledge we must seek to grasp its *ontic* reality in comparison to the way of being of other kinds of reality, such as things. (*Ontic* is here used in the sense of factual, in contrast to *ontological* which involves ultimate explanation in terms of the deepest ground of Being.) Scheler was concerned to lay the descriptive foundations of his position earlier in his career.[69] Such an undertaking inevitably involves more than phenomenological description of our own experience. In order to seize better the special sense of what we ourselves are, he contrasts our way of being with what we know of the rest of nature, sketching a global view of "Man's Place in the Cosmos," as the title of one of his last essays announces.

What distinguishes organic from inorganic existence, according to Scheler's mature view, is that the living thing has a center in itself. What distinguishes the animal from the plant is that, not only does the animal too tend to push out forcefully from itself as living center, but when it meets resistance from the other centers of force in its *Umwelt* it is able to distinguish itself from that other sufficiently to know it as an op-position, as a *Gegen-stand*. The given physiological-psychic structure of the animal, with the built-in distinction of nervous system and motor system, allows this gap between receptor and received to occur, permitting the animal to transcend to some determined extent the plant's total absorption in its here-and-now relation to what is *actually* given. Memory and anticipation are the cornerstones of intelligence, the ability to envision beyond the actual givens an end, itself given as need or impulse of the organism, and to use what is given as means to obtaining that end. In this sense, the animal has intelligence, for he is able to impose on things the forms which are characteristic of his *Umwelt*, in virtue of the givens of his nature. Thus the bee in building his hive transforms nature, imprinting it with his beelike presence. This biological-practical intelligence is found in man, highly developed but as such not *essentially* different from the instrument-constructing abilities of chimpanzees, of the sort reported by Wolfgang Kohler. "Between a clever chimpanzee and Edison operating as mere technician there is only a gradual (though very great) distinction."[70]

What then is different about men is not practical intelligence but rather a freedom in their intelligence which we shall term *Geist*—spirit. The animal is able to encounter "objects" in a definite *Umwelt* determined by his physiological-psychic structure. His interest is absorbed in those objects as presented. He manifests neither the tendency to reflect on the limits and sense of his own experience, nor the tendency to enlarge his horizons of encounter, to improve progressively his *Umwelt* (which he obviously lives in but does not reflectively dominate). Man's great essential difference—an ability which has nothing to do with the struggle merely to survive, an ability essentially different from that which assures him, as it does for the animal, a place in the world, an *Umwelt*—is the power to say *No* to things as they are primitively, "naturally" presented to him by his given psycho-physical makeup.

Primitively, like any organism, man exists as a hierarchy of drives which, when moving out into the world, encounters resistance from centers of force of all kinds. Indeed—and this suggests how, from the transcendental viewpoint, we can know there are *other* things—that resistance to my impulses is the primitive encounter with the foreign *Dasein*. That foreign existence is presented to me (as it is to the animal) as a given sort of thing, a *So-sein*. How is the form of that "whatness" determined? It is the encounter of the given structures of the sensing-knowing organism with what they allow to be known of the surfaces of the real things' own structures. The animal never goes any further than that. He never reflects on the nature of his own forms, or even that he is the source of the *a priori* forms of his experience. He is limited to dealing with things just as they spontaneously present themselves in the initial interweaving of *Umwelt* horizons and stimuli.

But man can rise above this *So-sein*, he can raise questions about the essential structures in themselves, i.e., about the very nature of the forms he brings to experience, about their adequacy in penetrating beyond the surface of what is most immediately given. The *phenomenological* reduction proposed by Husserl, with its goal of favoring a *Wesensschan* is only the most recent of a long series of historical attempts to seek the sense of what appears by first realizing methodically the extent to which what appears is dependent on that which permits the appearing in the first place.

What ought to be suspended in the reduction, however, is not belief in the existence of the things in the world. That is indeed just what cannot be called into question, the phenomenon of my spontaneous impulses' encounter with a *resisting* other constituting an ultimate and irreducible fact. Rather what can be questioned is the *naïvete* of the *So-sein*—what does it mean for things to be *this* way? *How* can they be this way? Can they be any other way? Such an inquiry tends to reveal the status, the hierarchy, the dependence of our spontaneously deployed *a prioris*, to bring out the more *fundamental* "essences" among them, those that tend to reveal the deepest, most universal and least alterable aspects of our nature. It should be seen that such an inquiry is not, as Husserl tended to suppose, an *ideal* inquiry into forms of experiencing, but an inquiry into *experience*, which concerns itself with the totality of what is given, whether in the order of thought or of feeling; the *a priori* are discoverable in reflection on the *So-sein* as initially given, rather than deduced from the notion of a formative *Denktätigkeit* as the *Critique of Pure Reason* tended to imagine.

We shall return to consider later the nature of these *a prioris* and their importance as ground of our ultimate ontological and ethical knowledge. For the moment, however, and against the background of what we have now learned about the nature of our encounter with the world and the possibility of rising above its givenness to reflect on its sense, we can see that human knowledge, taken globally, serves three sorts of goals of becoming, reflecting both man's animal-givenness and his super-animal spirituality. (1) The lowest is the practical command and transformation of the world in keeping with our human goals, the kind of knowing most resembling the activity of the higher animals, which pragmatism very one-sidedly keeps exclusively in sight. (2) "*Bildungswissen*," the development of the spiritual individual into a "microcosmos," capable of participating in the main structures of the world as fully as its individuality will allow, and in a way that is in keeping with its own personality. (3) "*Erlösungswissen*," literally "redeeming knowledge," knowledge in which the core of our personality participates in the *highest Being and Ground of things*; or in which the ultimate ground of things, insofar as it knows through us, seeks to come to some form of unity with itself, to the "redemption" of a kind of tension, of fundamental opposition which characterizes its struggle from the start. In his religious works, Scheler is very much concerned to describe the forms and appearances of this struggle of Being to comprehend itself through us, an effort in its ultimate goal comparable to Hegel's, but a fresh and original inquiry, quite unhampered by the familiar idealistic prejudices, much influenced by strains of

Christian mysticism, an altogether unique and unusual series of reflections.[71] In his critique of the pragmatic philosophy, however, these higher goals are mentioned only in order to suggest that the existentialist notion that knowledge seeks a goal which itself is no mere knowing, but a loving, a living, a real becoming, is not one with the narrow pragmatist conception of goals.

Scheler is prepared to go far to save the partial truth of pragmatism; but he attacks vigorously those who would make of it an exclusive truth. Thus he not only agrees that the practical handling of the world is fundamental, he makes of this form of knowing an *a priori*, "a general-biological and practical conditioned law of the "natural world-view of men, and thus grounded in natural perception."[72] But it is *a priori* only for experience which is motor-practically important, not for every kind of knowing of the world; thus it is not a rational *a priori*, as Kant suggested, nor an *a priori* of man in general, but only of man as *homo faber* or as "practical-intelligent animal," which is far from exhausting, or even approaching the center of human activity as such. And thus the formal-mechanical natural laws that are derived from this kind of knowledge do not have *ontic* significance, but rather only a biological-practical relative value.[73] There are other kinds of natural laws which are not biologically conditioned and practically limited, namely (1) the formal-ontological laws, founded by pure logic (Scheler here shows to what extent the Husserlian influence remains, even in a late work); (2) the laws of analysis and of geometric topology (i.e., pure mathematics); (3) the physical, chemical, and biological *Gestalt* laws of nature; (4) the material essence-composites, which limit the possibility of the contingent and arbitrary "images" we can have of concrete bodies.[74] This catalogue illustrates admirably the extent to which the Schelerian "essences" are neither empirical nor formal, but rather necessary, universal configurations which arise only in concrete experience. The "things" which present themselves to us in "images" (*Bilder*), and which are structured by these various sorts of possible *a prioris* are then "objective" without enjoying an "absolute existence" independent of any knower. They do not depend on me, individual center of free initiative, but they depend for their phenomenal form on the *a prioris* of human perception as such.

This appeal to the hierarchy of *a prioris*—the other kinds of "natural laws" being less restricted in scope than the biological-practical—is characteristic of Scheler's brand of "essential analysis," or phenomenological *Wesensschau*. We

III. Beyond Positivism and Psychologism 141

glimpse in it his fundamental ontology: Being may be the encounter of the human existent with the things that are, but neither those things nor the forms of the experiencing existent are arbitrary; they are the given real structures of the world. That means that even the forms of our experience—the conditions for the possibility of there being anything at all, as Kant might say—are themselves not merely formal, but also material, that is to say, that either they are one with the real structures of things as they are in themselves, or they are, in other cases, manifestations of what we ourselves are.

the a prioris

What does Scheler wish to affirm when he terms such structures "*a prioris*"? A signification is termed "*a priori*" when it offers itself to intuition as evident, without its having to be predicated of a particular object. It cannot be known "better" or "less well," but rather is either *seen*, or not *seen* (*angeschaut*).[75] The *a prioris*' independence from "experience" (*Erfahrung*) affirms that they neither arise in, can be made clearer by, nor in any other way depend on "observation," "induction," or any other such empirical accumulative process, but rather make all such experience possible and guide it along its way. However, the *a priori* is *for* the sake of the experience, it belongs to the objective sphere, it has its sense only in being "filled up" (in Husserl's sense) by "the facts."[76]

Why does Scheler insist so strongly on the "empirical nature" of his *a priori*—the fact that it is intended to be filled up with experience? Because he wishes above all to reject Kantian "formalism," i.e., any suggestion that the *a prioris* are mere forms, activities of spirit structuring a sensible "matter" which itself is without meaning. Rather he would have us see that every experience has its "formal" and "material" sides, the more universal, the less changing categories in the experience are as "form" to the "matter" of more particular sensible aspects; yet those more universal, more "formal" aspects are but the sense of the matter, and are perhaps particular to still more general insights. "We have to do here with an empiricism," but not of the truncated Humeian kind which arbitrarily restricts experience to a flow of discrete *sensibilia*. "These foundations [of our knowledge] are facts and exclusively facts, not constructions of an arbitrary 'understanding.' ... But the pure phenomenological fact does not receive its first determination from a 'principle' which would be its ground... nor could it be cut out of a pretended 'chaos' of *data*. The *a priori* given is itself made up of intuitive constituents, not of constituents supposedly 'projected' or 'constructed' by thought upon the facts themselves."[77] Indeed, nothing has so paralyzed the development of the theory of knowledge as the arbitrary notion that all knowledge must consist of an ensemble either of sensorial constituents or of ideas thought. Neither pure "thoughts" nor "sensation" could ever account for such conceptions as "force," "similitude," "resemblance," "effective action," "movement," "*esse*" "number," even "time" and "space,"[78] let alone the entire order of values. Rather than being derived from or imposed on sensorial experience, they are, declares Scheler, "acts" *guiding* the experience—they are presupposed by it and in turn it "fills them up" with particular content.

Such irreducible "pure acts" and "act-laws" are to be found in every department of our lives, in the emotions as well as the sphere of objective knowledge; for, as Pascal said, there exists an "order of the heart." If that "order" is to be something more than just rhetoric, then we must recognize that there exist *a prioris* that have nothing to do with thought.[79] They abound in the perceptive-affective order, where they are to be found in acts of preference, love, hate, in all acts of the will. "Feeling, preference and down-grading, love and hate of the spirit, has its own *a priori* content, as independent of inductive experience as the pure laws of thinking."[80] We have suggested already that Scheler was especially concerned with ethics. Not that he neglected the problems posed by the theoretical order; but because no other sphere had suffered so badly from the formalism growing out of a false theory of the *a priori*, he felt particularly compelled to restore to the practical order its lost substance.

a material ethics of value

Our "axiological intuition"—the basis of all ethical knowledge—yields insight into two correlated sorts of *a priori*: (1) the values themselves, and (2) the scale by which their relative worth can be assessed. Values and the order between values are not grasped introspectively (for introspection can tell us something only of the psychic), but in a "living and feeling" exchange with the world (whether physical, psychic or other), in love and hate, that is to say "in a movement meant to accomplish these intentional acts,"[81] values being after all essentially intentional.

Scheler distinguishes four classes of non-formal values. (1) *Values of the pleasant and unpleasant,* occurring in the objects which sensing beings can grasp. Due to the differences in senses, different things may appear pleasant and unpleasant to different individuals, but the values in themselves—what it is for something to be pleasant or not—remain unchanging. I may find strong mustard unpleasant, while you find it the delight of your life; for both of us, however, what it is for something to be pleasant is constant, and *what is pleasant* is always a certain kind of object. (2) *Values connected with vitality*, above all the "noble" and the "vulgar," differentiating higher and lower breeds of plants and animals, manifested by greater or lower health, youthfulness, etc. Scheler thus allows for Nietzsche's supreme values, but he places them in a subordinated position. (3) *Values of the Spirit*, including the aesthetic values of beauty and ugliness, the just and the unjust, and the values of pure knowledge—all clearly transcending the level of the merely vital interplay of organism and environment. (4) *Values of the holy and unholy*, found in certain "absolute objects," discoverable in the religious sphere, saintliness, divinity, etc.[82]

One might wonder, where are the moral values in this list? The moral act, Scheler explains, is essentially directed toward other values, its morality comes from the *rightness* of the act, that is, from its respect for the order among the values. The order of values, itself a matter of intuitive insight, is then all-important ethically. What are the marks of superiority as we ascend the scale just outlined? The higher a value, the more it tends to endure; a spiritual happiness, for instance, outlasts a fleeting pleasure. The higher the value, the less it is dependent on the subject's organism. The higher the value, the more personal it tends to be, yet—a seeming paradox—the more it can be shared with many other persons.

The hierarchy is to be taken this seriously: the most minimal participation in a higher value is preferable to very great participation in a lower.

It was said above that values are not discovered introspectively, but in a "living and feeling exchange" with the world. Scheler was very careful to develop phenomenologically his theory that, while some of our feelings are indeed mere vague states of depression or general anxiety, others are *intentional*, some telling us about our own reactions to situations, others revealing values. The feelings of value are genuinely cognitive, the agreeableness, the beauty, the goodness they reveal are objective values in things, to which the understanding is as blind "as the ear is to colors."[83]

By emphasizing the intentionality of all the acts which cannot be adequately described either in terms of traditional empiricism's "dust of impressions" sensation, nor of Kantian idealism's formalized "understanding," Scheler wished to give the world back its "fullness," without any loss of objectivity. Thus the way is opened to a blossoming of the spirit, dried up as it has been by its philosophic habit of turning in on itself to look for truth, and phenomenology is saved from the rationalistic framework in which Husserl tended to confine it by concentrating too exclusively on the objectivizing acts of consciousness. Instead of worrying about "what we can find in ourselves by internal perception in perceiving-affectively, in preferring, in loving and hating, in enjoying a work of art, in praying to God, let us rather pay attention to *that which*, in the affective-perception, in the preference in the love and the hate, opens up to us: the world and the axiological constituents of this world."[84]

scheler's personalism and pluralistic absolutism

The "value of all values" is the ineffable human person, whose glorification is the very sense of all moral order, and indeed "the sense and the ultimate value of the whole universe."[85] Scheler's personalism places him in conflict with those who like the Marxists consider man to derive his value from the place he occupies in the social whole. It places him in conflict as well with Kantian formalism, despite Kant's affirmation that the person is the ultimate consideration; for the Kantian person was really a universal reason, while Scheler's person is a unique individual, with an irreplaceable niche in the scheme of things, possessing, as each does, a kind of concrete value. The challenge met by Scheler's phenomenology is to describe a world in which persons, each unique, each an absolute, encounter values, general and concrete (e.g., other persons), which are objective and hence absolute, in a life designed to have a sense, answer a vocation, bring fulfillment, yet a life that is free and finite—as I am free, my will can be contrary to the objective values of things because I do not choose to use my faculties properly and hence do not allow the true values in their real order to present themselves to me clearly enough. Scheler makes an excellent case for the contention that objective absolutes and subjective error, real worth and worth ignored, are not only not irreconcilable, but that indeed they constitute the strong lights and obscuring shadows of which our experience is made up.

III. *Beyond Positivism and Psychologism*

Throughout most of his philosophical career, and only softening slightly in his last, increasingly pantheistic phase, Scheler never attempted to hide what we might term his pluralistic and personalistic absolutism—pluralistic in this sense, that there are many points of objectivity in the world that are not subject to a continuous making and unmaking relative to each other. That an ultimate Absolute, embracing and ordering the others, must cap such a system is obvious, and here again Scheler never hesitated, although tending at the end to reduce the *Welt-all* to a principle which can think itself only through the finite human consciousness.

Not only are the higher values grounded in and thus dependent on the realization of the lower ones, but, Scheler is convinced, the higher the value, the less certain is its realization, and the easier is its speculative denial. Only the truly personal act of a loving *Verstehen* can seize the value of the other person.[86] Normally true love tends to be substituted for by acts more proper to the merely vital level, like sympathy, which is then mistaken for it. The failure to achieve a certain dynamism on the lower levels breeds a stagnation, turns into resentment, and thus favors a way of life aggressively hostile to the higher, the personal, loving values.[87] The "love" of "humanity," the favoring of an "equality" in which all are dragged down to the merely practical level of the common mass, not only seeks to substitute for the Christian striving for value-uplifting, creative personal love, but they actually prove hostile to it. Scheler sees the whole history of the bourgeois class as dominated by resentment against the nobles, and thus as a systematic effort to substitute the mass (and merely vital) sentiments of "sympathy" for the suffering of mankind in general for a loving espousal of real persons for their individual worth. He criticizes technological civilization for its over-concentration on producing useful instruments as a manifestation of a mass lack of vitality, the extension of instruments being the sign of phylogenetic stagnation, whereas the sacrifices of real love are made precisely in the name of a creative uplifting of being to a higher level through espousal of the noblest elements in the individual.

Scheler acknowledges the debt owed Nietzsche for his discovery of the superman-oriented nature of genuine love. He criticizes the existentialist, however, for having mistaken bourgeois religion for genuine Christianity; real Christianity always keeps as its center "Love thy neighbor as thyself," rather than Comte's "Love all of humanity more than thyself." In his stubborn refusal to see the individual, spiritual person subordinated to the society, to nature, or even to altruism, Scheler is the genuine continuer of Nietzsche. But in his absolute refusal of voluntarism, in his intricate description of the objective *a priori* grounds of all value he leaves behind every trace of Nietzschean historism, if not to say nihilism, taking on the very difficult task of explaining how all the values of an era are historically conditioned, without yielding to the temptation of saying that the values themselves are subjective or relativistic.

Nicolai Hartmann

the knowledge problem
To the basic knowledge problem, namely, how can the subject go out of itself to grasp an object without ceasing to be itself, or, to put it the other way around, how can an object be absorbed into the structures of consciousness without having its essential transcendence compromised, there have been historically, according to Nicolai Hartmann,[88] three types of answers. The various *realisms* subordinate the subject to the object, which has the evident inconvenience of neglecting those sides of the experience of knowledge which modern philosophies have put so much in evidence—the *a priori*, the mélange of subjective and objective elements in all intuition, and the existence of various sorts of purely ideal knowledge. Yet realism enjoys the irreplaceable advantage of conforming with an ineluctable element of that natural knowledge which, after all, founds the acts of our everyday existence: it attests to the transcendence of the object, never losing sight of the fundamental truth that our knowledge is directed to a grasp of the other in its objective reality.

Idealisms have the advantage of eliminating the gap that would seem theoretically to separate a subject from an object conceived as constituted in itself independently of the structures of consciousness; this idealism accomplishes by attributing the origin of the object and of its structures to the same source that makes possible the ideal intuition of its reality. Fichte achieved the supreme idealist resolution of the problems of knowledge by postulating that the object owed its existence to a projection made by the subject to establish for itself an opposition that it could conquer in its discursive self-building. But the relative ease with which the post-Kantian idealists can explain the objectivity of a

III. *Beyond Positivism and Psychologism* 147

knowledge whose subjective and objective poles derive from the same source, and can make ontological sense out of the *a priori* by explaining how its anticipations of experience can be correct, does not offset the fact that idealist explanations of the subjective origins of the object cannot stand up against the force of our daily experience. For that experience convinces us the realists are right in maintaining the transcendence, indifference, and independence of an essentially heterogeneous objective order.

A third group of philosophers, the *monistic theorists* (e.g., Plotinus and Spinoza) have made a maximum and, in a sense, successful effort to maintain in their integrity and independence both the ontic and noetic orders while laying an ontological basis for their union in the perceptive intuition. But they have done so at the terrible price of "a maximum of metaphysics," meaning the most extreme leaps into speculative theory. Both Plotinus, in positing the "One" from which the *nous* and the realm of the physical thing emanate; and Spinoza, in positing the Infinite Substance of which thought and extension are only correlative attributes, leap deliberately and totally beyond all evidence and all hope of any corroboration of their theories beyond that of the internal consistency of their constructions.

The monists are right in trying to bring together a sphere of real things and the whole sphere of knowledge, with the *a priori* and the ideal not ignored but properly attended to. They are right, too, in seeing that some hypothetical theorizations will have to be resorted to, given our inability to penetrate totally the nature and conditions of our existence (which inability neither the idealists nor the monists seem ever to have been ready to admit). But theorization must pass through the cleansing fire of Kant's criticism. When reinstating the role of theorization in philosophy, as a necessary moment in the quest for an ontology that can found both what we know of the real world and what we know of *how* we know it, Hartmann proposes that it be theorization of the cautious sort, growing out of a maximum of phenomenological description, and never taking recourse to flights that cannot be in some way corroborated by any kind of experience.

The needed "metaphysics of knowledge" (or gnosio-ontology) must be more critical than Kant's philosophy, more phenomenological than Husserl's. It will avoid Kant's uncritical acceptance of idealist presuppositions if it succeeds in holding on to the experience of natural knowledge, which presents aspects of real things in their otherness and makes possible an ontology of the real world. It will be more phenomenological than Husserl by avoiding the sort of ontological theorization which led Husserl to reduce objectivity to a property of consciousness as positing activity organizing the structures of knowledge.

Hartmann shows by his evaluation of the status of phenomenological analysis that he is earnest in his intention to be "more critical than Kant." For, he contends, as phenomenological description moves toward its natural goals—the formulation of eidetic structures (i.e., the discovery of the essences and laws governing the way we encounter things experientially); and the formulation of *aporia*, the inescapable ultimate problems of knowledge and being which it is the very end of philosophy to pose and of the *theories* of philosophy to resolve as adequately as they can—it is subject, the moment it moves interpretatively toward the formulation of an *eidos* or a problem, to the inevitable influence of this metaphysical theorization. This Husserl, with his talk of "philosophy without presupposition," did not see clearly enough; worst of all he did not see, and therefore could not criticize, the *theory* governing the whole of his own speculations. The question, then, is not whether, once it is realized that epistemology cannot exist independently of ontology or vice versa, one's ontology and epistemology should be kept free of theory. Rather the question is, *what kind of a theory* should be allowed to govern one's elaboration of an essential conception of the structure of knowledge and being. To be admissible, a theory must meet one criterion—namely, that it will always submit to some, even though it may be very indirect, experiential corroboration.

Let us see more concretely by examining Hartmann's most basic work. *The Principles of a Metaphysics of Knowledge*, what kind of problems (*aporia*) are raised by an ontology of knowledge, and what kind of a legitimate theory Hartmann would admit to guide us toward a tentative solution that slights neither the reality of the *a priori* and of ideal knowledge, nor the objective independence of the concrete thing.

the metaphysics of knowledge

Knowledge is oriented toward two different spheres of objects: real objects and ideal objects (e.g., the mathematical values and essences; also the realm of values). The problems of knowledge concern both spheres; the reason that

III. *Beyond Positivism and Psychologism* 149

so much difficulty has arisen from these *aporia* is not only the natural limits of our knowledge, but also to some degree the mishandling, by each school of philosophy, of aspects of one or the other of these spheres. Hartmann points the way to theoretization which could resolve each major *aporia*, precisely by underscoring the aspects of experience which now one philosopher and now another has had the misfortune to overlook when trying to solve them.

1. *The general* aporia *of consciousness*.[89] The dominant problem—the knowledge problem—is, of course, the central difficulty of explaining how a subject, constituting a reality enjoying self-determination and interior life, can grasp the structures of things which transcend it and exist in themselves. To respond to this problem, a theory must slight neither (as the realists do) aspects of ideal knowledge, nor (as the idealists) the transcendence of the object. Hartmann's hypothesis is that some of the categories of our consciousness must have enough in common with some of the categories of the transcendent object to account for the idea's being able to represent the reality. Because both the conscious life and the real category of the object are participants in that *being* common to all things, conscious or not, the subject can find in itself enough affinity with the object to make it possible, through a system of symbols organized out of the categories of its own consciousness, to represent all that it intuits mediately of various categories of the real. If we are able to grasp the relations, causality, substantiality, unity, multiplicity, etc., in transcendent objects, is it not because we ourselves possess these very traits in the categories of our consciousness?

As a critical philosopher enjoying a clear grasp of the implications of the transcendental viewpoint, Hartmann is aware that our knowledge cannot be simply a grasp of the "thing-in-itself"; were the categories of our knowing one with the categories of the thing itself, there would be no possibility (a) of error; (b) of distinguishing my knowing from the thing known; (c) for the existence of ideal being without counterpart in the real world. On the other hand, however, were my knowledge not to coincide at least partially with the thing-in-itself, then it would simply not be *true*. The phenomenon then must offer at least something of the Being-in-itself (*Ansichseiende*). "One can in no way grasp phenomena without to some extent also knowing the *Ansichseiende* which appears in it."[90] Yet the phenomenon is, of itself, "Being-for-us." "It is not the thing itself but only its counterpart (*Gegenbild*) and this can deviate from the thing (*Sache*). Never can we see to what extent an appearance is real 'phenomenon' and to what extent *merely* appearance (*Schein*). Therefore all awareness of the thing as it is in itself must begin by a critical clarification (*Deutung*) of the phenomenon."[91] How is this possible? How can the aspects destined ultimately to prove themselves faithful representations of categories of the thing-in-itself be distinguished critically from those which are in fact mere *Schein*? Hartmann's whole *Kategorienlehre*, pursued unrelentingly for thirty years, is devoted principally to the effort of making some progress toward resolving this "antinomy."

2. Aporia *of perception and the given—the* a posteriori. The basic difficulty raised by "the overlapping categories" approach is manifest. It suggests that ours is somehow only an *indirect* knowledge of the thing-in-itself; yet does not the experience of perception carry with it the conviction, unshakable for the ordinary man in his natural knowledge, that in our *a posteriori* knowledge we attain directly to the concrete, individual existing thing? Moreover, our grasp of ideal objects carries with it a sense of the immediate possession of the object by the spirit.

The first step in making some progress with this time-honored *aporia* is to distinguish *a priori* and *a posteriori* knowledge carefully, while admitting of course the reality of both. Then we must observe what it is that *a posteriori* knowledge yields to us. Sensation attains the material object directly and concretely, but only phenomenally. The sensible qualities are however rich, varied, constant (with a psychological constancy, due to the whole body's devotion of all its sense powers to grasping the thing). In the core of its being, however, the thing remains transcendent; it is known only indirectly through the sensations, which the subject organizes categorically into an object, taking the sensations as symbols of the thing-in-itself, which are then interpreted, according to their constant sense, by means of the categories of consciousness—categories of relation, causality, multiplicity, unity, etc.—formed, that is, into a system of symbols that stands for the thing. Such a system of symbols is not subjective, not arbitrary, but strictly *objective*; it enjoys a transcendent value for two reasons: (i) the sensations themselves attain mediately, through the sensing organism, to real aspects of the real thing; (ii) the categories of consciousness that are used to organize the sensations into an object are, like the hidden depths of the thing-in-itself, *principles of being*; principles of being in consciousness can

III. Beyond Positivism and Psychologism

serve as symbols for principles of being in the real world while it remains partially hidden from us.[92]

We can see now how perceptual knowledge can yield *a priori* knowledge, i.e., knowledge with a universality and necessity that transcends the concreteness and contingency of perception; and why such knowledge can be universal and necessary: because they are *of* being, the categories of consciousness can be sources of universal and necessary knowledge that can be applied perceptually to every sort of concrete thing.[93]

This suggestion, far from dissolving the basic *aporia* in the theory of knowledge, enhances the enigma of the ontological problem. The ontological question now becomes: *How* does the common root in being of the real categories of the thing-in-itself (which are hidden from us in their depths) and of the categories of consciousness make possible this knowledge of the one by the other? Is it by analogy, as some have suggested, that is to say do we, recognizing in perception signs of the existence of such categories, then feel authorized to project back behind these perceptions categories *like* the categories in consciousness to which we have direct access by reflection?

There are two difficulties in such a suggestion. (i) It implies that the applicable categories of consciousness are not really the same as those in the things, but somehow only like them—which leaves the problem of the *Übereinstimmung*, the correspondence of the categories—fully unsolved. (ii) It suggests, as the idealists have tended to maintain, that we have preferential experiential access to the categories of the understanding. But, Hartmann points out, all our knowledge is directed to a grasp of the things themselves, and it is only late in our reflective history that we even become aware of some of the *Denkformen* for their own sake. It is in the concrete phenomena that we must seek out the categories first—the real categories of the things themselves. The *Kategorienlebre* begins consequently as a phenomenology. It is only in the course of the descriptive analysis of experience that we begin to distinguish kinds of categories, categories of the real from categories of spirit, and among the categories of knowledge those which prove helpful in illuminating the sense of some of our concrete experience from those which obviously do not apply to the material order at all.[94]

Hartmann refuses to be deceived into thinking that any formula will simply solve the ontological problem posed by knowledge, revealing the profoundest secrets of being and of our consciousness to us. Fortunately, however, the use of knowledge does not depend on our first understanding what are its categories and how to apply them, although our more sophisticated knowledge does benefit from criticism—especially criticism of the misapplication of categories—and needs it to remain on the path of truth consistently. Meantime we can do little more theoretically than affirm the ultimate identity between the categories of being and those of thought.

As we continue to examine Hartmann's formulation of and response to the principal *aporias* of knowledge, the basic theory of categorical identity in the oneness of being will remain the key to every solution. It will tend to draw our allegiance, though not by becoming itself any more translucently evident, but simply through its virtue of making sense out of all the givens of our knowledge situation in a way that makes possible their reconciliation in a minimally speculative metaphysics faithful to all the evidence.

3. *The* aporia *of* a priori *knowledge.*[95] The *immediacy* which is so characteristic of the experience of the *a priori* is explained: it is rooted in the very categories of consciousness. The "objectivity" of that *a priori* knowledge which is united to *a posteriori* perception to give us knowledge of a universal "state of things" (*Sachverhalt*) is made possible by the "identity of categories."

The groundwork of applying our theory to the other basic *aporia* helps us dispatch those two problems quickly. But the *a priori* poses still a third problem which has proved particularly troublesome to philosophy (especially to recent philosophy) and which deserves also some attention. That is the problem of the status of ideal *a priori* knowledge. We saw just a moment ago that Hartmann invokes the existence of such knowledge—*a priori*, universal, ideal, not concrete and material, yet existing in itself—to help explain how some categories of consciousness can be identical with the categories of being in other spheres. What is it that leads Hartmann to hold (as Husserl and Scheler held) that there is a sphere of *a priori* ideas which can be confounded neither with an aspect of concrete material being (they are not "abstractions"), nor with the forms of consciousness itself?

A priori ideas are distinct from the forms of consciousness because these obviously must be the same in all men, otherwise there would be no foundation for the potential existence of the same *a priori* ideas in all men; but the *a priori* ideas themselves exist in all men only potentially; they must be learned—at least some of them. Granted, once they are known they are seen to be im-

III. *Beyond Positivism and Psychologism*

mutable and absolute, valid for all times and all knowers. But nevertheless they only come to be discovered at certain periods in history; the geometry of Euclid was not known in Homer's day. Their content and their gradual discoverability distinguish them from the forms of consciousness upon which they depend as a condition for their being, but to which they cannot be simply reduced. Moreover, numerous *a prioris* resist complete rationalization.

But *a priori* ideas cannot be reduced either to abstractions of forms derived from the sensually perceived concrete thing: like Husserl, Hartmann is convinced that the very nature of sensation is in every aspect the opposite of the *a priori*—the contingency, concreteness, flux, accidentally of sensations contrasting with the necessity, stability, essentiality, and universality of all *a priori* knowledge. That is why Hartmann and Husserl both tend to look upon *a priori* ideal knowledge applicable to concrete things in the real world as related somehow both to perceptual data and to the universal, necessary structures of consciousness.

Hartmann's position regarding the knowledge of real structures enjoying universal necessity in themselves can only be understood against the background of the long tradition maintained unbroken since Descartes, that it is nonsense to look in sensation for the experiential ground of the universal necessity of our knowledge.[96] But where Kant (and the Neo-Kantian school) was convinced that only a non-noetic ground could be proffered for the applicability of the *a priori* categories of the knower to the thing-in-itself, Hartmann, like Husserl, is convinced rather that our *a priori* intuitions of the necessary structures in being are an intuition of the *Ansichseiende*. No other explanation, they feel, can account for the overwhelming success with which our *a priori* knowledge matches with vast ranges of concrete fact, indeed with the whole sensible realm, which it could not organize, in depth as well as in extent, if merely imposed formally from above upon an unsuspecting matter, about which we ought to wonder why it has anything to do with it. Nor could we explain how it is possible to criticize *wrong* applications of categories to experience. But as the supposed phenomenal, "profiled," superficial, hopelessly partial nature of sensation remains virtually a "truth by definition," there is little alternative but to attribute the necessity of our universal judgments to the inherent possession of categorial insight which guides us in the deciphering of the signs of essential structures which sensation mediates to us.

4. *The* aporia *of the criterion of truth.*[97] It was necessary to introduce these brief background remarks to help bring out the nature of the problem confronting Hartmann when he raises the important *aporia* of the criterion of truth and of progress in knowledge. The problem of a criterion of truth arises here, as it does traditionally, the moment subject and object are considered in opposition, and when the subject's grasp of the thing-in-itself is considered, as it is by Hartmann, indirect. If our perceptions are organized about categories of consciousness which, in part, coincide with the categories of the things themselves, how are we to be certain which of our representations symbolize truthfully the object and which have no objective counterpart?

Whatever we find it to be, we can expect no criterion to yield absolute certainty about external objective knowledge; of this, both the representative nature of knowledge and the fact that the coordination of structures is only partial, warn us. Hartmann, convinced that different categories interlace to constitute the same thing, develops this cautious criterion: Every aspect of our grasp of a transcendent object should be confirmable by a different grasp of the same object through a heterogeneous part of our knowledge. Not only, for example, can the evidence of one sense be checked against the presentation of another, but the *a posteriori* data of sensation can be correlated with and checked against certain *a priori* structures having a bearing on the same objective sphere. Conversely, the *a priori* can be checked experimentally against the sensible data.[98]

Applied to the truth of an ideal representation, this theory of "the criterion of the two-fold liaison" becomes more complicated. When purely ideal objects are in question, the heterogeneity of *a priori* and *a posteriori* elements is obviously lacking. However, ideal intuition "does not content itself with being an isolated intuition of separated essences…it reconstitutes the connections which exist between the intuited essences."[99] To the "stigmatic intuition" of essential content must be added the "conspective intuition" of an ensemble of relations.[100] The verification of the isolated essence occurs in placing it in an ensemble with which it has to coordinate intelligibly. "The principle of contradiction plays here the role of criterion," and this in a double way: (i) by checking the absence of contradiction between the notes within the particular structure; and then, (ii) by checking the absence of contradiction between the particular structures within an ensemble, and finally between the ensemble and the whole sphere of the ideal itself.[101]

III. *Beyond Positivism and Psychologism*   155

5. *The* aporia *of knowledge of the problem; and the progress in knowledge.*[102] Another problem arises from Hartmann's refusal to identify being and knowledge, namely, how does he know in the first place that there *is* anything lying beyond the horizons of our knowledge? The very fact that we can pose the problem of knowledge is itself a problem in this order, for the very posing of the problem seems to suggest that somehow we are able to step outside the limits of our knowledge in order to view it as a problem—which of course we cannot.

This difficulty is closely linked with another—that of explaining how progress in knowledge is possible. We recall Plato's difficulty: how can we advance knowingly toward that which is not known?

To clarify the solution to these problems Hartmann asks us to see that the realm of both ideal and real being-in-itself divides into three spheres: (i) the horizon of objects known, i.e., the horizon within which an actual coincidence of categories of consciousness and categories of either real or ideal being has taken place; (ii) the trans-objective, the sphere of potential objects, the unrealized possibility for categories to coincide further and yield progress in knowledge; (iii) the trans-intelligible, that sphere of being-in-itself that will never become an object of knowledge. This distinction helps us to see that our problem really poses two questions: (a) how can we know now that here exists a being-in-itself which we can know possibly, but do not actually know? (b) and how can we ever know that there exists a trans-intelligible sphere which, by definition, we shall never know?

The very existence of such a problem confirms the existence of a transcendent being-in-itself. Were there a total coincidence of conscious and ontological categories, as many idealisms have supposed, the problem of the subject's grasp of an object could never have occurred to consciousness. Perhaps, too, if there were to exist a finite consciousness completely closed in on its own limited structures which were not themselves transcendentally oriented, as seems to be the case with the animals, there would be no suspicion that there existed something beyond the ken of its knowledge. But since it so happens that human knowledge is essentially transcendent and objective in its orientation, it does in fact make progress, which progress is its own evidence that there probably lies beyond our present knowledge more things that we could grasp. It is only a step further to the realization, that since being-in-itself goes on its own way not caring whether I grasp it as an object or not, there must certainly be areas of being for the intuition of which my consciousness is totally inadequate.

While this suggests how we can infer the existence of both the trans-objective and the trans-intelligible being-in-itself, it does not yet solve the problem of how any progress toward the unknown is possible. Were the trans-object perfectly isolated from the knower, then progress toward such a completely transcendent goal would indeed be impossible. But in fact we are linked to the trans-objective in two ways. First, the objects we already know are ontologically related to other objects of which we have not yet taken full conscious possession. Second, the subject is linked to the things in the world in many ways other than the particular relation of conscious knowledge. By physical, volitional, emotional relations we are connected with a world of objects of which our conscious knowledge may not yet have a full intuition. These two sorts of link with the trans-objective—through other things and through other than cognitive intentions—offer some explanation of the possibility of progress in cognition.

the new ontology and the foundations of a philosophy of nature

Hartmann's principle that the categories of consciousness and the categories of being are not totally coincident rules out an idealistic ontology whose categories can be deduced from reason.[103] His Neo-Kantian theory of perception rules out the traditional realistic ontology's direct intuition of the principles of being in the thing-in-itself[104]; indeed Hartmann is in complete accord with Kant that the ancient claim to intuit substantial forms and to read the teleological structure of the universe directly in the natures of things has been undermined by the critique of knowledge. Yet, for all that, an ontology—a theory of the fundamental categories of being—is indispensable; without it, there can be no epistemology, no psychology, no theoretical foundation for ethics.[105] But where and how is a new ontology—a truly post-critical ontology—to find its categories?

> The categories with which the new ontology deals are won neither by a definition of the universal nor through derivation from a formal table of judgments. They are rather gleaned step by step from an observation of existing realities. This method of discovery does not allow for an absolute criterion of truth....[106]

III. Beyond Positivism and Psychologism

But just to the extent that ontological categories do coincide with categories of consciousness, can they not, to that modest extent at least, be intuited *a priori*?

Even this modest hope proves deceptive. In the first place, we have no criterion to measure the extent of that categorial identity. And precisely where on practical grounds we are more or less certain of this identity—in everyday life and for our natural orientation in the world—this identity is philosophically worthless because it does not bear upon the problems of philosophy. But where these begin, it becomes extraordinarily questionable and soon fails us completely. Second, in our cognitive apparatus there is lacking one fundamental prerequisite for so exploring this identity: an immediate knowledge of our own cognitive categories.[107]

In fact, Hartmann adds, our knowledge, being directed toward objects, is concerned first with things; only later, reflecting on our knowledge of things, do we come gradually to discover some of the categories, not only of the things, but of our knowledge of the things. To the extent that we can know categories, then, we do so "through an analysis of objects to the extent that they are intelligible to us."[108]

The basic material of the new ontology is the whole of what is given, i.e., our entire experience in all of its aspects, including the results of the sciences. Hartmann rejects the notion that we should limit our concern to a primitive givenness. Interpreting "primitive" in a way that, I do not believe, the phenomenologists intended, i.e., as a layer of unsophisticated initial givenness such as children and primitive peoples enjoy, he shows that I can enjoy no direct access to such a consciousness.[109] More positively—and more justifiably—Hartmann places confidence in natural science as an indispensable way of access to the full range of what we *can* know of the things themselves. Perfectly conscious of the "categorial limitations" of mathematical computation, Hartmann at the same time, in defense of the kernel of truth in the Galilean conception of "primary" and "secondary" qualities,[110] considers the intuition of extension as providing an immediacy of access not enjoyed by the *a posteriori* experience of secondary qualities like color, taste and sound.[111] The latter, however, are, for all their mediateness, nonetheless just as *real* as the *a priori* mathematical intuitions. Moreover, science cannot exist without a mass of fundamental non-mathematical categories:

> Not every aspect of inorganic nature is quantitative determination; even here is the quantitative only one among a number of basic moments, and not in the least the most fundamental. All quantitative determinations depend on certain "substrates" through which they enjoy their reality…e.g., spatial extension, temporal endurance, movement, speed, acceleration, mass, force, energy.[112]

One of the novel features of Hartmann's *Philosophy of Nature* is his consistent underscoring of the incalculable nature of the "supporting substrates" which transcend mathematics and depend essentially on other forms of categorial knowledge, "even in inorganic nature."

Hartmann's tendency, at once to accept at face value the findings of science as quite unequivocally true, indeed as more reliable than the reports of most other kinds of knowledge, and at the same time to bring out with exhaustive painstakingness the vastness of the realms of things which essentially transcend the categorial possibilities of science and which we do know, results in his works in a unique combination of the findings of science with those of the categorial and intentional investigations of the phenomenologists.

The method for extracting an ontology out of this vast range of "givens" is "*rückschlagende* analysis," "a penetrating study," not loath to the cautious use of hypothesis to guide its inquiry, "backing up" toward the categories from out of the broadest possible base of data derived from the widest experience of every sort of being.[113] Such a science is still in "the cocoon stage," so the history of man's search for the categories of being holds precious hints for it, especially since we have to date been able to "stabilize" only very few individual categories. The rest we are continuing to evolve.[114]

Categorical analysis must search for its categories just where empirical science has gaps—not, of course, with the ambition of developing them into definitions through bold assumptions but with the opposite tendency of recognizing their irrationality and deliberately integrating it into the total picture. Perhaps there are no ontological categories without an irrational component. Even the well-known principles of substantiality and causality are, in their essence, not wholly knowable. What substance actually is, how it maintains itself through its incessant transformation, how a cause goes about producing an effect—all these things cannot be explained any further. Nevertheless a great number of phenomena can be explained on the basis of these categories.¹¹⁵

A good portion of Hartmann's philosophical efforts have gone into analyzing the *Construction of the Real World*, to borrow the title of one of his major works.¹¹⁶ It is impossible even to begin to summarize Hartmann's detailed and careful analyses of the various spheres of being and their interdependence, his "modal" analyses of "reality" and "possibility," his analyses of the categorial laws, of the various "levels" of reality and their "*Stufenbau*"—their step-like construction—with the higher dependent on the lower, but irreducible to them; nor of the "special categorial analyses" of the characteristics of the various spheres—the "spiritual" in *Problem des Geistigen Seins*, the inorganic and the organic in *Philosophy of Nature*, and the realm of values in his *Ethics*. However, this one thing can be said about the impact of all these analyses in general. Philosophers acquainted with the critical tradition are likely to be won over to Hartmann's analyses of the "real world" only to the extent that he has succeeded through his "metaphysics of knowledge" in laying a solid basis for an ontology that escapes definitely Kant's objections against ontological analysis that would pretend to speak in a universal way of the real world. Hartmann admits that there is no critically justifiable "proof" in the strict sense for the "reality" of the real world, and no absolute guarantee ever that our use of categories is in union with the way the things are in themselves. Therefore the task of criticism is a never-ending one, and our knowledge of categories must progress in a never-ceasing "dialectic," our ideas seeking to conform their increasing rational comprehension to the given "*Sachverhalt*"—state of affairs. "In contrast to the old dogmatic ontology, the new ontology must claim to be critical. And if perhaps the new ontology can only partly justify this claim, it must at least pave the way toward this goal, in order to better its claim as its work progresses."¹¹⁷

ethics

Hartmann erected on the basis of his gnosio-ontological theory a rich ethical analysis. Although we shall not pause here to scan the ethical details of Hartmann's work, we shall consider enough of the fundamental aspects of Hartmann's conception of values to throw some light on his notion of man as "spiritual being."

Because of their universal worth, ethical values, declares Hartmann, are evidently *a priori* and ideal, but differ from other ideal objects in being destined not for contemplation but for action.[118] One seizes a value directly by an emotional act, "an act in which one takes a position (i.e.) a sentiment."[119] Such an act always contains a gnosiological core; thus it always influences the consciousness and can become the object of a reflective contemplation which is capable of considering the nature of the value without reference to any particular concrete action.[120] Nevertheless its orientation is toward action with concrete things.

But how exactly does such an ethical act "transcend" toward the real world? Hartmann distinguishes in this regard three aspects of the ethical act: (1) the emotional consciousness' internal taking-a-position; (2) consciousness of the object to which the value is directed (justice or courage do not function in the abstract, rather as justice toward a neighbor or courage in the face of a specific dangerous task); (3) consciousness of the reason which determines the position taken. The second moment is manifestly a simple act of knowledge of the real, for here one apprehends a real person, an action, a situation, etc. The third is knowledge of the ideal, the intuition of values. The first of these three moments—the taking-a-position itself—the properly emotional part of the act, is manifestly conditioned by the two other aspects, consequently by two acts of knowledge.[121]

But what type of knowledge act is this grasp of the ideal mentioned as the third moment in the emotional act? Do "values" exist independently of concrete "exterior" reality, in a sphere of their own? If so, how are they related to the general axiological principles (general principles of ethical and esthetic value) known abstractly by ideal reason and bearers of the "transcendent ideality" which alone can found universality and necessity? Here the critical question of the status of the ideal is asked in the most meaningful and vital context, where obviously a solution is essential to a good theory of action. It would seem, hypothesizes Hartmann, that "behind the values there must exist axiological principles," and these must be open to some sort of "intuition capable of penetrating directly into the different particular axiological matters enjoying an existence-in-themselves of an ideal kind."[122] Such an intuition is admittedly "enigmatic, mysterious," but no more so than perception of the real and the basic "stigmatic intuition" of the ideal object.

III. *Beyond Positivism and Psychologism*

In the later *Ethics* and again in *Problem des geistigen Seins* Hartmann is more successful in suggesting what is the nature of this special realm, obviously neither dependent on "exterior" nature nor irrelevant to it. We see the realm of values as the sphere of encounter between the given structures of nature and a spiritual existent, enjoying the capacity of foresight and therefore of the projection and pursuit of ends, whose ends are conditioned, however, by the given nature he possesses and by his concrete real situation. But this existent, while dependent on the inorganic and organic nature which are subsumed into the higher forms of his spiritual way of existing, still can operate freely in respect to them.[123] In Hartmann's view, this freedom may reach its highest point in man but does not await this, the highest level of being, to first manifest itself. Values, we suggested, result from the encounter of a sense-giving, knowing existent with his world. The freedom of this sense-giving nature keeps the values from being compelling, the way the animal's *Umwelt* fascinates and absorbs him. There is "room" in the whole structure of spiritual encounter with the world for a development in our sense of values.[124]

Though he insists on the *a priori* nature of the axiological principles lying behind the intuited values, and on the internal intuition of a realm of ideal "being-in-itself" as a source of value-knowledge, Hartmann still emphasizes here again, as in his ontology, the distance between his thought and idealism. He invokes the multiplicity of ethical systems and the historical development of ethical positions both in the individual and in the race, all constituting a wide spectrum of values extending from materialistic interests on the lower end of the scale to morality in the top range.[125] This is evidence which accords poorly with the idealistic overtones of the *a priori*. The key to this paradox is the double face of the postulated "stigmatic axiological intuition." Looking toward the concrete thing or act with which it is concerned, it appears *a priori*, for the intuition reveals a state of values enjoying universal, absolute validity. Looking toward the whole ideal sphere of our system of values it appears *a posteriori*, because each such intuition adds to our treasure of insights into value.[126]

This echoes Hartmann's discovery of the possibility of progress in *a priori* knowledge. The "stigmatic axiological intuition" is a faculty of finite man grasping little by little particular aspects of that ideal being-in-itself which is revealed partially in every value. The individual does not know "value as such," the "good-in-itself." The exigencies of *situations* in time and place, confrontation with other persons and the things we must share with them, are at each moment in life and at each stage in history the particular occasions that incarnate now this value, now another. Particular systems of ethics grow from the complexus of axiological intuitions enjoyed by individuals.

With each person's experience a hierarchy of values begins to manifest itself: there are subordinate spheres of value—moral, vital, thingly value, and that set of *Lastaverte* which express the simplest and most fundamental needs of the living organism[127] or subordinate values within a given sphere. Within the sphere of moral values, to take the highest group, the good resides in the value most expressive of the realities of a situation, while oriented toward that "happiness" which consists in the realization of the individual's noblest possibilities—considered again, not abstractly, but in view of the individual's situation. The "good" does not reside in the abstract value of an act but, as in the parable of the widow's mite, in the quality of the effort.[128]

Hartmann insists on the objectivity, the universal validity, and the necessity of the values thus discovered in the heart of the concrete situation. But how am I to know that the values I have represented before me are the overriding ones?

Once again, there is no absolute criterion. Hartmann proposes instead a negative criterion, valid essentially for all spheres of value. Different individuals enjoy "organs of axiological perception" of different potency. Of those who are blind to many values, "one cannot say that they commit positive errors concerning values, for what they do perceive as having some value really does. Their error is rather negative; they are blind to many values that a more developed organ would have clearly felt,"[129] much the way a person lacking musical sensibility will not perceive the values incarnate in a Mozart sonata. Error enters, of course, into the interpretation and generalization that accompanies all systematization of ethical experience; but that is another question.[130]

The very complicated body of ethics examined by Hartmann in his extensive work on this subject consists, to be sure, of far more than mere commentary on the brief epistemological indications we have given here. Yet as long as there remain problems about Hartmann's theory of knowledge, the ethics can be no more free of suspicion of resting on unsecured foundations than will Hartmann's categorial analyses of the "construction of the real world." Despite

III. *Beyond Positivism and Psychologism*

the encyclopedic range, the care and insight of Hartmann's works, he has not enjoyed the world-spanning attention of a Heidegger or of a Sartre. Some will claim that it has only been their talent for dramatizing that has secured the existentialists their enormous audience. As we turn now to the first of the several German and French existential thinkers we are going to study, Heidegger, we shall hope to suggest that there are, on the contrary, some sound philosophical reasons for their deserving the attention they have had.

IV. Two German Existentialists

MARTIN HEIDEGGER

"fundamental ontology"

In the introduction to his fundamental work, *Being and Time* (1927) Heidegger[1] proposed to establish, by using a phenomenological method, a "fundamental ontology." Indeed, according to Heidegger, if we understand what "phenomenology" really means (etymologically it has to do with the *logos* of the phenomenon, of that which appears), we shall see at once that a phenomenology has to be an ontology, and the only valid ontology will have to be phenomenological. For to give the *logos* of the phenomenon is to explain *how* that which appears can appear,[2] it is to explain the Being of the things-that-are (*das Sein des Seienden*). Only in probing to the ultimate foundations, in the human existent, of the possibility of opening a transcendental, temporal horizon in which things come to be can we live up to Husserl's exhortation, *zu den Sachen selbst!*—"Back to the things themselves!" Like Husserl, Heidegger rejects naïve realism's belief that we can hope to grasp things authentically, if uncritically. The whole tradition of Western philosophy has been an effort to understand the Being of the things-that-are, an effort which has both revealed and dissimulated Being, and on the way has conclusively proved that nothing is more difficult to understand (what is nearest is farthest away, as Heidegger has well put it). Yet we cannot pretend to understand *things* profoundly without understanding their foundation—what it means for them *to be*: how they are constituted in a world of meaning, and what it is to *be a thing* within a transcendental horizon of meaning.

The key to understanding the meaning of things is understanding their Being; and the key to understanding their Being is understanding how the human existent (the *Da-sein*, the Being-there) founds a temporal "world" of mean-

IV. *Two German Existentialists*

ing in which there can be any *things* at all. Heidegger's *Sein und Zeit* explores the existent's opening of the transcendental horizon that lets the light of Being shine on things so that they come to be meaningfully, historically, in time. In four hundred pages of dense description Heidegger shows that the *Dasein* founds the "world" in which he lives with things by projecting, from the past he inherits, a future which gives meaning in the present to the things-that-are. Husserl had stressed the importance of protension and retention in the simplest act of sense perception. Heidegger probes behind this psychic condition to show *how* we anticipate the "not-yet" in the light of "the no longer there" that we retain, stressing the creative freedom of the process. He shows that instead of living rooted in the present like a tree is rooted in its soil—standing in its meadow the passive victim of (to it) meaningless things, the rain that pelts its leaves, the wind that sways its branches, the worms that eat its bark—man rather *ex-sists*. *Ex-sistence* implies a certain kind of non-involvement—a standing out from the present, which permits a creative relationship to present things. Man's fundamental act of knowing depends on this "freedom," this capacity to tend toward a future which he forges out of what he has discovered in the past to be genuine possibility. The meaning of the *Seienden* I encounter now is in part interpreted in terms of what I am looking forward to, which in turn is in keeping with my past experience. A tree can be for me a thing because it can have meaning for me as tree; but the meaning of tree can in one instance be that of a nuisance threatening to fall on my house, or, in another, the center of the landscape I am arranging in my garden. In both instances the way I visualize the tree, in the light of my standing-out toward the future, is made possible by my bringing, to the present *Seienden*, light from the past; which previously revealed past-possibility is made living and applicable now because of my projection of a future. The possibility of a tree's falling with unhappy results on my poor house does not occur to baby John, who can look at the tree but who can *see* nothing. When baby John's experience increases until he has enough of a past to begin to possess a future, and when enough objects have fallen on his innocent head to awaken a sense of a need to will to survive, he may be able to begin to live out ahead of the present enough to make of the light of the past something meaningful.

Our "world" of meaningful relations to things is more than a jumble of *ad hoc* manipulations of some instrument (*Zuhandensein*) for some limited practical purpose, or of odd collisions here or there with some object (*Vorhandensein*) that just happens into our path.³ These relationships of the moment are part of a larger personal history, which in turn is the continuation of a whole tradition that stretches back for centuries. Underlying the tissue of particular projections which course through my day is a kind of ultimate structure, based on the way I project the fundamental form of my life, which determines how I conceive my very relationship to things. To make this clear, let us contrast the two most radically opposed possible ways of conceiving the basic truth relationship, i.e., our relation to the things-that-are, and we shall see in them two radically different ways of existing.

The *realist* conception of truth and what Heidegger calls "inauthentic" (*ineigentlich*) existence go hand in hand. As a form of existence they shape our entire tradition from the Greeks to modern science, the *metaphysical* way of existing. The realist conceives truth as a conformity of the intellect and the thing. To the realist the "thing" is simply *there*, before me, an ob-jectum lying over against me, in opposition to the subject who is to conform his mind to the thing. The realist's answer to *how* the thing can be there, can be either Plato's, "the Idea makes it be there; it is a reflection of that super-thing, other worldly, outside time"; or Aristotle's, "it is caused by the super-thing, pure *energeia*"; or St. Thomas', "God, who is *Actus purus*, caused it, it is the product of the thingliest of things (*Seiendste des Seienden*)."⁴ The realist always looks *meta-ta-phusika*, out beyond the sum total of the things of our experience (*das Seiende im Ganzen*) for an explanation of their presence before me. So convinced are they that there is the thing-in-itself lying before me, already constituted as ob-jectum, that they are unable to see that the question, *how* can the thing be present, can have another and prior meaning: *how* can the human existent open the transcendental horizons of consciousness to make present that which is present? They do not realize that, because my horizons are *transcendental*—meaning that whatever can *be* for me has to be within those horizons, obeying the conditions for presence prescribed by the possibilities of consciousness, the problem of the Being of the things-that-are is the problem of elucidating what I mean by their Being for me, as things constituted the way *Dasein* makes things be. That is why realists have always and will always miss the significance of time and the meaning of history. They do not see that the Being of the things-that-are (*das Sein des Seienden*) is historical (*Geschichtlich*), unfolding as a tradition, a structure of interpretation, in which one generation passes on its conception of truth to the next, which in turn draws the very possibility of a way to relate itself to things from the limits and actuality of the previous moment of this destiny (*Geschick*).[5] That is why the realist will always view his own conception of the nature of things as a whole (*das Seiende im Ganzen*) as Being-itself, and all deviate conceptions as simply erroneous.

Failure to see that Being is not a thing (whether *Idea*, *energeia*, or God) nor the totality of things, but that *Sein* and *Seiende* are radically different even though one cannot be without the other, is disastrous, both for the tradition as a whole, and for the existence of the individual *Dasein*. Let us consider first where "inauthenticity" led the tradition, and then we can see its effects on the individual's life.

The conformity theory of truth, establishing a bipolarity between subject and object, is open to an easy change of pole, which is precisely what has happened in the movement of the Occidental tradition from Descartes to Kant, and paradoxically culminated in the voluntarism of Nietzsche and the humanism of modern technique. Because the tradition has never understood where really lay the problem of the presence of that which is present, it ended up unabashedly concluding—when it became aware that things are not just simply *there* over against me (ob-jecta), but rather have to be placed there before me (*vor-gestellt*)—that the represented ob-jecta (*die vor-gestellte Gegen-stände*) are placed there by subjective consciousness. Placed there how? In conformity with the needs of life. Post-Kantian idealists, still under the influence of twenty-odd centuries of metaphysical thought, of course conceived "life" as an Absolute, existing *meta-ta-phusika*. Even Nietzsche, who realized that finite will operating for its own sake was a quite adequate explanation of a life force and a good enough reason for an explanation of why and how things are placed before me; Nietzsche, whose conception of a *Wille zum Wille* fulfilled and ended the search *meta-ta-phusika* for the Being of the things-that-are, still absolutized the pattern of the interpretations of will through the doctrine of the Eternal Return, for reasons we shall examine more closely when we consider the problems confronting the phenomenological conception of Being.[6]

The contemporary form of *Uneigentlichkeit* (inauthenticity) which we inherit from this long tradition is the humanism of modern technique.[7] Science, industrial organization, totalitarian bureaucracies, scientific reorganization of the whole planet are all phenomena growing from the conception that man is to impose the order of his will on the world. Science regards the *Seiende* as a bundle of forces waiting to serve man; industrial organization harnesses these energies, transforming the face of the earth until nature is no longer recognizable. Bureaucratic organization musters the brute force of many wills to carry out the exploitation according to the dictates of a Super Will. To become planetary is the natural goal of such reorganization; because of its very nature, it recognizes no limit, no tradition, nothing sacred. Why should anything be sacred, and why should there be any mystery if everything is of, for and by *me*, or rather of, for and by the Powerful One?

Such a truth conception, such a conception of *things*, such a form of existence is in some ways closer to the authentic conception than the tradition has ever been, save in the beginning when the pre-Socratic thinkers began to wonder about the Being of the things-that-are. It is closest because it is "farthest away"; the perfectly inauthentic is always a total parody on the authentic; and the greatest absence of the sacred, of the mysterious, of authentic Being makes this very absence of the authentic most evident. If the authentic conception holds that the root of the Being of the things-that-are lies in the freedom of the *Dasein*, see how close such a conception is to the inauthentic exploitation of things for will by will! Modern humanism's refusal to look *meta-ta-phusika* for an explanation of the presence of what is present is close to Heidegger's call for an *Überwindung der Metaphysik*, a surpassing of metaphysics.[8] Yet between the modern "fulfillment of metaphysics" and Heidegger's call for "surpassing metaphysics" there is an abyss. We can see the nature of this abyss better if we consider the roots of this situation in the individual existent.

The abyss that separates the two conceptions is what Heidegger calls the Abyss of the Nothing (*der Abgrund des Nichts*).[9] It is because the authentic existent confronts the mystery of the nothing that, ironic as it may seem, he does not fall into the nihilism of modern technical humanism. The inauthentic existent—whether he be the merchant too occupied with daily concerns ever to think much about the presence of what is present, or the metaphysician who posits the existence of a superthing to account for the presence of things, or the scientist who may hold that things are there for what they can yield—always fails to see that those things are present for me because I can project a meaning through my freedom from out of nothing, thus bringing Being to be. Before

I can ever see this, I must be brought to see how the things-that-are depend for their Being on the founding of a world by my projection of transcendental horizons. Only a radical experience of my own dependence on nothing can make me see this. In *Sein und Zeit*[10] Heidegger shows how "anguish"—the realization that I am a being mysteriously "thrown" into the world and destined to die—can make me see that had I not been so "thrown" there would be "no thing," and that after my death, the entire world of my projections will be "no thing." Anguish before the reality of the radical contingency of the "world" is Heidegger's existential counterpart to Husserl's *epoché*: It is the radical experience that throws my whole "world" into relief, showing its dependence on the transcendental horizons of consciousness.

The anguish of the realization of death reveals to me that the way the things-that-are come into Being with a meaning in history is similar to the way I am thrown into the world; and that they have the same mysterious origin: they both come from "no thing." Every act of interpretation that gathers up the light of the past and uses it to bring meaning to things in the present, in the process of projecting a future, is an act of creation, and the "thing" that is thus brought to be opens marvelous new horizons, like the word of the poet or the quartet of the composer. Some thinking is little more than a reshuffling of things previously revealed.[11] Of this "calculative thinking" Heidegger warns that it "uses up" the meaning that has been stored in things by previous creative acts, just as a word becomes tired and trite when mouthed a million times in the market place.

In opposition to such destructiveness, the authentic existent who recognizes that the birth of meaning—the making-be the things-that-are—being creative, is always a kind of miracle, comes to "care for Being," to protect it, by treating as mysterious, sacred, and precious the "gifts of Being" that through the ages, in the acts of "originative thinking," bring things to be. For he realizes that such originative thinking is our only source of food for life; he recognizes that things only come to be when a creative *Dasein* captures in "the Word" the light that sustains things within our horizons. The essentially creative act of making things come to be in the Word Heidegger terms the act of *poeien*, poetizing.

the poetic conception of authentic being
Dichterisch wohnt der mensch auf dieser erde—poetically dwells man on this earth.[12] This word of the Romantic poet, Frederick Hölderlin, whose poetry

is the major inspiration of Heidegger's recent thought, is truly the *Leitmotiv* of the Heideggerian *Denken*. It is only man, the mortal (*der Sterblichen*), who "dwells." Animals cannot dwell, because animals are not mortal; they die, but they have no capacity for anticipating the future, they cannot foresee death, they cannot know that they are *Sein-zum-Tode*. The ability to conceive of life is, ironically, the fruit of man's "mortality." For to be able to conceive of life as a whole which I form by my free acts of projection I must be able to see where ultimately I am headed—and that is toward death, "*Dasein*'s ultimate possibility." That man conceives of this end which is "not yet" is indicative of the creativity of human existence which need not be the passive victim of present circumstances.

But man cannot simply dwell; he dwells "on this earth." In the essay, "On the Origin of the Artwork," Heidegger explains how the *Dasein*-projected world is rooted in things which are already there without our creating them, but which take on meaning only when they become part of a world. The Heidelberg Bridge leaps the Main to tie together the Schlossberg and the hill of the Philosopher's Way into a human landscape. Yet the bridge can be only because the earth is there to yield its stone, and it is into this earth that the strong pillars of the bridge are sunk. Only the mortal can dwell, but he must dwell "on *this* earth," which means, in the words of "On the Essence of Truth,"[13] by letting the things be what they are. For we do not create the things, we understand and interpret them, giving them "Being" in the historical "World." Our interpretations, unless they are to be pure fantasies, cannot be arbitrary, but, for all their creative "giving meaning," they must do so in a way that lets the *Seiende* be what it is. To use Heidegger's example: Cape Sounion now has a meaning it would never have had had the temple of Poseidon never been constructed there; but the temple can convey that meaning only by according with the site. Man's dwelling is an act of freedom; but that freedom is grounded in finitude. It is, says this same essay, *Notwendig*, which we must not too quickly translate "necessary," for Heidegger writes it, *Not-wendig*: it is a result of the finite existent's "wandering (*wenden*) in Need (*Not*)."[14] What is this "need"? It is the need to understand Being, which implies two corollary *needs*: the need for the *Seienden* and the need for the "gift of Being," the creative poetic light from out the Nothing that brings meaning to things in the World. This is what it means to say that man dwells *dichterisch* on this earth.

IV. *Two German Existentialists*

To understand the basis of authentic human existence is to understand how the thing comes to be. The thing comes to be because the mortal *dwells* on this earth. In the essay "Bauen Wohnen Denken,"[15] Heidegger explains that dwelling implies precisely "building the thing" in which we dwell, making the thing to be. Heidegger would have us see the connection between *bauen* and *bilden*, the thing being built, as it were, by the mortal's ability to *bilden*—recalling the Kantian discovery that the center where the phenomenon comes to be is the *Ein-bildungs-kraft*, the imagination. The important thing to understand, though, is that the product of the authentic *Einbildungskraft* is not a *blose Bild*, a mere image, but precisely *ein Ding*, a thing. The mortal dwells "on this earth" because the poet can build the thing "by which dwells the mortal."

The thing (*das Ding*) is neither an arbitrary image, nor is it just *Seiende*. The authentic *Ding*, built poetically by the dwelling mortal "on this earth," is rather the mysterious lingering of "the four-fold unity" (*Gevierte*), which is the unity of the three time-exstases in the one projecting *Dasein*—the mortal.[16] Heidegger (in "Das Ding" and again in "Bauen Wohnen Denken") gives the Hölderlinian name to the origin of each of these four that compose the thing: the mortal, the earth, the heavens, and the divine. In this way he is able to capitalize on the rich poetic meaning Hölderlin has woven about each of these terms. Heidegger's "mortal" recalls to mind the Wanderer in Hölderlin's "Homecoming"; for the mortal is the child of history, seeking now that he has enough experience to be fully conscious, to return to the homeland of authentic things by escaping from the "errance" of the long metaphysical tradition. The "earth" is the dionysiac fruitgiver, the sustainer of life, the ever-present, always necessary dark force, which not only gives but mysteriously takes back into its bosom what it has given. The heavens, in the moon's course and the sun's daily journey, bring us the light that has been and will be again. Heidegger does not have to decide too abruptly when he clothes his thought in Hölderlin's magnificent language, whether the destiny which produced us has an element of the necessary lying inevitably beyond men's wills, whether this destiny will inevitably return on itself or not. The basic tenor of many Heideggerian analyses leaves us with the impression that he would respond "no" to both questions. But Hölderlin would seem to say "yes." How far are we to subscribe to the original sense of these images?

The same kind of problem exists with regard to the "divine." *Unbekannt der Gott*—unknown is the God that dwells in us, says Hölderlin. Heidegger will term the creative element of the "always more" in *Dasein* that makes possible the mystery of new revelation the *divine*. But we must not see in such an appellation an invitation to restore the God *meta-ta-phusika* whose death Nietzsche has ringingly announced. The God is in us, and is *Unbekannt*. He will remain *Unbekannt* as long as Being is forgotten; and Being is forgotten as much by making *Sein* equivalent to the Thingliest of Things as it is when we make the coming to be of things into a subjectivism. All Heidegger would have us do is clothe in a sacred awe the mysterious source of the creativity in us—that future-projecting poetizing which draws the power to make things linger in the Word from out the Nothing—and for the rest fall silent. The mystery of the poetical building of the thing is best protected by a respectful silence in awe before the coming to be of Being.

Heidegger will emphatically deny that such a doctrine is nihilistic.[17] The thing is not built from the "nugatory nothingness" of arbitrary will for the sake of will. It is built of *Seienden*; of the carefully preserved and respected light of past poetic comings-to-be; and of the mortal's originative acts, which themselves are not nothing, even though "unknown is the God who dwells in us." And he will deny with utmost vehemence that it is a subjectivism. "Being is not a product of thought; rather the opposite, essential thought is an event of Being."[18] Being is not a product of an idealistic representation (*Vorstellung*); nor is it a projection of will-for-the-sake-of-will. For Being, we must remember, is a destiny (*Geschick*), and when the poetic act of originative thinking co-operates in the coming to be of Being, it does so by inserting itself into a tradition which it furthers but does not create, and it exercises freedom in order "to let things be as they are."

Still, the mystery remains: Whence the new element in the truly originative act that lets Being come to be? In choosing to remain silent before this mystery Heidegger certainly hopes to foster respect for a real world in which, though *Dasein* occupies the central position, we are not absolute masters of all destiny.

Can the ultimate principle of a philosophy be the enigmatic and the unnamed and still provide sufficient protection against the arbitrary and the nihilistic? Is the silence Heidegger invokes divine or diabolic, as Kierkegaard would ask? Such a question brings out the extreme importance of history for this "phenomenological ontology." History is our only guide, the reality of past revelations that have made things be becomes the only destiny that can give meaning to the future—a future that is death-directed. But in what sense is this a direction? How are we to interpret the sense of what we read there, since interpretation in its essence is an act of future-direction? How can the "God" within us if he remains "unknown" direct us down the dark corridor that stretches toward annihilation in death, providing the essential discrimination that can keep us from wandering further from the "forest trail"? *Holzmacher und Waldhüter kennen die Wege. Sie wissen, was es heisst, auf einem Holzweg zu sein.*[19] Does it really suffice to penetrate to the sense of our historical destiny, seeing it as the revelation-dissimulation of Being; does it really suffice to know where not to go, to become the woodcutter and forest dweller who can find the way? Or must the direction of vocation be more positive than that?

Karl Jaspers

Karl Jaspers[20] is as sensitive as Heidegger to the nihilism threatening Western civilization.[21] But Jaspers' answer to this threat suffers from no Heideggerian ambiguity in its affirmation of Transcendence. Since Nietzsche, whom Jaspers also respects enough to take most seriously, the quest for Transcendence needs to be more solidly secured in reason than Kierkegaard thought necessary, for it now must withstand the attacks of nihilism. Jaspers owes a great debt to Kierkegaard, and candidly admits his admiration for him. Yet he has no wish to be a Kierkegaardian in his way of seeking out signs of the Transcendent. In place of the "leap," Jaspers advances the cause of reason rooted in existence, of "philosophical" rather than religious faith, based in as much illumination of our situation and of Being as we are capable, so that ultimate convictions owe nothing to irrationalism, but instead bring reason to an encounter with the properly unthinkable.

Jaspers is as ready as Heidegger to admit that the quest for Being must take place within the limits of the human situation. But unlike his contemporary, he is unambiguous in stating that both the being which we are ourselves, and the Being which surrounds us and of which we are only a part, have a sense that points beyond the limits of our horizons. Whether we explore outwardly into the world of things, or inwardly into the roots of our own experience, we discover no resting place, "no standpoint or any sequence of standpoints from which a closed whole of Being can be surveyed."[22] Whether searching outwardly or inwardly we always discover, at the limits of inquiry, the Encompassing (*Umgreifende*).

the encompassing that we ourselves are

Rather than start with the exploration of encompassing Being, Jaspers prefers to explore first the Encompassing that we ourselves are; for it is there, within the horizons of our own consciousness, that all Being comes to be for us.[23] The illumination of our own reality is not attained by the application of a particular objective method, nor can the field of study be precisely delimited in advance. We are not "objects" for ourselves, awaiting disinterested exploration as though we were mere things. Rather, we gradually come to a knowledge of ourselves by a process of seeing ourselves in encounters with things and other people. The Encompassing that we ourselves are is discovered "in situation," deploying its reality in the world of things, in the world of consciousness, and in the destiny of history. Let us examine in turn each of these levels.

1. The primordial level of reality of that Encompassing which we ourselves are is *Dasein*, objective being in the world of things. (Note that Jaspers' use of the term is not restricted, as Heidegger's is, to the human existent, but is rather the normal German usage, designating concrete existence.) *Dasein* is a reality with a beginning and an end; it is a struggle, through extension of one's power over others, to assure one's endurance, and to achieve success in the quest for happiness and good fortune.[24] "Everything that is real for us must have an aspect according to which it is *Dasein*," declares Jaspers in a principle giving the full measure of his realism, and showing that the lesson of Nietzsche's attacks on idealism are not forgotten.

2. In order to be real for us, something not only has to be an object in the concrete world of struggle and time, but as experienceable it must, to some degree, be capable of becoming part of our world of meaning, i.e., it must be in part an object of consciousness. For the Encompassing which we are is also *Bewusstsein überhaupt*, participating in the noetic world of "general consciousness" whose content enjoys universal validity for all knowers in all times, and whose ideal is a truth that would be an intelligible One.

Sensual encounter with objective things that does not move toward consciousness is dark and meaningless; concepts of consciousness without reference to and roots in *Dasein* are empty and without effect in the real world. The

IV. Two German Existentialists 175

Encompassing which we are dwells in both worlds, and they fulfill each other. Just as Jaspers, in describing man's fundamental reality as *Dasein*, indicates the validity of realism's insistence on the basic ground of all existence in a world of concrete things, so in the description of "general consciousness" is he admitting a place for the Kantian confrontation of structures of consciousness with the "given" perceptual data. Unfortunately, like Kant, Jaspers prefers to accentuate the mystery of the meeting of the general and the particular, of the temporal and the timeless in human existence, rather than dwell on the details of how this comes about.

3. The third aspect of the Encompassing which we are points the way to understanding something of this meeting. For the temporal existent is also "spirit." As spirit, he is able to guide his way according to an enduring idea through the flux of events, things, and moments which constitutes life in the world. Spirit seeks to bring every aspect of its dynamic activity into the clarity of general consciousness; and, conversely, it seeks to make of the idea a reality effective in the world of time and space. The conceptions of general consciousness enjoy an atemporal validity; but the ideas of spirit—idea here being used in a sense that recalls Hegel—must descend into the world of concrete things and make their way among the forces of the market place, to provide them with a kind of unity, and to consecrate them to the higher ends of human history. The unity provided by idea as mediator between concrete and universal, temporal and timeless, concept and *Dasein*, is not a closed one; it implies a movement which never attains in this life total fulfillment, but for which idea can provide at least a direction.[25]

The meeting of the concrete (*Dasein*) and the universal (*Bewusstsein überhaupt*) in spirit (*Geist*) capable of giving unity to the concrete movements of history as Jaspers describes it would provide something of a Hegel-inspired solution to the problem of the universal and the particular if Jaspers did not insist on probing beyond spirit, which is shown in its turn to have frustrating limitations, to the level of existence itself, thereby discovering a principle upon which *Dasein*, general consciousness and spirit alike depend.

Signs of this dependence on the freedom of existence can be discovered in analysis of all three aspects of the Encompassing which we are.[26] Each level of freedom is revealed to be a unique way of communicating with reality; each, when it seeks to become autonomous, reveals its incapacity to stand alone;

each, then, needs the other two. All three levels of freedom are aspects of one fundamental unity, the freedom of existence, which is the basic sense of the Encompassing itself.

1. *Freedom on the level of* Dasein. From a very early age I discover myself as *Dasein* trying to make my way in a world of things, using knowledge as an instrument of my power over the obstacles that oppose me. (Objective science is for most just such an instrument.) Similarly my relations with other persons on this level are usually nothing more than *Gemeinschaft*—a power group bringing together individual wills to attain a goal of mutual self-interest. Freedom is used for domination over things, as I seek primitively to assure my minimal well-being.

2. *Freedom on the level of general consciousness*. Increased maturity brings with it a "sense of responsibility," which carries with it the realization that merely forcing one's desires on the world is no fulfillment for a human being. We come to see that man has moral obligations, revealed by the grasp we enjoy through general consciousness of the forms of human nature. The ethical man seeks universally valid goals to guide his actions. Freedom is exercised within the structures of duty.

The consciousness allowed to reign alone in its quest for clarity and universality will tend to regard *Dasein* as a mere starting point for its "superior" operations, and to consider spirit and history as the darkling plain where only confusion and obscurity reign. Freedom caught on the level of general consciousness is reduced to "obedience of universal law," much in the Kantian sense; and communication is reduced to timeless participation in the eternal sphere of the ordered and the clear.[27]

3. *Freedom on the level of spirit*. Only very great maturity brings the realization that participation in the world of history and of time requires that a life have its own unity and direction. The historical realization of an idea provides for an exercise of freedom that is more vital, more engaged, and more flexible than mere obedience to the eternal structures of consciousness, yet more unified, more embracing and more inspiring than freedom's power-group schemes on the level of *Dasein*. Men bound together in the common pursuit of an historical idea through family, profession, university, etc., bringing continuity to the efforts of generations, welding individual actions into the self-less organic development of a tradition, calling for the noblest sacrifice of individual desires

IV. Two German Existentialists

to the preservation of the living whole, contrast vividly with *Dasein* struggling in the collisions of selfish power groups. And the living, ever-transforming unity of the historical organism displays a vitality that is lacking in the general forms of duty with which consciousness is concerned.[28]

But for all its dynamism, unified direction, and noble purpose, freedom as spirit is no more self-sufficient than *Dasein* or consciousness. That the freedom of *Dasein* is limited is obvious, both in the frustration of its projects (the quest for "endurance" is thwarted by death, "happiness" by the resistance of other things to our efforts to control them to assure our well-being, and "good fortune" is constantly haunted by the specter of ill health), and in its need to be subsumed into the living structure of spirit lest freedom be stifled by an empty dogmatism. The insufficiency of spirit, however, is less readily evident. The fruitfulness of union with others in a common historical enterprise can disguise the fact that, to find meaning and even preservation itself, such fruit requires something beyond historical idea. The sad truth is that these ruling ideas are never fulfilled and never total, never one in the perfect unity of truth. That is why spirit, left on its own, yields to the temptation to complete its task by constructing a false, hasty unity. In the intellectual order, this can lead to a Hegel; in the political order, to the *Terreur* of the French Revolution; in any human life, to the blind imposition of a partial and inadequate idea to every aspect of life, as though it could provide the needed total unity.[29] The way beyond spirit to the discovery of the deepest level of freedom, that of existence itself, lies less in realizing the limitations of spirit, than in the positive discovery that it is always *my* act of freedom that makes possible all activity on each of the three levels of the Encompassing which we have been considering. But mature man who discovers for the first time the originativeness and fundamentally of his own act of freedom also faces a danger. He can be so taken by the realization that his will is inexorably unique that he will be tempted to withdraw into majestic solipsistic isolation. However, to yield to such a temptation would be to misunderstand what it means to be and how one becomes a self. I can only realize my proper selfhood in the midst of some kind of communication which puts me in contact with and throws me over against the other. Our previous discoveries of freedom on all three levels of existence already pointed to this fact: in each case freedom was a way to deal with the exterior.

In a manner reminiscent of Fichte, Jaspers points out that when the "other" I encounter is only *Dasein* (either things or other people approached as though they were only something to be manipulated), then I discover myself merely as life-force, as "soul," in short as myself a kind of thing. When my encounter with others takes place through our mutual participation in the world of general consciousness, it is only the "knower subject to general law" as such and not myself as a genuine individual that I discover. Joined to others in the life of the spirit, I find my attention monopolized by the reality of the whole, rather than by the foundations of the whole in my freedom. All of these discoveries concerning myself are real, for I am indeed in part all these things—*Dasein*, consciousness, spirit—yet none of them could be were it not for their ground in "the Truth that I myself am," the ultimate source of unity and direction for everything I do, whether I recognize it or not.

I only become aware of myself as truth when I encounter the reality of others as themselves living centers of truth. This implies an act of profound communication "from originative source to originative source," as one freedom encounters another freedom in the very act of making-be a destiny. Love indeed uncovers the supreme paradox: The truth which I myself am, which provides unity for the idea of spirit and a living context for the concepts of general consciousness, which guides my life as *Dasein* in the world, that truth which itself is one and which seeks oneness on every level, *is not the only truth. Du bist auch eine Wahrheit!* You, too, are a truth, seeking among the things of the world, in the categories of clear consciousness and through the historical realization of an idea, that unity which alone can be the Being of the things-that-are. Only in the "loving struggle" (*liebenden Kampf*) that brings together unique centers of truth in an effort to extend the lines of battle toward the one of absolute truth do I exist fundamentally enough to realize what I am, and to encounter in the paradox of these many living truths signs of the Transcendence of the Being "in which and from which I am" (*in dem und ans dem ich bin*).[30]

Jaspers puts great stress on the limits of the Encompassing that we are. An important section of the *Philosophie* is devoted to analyzing the existent "in situation," and in showing the limitations incumbent in all situations.[31] In analyzing the "general situation-limits" of human existence, he points out that I am always limited to being "in a determined situation" at one time, in one place, participating in only one part of history. This means, then, that my approach to

IV. Two German Existentialists 179

the other *Dasein* will always be limited to a particular *perspective*.[32] Added to this are the "particular situation-limits" facing each individual, namely death (which frustrates *Dasein*'s desire to endure), suffering (which contradicts any claim to a universality that would be above the limits of the real world), struggle (which results from the partiality of all ideas of particular spirits, each struggling to make itself total), guilt (by which Jaspers means that our finite existence is limited in all that it does, so that its every choice of a possibility requires the exclusion of many alternative possibilities).

This encounter with the limits of the Encompassing which I am directs the search for the one toward the other Encompassing—that Being from which I come and of which I discover I am only a part.

the encompassing as being itself: world and transcendence

"The encompassing which we are is not Being itself, but rather the genuine appearance in the Encompassing of Being itself."[33] The discovery of the situation-limit, the exploration of the Encompassing that we are to its outermost horizons has proven that Being "is not made by us, is not interpretation and is not an object"[34]; on the contrary, the limits of *Existenz* in a world it did not make suggest its subservience to a Being that transcends it in every way. Jaspers' declaration, above all the phrase "it is not interpretation," gives some measure of the distance separating his philosophy from Heidegger's. Heidegger agrees that Being is not made by us and is no object; but for him it is interpretation (*Verstehen*), in the sense that "Being" only comes to be in time within the "ek-static" historical horizons of the "*eksisting Dasein*." Jaspers emphasizes the transcendence of Being, in the sense that the Being we discover within the horizons of interpretation points in every way to a reality independent of those horizons. The glimmerings of this Transcendent which encompasses the Encompassing which we ourselves are take on the utmost importance in his philosophy. We meet them in greatest evidence at the root and at the end of our quest for the one of truth. At the root of our quest for truth—on the primitive level of *Dasein*—we encounter the limit of *fact*.[35] "Even though we create the form of everything we know (for, in order to be intelligible all *Dasein* must be subsumed under the categories of consciousness)…yet knowledge cannot create the least particle of dust in its empirical existence."[36] Hence our truth is dependent on experience for its "matter." On the other hand, when we seek to penetrate beyond the many appearances in which Being comes to us, to grasp in an adequate intuition their real ground, ultimate Being always recedes from us. Not only do the forms of consciousness never achieve formal unity, but what is even more striking an evidence that we do not attain the one of truth, you and I never live the same truth.[37] From this lack of totality is born the war of ideas that marks the history of spirit. The irreducible "otherness" and the multiplicity of fact, the lack of totality of the forms of general consciousness, the war of historical ideas all, then, spell out to us the same hard reality: That the Encompassing which we are, rooted in the individual's unique act of *Existenz*, and struggling with a truth that is "other," cannot be the ultimate basis of that truth nor even of its own personal reality.

the transcendent one

The quest for the one is the task of "reason." "Reason is not unity but the Encompassing that we are [viewed] as impulse toward the one, in an effort to realize unity through the understanding of all Being. Reason is unity as task and as the way. Movement is the proper way of being present for this unity which remains unfulfilled in objective time [*Zeitdasein*] but in each reason is actually palpable as originative source and as end."[38] Not only is the one "palpable" (*fühlbar*) as source, sustenance, and end of the unified and unifying movement of reason, but also as we have just seen, in the experience of all limits.[39] Both the reality of the impulse to unity and its frustration everywhere it turns must be read together dialectically as part of the same phenomenon; for this unfulfillment of the really fundamental urge in us is the greatest sign that we hold our Being in a Transcendent which alone can fulfill it,[40] while the fact that the Encompassing which I am seeks Being in unity warns us that the Transcendent is not sunk in the opaque struggle of dispersion and manyness.

Such meditations on the Transcendent, drawn from our experience of the encounter between the Encompassing-which-we-are and the Enconpassing of Being, need speak of the Transcendent in a language that is neither objective and compelling, nor unambiguous.[41] The signs of the ultimate are never more than "happened-upon accidents, indicators and glimpses," to be read in an interplay of the negative element of all limits and the positive element of actual, though limited, reality. This, says Jaspers, is God's way of protecting our liberty; He prefers to speak indirectly, uncompellingly, in the soft voice listened to only

IV. Two German Existentialists 181

by faith. Believe, and everything becomes a sign of the Transcendent; or doubt, and then the limits become the incursion of the nothing from which we temporarily rescue a Being destined to be dissolved again into the black night from which it came. This great "either/or" commands the ultimate principles of Jaspers' philosophy. "The experience of the situation-limits leads the way [either] to the nothing or to being."[42]

The reality and limits of the human situation, and of the Encompassing that is Being, can be read through the eyes of philosophical faith as "ciphers" (*Chiffern*) of the Transcendent, so that reason and existence, the two poles of the Encompassing that I am, can break through to a glimpse of the unseeable (can "think the unthinkable thought"). The embracing of this paradox is what separates the *Existenzphilosophie* of Jaspers from Heidegger's *Fundamentalontologie*. Although both thinkers move in that "Night following the evening of the eveningland," their thought is radically different in that the one believes that there is a star beyond, while the other insists that the light must be recreated uniquely from within. Before contrasting these dramatic alternatives offered by the contemporary philosophical scene through an analyses of the differences that touch even their methods, we must concentrate on the most characteristic feature in Jaspers' faith-guided philosophy, the discovery of the Transcendent.

The road to Transcendence is twofold:

1. As a road leading beyond this world (*als Weg über die Welt hinaus*), through mysticism, in "wordless and objectless love" (object here meaning the kind of thing encountered experientially in the world), in renunciation of this world—it is open only to the "exception" who succeeds in breaking through the world of objects and ego to the inexpressible, immediate standing-open of Being itself.[43] This way is prepared for the man of faith through participation in an objective, historical "model of redemption" (*Erlösungsvorgang*), the adequate imitation and fulfillment of which cannot be achieved in this world.

2. As a road *in* the world (*als Weg in der Welt*), it has two forms: Most men look for a paradise which they conceive as a kind of continuance of all they like in this world. The "Eternal return of the like" reflects this attitude, transformed by one who does not believe in life for the soul after death. The other form is the one Jaspers chose to explore in his own philosophy: Some men are capable of living *in* the world in such a way that they are able to glimpse through and beyond it (*hi der Welt gleichsam quer zur Welt*).[44] The movement along this road

is "the dialectic of rebellion and rest."[45] Constant revolt is necessary to keep man from embracing the false repose of the affirmation "by an abstract '*Ja*' of the whole as an undetermined life-feeling."[46] Against all forms of abstract, false mysticism the revolt stands ready to reaffirm the reality of the concrete, of struggle, of existence itself. Yet rest is necessary as an end of the process, or the struggle sinks into the blind combat of meaningless forces. In one of those moving passages in which, since the war, he echoes the language and music of the Lutheran chorales, Jaspers terms this peace "*die 'ewige Ruh in Gott dem Herrn'*"—eternal rest in God the Lord.[47] Of it he says that it must "grow out of the concrete process of things; it blossoms forth from love which illumines the most hidden core of Being itself, and moves reason whose limitless movement has its originative source in the quest for this rest."[48]

The revelation of Being that is achieved in the dialectic of revolt and rest is fulfilled through the three inseparable movements of authentic philosophic life: Reason, love, and transformation of things into "ciphers."

Reason, in contrast to the movement without end of understanding (*Verstand*), seeks the whole seen as the one by awakening all that is real.[49] Reason seeking rest in human love finds only loving struggle when, in the depths of human communication, the frustrating limits of all human intercourse become apparent; then reason turns towards Transcendence in its search for fulfillment. "When each form of truth remains for us a limit to the realization of communication…then truth can only have its fulfillment in Transcendence, which is however, no 'world beyond' in the sense of being…a better version of this world."[50] The deepest limits, then, reason encounters only in the deepest love; and it is there that the need for Transcendence becomes most apparent.

"*Love* is the soul of reason,"[51] because reason is ultimately encounter, not disinterested "objective" contemplation of a thing by a thing. The workings of this core-unveiling, *Ursprung*-revealing love is mysterious. "I love before I know that I love"; hence it is not an operation that 1 can set about willfully and methodically. "Love is the profound not-willing which first becomes the ground of authentic willing."[52] While all of man's other impulses seek only their own satisfaction, love seeks out the essence of the beloved. "Love is not satisfied by the satiation of a particular impulse, but through the inner becoming of Being itself that takes place in all that is essential."[53] Love manifests itself on each level of existence:

IV. Two German Existentialists

1. "Vital *Dasein*." On this level love is the unbounded desire for fruitfulness, for life and for oneness with nature, the force that would escape death forever by reappearing in ever-renewing forms.[54]

2. "Intellectual consciousness." In contrast to the dark force of vital love, love on the level of consciousness manifests itself as an "urge to seek evidence of the true as right and to find satisfaction in the experience of this evidence." With its vision of timeless intelligibility and of the unity of abstract conception, consciousness, under the impulse of love, rejects all easy solution, and its restless search for genuine unity becomes itself "a likeness of eternity."[55]

3. "Spiritual atmosphere." Enthusiasm for order perhaps best characterizes the impulse of love as spirit, reaching out to encompass and organize every existing thing, in that unity of timeless consciousness and temporal objective being which is the historical realization of the idea. Man seeks a kind of eternity through participation in the enduring forms of historical Idea.[56]

4. "*Existenz*." Existential love, which takes place through communication between me as "originative source" (*Ursprung*) and another unique "originative source," although in maximum contrast with the "general timelessness" of the universal concept, nevertheless touches the eternal in the ineffability of its uniqueness and fundamentally.[57] Its essence being the constancy and loyalty (*Treue*—a conception much like Gabriel Marcel's *fidélité*) which another freedom can will, it brings repose in the solidity, certainty, and isolation from danger which one feels in true love.[58]

In all these aspects of love, on every level, a bipolarity is manifest, a confrontation of the Encompassing which I am and the Encompassing that is Being.[59] In both poles are discoverable signs of a yearning to unite all levels of the Encompassing that I am in a fundamental act, and all fundamental acts—every *Ursprung*—in the absolutely originative Being that is the ground of every *Existenz*, and gives objective unity to the world. This ultimate principle Jaspers names the *Einzig-Allgemeine*: the individual-general. Only when we discover ourselves on the profoundest level, where the concreteness of *Dasein*, the generality of consciousness, the movement of spirit and the operations of reason meet in the ineffable origination of one free truth, and reveal every depth of communication with the Encompassing that is Being, can we possess even a hint of God's nature. The love of man, then, though opposed to God on any but the deepest level, becomes, when truly authentic, the very road to His discovery.⁶⁰ In its reality and its limits we can read signs of the need for God.

the reading of the signs of transcendence
Such reading of the signs of Transcendence (*Chifferschrift*) is the very heart of the philosophical endeavor as Jaspers conceives it. The reading of ciphers of the Transcendent is neither a subjective nor an objective, neither a transcendent nor an immanent, enterprise; or rather, it is all of these and more. The reading of ciphers begins equally well at either pole of the subject-object split in knowledge; for we seek God both as the ultimate knower, the Subject of all Subjects; and as the ultimate object, the Transcendent foundation of the world. The reading of the signs of Transcendence does not begin by turning inward to probe for the depths immanent to us, since what we seek is a reality enjoying objective validity. Nor can the ciphers of Transcendence be brought to shine forth automatically at the terminus of some method of objective analysis, for their language speaks only to the heart disposed by faith to listen. Jaspers distinguishes three manifestations of the Transcendent on each of the levels of the Encompassing which we ourselves are.

1. On the level of *Dasein*, the reading of ciphers begins as "a gift from the originative source of Being."⁶¹ Not in the form of metaphysical hypotheses which conclude to the nature of Being, but in the "liveliness" of the cipher, beyond which I cannot penetrate, does Being shine forth (*in ihr das Sein leuchtet*). Everything in nature in the richness of its concrete givenness can serve as *Chiffer*; its very givenness, its being-there, becomes transparent when grasped as reflecting the "miracle" that there is anything rather than nothing at all. The more general our experience, the less likely it is to speak of transcendence in this first way. Yet the more densely concrete this being, the less its message is capable of being translated into terms enjoying a compelling, universal necessity for consciousness in general. To be understood, the cipher demands that my whole existence open itself freely to its message not just as reason but as feeling, indeed on every level.

The ciphers of the Transcendent present in the concrete appear in two forms: Nature and history (the counterparts in Being of *Dasein* and spirit). In a long analysis establishing that nature without history is pure possibility or endless activity, and that history cannot become empirical without nature, Jas-

IV. Two German Existentialists

pers shows that this interdependence can itself be read as a sign that both nature and history are partial revelations of Being which is more than either or both of them together. The generality and temporally unchanging reality of the forces of nature as "that which is powerful by lasting in all time and yet is not any concrete thing (*Seiende*)," contrasts with the power of the historical as "that which fades away in time and yet is a concrete thing."[62] Here, then, is further indication of Transcendence: In reading the ciphers of nature, we seek to penetrate its sense as a whole (*Ganze*); in reading the ciphers of history we seek a beginning and an end. But in neither case are we able to find, immanent to our experience in any adequate, objective way, either the totality of nature nor any real beginning or end of history. There is also transcendent sense then in these other inadequacies, this over-unfulfilled demand to be seen whole, and this exigency for a beginning and an end.

2. Consciousness in general provides the cipher of number, of order, of the rigorous and exact. Transcendence shines through the light and joy of abstract order. The rational insufficiency of empirical being (nature and history) and the splendor of the ideal of truth can be read together as a sign of the unity of the Transcendent. But if the lucidity of the universal concepts of consciousness are a sign of the unity of Being, their poverty and emptiness reveal that consciousness as such is not Being. This realization too can serve as a negative indication of Transcendence. Consciousness in general, according to Jaspers, encounters its most definitive and telling frustration in the dialectical self-destruction of the great rational metaphysical systems.[63] Every metaphysical effort to view objectively all being as one fails, at least as far as direct rational cogency is concerned, because of the contradictions hidden at its base. Jaspers agrees with Kant that the antinomies of pure reason will plague every system that pretends to be objective and total. Yet every system also has value as cipher, once it is viewed as philosophical myth, mirroring, in its very strivings, something of Being's true unity. Jaspers would interpret the traditional proofs for the existence of God in this same mythical way. In keeping with the Kantian spirit of his criticism, Jaspers considers all forms of proof to be ultimately reducible to the ontological proof, which, from the cipher-reading point of view, is distinctly advantageous. For the very circularity and discursive weakness of this proof is evidence of its mythical force: Does it not in effect say, "That which is present as being in existential certitude must also be *real*, otherwise that certitude itself could not be"?[64]

The force of the proofs for the existence of God "resides only in the existential plenitude (*im existentielle erfüllten Gebalt*) of the presence of Being where Transcendence is perceived as cipher."[65]

3. The cipher "closest to Transcendence" is, however, the search for God not in metaphysical systems, nor in nature and history, but in man himself as *Existenz*. Mythical language expresses this truth splendidly when it says that "man is created in the image of God." As microcosm in which nature, history, consciousness meet in their common root—human freedom—man becomes a transparent of the unity of Transcendence. There is something very strange about that rooting of all things in man's liberty: Liberty alone of all principles is incapable, of its very nature, of being made into an absolute object. But the very fact that necessity is the supreme ground of liberty—that I am free only to become that which I am, and that what I am is *given* to me to develop—is, in the very heart of my presence to myself, a sign of Transcendence, a trace of God. The traditional notions of divine reprobation and divine grace express symbolically shining-forth the *reality* of this demand of my "possibility" on my freedom. And then the very openness, the very *disponibilité*, as Gabriel Marcel would put it, of man's existential situation to this message of Transcendence is itself an ultimate cipher. "Transcendence comes toward man according as man holds himself open to it; and this coming itself, joined to the manner in which man can hold himself open, is the cipher of Transcendence."[66]

That our existence as liberty is cipher of Transcendence signifies for Jaspers, negatively, that our invention of ourselves—our "self-creation"—is not purely creation on our part; and positively, that this creation escapes arbitrariness through reception of self from Being. For my self-creation to be authentic, I must "recall" the gift of my being. In Jaspers' Transcendence-oriented philosophy, the Heideggerian notion of our "being thrown" into the world is replaced by the notion that our appearance in the world is rather a gift—and a gift, of course, implies a gift-giver.

The later Heidegger speaks of "the favor of Being" (*die Gunst des Seins*), but only in a context that makes it impossible to determine whether the "one who favors" is in any way personal or superpersonal. Hence we are obliged to look upon his use of religious language with suspicion, fearing that his ultimate intention is to show that traditional language of God and grace finds its authentic meaning in the realization that it is the *Dasein*-centered revelation of Being that

IV. *Two German Existentialists* 187

is ultimate—and nothing more. Jaspers' unequivocal faith in Transcendence as something more than any combination of man's acts with the things of the world makes such suspicion in his regard unnecessary. Religion, along with philosophy and art, is for him unequivocally part of the "language of Transcendence"; and its mythical approach to truth is the key to all cipher-reading.

Each religion is an incarnation in time of eternal truth. This truth cannot be deciphered by methods of comparative religion. Rather each religion represents wholly and immediately, though in its own way, Transcendence itself. Each philosophy and each artwork enjoys a transparency similar to that of the great myths, each allows the whole truth to appear to one properly disposed by faith. The spell cast by a Van Gogh over a straw-covered chair and a clay pipe reveals a whole hidden world, the world of Being itself, viewed from a new aspect.[67] The philosophical speculation is a similar creation when it is understood as *Denksymbol*, intellectual symbol. "Speculation is a thought which in thinking tends to go beyond the thinkable; it is a mystique as far as the understanding, which would like *to know*, is concerned, but an *illumination* for the self that transcends by means of it."[68]

The transcendence of the Absolute can only be both present in and protected by the cipher if the following conditions are met: The message of the cipher must be direct; and it must be so expressed as to maintain inviolate the essential withdrawnness of the Transcendent. Jaspers shows us in the case of what he considers an ultimate sort of cipher—the conception of God as a person—how important it is that neither of these conditions be wanting. There is a directness and intimacy about the notion that God is personal which gives the Transcendence a reality and a richness without peer. Yet as cipher it is valid only if we go beyond it; accepting it at face value *objectively* would betray the Transcendent into our hands. Jaspers insists that personal intimacy with God—and he even means ordinary prayer—makes of Him an infinite super-ego whose overpowering presence on the same level as my own freedom dangerously compromises any meaning my liberty might have. "Against the divinity appearing as cipher itself, man must protect this right that the Transcendent Divinity gives him and confirms in him from the depth of His great distance. God wishes, as Transcendence, that I be myself."

For all this warning on the interpretation of the notion that God is personal, the One God, who is reality itself (*Wirklichkeit*) remains for Jaspers the ultimate end of all knowing. Never an "object" grasped in itself, always fleeing the capture of concept, myth, and revelation, He is fleetingly present nonetheless in every object, act of history, aspiration, and creation, as ground, end, unity, fulfillment, ultimate sense.[69]

> The one God is not to be (conclusively) attained by any exclusive way. Only in the Whole; from out the historical depths; in embracing everything thinkable and all that can be experienced, can we rise to the One. God is not less, not emptier, not abstracter than the World but encompasses it, letting each thing, in being related to him, rise to its highest possibilities.[70]

Jaspers rejects the pretensions of every revelation to speak for God, terming this "an usurpation of God's prerogatives by historical man"; he would retain from them only their cipher value as myth. And he vigorously rejects the either/or which Kierkegaard implies, the inescapable choice between Christian revelation, or acquiescence to what Jaspers calls the "abandoned, soulless, God-forsaken world" of the atheistic nihilists.[71] Rather he steadfastly maintains the possibility of a purely philosophical faith—a movement of reason toward affirmation of transcendence in the reading of ciphers.

Jaspers' philosophical faith is no romantic pious-wishing on the part of a spirit too weak to face the nothing as relentlessly as Heidegger. To ascertain this, one has only to contemplate Jaspers' analysis of the "last and deepest cipher," the cipher of "the failure of all things" (*Chiffer des Scheiterns*).[72] The mortality of man, the waste of deadening pain, the destruction of irreplaceable links with the past, the "tears in the heart of all things mortal," not only are not forgotten by this philosophical faith but become for it the ultimate crux. The *undeutbares Nichts* poses the question of questions—whether "from the depths of darkness itself, Being can shine forth."[73]

Jaspers' faith consists in believing that it does. Although he has the weight of the world and the sense of all things in it to justify his stand, he recognizes that from out the total wreck of all things mortal there arises the voice of no formulatable argument. "Only silence remains possible in the face of the silence that is in the world."[74] The words that mime this silence really say nothing, but merely repeat "It is, it is thus, being is, being…" But in the nothing that seems

IV. Two German Existentialists 189

at every turn to await the children of finitude, in the anguish born of its recognition, Jaspers finds the very atmosphere in which all signs of Transcendence can take on meaning for us. In the depths of this anguish we may find the peace of ultimate faith. Any faith without it is mockery and emptiness. The only true peace is the offspring of patience, born within sight of the most terrible and inexorable of spectacles—the wreck of finite being.

Jaspers' philosophy stands unflinchingly in the mainstream of the great German tradition of modern philosophy, both in its starting point—the transcendental viewpoint it accepts from the Post-Kantian tradition—and in its step-by-step construction of an impressive structure of thought dealing with Being itself. If, however, it does not solve satisfactorily, in the light of the constitution of Being itself, problems concerning the relationship of the universal structures of consciousness and the concrete world of singular real things, it is only because Jaspers has not always succeeded in remaining true to a program of adequate, systematic analysis. The lack of sufficient discussion of analytic method arouses the suspicion, in view of the abruptness of transition between levels in the analysis, that Jaspers' philosophy has not come to grips sufficiently with the epistemological problems of the tradition.

That is the main difficulty of Jaspers' philosophy: the lack of careful analysis of the exact relationship, first between the rich variety of "levels" within the Encompassing which we are, then between it and the Encompassing that is Being. Thus, though we are assured that "somehow" the key to the relationship between the concreteness of *Dasein* and the universality of the structures of consciousness in general lies in their relation to the dynamic unifying actions of spirit, we search in vain both the immense *Philosophie* and the immense *Von der Wahrheit* for a clear notion of what this means. Similarly, although it is quite convincingly established that the quest for the one truth must be grounded in the unique and ineffable *Existenz* of the individual person, it never becomes clear how, out of the "loving struggle" of such *Existenzen*, can come hope of progress in the quest for the one.

So, the lack of descriptive junctions throughout the whole analysis leaves us inadequately prepared for the conclusions toward which it is supposed to build. The *Chiffer* solution with its message of Transcendence appears on the scene before an adequate encounter with properly prior problems has been attempted. This accounts for the impression that the "reading of ciphers" is a bit gratuitous. This impression is strongest when we are brought face to face with the most far-reaching *Chiffer*, the "wreck of finite being." Jaspers' failure to point the way by careful description to a solution of the problems that have plagued this tradition leaves the impression that the wreck of finite being as he describes it could be due in part instead to the wreck of Jaspers' philosophy. The jump from the assertion of the "wreck" itself to interpretation of it as the ultimate silent voice of Transcendence is so little prepared that one is tempted to reinstate, despite Jaspers' protests to the contrary, the Kierkegaardian word "leap" to describe it. If Jaspers' philosophical faith in the Transcendent ultimately resides in such a leap, it would be better to say so as frankly as Kierkegaard, rather than disguise the fact with talk of reason, spirit, general consciousness, and *Gemeinschaft*.

This difficulty is all the more clearly felt because of the immensity of Jaspers' contribution. He has assembled descriptions of all areas of human existence, and of all the kinds of Being-analyses the modern German tradition has bequeathed the contemporary thinker. He has provided himself analyses of each, ruled by good sense and great personal sensitivity and experience. He has demonstrated a need for discovering a place for each—*Dasein*, consciousness in general, the historical reality of spirit, the freedom of *Existenz*, the one reality of Transcendence—in any future philosophical system. Jaspers may not succeed in convincingly relating them into an ontological structure, but he manages to present them together in a way that shows that all have validity and are probably somehow ultimately reconcilable within such a structure. This provides the future with more challenge than cause for despair.

PART TWO

FRENCH *and* ITALIAN PHILOSOPHY

by Étienne Gilson

INTRODUCTION

PHILIBERT Damiron, a good observer writing in 1828, submitted a satisfactory classification of the main tendencies at work since the beginning of the nineteenth century in French philosophical minds.[1] According to him three doctrines filled up that period. The first is what the French call *sensualisme*, an ill-chosen word on account of its unfavorable ethical connotations, and which we propose to replace by the ethically neutral designation of "*sensism*." Whatever its name, that school was the direct continuation of the method and philosophy of Condillac. It represented in the first third of the nineteenth century the heritage of the eighteenth. The second doctrine is that of what Damiron calls the "theological school," which declared itself at the time of the monarchic Restoration (1814–1830). The third doctrinal tendency is represented by *eclecticism*, a rather loose group whose activity extended far into the nineteenth century. Still dominated by the memory of the French Revolution, other doctrines thrived in the first half of the century, but these were sociologies rather than philosophies in the proper sense of the term. For that reason, those doctrines will be considered apart.

V. *Ideology in France*

THE form assumed by sensism in the first third of nineteenth-century France bears the name of "ideology." For those who first used it, the name carried no unfavorable connotations. It is, in fact, a well-chosen appellation. According to Condillac, all objects of human cognition, including sensations themselves, should be called "ideas." Moreover, it had become an accepted view, chiefly under the influence of Locke, that just as physics deals with material beings, metaphysics has for its proper object the study of the human mind, including the origin of all its "ideas" and mental powers or faculties. Locke and Condillac had made decisive contributions toward the solution of the problem, but the task had not really been completed. It is noteworthy that the chief representatives of that school were born around the middle of the eighteenth century: Destutt de Tracy in 1754; Laromiguière in 1756; Cabanis and Volney in 1757; Garat and Gall in 1758. On the other hand, all those eighteenth-century products were really nineteenth-century authors. All their works appeared between the last years of the French Revolution and about 1830. Their golden age was the reign of Napoleon I who, we might add, did not like the *Idéologues*, and publicly said so. The members of the school, for their part, were continuing the eighteenth-century French tradition; they disliked tyranny. After managing to survive the Revolution, they lived through the Empire as men well trained in the art of careful opposition.

CABANIS

Cabanis[2] was a professor at the Paris school of medicine, and interested as he was in philosophy, his own approach to it was scientific. In philosophy proper, he claimed Locke for his great predecessor. To Locke was due the fundamental axiom: that *all ideas come through the senses*, or *are the product of sensations*.

Condillac had developed and perfected the doctrine; disciples of Condillac, such as Garat and Destutt de Tracy, had bettered, and occasionally corrected, the doctrine, but there still remained obscurities.

According to Condillac, the whole structure of the human mind was reducible to transformed sensations, and since sensation was a passive state, there was nothing but passivity in the mind. But Cabanis was invited to challenge the sensism of Condillac by his own observations as a physiologist. Condillac had resorted to sensibility exclusively in view of explaining the possibility of judgments; but all the vital operations such as digestion, circulation, and the various secretions do not hang on anything like sensations and judgments; there must be therefore in man an active principle over and above the passivity of sensations. This aspect of Cabanis' thought led him finally to a sort of vitalism much more metaphysical in nature than his usually physiological point of view seems to warrant.

Within the psychology of Condillac itself, Cabanis attacked the fiction of a statue progressively acquiring the various classes of sensations. Condillac first endows the statue with the sense of smell; the statue is given a rose to smell and it says: I am the smell of a rose. Cabanis observes that, even at that early stage in his psychological life, man would be something entirely different from a statue able to smell. Man has a body; from the very moment of its conception, that body never ceases to be the seat of confused perceptions coming to it from all its organs, changing with age, variable according to sex and to countless internal as well as external conditions. The second and third of the "Mémoires" bear the significant title of *Physiological History of the Sensations*. The idea that sensations could have a history of their own and that their constant presence, even when they pass unnoticed, could affect the psychology of man, had been foreign to the mind of Condillac. Cabanis did not use the modern word "cenesthesia"; he speaks only of "internal impressions," so manifold indeed that, in the present state of our knowledge, it is impossible to number them and to classify them with accuracy, but he expressly attempted to follow their general history from the early formation of the embryo till the time of death.

Cabanis pointed out a third weakness inherent in the psychology of both Locke and Condillac, namely their failure to account for the apparent innateness of instinct. Newborn chickens unerringly pick up grain and flies; if there is nothing born in them, how and when did they learn? Asked the question,

V. *Ideology in France*   195

Locke had answered that he had not written an inquiry into the mind of beasts, but into that of man. This is a good answer for a press conference, but not so good for a philosophical discussion. Another famous answer to the question was that "their mothers tell them." Condillac himself had implicitly acknowledged the difficulty. In order to explain instinctive reactions in animals, he supposed the existence in them of extremely rapid reasonings that habit had made practically instantaneous. But observation does not bear out that supposition. On closer inspection, instinctive reactions seem to constitute an intermediate class of facts between physiological functions on the one hand and intellectual functions on the other hand. They seem to be destined to act as their common bond.[3]

Cabanis always hoped to reduce all those phenomena, plus those of moral and intellectual communication between human beings, to one common principle. He did not achieve that ambitious end, but his work left a deep mark on the history of the school. After him, it became impossible to forget that the human mind is tied up with a body. Condillac had reduced everything to *sensation*. Cabanis reduces everything to *sensibility*. By so doing, Cabanis feels that he is giving weight and substance to Condillac's rather abstract psychology and making scientific progress possible in the science of man by combining physiology, ideology, and ethics as three branches of one and the same science, which he thought could rightly be called *the science of man*.[4] In short, Cabanis refused to consider ideology as a self-sufficient discipline. By bringing it together with both physiology and ethics, he combined them into an integrated whole, anthropology.[5]

While dealing with essentially physiological problems, Cabanis never made an open choice between spiritualism and materialism. To him, the fundamental fact of "sensibility" was a double-edged one. Since it was possible to read it, indifferently, in the language of matter and in that of spirit, *irritability* and *sensibility* were to him two names for one single thing, the only difference being that irritability points out its physiological aspect and sensibility its psychological one.[6]

Besides his two volumes of memoirs on the relations of the physical and of the moral in man[7] Cabanis has left a curious document, the authenticity of which has been doubted, but which it is impossible not to take into account in assessing his contribution to ideology. The document is a *Lettre posthume…sur les causes premières* (*Posthumous Letter...on the Prime Causes*)[8] in which, without unsaying anything he had said, Cabanis approached for the first time the metaphysical problems he had so far carefully avoided. In the *Lettre*, Cabanis stresses the necessity of positing a soul, that is to say a vital principle. Soul must be considered, not as "the result of the action of the parts, or as a particular property attached to the animal structure, but, rather, as a substance, a real being which, by its presence, causes in the organs all the motions of which their motions are composed." Then he added that the soul keeps together the various elements employed by nature in the normal composition of organs and that it consigns them to corruption at the very moment it leaves them forever. His main reasons for this change of point of view was the impossibility of accounting for the birth and growth of living bodies without resorting to the notion of a vivifying force that animates them and keeps them together as long as nature wants them to last.

Just as it was going far beyond the physiology of the "Mémoires," the *Lettre* was committing Cabanis to unexpected theological conclusions. For indeed he was dealing with natural theology in establishing that there is a Prime and Universal Cause, endowed with intelligence and will. The purposiveness everywhere visible in nature left him no other choice: "No analogy, no verisimilitude can enable the mind of man to account for such a result; on the contrary, everything invites man to consider the works of nature as produced by operations similar to those of his own mind in the production of its most wisely combined works, with the only difference that, in the works of nature, the degree of perfection is a thousand times higher. This leads man to the idea of a wisdom that conceived such works, and of a will that executed them, but of the highest wisdom, and of a will most carefully attending to all details, wielding the most extensive power and exercising it with utmost precision." Cabanis had never written anything inconsistent with such views, but nothing in what he had written presaged such a development. Perhaps he had simply seen the end of his own science and he was beginning to think beyond it.

Destutt de Tracy

The typical representative of ideology was Destutt de Tracy.[9] He barely escaped death during the French Revolution; more fortunate than Condorcet, he was

V. *Ideology in France*

saved by the downfall of Robespierre. While in jail, he read Condillac's *Treatise of Sensations* and, becoming enthusiastic by his reading, he saw at once what his future life would have to be, supposing he were to have one. It would be devoted to the teaching, writing, publishing, and republishing of his *Éléments d'idéologie* (*Elements of Ideology*). In his preface to the edition of 1804, Tracy calmly declared that, in his candid opinion, he thought he had found truth, and no hesitation remained in his mind concerning the questions he had dealt with.

As Tracy understands it, "ideology is part of zoology," a part indeed of exceptional importance in the case of man. Locke was the first to observe and describe human understanding as being "just a remarkable circumstance of the life of an animal." With him the study of the human mind became a branch of physics. "Not that, before him, men did not form many hypotheses on the subject; one even boldly dogmatized on the nature of our soul, but it always was in view, not of discovering the source of our cognitions, their certitudes and their limits, but, rather, of determining the principle and the end of all things, to guess the origin of the world and its destiny. That is the object of metaphysics. We shall include it among the arts of imagination destined to give us pleasure, not instruction."

Some good minds followed in the wake of Locke. "More than any other, Condillac has increased the number of their observations, and he really has created ideology." Nevertheless, he let some errors creep into his work; besides, he has not organized his various treatises into one complete body of doctrine usable as a text for a lecture course. Tracy had ambitioned to provide such an all-comprehensive work under the general title of *Éléments d'idéologie*. Had it been completed, the work would have consisted of three main sections, each containing three parts, plus a tenth supplementary part by way of appendix. The plan is so revealing that we shall give it in its entirety.

> ÉLÉMENTS D'IDÉOLOGIE
> First Section: *History of our means of knowing*
> PART 1: Formation of Our Ideas, or Ideology Properly So Called
> PART 2: Expression of Our Ideas, or Grammar
> PART 3: Combination of Our Ideas, or Logic
> Second Section: *Application of our means of knowing to the study of our will and of its effects*

> PART 1: Our Actions, or Economy
> PART 2: Our Feelings, or Morals
> PART 3: The Direction of Both, or Legislation
> Third Section: *Application of our means of knowing to the study of beings other than ourselves*
> PART 1: Bodies and Their Properties, or Physics
> PART 2: Properties of Extension, or Geometry
> PART 3: Properties of Quantity, or Calculus

The projected appendix was to deal with the false sciences that are annihilated by the knowledge of our means of knowing, and of their rightful use. As was said, metaphysics is one of those pseudo sciences. However, Tracy never reached that part of his plan. Of those ten parts Tracy wrote only the first four and the beginning of the fifth one, namely: *Ideology Properly So Called, Grammar, Logic, Economy,* and the beginning of *Morals*. Of the five, *Ideology...* is the most important, providing as it does the basis for the whole structure. In Tracy's own words, the elements of ideology, or of prime philosophy, provided a "complete treatise on the origin of all our cognitions."[10]

The faculty of *thinking* is that of receiving a mass of impressions, modifications, and ways of being of which we are aware and which can all be comprised under the general denomination of *ideas* or *perceptions*. Since we feel them, they could as well be called *sensations* or *feelings* in the wider acceptation of the terms. In short, "to think, always is to feel something, it is, simply, to feel." The principle that thinking is feeling is the lifeline that binds Tracy to Condillac.

Divergences begin to appear from the very moment Tracy defines the various operations included under the notion of thinking. "The faculty of *thinking*, or of having perceptions, includes four elementary faculties that are called *sensibility*, properly so called, *memory, judgment,* and *will.*" This classification takes us far away from the linear deduction of all faculties from sensation attempted by Condillac. The Baconian spirit of observation is overcoming the Cartesian spirit of deduction in the mind of Tracy. This is the more certain as, at the end of his *Logic*, Tracy published his *Reasoned Abridgement of the Instauratio Magna or Great Renovation*, after the London edition of 1778.

Sensibility, described with a physiological precision under the influence of Cabanis, divides into the traditional external senses, but, under the same

V. *Ideology in France*

influence, Tracy adds that "over and above those external sensations, we still receive, by the extremities of those of our nerves that terminate at the different parts of the inside of our own body, a large number of sensations that we call, for that very reason, *internal sensations*." Such are those that arise from the functioning of the various organs according to the state of our health. It is needless to stress the importance of this innovation, whose consequences will become decisive in the doctrine of Maine de Biran.

Memory is a second species of sensibility; it consists in being affected by the remembrance of an experienced sensation. Memory presupposes sensation, and it is a particular mode of sensibility, but itself is not a sensation properly so-called; sensation is caused in the brain by an actual impression in another organ; memory is the effect of a certain disposition left in the brain in consequence of some previous sensation. It is essential to observe those distinctions if one does not want everything to get mixed up in the analysis of thought.

The faculty of judging, or *judgment*, is still another species of sensibility, for it is "the faculty of feeling relations between our perceptions." These relations "are internal sensations of the brain, just as memories." The faculty of feeling relations almost necessarily follows from that of feeling sensations. Note the slight hesitation in Tracy's language: "La faculté de sentir des rapports est une conséquence *presque* nécessaire de celle de sentir des sensations." But he boldly goes on to say that as soon as one distinctly feels two sensations, "it naturally follows that one feels their resemblances, their differences, their connections, etc." From those "perceptions of relations between perceptions" derive all our judgments. The affirmation of any proposition reduces itself to this, that the whole notion of the attribute is wholly included in the whole notion of the subject and is part of it, for all judgment always consists in "feeling that an idea is one of the component ideas of another one, and is part of it."

The fourth and last mode of sensibility is *will*. It can be defined as "the faculty of feeling desires." The desires are consequences of our other perceptions as well as of our judgments on them; but this is peculiar to them: by our desires we always are happy or unhappy depending upon whether they are fulfilled or not. Another remarkable peculiarity about them is that they condition the use of our mechanical and intellectual powers. Through desire we are a power in the world. To regulate our desire well is therefore of utmost importance; otherwise we cannot become the men we want to be, which of course makes happiness impossible for us.

Of these four distinct faculties in our power of thinking, the last three are consequences of the first one. From these four simple elements—*sensations, memories, judgments, and desires*—all our composite ideas are formed.

The main problem met by sensism had always been to explain how we know that our sensations are occasioned by beings that are not ourselves.

Tracy does not doubt that our internal sensations teach us nothing else than our own existence. He even adds that the same applies to smells, tastes, sounds, tactile perceptions, and even unintentional motions, in which nothing indicates to us why they begin and why they end, what opposes them, or if we have members and what sort of thing their movement is.

> But if to that sensation of movement we add the condition that it be voluntary, and with the desire to experience it again after it ceases, we are sure, when it does cease, that its ceasing is not of our own doing. We feel certain, at one and the same time, of the existence of ourselves, who are willing, and of that of something that resists; or else, if from the very first instant we do not perceive that second existence, countless experiences will soon assure us of it, by showing us that many impressions of different sorts are constantly ceasing when that feeling of resistance vanishes, and that they likewise reappear as soon as the same feeling is experienced again; for then we judge with certitude that those impressions are so many effects of the qualities of that being whose chief property it is always to resist our desire to feel the sensation of movement.

The reason this fundamental truth was overlooked is that, in the past, thought has been considered abstractly and not as related to body. Considered under this new perspective, man is seen as a much more complex reality. As a living being, man can raise weights a small part of which is enough to break his muscles after his death. As long as it lives, our body assimilates to its own substance the bodies on which it feeds; after death, the reverse happens and all its component elements are absorbed by the surrounding bodies. All this shows that "vital force is something." As long as it lasts, we live, that is to say,

V. *Ideology in France*

we move and we feel. There are in us many motions unattended by perceptions, but there never is in us any perception without some attending motions in our organs. So, in the last analysis, the action of feeling is in us a particular effect of the action of moving.

The frequent repetition of the same acts begets habit. Anticipating one of the main positions of Ravaisson, Tracy observes "[that] the more movements are repeated, the easier and more rapid they become, and that the easier and the more rapid they become, the less perceptible they are." The perception they cause in us then diminishes, to the point of completely disappearing, even though the motion continues to take place. This accounts for the existence of a prodigious number of inner movements and of intellectual operations of which we have no awareness, and also explains that, owing to their frequent repetition, our movements and our intellectual operations become swifter, easier and less perceptible, and that to a prodigious degree.[11]

The most precious of human inventions is that of signs, especially those that consist of the conventionally adopted sounds we call words. Thought always precedes the words that signify it, but language permits an extraordinary progress in the development of knowledge.

The reason is that most of the ideas we now have in mind are abstract and general ideas; as such they have in us no other support than the signs by which they are represented. Let us take a simple example, the notion of *six*. If we had no word to signify it, and nothing else than its image to represent it to our minds, we could hardly form a clear notion of it. Now, *six* is a very simple concept as compared with most of those we are usually dealing with. Where would we be without signs to help us in our intellectual operations? "The cause of that effect of signs seems to be as follows: our purely intellectual perceptions are very light and, by the same token, very fleeting, because the inner motions by which they are achieved affect very little the nervous system; by adding itself to them, the sign makes them share in the energy of the sensation it causes.... It becomes a formula which we remember easily, because it is sensible, and we employ it in ulterior combinations even though we have forgotten its mode of formation."[12]

The ideology proper dominates all the parts of his projected encyclopedia which Tracy had completed. Grammar is a sequel to the treatise of ideology and it is a preamble to logic. In Tracy's own terms, "I have inquired into the formation of ideas only in order to know well the theory of their expression. I shall examine their expression only in order to discover the laws of their deduction."[13] Conceived after the pattern of the "general grammars" of the middle ages, that of Tracy aims to reach, beyond the structure of some particular language, the universal rules swaying the expression of thought by the human mind in general. Logic has little to add to the combined results of ideology and grammar. It is noteworthy that Tracy deemed it advisable to add to his own logic a French translation of that of Hobbes (*De corpore*, vol. 1, p. 1), but he was simply completing his ideology. He himself says that, with his *Ideology Properly So Called* and his *Grammar*, his *Logic* makes up one single treatise: "According to common views, logic is the art of reasoning. Such as I conceive it, logic is not that; methinks it is, or it should be, a purely speculative science, which exclusively consists in the examination of the formation of our ideas, of the mode of their expression, of their combination and of their deduction, and that from that examination follows, or will follow, the knowledge of the characters of truth, of those of certitude as well as of the causes of uncertainty and error."[14]

Tracy had waited for the completion of his *Éléments*, including *Grammar* and *Logic*, in order to be able to dedicate the whole work to his excellent friend Cabanis. In his opinion, his own *Éléments* and the *Rapports* of Cabanis were two aspects of one and the same truth. Tracy regretted not to have been able to establish more intimate bonds between ideology and physiology, but neither his plan nor his competence permitted him to do so. He was hoping that his friend Cabanis would perform that supreme task, as if one and the same man could own two different minds.

Maine de Biran

At the burial of Maine de Biran, in the presence of Victor Cousin, Royer-Collard remarked: "He was the master of us all." Still, at that date, the departed philosopher had published practically nothing, but he was leaving behind countless works, or fragments of works, all of which unmistakably bear the mark of his pen, although few of them were brought to completion.

V. *Ideology in France*

the data of the problem

Different reasons account for the failure of Biran to complete most of his more important works. In the first place, he was not a professional, that is, a teacher. His whole career was that of a government official and politician. Nor should the fact be deplored; for such a mind, teaching would have been a greater impediment to philosophy than politics. His functions did not prevent him from philosophizing, but they prevented him from writing.[15]

A second reason was the very nature of Biran's philosophical undertaking. Taking his cue from the ideologists, and even, in a sense, from Condillac, he engaged in the task of achieving a thorough analysis of the mind,[16] that is, of resolving it into its constituent elements.[17] Locke, Condillac, Cabanis, Destutt de Tracy, and Laromiguière[18] had successively attempted the task; every one of them had carried it to completion, but not one of them had been satisfied by the results obtained by his predecessors. And indeed, anybody can decompose the mind into elements, and do it successfully, because it can be done from any number of different but equally plausible angles. Perhaps the greatest merit of Maine de Biran was that he perceived the artificial character of those ideologies. Because they contented themselves with imagining possible structures of the mind, they never pierced deeper than the level of abstract analysis and of a dialectical arrangement of notions. The proper contribution of Biran to ideology was his early decision to apply to the study of the mind the method applied in physiology. When a scientist says "muscle," or "nerve," he can describe the inner structure of the things in question, but what philosopher, after saying "sensation," ever stopped to submit it to the searching and exacting analysis required for its objective description? By thus attempting to turn ideology into a true science of observation, Biran was deciding the future of a large part of French philosophy in the years to come, but he was undertaking a task far beyond the possibilities of any one individual.

A third reason for the fragmentary character of the results is the very nature, not, this time, of the method, but of the object at stake. By turning into an object of observation the mind that, so far, had rather been a subject of conversation, Biran was entering the obscure region of deep psychology where objectively defined results are equally hard to obtain and to communicate. A dialectically conceived book is always easy to complete; he is a poor dialectician who cannot "arrange" a conclusion; but Biran was after something else, and he knew it: "I know all the weakness of my means; I feel how out of proportion they are to the very scope of this essay [on the foundations of psychology]. I am leaving port, I shall dive into an underground sea, but without hoping to reach its faraway shores and to be able to shout: Italy! Italy!"[19]

the inner sense

The only instrument at the disposal of Biran for probing the depth of the human soul is what he himself calls "inner sense": *le sens intime*. That sense within should not be imagined after the pattern of any one of the external senses. Inner sense is consciousness, an awareness of what is going on within our own thought; its effects are similar to those of sight and of touch when those senses inform us about what is going on outside of us. This direct information we have about ourselves is our only chance to contact absolute reality. But how far does it take us?

In applying to consciousness as to the source of philosophical knowledge, Biran simply prolongs the tradition of Descartes, but between Descartes and Biran, there is Kant. In Descartes, Biran recognizes his own project to resort to inner observation as the only place where the true principles of science can be found. Moreover he agrees with Descartes that the knowledge of the *ego*, as a fact of consciousness, is distinct and separated from the representation of all objects perceivable by sense or conceivable by imagination. "Lastly Descartes proved, I am not saying the absolute separation of the substances, but the essential distinction there is between external and internal phenomena, or between the faculties specially appropriated to the ones and to the others." Descartes thereby became "the creator or the father of a science which, under some title or other, must found itself on inner observation." Inasmuch as it thus insures the specificity of inner knowledge as well as that of its object "the philosophy of Descartes must be considered as the true *doctrine-mère*." It gives to the science of the principles the only basis it can have, namely the primitive fact of inner sense.

This, however, is the point where, for the first time, Kant will leave his mark on the evolution of a French philosophical mind. For a time, Biran had felt inclined to identify the immediate apprehension of the *ego* with that of the very substance of the soul, but, as he himself said: "I am indebted to Kant for having made a necessary distinction between two terms which all metaphysi-

V. Ideology in France   205

cians, including Descartes, have confused, which is one of the greatest causes of obscurity and of embarrassment in metaphysics. We feel our phenomenal individuality, or existence, but we do not feel the very substance of our soul, no more than that of any other one."[20]

This docile acceptance of one of the main conclusions of the "Transcendental Esthetics" of Kant is the more noteworthy as it is presently followed by what will be a reaction of several nineteenth-century philosophers to the *Critique of Pure Reason*. No doubt, they will say, Kant is right, but it should still remain possible for us to have a metaphysics.

To the criticism directed by Kant against the transcendent use of the categories of understanding abusively made by dogmatic metaphysics, Biran replies that there can be no foundation for that which is conditional and contingent, other than a free cause, a free being, by which variable and fleeting phenomena are produced.[21] The point Biran wants to make is that "since one cannot conceive an act, or its phenomenal result, without thinking of a being by which that act is produced, it necessarily follows that the relation of *causality* comprises the notion of substance." If there is no causality without substance, the being which we posit as absolutely necessary in itself, apart from the relation of causality which determines it, is not a mere logical abstraction but an actual being. In short, Biran is maintaining that an absolute can be given in a relation.

In order to substantiate his criticism, Biran had to show that "in their notions as well as in the primitive fact that is their origin, existence and causality, or being and cause, are not absolutely identical, or, at least inseparable in the mind."[22] In a way, this was to undertake an almost impossible task. After conceding to Kant that inner sense does not reach the substance of the ego such as it is in itself (against Descartes), how could the mind reach, within its own experience of relation, a being in itself posited as an absolute?

Biran does not consider it impossible. In the first place, Kant himself had done it. How otherwise could he infer from the existence of given phenomena that of non-given noumena, which precisely are their causes? Next, Biran feels himself in possession of an important truth overlooked by Kant. He knows of an inner experiment in which, reaching himself, at first, as a merely phenomenal ego, man soon apprehends himself as a noumenal force, independent, acting upon organs that obey it. Should it be possible to establish that truth, consequences of decisive importance would follow. For indeed, if there is such a force, it is the origin of the perception of all existence, including that of understanding itself. Descartes had said: I think, hence I am; Condillac had said: I feel, hence I am; Biran would prefer to say: I will, hence I am. But only inner sense is qualified for performing that experiment.

the primitive art

Biran is in quest of the primitive mental act from which, dircetly or not, the whole mental life can be reconstructed. Condillac says: sensation. He makes his imaginary statue say: *Je suis odeur de rose*, but, insists Biran, that is impossible, for in the sentence under consideration, there is at least one word unaccounted for, namely, *I*. The observer knows the meaning of *I* at this early stage of the mental experiment, the statue does not; so it cannot say, *I am*. Even letting aside the capital notion of existence—in fact, inseparable from that of the ego—the hypothesis of Condillac is an absolute impossibility.

Trying to do the experiment all over again, what do we suppose the statue would say? Not *I*, but would it say at least: rose smell? A sensation is nothing unless it be perceived, and if there is no *I* to perceive it, the sensation at stake does not exist. There can be no such thing as the smell of a rose floating in emptiness without any subject to perceive it. There would in that case be neither perceiving subject nor object to perceive. It is an illusion to imagine that, of itself, the presence of a sensation gives rise to the apprehension of a subject. When I am suffering a pain or enjoying a pleasure, I do not identify myself with either pleasure or pain. I do not mistake myself for my headache. The question then remains: what is the primitive fact of consciousness from which all the rest follows or, at least, which is presupposed by all the rest?[23]

From what precedes, it is already clear that, for us, the primitive given cannot be any sensation as such. Since it has to be perceived in order to be a fact of consciousness, the primitive given must needs be at least the *idea* of a sensation. Now the idea of a sensation always belongs to a knowing subject. It is somebody's idea at the same time as it is the idea of something. The primitive given, whatever name we give to it, is necessarily tied up with the personal individuality of the ego.

What is wrong with all the previous answers to the problem is that they ask it in terms of the substance-accident relationship. Not only Descartes and Condillac, even Kant fell a victim to that delusion. The gist of Biran's philosophy is

V. *Ideology in France*

that, by observing himself, he was led to ask the question, not in terms of substance-accident, but in terms of cause-effect. That was a far-reaching decision; in a sense, all the so-called "philosophies of action" owe something to Maine de Biran. And it was not an arbitrary decision; on the contrary, Biran was led to it by the remark that, since there is in us a principle of activity, it must be included in our primitive constitution. Now such a principle cannot be an idea. Just as the idea of substance, the idea of force is an abstraction several times removed from what should be a primitive fact of consciousness. Prior to the notion of force, there is the "immediate feeling of force and that feeling is no other than that of our very existence from which that of activity is inseparable."[24]

Biran has often described the fundamental and primitive experience in which "inner sense" apprehends the ego as an efficiently acting cause. Since, as was said above, we cannot feel we are acting, and causing, without feeling that we are, the experience of the ego is one with that of our own causality. Now the inner sense experiences in us the presence of such causality: "We cannot know ourselves as individual persons, without feeling ourselves as causes with respect to certain effects or movements produced in the organic body. The cause, or force, actually employed to move the body is an active force which we call *will*; the ego identifies itself with that acting force completely. Now the existence of that force is for me a fact, only inasmuch as it exerts itself, and it exerts itself only inasmuch as it can apply itself to a term either resistant or inert. The force therefore is determined or actualized only in the relation to its term of application, just as this term itself is determined only as resisting or as inert in relation to the force actually moving it, or tending to impart movement to it. The fact of that tendency is what we call *effort*, or *willed action*, or *volition*, and I say that that effort is the true primitive fact of inner sense. No other fact unites all the characters and fulfills all the conditions previously analyzed."[25]

Having thus determined the primitive fact of inner sense, it becomes possible to deduce from it a true science of the principles. It is the origin of the principle of causality—a point that seems to have escaped Kant—since the abstract notion of cause and the very category of causality have no other possible basis and foundation besides the awareness of our own force, or, in Biran's own words, of the effort that is ourself (*ou de l'effort qui est nous-même*). Now, as was already observed by a very judicious philosopher, the principle of causality is the *father of metaphysics*[26]; all the other metaphysical notions therefore find in the feeling of effort their true origin. In clear awareness of the philosophical operation he was performing, Biran defines its nature with utmost precision: it substitutes *cause* for *substance* as the fundamental metaphysical notion; since philosophers had always used substance as the key notion in philosophy, it was to be expected that another philosophy, another analysis of sensations and ideas, another genealogy of the faculties, would result from that new primacy of causality.

Going over the results of his analysis, Biran notes with satisfaction that his answer covers the data of the problem. Effort is a *fact*[27] since the force, or power, whereby the motions of the body are effected is necessarily distinct from the *inert* object to which it applies. That fact is *primitive*, since even external sensations, in order to become our first cognitions, must be caused to operate by that very same individual force that causes effort. That primitive fact moreover is a fact of *inner sense*, since it is known by self-awareness, without any special organ being required for our knowledge of it.[28]

Why is not the *I think* the primitive fact of inner sense? To this question, the excellent historian who asked it has given the perfect answer: "because Cartesianism is a philosophy of substance and not a philosophy of cause."[29] One could also ask, why did not Biran stop short before the barrier raised by Kant on the way to metaphysical speculation? And the answer would be the same. Our representation of the inner force which we are may well be given to us in *a priori* categories of understanding, as a fact of inner experience, however, and irrespective of all representation of it, effort is grasped in itself. And no wonder, since that effort is I myself, immediately apprehended as a factual reality.[30]

the reflexive method

In the preceding exposition of the doctrine, the word *metaphysics* was freely used. To avoid it was hardly possible. Besides, it is a correct denomination, but the way Biran practiced metaphysics was so influential on the development of French philosophy that it is necessary to pause a moment in order to consider it attentively.

Biran has no objection to metaphysics, but there is a sound one and a wrong one. All depends on the method used. As Biran conceives it, sound metaphysics is a science like all the other sciences of nature; like them, it deals with facts known by observation and connected by necessary relations found-

V. *Ideology in France*

ed upon their very natures. The only difference is that prime philosophy deals with internal facts, known to inner sense, and objects of an experience given with and in the immediate apprehension of the ego. As was later the case in the doctrine of Bergson, the immediate data of consciousness are the last ones to be perceived. Covered as they are by thick layers of more superficial facts, they are first in themselves, but they do not fall in the first place under our apprehension.

The method used to discover them is what Biran calls "reflection." The French philosophers who later advocated the use of a "reflexive method" were all, to that extent, continuators of Maine de Biran. Such as he himself understood it, reflection was a direct application of inner sense to facts of consciousness in order to observe them with precision. Reflection then does not deal with general ideas, or with abstract notions, as happens most of the time when, indulging in the pleasure of connecting ideas, a man imparts to us the result of his reflections. The reflexive method essentially is careful inner observation; if it abstracts, it does so only by distinguishing observed objects, that is, by considering apart that which actually is something apart. Scientists do not proceed differently. The problem is to adopt toward facts of consciousness the methods of observation so successfully applied by science to the external world. To do so is far from easy, but no other method will yield satisfactory results.

That notion of a scientific philosophy, in the sense of a philosophy proceeding in the exploration of the ego exactly as science does in the exploration of the material world, has remained one of the constants of modern French philosophy. At the same time, all the representatives of that tendency (already present in Descartes) strived to attain truly metaphysical conclusions. Whether the undertaking is possible or not is another question. But we should at least try to understand what such men have in mind when they say that inner experience can lead them far beyond the conclusions of the sciences of nature. They do not mean that inner sense will give them supplementary information concerning the objects of the sciences of nature. They rather think that the reflexive method of inner sense will impart to them the knowledge of objects altogether different from those of physics and of physiology. Scientific by its method, inner reflection is trans-scientific by its objects, and vice versa. A truly unscientific attitude in philosophy would be to apply to the study of the ego and of its modes the conclusions obtained in the study of the material world of external objects.

When it succeeds in grasping its own objects, inner experience differs from external experience *toto genere* and *tota natura*. It is infallible, it entails the impossibility for the thing to be otherwise than it is and, in the particular case of causality, the impossibility for it not to be attended by its effect. How could it be otherwise since, in the experience of inner sense, its immediate datum is the very connectedness of its objects?

This is where Biran feels entirely different from his predecessors, including even Kant. Ontology, or metaphysics properly so called—the metaphysics of Wolff in particular—but also mathematics and general physics, all deal with abstract notions, that is, with general notions, not with observable facts of consciousness. The result is that, in all matters, they follow the law of logical necessity, for instance: every effect has a cause, every consequence has its principle (principle of sufficient reason). The very name of the principle reveals its abstract nature: what the philosopher is interested in is a "reason" (a principle of intelligibility) not a cause (a principle of existence). Inner sense, too, attains necessities, but they are necessary connections between facts; for instance: a motion felt and interiorly perceived as free can have no other cause than the willed effort, or the *I* that makes it begin; in consequence, all passive modification, every event which begins (outside of me) has a cause (non-ego) that makes it begin; again, all efficient cause in the intellectual and moral order consists in the will of a free agent; all efficient cause, even in the physical order, is an immaterial force, essentially different in nature from its effect and incapable of being represented, as that effect can be, by appealing to material images.[31]

The sciences founded on inner sense and elaborated by means of the reflexive method are psychology, ethics, and natural theology, this last being a science dealing with experienced facts and an actual being, God, very different therefore from the ontological metaphysics of Leibniz and Wolff. In a passage where several nineteenth-century French philosophies are anticipated, Biran remarks that "psychology, ethics, natural theology only acknowledge a necessity given in consciousness, and are wary of that formal necessity which logic is always tending to force upon them. Having no other basis than consciousness, and distinguishing itself from the principle of contradiction as well as from that of sufficient reason, the principle of causality preserves, in all its applications, the infallible certitude and the necessary evidence of its source. From the person a free cause, creator of modifications, understanding raises itself by the

V. *Ideology in France*

chain of the secondary causes, themselves conceived after that internal model, up to God, creative cause of existences, cause of causes. I and God, such are the two poles of science, the two foci of the indefinite curve in which the intelligence of man is destined eternally to circulate without fear of aberration, so long as it does not wander away from those two poles."[32] Had Biran intended to summarize his whole philosophy, he could not have done it better.

A typical feature of all the philosophies of inner sense is that their conclusions cannot be communicated. Every philosopher has to go through all the moves of the reflexive method and to do it for his own account. Such is already the case with Biran. In this respect, he is fully aware of the advantages enjoyed by the notional philosophies, whose proper instrument is logic and which, for that very reason, are easily transmissible from mind to mind. "Interior psychology," as Biran sometimes calls his own science of the inner man, obtains results "often incommunicable and locked within the limits of the consciousness of each one of us." He even admits that such results "always suffer some loss in trying to manifest themselves outside." We are here touching one of the more intimate aspects of Biran's obstinate silence. Why talk and publish, if the price to pay is a loss of truth? To be sure, the silent philosopher will not attain glory, but "one must choose between that world and the inner world. He who lives within himself must renounce all the advantages of exterior life, among which the first no doubt is glory; yes, he who has more deeply studied than others the faculties of his own mind, ought perhaps, for that very reason, renounce much place in the mind of others."[33]

the philosopher and his philosophy

Biran was the very reverse of a man whose personal life would remain foreign to his intellectual speculation. All the relations of soul and body which Cabanis had described with the objective detachment of a scientist, were for Biran, with his very sensitive temperament, as so many personally experienced facts. The first item of the practical philosophy he deduced from his psychology naturally was: *Know Thyself*. Likewise, natural theology,[34] which we saw him include among the privileged sciences of inner experience, was from the very first for him the normal expression of his religious feelings. The remark applies to the whole of his philosophical career, till the end. Even in the very last months of his life, when he practically ended in confessing the truth of Christianity, Biran continued to think of God in terms of the Cause of Causes. He was certain there is a God on the strength of his inner experience of causality.

On the other hand, while that philosophical certitude gave him intellectual satisfaction, it did not perfectly answer his moral needs. One of the reasons Biran attached so much importance to the will is that, in his own sight, he himself had too little of it. Not as an individual, for he was not a weak man, but as a human being, Biran resented the disproportion between what he could obtain from himself and what he would have liked to be able to do. According to his own doctrine, the "hyperorganic" force of his will should have ruled his body without meeting with any insuperable resistance; as a matter of fact, his *Journal* often shows him distressed at his inability to achieve self-mastery in the conduct of his inner life. Like Rousseau, Biran then felt himself passively submitted to all external influences from nature and society, always in danger of losing his own ego and constantly fighting to preserve it.[35]

At a later stage, when he began to fight for actual self-mastery, Biran turned his mind toward the Stoics. He was hoping to learn from them the secret of a life free from the vicissitudes and tyranny of external influences. For some time he toyed with the idea of emulating Epictetus and Marcus Aurelius, but he soon found that stoicism was a remedy only for very healthy persons. Self-mastery cannot be achieved by means of self-mastery. The great harm done by passions is that they prevent us from using reason and will; how then could we resort to them in order to sway our passions?

These and similar reflections led Biran to the conclusion that there was a still higher level of inner life. The last pages from his pen were devoted to a sort of philosophico-religious conspectus of the various degrees of inner life. Biran's so-called doctrine of "the three lives" is the final expression of his religious thought.

> Man is intermediate between God and nature. He is related to God by his mind and to nature by his senses. He can identify himself with nature by allowing his ego to be absorbed by it, along with his personality, his liberty, and by giving himself up to all the appetites, to all the impulsions of the flesh. He also can, up to a point, identify himself with God, by letting his ego be absorbed in the exercise of a superior faculty, which the school of Aristotle has entirely overlooked, but which Pla-

V. Ideology in France

tonism has discerned and characterized, and which Christianity has perfected by bringing it back to its true type.

The life of man can be lived at three different levels. At the lowest as well as at the highest level the soul loses its personality; at the lowest level, that of the sensations, desires, and passions, the soul loses itself in creatures, whereas at the higher level it loses itself in God. The intermediate state is that in which man preserves his personality along with his liberty of acting. "This is the proper and natural condition of man, that in which he exercises all the faculties of his nature, develops all his moral power in fighting the unruly appetites of his animal nature, in resisting the passions as well as all the allurements, all the strayings of the imagination. Above and beneath that state, there remains no struggle, no effort, no resistance, consequently no *I*; the soul is in that state of alienation, sometimes in deifying, sometimes in animalizing itself."

In such a doctrine, ethics is intimately tied up with religion; not, however, in the sense that the rules of morality would hang on the will of God or on our knowledge of his nature, but because, in fact, man progresses in his union with God as he is progressing in moral perfection. The two ways are one. "The relations that exist between the elements and the products of the three lives of man are the more beautiful, but also the harder subject of meditation." Man has no effort to make in order to live his animal life; on the contrary, he only has to let himself go. The intermediate life requires strenuous efforts, for it is a predominantly active life, as befits a being whose very substance is that of a will. Stoicism is the highest there can be in active life; in its perfection, it is the triumph of the human will, but, on the one side, it abstracts from the animal nature of man and, on the other hand, it wholly overlooks the higher life of the mind. The result is that its "practical morals" exceed the forces of human nature. And indeed stoicism forgets to take into account the obstacles opposed by sensations, imaginations and passions to the free display of the moral will; as it fails to see that man cannot achieve that moral liberty without raising himself up to the third and higher life, it leaves him betwixt and between, struggling in an uncomfortable middle where he cannot possibly stay. Only Christianity embraces the whole of human nature; it knows man's lowest nature, it also knows the possibilities of man's will, and it even avails itself of the deficiencies of man's nature in order to lead him to his highest end.

As he was nearing the end of his life, Biran thus was discovering the Christian notion of grace. At the same time, he was feeling more and more in sympathy with the great exponents of the Christian philosophy of man: Pascal, Fénelon, and the author of the *Imitation of Christ*. They all took him back to Scripture, especially the Book of Job in the Old Testament and the Gospel of Saint John in the New Testament. Only, as a philosopher, he could not give up his personal method in approaching those ultimate problems: observation by means of the inner sense. So he could only strive to experience in himself that higher life of union with God, but there were two difficulties: how to obtain grace, how to be sure one is in possession of it?

Biran there found himself at grips with the same difficulty that was later to plague Bergson: how to attain the God of religion by merely philosophical means? In a striking passage of his *Nouveaux essais d'anthropologie* (*New Essays of Anthropology*), describing that ideal state in which intellectual life would remain wholly unconcerned with body, Biran adds: "That is the miracle of the Man-God; stoicism cannot go as far as that." The Book of Wisdom, Saint Augustine, the mystics, offer to him the ideal of a "pure love" which at once "identifies itself with a sort of intuitive knowledge wherein one sees truth without seeking after it, in which one knows all without having studied, or, rather, in which one despises the whole human knowledge because one finds oneself above it. At that ultimate degree of elevation, love and knowledge become one; but that is more than a human knowledge." Visibly, Biran is nearing the goal: "God is to the human soul what soul is to body." Our soul has faculties and exercises operations of its own; over and above these, however, "it has faculties of operations due to a principle higher than itself, and those operations take place in its innermost, without the soul being aware of them. These are intellectual intuitions, inspirations, supernatural motions wherein, disappropriated from itself, the soul is wholly under the action of God and is absorbed in him." It is not right, as mystics do, to wish to reduce everything to that higher order, but there certainly is no higher one. The problem is to reach it.

We read in the Gospel of John: "He who sees me, sees my Father" (14:8–9). "This becomes clear when one distinguishes being, the divine spirit, the father of lights, from the *I* which is a manifestation of him. We only can see being in its manifestation, the Father in the Son. At present the divine spirit enlightens the soul by the reflection of the *I*, and not directly."[36]

V. *Ideology in France*

Did Biran ultimately go beyond the highest point accessible to human reason unaided by faith? History has no answer to such problems. One thing at least is certain. With Biran, ideology was achieving a twofold progress. First, it was substituting for clear but superficial descriptions of the mind a searching exploration of its innermost depths. Next, it was attempting to turn itself into a means of metaphysical inquiry. In writing "To be, to act, to will is the same thing under different names," Biran was taking ideology far beyond its natural limits which, normally, did not exceed those of an analysis of the human mind. With him, ideology was dying of its own triumph, but its successor was already born. It was a curious hybrid, a sort of positive metaphysics, conceived as a science of observation, yet capable of transcending experience, so to speak, from within.

VI. *Ideology in Italy*

THE French school of ideologists formed a well-knit group of philosophers. Especially at its beginning, when men like Cabanis and Destutt de Tracy were personal friends, their relations amounted to a quasi-collaboration. In Italy, ideology was the free choice of independent personalities; there was no school; besides, the Italian ideologists followed ways independent of those of their French predecessors.[1] Nothing would be more wrong than to consider the best among them as a mere reflection of the French movement. Of course, French influences are visible in Italy, but much the same way English influences were at work in France. The truth of the case is that, in both countries, the leading influence was that of Locke.[2]

Francesco Soave

Condillac had spent ten years, from 1758 to 1767, in Italy, at the court of the duke of Parma, as a preceptor to the young prince. There was at Parma a famous institution, the Alberoni College, whose masters naturally became acquainted with, even influenced by, Condillac,[3] so that even outside of Parma his influence was felt. Opposition was not wanting,[4] but the translation of Condillac into Italian, followed by works of Destutt de Tracy and of Laromiguière (between 1815 and 1821) helped to popularize the French brand of sensism.[5] On the whole, however, it would be more just to connect Italian ideology with the *Inquiry* of John Locke than with the *Treatise* of Condillac.

This is eminently true of the doctrine of an errant professor of philosophy, too often a victim of political perturbations in Italy, but always teaching somewhere, the "good" Soave, a religious of the teaching congregation of the "Somascs" (because their mother house was in the city of Somasca). Let us call him the "good" Soave,[6] as they do, but not without stressing the fact that his

VI. *Ideology in Italy*

goodness was not meekness, for he was quite a fighter. Soave always fought on three different fronts, against Kant, Erasmus Darwin, and Destutt de Tracy. His opposition was not an impersonal one. On the contrary, Soave never hesitates to quote chapter and paragraph of his own *Istituzioni di logica, metafisica ed etica* (*Institutions of Logic, Metaphysics and Ethics*) as the proper place to find competent refutations of his adversaries.

Soave's criticism of Kant has been judged superficial, even slightly ridiculous. He had but an indirect knowledge of the doctrine through the book of Charles Villers, *Philosophie de Kant, ou principes fondamentaux de la philosophie transcendentale de Kant* (Metz: Collignon, 1801), but Soave needed nothing more in order to realize that, from the point of view of traditional empiricism, the *Critique* of Kant was introducing a new form of idealism, and, consequently, of skepticism. Kant's true intention was a twofold one; in his own words, it was to limit (*begrenzen*) in order to found (*begründen*). In other words, Kant intended to restrict the domain of knowledge to the kind of objects we can really know. On the other hand, the "limiting" part of the operation necessarily appeared to metaphysicians as a victory gained by skepticism. Soave then was well founded in denouncing the catastrophic consequences of the *Critique* of Kant in the domain of metaphysics. This he did in no uncertain terms: "Persuaded that the existence of bodies cannot be known, the Prussian philosopher declares that, in the universe, all is for us an illusion; that the ideas we receive from external objects all are phantasms of our own making which nothing real answers outside of us, and that no other real existence is known to us, beyond that of the being that thinks within ourselves." That Kant never explicitly maintained those conclusions is quite clear; but that they rightly can be deduced from his authentic doctrine is another thing. Soave was only maintaining that those consequences logically follow from Kant's criticism, which was a debatable point, but not an absurdity.

His second adversary was a biologist whose personal name has now become eclipsed by that of his illustrious grandson. Erasmus Darwin (1731–1802) was the author of a half scientific, half philosophical *Zoonomia* dealing with the laws of organic life. Right after criticizing the "Prussian philosopher," Soave adds that, "on the contrary, the English philosopher does not recognize, outside of the supreme author of nature, any other being than that of the corporal and material substances, just as he makes corporal movements of ideas, perception, sensation, will, memory, and all that which concerns thinking being. Nor does he attribute all these operations to men only, or to animals only, but, extending them up to vegetables, he here seems to be trying to revive the condemned madnesses of those who make man a machine, or a plant."[7]

In answer to Destutt de Tracy, Soave has devoted a critical study which offers the best exposition of his own philosophy because, on every point, it pits the truth of his own position against the errors of Tracy. Incidentally, Soave protests against de Tracy's contention that the founder of ideology was Condillac. Its true founder was Locke; Condillac only amplified it. It is true Condillac has turned the doctrine of Locke into a unified system; he shared that questionable honor with Helvetius. After so aptly criticizing the passion of philosophers for systems (in his *Treaty of Systems*) Condillac himself finally made one. This should not be counted to him as a merit, but, rather, as a demerit.[8]

The gist of Condillac's and Tracy's errors was their fundamental thesis that "to think is to feel, and nothing else than to feel." Against that position, Soave pits his own as exposed in his *Istituzioni di logica*, §11, chap. 2. To feel is a passive state; we are not free to feel or not to feel while external objects are acting on our senses. Against Condillac, and with Locke, Soave admits a twofold source of knowledge, sensation, and reflection. Apart from sensation, all knowledge is active: "The soul is most active (*attivissima*) in paying attention, reflecting, comparing, judging, reasoning, and willing; for the volition, or act of the will, which is an active determination of the soul to accept or to reject a proposed object and, between two things, to choose one rather than the other." The power of thinking, then, cannot be confused with mere sensibility, nor can it rightly be said that to think is nothing else than to feel.

To Tracy's vague word "sensation" Soave proposes to substitute the more complex panel of two couples of terms: *modification* (includes pleasure and pain), *representation* (without pleasure and pain), *sensation* (I *feel* a rose), *perception* (I *look at* the rose). Another mistake is the indiscriminate use of the term *idea* made by ideologists after the example of Condillac. From its very etymology, an *idea* is an *image*. The word should therefore be reserved for all the objects of thought that can be imagined. These are the thoughts connected with space; all the others should be called *notions*. Notions are smells, tastes, feelings of heat and cold, faculties and operations of the soul, truth and error, cognitions or ignorances, in short, "all intellectual and moral entities." Had he

VI. *Ideology in Italy*

but known this, Kant would not have made the mistake of defining "ideas" as "concepts of concepts."

As to will, how could it be identified with the mere "feeling of desires"? A desire is a tending of the soul toward a good that is proposed to it. I am feeling a pleasure, I wish it would last. Will, therefore, is not the faculty of feeling desires, it is the faculty to second them or to suppress them. We second them if they tend toward a true and real good; we curb them if they tend toward an apparent or a false good. The power the soul has to choose, to embrace, or to reject, is an eminently active one.[9]

Soave has clearly discerned in Tracy a tendency which took him far away from Condillac. According to him, sensibility is a faculty of our organization, in fact, and according to all philosophers of repute (Locke, Condillac, Bonnet, d'Alembert, etc.), it is a faculty of soul. By attributing sensibility to our physiological organization, Tracy is courting epicureanism, in itself the most absurd, and to morals the most dangerous, of all systems. Besides, Tracy does not go to the trouble of proving the existence of a thinking subject in us. In fine, if our organism feels, why should not plants and minerals feel as we do?[10] From Tracy to Erasmus Darwin the distance is not as great as it seems.

Given this opposition to Tracy, in what sense can Soave still be called an ideologist? The justification for that appellation lies in the fact that his own aim and scope is the same as theirs, namely, to decompose thought into its component elements. Only Soave does it in his own way. According to him, our faculties are six in number: to feel (*sentire*), more passive than active, in that it does not depend on the will; to reflect (*riflettere*), a fully active power of fixing one's attention on a certain object of thought and of transferring it to another at will; to know (*conoscere*), that is, to compare ideas, to judge and to reason[11]; to remember (*ricordarsi*), a sometimes passive and sometimes active faculty, depending upon whether memories spring up of their own accord or, on the contrary, are intentionally recalled and recognized as such; to will (*volere*), in which the soul is always most active in determining itself to will or not to will, as well as to will this and that; to operate (*operare*), that is to say, the power of initiating all internal operations and all external movements of the body. From these six fundamental faculties are derived: (1) the self-awareness of the subject's own existence, which every man achieves by repeatedly performing operations whose only possible cause is himself; (2) by reflecting and variously applying attention to diverse ideas, or to various parts of them, man can abstract, generalize, combine, or separate ideas, which constitutes the very substance of intellectual life.[12]

There is nothing to be gained by comparing Soave to other philosophers, and not much more by putting any label on his doctrine. Without being deep, his thought is consistent and most of the self-contradictions he is sometimes reproached with come from applying to his doctrine rules of judgment he would not have accepted. The flexibility of the notion of ideology clearly appears in his doctrine, for he agreed neither with Locke, nor with Condillac, nor with Tracy; still, in a way, he was one of them, enjoying their common freedom to analyze the mind each in his own way.

Melchiorre Gioia

Melchiorre Gioia[13] is a good representative of the tendency, perceptible in Italian philosophers of that period, to make philosophy serve practical ends. Ethics naturally was such an end, but economics, law, and public administration were not forgotten. One reason was that, in the troubled early nineteenth century, many Italian philosophers actively shared in the political and administrative life of their time. Here, as in the case of France, it would be interesting to know the amount of philosophical speculation for which we are indebted to political failure, jail, and premature retirement. The tradition of the *consolatio philosophiae* is an old one. Gioia was fortunate in that his intellectual hobby was statistics, a matter which provides openings on political jobs as well as on philosophical speculation.

In fact it would be difficult to find something in which Gioia was not interested. In philosophy proper he began by writing *Elementi di filosophia* (*Elements of Philosophy*) for schools. At that time his thought still was strongly influenced by the sensism of Condillac. Judgment still was a "secondary sensation," that is, a sensation under a derived form; human life itself appeared to him as "a continuous movement of sensations." Without overstressing some formulas used by Gioia in what was a mere philosophical introduction, one can observe his tendency to consider the difference between man and animals as chiefly organic in nature. Erasmus Darwin, whom he was later to oppose, seems to have impressed him at that early stage of his philosophical reflections.

VI. *Ideology in Italy*

In his *Ideologie*, Gioia adopts a different attitude. The very title shows his intention to join the group of the ideologists, but his first care was to submit their work to a searching criticism. As he saw it, ideology had become a sort of harmless game consisting in finding out how many elementary faculties there are, and which they are. Are those faculties two, or three, or five or six in number? Each ideologist makes his own choice, and nobody can prove he is wrong, but he himself cannot prove he is right. What are the causes of the disorder and how can they be remedied?

The root of that evil is a threefold one.

First, there is an *excess of useless research*. The works of German as well as French philosophers are plagued with it. German books are devoted to the discussion of abstract terms whose elucidation leads nowhere. They all are about unity, plurality, and totality, or about identity and diversity, or causality, that is, about abstract notions empty of substance. The French philosophers elegantly discuss subtle points and content themselves with giving them verbal answers. In his *Leçons de philosophie*, for instance, Laromiguière wonders if, at the very first instant it begins to live, the statue made by Pygmalion would be able to say, *I?* Condillac makes his own imaginary statue say: *I am rose scent*, which means he answers the question in the affirmative; Laromiguière himself wonders; after discussing the problem at some length, he concludes to his own satisfaction that "the soul has the *feeling*, but not the *idea* of its own existence." To which he adds: "The choice of these two words, and the nature of their opposition, has settled the dispute." To all of this Gioia comments: "Let us pity the fate of the youths condemned to busy themselves with such silly trifles."

The second cause of disorder in ideology is *the want of necessary research*, meaning the fact that certain research that ought to be made is being neglected because philosophers waste their time on idle problems. Instead of wondering how many faculties there are, why do they not define the meaning of the word "faculty"? Some indeed do attempt to do so. The same Laromiguière declares that "the diverse *modes* of action of the soul precisely are what we call faculties." Now, were the number of our faculties to be deduced from the diverse "modes of action" of the soul (i.e., the different ways in which soul operates) faculties would not be two, or six; there would be at least one thousand of them. We do not attribute to a dancer as many legs as there are steps in his dance. Such verbal inquiries should be discarded to make room for a proper investigation of reality.

The third main defect of ideology, such as it is being practiced, is *its most arid and abstract mode of exposition*. This sets readers against it. Always interested in concrete results, Gioia wants ideology to be intelligible to all sorts of persons, the more so as there is no reason why it should be hard to follow, since all its objects are facts within the human mind.[14] In fact, Gioia's own theory of faculties is very simple. In other ideologies, it constitutes the very subject matter of the book; in that of Gioia's it is but one among many other problems. Twenty pages are enough for him to explain what he has to say about memory, imagination, and intelligence.[15] His real interest lies in another direction.

Despite his excellent intentions, Gioia cannot avoid the pitfall of all ideology, which is to begin by setting up an arbitrary classification of elementary psychological facts. The trouble is not that such sets of definitions are not legitimate; on the contrary the trouble is that they all are equally legitimate, though different. In Gioia's proposed language, all the impressions we are conscious of are called *sensations*; among sensations, those innocent of pleasure and pain are called *ideas*; sensations blended with pleasure or pain should be called *feelings*. In all this, however, Gioia's intention is not to innovate, but to simplify. Fully conscious of coming at the present extremity of a long line, he sees himself as the successor of Aristotle, Locke, Condillac, Helvetius, Destutt de Tracy, and other recent French philosophers. Cabanis, however, followed a different line; he "modified the idea of Condillac" by proving that one cannot explain everything only by the action of external senses. That was not particularly important; yet, Cabanis was the first French philosopher to handle ideology without losing contact with facts, and that at least was important. Ideology itself must be cultivated in view of physiology, ethics, medicine, and law, "for such is the true aim and scope of the study of human nature, namely, the knowledge of the rules necessary for the conduct of man."[16]

The general trend of Gioia's ideology is quite spiritualistic. The fact must be stressed precisely because his doctrine attaches so much importance to the problems of physiology raised by Cabanis as well as to those of zoology discussed in the *Zoonomia* of Erasmus Darwin. The main concern of Gioia is to prove that man is far superior to brutes; as compared with them, man stands alone. Hence his statistical tables of comparison between animal organs and human organs of corresponding function and denomination. In his own words, "I demonstrate that the quantity and the quality of the ideas and feelings cor-

VI. *Ideology in Italy*

respond neither to the number nor to the perfection of the external senses." In short, his professed intention is to set into relief the immense distance that separates man from brutes: *dar risalto all' immensa distanza che separa l'uomo dai bruti.*[17] This being said, however, it must be noted that, according to Gioia, that superiority of man over brutes is all a matter of inner organization. Animals can have finer sensations than men; women too, for that matter, and yet did any woman ever surpass Voltaire, Milton, Boileau, Smith, Newton, and Kepler? So Erasmus Darwin and Helvetius are wrong in reducing all problems to material ones, but, at the same time, there is no doubt that inner organization is the prime cause of the difference of perfection between animals and man. It is just as with clocks. Some mark the hours, others mark them and sound them, still others do all that and are alarm clocks besides; the cause for those differences lies in more or less complex inner structures, and such also is the case for the difference of beasts and man.[18]

As was seen in connection with Locke and Condillac, one of their weak points was their failure to account for instincts. Gioia accepts them such as they are, but an original feature of his doctrine is that he adds to animal instincts a set of intellectual instincts proper to man, namely: curiosity, the need of being appreciated, the need of exercising power and the so-called instinct of sociability.[19] His short but adequate descriptions of those inner tendencies naturally common to all men were something comparatively new; with them ideology was widening the scope of its inquiries.

A still more remarkable feature of the new ideology was the importance it attributed to psycho-physiological problems. Condillac had been a psychologist, Cabanis had been a physiologist, Destutt de Tracy had declared that he regretted not to be a physiologist as well as a psychologist; in consequence, he had directed his readers to Cabanis for further scientific information; Gioia did his very best to unite the two disciplines in his own work. From this point of view, his discussion of the relation of stimuli to sensations and vice versa was without parallel in the works of his predecessors. What Gioia calls the "laws of intensity," despite a lack of scientific precision more than excusable at that date, were opening new fields of research.[20] More original was Gioia's decision to consider that sort of investigation "psychological." Similar remarks must be made concerning Gioia's treatment of passions, their causes, their qualities, their species, their degrees of intensity and of stability. Here, however, Gioia was treading more familiar ground. The psychology of the classical poets had already explored the nature, varieties, and effects of the passions. Their relation to the body had been studied by Descartes. Gioia centered his interest on a point in which modern novelists have found an inexhaustible source of inspiration, to wit, the influence of affections and passions on the apparent value of things. The fact was well known; Lucretius had already noted it, but Gioia submitted it to a more attentive ideological analysis in describing the many ways in which feelings unbalance our judgments about reality. Among the eases examined in his treatise let us note his study of the effects on judgment of sensual pleasures, love, vanity, pride, ambition, avarice, pedantry, party spirit, the timely use made of respectable names whereby we hope to impress others, or they hope to impress us. Superstition too is such a force. But the problem of error has received at the hands of Gioia a much more extensive treatment.[21]

The *Esercizio logico* (*Logical Exercise*) is the most personal of his books; in fact, no other book in logic looks in the least like it. His starting point was that, just as the right place to learn medicine is a hospital, so also the appropriate way to learn logic is to observe men in the very act of being mistaken. In order to facilitate such clinical observation in matters of reasoning, Gioia undertook to show, within the compass of one single book, and always resorting to concrete examples, quoting names, books, and sentences, how logic was and actually is being violated by authors. His detailed and well-ordered analysis investigates three main fields in which errors are generally committed: Style, Order, Ideas.[22] There is a Baconian inspiration about this hunting for causes of error, but Gioia seems to agree with a remark made by Joseph de Maistre, that unless you come to personalities, you do nothing against error. Having to deal with logical ailments, Gioia names patients, describes ailments, and localizes sore points. Nor are his victims men of small stature: Lamarck, Erasmus Darwin, Barthez, Pinel, Cabanis, Virey,[23] all come in turn for their share of criticism. In the usually close atmosphere of ideology, Gioia is like a breath of fresh air.

Giandomenico Romagnosi

The stormy career of Romagnosi[24] was that of a professor of law, and by far the better part of his reflections had the philosophy of law for their object. It would perhaps be still more exact to say that he was teaching law in a philosophical

VI. *Ideology in Italy*

way. Such, for instance, was the case with his *Introduzione allo studio del diritto pubblico universale* (*Introduction to the Study of Universal Public Law*).[25] This tendency to generalize was the sign of a philosophical vocation. He was practicing law when, in 1795-1796, he wrote up a memoir on a subject proposed by the Academy of Mantova: *Ricerche sulla validità dei giudizi del pubblico a discernere il vero del falso* (*Research on the Validity of the Judgments of the Public in Discerning the True from the False*).[26] A lawyer had good reason to feel interested in the subject, but only a born philosopher could handle it with the mastery and, above all, the accuracy in method which characterize Romagnosi's essay.

At that early date in his philosophical career, Romagnosi understandably followed the method of the ideologists. To define notions with accuracy and to order them according to their actual relations in reality, in short, *analysis*, is the only method not only in philosophy, but in all sciences. Romagnosi more precisely says *un a minuta e ragionata analisi*[27] (a detailed and reasoned analysis), a phrase which could well serve as a definition of the method of Condillac.

The discussion of the problem provides Romagnosi with many opportunities to express his own philosophical views. From the outset it is visible that he does not favor a merely passive conception of the human soul. Against Helvetius, he maintains that judgment is *not* a mere way of feeling. Sensations are realities rather than truths. One cannot account for truth without resorting to judgment, and judgment itself is impossible without an active power of the soul. Even before judgment, the soul is active in abstracting and generalizing. There is nothing particularly original in those early views of the young lawyer, except that they lead him to a kind of methodological idealism, already inherent in Condillac, but which Condillac had rather toned down, whereas Romagnosi obviously feels very much pleased with it.

Romagnosi calls his own attitude "a new way of considering ontology."[28] Thus understood, ideology and ontology are practically one and the same discipline: "Ontology, that is, the science of being in general, or of being *qua* being, precisely is nothing else than the science of the operations which the human soul perpetually and invariably performs in the exercise of his faculties of feeling." In an impressive formula, Romagnosi adds that ontology "is a natural and eternal reasoned story of the operations of human knowledge."[29] This entails two consequences. With regard to philosophy, the denominations used in ontology become a sort of dictionary of the affections and operations of the soul in its effort to perceive and to know. The complicated reasonings of the philosophers to analyze soul into its component faculties simply mean that, while one of its operations is taking place, there is no room left for another one. With regard to the very object of knowledge, it follows that, considered in their relation to man, "beings properly are nothing else than his ideas." Let us note the wording of the phrase: *a riguardo dell' uomo*. Romagnosi does not say that, in reality, beings are nothing else than our ideas of them, but he holds the view that, *to man*, beings are nothing else, and this inspires him with the pleasant idea that, henceforward, all the beautiful speculations of the philosophers, ancient and modern alike, concerning the existence of the external world, are completely ruined. Of course, there is an external world; but, to us, it is nothing else than our knowledge of it.

This attitude deserves to be noted in view of Romagnosi's future reaction to Kant. In 1796, he already feels certain that the external world exists in itself, independently of our knowledge of it. Romagnosi does not simply feel it, he knows it. Idealism is wrong, because the necessity there is for us to perceive successive and particular impressions in order to think implies the existence of external objects by which our ideas are caused. We first acquire the feeling of the presence and unity of our own being as source of our own operations, after which, applying that notion of a subject to other things besides ourself, we conceive them as the causes of our ideas. Romagnosi expressly rejects the position of d'Alembert, who accounted for our certitude of the existence of the external world by a sort of "instinct safer than reason itself." Romagnosi considers that conclusion as following from a causal inference. The reality of the world then is a rational certitude, but we know nothing else about it than our ideas of it.[30]

It has often been remarked that such a conclusion predestined Romagnosi to become a disciple of Kant, but he never did. His refusal to become a Kantian has been explained in the usual way: Romagnosi did not read Kant in the German original, he was misled by some commentaries of Villers, etc. Such explanations are partially true, but they are not sufficient. Like Soave and a few others (among them Auguste Comte), Romagnosi could very well understand the meaning of Kant's philosophical reform without studying it in its detail. The truth of the case seems rather to be that, because the prodigious arbitrariness of Kant's critical decision was to him unimaginable, Romagnosi tried any other

VI. *Ideology in Italy*

interpretation of the doctrine rather than the true one. Incidentally, it is noteworthy that although all agree that the criticism of Kant is a landmark in the history of philosophy, no philosopher of of note ever contented himself with subscribing to it.

Romagnosi expressed himself on Kant in two articles: "Historico-critical Exposition of Kantism and of the Consecutive Doctrines," published in the *Biblioteca italiana*, 1828–1829. He clearly discerns the character of instrumentality proper to the criticism of Kant (it does not establish any truth, it is only about the way to know truth). More important still, Romagnosi clearly realizes that, in the last analysis, Kant stands on exactly the same ground as Condillac and himself: whether we raise ourselves up to heaven or go down to probe abysses, we never get out of ourselves. When Romagnosi adds to those correct remarks the reproach, directed against Kant, of not having *empirically* justified his conclusions, he completely misses the point, but of course that was where he could not believe that Kant really meant what he was saying.

Leaving aside the good-natured jokes of Romagnosi about the unreality of the Kantian philosophical universe, it is noteworthy that, following his own reflections, he had reached a conclusion very similar to that of Maine de Biran on the same subject. There is a sophistical substitution of points of view in the implicit reasoning of Kant: *We cannot know the external objects in themselves; therefore we only possess figments purely ours.*[31] The two philosophers agree that the consequence does not follow, and their remark is the more justified as, in point of fact, Kant himself does not hesitate to make a transcendental use of the category of causality in affirming the existence of things in themselves, of which we only know that they are, although we cannot represent to ourselves what they are.

This being said, it must be conceded that the very inability of Romagnosi to take Kant at his word made it impossible for him to realize the true meaning of the doctrine and the reason for its fantastic success. In Italy as well as in France, Kant then was becoming the fashion and without going quite "as far as that," it began to be admitted that, on the whole, Kant was right. Romagnosi simply maintained, against the formalism of Kant, the rights of psychological analysis and of empirical observation in all cases when the actual structure of the mind is at stake. It is permitted to wonder if, in this, the Italian philosopher was not justified, for indeed, even granting the necessity of deducing the categories of the human mind, it does not follow that their deduction should be an *a priori* deduction. The *a posteriori* method initiated by Aristotle in the fourth century B.C. remains, at the very least, an open possibility.

It was only in the last years of his life, when he was wholly destitute and mostly living on the generosity of a noble friend, that Romagnosi formulated the philosophy underlying all his preceding speculation about Kantism, the foundations and value of public opinion, and even law. Like those of Locke, Condillac, Tracy, Laromiguière, Soave, and others, Romagnosi's philosophy is a particular brand of ideology. As with all of them, especially Maine de Biran, Romagnosi aimed to overcome the limits of ideology by making a better and a new use of its method. That the method itself—that of psychological empiricism—might be an insuperable obstacle, does not occur to his mind. Like all the other ideologists, he clearly realized that the mind cannot be purely passive in its operations. Hence a personal and interesting series of modifications brought by Romagnosi to the general scheme of the received doctrine turned it into a philosophy of his own.

The primitive element is, of course, sensation, but by a complete reversal of the ideological tradition, Romagnosi makes sensation an active state, due to the co-operation of two powers contributing to a common effect. This effect—sensation—thus appears as the indivisible effect of two acts, to wit, the active causality exercised by the external object, and the active reaction exercised by the soul in answer to its action. In a way, Romagnosi was rediscovering a too-often-neglected aspect of the authentic doctrine of Aristotle: sensation is the *common act* of the feeling and the felt.

This initial co-operation of two distinct powers communing in the production of the effect provides Romagnosi with a general pattern for the analysis of the mind. At the origin of all its operations, Romagnosi places its power to deal with all sensations. Far from its being transformed sensation, the mind is rather the natural aptitude to transform it; in short, it is what Romagnosi calls a logical sense, or a rational sense, that is, the inner power whereby we turn the data of sensations into rational products. What it is in itself, we don't know, but we do know that it exists and that all that which our mental activity comprises, beyond bare sensations, is due to it.[32]

What is the origin of those additions which the mind contributes to the empirical data of sense? The "logical sense," or "rational sense," draws them out

VI. *Ideology in Italy*

of its own substance; they are, so to speak, its natural functions. Using a general denomination for all those contributions of the logical sense to knowledge, Romagnosi calls them "reasons" (hence the name of "logical" sense, from *logos*, reason); all cognitions arise from the transformation of sensory data by those rational factors contributed by our soul.

It almost looks as though Romagnosi was fighting to keep away the word "categories," which would so well fit his doctrine, but he has good reasons to avoid it. No more than Kant does Romagnosi attribute to us the knowledge of things such as they are in themselves; we know them such as they are as known; but they would not be known such as they are being known if, in themselves, they were not that which they are. Here again, as in the primitive fact of sensation, knowledge arises from a composite power, a "com-power." If this is idealism, it is a very peculiar brand of it. Romagnosi himself calls it an *associated idealism*, or a "*compotential idealism*," meaning thereby that while we cannot reach objects beyond our knowledge of them, we know things only because they do exist, and our knowledge of them is that which it is only because their natures actually are that which they are.[33]

The general ideology of Romagnosi provided him with a convenient tool to analyze moral ideas, to order them, and, above all, to find them an objective as well as a subjective justification. In ethics as in gnosiology, it is equally wrong to think that everything comes from without or that everything comes from within. Man is neither a mechanical agent determined from without as well as from within, nor is he a God freely decreeing what is good and what is evil. In this respect, man is a liberty conditioned by norms founded in his own nature as well as in that of external reality. The love of happiness is the supreme law of moral life. Good and evil are determined by reason from the positive or negative relations of things to that end. Happiness itself consists in the more successful preservation and in the more rapid improvement of ourselves. The law of perfectibility, so important to the philosophers of the late eighteenth century, still remains present to the mind of Romagnosi. Only man is perfectible, and he alone is perfectible on account of his rational power; to achieve perfection in all orders of knowledge, of morality, and of action would also be to attain the "supreme good." No single man can hope to attain it. To the limited extent to which it is attainable, the supreme good is the proper goal of social and political life. To pursue it is what Romagnosi calls "the law of duty." In accordance with his eminently concrete approach to philosophical problems, Romagnosi describes it as including all that which the nations had, have, or will have a duty to do in order to be in a better position to discover the good and the useful, to build up, within the shortest possible delay, the best and most durable institutions possible. The collective fulfillment of that duty by society is what Romagnosi calls *civilization*, the process whereby the State progressively actualizes the conditions required for a cultivated and a happy community life.[34] Remembering that Romagnosi spent the better part of his life studying laws, institutions, and constitutions, one will not fail to understand those words in the more concrete sense they can bear. In ethics, the great civilizing powers of Greece and Rome are the true sources of Romagnosi's inspiration.

Melchiorre Delfico

Like many Italians in the first third of the nineteenth century, Melchiorre Delfico[35] resorted to philosophy as to a refuge from the vicissitudes of a troubled political life. His general tendency was similar to that of the other ideologists, especially Cabanis, with this reservation, however, that his scientific notions were those of a philosopher instead of, as was the case with Cabanis, his philosophical positions being those of a scientist.

Delfico's major contribution to ideology was his wholly justified insistence on the significance of imitation. In order to give it more scientific weight, Delfico presents it as a physiological function and calls it *imitative sensibility*. By relating it to sensibility, he was insuring the continuity of his doctrine with the sensism of Condillac. Being a sense, or sharing in the nature of sense, the tendency to imitate must have an organ of its own and an organic seat. The location of that seat is not known but it is enough for us to be certain that imitation is an inner sense that chiefly operates through two outer senses, hearing and sight. From both points of view man essentially is an imitating animal.

Sounds are perceived by hearing and imitated by voice. Hence imitation becomes the origin of language. The simplest of all cases is onomatopoeia. By imitating a sound associated with a fact (*bang* for an explosion), or a thing (*seesaw*), or a being (a *cuckoo*), a name is spontaneously formed. Onomatopoeia is particularly active at the early stage of the formation of a language; it soon becomes antiquated, but there still remains in many names a sort of kinship be-

VI. *Ideology in Italy*

tween the sound and the meaning. Soft-sounding words often remain associated with sweet feelings and harsh sounds with harsh feelings.[36] In all such cases, one must admit that the phenomenon has a cause, that is to say, "a proper organ for the imitation of the sensations coming to us through the ears."

At a higher level of discussion, Delfico disagrees with Buffon, according to whom men talk because they think; on the contrary, men think because they talk.[37] Usually, Delfico operates at a more modest level. Normally he sticks to intelligent obviousness: when smiled at, babies smile back, children play at having marriages and funerals as well as at being soldiers, in imitating the movements made by the lips of talking persons. The point of these examples is that they manifest the character of organic automatism proper to imitation. The fact is still more evident in the case of birds that learn to sing musical airs and to articulate words by simply hearing sounds and trying to reproduce them. Will has no part to play in such cases; it simply happens that sounds provoke vocal imitation and repetition generates habits.[38]

Passing from psychology to ethics, we are invited to use imitation as a solid and objective basis for the notion of "sympathy." No feeling is more effective in shaping human relations. Now to "sympathize" is to "feel with," and thus spontaneously to share in the emotions of pleasure and pain expressed by another man, and this is a clear case of imitation. Laughter is infectious; a sad mien makes us feel sorry without our knowing why. This is therefore a purely physical phenomenon and "physical sympathy" would be better called "consensibility." If this be true, imitative sensibility becomes the real basis of social life, or, in Delfico's own words, "the true moral sense of man." To turn a moral sense into a physiological sense, or, at least, to look for its basis in some organic cause, is typical of the general trend of the doctrine. For instance, a particularly "moral" form of sympathy is compassion. Now compassion is observable in practically all animal species; it is natural for an animated being to feel pain at the sight of other beings in pain; the rise of the social condition of man is made possible by compassion, and the starting point of the whole process is found simply in an inner sense organ: "just as it is a daughter of imitative sensibility, compassion is the mother of those feelings of humanity that lead men to live in society and insure the duration of the body politic."[39]

At that point, Delfico makes bold to generalize his conclusions. If what precedes is taken for demonstrated, "imitative sensibility" is only one of the parts of inner sensibility; it operates by a system of organs (especially hearing and sight) as can easily be observed; moreover, man is naturally able to impart certain directions to such imitative reactions and to order them in view of premeditated ends. Granting those points, a very general consequence follows at once: the whole human knowledge and all the human arts being as many results of sensations, and since sensations can be moderated, strengthened and even, by means of repetition, brought to a point where they seem to give rise to new faculties, it is logical to think that the same will be true of the impressions that come to us from "the organs of imitation."

These remarks assume their full meaning in connection with the problem of education. A major concern with most of the eighteenth-century philosophers, education is always present to the mind of Delfico. He thinks that, in consequence of his own discoveries, the heretofore unexploited resources of "imitative sensibility" shall have to be harnessed and put at the service of pedagogy. We still have much to learn in that field. Comparative studies should be made on the corresponding variations of repetition and of imitation in the various kinds of impressions. By observing facts and seeing how they condition one another, it will become possible to construct a "philosophy of reality," without getting entangled in the "metaphysic of ideas." Delfico understands by this a metaphysics which, "creating beings and relations between beings all situated beyond the reach of sense, carries us into a world of its own making."

In that educational task, Delfico sees Rome as entrusted by history with a particular mission. Already a world art gallery, it should more and more become a center of studies for all the nations of the world, especially for all that concerns the fine arts. "Such a university would be more useful than one thousand colleges; once turned into a school of beauty and a place of noble pleasures, it would make us forget the ancient wrongs done to morals and to reason."[40] The anti-historicism of Delfico and its opposition to the old Roman tradition are more traits inherited from the eighteenth-century cult of progress, but his personal contribution remains the same and he never loses sight of it. On the strength of his own doctrine of imitation conceived as one of man's sense powers, disciplines condemned to vagueness and inefficiency will be turned into precise and efficacious techniques: "With such principles grounded in nature, education will acquire a physical basis and, without enjoying the precision of a calculus, it will become susceptible of a much higher certitude in its handling."[41]

VI. *Ideology in Italy*

Similar notions dominate Delfico's inquiry into the nature of the beautiful. Following the general line of sensism, he asks how the abstract notion of beauty can arise out of simple sensations. His doctrine of imitation admitted of only one answer to the question. The beautiful must first be given in nature, where it is indeed abounding. Its perception by sense fills us up with delightful feelings. That pleasure is for man an invitation to emulate nature and even surpass it. The beauty thus conceived by man in his desire to surpass natural beauty is called "ideal beauty." It adds to natural beauty both grace and sublimity.[42]

It is noteworthy that the Italian ideologists constitute a generation roughly contemporary with that of the French ideologists; in both cases the doctrinal filiation is the same. Delfico describes it as "the philosophy of Locke, enlarged and brought to good use by Condillac, Bonnet, and Tracy, and which the more loyal friends of reason made their own."[43] He also calls it "a philosophy of reality grounded on the theory of sensations,"[44] and indeed ideology was just that. Quite a few others adopted it as a method besides those whose writings have been quoted,[45] but it is remarkable that, with Delfico, ideology proved eminently faithful to its own spirit. He would have lived most congenially in the society of the encyclopedists and, in his own time, he would have enjoyed the company of Cabanis. But, precisely, this might well serve as an illustration of the limits which ideology could not overstep. Its true possibilities lay in the direction of psycho-physiology rather than of metaphysical speculation.

VII. The Christian Reaction

THE history of Christian philosophy during the French Revolution is not well known. The received view that, for a time, it ceased to exist, might well be true, but there are a few signs that a sort of secret stream of Christian thought continued to flow during those troubled years. Scholasticism had then become a strange mixture of all sorts of doctrines. Surrounded by philosophies either hostile to Christianity or foreign to it, the Christian authors of philosophical textbooks seem to have attempted to modernize the teaching of the traditional philosophy by resorting to any doctrinal position that was not incompatible with it. A remarkable witness to that state of mind is the famous *Philosophia Lugdunensis*, an anonymous textbook whose success was incredible.[1] What surprises us most in it today is that such a mixture of Aristotelianism, of Cartesianism, and of ontologism was imposed by the Catholic hierarchy, in more than one French diocese, as the standard work to be used in classes of philosophy.

Under those circumstances, it is not surprising that other ways were attempted by the first Christian thinkers who, soon after the political hurricane of 1789, undertook a philosophical restoration in the sense of the Christian tradition. Their effort is usually called "traditionalism." Just like the word "ideology," traditionalism is a vague denomination that covers different attitudes. Nevertheless, just as all ideologists had in common their ambition to establish a genealogy of thought, starting from sensations, and to substitute that analysis of the mind for metaphysics, so also it will be seen that all the traditionalists aimed at founding philosophical knowledge and metaphysical certitude on some primitive communication of truth revealed by God to man. Apart from the inner structure of the doctrines at stake, two points are worth considering about them. Why did several philosophers spontaneously adopt that attitude? Why did the Church finally disavow some of those men, its most loyal and ardent supporters?[2]

VII. *The Christian Reaction*

Louis de Bonald

An immediately apparent fact about de Bonald[3] is that his whole thought bears the mark of the French Revolution. From beginning to end it is a reaction against it. Having witnessed the destruction of the political and social order in which he had first lived, confronted with the bloody excesses of the revolution, with its frightening ability to destroy the old and its inability to create the new, himself an exile from his own country or, as we would say today, a "displaced person," de Bonald had made society, its nature and its origin, the permanent object of his reflections. He himself has defined in one sentence the aim and scope of his philosophical undertaking. As is usual with him, the style is somewhat heavy, but the meaning is clear. "I have inquired, in the light of reason only, and by means of reasoning, whether there is one fact, unique, evident, tangible, proof against all objection, that is the generative, or, at least, constitutive principle of society in general, as well as of all the particular societies, domestic, civil, and religious."[4]

In view of the general character of his philosophy, everywhere eager to serve the interests of society by serving those of religion, it will be well to note that de Bonald intends to appeal to reason only. He is a philosopher, not a theologian. If he can be said to theologize, it will only be in the field of natural theology. A second character of his doctrine is its unified, systematic nature; in an entirely different order of ideas, de Bonald proceeded, like Descartes and Condillac, on the basis of one single principle. Third, and this is the Baconian side of his thought, that principle is not an abstract generality, but an observable fact. This point is so important in the doctrine that it deserves special consideration.

The answer of de Bonald to his own question is in the affirmative. There is such a fact, but for it to be tangibly evident, it must not be found in feeling, nor in the testimony of man's conscience. To allege the testimony of some voice of conscience speaking to the inner man is to risk the objection that such personal conviction is valid only for those among us that experience it. Now it has been well observed by Damiron that the philosophers of that school refuse to appeal to the subjective testimony of personal conscience. Their starting point never is the ego; when they say "man," they do not mean *I*. What they are interested in is man as an observable fact. Now there is an outer man just as surely as there is an inner one. That exterior man is "social man," that is to say, society itself. Since what we are after is a visible principle and cause of societies, we cannot hope to find it elsewhere than in society itself. That principle and cause is "the primitive and necessary gift of language made to the human kind."

Language exhibits all the characters required from a philosophically valid starting point. First, it is an externally observable fact, for society is such a fact, and language was given to man in view of making social life possible. It has no other conceivable use and there is nothing subjective about it.

On the other hand, considered as a fact, language is both external and internal. It is internal inasmuch as it expresses the moral man and results from that which is innermost in him, namely thought. At the same time, inasmuch as it is voice, language results from the action of material organs belonging to external and physical man.

In fine, language is an absolutely primitive fact. Since it began with society, it is impossible to go farther back in the series of causes. It likewise is absolutely general and perpetual, since it is observable in all places where there are two human beings and cannot be conceived of as coming to an end as long as there are men. Language is both common and usual, since all normal and free men can talk, even those still living in primitive societies. Such then will be de Bonald's initial fact, and his central position about it will be that *man cannot possibly have invented language; consequently language must have been given to him by God.*

The reason for this thesis is that, in order to invent language, man would have had to use reason without using words, which is impossible. In itself, reason is prior to language; de Bonald will make this abundantly clear. Unless there be thoughts to express, there can be noises made by the mouth of man (or of parrots) but there can be no words. On the other hand, there can be no thought if there are no words to express it. Man cannot think, even silently, without talking to himself and telling himself what he thinks. To think then is to talk to oneself, just as to talk is to think for others. In both cases, "it is necessary that man should think what he says before saying what he thinks."[5]

If this is true of man as such (as being founded in his very nature of *homo loquens*) it must also be true of man as a social animal. Society cannot be the cause of language, for the reason that, without language, there can be no society. The simplest of social groups, family, becomes a society worthy of the name only when its members begin to exchange simple expressions of elementary needs and feelings. Later, when the domestic society acquires the form and size of political society, writing multiplies the possibilities and efficacy of language as a social bond, but it only exploits resources virtually contained in a primitive gift. Since language can have for its cause neither individual man nor social man, its only conceivable origin is a gift of God.

It has been remarked that de Bonald does not say how that gift was made. This is true, but in saying that God gave man language, de Bonald simply means that God created man a thinking and talking animal. There was no particular moment when man was given language because, before he was able to talk, man was not able to think; he was not a man.

This notion of language is tied up with the peculiar way in which de Bonald conceives the origin of human knowledge. In a doctrine where man cannot think unless he talks, God must have given man thought in giving him language. This is the meaning of the brand of traditionalism proper to de Bonald. Its import is that, just as language itself, thought cannot have been instituted by man. From the very beginning God has implanted in the human mind fundamental truths by creating man able to talk. In this sense, truth can never be new in the world. Error always is something new, not truth. To create man, human speech, intellectual truth and human society was for God one and the same thing.[6]

Just as language is primitive in thought, power is primitive in society. Exactly as he opposes the theory that language results from man-made conventions (since where there is no language there is no man), de Bonald rejects the theory that society results from a freely established contract, because in order to establish a contract men have first to live in some sort of society. A contract can modify the form of a society, not create it. The primitive fact in society is not contract, it is power. Where there is power, there can be law and, by the same token, there can be society. The origin of political power is the same as that of language. It is divinely instituted: *omnis potestas a Deo est* (Rom. 13:1–2). God did not create man, then power, then again society; God created society in creating man a talking animal and he created power in creating society because, in fact, they are one and the same thing.

This "theory of power" is tied up with a theory of what de Bonald calls "primitive legislation." Both rest upon the same fact. God has created all men alike, but he also created them similar to himself, and just as to be similar to God is not to be equal to God, so also for men to resemble one another is not to be equal among themselves. They are similar in both will and action: they want similar things and they perform similar acts, but they are not equally able to will and to act. In short, contrary to Rousseau's famous pronouncement, men are created unequal. This is what makes society both possible and necessary. It is possible because, created similar, men can unite in view of the pursuit of similar ends obtainable by similar means; it is necessary because, created unequal, men must enter a system of necessary relations between stronger and weaker, which is society itself. Without such a system of inequalities, all would be strong or all would be weak; there then would be a mere juxtaposition of unrelated beings and, therefore, no society.[7]

Since society demands the relationship of power to weakness, the unity of society requires the unity of power. There are two kinds of society, that of man with God and that of man with other men. These two societies both produce and preserve. Religious society produces and preserves in man the knowledge of God. Human society produces and preserves the very life of man in the temporal order. In each of these two societies, it is necessary to introduce a distinction overlooked by Rousseau, by Hobbes, and so many others, not without tragic consequences. One must distinguish between the *native* state and the *natural* state of beings. The acorn, the child, are the native state of oak and man; but to be a full-grown tree is the natural state of an oak, as to be an adult is the natural state of a man. In each one of the two main types of societies the *native* state is related to the production of beings, the *natural* state is chiefly related to their perpetuation and conservation.[8]

The *native* state, or condition, of man is not the loose condition of men not yet related by social ties; on the contrary, it is a society, to wit the domestic society composed of three persons both unequal and alike: father, mother, and child. There is in it unity of power, that of the father which, through the mediation of the mother, reaches the child. The bond of domestic society is marriage; through marriage, two persons become parts of a whole, the domestic society to which they belong, and which does not belong to them. Men then are born in a native condition that is, at the same time, a social condition. In this sense, there are no individuals, or, at least, men never find themselves in the condition of mere individuals. This is what makes divorce impossible. Individuals could divorce; they could dissolve a society they had made; but if domestic society is the native state of men, it does not belong to them, they belong to it.[9]

VII. *The Christian Reaction*

The *native* state of religious society is tied up with the native state of civil society. The first state of religion is not at all an inner emotion experienced by an individual in the presence of nature, it is that of a religious social group, the family, in which a domestic cult is rendered to God by the father, acting as a priest who celebrates for all the members of the family. The main act of the domestic cult is a sacrifice, either that of animals or that of fruit. There is a deep meaning in sacrifice as a form of worship. It is self-denial expressing love, and the love of God is the very essence of religion.

The *natural* states of these two forms of societies do not alter their essences, but, rather, they consolidate them and perfect them. The respective structures of all societies are alike. Every society consists of three distinct persons, whom one could call "social persons." These are: Power, Minister, Subject. In domestic society, the three social persons are called: Father, Mother, Child; in religious society: God, Priests, Faithful; in political societies: Kings or Sovereigns, Nobles or Government Officials, Subjects or People.

There is no society without Law. "Law is the expression of the will of the sovereign, promulgated by power, to be the rule for subjects." Some say it is the will of men, others say it is the will of God, and all are right, for if it is just, Law is the will of God, *spoken* by man, in order that it be *heard* by men. The import of the various laws is determined by the natures of the things which they bind together, be it in the physical or in the moral order. It has been rightly said by Montesquieu that those relations are necessary, and that they follow from the nature of things. Indeed, without them, things could not be. They are not only necessary, but perfect, since it is owing to them that the perpetuation of physical beings is assured and order preserved between moral beings. At the same time, it must not be forgotten that "those natural, necessary and perfect relations are the work of the will of God himself who, by freely creating beings, has produced the necessary relations existing between them."

There is a hierarchy between those societies as well as between the respective systems of relations they constitute. Since all power is from God, religion is the constitutive basis of all social state. "Civil society is composed of religion and of the State, just as man, a rational being, is composed of intelligence and of organs." Moreover, "man is an intelligence that must make its organs serve his happiness and perfection which are his ends. Similarly, civilized society is nothing else than religion making political society serve the perfection and happiness of the human kind." Such being the situation, political administration has its rule in morality, by which only it can foster the interests of religion. The most perfect society therefore is that in which the constitution is most religious and the administration most moral. "So religion must constitute the State, and it is against the nature of things that the State should constitute religion. But in order that the State be constituted by religion, it is necessary that it should regulate the ministers of religion, whose passions could alter religion and thus shake the constitution of the State. So the State must obey religion and, in turn, the ministers of religion have a duty to obey the State in all those of its prescriptions that agree with the laws of religion, and religion itself should prescribe nothing that is not conformable with the just laws of the State. Where that order of relations is respected, religion defends the power of the State, just as the State defends the power of religion."[10]

De Bonald saw eighteenth-century philosophy as a sort of organic whole and he seems to have been the first to present it as a historical entity enjoying a unity of its own, at least in its inspiration and spirit. That tree had to be judged by its fruit. To de Bonald, the fruit was bad, since it was the French Revolution of 1789. Despite personal divergences, the encyclopedists had all cultivated an anti-metaphysical attitude, substituted the critical exercise of reason for the interpretation of facts in the light of the principles, reduced the life of the mind to mechanical associations of passively undergone sensations and images, so much so that, even those among them who did not consider it material dealt with the mind exactly as with a living organism subjected to the laws of matter. The kind of man Condillac conceived of directly led to the "social contract" of Rousseau, that is to an artificially made society which its founders are free to unmake exactly as they first were free to make it. Societies made at will can be changed at will. In the philosophy of de Bonald, on the contrary, everything comes from God and is created by Him alone; with the organic structures, physical or moral, to which it belongs. This is particularly true of man. Created a social animal, born a member of the social unit we call family, man demonstrates by the very mode of his propagation that even society is a natural fact. Just as he is created endowed with reasoning power, principles of knowledge, and language to express it, society is created along with power, authority, structure, and order. For the social reformers soon to come, de Bonald was to remain the very embodiment of the organic and conservative spirit as opposed to the

VII. *The Christian Reaction* 241

spirit of restlessness that had dominated the eighteenth century.[11] To Auguste Comte in particular, de Bonald will remain the very model of the "organic" way of thinking which the nineteenth century had to oppose to the vagrancies of the merely "critical" mind.

Joseph de Maistre

Joseph de Maistre[12] himself has expressed his surprise to find that, unbeknownst, de Bonald and he had spontaneously hit on the same truths and upheld practically identical conclusions. The style of de Maistre, however, is very different from that of de Bonald, even as a style of thought. He is less a purely speculative philosopher than an apologist of Christian truth and his personal vocation seems to have been to justify, by essentially rational means, the most unpopular parts of the Christian doctrine.[13] He had a gift for it. Above everything else, de Maistre had an extraordinary aptitude never to let himself be disconcerted by any objection. No objection against a truth can itself be true. In such cases, just face the objection, submit it to the light of reason and you will see it dissolve under your very eyes.

Another distinctive trait of de Maistre is that he was very personal in his attacks against error. Reproached with his taste for attacking persons instead of contenting himself with refuting doctrines, he replied that, indeed, nothing has been done to refute error so long as, behind the erroneous doctrine, criticism has not reached its author. De Maistre always plays the man. His *Examen de la philosophie de Bacon* (*Examination of the Philosophy of Bacon*) (1815) is largely directed against Francis Bacon himself whom he reproaches, among other things, with not having known as much science as his thirteenth-century namesake, the English Franciscan Roger Bacon.[14] It is difficult to say whom he detests the most—Bacon, Locke, or Hume. In point of fact, although he seems to consider Hume the more venomous, his favorite target is Locke, no doubt because of the sort of dictatorship he had exercised over the minds of a whole century. De Maistre protests he has nothing against Locke personally. Everything about him was right, except his philosophy. In this Locke resembled the dancing master of whom Swift once said that he had all the good qualities conceivable, except that he was lame. Even the philosophy of Locke would no doubt be excellent had its principles been true.

Locke embodies for de Maistre the "bad principle" which reigned in Europe ever since the time of the Reformation. It is "the principle that denies everything, shakes everything, *protests* against everything: on its bronze forehead is written, No! and this is the true title of the book of Locke which, in turn, can be considered as the preface to the whole philosophy of the eighteenth century, itself purely negative and therefore, null."[15]

Still more openly than de Bonald, de Maistre considers "the philosophy of the last century" as a kind of doctrinal whole which "will remain in the sight of posterity as one of the more shameful epochs of the human mind." It had a favorite purpose, not to say a unique one, namely to detach man from God: "All that philosophy was only, in fact, a system of practical atheism; I have given that strange disease a name: I call it *theophobia*."[16]

The main symptom of theophobia is a constant and marked tendency to resort to any solution rather than God in answering any problem. The symptom can be observed in all philosophical books of the eighteenth century. They would not frankly say: *There is no God*, for fear of getting in trouble with the law, but they would say: *God is not there*. God is not in man's ideas: they come from sense. God is not in our thoughts: these are but transformed sensations. God is not in the plagues that afflict mankind (for instance, the deluge): these are but physical phenomena like all the others and they can be accounted for by means of well-known laws; God does not think of you, nor, for that matter, of any other man: the world is made for the sake of insects as well as of man; in short *no physical event can have a cause related to God*.

Against that general attitude de Maistre undertakes to show that, on the contrary, the explanations of natural and historical facts by the intervention of a supernatural agent acting in view of supernatural ends are the only satisfactory ones. Nothing is more unlike cheap apologetics than the reasons developed by de Maistre. He has a gift for revealing the presence of the preternatural in familiar historical and social facts such as the striking difference there is between the peculiar condition of the public executioner, the most unglorious of men, and that of the soldier, a killer admired by all. De Maistre shows in original sin the only rational answer to many otherwise unexplainable facts. There is a kind of pre-Chestertonian touch—though of a much heavier kind—in the never flustered assurance with which de Maistre makes reason testify in favor of transcendent and revealed truth.[17]

VII. *The Christian Reaction*

Among the philosophers whom de Maistre likes are Thomas Aquinas, whom he does not know too well, but to whose authority he resorts in order to maintain against Locke that there are in man innate cognitions. He also admires Malebranche, a great mind which France is unworthy to possess. But the philosopher whom de Maistre calls "the best of his friends" is François de Cambrai, that is, Fénelon.[18]

On the positive side, de Maistre favors a traditionalism grounded less in an oral revelation of truth made to man by God than in an exceptionally high intuitive power granted by God to primitive man, and now well nigh lost. According to his own views, God created man endowed with a learning not only greater than our own, but different in kind. In the beginning, man knew effects in their causes; today, men painfully strive to rise up from effects to causes or, rather, they content themselves with effects; they do not bother any more about causes; they do not even know what a cause is.[19] To the favored eighteenth-century theme of the continuous advancement of learning de Maistre thus opposes the contrary certitude that mankind has unlearned what it first knew and is now engaged in the slow work of recouping part of the loss.

The problem of language is the same as that of knowledge; "language is eternal and every tongue is as old as the people that speaks it." The notion that all languages were poor in their beginnings is only one more gratuitous supposition made by the philosophers. It is true those primitive languages have disappeared, *etiam periere ruinae*, but they did exist, because man cannot have received knowledge without at the same time receiving language.[20] The problem of the "origin of ideas," so dear to philosophers (e.g., Condillac) is therefore absurd: "thought and language are but two magnificent synonyms."[21] Both come to man by way of revelation and rest upon authority.

On the problem of society and its principle, de Maistre was at one with de Bonald, not because he was borrowing anything from him but on account of what he himself considered their quasi-miraculous agreement. Man is not the maker of things; he finds them already made and endowed with natures it is not in his power to change. "Man can modify everything within the sphere of his activity, but he creates nothing; such is his law, in the physical as in the moral realm. Man can of course plant a seedling, grow a tree, and perfect it by grafting and pruning in a hundred ways; but he has never fancied that he has the power of making a tree. How has he come to imagine that he had that of making a constitution?"[22]

For all his rationalism, de Maistre had a soft spot for mystical doctrines related to the notion of divine illumination. The more remarkable feature of his doctrine in this respect was that, as he himself saw it, science was already striving to recall men from matter to spirit. This seemed evident to him when he thought of Newton, whom he absolutely refused to put in the same class with Locke. Only men like Voltaire dare to say: Locke and Newton, as if any comparison were possible between the two names! Scientists are always speaking of "mechanical laws" and of "mechanical principles" while, in fact, there is nothing really mechanical about the notions they have in mind. They are unwilling to acknowledge the fact, but scientists are now behaving like a secret sect enjoying the monopoly of truth and hoarding secrets hidden from the public. They seem to forbid other people to know more things, and to interpret them otherwise than they themselves do.

De Maistre foresees the coming of a new era. Introducing in one of his *Soirées de Saint Petersbourg* (*Evenings in St. Petersburg*) a curious personage, different from himself, but with whom he obviously feels in sympathy, de Maistre has him announce that the proud science of the day will soon find itself humbled by an *illuminated* posterity which will blame it for its inability to draw from the truths God has given to it consequences more precious for the happiness of man. "The face of the whole science will then be changed; long dethroned and despised spirit will recover its place. It then will be demonstrated that all the ancient traditions are true; that even paganism was only a system of truths corrupted and out of their respective places; that it is enough to clean them up, so to speak, and to restore them to their places in order to see them shine again...."[23] As we said, all of this expressed the position of some illuminists rather than that of de Maistre himself. Yet he never wholly disapproved of them. Disliking as he did their tendency to join secret sects and to separate themselves from the Church, he felt that their minds were moving in the right direction, from a revelation lost by man's rebellion, to a revelation regained, under God's guidance, by the patient effort of human reason.

Félicité de Lamennais

All the great themes of traditionalism meet in the doctrine of Félicité de Lamennais[24] but are formulated in a new spirit. Like de Maistre and de Bonald,

VII. *The Christian Reaction*

Lamennais takes a stand against the critical rationalism of the eighteenth century, and for the same reasons. Society needs peace; there is no peace in the heart of any man in which there is no truth, and the same applies to social bodies: there can be no peace in a society in which there is no truth. Truth here means intelligible propositions to which men cannot refuse unconditional assent. The aim and scope of Lamennais' doctrine was to determine the nature of such truth and its source, and thereby to restore order and peace in modern societies.

Two features of his doctrine should be underlined as typical of it. They are the two causes of the dramatic evolution which was to lead this zealous priest, the very apostle of submission to the authority of the Church, later to rebel against that authority and ultimately to leave the Church.

The first is his complete denial of the aptitude of man to achieve any certitude by means of his natural powers of knowing. In so far as *individual* man is concerned (the reason for this restriction will be made clear) certitude is impossible. In this respect, the skepticism of Lamennais is complete. Knowledge comes to us from three sources—sense, feeling, and reasoning. The deceptive nature of sense knowledge has been stressed by many philosophers and Lamennais simply takes up their main arguments. One of them ought to suffice: since I can suffer hallucinations, I cannot even know with certitude whether I am perceiving or not. Consider what happens to those who rely on the certitude of sense in philosophy: Hume, who does not know if there is causality in the world, and Berkeley, who does not even know there is a world. Next comes feeling. By this word, Lamennais signifies that sort of inner voice which some philosophers, Rousseau for one, profess to trust much more than reason. True enough, evidence is such a feeling, but we can observe that individual feelings of evidence result in many contradictions, oppositions, and controversies. Besides, feeling contradicts itself, since we feel that which we think we feel, whether or not a reality answers our feeling. Last comes reasoning, but since neither sense nor feeling carry any certitude, reasoning has no reliable foundations. Hence a rule emerges that can be considered universal, namely that men don't agree. "Two minds starting from the same point and walking to the same goal cannot take four steps without parting company." Nay, the very same mind, taken at two different moments, will not agree with itself. To conclude, if man remains in isolation, he condemns himself to complete and incurable skepticism. Let us carefully note this first feature of the doctrine: the traditionalism of Lamennais rests upon the utter powerlessness of individual human reason to know any truth with certitude.

Although knowledge is denied to individual reason, another way to it remains open. Men act as though they were certain of many things. They might profess skepticism in words, but their conduct gives the word the lie: "Man acts, hence he believes." The truths that are the more necessary in view of action are also those we are less able to prove. The necessities of life thus make us form in our minds a certain number of unshakable certitudes. We call them (note the influence of Thomas Reid) truths of common sense. Those commonly received principles of action presuppose commonly received rational conclusions; for indeed, in order to act, one must think, that is to say, one must affirm and deny, in short one must judge. Here again common sense (in the Reidian sense of opinions commonly assented to) is for us the only criterion of certitude. When several individuals disagree in their judgments, there is no certitude; as soon as their conclusions agree, they all feel safe. Common assent is in fact for us the only safe criterion of truth. Hence comes the second characteristic feature of the doctrine. The common consent of the human mind to certain conclusions of human reason is the only criterion of truth there is, and that criterion is quite sufficient.

Such is the gist of the doctrine. Neither man nor society can exist without certitude; certitude is the absolute impossibility of doubting; the condition for that impossibility is the conformity of our personal judgment to common sense (or common sentiment of other men); this aptitude of common sense, or consent, to guarantee our personal certitude is called *authority*. In the last analysis therefore, the only criterion of truth is authority.[25]

So far it has been proved that, *in fact*, only authority gives man certitude; can we go one step farther and prove that there are objective reasons why it should be so?

In order to answer that question, we must look for a fact containing in itself its own justification and, at the same time, the justification of all the others. In other words, we must find an authority able to guarantee both its own certitude and all the other certitudes. Does the common consensus of men offer such a self-sufficing primary certitude and authority? Yes, the existence of God. All our knowing powers contribute to ascertain it: memory, for it comes to

VII. *The Christian Reaction*

us through the immemorial tradition of mankind; sense, since God has made himself visible to man; feeling, as is attested by the universality of prayer and of men's desire of beatitude. I am as sure of the existence of God as I am of my own existence, and for the same reason; in both cases, only common consent to the truth of those conclusions makes me sure they are true. Despite what atheists say, one cannot *really* doubt the existence of God: "one only can deny it by violently opposing nature which urges us to defer to universal consent."

This still is only a fact, but it can be turned into an intelligibly justified truth. The idea of my own existence does not carry with itself any necessity; I am not to myself the cause of my own existence. Nor is any other contingent being the cause of its own existence. If we stay locked within ourselves and even within the world, we may well wonder if it is not all an immense dream. Not so when we think of God. His notion in us is that of a supreme being. Now it is universally recognized that, of itself, Being is necessary, perfect, self-sufficient, and containing in itself the reason for its own existence. As it needs no other being in order to exist, that Being is the absolutely first principle, origin, and cause of all other existence and of all other truth.[26]

We are nearing the goal. Since God is the supreme and only reason for all the rest, human understanding itself is but a possibility to be actualized by God. Our reason cannot actualize itself except as a participation in the supreme Reason. To be certain is to be certain that God is, that we are by Him, think by Him, and know by Him. The life of man's understanding is to participate in God. How is that participation effected? By revelation, which is the spoken word of God. By speaking to man at the time of creation, God gave him, at once, the first truths and the first seeds of reason. To conclude: "That first revelation, by explaining our existence, unintelligible in any other way, also accounts for our understanding; it shows us its foundation in the essential truths originally received by man, and invincibly believed on the testimony of God, whose authority thus becomes the basis of our certitude and the reason of our reason."[27]

The tendency to blend traditionalism with an epistemology based on the notion of a primitive revelation was nearly irresistible. At any rate, Lamennais did not fail to denounce the pernicious influence which, as he himself saw it, the philosophy of Descartes had exercised on the theology of the seventeenth and eighteenth centuries. One of the practical consequences of his own doctrine was the imperative necessity to substitute authority for rationalism as theological method.[28] Christian theology had all the qualities required from a universal criterion of truth. If there is a God and if we know truth in knowing God, the only way to reach certitude is to obey God's authority.

God is reached through religion. By "religion" we mean the ensemble of relations there are between God and man. Now since such relations follow from the nature of things (reminiscence of Montesquieu), they are necessary; consequently, there is only one good way to conceive those relations, there is only one true religion. That religion must be the one whose claim to authority is both the most universal and the most justified. Not Protestantism of course, which stands for free examination against authority; nor Judaism either, which is tied up to a nation; there is one universal church, the Catholic Church; hence the authority of the Pope.[29]

Here, however, an important point must be made. Precisely because it is a traditionalism, the doctrine of Lamennais must identify Catholicism with the substance of the primitive revelation of truth made by God to mankind at the time of creation, and hence it is necessary for him to conceive of Catholic truth as the epitome of all that which has ever been true in the religions of the past, minus, of course, their errors. Catholicism thus becomes a sort of general reason, universal and common to all those who share in the light of reason. In a sense, this was exactly what Lamennais wanted to obtain. A man of his own times, he felt (and he said) that unbelief and atheism had to be fought with modern weapons. If you quote Scripture and allege miracles, people simply do not listen. The real enemy to be destroyed is individual and particular reason; hence the necessity of substituting for the false authority of individual reason that of the universal, impersonal, and divine reason of the Church. The peril latent in the doctrine is visible at once: even if universal reason is the Church, the Church is something other, and more than, universal reason.

Such positions could not please the representatives of traditional theology which, whatever else it may be, certainly is not a traditionalism grounded in a radical skepticism concerning the power of personal reason to find truth. Moreover, a large section of the French hierarchy at the time was Gallican, and the uncompromising ultramontanism of Lamennais could not please them. Still less could it please the French government to see the Sovereign Pontiff endowed with the privilege of being the very embodiment of truth and authority in all matters. Lamennais there found himself in the same situation as Tertul-

VII. *The Christian Reaction*

lian. Eager as he was to insure the absolute independence of the Church from the State, he unleashed in his paper *l'Avenir* a resolute campaign in which he held the view that to be separated from the State is for the Church an essential necessity. As a corollary of the slogan, a free church in a free state, he imposed upon the Church the duty never to meddle in temporal matters and therefore to approve, for the State, of the freedom of the press (freedom, for the press, to teach and to spread error), a position of which the Church will never approve. Rome saw at once that, by thus absenting itself from social and political reality, Catholicism was betraying its duty, nay, its very own mission, to teach the world and to save it. Hence the encyclical of August 15, 1832,[30] in which Pope Gregory XVI condemned as erroneous, absurd, and almost delirious Lamennais' opinions that the Church should not worry what cults the state encourages, what doctrines it teaches in its schools, what opinions the press circulates. Lamennais first accepted the censure, but he retired to his country estate and began to brood over his exasperation. The result was *Les paroles d'un croyant*. From that time on, Lamennais was out of the Church; with *Les affaires de Rome* he ended in announcing a universal religion, one, eternal, and transcending all its transitory forms and through which Christianism would be rejuvenated.[31]

Christianism has a marked preference for rejuvenating itself. All the disciples of Lamennais deserted him, leaving him with a broken heart.[32]

Louis Bautain

The similarity between the various forms of "traditionalism" testifies to the presence of a philosophical situation independent of their respective authors. As the traditionalists saw it, the naturalism of the eighteenth century was responsible for the revolution of 1789; the philosophies of Condillac, Locke, and Descartes were responsible for that naturalism; at the origin, the Reformation was responsible for the rise of a philosophy like that of Descartes extolling the rights of individual reason and of private judgment. The battle then was between philosophy and religion. Reason had to be humbled, if not downright destroyed, in order that religion could live. All the anti-rationalisms known from the time of Pascal had thus gathered in the doctrine of Lamennais.[33] The philosophy of an admirable priest, the abbé Louis Bautain, exhibits the same character. The difference lay in the man rather than in the spirit of the doctrine, for after modestly submitting to the censure of Rome, he died in the communion of the Church, surrounded by the converts he had made.[34] This personal contrast dramatizes the impersonal nature of the forces at work behind the spreading of traditionalism.

Among the many writings of Bautain one stands out as an irreplaceable document in the history of nineteenth-century Christian philosophy. It consists of a correspondence between Bautain himself ("The Master"); one Adolphe Carl ("Adolphe"); Theodore Ratisbonne (significantly called "Adéodat"); Isidore Goschler ("Julien") and Jules Lewel ("Eudore"). These four young men had constituted the whole audience of his private lecture course in Strasbourg; three of them (Ratisbonne, Goschler, and Lewel) were Jews; all three became converts to the Catholic Church at the end of that private correspondence; one of them was the future Père Marie-Théodore Ratisbonne, founder of the Society of Priests and of the congregation of the Sisters of Notre-Dame de Sion; that exchange of letters was published by the future Cardinal Henri de Bonnechose, with an introduction of his own, at the time when a condemnation of certain aspects of the doctrine looked imminent, and indeed one could not easily imagine a more convincing proof of the apologetical efficacy of the doctrine. Still, after its protracted examination by Rome, Bautain was invited to retract. Had he refused to comply, the situation of that saintly priest would have been the same as that of Lamennais, a redoubtable warning to all Christian philosophers that even utmost sincerity and ardent zeal are no valid substitutes for doctrinal truth.[35]

The history of the evolution which led from the *Cogito* of Descartes to the final skepticism of Hume was a common good of the traditionalist school. Its exact meaning was not that, starting again from Descartes, philosophy could fare better; on the contrary, the point of the story was that, starting with Descartes from private judgment, philosophy was bound to reach identically the same conclusions. On this point, Bautain added nothing to the doctrine of the school, except that he told the story in greater detail and included Kant in his own version of it.

As Bautain read its history, philosophy under the pagan Greeks relied on nothing but reason, and hence was a chaos of mutually contradictory doctrines. Then came Christian revelation, followed by an age of Christian philosophy represented by the Fathers of the Church: informed and led by revelation, rea-

VII. *The Christian Reaction* 251

son attains certitude and achieves doctrinal unity. A third stage is marked by a comeback of Greek rationalism. The rational method begins to introduce itself into Christian speculation around the twelfth century; the movement reaches its climax with scholasticism, when "theology and philosophy, delivered over to the dialectics of Aristotle, still find a support in the revealed word." Then, with Descartes, still another era begins; become pagan again, reason destroys everything and progressively leads philosophy to the conclusion that no metaphysical conclusion can be known with certitude. If religion is to survive, it will have to find support elsewhere than in the natural certitude of reason.

Bautain thus wholly agrees with the negative conclusions of Kant's *Critique of Pure Reason*. This is no historical inference. The Thirteenth Letter of the Master, directed to Adéodat, is explicit on this point, where, of course, many of the main themes of traditionalism meet. The rationalist says, "My reason is I myself"; no, reason is not *you*, it is *yours*. Placed above sense, but lower than intelligence, it receives truth *ex auditu*, from language, and because it believes in what it is told. This is what happens when man is informed about the existence of another world superior to that of sense, but it is in the same way that "it receives data and principles which cannot be proved by reasoning. When the will adheres to those principles, they become the support of reason, the rule of its judgments. On the contrary, when reason pretends to be to itself its own rule, or to receive it from itself only...it has no basis left, no method; it loses itself in hypotheses, it engages in a maze of contradictions and ends in absurdity."

What gives Bautain's position its particular flavor is that, according to him, this is precisely the meaning of Kant's *Critique*. The doctrine of the antinomies of pure reason signifies exactly that the natural reason of man is powerless to demonstrate *any* metaphysical proposition. That conclusion is true and, moreover, it is excellent. By killing the very possibility of metaphysical certitude in general, Kant eliminates scholasticism. The harm done to theology by the introduction of the philosophy of Aristotle into the sacred doctrine can now be undone. From this point of view, the greatest merit of the Philosopher of Königsberg is to have decisively established "the powerlessness of reason peremptorily to solve a single metaphysical problem." Whereupon, recalling the "celebrated antinomies of pure reason," Bautain notes with great satisfaction that not one of them can be solved: there is a God and there is no God, the soul is spiritual and it is not spiritual, the soul is immortal and it is not immortal, man is free and he is not free, the world is eternal and it is not eternal, there is for us no decisive reason to make a choice between these contradictory conclusions. Arguments of that sort, therefore, are of no philosophical value[36]; if there is a truth about God, philosophy will not tell us what it is.

That metaphysical skepticism was a flat philosophical conclusion, but, in the mind of Bautain, there were religious motives behind it. Kant had wanted to limit philosophy in order to found science; Bautain wants to set limits to philosophy in order to found religious knowledge, and this was for his doctrine the source of many obscurities.

At a first level, Bautain maintains that reason should not pretend to justify the revealed truths which, of their very nature, transcend the power of created understanding. All theologians would agree. Going farther, Bautain upholds a much more complicated position. There is no true God but the Christian God; philosophy can know nothing of the Christian God taken precisely *qua* Christian; consequently, philosophical reason can know absolutely nothing of God.[37] But he does not stop there. Bautain only subscribes to the negation of metaphysical certitude by Kant in order to justify the wholly un-Kantian notion of a metaphysical knowledge made possible by the Christian revelation. "No metaphysical science is possible for reason left to itself and reduced to its natural means," but such knowledge becomes possible with the help of religious revelation. Boldly commenting on Scripture, Bautain affirms that his conclusion was already formulated by Saint Paul (2 Cor. 2:14), for indeed "the *animal man* of Saint Paul is the same as the rational animal of Aristotle, and the *spiritual light* of which the Apostle speaks is that which comes from the metaphysical world in order to enlighten our intelligence; it is a light which, here below, reason only sees in its last reflections." The ultimate conclusion of Bautain is thus not that human certitude is impossible but that it is possible only within revelation and religion: "Outside of Catholicism there is no science worthy of the name, no certitude, nothing but arbitrary opinions, human systems."[38]

The doctrine thus concludes with one of the less felicitous expressions of the ill-fated notion of "Christian philosophy." "In his present condition, man is incapable of rising by himself to the certitude of any principle."[39] Even being is not clear to him. Unable to think of it apart from the notion of some particular existent, man can conceive of it only under the form of his own being. What then shall we say is the source of our certitudes? The answer is "common sense."

VII. *The Christian Reaction*

As usual, the problem is to know in what sense that too flexible notion should be understood.

The only thing to do here is to listen to Bautain's own explanation; it is not a masterpiece of precision and clarity. Common sense is called "common," because it is found in every human individual. "It alone is the capacity of understanding the truth of Being, the meaning of the Word when Word and Being are announced to us. It is the comprehensive form of language; it is understanding, or, if you prefer, it is our natural reason first excited by the sight of natural phenomena, then developed, formed, determined, and exercised by the language of our fellow men."

The first part of that description suggests that, to Bautain, common sense can be said to be any cognitive power, provided it be not understood as private. This proviso shows him in the very act of identifying the two notions of common sense and of revelation through that of language. Indeed, we think only because we are being talked to: "It is the action of living speech that makes us reasonable, able to think and to speak." Consciousness and reason can be developed by language only: "That law is general for all the children of Adam; I shall even make bold to say that it is the law of all created intelligence (i.e., angels). It always is a higher light which illuminates and fecundates the mind. Consequently the reason of the first man, as well as that of all his descendants, must have been stimulated by a higher word that set it working. Now who could address the first word to created intelligence, to the reason of the first man, if not the Creator of man?"[40]

Having thus attained the theme of language, Bautain goes over to another and no less known major theme of traditionalism. Since the words spoken to man by God cause in him the awareness of himself as well as of God, the *authority* of God is in us the cause of all knowledge: "The awareness of the authority of the speaking being, and of the necessary subordination of the listening being, such is the foundation of common sense, which is truly common to all men, since it is the essential character of mankind."

Conceived as a mere awareness of the authority of the first revelation of God to man, common sense was in danger of losing all psychological reality as a concrete power of knowing. Bautain felt the danger and this led him to a supreme effort to restore some substance to the highest cognitive power of man. Common sense is not a being of reason; it is neither an abstract nor an imaginary form, nor a contingent modification of the mind, nor a collective or general unit existing outside of the mind and exerting its authority over it. No, common sense is in every one of us "the capacity of knowledge and of science; it is the mother-idea which conceives the truth of being, of the word and the reality of the existences of all degrees. I say the mother-idea, because that common or general idea is waiting for the excitation, for the fecundation in order to develop into a living form; it is then that the idea, fundamentally the same for all men, becomes diverse in its form and in its dignity, according to the influence which man undergoes and to the word which he hears and receives."[41] Hence this provisorily last conclusion that "common sense, however common it fundamentally is, is nevertheless different in individuals."[42]

Bautain's meanderings are not without constancy in their general direction. His inability to recognize the existence of a metaphysical knowledge of God, limited and imperfect, yet certain and valid as far as it goes,[43] sets him in opposition to the teaching of Saint Paul concerning the pagans who, "having known God," did not duly worship Him (Rom. 1:21). Hence, in spite of the universal respect inspired by his religious zeal and the efficacy of his apostolate, Bautain had to submit to very explicit and appropriate recantation. In docilely subscribing to everything, he showed himself a better Catholic than Lamennais.[44] Bautain never ceased to write, but his interest turned from metaphysics to psychology[45] and ethics. The only message he had really wanted to deliver had not found in his mind its proper form. There was something broken in him. His work remains for us an exemplary instance of the disorderly condition prevailing in the minds of Catholic philosophers around the middle of the nineteenth century. There never were better Christians; only, like Tertullian, they did not know the meaning of *sapere ad sobrietatem*.

From Traditionalism to Christian Philosophy

Traditionalism was a reaction against the anti-Christian philosophism of the eighteenth century and what the times considered its disastrous political consequences. For those who opposed it, nothing was more natural than to advocate a general return to the fundamental truths of Christian faith. The trouble visibly was that, in doing so, the tenants of the Christian tradition were tempted to pit religion against philosophy, revelation against reason. Thus was undone the

VII. *The Christian Reaction*

work of many generations of Christian thinkers who stressed, on the contrary, the intimate accord they saw between the teaching of Christianity and the innermost aspirations of human reason. After the masterpieces of Saint Augustine, Lactantius, Saint Hilary of Poitiers, and other Fathers of the Church, the painstaking efforts of the schoolmen had turned out philosophical commentaries on Scripture, conceived in a different style, but of no less importance for the solution of the problem. As the traditionalists conceived them, their own answers to the problem presupposed the nullity of that century-long effort of Christian speculation. They all took it for granted that after Descartes, Bacon, and Locke, scholasticism had become a thing of the past. In short, be it ignorance or prejudice on their part, the post-revolutionary Christian thinkers seemed to agree that the seventeenth-century condemnation of scholasticism was fully justified.

The second third of the nineteenth century witnessed the beginning of a new effort to redress the situation. A revival of genuine scholasticism then began to take place. No doubt, scholasticism had never been quite dead; a detailed history of its revival would show various influences at work to bring about a revival that resembles today a resurrection. By and large, however, its birthplace seems to have been Italy, and one of its first notable representatives was Gioacchino Ventura de Raulica.[46]

At the time of his youth, Ventura fell under the influence of de Bonald. He even helped propagate de Bonald's philosophy by translating into Italian one of his works. To Ventura, de Bonald's doctrine was "a flash of light in a deep night." Fortunately, Ventura came to realize in time the peril latent in the doctrine. We are indebted to him for the first searching criticism of traditionalism.

A first reproach leveled by Ventura against de Bonald is the extraordinary naïveté of his doctrinal position. According to Ventura, there has been no Christian speculation worth speaking of since the destruction of scholasticism by Descartes and Bacon. Scholasticism itself had been of no value and it had been justly condemned by modern philosophers. Consequently, de Bonald had to be believed when he presented himself as the first to reveal to the world a valid form of Christian philosophical speculation. Moreover, in tracing back the corruption of scholasticism by the influence of the pagan philosophy of Aristotle and other Greeks, de Bonald was practically presenting himself as the discoverer of the first valid philosophy for about three thousand years. If this was not impossible, it was at least unlikely.[47]

A second reproach to de Bonald is his complete ignorance of scholasticism. More exactly, Ventura does not reproach him with ignoring it, but, quite precisely, with condemning it without knowing it. The reproach was well founded. De Bonald was largely excusable for making such a mistake. Had Ventura lived at the time of de Bonald and personally experienced the complete absence of Christianity in intellectual circles in the last third of the eighteenth century and the beginning of the nineteenth, Ventura himself would not have thought of advocating a return to scholasticism. During those years, scholasticism was not merely antiquated, it was ridiculous in a country like France, where it is an admitted fact that "ridicule kills." Had not Ventura himself, a priest and a theologian, begun by translating de Bonald as an antidote to the philosophism of the times? Still, in point of fact, it always is wrong to blaspheme something one does not know.[48]

A third reproach, much more serious, was leveled at the very substance of de Bonald's traditionalism. Ventura accuses it of being a "rationalism" not so different, after all, from that of the eighteenth century which it aimed to destroy. In point of fact, we ourselves could not expose his doctrine without signaling its ambiguity on that point. Let this be one more occasion to remember that although philosophies endure in an *aevum* of their own, the philosophers themselves always are (to use existentialist language) "in situation." In his *Contra Gentiles*, Thomas Aquinas had felt it necessary, addressing philosophers, to speak to them in the language of philosophy. All the great schoolmen had done the same thing. Then two curious things happened. On the one hand, scholasticism was reproached with turning religion into a philosophy, a reproach well known to Thomas Aquinas; on the other hand, its adversaries undertook to do the very same thing. As Ventura interprets it, the doctrine of de Bonald, with its pretention of justifying Christian truth in the light of natural reason only, had made that very mistake.[49] Of course, de Bonald had only wanted to demonstrate the necessity of revelation, not its content, but at the time of Ventura traditionalisms were beginning to fight one another.

In order to clear up the difficulty, Ventura distinguishes between two sorts of philosophy: the *inquisitive* philosophy and the *demonstrative* philosophy. Inquisitive philosophy consists in seeking after truth as after something still unknown and which stands in need of being discovered. It is a "seeking philosophy" (*une philosophie cherchante*) which, since it presupposes no already

VII. *The Christian Reaction* 257

known truth, relies upon reason alone in order to discover it. Already practiced by the Greeks, that method had been renewed in modern times by Bacon and Descartes. The upshot could not fail to be the same: starting from nothing, such philosophers always seek and never find; their conclusions are mutually contradictory and, by the same token, mutually destructive. Inquisitive philosophy is responsible for the destructive consequences of eighteenth-century speculation.

Demonstrative philosophy is quite different. Instead of striving to discover truth as something unknown, it aims to demonstrate it as something whose truth is already felt but still awaits rational elucidation and confirmation. Since it presupposes the acceptance of a truth already given to the mind and obscurely grasped by it, demonstrative philosophy is a "believing philosophy" (*une philosophie croyante*). For several centuries, demonstrative philosophy was that of the Fathers of the Church and of the Doctors of the Church. Its two most illustrious exponents were Saint Augustine and Saint Thomas Aquinas. That "philosophy of faith" is not only good, it is excellent. The distinction and opposition of those two philosophical attitudes is well summarized by the very title of Ventura's pamphlet *De la vraie et de la fausse philosophie*.[50] Well founded or not, his attack against de Bonald has at least provided Ventura with an excellent opportunity to define his own position.

When speaking for himself, Ventura gives to demonstrative philosophy its proper name: Christian Philosophy. Since its greatest exponent is Thomas Aquinas, and since scholasticism is its perfect expression, "true philosophy" could be nothing else. And indeed, scholasticism is a demonstrative philosophy in virtue of its very notion. Starting from revealed truth, it only aims to elucidate the meaning of that which the Christian already knows to be true and, if need be, to show how deeply revelation agrees with the natural light of reason. Ventura thus became one of the first and more resolute tenants of the notion of Christian philosophy. The fact is important to know because the necessity of clearing up the difficulties with which the notion is fraught largely accounts for the later attitude of the Church toward it.

The more apparent of those difficulties is such that even Ventura himself could not fail to notice it. If philosophy is true because it is demonstrative only, and if what it aims to demonstrate, or to elucidate, is the faith of the Christian revelation, then it is not a philosophy at all. Besides, Ventura seems implicitly to acknowledge the fact when he quotes Saint Thomas Aquinas as the greatest philosopher there ever was. What is the *Summa theologiae* if not a conspectus of Christian theology? No philosophy worthy of the name can start from the data of revelation, it can start only from the first principles of reason.

Ventura would not accept the objection, but still it is not easy to see how he can avoid its consequences. The general title of his Paris conferences well expresses his answer to the difficulty and his inability to cope with it: *La raison philosophique et la raison catholique*. A Catholic usage of reason is no doubt possible, but is "Catholic reason" a possibility? Ventura must maintain that there is such a thing. If there were no "Catholic reason," no Catholic philosophy would be possible; it must be the work of a believer in order to be Catholic and, in order to be a philosophy, it must be the work of reason.[51] On the other hand, Ventura cannot uphold this view without forming a notion of reason wide enough to include, along with the principles naturally known to it, the fundamental truths revealed by God in view of man's salvation. The thing can be done and, in a sense, the plague of traditionalism is that, under one form or another, it ultimately has to attempt an operation of that sort.

This is where the inner necessities of philosophical thinking were reserving for de Bonald a well-deserved consolation. Reduced to its essentials, Aventura's problem was the same as de Bonald's. Both had to find a philosophy inquisitive enough to deserve the name of philosophy, and "believing" enough to be justified in calling itself Catholic. There was a solution to the problem, but there perhaps was only one; de Bonald had already found it and we must remember that, before his conversion to the "Christian philosophy of Saint Thomas Aquinas," Father Gioacchino Ventura had translated into Italian, along with *Du Pape* of J. de Maistre, *La législation primitive* of de Bonald. It is no wonder that, when he himself attempted to handle the problem in his own way, he simply fell back on one of the possible variants of de Bonald's solution.

The simplest way to solve the problem is to include both reason and faith under the wider notion of revelation. Ventura did so in his late work *La tradition et les Semi-Pélagiens* and, of course, he resorted to the notion of "language" in order to solve the difficulty. The curious point about his own answer is that he managed to place it under the authority of Saint Thomas Aquinas.

It is a constant doctrine of the Angelic Doctor that man can think only with images. Aristotle had already said so and, so far as our notions of materi-

VII. *The Christian Reaction*

al objects are concerned, there is no problem. If it is a question of conceiving notions of immaterial things, there is a difficulty. There are no phantasms of incorporeal things. Thomas Aquinas himself so admits (*Summa theologiae*, I, q. 84, a. 7, ad 3). Since, in physical nature, nothing informs us about incorporeal realities, the first phantasms enabling us to conceive them must needs come to us from the moral world, not from the world of nature, but from that of man. In this case, the moral world is represented for us by "instruction, teaching, domestic revelation." Through the ministry of ears or of sight, language reaches imagination, and it is by looking, at one and the same time, at the particular notions signified by language, and at the phantasms in which language is included, that intellect first can make intelligible to itself the immaterial objects of its conceptions, and then reason about them. "Hence the conclusion that the *name* of immaterial things, provided by the social environment, is as necessary for the knowledge of immaterial beings, as sensations are necessarily required in order to manifest the existence of bodies." Obviously, this amounted to placing language at the origin of all the notions of the human mind having as objects things imperceptible to sense. The revelation of intelligible truth to man by language thus becomes the only source of all revelation both natural and supernatural. Of course, Christian dogma provides material for such a doctrine: *fides ex auditu*.... Just as God was to Moses, the mother is to her child the source of a revelation. By teaching him to speak, she teaches him to think. In Ventura's own perspective, and complicated as it is by the impossibility he sees for man to abstract from sense knowledge *any* intelligible concept, traditionalism entails extreme consequences in theology as well as in philosophy: "That man, who never had heard one word about God...could by his own resources, raise himself up to such a cognition, to such an idea, that is not only difficult, it is downright impossible. That would be to attribute to man a power of transporting himself, in a single leap, from the corporeal world to the spiritual world which is separated from it by infinity." What would Thomas Aquinas say of such a doctrine? Are the *invisibilia Dei* of Saint Paul to be understood as meaning the words spoken to man by other men and by God? The fact is that, looking at the phantasms impressed in us by the corporeal objects of sense knowledge, Ventura cannot see how the agent intellect could abstract from them the notions of purely intelligible beings, such as God. Let us carefully note the point: there is *nothing* in corporeal creatures to suggest to the mind the notion of God.

To hold the contrary view is to attribute to man "the power of building without material, of operating nothingness."[52] This was not to refuse to man the power of attaining a true certitude concerning the existence and nature of God, but it certainly was one of the many ways to refuse to man the power of naturally raising his mind to the notion of God starting from the sense experience of material things.

Ventura was prompted by a right feeling of the true nature of the problem. By associating the name of Saint Thomas Aquinas with the notion of "Christian philosophy," he was anticipating the teaching of Leo XIII in his encyclical letter *Aeterni Patris* but, at the same time, by including Christian philosophy in the same genus as philosophy pure and simple, he was raising dangerous obstacles on the way to a complete elucidation of the notion. When Ventura says he "will turn science into a commentary on faith," he accurately describes the scholastic *theology* of Saint Thomas Aquinas rather than the Christian use of *philosophy* which Leo XIII recommended as the best way to philosophize after the model of Saint Thomas. But nevertheless even the imperfect notion of the Christian philosophy developed by Ventura was to help. Many others, besides him, then found themselves engaged in difficulties like his, or worse.[53] The significance of Ventura remains in the fact that he was the first of the traditionalists to look for an answer to his problems in the doctrine of Saint Thomas.

VIII. *The Philosophical Reaction in France and Italy*

By "philosophical reaction" here is meant the opposition to sensism and to the spirit of the eighteenth century which expressed itself under the form of philosophical doctrines. In most of them, especially on the Italian side, religious motives were still visibly at work, but not necessarily so and, at any rate, the last word in them belonged to reason, not to faith.

French Spiritualism: Victor Cousin

The French philosophical reaction was inspired by a generalized feeling that philosophical anarchy had something to do with social and political unrest. That feeling accounts for the mixed careers of several men who, while being essentially politicians, deputies, and at times ministers, availed themselves of periods of political inactivity, in order to elaborate conservative philosophical doctrines. Not very important as philosophies, the fruit of their philosophical reflections is nevertheless a link in the chain of philosophical speculation that connects the French eighteenth century to the twentieth.

The name of Royer-Collard still survives as that of a philosopher-statesman who resolutely attacked sensism as paving the way to skepticism, itself the forerunner of political indiscipline.[1] One of his students in Paris was young Victor Cousin. Another case of philosophical reaction was that of de Gérando.[2] Not too good a writer (Sainte-Beuve once observed that, like spaghetti, his sentences never seemed to reach the breaking point) de Gérando deserves to be mentioned as the first French philosopher to take an interest in the history of philosophy. Germany already had Georg Brücker,[3] but there was in France nobody at that time to represent a discipline which, owing to the multiplication of doctrines with time, was becoming a necessity. De Gérando saw a deeper reason, and a properly philosophical one, in favor of that form of history. The knowledge of various philosophies permits their comparison and their critical examination. In this sense, history of philosophy can be considered as a philosophical experience and a source of philosophical progress.[4] Such was to be, to a large extent, the method advocated by the founder of eclecticism, Victor Cousin.[5] The preface to the second edition of Cousin's *Fragments philosophiques* abounds in information concerning the French philosophical situation around 1810.

The philosophy of Locke, as perfected by Condillac, reigned supreme in France till that date, but Cousin observes that a reaction against it was setting in. Predominantly critical and destructive, that philosophy was largely responsible for the devastating violence of the French Revolution. The tyrannical influence of sensism at that date is illustrated by the fact that, in Cousin's sight, a simple critical discussion of Condillac by Laromiguière in his *Leçons de philosophie* (1815–1818) appeared as a distinct symptom of a new state of mind on the part of the philosophical public. That Laromiguière had dared to disapprove of Condillac's method was to Cousin the proof "first, that a philosophical revolution was obscurely taking place in minds: next, that that revolution was already prepared in public opinion."[6]

A mere glance at the French systems elaborated since the end of the revolution confirms Cousin's view. Not only the sensists or ideologists, but the traditionalists as well, agreed that the one problem to solve was that of the origin of our ideas. The importance attributed by de Maistre, de Bonald, and others to the relationship of thought and language had no other origin. Strangely enough, even the spiritualist reactions against the philosophies of the recent past will not completely free themselves from that spell. Even Kantianism will be considered a sort of ideology dealing with the origin of man's knowledge. Hence the curious attitude of Cousin toward Kant. "Let us examine ourselves well," Cousin says, "we men, and particularly we Frenchmen of the nineteenth century. The spirit of analysis [read: Condillac] has caused a great deal of wreckage around us. Born surrounded with ruins in all domains, we feel the need of reconstruction."[7] Now, the revival of idealism initiated by Kant could facilitate that metaphysical restoration. So Cousin will claim Hegel and Schelling for his masters[8]; at the same time, Cousin will insist that his doctrine is not theirs and indeed it is but too visible that he is going his own more modest way.

He himself had chosen to call his philosophy an "eclecticism." In his own

VIII. The Philosophical Reaction in France and Italy 263

mind, this was the name of a method to be applied to all philosophical problems. As he described it, eclecticism is nothing else than the very method used by scientists. It consists in discussing each of the results obtained by scientific investigation, to set apart that which is true in order to be retained, and that which is false in order to be eliminated. By constantly adding true results to true results, a body of demonstrated knowledge is progressively constituted. Eclecticism thus consists in choosing the true and rejecting the false. There is no reason not to apply the same method in philosophy.

Cousin did not single out such an ambiguous name without anticipating many misunderstandings. He has done his best to eliminate the more damaging ones. For instance, he stipulates that eclecticism is not a syncretism mixing together all systems. On the contrary, it leaves no system intact, since it breaks down each particular system into two parts, the one false, the other true; it destroys the first one and only employs the second in its work of recomposition. Again, eclecticism is not the absence of all system; on the contrary "it is the application of a system, it starts from a system," for indeed, in order to gather together all the truths and to keep out all the errors with which truths are mingled, one should be able to discern truth from error; in other words, one should oneself be in possession of truth. This is to say "that one must have a system in order to judge all systems." Eclecticism is a system that constantly enriches itself by feeding on other systems. Its own truth is the sum total of all their truths.[9]

This authentic notion of eclecticism is a fruitful subject matter for philosophical reflections. Is true philosophy obtainable from a mere bringing together of partial philosophical truths? As a matter of fact, is it certain that even science proceeds exactly as Cousin says it does? At any rate, the founder of French eclecticism does not pretend to initiate an absolutely new type of philosophical speculation. On the contrary, he says that eclecticism already existed in the mind of Plato in antiquity, and that, in modern times, it was the constant practice of Leibniz. Still, Cousin attributes to his own school a particular place in that tradition: the particular merit he claims for it is to have assigned to it not only a name, but a method.

Cousin is well aware of the continuity there is between his own philosophy and that of his predecessors, even those he expressly opposes. His undertaking is deeply imbued with "the spirit of the modern philosophy which, ever since Descartes and Locke, recognizes experience only and places the science of human nature at the head of philosophical science." This open confession of "psychologism" accounts for the permanent inability of the nineteenth-century French school of philosophy to recapture the spirit and methods of metaphysics which, on the contrary, the Italians Rosmini and Gioberti restored to the fullness of their rights.

In the famous lecture course of 1818, the question at stake was: "Are there ideas that are neither the knowledge of bodies, nor the knowledge of ourselves, and what is the foundation of those ideas?" We are sure of ourselves and of the existence of bodies, but what about the rest? Outside of my own thought, what is that which I call space, time, justice, ideal, and God? Philosophers want to account for everything by the notions of nature and of the ego, but can this be done? After re-establishing nature and ego as two distinct elements, Cousin notes the existence of ideas that find their origin in neither one of these two elements, that is, of ideas that arise neither from sensation nor from reflection. Such ideas present two distinctive characters: universality and immutability. As universal, they transcend the individuality of the ego; as immutable, they transcend the perpetual variability of nature. Kant has listed those ideas, which Cousin calls "absolute." Their list can be reduced to two fundamental ideas: (1) that of *cause*, which includes, or entails, those of phenomenon, accident, multiple, particular, individual, relative, possible, probable, contingent, diverse, and finite; (2) that of *substance*, which includes being, unity, absolute, eternal, universal, similar, and infinite. And indeed, the universe itself can be defined as something that changes and does not change, but the something that does not change evades observation; our reason makes us conceive its existence, but not its nature. "Infinite being," Cousin says, "manifests itself to our mind only by the ideas of *true*, of *beautiful*, and of *good*, which are immutable as being itself is, but are more easily accessible to our human reason." In this way, "absolute ideas" find themselves reduced to "the ideas of cause, or phenomenon, on the one hand and, on the other hand, to that of substance under the threefold form of true, beautiful, and good."[10]

Absolute truth consists of the axioms that preside over all the sciences. Those axioms need a basis. Cousin places it in God himself whom, besides, religion presents as the source of all truth. Of course, Cousin has to prove that this affirmation of God as absolute truth is a necessity for the human mind. In exposing the doctrine, Adolphe Garnier observes that this concession to empiri-

VIII. *The Philosophical Reaction in France and Italy*

cism seems to turn the idea of God into a mere product of the human mind, but Cousin himself stipulates that this "necessary belief" is a "reflected belief," that is, a product of reflection. The mind becomes aware of the constraint imposed upon it by truth only when it reflects upon itself and struggles, so to speak, to free itself from the bonds of that truth. Now, every reflected state presupposes an anterior and unreflected state wherein the ego has not yet returned upon itself, has not yet perceived itself in perceiving truth, and has thus obtained what Cousin calls a *pure apperception*, free from all imprint of subjectivity. Truth imposes itself on reason, and it is not reason that makes truth.

Cousin stresses the non-empirical character of the notions thus given in pure apperception. Obviously, he is striving to find some equivalent for the pure *a priori* character of the Kantian categories. As he does not dare deny that the ideas of cause and substance have indeed an empirical content, Cousin distinguishes between the *ideas* of cause and of substance, which apply to finite and contingent objects, and the *principles* of substantiality and causality which, on the contrary, give us possession of external objects both necessary and infinite. Such principles offer themselves to the mind completely formed. It is therefore impossible to account for them by means of any sensation or of any previous reflection. Generally speaking, ideas do not precede judgments, but, rather, they are given to us already correlated by judgments. Thus understood, judgment is found at the beginning of our intellectual operations, the principles being the only primitive judgments and the origins of all the correlations established between ideas by other judgments.

The good follows from the true. Absolute truth comes first; it puts our freedom under obligation. Truth demands to be practically enforced, an exigency which becomes the source of both duty and authority. "Moral obligation" is the will practically to achieve the true; the idea of duty then derives from that of good, not inversely. Hence follows the series of moral duties. But their fulfillment is made possible only by the existence of society. As a necessary prerequisite for the possibility of duty, society is predestined, necessary, inevitable; it is given *a priori*. Government itself is there for the sake of society, whose proper end it is "to maintain the fulfillment of truth." The notions of merit and demerit, of reward and punishment, find their justification in that mission imparted to society. Good and evil determine merit and demerit, which, in turn, determine and justify rewards and punishments. To conclude, law comes neither from sensibility nor from liberty; its origin is "reason, which establishes communication between man and absolute truth, whose *pure apperception* conditions the *necessary conception*."[11]

The remarkable importance attributed by Cousin to his discussion of the beautiful is explainable by the influence exercised on his philosophical reflection by the esthetic theories of Winckelmann (1717–1768), developed and systematized by Quatremèrc de Quincy (1755–1849). The mark of that influence is visible in the 1818 dissertation of young Cousin on *Le beau réel et le beau idéal*. Based on a conventional interpretation of Greek art, known only imperfectly and not in its best monuments, the esthetics of those archaeologists considered ideal beauty as incompatible with concreteness, individuality, reality. While reality is particular and concretely determined, the beautiful is undetermined, general, abstract. This was to mistake the great art of the Greeks for the estimable art of Canova. Cousin fell under the spell of those ideas: "The ideal in the beautiful, as in everything else, is the negation of the real." Less radical in the lecture course of 1818, especially in its revised form,[12] Cousin never gave up his early conviction that, in all domains, the "idea is the pure generality."

It has been maintained, and rightly so, that the whole doctrine of Cousin bears the mark of that esthetic view of Greek art.[13] As he intended to oppose Locke, Condillac, and the ideologists for teaching an empiricism verging on skepticism, Cousin had reproached them with overlooking the presence of necessary truth in the pure apperception of the ego. He also intended to avoid the arbitrariness inherent in the philosophies of Kant, Fichte, and Hegel by grounding the principles of human knowledge on an analytical description of their inner necessity. This is what he himself called his "psychological method," but, precisely, the difficulty inherent in his own doctrine was that of finding in a mere psychological observation, which cannot go beyond the givenness of facts, the justification of a metaphysical necessity. Consciously or not, Cousin and his disciples, such as, for instance, Théodore Jouffroy,[14] were simply continuing the long tradition of French philosophy since the time of Descartes. It consisted in looking at the ego for a means to transcend it. Thus to substitute psychology for metaphysics is to suppose that inner experience enjoys privileges refused to external and sensible experience. The decisive reaction against psychology in metaphysics was not to come from France, but from Italy.[15]

The Italian Metaphysical Revival: Antonio Rosmini and Vincenzo Gioberti

The historical period called *Risorgimento,* because it witnessed the first political reunification of Italy since the time of the Roman Empire, was also an era of philosophical activity.[16] Its two greatest names were those of Rosmini and Gioberti.[17] Both were metaphysicians equally interested in the task of restoring to the fulness of its rights the traditional philosophy of Christianity. Both were priests in a time when it was practically impossible for a Christian philosopher in Italy not to feel divided by a twofold allegiance to Church and to country. Both wanted to offer an opposition to the rising tide of rationalism, not a theology of scholastic inspiration, but a philosophy standing on its own ground, yet attuned to the teaching of the Catholic theology. Rosmini and Gioberti disagreed between themselves, they criticized and were criticized; finally, their two philosophies became a bone of contention for their contemporaries and for their Italian successors. At any rate, owing to them, Italy then shared with Germany the merit of being the seat of a metaphysical revival.

Antonio Rosmini

Rosmini was an authentic philosopher, endowed with uncommon intellectual and literary gifts and the author of an extremely abundant philosophical production.[18] A saintly priest, he devoted his talents to the elaboration of a philosophy, both modern and Christian, capable of counterbalancing the anti-metaphysical and anti-theological influence of Kant. His erudition was enormous, but it never prevented him from going his own way. This, which in a philosopher is a great merit, can become a cause of trouble when the philosopher aims to speak on behalf of a Church whose very essence it is to be a common tradition.

the notion of being

While still very young, Rosmini made a very old discovery. He discovered the Porphyrian Tree which, rooted in the perception of individual beings, and ascending from species to genus, posits the supremely universal genus at the top of their hierarchy. The medieval logicians used to call it the *genus generalissimum*; it was so absolutely general, in fact, that it could not be anything more than a logical notion; its name was being.

In one of his autobiographical writings,[19] Rosmini recounts how, at eighteen, while walking home and letting his mind wander from object to object, he realized that all those various objects were as so many determinations of one more universal and determined object which included them all. Going over his analysis of particular objects of thought, he concluded that, "whatever his starting point, he invariably arrived at the most universal of objects, ideal being, free from all determination. Again, I saw that I could not take away anything from that object without annihilating thought itself, and at the same time I saw that that object included in itself all the objects to which I already had applied my mind. I then undertook to find out the first possible determinations of indeterminate being, then the following ones and so on till the end. By this means I discovered that synthesis was gradually bringing back under my eyes all the objects which analysis had gradually eliminated. I then was convinced that the ideal indeterminate being must be the prime truth, the prime object grasped by an immediate intuition, and the universal means of acquiring all knowledge, either perceptive or intuitive."

In this account of his initial philosophical experience, Rosmini mentions two points that deserve particular attention. Having reached the notion of being, he saw that he could not remove from it anything "without annihilating thought itself." Let us keep this point in mind; the identification of the knowing mind and the known idea will appear to us an absolutely fundamental element of the doctrine and perhaps the main source of the difficulties one has to overcome in interpreting it.

The second point is easier to grasp. In striving to find out the essential properties of being *qua* being, Rosmini could do nothing more than rediscover the ancient and, indeed, the eternal doctrine of Parmenides. Unless he makes the rediscovery for his own account, one will never become a metaphysician.

What is being? "From the very fact that it offers itself to the mind, the pure essence of being is known immediately and in itself, so that no human intellect can remain ignorant of what being is; nor could anybody teach it to a man who did not know it." Hence Rosmini's fundamental principle: "to ignore being is to be deprived of intelligence"; for indeed, as old Parmenides once said, thinking and the being that is thought are one and the same thing.

Following this Parmenidean trend of thought, which is one with the fundamental necessities of the human mind, being appears as necessary: being is,

VIII. *The Philosophical Reaction in France and Italy*

and non-being is not. There is no getting away from that principle. Secondly, and for the same reason, being is eternal. For indeed, to say that being came from non-being is absurd; but to say that being first came from being is no less absurd: if it came from being, then being already was there. In itself then, being is absolutely eternal and uncreated. To say that it is necessary, and to say that it can neither begin nor end and that it cannot *not* be, is to say the same thing.

For the identical reason being is immutable. This, at least, is true of being in itself and of itself. Whence could any change arise in a being that necessarily is that which it is? Since it is immutable, being in itself is absolutely simple: any inner diversity only could have happened to it, so immutability implies simplicity. Since it is simple, being is indivisible, for division is impossible in a perfectly homogeneous being.[20]

From those classical attributes of being *qua* being, Rosmini proceeds to describe a rather different attribute, one which is characteristic of his own philosophy: being is "objective." This means, according to Rosmini, that it is of the essence of being to posit itself before the mind as an object endowed with a reality of its own, distinct from that of the mind. Being, therefore, is given in the mind as something other than the mind. To understand this point is important, because it accounts for the otherwise paradoxical fact that Rosmini's essay on the ideas is at the same time an essay on being. In other words, it permits us to understand one of the features of the doctrine which Gioberti will oppose, perhaps not without misconstruing it, to wit, that the metaphysics of Rosmini can be a gnosiology. In Rosmini's own mind, there was nothing wrong with such a doctrine because, to him, gnosiology also was a metaphysics.

The notion of being is considered by Rosmini as the proper object of intellect. In saying this, he is conscious of following a perfectly safe tradition since, in his *Summa theologiae*, Thomas Aquinas says that *objectum intellectus est ens vel verum commune* (I, q. 55, a. 1). True enough, in that passage, Thomas Aquinas speaks of angels, a point which Rosmini fails to mention, but one must concede to him that, in a sense, the same is true of man. The all-important difference to be noted between the two doctrines is that, in the gnosiology of Rosmini, the idea of being is innate. It is not innate in Saint Thomas' sense, namely that our intellectual power of forming it is innate and spontaneously forms it at its first contact with objects of sense perception. According to Rosmini, it is innate in the sense that it is present to us and seen by us from the very first moment of our existence, even though it can take us a rather long time to become aware of it.

That conclusion can be demonstrated by eliminating all the other conceivable explanations of the origin of the idea of "being in general." It is not contained in sensations, which all have particular objects; it cannot be extracted from sensations, since universal being is not contained in particular beings; it cannot be an emanation of our soul, for it could not emanate from it unless it first were innate in it. Generally speaking, there is a decisive reason why the idea of being cannot be derived from any other one; it is that, on the contrary, we cannot think of anything except as of a being. This is what is meant by saying that the notion of being in general is "necessary"; it is an idea that necessarily enters the formation of all our ideas. It is, therefore, an antecedent condition for the possibility of all knowledge; and this is the decisive argument in favor of its innateness.[21]

We have said that the idea of being was an object; what does that object present to the inner eye? Only that which is left in any other object after it has been mentally stripped of all its determinations. Let us call it the "beingness" of being. It is the bare notion that represents to us all beings as not being nothing. In this sense, and because it presents to the mind a mere abstract property common to all that which is, the innate idea of being is that of "possible being" only. Hence the complete definition given by Rosmini: "possible being is present to us and contemplated by us from the very first moment of our existence, although we do not advert to it until much later."[22]

The assertion of the idea of being is fundamental in the doctrine of Rosmini. The presence of that idea is in us the source of all *a priori* knowledge: because that knowledge is *a priori,* we are free from Locke, from Condillac, and from the whole sensism influence under all its forms; because that *a priori* is a knowledge of being *qua* being, it frees philosophy from the Kantian *a priori* and its skeptical consequences. No *a priori* can be more dogmatic in the Kantian sense of the term than that of Rosmini.

being and intellect

Every time Rosmini describes the process of abstraction at the term of which intellect finds itself left with the sole notion of *beingness* in general, he casually adds the remark that abstraction cannot proceed any farther, because, if the

VIII. *The Philosophical Reaction in France and Italy*

abstract notion of possible being in general is removed, there is nothing left. Nothing, that is to say, no object, nil, but, at the same time, this means that there is no knowledge, no intellect, no mind. In following Rosmini's essay on the origin of ideas, one feels tempted to interpret his doctrine as a variety of idealism; and indeed he proceeds to an analysis of the ideas which recalls the general method of the ideologists; at the same time, it is impossible to imagine a more realistically minded philosophy because, in it, the intelligible objects are not only the cause of our intellections of them, but of our very power of intellection. Rosmini seems to think that, since intellection begins with the presence to the mind of the prime intelligible object offered to it, and since it could not possibly function if that same intelligible were taken away from it, the idea of being in general is the cause, not of intellection only, but of the intellect as well. As this is one of the main sources of difficulties in interpreting the doctrine, some effort of attention should be made in order to grasp the point.

In the doctrine of Rosmini, there is no difference between explaining the origin of acquired ideas by means of the general idea of being, and explaining the formation of human reason. There can be no difference since "the idea of being, present to our spirit by nature (as innate in it) is that which constitutes the two faculties of intellect and reason." The whole doctrine rests upon this remarkable principle. Here is its Rosminian justification. We receive from sensations the matter of our cognitions; that matter becomes cognition "when the form, that is to say *being*, is added to it." Being can be added to it because the soul is at once sensitive and intelligent; so "it considers that which it feels by means of the sense, in relation with the *being* which it sees with the intellect, and finds in the thing felt a something (a being) acting upon it." Such then is intellect: "the faculty of the intuition of indeterminate being"; remove indeterminate being, no intuition of it is possible; there is no intellect left. On the other hand, reason is the faculty of applying being to sensations; if being is removed, reason has nothing to apply to sensations, it therefore ceases to exist. It is being therefore which, offered to the soul as an object, elicits from it the essential acts which we call intellect and reason; in short, those "two faculties exist in us only because we are endowed with the permanent intuition of being."[23]

The immense erudition of Rosmini could not let him ignore that he had some well-known predecessors to reckon with in the discussion of that problem. In fact, he goes as far as saying that the doctrines of Saint Thomas and

Saint Bonaventure "seem" to him to agree with his own solution of the problem. This point being a bone of contention between Rosminians and Thomists, it will not be amiss to dwell on it.

Rosmini himself begins by recalling the text of Thomas Aquinas concerning angels (*ST* I, q. 55, a. 1): "The proper object of the intellect is *common being* or *truth*." In speaking of *being*, Thomas himself "uses the substantive word (*ens*)," whereas, Rosmini adds, "when I say simply *being*, or *being in general*, I take the word in the infinitive sense (*to be, esse*)." He clearly realizes the difference between these two terms, but he deems it enough to observe "that the ancients often used them indifferently one for the other." It should therefore be kept in mind that, to Rosmini, the terms *ens* and *esse* were practically equivalent. Consequently, when Thomas says that being is the object of intellect, Rosmini understands that *ens*, or *esse*, taken in their most abstract generality, are the object of intellect.

On the other hand, "Saint Thomas teaches that the nature of a faculty is determined by its object; to him, therefore, *being* contemplated by us was that which made the intellectual faculty what it is." So, instead of considering the intellect as the immaterial power of knowing that belongs to an intellectual substance, the soul, and which, owing to its very immateriality, is able to abstract from sense data what of intelligibles it contains, Rosmini understands intellect as resulting from the information of the soul by the first intelligible, common being. Thomas teaches that the intellect is informed by the first intelligible; here, instead of knowing the first knowable because it has an intellect, the soul has an intellect because it is informed by the first knowable, being.[24]

It must be conceded that, on this point as on some others, it is difficult to obtain from Rosmini an absolutely clear statement. His first expressions obviously mean that intellect and reason are not faculties, but "essential acts" elicited from the soul by the presence to it of common being. He then confidently writes: "In short, the idea of being united to our soul is that which forms our *intellect* and our *reason*; it is that which constitutes us intelligent beings and rational animals." Does he mean just that? Or is Rosmini playing on the duality of sense which authorizes the use of the verb "to form" in the sense of "to inform"? At any rate, this is what enables him to consider himself in full agreement with the teaching of the "great Doctor of Aquin." And indeed, texts wherein Thomas Aquinas says that, as an intelligible form, being *informs* the intellect, are not hard to find. The question is, does Rosmini want to say what Thomas Aquinas himself says, or does he want to make Thomas Aquinas say what he himself considers true? *Adhuc sub judice lis est.*[25]

being and knowledge

All the difficulties of interpretation and of appreciation of Rosminianism arise at the confluence of the two notions of intellectual knowledge and of being. Taken separately, they create no difficulties; when they join, difficulties abound.

On the side of knowledge, it has just been said that the intellect seems to be constituted by the soul's intuition of being. That interpretation is confirmed by the Rosminian identification of intelligible being with the natural light of reason. To Rosmini, the abstractive illumination of the phantasms by the agent intellect in the doctrine of Saint Thomas, with the ensuing universalization, really consists in the addition to phantasms of the idea of being.[26]

On the side of being itself, it has been said above that *ens commune*, or *esse*, conceived of as the universal genre of possible being, is the immediately informing object of intellect. Since "all acquired ideas proceed from the innate idea of being," and since our cognitive power exists only "in virtue of the union of the idea of being with our spirit," it follows that the idea of possible being "is also the informing principle of all the ideas which the same faculty is capable of acquiring."[27]

Since it is an object of intuition, being is perceived by an intellectual sense. In the corporeal sense, the thing does not communicate itself as an object, but as an agent; in the intellectual sense, the thing communicates itself as an *object*; it is only present or manifested to us. As manifestation of an object the known thing is an *idea*. Such is the status of being in general. It is an idea, "but from this idea, the subject who has an intuition of it, *produces for himself* what we may term intellectual sensations."[28] "Ideal being," or being as idea, is the prime object and form of our intellect. Because it is not real being, it has been called by us "possible." The relation of these two terms is important to understand.

"Ideal being is an entity of a nature wholly peculiar, not to be confounded either with our own spirit, or with bodies, or with anything pertaining to real being." At this point, we should foresee that Rosmini is going back to a notion of being familiar to all the great ontologies of essence. When they are true to type, these philosophies uphold a certain univocity of being, which they can do without falling into pantheism because, for them, univocal being is not "real being" (an actual reality owned in common by different subjects); rather, it is "possible being," that is being manifested to the mind under the form of an intuited notion. Now, in such doctrines, the point is that, although ideal being is not a real thing, it is not nothing. To give it its technical name, let us call it "possible" being. Rosmini here is joining the large family of the philosophers and theologians for whom possibility is a medium placed halfway between actual being and mere nothingness; as they usually express themselves, possible being is an "entity." It is, Rosmini says, "a most true and most noble entity." We cannot analyze it, precisely because it is the light of our spirit, and what could be clearer than light? "Put out this light, and you have nothing but darkness." Nevertheless, as a manifested idea, possible being is just seen; it neither affirms nor denies; rather, it constitutes the possibility of all affirmation or negation.[29]

Affirmations and negations are judgments. All judgments depend on principles, themselves grounded in the very intuition of being. These principles are as follows: the principle of cognition ("the object of thought is being"); the principle of contradiction ("being and non-being cannot be thought simultaneously"); the principle of substance ("the accident is unthinkable without the substance"); the principle of causation ("a new entity is unthinkable without a cause"). It is noteworthy that these principles are nothing but "applied ideas," a feature of the doctrine which insures the perfect continuity of scientific knowledge in the light of ideal being. All the fundamental ideas of unity, number, possibility, universality, necessity, immutability, and absoluteness are pure ideas, because they owe nothing to sense; as has been seen, they can be obtained from a direct intuition of ideal being. They are its essential properties.[30] In Rosmini's oft-quoted saying, being is, of its very essence, manifested, manifesting, and manifest.

In order to obtain a further definition of the nature of ideal being as object of the mind, we must investigate its essence. What is essence? It is "that which is contained in any idea whatsoever." In other words, "the essence is what we think in any idea." All our ideas but one are determinate; what we think in them are either the specific essences (ideas of species) or the generic essences (ideas of general). Besides these, however, there is one which is wholly indeterminate because it answers absolutely indeterminate being. "What we conceive through this most universal idea may be called *the most universal essence*, or simply *es-*

VIII. *The Philosophical Reaction in France and Italy*

sence (from *esse*, *to be*). It is often so called by Plato."[31] And in this Rosmini is right, he simply is rediscovering the authentic meaning of Plato's *ousia* and, in a sense, that of the Augustinian *essentia*, with this difference, however, that he is turning idea and essence into a mere possibility.

being and God

We are reaching the point where Rosmini's philosophy became an object of ecclesiastical censure.[32]

The starting point of Rosmini's reflections seems to have been that, as early as Parmenides, philosophers have endowed being with attributes that fit the notion of God. Being is necessary, immutable, eternal, one, and simple; we cannot conceive being differently, nor can we speak differently of God. There is therefore in all that which is (precisely inasmuch as it is) something similar to God. Rosmini calls it the "divine." The word is employed by him in a sense similar to that of the Greek *theion*. Most of the Greek philosophers thought there were "divine" objects, in this sense at least that, without themselves being gods, they somehow shared in the attributes of the divinity. All Christian theologians admit at least the intimate presence of the divinity in nature; nature itself is not divine, but the presence of the divinity in it is divine. Few theologians, if any, succeed in avoiding that notion of a *divinum quid* that is not God, and whose presence to us makes us to be. Guided by what perhaps is a sound instinct, they avoid defining it. Rosmini, bravely but perhaps recklessly, undertook to turn the divine into a definite philosophical category. He specialized the name to signify that in nature which immediately attests the presence of God. As a Christian philosopher, he likewise undertook to use the presence of the divine in nature as a means to reach the knowledge of God. From this point of view, the whole doctrine of Rosmini can be said to have found its program in the well-known passage of the Acts of the Apostles (17:27–28): men were so created "that they should seek God, and perhaps grope after Him and find Him, though He is not far from any one of us. For in Him we live, and move, and have our being." God, inasmuch as he is not far away from us, Rosmini calls the divine, and his natural theology consists in an effort to go from the divine to the Divinity.[33]

From what precedes, it is immediately apparent that, among all the objects of thought, there is one that eminently exhibits the characters of the "divine"; it is being. It can rightly be named "divine" because: (1) it has all the main attributes of God; (2) it is *not* God. The first point has been abundantly established; both being and God are necessary, one, simple, immutable, eternal, etc.; what is more, they equally possess those attributes because they are beings. Let us add that, besides being itself, nothing else is possessed of those attributes. Beings given in sense experience are neither necessary, nor simple, nor immutable and eternal. If there is something divine in them, it is due to the fact that they finitely and contingently share in the nature of being as such. The divine *par excellence*, therefore, is the idea of being. But the second point is no less certain: the notion of being is *not* God. What is being *qua* being? An idea; God is not an idea. Being is possible, God is pure act. As a notion in the mind, even the idea of infinite being is finite, God is infinite. In short, possible being, such as it is in the mind (and it can be nowhere else) is infinitely different from being (*ipsum purum esse*), which is God.

This is not a concession made by Rosmini; if the point is overlooked, his whole doctrine makes no sense. Two sure signs guarantee the truth of the remark.

First, it is the constant teaching of Rosmini that the *natural* sight of God is impossible for the human mind.[34] Second, the very notion of being, on account of which he is blamed for teaching a certain form of pantheism[35] was expressly intended by him as a safeguard against that peril. This is beyond doubt, but even if it is granted, the question remains to know how such a radical misunderstanding of the meaning of his doctrine has been possible. One reason for it was his own insistence on proving his substantial agreement with the doctrine of Saint Thomas Aquinas. As neither his notion of being nor his notion of intellectual knowledge agrees with those of Thomas Aquinas, it is only too easy to prove to him that, on this point at least, he is wrong. Hence the natural consequence: you say that your doctrine is the same as that of Saint Thomas, but it is not; and since you say so in order to justify it, your doctrine must be wrong.

Another reason, more philosophical, goes to the root of the problem. Possible being is a univocal notion; so it applies to being and to beings in the same sense. Moreover, the essence of a thing is that which our mind apprehends in its notion of it; consequently, in Rosmini's philosophical language, there is no harm in saying that, in forming the notion of the *beingness* of being, I form the notion of the very essence of being. Again, if ideal being is the divine, then the divine is included in reality from the very fact that common or ideal being is included in it. To Rosmini himself, all this entails the consequence that God is *not* immediately apprehended by the mind, that God is *not* included in given finite reality, in short, all this Rosminian language is intended to insure the absolute transcendency of God. Unfortunately, to the ears of most of the theologians, all that which Rosmini was saying of the essence of possible ideal being sounded as though it were being said of the actual existence of real being. That is how in fact he was interpreted, and it can be said of Rosmini that, playing as he himself often did with so perilous an ambiguity of language, he had done a great deal to expose his thought to misinterpretation.

These remarks are not extraneous to philosophy; on the contrary, they pave the way to a correct understanding of Rosmini's proofs of the existence of God. The very fact that there are such proofs in his doctrine is a sufficient indication that his intuition of ideal being is in no way an intuition of God. If we saw God, we would stand in no need of proving his existence. Now it can be said of Rosmini that he welcomed all the proofs of the existence of God offered by the great philosophers and theologians of the past. The *a posteriori* demonstrations, from God's effects, were acceptable to him. What is particular in his attitude on that problem was his marked preference for the *a priori* proofs, especially those that appealed to the notion of being. The genuinely Rosminian proofs of the existence of God rest upon the essential properties of ideal being as known to the mind; they argue from possible being to actual being or, in other words, from the divine to God.[36]

In approaching that key problem, let us remember that, in Rosmini's doctrine, the notion of being is neither given by sensation *nor formed by abstraction*. It is innate in us and, for that very reason, it is in us antecedently to all experience. If we add that the first principles are nothing but the idea of being considered in its applications, it will become apparent that, in such a doctrine, *a priori* reasoning about being is not only possible and legitimate, but necessarily required and therefore valid.

As early as the *Nuovo saggio sull' origine delle idee*, Rosmini inferred from what precedes the following consequence: "It is possible, then, to form a reasoning with no other datum than that of the idea of being; and this is truly a pure *a priori* reasoning, inasmuch as it requires only a datum evident through itself, and not acquired through experience. Now I believe also that with the sole datum of the idea of being, it is possible to work out a rigorous and irrefragable demonstration of the existence of God; which would therefore be a pure *a priori* demonstration."³⁷ As Rosmini himself has attempted to summarize his complex demonstration, it seems advisable to report verbatim his own version of it:

> *Being taken in general*, which naturally shines to our mind, is, as I have said, of such nature that, whilst on the one hand it reveals to us no subsistence outside the mind and on this account may be called by the name of *logical being*, on the other hand, it would be absurd to view it as a modification of our spirit. Nay the fact is that it exhibits an authority so overwhelming, that our spirit cannot help being entirely subject thereto. We are conscious of having no power to effect the least change in it.³⁸ Moreover, being is absolutely immutable; it is the knowableness of all things, the fount of all cognitions. It has none of that contingent nature which belongs to us. It is a light which we always see, but which has dominion over us, vanquishes us, and, by completely bringing us under subjection to itself, ennobles us. Besides we can think of ourselves as nonexistent; but it would be impossible to think that being in general, namely possibility, truth, are not. Truth was truth before we came into this world, nor could there ever have been a period when it was not such. Is this nothing? Now the nature of that truth which shines within me, binds me to say, "This is"; and even were I to refuse to say it, I would still know that, even in spite of me, the thing *is*. Truth, therefore, being possibility,³⁹ presents itself to me as an eternal and necessary nature, such as no power can undo, since no power can be conceived of as undoing truth. And yet I do not see *how* this truth subsists in itself; but I feel its unconquerable force, the energy which it displays within me, and by which it irresistibly, yet sweetly, subdues my mind, and all minds. I feel this as a simple fact, against which no opposition could be of any avail.
>
> This fact, therefore, this truth, which I always see and is my intellectual light⁴⁰ informs me (1) that there is in me an effect which cannot be produced either by myself or by any finite cause; (2) that this effect consists in the intuition of an object intrinsically necessary, immutable, independent of my mind, and of every finite mind.⁴¹

VIII. The Philosophical Reaction in France and Italy

These foundations of the proof are its main moment. From the first point (the irresistible binding force of the idea of being), and by applying to it the "principle of causation," we must conclude that "there exists a cause which manifests an infinite force, and which must therefore itself be infinite." From the second point (the presence of the idea of being in my mind), I conclude that "it is of the nature of this infinite cause to *subsist* in a mind, namely, to be essentially intelligible; and if it must necessarily subsist in a mind, this mind must be eternally intelligent." Hence the conclusion "there exists an eternal mind which has the property of being *per se* intelligible,[42] and of communicating intelligibility to other things, and as such, is the *cause* of the infinite force manifested in our minds, as well as of our cognitions."[43] The proof therefore rests upon an application of the principle of causality to the binding necessity of the general idea of being considered as an entity innate in the mind.

The metaphysical background of the proof is the univocity of being, which Rosmini borrows from Duns Scotus,[44] but instead of arguing, as Scotus did, from the intrinsic modalities of being as such (causality, perfection, etc.), Rosmini appeals to his own *principle of absolute subsistence* (immediately derived from being), which runs as follows: "That which exists relatively supposes that which exists absolutely." On the strength of this principle, the mere fact that ideal being exists relatively in the mind entails the consequence that actual being must be found in absolute subsistence.[45] This does not make the existence of God self-evident. It is a proof, in that it is a rational inference from a datum given in the mind; *if one accepts the univocity of being*, the proof is even metaphysically correct, since it infers from the finite mode of being in reality. Nor is this *processus* arbitrary; since the finite mode of being in the mind is not nothing, it is something; then it should have a cause and since such a cause must exist absolutely, it can be no other than the absolutely subsisting Being.

being and ethics
Principii della scienza morale (*The Principles of Moral Science*)[46] contains a complete exposition of Rosmini's ethics.

The moral law is a single notion of the mind whereby we judge of the morality of human actions, and in accordance to which, therefore, we must act. The idea of being is of course the supreme rule of all the judgments of the human mind; it therefore is also the supreme rule of the moral judgments, or, more exactly, it is the first and the more universal of the moral laws. Brought down to its simplest formula, that law runs as follows: "Follow the light of reason." As such, that law applies to all judgments, the speculative as well as the practical, but since *being* and *true* are one and the same thing, the notion of being specially is the principle of all the sciences that treat of good. Since, however, we are dealing with the good of man, we must first determine the notion of the subjective good of man, which is happiness. In technical language, this is the science or doctrine of *eudemonology*.

The idea of being is the principle of eudemonology. It is the supreme principle of the science that treats of human happiness. The good of man, upon which his happiness depends, is a good of existence or a good of perfection (classical distinction between *esse* and *bene esse*). The good of existence for man is his own existence, whereby Rosmini means to say, his own human way of existing: human nature. What is man's good of perfection? Since he is a dual being, made up of two substances (corporeal and spiritual) subsisting together in one single subject (the *ego*) which is man, he needs two different kinds of good. As an animal, man can enjoy only corporeal and particular bodies; as an intelligent subject, man also can attain the universal and the absolute, including the supreme term of intelligence, God. In this life, God is the ultimate object of Christian hope; he is not seen, but believed; the sight of God in future life should not be called happiness, but beatitude. Eudemonology therefore stops short of that lofty ideal. Strictly speaking, it deals with the various techniques by which man can achieve the satisfaction of his natural wants, corporeal as well as intellectual. Even at that modest level, there is a hierarchy to observe. The good of perfection of the intellectual part of man is higher in dignity than that of the animal part. With respect to the good of the body, the good of intellect is in the relation of end to means. Inasmuch as it is ordained to the good of intelligence, the animal good participates in the dignity of intellectual good. Man is one subject. It is one and the same ego that receives corporeal sensations and that reasons about them. All the good belonging to an intelligent subject, mediately or immediately belongs to intelligence, the supreme part of man.

Because it has man for its proximate object, eudemonology deals only with the subjective good of man. For this reason, it must be distinguished from *ethics,* which is the science of objective and universal good. Just as sense is the source of subjective good, intelligence is that of objective good. Indeed all *sen-*

VIII. The Philosophical Reaction in France and Italy

sible good is subjective, because it is good for the subject that unites itself with it and feels it. On the contrary, known intelligible good is objective of its own nature, because man does not apprehend it by intellect as belonging to himself, but such as it is in itself, the same for all. Objective good therefore is absolute good, itself one with absolute being.

The moral law for man then is to follow the light of reason in pursuing the objectively moral good. In this life, the objective good originates the moral good just as the subjective good originates the eudemonological good. Objective good becomes moral when it becomes the object of a will. When the subject wills the objective good known by the mind, and at the very moment it begins to be willed, that objective good becomes a moral good. Hence this definition of moral good: "Objective good known by the intelligence and willed by the will."

There is no being without order, which is the relationship that obtains between the various degrees of perfection, that is of being. Since order implies perfection and good, the will that loves good also loves order. It is therefore just to set up order as the principle of morality, but this is true only if order is identified with good and, through good, with being. "So man sees being with his intelligence; seeing being, he sees the order of being, and that being is the good; the will that loves being and the order of being is the good will, the will that wills the good and, by willing it, makes it a moral good." Thus completed, the formula of ethics loses some of its vagueness; it can be translated as follows: "Act well and love being everywhere where you know it, and love it following the order in which it presents itself to your intelligence."

Such is the great principle of Rosmini's ethics. To his own mind, it necessarily follows from the first principle of all philosophy. For indeed, since being is the proper object of reason, to follow the light of reason is to follow the light of being; so the will should pursue being; one must love being wherever it is found, and, finding at last the perfect formula of an ethics pure *a priori* like that of Kant, yet realistic like that of Thomas Aquinas, Rosmini makes bold to propound this formula of well-understood moral duty: "One must love being everywhere where one perceives it, one must love all being *because it is such*."

One adds nothing to that remarkable formula of a realistic moral imperative by specifying that the love of being must follow the order of beings, for indeed order is nothing else than a degree of being; "Whoever loves being, loves it more according as it has more being; he loves being, therefore, in *an ordered way*."

By following the notion of ideal being to its moral consequences, Rosmini has achieved a philosophical system equally remarkable by its unity and by its universality. His ethics betrays the same desire as the rest of his doctrine, which seems to have aimed at achieving an organic synthesis of what was true in the traditional philosophy of the Greeks, as perfected by the Christian doctors, and of what was justified in the aspirations of the best among the modern philosophers. An ethics in which "obligation" and "duty" find their foundation in the apprehension of ordered being by the natural light of reason is not a blind categoric imperative, but the free love of good acknowledged by intelligence and determined by reason. Here is the basis for a society organized in view of the fuller development of moral persons. In short, Rosmini envisaged a universe finding its end in the moral perfection of intellectual creatures, through whose knowing power it communicates with God, indeed a noble conclusion to a noble philosophy. It also was the expression of one of the most beautiful souls that ever dedicated themselves to the quest of Christian wisdom.

Vincenzo Gioberti

Like all the Italian philosophers of his time, including Rosmini himself, Gioberti got caught in the turmoil of the Risorgimento. It can even be wondered if we are not indebted to his political misfortunes for the better part of his philosophical production. At all times and in all countries, exile and jail seem to favor philosophical reflection.[47]

By temper, however, Gioberti was a fighter, even in philosophy, and he was well aware of the fact.[48] And this quality paid off philosophically, for his metaphysics has greatly benefited by Gioberti's natural disposition not to permit error to go unchallenged.

ontology vs. psychology

Gioberti wanted his philosophy to be an "ontology," understood in the sense of "a science of being." He rejected those doctrines that start from something other than being or, at least, from something posited in itself and as separated from being. Unless you begin with being, you never get back to it, and if philosophy

VIII. *The Philosophical Reaction in France and Italy*

does not deal with being, it can deal only with non-being; in short, it then has no object.

Gioberti's principal "no" is aimed at psychologism, that is to say, at any doctrine that, intentionally or not, substitutes the method proper to psychology for the method proper to ontology, or science of being. The two sciences must use different methods because their objects are different. Psychology deals with *cognitions* (sensations, facts of consciousness), while the objects of ontology are *realities*, namely the very objects apprehended by such cognitions. The two moments of ontological knowledge are: (1) intuition, that is, the intuitive direct and immediate apprehension of reality, also called ontological intuition; (2), ontological reflection, which should never be confused with psychological reflection.

The doctrine Gioberti here has most in mind is the eclecticism of Victor Cousin, the most salient feature of which was its avowed intention to lead the mind to metaphysics by means of a psychological reflection on the content of intellectual knowledge. The true object of ontological intuition is the intelligible. Of itself, it is a contemplation by the mind of an object similar to the kind of reality Plato called Idea. Thus understood, ontological intuition constitutes the first degree of contemplation; "it provides ontological knowledge with the very object on which it will operate, with the principles from which it will start and with the method that will govern its inquiry." As was said, that object is something like an Idea, but the intelligible object given in intuition is not intuition's own apprehension of it. To think that way would be to relapse into the psychologism of Cousin. The object of intuition is the ontological reality that constitutes the proper object of metaphysical knowledge.

Gioberti's opposition to Cousin's psychologism accounts for his harsh criticism of Rosmini's doctrine of knowledge. Its first defect precisely is to be a doctrine of knowledge that mistakes itself for a doctrine of being. In Gioberti's interpretation of his doctrine, Rosmini had aimed to oppose to the criticism of Kant a theory of knowledge leaving open the possibility of metaphysical knowledge. For that very reason, his own philosophy remained a gnosiology. To Rosmini, being is an idea, and he conceived it as "the ultimate possible abstraction and the more abstract of all ideas"; the supreme object of his philosophy thus remains "a mental being, and not yet a being subsisting outside of the mind." In fact, if not in his intention, Rosmini opposes Kant's idealism with another variety of idealism. The result is bound to be that, since there is no real being at the beginning of his philosophy, there will be no real good at the end. Immoralism necessarily follows from such a metaphysical principle.[49] What is needed is a psychological Prime that is, at the same time, an ontological Prime. Gioberti's doctrine aims to provide it.

What is the ontological Prime? According to what precedes, it only can be an idea, and that first idea can be no other than that of being. In itself, however, being is but an intuition; in order to turn it into a truth, we need to form a judgment. The judgment whose function it is to reveal the nature of the first Idea can be called the formula of the Idea, or, in Gioberti's own terms, the "ideal formula" (*formula ideale*). If it is found, that formula will be, at once, the *primum psychologicum* and the *primum ontologicum*; by the same token, it will provide us with the *primum philosophicum*.

the ideal formula: first cycle

In order to be a judgment susceptible of truth, the ideal formula must comprise three terms, that is to say, two terms bound together by a third one. Moreover, in order actually to be true, that judgment must join the two terms at stake by a relation grounded in the nature of the first. The question is: can such a judgment be formed, starting from the sole notion of being?

In trying to follow Gioberti, one cannot avoid stumbling upon a preliminary difficulty. According to him, philosophy is ontology; if we want to avoid idealism, we must posit at once that the first idea also is the first thing. The first idea and the first thing are those on which all the other ideas depend in the order of knowledge as well as in the order of reality. Because the psychological prime is identical with the ontological prime, their union constitutes the philosophical prime. If this be true, the ontological intuition of being necessarily is that of being itself at the same time as it is the intuition of its idea. By refusing to disjoin the psychological prime from the ontological prime, Gioberti avoids psychologism, which is the ruin of philosophy.[50] On the other hand, by uniting these two primes to the point of identifying them, Gioberti places himself in a position where it becomes for him difficult to avoid ontologism. There are many ontologies (metaphysics of being) innocent of ontologism. What is called ontologism by the theologians is any metaphysics in which, under any form whatsoever, the first act of human knowledge is an intuition of being, partially

VIII. *The Philosophical Reaction in France and Italy*

or totally identical with being, that is to say, with God. Gioberti did not want to commit such an error; however, could he possibly avoid it?

Let us observe that Gioberti himself makes profession of teaching an "ontologism." As early as his *Introduzione alla studio della filosofia* (*Introduction to Philosophy*), he did not hesitate to write that, "strictly speaking, God is the first philosopher, and that the human philosophy is the continuation and repetition of the divine philosophy." Interpreting in a new sense the Augustinian doctrine of the "inner master," Gioberti draws the conclusion that, since the philosophical labor does not begin in man, but in God, "it does not ascend from the spirit to being, but, rather, it descends from being to the spirit." Whereupon, in a revealing formula, Gioberti adds this remark: "There is for you the deep reason, which clears up the truth of ontologism, and the absurdity of the contrary system. Before being a work of man, philosophy is a divine creation. The psychologists deprive philosophy of its heavenly support and turn it into a mere human artifice by separating it from being; they thus condemn it to a distressing doubt and they assign to it nothingness as its principle and its end."[51]

There is therefore little doubt that, in starting from being, Gioberti intends to start from God. On the other hand, that tendency is opposed, in his own mind, by a no less strong one. At the same time that it is an "ontologism," his doctrine is also a "creationism." The easiest way to reconcile those two aspects of his thought is to admit that, as seems to be the case, Gioberti perceives at once his own being as a finite, contingent, and partial being. As such, man apprehends himself as caused by the very being whose idea is the first object of his mind. Anticipating the philosophical language of our own times, Gioberti says that he perceives himself, not as being, but as an existent caused by being. The object of the ontological reflection is to explicate (to unfold) that primitive relationship between being and existents. Critics do not agree on the final interpretation Gioberti himself gave of his own thought. Perhaps some of them want to make him as much of a pantheist as they themselves are. It is however certain that, especially in the *Introduzione alla studio della filosofia*, which is the most systematic exposition of his thought, Gioberti was careful to distinguish God in Himself from God in our being and even in our thought. The notion of a primitive revelation helped him to formulate the necessary distinctions. "Between the primitive and divine judgment, and the human and secondary judgment, *that is between intuition and refection* [italics ours], there runs the medium of language by which the intuited true makes itself accessible to the reflecting power of man. So man is able to repeat to himself as well as to others the judgment of God. Now language, which expresses the reality of being, was created by being itself; it is a second revelation, or, more exactly speaking, it is the primordial revelation clothed in a certain form by Him who revealed it. That form is a proposition which humanly expresses the divine pronouncement."

This point should be kept in mind in striving to understand how Gioberti could pass from his ontological intuition of being to the "ideal formula" such as it will presently be reported. At the origin of his reflections on the subject, the word of God speaking to us in Scripture appeared as the connecting link between the intuition of being and its ideal formula. God himself says that he created heaven and earth. "Equipped with that objective proportion (between the human pronouncement and the divine pronouncement) reflection appropriates to itself the corresponding judgment, it repeats it, explains it, and owing to it, it elaborates its scientific work."

Revelation through language, and received *ex auditu*, explains the origin of the philosophical prime. In Gioberti's own words, "the divine judgment is expressed by an equally divine proposition, in the reflective repetition of which the principle of the human philosophy consists, just as the unfolding of that philosophy consists in the unfolding of the same divine proposition." Hence the ideal formula: "Being creates the existent." The formula is organic, as can be seen from the intimate relation there is between its two terms. *Existence* points out the operation by which a certain thing, first merely potential, becomes actual. That was its primitive meaning. In modern language, it points out the condition of that which is because it has been produced. Let us define existence as "the reality proper to an actual substance, produced by a substance distinct from it, that contains it potentially, inasmuch as it is apt to produce it." The idea of existence therefore is inseparable from that of being. Whether we perceive ourselves as caused beings, or we simply learn from God himself that being is our cause, we know from the very moment of reflection that the whole structure of the universe is a relationship between existents and their ontological cause, which is God.[52]

The unfinished *Della Protologia* does not seem to justify any other interpretation of Gioberti's doctrine. At that later date, "nature, providence, and revelation" still express various aspects of one and the same reality. The notion

VIII. *The Philosophical Reaction in France and Italy*

of creation still remains for him the central point of the doctrine. As to the creative act, it still remains "a passage: the passage from being to the existent." That passage is an infinite; exactly, it is the infinity of the divine all-powerfulness, manifesting itself in the production of finite being. The term of creation is finite, but creation itself is infinite because it bridges the infinite distance there is between being and nothingness: "the creative act is actually infinite inasmuch as it implies the passing from nothingness to existence. At the very point where act proceeds from being to the existent, it draws the existent from nothingness." It is therefore no wonder that the existent exhibits a tendency to achieve the fulness of being, which is its origin. But the thing cannot be done. The finite existent cannot equal infinite being. There is in it, however, a sort of potential infinity, in that the existent tends to attain God, being, or the creative act, in a threefold way: by knowledge, by love, and by a substantial union which is nor possible in this life. The union of the finite with the infinite is the supreme object of the second cycle, the ascending creative cycle, whose term is the same as the principle of the descending creative cycle. A doctrine of good thus completes Gioberti's doctrine of being.[53]

the second creative cycle: ethics

Good is the leading notion in ethics; the scientific basis of good can be found in the absolute, and nowhere else. The doctrine that deals with the first lineaments of the absolute is prime philosophy, or metaphysics. Prime philosophy has to be both axiomatic and universal: axiomatic because, otherwise, it would not be prime; universal because, otherwise, it would not provide other sciences with their necessary foundation.

At the point of justifying his own conception of ethics, Gioberti restates in the shortest possible way the elements of his personal metaphysics:

> The First Science must rest upon a capital axiom, which comprises in its universality all propositions of more restricted application. In virtue of their special nature, these must derive from a primary and universal axiom that contains them in itself. Moreover, prime science must rest upon the concrete, because only the concrete can impart objective value and fecundity to abstract propositions, and lay down the matter upon which the abstracting spirit can fruitfully exercise itself. Now that

universal axiom, founded on the concrete, and able to serve as a protological and encyclopedic axiom, is the ideal formula elsewhere cleared up and expressed by me in the following terms: *Being creates existences.* The formula is first because we cannot have the least thought, nor form the least judgment that does not presuppose it and is not included in it; it is universal because all the special axioms derive from that formula; it expresses a concrete, because, in signifying it abstractly, according to its own nature, the reflection operates upon the intuitive concrete that precedes it, and without which that very reflection could not take place; that formula is supremely fecund because, besides generating all the special axioms, it provides the concrete matter of and the data of the various sciences, their methods, their ends and, in fine, the inductive and deductive consequences that flow from the scientific materials fecundated by that formula and cultivated by the specialized disciplines and faculties.[54]

Ethics stands in regard to the prime science in the same threefold relation as the other disciplines. The three elements are the cause of good, good itself, and the effects of good.

The prime cause of good is God himself. The idea of creating being, which is the organic principle of the ideal formula, provides the prime cause of good, the law that constitutes it and the principle of obligation that attends it. Being is the prime cause of the good act because it creates, conserves and moves the agent which, of itself, cannot operate without the assistance of the creative and absolute cause. The creative act is not transitory, but continuous and immanent. Although it produces not only the power of acting present in secondary causes, but their very efficacy, the intervention of the first cause does not hamper human liberty, but rather, it directs it and informs it, because a created spirit cannot be free except inasmuch as God made it to be such and moves it to operate freely. In moving free will, being likewise actuates the reason of the secondary cause and it uncovers to it the universal reality in the two orders of the necessary and the contingent, as well as in their reciprocal relations. The human spirit offers that "great concrete" through intuition, and it is the concrete of the ideal formula which, embracing the whole real, embraces by the same token the whole intelligible.[55]

VIII. *The Philosophical Reaction in France and Italy*

These considerations clearly show the central place occupied by the notion of creation is the doctrine of Gioberti. More exactly, what is at stake is the principle of the essential creativity of being, itself grounded in the pure actuality of being *qua* being. In this sense, Gioberti's metaphysics and ethics remain intimately related to the great tradition of the Thomist metaphysics of being. The contingent has neither reality nor intelligibility except by mode of participation. This participation does not flow from an emanation, it results from a creation. Were it not so, the receiver would be substantially the same as the giver; it would not be contingent as, in fact, it is.

Gioberti also remembers the great Augustinian tradition of Malebranche, kept alive in Italy by Gerdil, but he himself has observed that the doctrine of the vision in God had left out an important point. "Guided by the doctrines of Saint Augustine and of the realists, Malebranche has shrewdly realized that human knowledge has no value except as a participation of the divine thought, and in this the celebrated theory of the ideal vision consists. But he did not realize that if the spirit only saw the eternal ideas, it would not truly participate in the thought of God, who, besides being intelligent, also is a free agent and a creator." In order to remedy that defect, Gioberti adds to the intuition of the intelligent and all-knowing being "the imperative of the intuition of being, as endowed with an all-powerful will which individuates the ideas by a free act of creation."[56] Hence the moral law, founded in the divine intellect, and the moral imperative founded in the divine will, both identical in the unity of the creative act, itself identical with the divine essence.

Only from this point of view does one realize the ultimate reasons for the obstinate opposition of Gioberti to Rosmini. Gioberti's philosophy is intensely creationistic. After the first creative cycle, which is that of the divine creation, man initiates a second creative cycle effecting the return of man to God as to his ultimate end. God does not only create the existent, he re-creates the existent by a sort of "second creation," purely supernatural in its essence, and which constitutes the order of grace. *L'ente redime l'esistenti*, the traditional doctrine of the *opus creationis* and of its free restoration by the *opus recreationis*, here finds its equivalent in the philosophy of Gioberti.

Whatever its nature, either merely natural or partially supernatural, the moral activity of man can find its justification nowhere else. As a science, ethics must be able to operate a synthetic reduction of its various elements to one single judgment, which includes them all, and is in germ that very science. That judgment runs as follows: *Being, through the choice of man, creates the Good.* In this new formula: *Lente, per mezzo dell'arbitrio umano, créa il Buono*, Gioberti is conscious of making a partial restatement of the ideal formula, inasmuch as it accounts for the order of morality.

As has just been seen, the ideal formula initiates two cycles, a first creative cycle that causes man to be, and a second creative cycle that brings man back to his origin. According to these two cycles, the ideal formula divides into two pronouncements, the one concerning virtue, the other concerning beatitude, which are the two poles around which the notion of good revolves.

The first of these pronouncements is as follows: *By subjecting affections to law, choice produces virtue.* This answers the first creative cycle, because, by sacrificing his personal preferences in order to conform his will to the supreme law, man imitates the creative act by which nature itself was first constituted in conformity with the divine ideas. The second cycle of ethics likewise answers the second creative cycle. It can be formulated as follows: *By reconciling affections with law, virtue produces beatitude.* The two cycles of ethics insure the completion of the moral cosmos just as the two cycles of creation insure that of the universal cosmos: "And exactly as the latter cycle includes both time and eternity, heaven and earth, so also this second cycle of ethics comprises the two divine kingdoms, the Church and paradise." In fine, "just as, in the two creative cycles God is the principal and only agent, so also in the two ethical heavens, man co-operates with the divine work, imitating it and showing himself careful to elaborate, under the guidance of the divine art, his own goodness and his own felicity, and in this does consist the divine resemblance which his Creator bestowed upon him."

Those considerations take us to teleology, the ultimate science, or science of ends, just as protology is the science of the principles. Teleology is the summit of the scientific pyramid while protology is its base. Among all the ideas, the only one that has the reason of end is that of the well done, the only one that can constitute the ultimate end is that of the good. Because the good is the only possible ultimate end of moral operations, ethics, which treats of the good, is intimately related to teleology, just as logic, which treats of the true, is particularly interlocked with the prime science, or protology.

All the human faculties thus find themselves related to principles, for they

VIII. The Philosophical Reaction in France and Italy

all reduce to two, cognition and action, art being but the bond of contemplation and action. As it insures the passage of the one to the other, teleology shares in the nature of art. It applies speculation to action, owing to the mediation of the doctrine of the ends: "It translates the absolutely universal formula of the prime science into a more particular and immediately applicable one, according to the various orders of things to which man intends to apply it."

It is therefore necessary to find middle formulas mediating between the two extremes of protology and teleology. Such formulas may vary with time and circumstances. Generally speaking, however, every nation has to submit to universal conditions valid for all peoples. When applied to human society in general, the protological formula, *being creates existences*, yields the following mediate principle: *religion creates the morality and civility* [civilization] *of the human kind.*

History witnesses to the truth of that statement. At all times and in all places the civil orders were born of the sacerdotal orders, the cities of the temples, the laws of the oracles, the philosophies of the theologies, education and culture of religion. Indeed, "religion is to the other institutions what being is with respect to existents, the prime science with respect to the secondary sciences, the cause with respect to effects, that is to say, the dynamic and organic principle which produces them, conserves them, restores them, and perfects them." This is particularly true of Christianity with respect to Italy. For Christianity has created all the nations of Europe but, because it chose that nation before any other one, *the Catholic religion has created the morality and the civility of Italy*. Hence the proper vocation of Italy is as a civilizing power and as a force for the redemption of the nations. "Italy is the sacerdotal nation in the great body of the redeemed peoples (Ex. 19:6, 1 Pet. 11:9); Italy is the head of Christianity as the other nations ought to be its arm." In fact, the Italians were just that in the long fight of Europe against the Saracens. The inhabitants of the peninsula enriched the other peoples not only with the supernatural gifts of Christianity, but with civilization as well. "All the great European intellects that illustrated their own countries with any kind of splendor were lit by the living flame of the Italian genius."

Such is the mediating formula proper to Italy: to gather nations together, to resurrect that which seemed to be dead and to do so by recalling men and things to their principle. Protestantism has failed to corrupt it; Cartesianism, the ruin of religion and philosophy in France, would also be that of Italy if that venomous weed were not in good time extirpated from the happy garden of Italy, that new Eden which, having a pure source to quench her thirst and the tree of life to feed the minds, can do better without importing wild fruit from foreign lands. "It is vain, ridiculous, absurd to want to find out or to invent the principles, because all inquiry, all reasoning, all discovery presupposes them." The principles are given by language, which is authentic only if it comes from God and can show the titles of its divine origin. At the end of his ethics, Gioberti thus gathers together the classical themes of traditionalism: revelation, language, authority, and so on. "I believe in good and reasonable progress because I believe in Christianity and in the Church as the preserver of the divine germs, of which every improvement is born." But the ultimate justification for such positions lie, with Gioberti, much deeper than they do in traditionalism. He would doubt the possibility of human perfectibility if the Church were not immutable. It is immutable, however, and this is why it can apply to changing circumstances the unchanging essence of the Christian notion of good. Whence does the good example come? From Italy. "Dante, Michelangelo, Galileo, Vico, Muratori, that is to say the five greatest names ever produced by the Peninsula in literature, in the fine arts, in experimental science, as well as in those of calculus, of philosophy, and of erudition, all were sincerely Catholics. Why should the learned men of today feel ashamed to follow in their wake?" And whence does the bad example now come? From France, and from nowhere else. Not indeed from ancient France, the elder daughter of Christian Rome, but of that half-learned, arrogant, and frivolous France, such as she came out of the hands of bad philosophers. The rabid incredulity of the past century is now being replaced in France by a mild indifference and by a nerveless, spiritless philosophy, a philosophy without doctrine which some want to acclimatize in Italy; "for my own part, I shall never accept that the mother of civilization and of universal Christianity should become a philosophical satellite of France."[57] *Instaurare in Italia la vera idea del Buono* is a legitimate intention indeed, and the more justified as Gioberti wanted it to be a truly metaphysical instauration.

The influence of Gioberti has been very wide. Even among the Jesuits, whom he detested, there were men to adopt some of his ideas, not however without correcting his language and rectifying some of his positions.[58] His metaphysical terminology remains visible in the very title of the well-known

VIII. The Philosophical Reaction in France and Italy

opuscle of Albert M. Lepidi, O.P.: *De ente generalissimo, prout est aliquid psychologicum, logicum et ontologicum.*[59] One should not wonder too much at such a fact. In the first place, the polyvalence of the notion of being is a fact, and the distinction of its three orders (psychological, logical, and ontological) raises problems that cannot be ignored. Next, there is in Thomism an all-important notion of being, and Thomists will always feel interested in a doctrine which, identifying it with God, posits it as the *primum ontologicum*. The danger point in such doctrines is always reached where, in some way or other, the *primum ontologicum* is identified with the *primum psychologicum*. Theologians always will mistrust such doctrines as courting the peril of "ontologism." In such cases, they always will remind readers that in metaphysics, and particularly in natural theology, our notion of being remains an abstract concept; it is not an intuition of intelligible being itself, and indeed such an intuition would be hard to distinguish from a confused, yet immediate, sight of God.

The Spreading of Ontologism

Ontologism is an ambiguous word. It is given as the name of a theological error several times denounced and condemned by the authority of the Catholic Church. Even so, the condemnation does not concern ontologism as such; it always points out "a certain form of ontologism." Such was the case with an important theological consultation, the *Request to the Vatican Council on the Subject of Ontologism*; it was the joint work of Riario, Cardinal Sforza, of Naples, and of Joachim Cardinal Pecci, of Perugia, the future Leo XIII.[60] The request is directed against "that form of ontologism which openly contradicts the Catholic doctrine." Its definition is as follows: "The direct and immediate knowledge of God is natural to man." The *Postulatum ad Concilium Vaticanum de Ontologismo* denounced the thus understood ontologism as a corollary to pantheism in the doctrines of Spinoza, Schelling, and Hegel; then as its "immediate principle in the system of Malebranche and of his disciples up to Gioberti" (p. 575).[61] Eclecticism follows from ontologism, "for if we know everything in God, our mind is incapable of error, so the various and opposed opinions of the philosophers always are certain parts, or aspects of, truth, which is what the eclectics say." A last note is directed against Gioberti: "et Giobertius ex hac philosophia intuitus infert, naturalem ordinem et supernaturalem re non differre, Theologiam esse progressum naturalem philosophiae, imo utramque esse unam eamdemque scientiam etc."

This was but an expert consultation. In 1861, propositions borrowed from the doctrine of ontologists had been formally condemned. Five of them defined straight philosophical positions: (1) the immediate cognition of God, at least the habitual knowledge of Him, is essential to the human mind, so that without it we can know nothing; indeed that cognition is the intellectual light itself; (2) the being which we know in all things, and without which we know nothing, is the divine being; (3) considered on the part of things, the universals are not really distinct from God; (4) the innate cognition of God as pure and simple being involves all other knowledge, so that, by it and in it, everything else is implicitly known to us; (5) all the other ideas are but modifications of the idea by which God is known to us as simply being.[62]

In a much wider sense, the word "ontologism" signifies a loose group of doctrines which rest upon the observation of a fact, namely, that when applied to metaphysical being, the description of being given by Parmenides around 500 B.C., remarkably fits the theological description of the Christian God. All Catholic theologies are obliged to take that fact into account. To the extent that they identify God with being, Christian philosophers cannot fail to feel tempted to pass directly from the notion of being in their minds to the cognition of God in himself. As early as the thirteenth century, Saint Bonaventure remarked in unforgettable terms that there is such a thing as a contemplation of God in the notion of being (*Itinerarium*, ch. V). It is no wonder then that those who were reproached with teaching ontologism, in the theological sense of the term, always found texts in Bonaventure, Thomas Aquinas, and other irreproachable authorities to quote in favor of their own positions. Whether such and such a doctrine falls under the theological note of "ontologism" is something historians as such are not competent to say. At any rate, the notion of "ontologism" in general is too abstract and too vague to be the object to a doctrinal condemnation. Every ontology is exposed to the risk of ontologism. In Belgium and in France, several priests endowed with good philosophical minds experienced the intrinsic difficulties of the position.[63]

Just as the presence of Condillac at Parma had left behind a wake of sensism, the presence of Gioberti in Brussels, where he taught, wrote, and published, acted as a ferment of ontologism. The center of the doctrine was Louvain.[64] In its origin however, the movement was a reaction of the Christian mind against the atheistic rationalism of the early nineteenth century; just as on the Italian side, Belgian ontologism blended with various forms of traditionalism. Strictly speaking, one should have made a choice between traditionalism (all knowledge is a divine revelation) and ontologism (all knowledge is included in the innate notion of being, even our knowledge of God); in fact, however, it was tempting to understand our knowledge of God as born of a confluence between our innate notion of being and the revealed truth that God is being.

The Louvain professor Ubaghs taught such a combination of traditionalism and ontologism which was denounced by Rome[65] under the form of five propositions: (1) We cannot succeed in knowing any external metaphysical truth (that is, a truth concerning that which does not fall under our senses) without being instructed by someone else, and, in the last analysis, without the divine revelation; (2) external metaphysical truths cannot be properly demonstrated (Ubaghs, *Theodicy*, p. 220, n. 4, 13ff.); (3) the existence of God cannot be demonstrated. We deny that one can demonstrate that God exists (ibid., p. 73); (4) the proofs of the existence of God are reducible to a certain faith, or are grounded in that faith, by which we see less than believe, or feel naturally persuaded of the faithfulness of that idea, a thing which cannot be seen by mere internal evidence (ibid., p. 73); (5) the author reduces to common sense all the proofs of the eternal metaphysical truths.[66]

The composite nature of those propositions mirrors that of the doctrine. Of course, Ubaghs would not content himself with saying that the existence of God cannot be demonstrated. For him, demonstration meant demonstration through the cause, and since there is no cause of God there can be no demonstrations of His existence. But that which cannot be demonstrated can sometimes be proved, and Ubaghs repeatedly affirmed that the existence of God can be proved. His proofs of it were of the traditional type, and he holds them to be valid, although the value of none of them is absolute unless the ontological argument is added to them. The gist of the argument is that we naturally see God inasmuch as we see the eternal truths, which are God. Nevertheless, that intuition of God in the eternal truths is radically different from the beatific vision. The beatifying intuition has for its object the very essence of God, the natural intuition of God bears upon the attributes of God seen by the mind in its own idea of being.[67]

Despite the explanations given by Ubaghs and the modifications to which he submitted certain of his formulas, the doctrine was finally declared to be unsafe in itself and unfit to teach. What was denounced in the teaching of Ubaghs was "the doctrines of the absolute necessity of revelation and of the absolute impossibility there is to give a proof of the existence of God that is not ultimately reducible to something like an act of faith."[68]

At the same time, a similar movement was developing in France, where it could find many pre-existing seeds waiting for an opportunity to revive. Malebranche provided all the necessary starting points for an undertaking of that sort. Even the upshot could be foreseen. Put on the *Index librorum prohibitorum* as early as 1689, 1707, and 1712, the main writings of the great Oratorian, partially vindicated by Cardinal Gerdil, could still be consulted by a teacher universally respected, the Sulpician Branchereau.[69] Designated to teach philosophy at the seminary of Clermont, Branchereau anonymously published a complete course of lectures in 1849, the *Praelectiones philosophicae* (1849). Following the Wolfian tradition, the three volumes of the first edition divided philosophy into *Ontology, Natural Theology, Cosmology, Anthropology,* and *Esthetics*. A short *History of Philosophy* completed the work. The doctrine starts, in the Cartesian way, with the "I think."

> I cannot think without thinking of something. So, since thinking is the primitive fact, all that of which I am thinking necessarily has some reality. Now I think of two sorts of truths, or objects of thought, the ones necessary, the others contingent. But how to found that object of thought, especially the contingent one, which does not impose itself on my mind? Is it truly outside my mind? Has it got a being independent of my thought? And how are we to solve the problem raised by Kant, and solved by his relativism, itself a form of skepticism, or else declared impossible to solve by other rationalists such as Jouffroy? We shall solve it only by hanging the chain of the contingent truths on the divine absolute such as Malebranche understood it, and by realizing that perceived being, such as the exterior world (a being that is possible, since it appears to me) rests in its reality upon an idea, which is found in God; so we see the relative beings in the light of the absolute being.[70]

VIII. *The Philosophical Reaction in France and Italy*

Like Malebranche himself, then, Branchereau is less interested in the "I think" as an immediate apprehension of the ego than in the ideas apprehended in it. After the 1861 condemnation of the propositions forced upon Rosmini, Branchereau summed up his doctrine in fifteen propositions which he volunteered to submit to the judgment of the Holy See (1862). Every cognition is a relation of subject and object. Object itself divides into absolute being and relative being.

Absolute being is real, concrete, infinite, and perfect; it is not the abstract notion of being in general, but rather it is being itself in its fullness, in short it is the being we call God. From the preceding inspection of its idea, absolute being appears as necessarily existing. The so-called ontological argument cannot be rejected, the more so as, in affirming that God is, it simply recognizes a fundamental exigency of reason, its principle of identity.

Relative being can be conceived as possible or as actual. Conceived as possible, it answers an eternal and necessary idea, which is its essence. As an intelligible idea, its essence is in God. The Word is the "place of the possibles" (Malebranche). All contingent beings, therefore, have in absolute being the objective foundation of their intelligibility. Since, as essences, all conceived things are real in God, to know them is for us to see them in God. To say that our thought is directly related to something divine merely acknowledges the ultimate foundation of the objectivity of our knowledge of possible beings.

Conceived as actual, relative being no longer has its foundation in the vision in God of its essence; the principle of its intelligibility then is its creation by God. The existence of created things is perceived neither in their ideas in God nor in the ideas of their own essences in themselves; the cognition of their existences results from: (1) sense perception (internal or external); (2) an invincible judgment affirming the reality of their created existence. Created things, precisely *qua* created, are therefore in God in no sense of the word. Only the idea of actually existing things is eternal and part of the divine essence; actually existing things themselves are not so.

Branchereau thought he had efficaciously protected himself against all doctrinal risks. As he understood it, the vision in God only related us to the intelligibility of the Word, not to the reality of his unfathomable essence. As to our knowledge of actually existing things, it presupposed the free decision of a creative act causing them to exist *ex nihilo*. No pantheism was to be feared.

Still, in 1867 and despite all his explanations, Branchereau failed to obtain an approbation of his doctrine. This was, for others as well as for himself, the end of ontologism as a distinct doctrinal line.[71]

The lesson of those events was well expressed by Father Ramière, S.J., in his book *On Unity in the Teaching of Philosophy Within the Catholic Schools* (*De l'unité dans l'enseignement de la philosophie an sein des écoles catholiques*, 1862). Ramière clearly discerned what was at stake. The French ontologists assuredly were very prudent, moderate in their views and safe against the imputation of pantheism, but that was not the point. Around 1860, the Catholic Church was anxious to restore doctrinal unity in the schools as well as in the minds of individuals. The times were ripe for some doctrinal intervention on the part of Rome, setting up a standard theological doctrine and bringing doctrinal disorder to an end.

IX. French Positivism

THE positivism of Auguste Comte is one among many efforts made by self-appointed reformers to bring to an end the mental and social disorder caused by the French Revolution of 1789. One of them was Charles Fourier,[1] who considered himself the Newton of the social world. His was a utopian doctrine, which divided society into groups of about eighteen hundred persons (a *phalanx*) living a communitarian life in "phalansteries" (i.e., phalanx-monasteries). The movement was quite a success. It even reached America, where a very active disciple of Fourier, Victor Considerant,[2] established in Texas a phalansterian community.

Another utopian reformer, Saint-Simon,[3] the founder of the very influential movement called Saint-Simonism, preached the gospel of production (*Du système industriel* [*The Industrial System*], 1821). His intention was to restore social and political order by rebuilding society on the basis of a scientific truth (reduction of the whole body of science to the Newtonian law of gravitation) as well as of a religious truth (the Christian law of charity understood as a purely natural truth). The religious aspect of all those doctrines manifested a survival of French Revolution deism, with its cult of Reason and its humanitarian aspirations. Saint-Simon considered himself a prophet destined to found a New Christianity; indeed, Saint-Simonism was an influential movement combining religion, banking, and industry. Its main figure was Enfantin (1796–1864), a mind full of many projects, including even those of the Suez Canal and the Panama Canal. For some time Saint-Simonism was an active religious formation of little philosophical significance, but one disciple of Saint-Simon was to organize a religion of his own. His name was Auguste Comte, the founder of philosophical positivism and of the positivist cult of Humanity.

Auguste Comte

No name compares in importance in the history of French positivism with that of Auguste Comte.[4] A man with a social mission, a philosophical, political, and religious reformer, Comte has abundantly explained himself and never more clearly than in his early *Plan des travaux scientifiques nécessaires pour réorganiser la société* (1822). His future "positivism" was already in germ in that essay.

the goal and the way

Like most of the French philosophers we have met during the first third of the nineteenth century, Comte was living in the shadow of the French Revolution. His proximate goal was to "terminate the Revolution." This could be done neither by the disciples of the eighteenth-century philosophers nor by the traditionalists. The critical philosophy of the eighteenth century had destroyed the metaphysics and the theology of the past, but its purely negative principles did not permit it to rebuild anything. It could destroy, it could found nothing. So society found itself in a doctrinal vacuum. Only a new doctrine, as acceptable to all as theology had been to the men of the middle ages, could become the common bond of a new society.

Such then was the situation. Comte admitted that there had existed a really organic society in the middle ages, and that the social bond had then been provided by the common acceptance of one single system of ideas, namely, Christian theology. European unity then was the unity of the Christian dogma and of the common belief in its truth. Protestantism was responsible for having wrecked that religious unity; the philosophy of the succeeding centuries had done the same with the intellectual unity of the West. The medieval system of ideas (Christian theology) being no longer acceptable, it was necessary to establish a new one. In modern times, only scientific truth is universally acceptable. The problem then was for Comte to elaborate a new philosophy borrowed from science and to use its truth as the unifying bond of the new society. Hence the two parts which, without undue modesty, he himself distinguished in his future career; in the first half, he had to be Aristotle; in the second one, he would be Saint Paul.

The very nature of the project implied a twofold conviction; first that the world is swayed by ideas; next that the highest expression of the world-swaying ideas is philosophy.

IX. French Positivism

On the first point, Comte showed himself the heir to the great rationalist tradition of the eighteenth century. In a sense, his own work was to remain a vastly improved version of the prospectus of Condorcet describing the progress of the human race as one with the progress of human knowledge. If Marxism can describe itself as a historical materialism, Comtism could not unfittingly be described as a historical idealism. In the very first lecture of his *Cours de philosophie positive* (*Course in Positive Philosophy*), Comte simply takes it as evident that "ideas govern and revolutionize the world, or, in other terms, that the whole social mechanism ultimately rests upon opinions." Intellectual anarchy was the cause of the French Revolution. To terminate that revolution and to set up a system of ideas able to wipe out the deep divergences then obtaining between individual intellects, was to Comte one and the same thing. The remedy for that political situation does not rest with politics, only a doctrine can provide it. Since the evil lies in the mind, the mind should first be healed. "As long as individual intelligences will not have adhered, by a unanimous assent, to a certain number of general ideas capable of forming a common social doctrine, one should not blind oneself to the fact that, of necessity, the state of the nations will remain an essentially revolutionary one. Despite all the political palliatives adopted, there will really be nothing more than provisional institutions." In more concrete terms, since ideas direct the world, only a new system of ideas can provide the common doctrine destined to restore social order and peace. Revolutions, republics, empires, monarchical restorations will never provide the right answer to the problem. Auguste Comte himself will terminate the revolution by providing the common social doctrine which will establish order in society by first establishing it in the mind.

Second, according to Comte, the saving truth must be a philosophy. The whole substance of positivism will be borrowed from science, but intellectual unity requires a systematic ordering of truth. Now science itself does not constitute a system of ideas. On the contrary, the natural tendency of sciences is to multiply without end and that of the scientists is to specialize more and more in the study of more and more restricted subjects. Overspecialization is the curse of scientific research, and this alone justifies the prediction that science as such will never provide societies with the system of ideas required for their unity.

Philosophy, on the other hand, normally aims at systematization. On account of its social destination, positivism shall therefore assume the shape of a philosophy. In order to be a system, it will have to make a choice among the countless conclusions of the various sciences. Naturally, it will limit its choice to the most general conclusions of each science. Moreover, it will have to make a choice between the sciences themselves; some sciences are fundamental, some are not. Positive philosophy then will be something specifically other than positive sciences. It will be the specialty of the scientific generalities: *la spécialité des généralités*. Brought together by philosophy the ultimate conclusions of the fundamental sciences constitute a systematic interpretation of the world.[5]

Such was at least the initial conviction of Comte: whereas the purely scientific mentality makes for increasing dispersion, the mental attitude of the philosopher well versed in science is to see them spontaneously tending to unity. With the passing of years, Comte will more and more wonder if it is not necessary to set up a center of reference exterior to science itself in order to extract from it a philosophy worthy of the name. Comte's answer to the question will remain tied up with his personal notion of sociology as a science; the notion itself is inseparable from the general classification of the sciences which is the backbone of positive philosophy.

science and philosophy

Like all great philosophical doctrines, the system of Comte goes full circle. Its exposition could start indifferently from the positivist classification of the sciences or from the Law of the Three States. In the last analysis, to understand the doctrine is to realize the unity of that twofold truth.

The sciences are susceptible of receiving a certain systematic unity, under two conditions. First, one must distinguish between the fundamental sciences and the secondary or related ones. For instance, biology is a fundamental science because it deals with a general fact, life; mycology and entomology are not fundamental sciences, because their objects are particular cases of the general laws of life. Comte unhesitatingly assumes that there is an order of the sciences because there are distinct and ordered layers of reality. He would not say he assumes it, he would rather say he sees it is so.

Second, we must realize that, by and large, the *systematic* order of the sciences coincides with the *historic* order of reality.[6] This is perhaps the boldest metaphysical assumption common to all the positivisms founded on the rejection of metaphysics. They assume that there are such things as *more or less*

IX. French Positivism

general facts, as if generality were not a thing of the mind. Having thus put metaphysics into physics from the very first moment of their undertaking, they naturally find it easier to handle essentially metaphysical problems in an apparently scientific way. But we must follow Comte if we wish to understand his doctrine.

According to what precedes, positive philosophy presupposes that a choice be made among the sciences: only the fundamental sciences will be retained. Moreover, the systematic order of those sciences will coincide with their historical order of succession. The simplest ones were the first to appear; the succeeding ones followed in an order determined by the increasing complexity of their respective objects. If their systematic classification follows their historical order of formation, sciences will be classified according to an order of increasing complexity. On the other hand, the simpler the object of a science, the more general it is. We call it "general" because, of its nature, it is implied in the objects of all the following sciences, whereas it itself does not imply their own objects. The object of mathematics is implied in that of biology, but the reverse is not true. Biology is less general than mathematics precisely because its object is more complex. Consequently the fundamental sciences will naturally find themselves classified in an order of decreasing generality and of increasing complexity.

The resulting classification is as follows: (1) mathematics; (2) astronomy; (3) physics; (4) chemistry; (5) physiology. Here, however, the philosopher finds himself confronted with an empty place. So far, there have been sciences for all the different orders of reality, with only one exception, the social facts. Writing after Montesquieu and Condorcet, Comte could not easily overlook the empty place left in the system of the sciences by his predecessors. Besides, Saint-Simon and others had already thought of filling it up by imagining a social science based on the universal law of attraction established by Newton. Comte felt therefore obliged to create sociology conceived of as a positive science dealing with the social facts. More complex in its object than all the other sciences, sociology also is less general; it combines the minimum of generality with the maximum of complexity. It had to come last because its object implies all those of the less complex and more general sciences. They had to be constituted first in order that sociology become possible. Owing to Comte, at last, the general scheme of the fundamental sciences has been completed.

The notion of a "social physics" then assumed a decisive importance, for indeed, to him, that was exactly what "sociology" actually was. It became the keystone of his philosophy. His ultimate goal was to provide mankind with a system of ideas capable of uniting all men in a common assent to it; the substance of that system had to be borrowed from science; for that very reason, the philosophical bond of all men could not be formulated before the system of the sciences had been completed; by completing the system of the sciences, then, the discovery of sociology was making it possible to terminate the revolution. By the same token, it was answering the question: on the basis of what system of ideas can a truly organic society be organized in modern terms? Positive philosophy was the answer, and since only the foundation of sociology as a science had made it possible, the vocation of Comte as a social reformer was one in his own mind with his vocation as a creative genius in the field of science. Because he had been another Aristotle, he could become another Saint Paul.

positive philosophy and positive spirit

In order to understand what follows, a new element must be added to the data of the problem. Comte did not only think he was founding sociology as the last and supreme positive science, he also thought that he had practically completed it. This illusion can be accounted for by the deep impact of Newton's physics on the minds of his contemporaries and immediate successors. He did not seem to them to have merely discovered an astronomical law, but rather, they considered him as having provided an answer to all the problems which could be asked by the human mind. The notion of attraction was supposed to be the key to all difficulties. When Comte decided that he had founded sociology, he could easily imagine himself as having also found the universal law in the light of which all the social facts would become intelligible. At any rate, that is what Comte did. In the last volume of his course in positive philosophy, he did not only announce the creation of sociology as a science still to be constituted with work, resources, and time, he simply proceeded to an exposition of the fundamental law from which all the rest would necessarily follow. He taught sociology as a reality in being from the very moment he discovered it.

The fundamental law of sociology is the so-called "law of the three states." Starting from a chance remark made by a physician, Dr. Burdin, Comte had

IX. French Positivism

the intuition that, in all its various spheres of activity (and not in the order of knowledge only), the human mind was subject to a general law of development. This was not to him an arbitrary intuition. On the contrary, Comte considered it as susceptible of a twofold confirmation: on the side of biology, the physiological organization of man could account for it; on the side of history, massive evidence was in favor of it. He stated the great law as follows: "Each and every one of our main conceptions, each branch of knowledge successively passes through three distinct theoretic stages: the *theological* stage, or fictive stage; the *metaphysical* stage, or abstract stage; and the *scientific* stage, or positive stage. Each one of those three stages expresses itself in a distinct way of philosophizing." Those three general systems of conceptions concerning phenomena as a whole exhibit two striking characters—they are mutually exclusive, yet they follow each other in a necessary order: the first one, theology, is the necessary starting point of the human mind; the third one is its fixed and final stage; the second one, the metaphysical stage, is a merely transitional one. Metaphysics is a shadow theology; still, the human intelligence necessarily has to go from theology to science through metaphysics.[7]

In the theological stage the mind directly aims at knowing the intimate nature of things, along with the prime and final causes of that which exists. In short, all its knowledge must be *absolute*. This leads man to account for everything by resorting to a certain number of supernatural agents whose arbitrary intervention explains all the seeming irregularities of nature.

In the metaphysical stage, the supernatural agents are replaced by abstract forces; these are veritable entities, that is "personified abstractions" conceived by man as "inhering in the various beings of the world and as capable of bringing about by themselves all the observed phenomena, so that to explain them then consists in assigning to each one of them its corresponding entity."

In the positive stage, in direct opposition to the theological stage, "nothing is absolute, all is relative," and not ideas only, but things. Renouncing the aim of knowing the origin, substance, and end of things, the intelligence exclusively aims at discovering, by appropriately combining reasoning and observation, the actual *laws* of the phenomena. By the word "laws" Comte means "the invariable *relations* of succession and similitude between phenomena." Whereupon, yielding to another intuition, Comte adds, as if his statement raised no problem, that in the positive stage, the explanation of the phenomena consists only in the bond established between some particular events and some general facts (*faits généraux*) of which the progress of science tends progressively to reduce the number.

History reveals the continuity in development according to that law. The theological system reaches its point of perfection when it substitutes one single god for a multiplicity of divinities; compared to polytheism, monotheism is an almost metaphysical explanation. In the metaphysical stage, after explaining everything by means of a plurality of forces and of causes, the human mind unifies them under the general notion of nature, conceived as the unique source of all phenomena. Nature is an almost scientific notion. "Similarly, the perfection of the positive system, to which it ceaselessly tends, although it is very probable that it will never reach it, would consist in being able to represent to oneself all the diverse observable phenomena as so many particular cases of one single general fact, such as gravitation, for instance."

That last remark gives to the doctrine its true meaning. At the core of that evolution, we find at work only one single force, namely, the positive spirit, which is one with the very essence of the human intellect. The three mutually incompatible philosophies are its work; its presence from the very beginning of that evolution explains the very succession of its three stages, as if the positive spirit were progressively revealing itself to itself through the different stages preparing its final pure manifestation.

Wholly unrelated to Kantianism, the positivism of Comte nonetheless leads to a similar philosophical conclusion: it substitutes the search for laws for the search for causes. In other words, it substitutes science for metaphysics.

Thus understood, positive philosophy exhibits four main characters. First, it is an experimental manifestation of the laws followed by the human mind in the performing of intellectual functions. By the same token, it yields a method, that is, "the precise knowledge of the general rules permitting safely to proceed in the quest of truth." Comte then is a new Descartes.

A second character of positive philosophy is that it will permit a general reorganizing of the system of education. Comte thus falls heir to the eighteenth-century feeling of the need for a new pedagogical ideal. A still theological, metaphysical, and literary education must be replaced by "a positive education, conformable to the spirit of our times and adapted to the needs of modern civilization." General education necessarily rests upon a general and systematic body of human knowledge. Positive philosophy will therefore provide the possibility for a rational education, itself a prelude to social regeneration.

The study of the scientific generalities is not only destined to reorganize education, it also will contribute to the particular progress of the various positive sciences. This mission, imparted to positive philosophy, to improve the positive sciences clearly shows how distinct the two notions of science and of philosophy remain in the doctrine of Comte. Positive philosophy thus assumes the traditional function of wisdom conceived as a judge of the particular disciplines. Exclusive specialization is one of the evils philosophy has to contend with in the minds of modern scientists. To learn all the sciences as if one wanted to know each one for itself is an impossible undertaking. In this sense a truly scientific education is today impossible even for the best possible minds placed in the best possible situation to learn. By reducing the ultimate conclusions of the sciences to one systematic whole, positive philosophy therefore makes possible an integrated system of education.

The fourth and by far the most important character of the new philosophy is that "it can be considered as the only solid basis for the social reorganization which must bring to an end the state of crisis in which the more civilized nations have found themselves for a long time." This social function of Comte's philosophy exactly fits the certitude he had of having invented sociology as a science. It also justifies his intervention in the structure of the positive sciences in order to ordain them to the practical end of the doctrine. This is what prevents Comte's positivism from being a mere scientism. In short, it is this feature that justifies calling the positivism of Comte a philosophy.

positive philosophy and positive politic
We are now reaching the core of Comte's philosophical difficulties. Can a philosophy be extracted from science without betraying either science or philosophy?

As Comte conceived it, positive philosophy was to be a philosophy innocent of metaphysics; hence his decision to borrow its substance from science. One of the permanently significant parts of his doctrine is the discovery he made that, such as he found it, science itself was full of metaphysics. An instance of the fact is the mathematical notion of infinity, which means one thing for Leibniz, another thing for Newton, still another one for Lagrange, and so on. In discussing its concept, Comte reaches the conclusion that the demonstration given by Leibniz was very confused and unsatisfactory; on the other hand, the conception of transcendent analysis by Lagrange was of an admirable simplicity; in fact, however, the conception of Leibniz, which rests upon the wrong idea, shows itself far superior to that of Lagrange when it is a question of applying it to the solution of a given problem. Despite its intrinsic superiority, "the conception of Lagrange nevertheless remains, on the whole, essentially unsuitable for applications."[8] Science itself then still stood in need of undergoing a positivist purification, and it was not going to be an easy task, since, in some important cases, error seemed to be in it a condition of its very fecundity.

Another consideration entailed still more decisive philosophical interventions in the body of positive sciences. The question was for Comte to extract from it an encyclopedic system of ideas systematized and graspable by one single mind. In consequence, Comte strictly limited not only the number of the fundamental sciences but also that of the questions to be handled within each one of them. To be eliminated were all the questions not susceptible of positive answers, that is to say, of answers justifiable by logical reasoning about observable facts. For instance, Comte did not approve of any inquiries concerning the composition of the planets; because, in his own time, spectroscopy did not exist, he considered vain all suppositions concerning such objects. For the same reason of intellectual economy, he wanted to simplify the unnecessarily complicated sciences. For instance, he thought that chemistry could, and should, be reconstructed on the basis of two elements only. But the decisive intervention of philosophy in scientific knowledge was tied up with its ultimate social destination.[9]

The last constituted science was sociology. In the mind of Comte, this meant that the science of human facts was the best vantage point from which to systematize the ultimate conclusions of all the other ones. As the most complex order of facts, the social facts cannot be understood apart from all the preceding order of facts. Consequently, in the study of the other fundamental sciences, preference should be given to that which, in their objects, prepares the way for sociology. For instance, in astronomy, there is no point in studying stars and planets the knowledge of which has no practical bearing on human life. By limiting itself to the study of the sun and of the moon, astronomy would serve its only useful purpose, because those are the only astronomical bodies that directly affect the "human planet," earth. It can therefore be said that positive

IX. French Positivism

philosophy spontaneously oriented itself toward man and his habitat as toward its objectively given end. Whether or not that primacy of man in nature can be considered a fact, and a scientifically observable fact, is another question. At any rate, Comte himself entertained no doubts on the point.[10]

In order to fulfill the second part of his life program and to complete the new Aristotle by a new Saint Paul, Comte had always foreseen that two more conditions should be fulfilled, but he could not foresee under what particular circumstances their fulfillment would take place. He had always known that to the force of truth, conceived of as the common bond of society, there should be added the force of love. In the second part of his career, in consequence of his violent love for a young woman whose consent he failed to win, and who died a premature death, Comte more and more stressed the primacy of feeling over knowledge.[11] One gets tired of knowing, Comte would then say, one never tires of loving. Hence his ceaselessly repeated assertion that, after positive philosophy has been formulated and completed, feeling and heart must take precedence over knowledge and understanding.[12]

A society of all the nations having already reached the positivist level of mental development should therefore be organized. Its motto would be: Order and Progress. Order would then be provided by the truth of positive philosophy, the sole system of ideas capable of winning the universal assent of all men. The revolution would thus be effectively terminated. Just as order would be the means of establishing such a society, progress would be its end, for indeed progress is the unfolding of order. The active force of that development naturally had to be love, that is to say the love of man for man. Not however for any particular man, but rather for humanity as a whole. Humanity first was to Comte the collective body of all men[13] past, present, and future, who have reached the positive level of intellectual development defined by positive philosophy. Humanity consists of a much larger number of dead men than of living men; it is a City of Man, a kind of positivist duplicate of the Christian City of God.

In the last part of his life. Comte completely subordinated the positive philosophy to its social and political end. He went so far as to turn it into a religion. Since the law of the three states is irrevocable in its effects, there was for Comte no going back to the god of the theological state nor to that of the metaphysical state; so there was to be no god at all; mankind needed a religion in order to be really organized and united, but it only could have a godless and atheistic religion. In fact, according to the doctrine itself, the only possible object of worship for man is man. Accordingly, Comte finally raised the human race to the dignity of the Great Being; positivism itself became a religion and a church in which a body of learned men (neither theologians nor scientists but Positivist Philosophers) took the place of the Catholic clergy and provided the "spiritual power" necessary for the guidance of mankind to its natural and temporal end. The *Catéchisme positiviste* (*Positivist Catechism*) of Comte, along with its program of positivist sacraments, of positivist feasts celebrated according to the positivist calendar set up by Comte himself, and even with its ritual to be some day adopted by all the nations of the earth, is a concrete expression of Comte's earnestness in his effort to replace the worship of God by the worship of Humanity.

The lesson to be drawn from his last writings is a twofold one. First, that science can provide no unified set of conclusions unless its observer adopts on it a point of view exterior to the body of scientific knowledge. In short, there can be no such thing as an objective scientific synthesis. Hence the title of the last and unfinished work of Comte, *La synthèse subjective*. The conclusions of the various sciences can be unified only from the point of view of the love of man for humanity ordering them with reference to mankind. This is a usage of science which science itself neither prescribes nor teaches. Second, even for a positivist mind, it is not easy to invent a new religion without copying an old one. The cult of Humanity and the positivist church were little else than a shadowy duplicate of the religion of Christ embodied in the Catholic Church. The last years of Comte show him wholly lost in his dream of a future universal society of men, with its nucleus constituted by an Occidental Republic, its capital first in Paris, later on in Constantinople, with a money and a navy of its own, living in peace under the spiritual leadership of its positivist clergy and of its positivist pope, the High Priest of Humanity, rightful successor of Auguste Comte.

the disintegration of french positivism

Comte left behind him a complex situation. His immediate influence was very restricted. Neither a professor of mathematics nor a professor of philosophy, he taught his doctrine to a mixed public in which noted scientists sat side by side

IX. French Positivism

with small employees, shopkeepers, and even a few workers. But there was in his doctrine a wealth of ideas that could not fail to attract attention.

The doctrine intended to be "positive," that is to say, affirmative, in opposition to the negative and predominantly critical philosophy of the preceding century. Moreover, it was anti-metaphysical, its positive nature consisting in accepting no conclusion that was not logically justified and supported by scientific observation.

On the other hand, the doctrine intended to be a philosophy, even a wisdom exercising all the prerogatives traditionally attached to the title, to wit, to order and unify the various sciences by relating them to one and the same end. Incidentally, the positive philosophy had a right to submit the sciences to a constructive criticism in order to insure their perfect positivity.

In elaborating his doctrine, Comte had had to take for granted many notions he finally left unexplained. His main assumption was that the world of positive philosophy is composed of hierarchically disposed layers of reality, a higher one always including all that was included in the lower ones, plus a new element proper to itself. Comte considered this feature as essential to his doctrine; its rejection was what he called "materialism," which he defined as an attempt to account for the superior by the inferior in all domains. As a positivist, Comte could take that huge fact for granted; as a philosopher, he could not very well leave it unexplained, and some of his successors will start from there in effecting their return to metaphysics.

In fine, Comte had crowned his positive philosophy with a project for the unification of mankind under the leadership of a new "spiritual power," the priests of positivism, themselves submitted to the High Priest of Humanity. This is where the tension between Comte and his first disciples first reached its breaking point. Among the best ones, many who had willingly followed him as long as he was elaborating a positive philosophy, refused to accept his positive politics, and, of course, his positive religion. Among the rebels was John Stuart Mill, whom Comte called his "eminent friend." After the publication of Mill's *System of Logic Ratiocinative and Inductive* (1843), Comte considered him as "henceforward fully associated to the direct foundation of the new philosophy," but Mill himself finally parted company with Comte. In France, Emile Littré likewise refused to follow.[14] Comte was deeply disappointed by those defections. He really believed in his religious mission. As he once wrote to a friend:

"I feel persuaded that, before the year 1860, I shall be preaching positivism in Notre Dame as the only real and complete religion."[15] Things did not work that way and, today, little more is left of Comte's religion than the original positivist chapel in Paris and the positivist motto, *Order and Progress*, on the Brazilian flag.

Soon after Comte's death, the very body of positive philosophy began to disintegrate, each particular science reasserting its independence and separating itself from the others. In France, the movement took two directions, psychology and sociology.

Positive Psychology

As has been said above, Comte did not recognize the existence of psychology as a distinct science. He even objected that its method was impossible by definition since, in order to observe himself by introspection, a man has to be both observing and observed at one and the same time, which is impossible. But he could think of a positive study of man as a living organism and as a fellow of human society. This was inviting a return to Cabanis and to the tradition, deeply rooted in France, which links psychology to physiology and to medicine.

Hippolyte Taine[16] spontaneously entered that way. He was no disciple of Comte, but he provides an excellent example of the kind of positively minded speculation whose general tendency it is to reduce philosophical thinking to the methods of straight scientific reasoning. The temptation is irresistible. Science has progressively mastered so many fields of research hitherto exploited by conventional philosophical speculation that one wonders why all problems should not be handled in a scientific way. You never can tell till you try. Taine's first significant book had the value of a manifesto. In attacking, with great literary talent and philosophical insight, the "philosophers of the nineteenth century," he sounded the death knoll of what could be called the literary, or eloquent, school of French philosophy.[17] The book presented itself as "a book of refutation, not of theory." It started from the fact that in France (as well as in England and Germany) there were two types of philosophy: spiritualism, for the use of men with a literary culture, a philosophy which considers "causes" or "forces" as distinct entities permitting the taking account of the nature and structure of beings; and the philosophy of the scientists, who account for everything by

IX. French Positivism 313

resorting to observation and logical reasoning. Thus far, Taine was merely repeating Comte, but he had an objection even to the scientific part of positivism. Comte had considered metaphysical the notions of cause and of force; as metaphysical, they had to be expelled from positive philosophy; consequently, Comte had declared impossible and without an object the investigation of natural forces and natural causes. Taine felt unwilling to follow either the spiritualists in their attempt to duplicate the real world of beings by an imaginary world of causes and forces, or the positivists in their decision never to ask questions about such problems as the cause of life, the cause of the universe, etc. The thing to do was to identify the causes with the facts. Were it proved that the causes are the facts, spiritualism and positivism would be refuted at once; one single notion would then be substituted for the older methods of explication. Hence, in Taine's doctrine, the importance is attributed to the notion of "general facts."[18]

Since they account for other facts, "general" facts are causes, and since they are facts, their notion is innocent of metaphysical implications. Here, however, two remarks should be made. First, the notion of general facts was already familiar to Comte. Next, it was not growing more precise in passing from Comte to Taine. Like all the philosophical notions borrowed by scientism, it does not become scientific simply by losing its philosophical meaning. The influence of the book on the teaching of philosophy in France was deep and lasting. The spiritualism of Cousin became at once a sort of antiquated and slightly ridiculous way of thinking. Taine made it possible for teachers of philosophy to present themselves as the supporters of a "positive" philosophy without getting entangled in the personal system of Comte, and, above all, his religion.

Apart from his critical survey of classical spiritualism, Taine attempted to provide a scientific description of the functioning of the human mind. His book, now known under the simplified title *L'intelligence*, was in fact a new version of the kind of analysis of mind several times attempted by Locke, Condillac, Destutt de Tracy, and many other ideologists. This time, however, the task was supposed to be carried out in a genuinely scientific spirit, using all the resources physiology had placed at the disposal of psychology since the death of Cabanis. Of course, no metaphysical notion was to be admitted.

In Taine's own language, "intelligence" means the "faculty of knowing." By faculty, or power, or capacity, nothing more should be understood than all the facts belonging in the specific class designated by any one of those words. There are "general characters" signified by general ideas. They constitute the "fixed and uniform portion of existence. They are not mere abstract conceptions or fictions of our mind. The more general they are, the more abstract they are."[19] Contenting himself with this classical description of abstract and general ideas, Taine proceeds to his own description of the nature and functions of the mind.

The method will be "analysis." The word recalls Condillac. In fact, in his Preface to *L'intelligence*, Taine expressly noted that the best interpretation of the right method had already been suspected by Condillac but forgotten ever since.[20] For once, however, Taine acknowledges that the analysis of intelligence raises the "metaphysical" problem of the existence of the external world. For indeed we affirm it, and it is not clear on what ground. But perhaps there is a way out of the trouble. Mathematicians admit that real quantity is but a particular case of imaginary quantity. Could not we imagine that real existence is but one particular case of possible existence? Cannot we suppose that actual existence is the particular and singular case occurring when the elements of possible existence fulfill certain conditions that are lacking in other cases? "Should this be granted could not we seek after those elements and those conditions? Here we find ourselves on the threshold of metaphysics. We shall not enter it."

The answer to that metaphysical problem would be the keystone of the whole structure, but intellectual knowledge can be described without it. It essentially consists of judgments. Those judgments are couples of general ideas which themselves are mental images exhibiting an aptitude to evoke a certain class of memories. A mental image is a spontaneously reviving sensation; each sensation is made up of smaller elementary sensations and so on indefinitely. We are therefore well founded in admitting the existence of infinitesimal sensations, all alike and which, by their various arrangements, produce the diversity of the sensible world. It is enough to conceive of those elements as bound together by the elementary laws of the association of ideas in order to account for the whole structure of intelligence.

Such is, at least, the point of view of intellectual knowledge on intelligence, that is to say, in the last analysis, on itself. But instead of looking at intelligence from within, we can consider it from without. We then apply to the external, but objective, testimony of sense. According to it, all the preceding events consist of molecular movements of the cerebral cells. In both cases however, if we proceed to analyze the whole bulk of intelligence into its component elements,

IX. French Positivism 315

the result is the same. By successive decompositions, analysis leads to the ultimate elements of knowledge, after which it becomes easy to see how they combine. Made up of groups of elementary sensations, the global sensations are duplicated (Taine says *repeated*) in the cerebral lobes under the form of their own images.

> Enjoying the property of reviving spontaneously, those images associate and evoke one another according to their more or less strong tendency to revive. By associating, they form groups. Those groups themselves are more or less complex, but in all cases they are tied up with certain sensations, or they are tied up with one another. According to the nature and degree of their respective affinity or of their antagonism, those complex groups of sensations, of memories, of previsions, or of simple concepts constitute what we call the acts of consciousness properly so called. At the end comes the sign, which stands for the concepts and permits the formation of general ideas and of general judgments. It is just about the same as in the case of a cathedral. In the last analysis, a cathedral is just a heap of sand; but the grains of sand are pressed into stones; by counterbalancing their opposite weights, those stones remain attached two by two and group by group until they make up the cathedral. So also, in us, all those associations, all those pressures order themselves into a vast harmony.[21]

This easily satisfied conception of man's intelligence, especially in its association with the psychology of Spencer, will constitute the background of the Bergsonian reaction. Of course, it is tempting to achieve a purely mechanistic interpretation of intellectual life, but in the case of a cathedral, besides sand, stone, and forces, there is an architect. In Taine's supposition, the architect himself is but another spontaneously formed cathedral and so on indefinitely. Such mechanistic interpretations of nature sometimes look like truncated demonstrations of the existence of God.

The same tendency to reduce the complexity of reality to that of a complicated mechanism makes itself felt in Taine's *La philosophie de l'art*. A large part of his philosophical reflection was a long and ceaselessly renewed effort to identify the causes of the masterpieces bequeathed to us by the writers, sculptors, painters, and other artists of old. Music does not seem to have detained his attention with the same intensity as literature and painting. Whatever the subject he happened to handle, the method was the same. It was for him a question of analyzing the work of art into elements, each of which had to be related to a certain cause. At the end of the process, the work of art had been explained away.

In Taine's own view, his esthetics was "modern," and it differed from the old one in that it was historical, and not dogmatic; it was not prescribing precepts; simply, it was taking stock of laws. At the beginning of his lecture course on the history of the arts, Taine specified the way he would understand his task: "My only duty is to expose before you facts, and to tell you how those facts came to pass. The modern method which I am trying to follow, and which begins to introduce itself into all the moral sciences, consists in considering all the works of man, especially the works of art, as so many facts. They are products the characters and causes of which we must set down; nothing more. Thus understood, science neither prescribes nor forbids; it takes notice and explains."

Generally speaking, a work of art is calculated to cause in us a pleasurable sensation. The cause of the pleasure it gives us is beauty. The beautiful therefore is relative to our aptitude to perceive it. Availing himself of his general conception of nature and intelligence (the perception of "general facts"), Taine describes the work of art as "aiming at manifesting some essential and striking feature, and therefore some important idea, more completely than is done by natural objects. In order to achieve that end, it employs an ensemble of connected parts, whose proportions it systematically modifies. In the three arts of imitation, sculpture, painting, and poetry, those ensembles correspond to real objects."

Such being the object of art, artistic production observes the following law: "The work of art is determined by an ensemble which is the general state of the mind (*l'état général de l'esprit*) and the surrounding way of life." The philosophy of art thus becomes a particular case of the general philosophy of history and of civilization. At every moment of history, the institutions and the genius of a particular people are determined by three main factors: the race, the social environment (the *milieu*), and the moment. Historical analysis permits the determination of the value of each one of those factors for each and every one of the forms of art recorded by history. Taken together, those factors determine a state of mind proper to each successive period in the history of a society; on account

IX. French Positivism

of its peculiar state of mind, each society also has a "preferred pleasure" at each typical moment of its history; the works of art produced during one of those historical periods aim at causing the kind of pleasure contemporaries desire to feel. By applying that method to all the favorable cases, which are obviously many, Taine established its truth for the history of the arts in antiquity and in modern times.[22]

Who would deny the too-obvious fact that the works of an artist bear the mark of the general condition of culture proper to his epoch and to his country? The method of explanation is not only legitimate, it is unavoidable. The question remains, however, of whether it does not leave out the essential data of the problem, namely, the artist. As has been observed, the race, the *milieu*, and the historical moment were the same for a great many contemporaries of Shakespeare, yet there was only one Shakespeare. To fill up the gap, Taine resorts to what he calls a "dominant quality"; in Shakespeare's particular case, imagination; but many contemporaries of Shakespeare were not wanting in imagination; only they did not have the imagination of Shakespeare, and how is our esthetics going to account for that?

Taine had lost his religious faith at the age of twelve; science then had offered him a sort of vicarious system of beliefs. In order to find some satisfaction in it, he had had to resort to a rejuvenated form of naturalism as well as to the optimism which permits only the discovery of intelligibility and order in the scientific description of nature. His psychology precisely expressed his confidence in the aptitude of reality to organize itself in an intelligible way. His esthetics presupposed that beauty is in nature before being in art, so much so that the ideal beauty of nature ultimately remains in his doctrine the source of the ideal beauty in art. Through Comte, and beyond Comte, Taine goes back to the naturalistic optimism of the eighteenth century.[23]

After Taine, psychology more and more strongly stresses the part played by physiological information and by the clinical observation of mental cases. In this respect, Taine certainly anticipates the psychology of Ribot[24] and of his modern French successors, such as Pierre Janet, Georges Dumas, Charles Blondel, and others, all fully qualified physicians and specialists in mental pathology as well as professional philosophers.[25] The very continuity of that medical trend in French psychology probably accounts for the more lukewarm welcome given in France to Freud and to his doctrine. Freudism has mainly been in France a theme reserved for novelists and for art critics; psychologists could not forgive it the arbitrary and shifting nature of its fundamental notions and explanations.

Positive Sociology

The keystone of Comte's positivism had been his foundation of sociology as a positive science, that is, in his own words, of a "social physics." His successors undertook to free sociology as a science from its cumbersome connections with positive religion and positive politics. They likewise observed that, even supposing Comte had correctly understood the nature of sociology, he could not possibly have been right in imagining that he himself had completed the new science at the very time he had founded it. There was no reason why the development of sociology should not require as many centuries as that of mathematics and physics. Dealing with more complex objects, it should have required a still longer time in order to build up the complete structure of the new science. One should perhaps rather say that, as is the case with every new science, Comte should have foreseen for sociology a future of indefinite progress.

In France, the notion of sociology conceived of as a positive science still to be constituted by observation and scientific demonstration first appeared toward the end of the century with Emile Durkheim.[26] His *Règles de la méthode sociologique* (*Rules of the Sociological Method*) established him as the head of a new school of thought whose official organs were the *Année sociologique* and the collection *Les travaux de l'année sociologique*.

Durkheim felt justified in considering sociology as a positive science because it dealt with an objective order of facts. Facts are objective when they exhibit a nature which remains stable in itself independently of the observer. Social phenomena are like that. Every man finds himself inserted in a social group from which he holds his general view on the world and his general rules of conduct. In fact, he owes that social group all his tastes, all his spontaneous convictions as to the proper ways of feeling and of acting. As societies grow more complex, man usually belongs to several social groups at one and the same time. Conflicts of loyalties are then bound to arise. There is not one of us that does not belong to at least two social groups, his family and his nation. His church usually comes as a third group, but there are many others. The gist of

IX. French Positivism

Durkheim's sociology is that each and every social group naturally produces, as a sort of secretion, collective representations, beliefs, and rules of behavior which constitute the very substance of what we call the individual minds. In this sense, man does not make society, but rather society makes man.

A mere glance at the human condition shows that Durkheim's views are at least partially justified. Peoples, professions, families, and individuals differ because each group is definable by a set of intellectual, moral, and social ideas and habits which make it the particular group it is. Individuals all are more or less representatives of one or several such groups. The collective representations (views of the world) and the social imperatives (collectively adopted rules of conduct) are the social facts. They are objective facts because we find them ready-made for us, we cannot change them at will, rather we are subjected to them as to a binding authority. The proof of it is that any attempt to violate such imperatives is attended by some punishment, just as, on the contrary, docility to the social code of thought and conduct is rewarded by recompense. The importance attributed by Durkheim and his school to the study of primitive societies is due to the fact that, in them, such notions as that of taboo clearly reveal the true nature of social facts. To violate a taboo is to risk punishment; but even civilized men live surrounded with taboos, as we know from bitter experience.

The objective reality of social facts lies in their compelling force, and that force itself is evidenced by the sanctions which make them respected. Sanctions are twofold in kind, retributive or punitive. Retributive sanctions are here understood in the sense of rewards destined to acknowledge merit, or of any system of equity insuring the respect of justice in human relations. Punitive sanctions themselves divide into two classes: the organized sanctions, intentionally set up by society for the repression of crime (death, prison, fines, etc.) and diffuse sanctions, which are spontaneous reactions of the social group against the infringements of its own code. A simple example of such diffuse sanctions is the ease of "ridicule." The nonconformist in dress, in manners, in speech, and in opinions can expect to be punished by the unpleasantly manifested disapproval of his group. One always can do what "is not done," but there is a price to pay for it. Social customs, traditions, received conventions, have a way of asserting their own existence and of making themselves respected. Whatever their particular forms, sanctions always attest the objective reality of social facts.

From the very beginning, Durkheim was aware of raising a new problem whose solution was not easy to find: if human rules of opinion and conduct are determined by the social groups, what will become of ethics? Each member of the sociological school applied himself to the problem. Lucien Lévy-Bruhl[27] solved it in a very simple way. Sociology, according to Comte, is another name for social physics. Now in physics do we ask what the laws of nature ought to be? No, the question would be absurd; we only ask what those laws actually are. The same remark should apply to all the so-called problems of morality. If sociology is duly constituted, ethics (*la morale*) will be replaced by a *science des moeurs*. To the question, What should I do? there is no answer. Societies tell us what to do; moral obligation is a given and an empirically observable fact. Another friend of Durkheim, Frédéric Rauh[28] never contented himself with that answer. His point was that, even in dealing with physical nature, science is not enough; there is an art of using our knowledge of physical laws and of imagining the various ends we should have in view in pursuing their possible applications. The problems besetting the use to be made of our knowledge of nuclear physics well show the nature of the difficulty. Lévy-Bruhl was of the opinion that society would solve the problem for us. Rauh preferred to think that a sort of moral engineering, or of moral art, would remain necessary even after the constitution of social physics.

Durkheim himself always believed that there was no problem. A born moralist, he did not feel interested in building up a speculative structure without practical applications. Sociology should help man to better his life at least as much as physics and biology were helping him to do so. Far from seeing any opposition between the scientific nature of sociology and its practical usefulness, Durkheim insisted that sociology would help *because* it had become a science. Whether or not ethics had a transcendent end inaccessible to observation was to him a metaphysical problem with which he was in no way concerned, for indeed, social facts being what they are, sociology could not possibly be modified by any answer given to that problem. On the contrary, Durkheim was very much concerned with the practical consequences of the new sociology: "From the fact that our first intention is to study reality, it does not follow that we do not intend to better it. Our research efforts would not be worth one hour of trouble if they had no other interest than a merely speculative one. If we carefully separate the theoretic problems from the practical ones, the reason is not

IX. French Positivism

that we are not interested in the latter; on the contrary, it is in order to be able to find for them a better solution."

The problem remained, however, to pass from the objective description of sociological reality to the formulation of rules of conduct in view of a better future, and here the example of physics is not enough because, precisely, the problem of how to make use of scientific knowledge in the order of physics or biology is included within the wider problem of how to make a morally good use of it.

Durkheim's answer is that "science can help us to find the direction we should follow in our conduct and to determine the ideal toward which we are confusedly tending; we shall raise ourselves to that ideal only after duly observing reality and extracting its notion from it." In the last analysis, the justification Durkheim invokes for his attitude is that we cannot do otherwise. The ideal has no basis except reality; the idealists themselves start from some aspiration of their heart, which is but a fact, and they turn it into an imperative to which their reason bows. Of course, they want us to bow to it too; why should we not wish to study the nature of that fact before concluding that it provides the legitimate foundation for a moral duty?

How then are we to find the rules whereby to judge the facts? Such rules will reveal themselves through contact with sociological facts. We need no special rules to judge whether an organ is healthy or not; physiology tells us what it is for an organ to be healthy and medicine tells us what to do in order to restore organs to a healthy condition, if need be. There also is a state of moral health, and we know very well what it is. Science can determine for us its conditions, and since it is never found fully realized, one already can consider an ideal our desire to achieve and to perfect it. Moreover, the conditions of moral health change because societies themselves are changing. The more difficult moral problems we have to solve consist precisely in determining what the new moral ideal should be in terms of the changes that took place in the social environment. By providing us with the knowledge of similar variations that already took place in the past, science makes it easier for us to anticipate those that are now taking place. Lastly, by comparing the normal with itself, we shall realize that it contains some contradictions, that is to say, some imperfections. To redress them or to eliminate them is another task for sociology to fulfill. It is a strictly scientific one, and we need no other foundation for ethics.[29]

This at least can be said in favor of Durkheim's position, that his sociology certainly implied for him a definite system of ethics. Whether or not he was philosophically justified in thinking that, provided only man wants to live, things should be just as they are, is another question. The fact is that this simple observation opened to him a vista of moral obligations attended by perfectly legitimate sanctions. Man not only *is* engaged in groups, but since he is he *ought to be*, and the more he is the better. The first book of Durkheim, *De la division du travail social*, dealt with the evident fact of the increasing division of work in societies. It is a necessity, therefore it is good. Durkheim wanted to establish that far from progressively leading to the destruction of personality, the always more marked specialization of human activities makes for more unity at the same time as it makes for more diversity. Durkheim envisioned a society whose main duty would be for it to be itself as perfectly as possible, and for each one of us to find his own place in it and to fill it well. The exclusive duty of man no longer is to achieve the qualities of man in general; he also is bound in conscience to achieve the qualities proper to his own employment in society. Linder its social aspect, the categoric imperative of moral conscience is progressively assuming the following form: *Render yourself capable of usefully fulfilling a determined function.*[30] As a matter of fact, all the members of the Durkheimian school whose political affiliations are known were socialists. Taken in itself, even that was a sociological fact.

An interesting by-product of Comte's positivism, the sociology of Durkheim itself disintegrated into still more positive sciences. Its more recent representatives seem to have exchanged sociology for ethnology, a legitimate and interesting development indeed, but which has for its result that, in France, sociology now belongs in the history of science rather than in the history of philosophy.

Philosophical Reflection on Science

Comte's effort to demetaphysicize the sciences of his own times had led him to some of the most interesting conclusions of his philosophy. As he was hastening to his sociological conclusions, he did not dwell on the subject. After him, many French scientists, or philosophers with a good scientific foundation, undertook to formulate philosophical conclusions on the basis of what positive

IX. *French Positivism*

science says about man and the world. It is typical of such thinkers that, without a philosophical system of their own, and simply carrying beyond the field of science their scientific methods of thinking, they contented themselves with saying what it is sensible for a scientist to say when he asks himself certain philosophical questions. Their attitude is very different from scientism; they do not reduce human knowledge to scientific knowledge, but, rather, they question the nature and value of scientific knowledge, especially in its application to its own objects and to nonscientific objects as well.

Since not all of them can be quoted here, we wish to single out the name of Cournot,[31] a scientist and philosopher from whom every man interested in philosophy has a great deal to learn about the true nature of scientific knowledge.

As Cournot sees it, philosophy is a reflection on science. In this sense, it is a sort of positivism, but it differs from that of Comte in many ways. First of all, it is not a system. One could perhaps say that it is less philosophical than the positivism of Comte, in that it more closely adheres to science. For the same reason, the doctrine of Cournot does not aim to reform society; its only scope is to coordinate and to classify the highest conclusions formed by reason at its best, that is to say, of science.

All knowledge unifies by ordering. Cournot likes to quote the words of Bossuet: "The relation of reason and order is intimate. Order is the friend of reason and its very object." On the other hand, yielding to one of the deepest aspirations of metaphysical realism, Cournot considers the order present in minds as a reflection of the order there is in things. More precisely still, reason itself is in us an effect of what of order there is in the material world. In short, and always for the same cause, the order in the mind cannot be different in kind from the order in things. As Bacon said, in a sentence which Cournot is not less fond of quoting than that of Bossuet, human knowledge must be conceived by analogy with the universe, *ex analogia universi*.

Applying this principle to his philosophical interpretation of science, Cournot sees probability as the proper nature of human knowledge. This is indeed a philosophical conclusion, not a scientific one, because science has for its object relations between extended, determined, and measurable objects, whereas philosophy deals with the conclusions and the methods of the sciences, which are not objects of that sort. At the same time, it is a conclusion founded on science, and, through science, on reality.

There is probability in science because probability first is in things. It is there under the form of *chance*. Most of us consider chance as the result of some imperfection in our cognition of reality. Chance is something deeper and more real. Rather than our ignorance, it signifies (as Aristotle had already pointed out) that which follows from the meeting of mutually independent causes. There is not enough chance in the universe to make laws impossible. In point of fact, regularity prevails, which indeed is why there is a universe. However we may produce irregular and conflicting motions, in air and water for instance, regularity and uniformity will set in of their own accord. "Now wherever there is regularity, constancy, order, there no doubt is a reason, that is a law; for if it were chance, the chance would be prodigious, unbelievable. If, beyond what we have been able to observe, there is a law, facts will still conform to it; they always will, and this is verified by experience. On the other hand, if there is any chance in the world, in no case will knowledge be perfectly certain; it will never be more than more or less probable. Probability can be, so to speak, infinite; and infinite probability, physically speaking, amounts to reality, just as the contrary probability, if it is infinite, is the physical impossibility; still, logically speaking, it is only probability."

The great merit of Cournot was to realize the utmost importance of the two notions of probability and of statistical knowledge, whose scientific importance is evident today. He had no intention of denying world order nor of substituting mere probability for certitude. Cournot simply wanted to make it clear that there remains an element of probability in all certitude, because there always is room for a measure of chance in the objectively given order of things. In his own mind, this was to rationalize chance much more than to deprive rational knowledge of its necessity.

Cournot is a good example of what can be the view of the world suggested to the mind of a scientist by his own interpretation of scientific knowledge. His own critique is a probabilism, or, rather, a "probabiliorism." To him, all knowledge is relative, just as was the case with Comte and Kant. But the reason for his relativism is not, as it is in positivism, that knowledge bears upon relations only; nor is it, as in Kantianism, that knowledge is *a priori* determined by the two forms of sensibility, space and time; on the contrary, probability is all in favor of their objectivity. Nor is there any probability in the *a priori* nature of the so-called "categories." These are known *a posteriori* and should rather be

IX. *French Positivism*

called "fundamental ideas" as being the more general among the ideas discovered and experimentally confirmed by science. They are called "fundamental" with respect to scientific knowledge. The fundamental ideas also differ from categories in that they are not the same in all the sciences. From mathematics to mechanics, astronomy, physics, biology, and sociology there is an addition of one fundamental idea every time one passes from a lower science to a higher one. In each particular case, science has empirically to ascertain which ideas can be extended from one order of reality to another one. This careful probabilism justifies Cournot in maintaining that the truth about man's destiny cannot be accounted for in terms of what is true for the orders of reality known by positive science only. The fundamental ideas valid for the order of nature do not apply to the supernatural order.

A more recent witness to a similar state of mind was Emile Meyerson.[32] In a succession of books all leading to the same conclusion, Meyerson has attempted to establish that scientific explanation is dominated by the mind's obscure desire to equate intelligibility and identity. His critical examination of the leading scientific hypotheses is very impressive indeed. The title of his best-known work, *Identité et réalité* (1908) clearly defines the problem he never ceased to scrutinize. Science investigates reality, and it expresses its findings in terms of equalities and, in the last analysis, of identities. But identity cannot be the last word about reality, otherwise nothing would happen and there would be neither causality, nor quality, nor novelty in nature. The likely metaphysical implication of Meyerson's criticism of science was a realistic ontology anxious to vindicate against idealism the rights of causality and quality. In fact, Meyerson seems to have intentionally avoided committing himself on such metaphysical points. When asked by friends about the possible metaphysical implications of his own interpretation of science, he simply refused to answer. But metaphysicians are not hampered by such scruples and they can find in Meyerson many a fruitful subject of reflection.

X. *Maine de Biran's French Posterity*

In a letter to Paul Janet, Paris, December 8, 1891, Jules Lachelier called to his attention the part played by Ravaisson in the French philosophical movement of the times. "It seems to me," Lachelier said, "that it was Ravaisson who taught us all to conceive of being, not under the *objective* forms of substances and phenomena, but under the *subjective* form of spiritual action, whether, by the way, the latter be ultimately conceived of as an action of thought or as an action of will." To which Lachelier added: "I believe you would find this notion in M. Bergson, and even in M. Ribot, as well as in M. Boutroux and in my own doctrine. That might well be the only notion, common to us all, that gives its unity to the philosophical movement of these last twenty years. I need not remind you of the article in the *Revue des deux-mondes* where M. Ravaisson said this in 1840. He then traced back the movement to the philosophy of Maine de Biran. There is there, I believe, a starting point."[1]

The same view can be supported from another angle. The nineteenth-century French philosophers roughly divide into two groups according to whether their first formation was predominantly mathematical (École Polytechnique, Paris): Comte, Renouvier, Cournot, etc.; or philosophical (Sorbonne, École Normale Supérieure): Cousin, Lachelier, Boutroux, Bergson, etc. Maine de Biran had been a free lance. Of the latter group, not one was wanting in scientific knowledge; some of them, like Boutroux and Bergson, were well versed in the science of the time, but they did not metaphysicize from positive science as a base.[2] All of them were looking for the starting point of their philosophy in an inner act intuited by the subject.

X. Maine de Biran's French Posterity

Félix Ravaisson

The example set up by Maine de Biran was followed by Ravaisson[3] in a small number of writings whose influence has been decisive in the history of French philosophy. The knowledge of self gained by introspection remained for him the fundamental method in philosophy. By the word "self," however, one should not understand the mind, or the soul, to the exclusion of the body. Again like Maine de Biran. Ravaisson is well informed on the works of Bichat (*Recherches physiologiques sur la vie et la mort*, 1800), but his preference goes to the writings of the "vitalists" even though, as is often the case with this class of biologists, their speculation leans toward occultism. Three names frequently reappear under the pen of Ravaisson: J.-B. Van Helmont, a Belgian (1577–1644); G. E. Stahl, a German (1660–1734); and P.-J. Barthez, a Frenchman (1734–1806).

Of Van Helmont's works, Ravaisson quotes the *Ortus medicinae* (1618), especially that part of it which deals with the "archean principles" of diseases (*De morbis archealibus*). According to Van Helmont, each particular physiological function is directed by a sort of secondary soul, or *archaea*. Of G. E. Stahl, Ravaisson quotes the *De motu tonicovitali* (1692), the *Theoria medica vera* (1707), and the *Negotium otiosum, seu skiamakhia* (1720), written in defense of his own doctrine against Leibniz. Stahl replaces the "archean principles" of Van Helmont with one single soul which, being the principle of life, is also the most important agent in curing diseases. Of his compatriot Barthez, Ravaisson knows the *Nouveaux éléments de la science de l'homme* (1778) and the *Traité du beau* (1807). According to Barthez (and his "school of Montpellier") everything in man depends on one single "vital principle," vital unity being, in every living organism, not the effect, but the cause of its perfection.

Nevertheless, the single deepest influence undergone by Ravaisson was that of Aristotle, whose philosophy he not unrightly understood as a sort of universal dynamism wherein forms and souls are attracted toward one single supreme principle of cosmic love.[4] His interpretation of the Philosopher is found in the two volumes of his *Essai sur la métaphysique d'Aristote* (1837, 1846). It cannot be said that Ravaisson ignored Kant, whom he occasionally quotes, but his mind remained untouched by the Kantian denunciation of metaphysics as a pseudoscientific knowledge. Nor was this indifference to Kantian criticism a mere oversight. In his *Rapport sur la philosophie en France au XIXe siècle* (1867), Ravaisson places under the conjoined authority of Maine de

Biran and Kant a thoroughly metaphysical view of the world which in fact was entirely his own: "Liberty is the last word of things; under the disorders and the antagonisms that disturb the surface where the phenomena happen, at the bottom, in the essential and eternal truth, all is grace, love, harmony." How can one go beyond the phenomena and, in spite of Kant, reach this deeper metaphysical level? Ravaisson has defined the method which, according to him, philosophy was henceforward to follow, and not only the method but the goal it would pursue: the constitution of "a spiritualistic realism or positivism, having for its generative principle the awareness, achieved by the mind in itself, of an existence from which it knows that everything else is derived and on which he knows that everything else hangs. This is nothing else than its action."

This was an astoundingly correct prophecy. From Maine de Biran to Bergson, through Ravaisson and Lachelier, there runs an unbroken chain of metaphysical speculation. This speculation can be called a spiritualistic realism, because it ultimately rests upon the direct observation of inner life and always builds on facts, never on abstract concepts. Lastly, it always aims to attain, within the mind, a trans-subjective reality, generally situated beyond the order of passivity and of understanding.

Simple facts witness to the continuity of the evolution. Four doctorate theses stake out its course. In 1838, there is that of Ravaisson, *De l'habitude*; in 1870, that of Lachelier, *Du fondement de l'induction*, dedicated to Ravaisson; in 1874, that of Boutroux, *De la contingence des lois de la nature*, also dedicated to Ravaisson; in 1889, that of Bergson, *Essai sur les donnés immédiates de la conscience*, dedicated to Lachelier. The doctrinal continuity finds in such facts its concrete expression.

The personal contribution of Ravaisson to the movement is his thesis *De l'habitude*, short (48pp.), elliptical, and written in a deceptively easy classical French style. From the very beginning, the notion of habit is defined in terms comprehensive enough to apply to the totality of being.

Reality divides into inorganic and organic. Inorganic reality is the realm of mobile extension, which is the general character of body. Its universal law is the tendency to persist in its mode of being: inertia. Since it belongs to all that which is, the effect of inertia is self-annulling. By persevering in its own motion, each mobile piece of extension annuls different motions in which other bodies likewise tend to persevere. If they do not annul each other, they lose

X. Maine de Biran's French Posterity 329

themselves in a common resultant different from its elements. In short, mobile extension is the seat of only three possible kinds of interactions: (1) mere changes in reciprocal relations (mechanics); (2) reciprocal annulling resulting in a sort of equilibrium of forces (physics: positive and negative electricity); (3) production of a common resultant different from its elements (chemistry: chemical combination). In all three cases the result is a homogeneous whole, always divisible into integrant parts similar to each other and to the whole. There is in it no determined substance, no distinct center of energy and of individual power wherein a habit could be generated and preserved. Habit is impossible in the inorganic order of reality.

Organic bodies are not homogeneous, nor are they divisible into similar parts. Organized beings are "heterogeneous units in space," this being the very definition of organization. It takes time to achieve organization: the permanent unity preserved through time by a growing organism is Life. With succession and organization, individuality begins. A heterogeneous whole is not merely being, it is a being: "Ce n'est plus seulement de l'être, c'est un être" (I, 2). An individualized subject developing, under various forms and at various moments, its inner energy offers all the conditions required for the possibility of habit. The inorganic order is that wherein nothing has any individual subsistence; it is the order of Destiny. Only the living being is a distinct being, a distinct nature; the organic order is the real order of Nature. So habit only can begin where nature itself begins.

In its widest acceptation, habit is a disposition, with regard to a change generated in a being by the continuity or the repetition of that same change (I, Introductory Remarks).

Life is superior to inorganic being, but it presupposes and requires inorganic existence as its condition. The effect of habit is different according to whether it affects that which is inorganic in organisms or that which is organization itself—nature. At all levels of existence the effects of habit obey one and the same law: "Receptivity decreases, spontaneity increases" (I, 2). For instance, a repeated change passively undergone by a living being either destroys it or else it ceases to be perceived. On the contrary, the more frequently and the longer a living being reiterates a change whose origin is in itself, the more intensely this being will reproduce the same act or, at least, tend to reproduce it. In short, habit lowers passivity and excites activity.[5]

This organic activity grows in spontaneity and in intensity as analysis ascends the series of living beings, from those that only move by parts (plants) to the wholes that move themselves in space (animals) and, in short, to the intelligent being that knows, foresees, calculates, and judges its own motions (man). This being we know well enough, and we know it from within; it is ourselves. In this privileged case, the author, and actor, and the spectator of the play are one and the same person. Habit can be observed and known from within.

The result of this observation is to show Nature as the battlefield of two opposite tendencies or, rather, as a self-developing Life that moves between its inferior level, whose lowest limit is necessity, or Destiny, and a superior level, that of the spontaneity of Nature, whose highest limit is the Liberty of understanding. Habit descends from the one to the other of these two levels and, by bringing them together, it reveals, along with their intimate essence, their necessary connectedness (II, 4).

This probably is the most important among the conclusions of Ravaisson. When observed in man, habit is seen as progressively reducing thought, will, and motion to a condition of uniformity, of passivity, and of determination. Hence the profound remark made by Aristotle, that "habit is another nature."[6] The remark is deep because this is a convertible proposition: Nature, in turn, is a sort of habit. As such, Nature is a condition of passivity and of determination; exactly, it is the condition defined by what we call the Laws of Nature. On the other hand, this passive and self-repeating uniformity is the effect and, so to speak, the residue of a free and intelligent activity.

Hence the two characters of Nature. Even considered in its passivity, Nature remains intelligible and constitutes a fitting material upon which an intelligent activity can act. Thus, in human deliberation, the will always starts from some indistinct and spontaneous idea, which provides its occasion and material for deliberation and reflection. It is noteworthy that, here again, Ravaisson refers his reader to Aristotle, *Eth. Eudem.*, VII, 14, and to the remarks made by a late Peripatetic, "the deep metaphysician Cesalpini, *Quaest. Peripatet.*, II, 4."

The second character of Nature is a corollary of the first. Even in its passive element, made up of acquired habits, Nature shelters a remnant of the spontaneity from which it flows, a confused but real aspiration to the good, always more or less ready to answer the call of liberty. Nature is wholly engaged in its desire, and, in turn, its desire is wholly engaged in the good that attracts it. In the acute words of Fénelon: "Nature is predisposing grace." Nature is God in us, hidden from us because He resides in that most intimate part of ourselves where we cannot descend since, in Augustine's own words, He is more inward to me than my most inward part: *Intimior intimo meo.*[7]

Remarkably enough, Ravaisson is here finding himself at the meeting point of Christian Wisdom and of Greek Wisdom. In a way, Aristotle says, "the divine in us is that which moves all things" (*Eth. Eud.*, VII, 14). What is new, in Ravaisson's doctrine, is his notion of Nature conceived as what is left of a former thinking and desiring activity. Owing to the progressive influence of habit, which reinforces its passivity, knowledge becomes in nature a sort of immediate intellection, a concrete thought wherein idea is merged in being. Likewise, the will becomes immediate in nature where it is desire itself, or rather love. "This knowledge and this desire, this idea substantialized in the movement of love, is Nature itself" (II, 5).

Thus understood, nature is the very continuity of concrete reality. Taking a view of the universe whose influence was to dominate in the philosophy of Henri Bergson, Ravaisson sees both understanding and will as tied up with discontinuity. The intellect knows by conceiving its objects as defined and distinct. The will only tends to definite ends posited as distinct by intellect. Hence "understanding and will determine nothing that is not discrete and abstract. Nature makes up the concrete continuity, the fulness of reality. The will tends toward the ends; nature suggests the means. Art, a work of the will, gets a hold over exterior limits and surfaces only…nature works from within. Science, a work of understanding, delineates and constructs the general outlines of the ideality of things. Only nature, in experience, yields their substantiality. Science circumscribes, under the extensive unity of logical or mathematical form. Nature constitutes, in the dynamic, intensive unity of reality" (II, 6).

The secret of this concrete fecundity of Nature lies in its very origin. Continuity or repetition depresses sensibility and passivity; it exalts motility, "but it exalts the one and it depresses the other in the same way, for one and the same cause: the growth of an unthinking spontaneity, which more and more penetrates the passivity of the organization and settles itself in it, outside, and beneath the region of will, of personality and of consciousness" (II, 3). In short, the history of habit represents the way Liberty is returning to Nature or, rather, the invasion of the domain of Liberty by natural spontaneity (II, 6).

From Victor Cousin to Ravaisson, a distinct progress has been achieved. In setting up observation and induction as the two valid methods of knowledge, Francis Bacon had been the spokesman of the modern scientific spirit. Victor Cousin and his school had still conceived philosophy as an application to inner experience of the Baconian methods of observation and induction. The result could be but a sort of physics of the mind in which the very necessity of necessary knowledge could be nothing more than a fact.

Dissatisfaction with that state of affairs was first marked by Ravaisson in an early article "Contemporary Philosophy," published in the *Revue des deux mondes* (1840). The occasion was the recent publication of a French translation of Hamilton. Ravaisson made two decisive remarks. First, that the maxim of the Scottish school and of Victor Cousin, according to which we have no immediate cognitions beyond those of phenomena, was lagging behind the final conclusions of Maine de Biran. And indeed, as was said above, Maine de Biran had hoped to attain an absolute as given *in* the relative of experience. The active force attained by Biran in the experience of muscular effort was conceived by him as "hyperorganic" in essence; it therefore had a "cause" transcending the body, and the very possibility of such an inference implied the presence, in reason, of a power of knowing, if not the nature of substances, at least their existence. In the same article however, Ravaisson added that, "in placing, beyond the active force of which we are aware, the absolute of our own substance, even Maine de Biran had not yet attained the inner point of view where soul apprehends itself in its depths, which is all activity, so that it is neither necessary nor, in fact, possible, still to imagine as inert the substance that supports it." The decisive conclusion of the article was that, even though we might refuse to go beyond the actual position of Maine de Biran himself, it at least had become necessary "to give up the specious parallelism that had once been established between the method of the physical sciences and that of philosophy."[8]

At the end of his own career, Ravaisson himself resolutely went beyond the cautious metaphysical empiricism of Biran. He did so, no doubt under the influence of Schelling, but also, let it not be overlooked, under that of Aristotle, whose Prime Mover moves everything inasmuch as he himself is a universal object of love. "Today, after so much research accomplished and so much experience accumulated, we see more clearly than ever, that the inside of reality, so to speak, is the soul, and that the inside of the soul is will. Knowing those things, how could we fail to acknowledge that it is in that which constitutes the innermost recess of the will itself, that is hidden the deep source from which all science flows? True love, that is to say the love of that true good which itself is no other than Love, is that not, in effect, wisdom?" Obviously, even with Ravaisson, intellect still was under a ban; its disqualification still seemed to be required for a rehabilitation of metaphysics.[9]

Jules Lachelier

While still a student at the École Normale Supérieure, young Lachelier[10] wrote a composition on this saying of St. Francis de Sales: "A good way to learn is to read; a better one is to listen; the best of all is to teach."[11] The influence of Lachelier as a teacher has been both deep and wide reaching; some of his best-known pupils (Boutroux, Séailles) agree that one can form no idea of his character and thought from merely reading what little of his doctrine he published.

The thesis of Ravaisson had for its motto one line from Aristotle. That of Lachelier, *Du fondement de l'induction* (1871) is borrowed from Parmenides: *Thinking is the same as that which is being thought.* Nothing can more clearly show the part played by Greek philosophy in the nineteenth-century French revival of metaphysics.[12] Lachelier was far from ignoring Kant; on the contrary, he has made extensive use of his writings, but, strangely enough, his interpretation of Kant has been still more deliberately dogmatic (i.e., indifferent to the true spirit of criticism) than that of Ravaisson. The two main parts of Lachelier's *Fondement de l'induction* rest, the first on the *Critique of Pure Reason*, the second on the *Critique of Judgment*, as if the two critiques fulfilled the same functions in the philosophy of Kant. Moreover, Lachelier uses the criticism of pure reason to show that, by one of its aspects, reality truly is mechanism and necessity; then he uses the criticism of the power of judging in order to establish that, at a higher level, reality truly is purposiveness and liberty. To Lachelier, Kant was a standing invitation to practice the reflexive method in philosophy: if the *I think* does not accompany all my representations, these are not really mine. On the other hand, what had been to Kant an object of critical reflection (experienced thought) was to remain for Lachelier, in virtue, not of a misconception, but of a deliberate choice, a psychological experience naturally leading to metaphysics. Boutroux relates a saying of Lachelier which throws a vivid light on this fundamental aspect of his thought. Discussing with colleagues the question whether psychology can become a strictly positive science, that is, a science completely separated from metaphysics, Lachelier concluded: is it not more correct to say that true psychology precisely is metaphysics?[13]

Used in this spirit, as a method to investigate reality by a reflection of the soul on self, the criticism of Kant yields unexpected results.

The two main notions of cause (*Critique of Pure Reason*) and of purposiveness (*Critique of Judgment*) are, in fact, principles. Against Aristotle's well-known position on this point, Lachelier thinks that even principles need to be demonstrated. Of course, what Lachelier here has in mind are the primary notions to be used as starting points in philosophy, not the formal notions of being and identity. More precisely, the notions to be demonstrated are those of cause and of end. The reflexive method (reflection of the mind upon itself) permits such demonstrations.

In this hypothesis (suggested by the method of Kant) "the highest of our cognitions is neither a sensation, nor an intellectual intuition, by which thought immediately grasps its own nature and the relationship to phenomena it sustains; it is from this relationship that we can deduce the laws it imposes on phenomena, and which are nothing else than the principles" (p. 44).

Lachelier applies this method to the problem of the principle of induction. By induction is meant the inference of a universal and necessary law from particular and contingent facts. No empirical explanation of this operation is acceptable (against J. S. Mill). Its possibility rests upon the preceding principle (the truth of the reflexive method), which itself divides into two distinct laws: the first, according to which each and every phenomenon is included in a *series*, wherein the existence of each term determines that of the following; the second, according to which every phenomenon is included within a system, wherein the idea of the whole determines the existence of the parts (p. 48). If these two laws did not exist, human thought would not be possible.

First the law of efficient causes explains, at once, the possibility of our own knowledge of phenomena and the existence we attribute to them, for indeed nothing exists, at least for us, except as one among other objects of thought, while, conversely, it is proper to thought to conceive it and to affirm the existence of its objects (p. 60). The very nature of these objects can be deduced

X. Maine de Biran's French Posterity

from this law. Inasmuch as things fall under the law of efficient causality, they constitute a world subjected to universal mechanism and, thereby, to universal necessity. This applies even to man and his mind. Nothing happens, not even a thought or desire, whose cause is not to be found in some other thought or desire. The only conception resulting from what we know of the essence of thought, conceived of as an aptitude to think of the world in terms of efficient causality only, is a sort of "idealistic materialism" (p. 77), that is, an ensemble of necessarily determined but uncoordinated movements.[14]

Such a physical universe would provide no ground for the possibility of inductive reasoning. Efficient causality does not account for the coordination of several different series of movements. Inductive reasoning does not go from parts to wholes, but, rather, from wholes to their parts. Induction can foresee, from that which happens, that a universal law of nature is true, but it can do so because, in fact, it infers from the truth of the law to that of the particular cases. Thus to argue from wholes to parts is the same as to argue from the point of view of final causes. The law of final causes is the characteristic element that makes induction possible (p. 78).

There is, however, a twofold difference between these two laws: the law of efficient causes gives rise to hypothetical, yet, within their own limits, absolute judgments. Consequences will follow only *if* their antecedent conditions are present, but, if these are given indeed, consequences infallibly follow. In the order of final causality, there certainly must be a certain harmony between the antecedent conditions, but these need not always be the same, nor can we be absolutely certain that identically the same effect will necessarily follow. Scientific mechanism, where it can be achieved, goes to the bottom of reality, induction rather consists in guessing, by a sort of instinct, the variable processes of the art that is playing at the surface of things (p. 82).

The reality of final causality can be demonstrated, for indeed, even granting that mechanism could account for the existence and unity of certain series of phenomena, it still would not account for the existence of a "system" endowed with a unity of its own. Mechanism can account for the series; the convergence of certain series tending to a common goal cannot be accounted for otherwise than by resorting to the notion of "ends," or final causes (p. 85). Now, the agreement between different parts of nature can result only from their dependence with respect to certain wholes; it is therefore necessary that, in nature, the idea of the whole should have preceded that of the parts. This is to say that nature must be subjected to final causes (p. 88).

Things then can be said to *exist* on two accounts. First, inasmuch as they necessarily follow from other things as from their efficient causes; next, and in a much higher way, inasmuch as, especially in the realm of life, they constitute units made up of various elements gravitating toward a common end: "Thus nature is possessed of two existences, both grounded upon the two laws which thought imposes upon phenomena: an abstract existence, identical with the science whose object it is, that rests upon the necessary law of efficient causes; and a concrete existence, identical with what one could call the esthetic function of thought, which rests upon the contingent law of final causes" (p. 90). In this sense, the teleological unity of every being is (without prejudice to the mode of intuition to which we shall be elevated in another life) the veritable *noumenon*, of which the phenomena only are the manifestations.

Harmony is a degree, however modest, of beauty. Since final causes account for the true being of things, a truth without beauty would be a mere logical play of the mind. So, the only truth both solid and worthy of the name is beauty (p. 92). In this view, every thing is given as true and real in virtue of the place it occupies and the function it fulfills in the harmonious structure of a whole. As such, every thing is an intermediary end and provides understanding with a provisional term that makes possible the progress of thought. The sequences of efficient causes go to infinity; they are unthinkable because thought does not know where to stop in following them. But thought finds stopping points in progressing toward the ends. So, "the ends are the true reasons of things, and the ends constitute, under the name of forms, the things themselves," both matter and efficient causes being only necessary hypotheses, or, rather, necessary symbols by means of which we project, into space and time, that which in itself is superior to both (p. 95).

In the world of Lachelier, not universal necessity, but, rather, universal contingency is the true definition of existence, the very soul of nature, and the last word of philosophical thinking (p. 95). For the same reason, every movement in it results from a spontaneity tending toward an end; in other words, its cause is a tendency and a tendency that produces a movement is a force. So "every phenomenon is, not a force, but the development of a force" (p. 97). In a world made up neither of sensations nor of abstract notions but of real and physical actions, force is the connecting link between the extensive diversity of movement and the intensive unity of the mind.

The part played by the notion of final causes in the doctrine is therefore essential. Purposiveness is the condition for the very possibility of mechanism, not the reverse, so that all the mechanism at work in nature does not preclude the possibility of contingency. On the contrary, it presupposes its presence in the physical world. In man, this contingency manifests itself under the form of freely chosen ends, which is the very essence of liberty.

"The miracle of nature, within ourselves as well as without, is the invention, or the production of ideas, and this production is free, in the strictest sense of the word, since every idea is, in itself, absolutely independent of the preceding one[15] and is born of nothing, like a world" (p. 109). Assuredly, such creations follow a certain order, and the liberty that causes them is not arbitrariness, for the will of man is neither a thing in itself, nor a concrete and active power of the mind: "it only is the reflection of a tendency upon itself" (p. 111). In a formula that anticipates one of the essential features of Bergsonism, Lachelier says: "It is by a sort of idolatry of understanding that we seek in such a reflection the principle of the action it enlightens." The world of Lachelier is made up of causal necessity ordered and even created by intelligible purposiveness, and this is the reason such a world is essentially free. But "only invention is free, because it depends upon itself only and decides on all the rest: and that which we call our own liberty precisely is the consciousness of the necessity in virtue of which an end conceived by our mind determines, in the series of our actions, the existence of the means which, in turn, must determine its own" (p. 111).

In concluding his treatise, Lachelier observes that this true philosophy of nature is a "spiritualistic realism,"[16] itself independent of all religion; but, he added, because it subordinates mechanism to purposiveness, it prepares us to subordinate purposiveness itself to a still higher principle, and to overstep, by an act of moral faith, the limits of thought as well as those of nature. How Lachelier would have carried his conclusions up to this supreme one we do not know, except in an indirect way by reports come to us from his pupils.[17] There is no doubt, however, that the last words of his main work are an invitation to consider his philosophy as a preamble to religion.

Emile Boutroux

Emile Boutroux is, after Victor Cousin, the second French philosopher of note to have devoted a considerable part of his activity to the history of philosophy.[18] Germany had paved the way and Boutroux can be considered as having imposed this discipline in French university teaching.

In his own mind, history of philosophy had a philosophical significance. His secondary thesis dealt with the problem of the eternal truths in Descartes[19]; in it he showed his interest in a doctrine which considers the so-called eternal and necessary truths (i.e., the principles) as radically contingent and hanging on the free will of God. In an introduction (c. 1877) to the first volume of Zeller's *Philosophy of the Greeks*, Boutroux stressed the contingent character of the development of philosophy, against the tendency of Hegel to reduce its history to the unfolding of one grand law. Probably the best illustration of this aspect of his activity is to be found in his course of lectures at the Sorbonne, in 1896–1897, on *The Philosophy of Kant*.[20]

In this remarkable work, Boutroux clearly showed the nature of the philosophical revolution achieved by Kant. Ever since the time of the Greeks, philosophers had considered philosophy to be the knowledge of being. Some would say being was matter, others would call it spirit, but they all agreed that the object of philosophical speculation was "that which is," or given reality. Kant's critical philosophy interposed science and ethics between philosophy and being. With him, the object of philosophy became a question of understanding how these two disciplines are possible. This change in perspective became for modern philosophy a source of grave difficulties when the problem arose of proceeding from thought to being. But even apart from these difficulties, Kant created an inextricable situation. Having decided to start from science, not from things, Kant has set up an absolute notion of science and of ethics as though these two disciplines were something immutable and perfectly determined.[21] Moreover, Kant identified knowledge with the determination of that which is universally and necessarily true, thus excluding from philosophy all the contingent elements present in nature as well as in man. Is this legitimate?

In order to show that philosophy must be something more than an explanation of some product of the human mind, Boutroux, in a picturesque page of his study on Kant,[22] opposes to the attitude of the Greeks, whose philosophy directly applied itself to things, what he thinks was the attitude of the Scholas-

X. Maine de Biran's French Posterity 339

tics, particularly that of Saint Anselm, when they substituted for things certain doctrines and dogmas and undertook to rationalize and systematize them by ordering them under their own principles. *Fides quaerens intellectum*, Saint Anselm had said. Has not Kant done for science what the Scholastics had done for faith? Could not his own motto be something like: science and morality seeking to understand themselves? Did not Kant institute a new scholasticism on the basis of science and morality such as he had found them, ready made?

Disregarding the oversimplified view of scholasticism implied in these remarks, one can keep all this in mind as a good introduction to the personal philosophy of Boutroux himself, such as it is exposed in his chief work: *De la contingence des lois de la nature*. Its epigraph again was borrowed from Aristotle (*De part. anim.* I, 5): *and thereby to be gods*. By these words, Boutroux openly declared his intention, in spite of Kant, to go beyond science to metaphysics and even, beyond metaphysics, to religion. Moreover, Boutroux was acutely conscious of the nature of the task he was undertaking. Kant had substituted science for nature, and morality for man; hence the view favored by Kant and accepted by many, which sees nature as a system of necessary relations between phenomena. Boutroux wondered, is this a view of nature, or is it a view of science? Does this express what reality itself is, or, simply, what science abstracts from reality in order to turn it into a fitting object of knowledge?

Boutroux's general answer is that reality comes first. Nature does not follow any laws, but, rather, laws follow nature. Already Ravaisson (to whom, as has been said, the thesis of Boutroux is dedicated) had suggested that the scientific laws correspond to what could be called "habits of nature." Boutroux expressly and forcibly draws this conclusion, which becomes the very center of his own philosophy: "The laws are the bed in which passes the torrent of facts: they have dug it, although they follow it."[23] True enough, every attempt to account for phenomena sooner or later confronts us with what is called "the nature of things," and it can be said that, if the torrent digs its own bed, it is because, of itself, it flows this or that way. And there is indeed a nature of things, but how do we know that that nature is a strict necessity? It is not true to say that the laws rule the phenomena, or that the phenomena obey the laws. The laws are not posited before the things; on the contrary, the laws presuppose the things; they only express the nature of things previously realized. Of this nature itself we only know the average manifestations. In a remarkable passage which anticipated by some seventy years the modern statistical notion of physical laws, Boutroux was already observing that the regularity of the laws of nature does not require the absolute regularity and necessity of all the causal relations between phenomena.

What is a natural phenomenon, a natural fact? Where exactly does it begin and where exactly does it end? All experimental observation consists in narrowing, as much as possible, the limits within which the measurable element of phenomena is contained, but these limits always remain a little too wide. What we see, in natural laws, are the containers of things, not the things themselves: "We do not know if things occupy, within their containers, an assignable place. Supposing the phenomena were undetermined, but in a certain measure only, and supposing this measure invincibly escaped our gross means of observation, appearances would none the less remain exactly such as we see them. We are therefore attributing to things a determination that is purely hypothetical, if not downright unintelligible, when we believe implicitly the principle according to which a particular phenomenon is bound with another phenomenon. The term 'particular phenomenon,' strictly understood, does not express an experimental concept; it might well even be contradictory with the very conditions of experience."[24]

Paradoxically enough, the rights of contingency are justified by a dialectical method whose strictness almost equals that of a mathematical demonstration. The whole argument rests upon a definite notion of "necessity." Absolute necessity would exclude all relation subordinating the existence of a thing to another one as to its condition. But this would be to exclude all possibility either of *things*, or of *laws*, and since we are inquiring into the presence of necessity in this given world, full of interconnected things, absolute necessity is out of the question.

What about relative necessity? By this is meant a "necessary relation" between two things. The only relation of this sort in the order of analytical knowledge is that of identity, $A = A$. But no knowledge can be acquired by this sterile repetition of one and the same term. The syllogism, which is as analytical as any actual reasoning can be, does not affirm an identity of terms; it does not say that $A = A$, but rather, that A *is* B. In propositions of this type, the predicate differs from the subject; in fact, such propositions say that the predicate is part of the subject. Where there is not perfect analytical identity of terms, there necessarily is a measure of synthesis. All the propositions implying a certain progress of knowledge, then, are synthetic propositions. Experience does not provide universal cognitions in space and time; it only lets us know external relations between things, and these relations are given to us as constant, not as necessary. The note of necessity is attributed to them by the mind; so, as Kant rightly says, in order to be necessary, a synthesis must be known *a priori* (i.e., must be posited by the mind). As such, however, it is only a subjectively necessary synthesis; how can we know that it is also an objectively necessary synthesis (i.e., necessary in things themselves)?

Only two classes of judgments can be objectively necessary, those that express relations of efficient causality, and those that express relations of causality in the order of ends (final causes). But there is no end of which one can say that it must be realized necessarily, for no single event is, all by itself, the only possible one. Moreover, when a certain end is posited as something to be realized, it can always be realized by different means, just as every goal can be reached by different ways. There is then no absolute necessity in the order of final causes.

In spite of appearances to the contrary, the same is true of efficient causes. There is, of course, an element of necessity in their relations. There is enough of it to account for the possibility of science, but science does not require absolute necessity. In every relation of efficient cause to effect, the effect must be somewhat different from the cause, otherwise nothing would be produced. Now, however slight the difference, its consequences can be considerable for the future of the species. Unnoticeable variations are likely to have initiated the formations of the types now found in the inorganic as well as in the organic world.

On the strength of these conclusions Boutroux establishes that there is an element of contingency in causal relations at all the levels of the hierarchy of beings. Concerning being itself, possibility does not necessarily entail actual existence (ch. 2). At the level of genus, it is only a question of abstract and logical notions, posterior to concrete individuals and determined by them rather than determining them (ch. 3). Just as being receives logical form in a contingent way, so also space, time, and movement, which are the formal determinations of matter, do not exhibit, *in concrete reality*, the necessity they have as notions in the mind. Spaceless, timeless, and motionless beings are not impossibilities. Even conceived as determinations of material being, such notions imply quality at least as much as quantity, and there is no conceivable relationship between the quantitative element to which one wants to reduce the material substance of things and the qualitative element which often constitutes that which is highest in nature.[25] Having thus reached the level of bodies,[26] Boutroux finds it easy to show that even the physical universe is not immutable. Now, if the general laws can vary, however little, even though their variations cannot be observed during our short life in the corner of matter where we are, "the whole structure of destiny crumbles down" (p. 84).[27]

Within the order of life, we attain to beings whose parts are hierarchically related so as to constitute individual wholes. No doubt, all the elements entering the structure of living organisms are physical and chemical in nature, but these are ordained, harmonized, and so to speak disciplined by a superior intervention. "Life is, in this sense, a veritable creation."[28]

From life to human life, more contingent degrees of being can be observed. There is life without consciousness; there is consciousness without self-awareness; there is self-awareness without the privilege of organizing actions in view of freely chosen ends. In other words, neither the existence of an *ego* nor liberty are necessary consequences of physiological life. They are not necessarily tied up with it, neither by right, nor, as can be seen, as a matter of fact.[29] On the contrary, the emergence of man as a being conscious of his own existence cannot be accounted for by the mere interplay of physical and physiological laws. Moreover, man's interventions in the order of nature, owing to his understanding and will, bring about results for which nature itself cannot account.[30] There is no necessary relation between the quantity of physical energy spent by a human nervous system and the effects of the mental energy that attend it. In short, it is impossible to conceive the decisions of will after the pattern of effects resulting from causes.[31] Bergson, who was to carry his own analysis of will much farther than Boutroux, may well have found in this first discussion of the nature of "deliberation" an incentive to undertake his own investigation of the problem.

Summing up his own view of the world, Boutroux remarks that the existence of degrees of being is necessary neither by right nor as a matter of fact. Every given order of being[32] enjoys, with respect to inferior orders (or "worlds") a certain amount of independence. It can, in some measure, exploit their own laws and intervene in their own development.[33] In the last analysis, there is not one single real relation of antecedent to consequent, however general it is sup-

X. Maine de Biran's French Posterity

posed to be, that can be conceived as necessary[34] because necessity is inconceivable in the order of the variable and perfectible; no repetition of quantitative relations can account for qualitative differentiation and progress. In short, the threadbare saying "Nothing gets lost, nothing is created" has no absolute value"[35]: continuity, heterogeneity, hierarchical organization, life, consciousness, liberty, are so many additions to bare existence.[36] There is therefore in the world a measure of creation.

An important consequence follows from this conclusion. Were it true that nothing new is ever created in the world, *static* sciences could sufficiently account for given reality. As it is, since there is contingency and progress in the world, *dynamic* sciences should be constituted over and above the static ones. One character of these new sciences is that they should constantly resort to observation rather than to deduction: "If it be true that, along with a principle of conservation, there is a principle of contingent change, to neglect experience always is dangerous, always illegitimate."[37] Another characteristic of such sciences should be to attribute an extreme importance to problems of development: "Not the nature of things, but rather their history, must be the supreme object of scientific research."[38] Not scientific knowledge, but, rather, the pretension of science to deduce rather than to observe is what Boutroux considers the target of his criticism. There are laws, and these can be true; the only point is: their truth has not the mark of absolute necessity. And how do we know this? Simply because, if being were the seat of absolute necessity, there would be no world.

If the last word of nature is "liberty," only a supreme liberty can account for its existence and structure. The philosophy of Boutroux is the most elaborate modern version there is of a proof of the existence of God by the degrees of being. Instead of arguing from a static hierarchy of beings (in accordance with the uncreated static universe of Aristotle) Boutroux argues from a dynamically constituted hierarchy of beings (in accordance with the trend of modern science). But one should not interpret his theology as a doctrine in which God appears at the term of a progressive evolution. In the metaphysics of Boutroux, just as in that of Aristotle, act always is prior to potency; the best always comes first.

As Boutroux understands him, God is the being whose creative action we feel at the very core of ourselves, in the middle, so to speak, of our efforts to draw closer to Him. God is perfect and necessary being. In Him, power, or liberty, is infinite; "it is the source of His existence which, for this reason, is not subjected to the coercion of fatality. The divine essence, being co-eternal with power, is *actual perfection*. It is necessary in virtue of a practical necessity, that is, it absolutely deserves to be realized, and it can be itself only if it is realized freely. At the same time, it is immutable, because it is fully realized, and under such conditions a change could only be a decadence. Lastly, the condition resulting from this excellent and immutable act (the spontaneous act of infinite power) is unchanging *felicity*."

Liberty, actual perfection, and felicity, no one of these three natures precedes the others in the divine essence. Each one of them is absolute and primordial; indeed, they are one.

God is the creator of the essence and existence of beings. Moreover, it is His action, His providence, that gives to higher forms the faculty of using, as their own instruments, the inferior forms. Besides, there is no reason to consider a special care of his creatures as more unworthy of God than his creation of changing, contingent, and particular beings.[39]

Such is the universe of Emile Boutroux. In it, all beings are striving to imitate God and to resemble Him. Each and every one of them does so *in* and *by* its own nature. Each and every one of them, according to its nature, is given by God the measure of spontaneity it needs to be able to get beyond itself. The higher the being, the wider its liberty, which is for it the means to proceed to its end. This end is the good. Through personal and social life, man is striving to attain it.

Henri Bergson

Henri Bergson[40] used to say that it takes some time for a philosopher to know what he is going to affirm, but that, often enough, he knows pretty soon what he is going to deny. In saying this, Bergson was speaking from experience. He himself has several times explained what it was he first said "no" to, and why. He first said no to Herbert Spencer, and his reason was that the philosophy of Spencer is an evolutionism in which time plays absolutely no part. World evolution is supposed to have taken millions of years, but supposing a universal acceleration of motion in the process of evolution, world history could have taken place within the limits of one year, of one day, or of one minute. Its history would have been very short, yet if the philosophy of Spencer is true, that history of the world would remain substantially the same. Spencer's is an evolution without duration, which does not sound right.

Looking for the cause of this strange interpretation of universal change, Bergson noticed at once that, just as in the case of Kant, what Spencer called time was really but another name for space. This attracted his attention to the natural tendency of intellect to eliminate from its representation of reality the fact of duration and to substitute for it its expression in terms of numbers, of places and, in short, of space. Bergson wondered why it should be so. In discussing this important problem, he naturally availed himself of the general conclusions already formulated by Boutroux, Lachelier, Ravaisson. In a sense, Bergsonism can be considered the last word of spiritualistic realism. The very title of his doctorate thesis suffices to establish the fact: *Essai sur les données immédiates de la conscience.* From this alone a jury could guess that the starting point of the candidate was to be the same as that of Maine de Biran's. However, not effort, but, rather, the continuous stream of consciousness was to be for Bergson the preferred approach to the nature of duration and, by the same token, of reality.

method
Bergson himself has said that any interpretation of his doctrine that does not place duration at its very center is sure to miss its true meaning. He surely knows best. But the core of a doctrine also is the *locus* of its difficulties. An exposition of the doctrine cannot begin with what is most secret in it. In approaching it from another direction, however, one should keep in mind that this is the goal Bergson is trying to reach. The final cause of the doctrine undoubtedly is duration.

The very existence of philosophy, as a discipline distinct from the sciences of nature and of mathematics, presupposes the existence of a mode of knowledge specifically distinct from the scientific method. The best way to realize what scientific knowledge actually is, is to observe it in its origin, which is vulgar knowledge as found in ignorant people, in children and, to a point, even in brutes.

Knowledge begins when a living being begins to discern "things." We know what it is to be in a dark place and to "get used" to darkness. At first, one sees nothing; little by little, one begins to discern objects. In like manner, a living being must get used to nature and progressively discern things in what, at first, is but a chaos of sensations. The child does this by means of sight, touch, and motion. By trial and error, he gets acquainted with groups of sensible qualities regularly given together. To each of them, he gets used to giving a name: table, dog. By exploring reality through a succession of acts the child finally "cuts out," within the continuous material provided by reality, what we call "a thing," an object. Our concept of the thing signifies the sum total of our active experience by which it has thus been constituted.

Let us generalize the conclusion. We shall say that man creates objects by acting. Our concept of an object points out that which can be done with it or, at least, what our attitude should be with respect to it. For every normal being, to recognize an object is to know how to handle it, or how to behave toward it. In the mental disease of *apraxy*, the subject is, at once, unable to recognize the object and to handle it.

For thousands of years human reason has formed itself by repeated efforts of this kind. It has progressively constituted itself as a power to "cut out" from the continuous tissue of reality objects extended in space, distinct from each other, occupying a certain place and susceptible of being counted. Science simply continues, prolongs, and betters the method spontaneously applied by vulgar knowledge. To provide a scientific account of reality consists in cutting out, within its continuity, distinct objects and in describing their properties. This science does in mathematics, in physics, in biology, etc.; its method is more accurate than that of vulgar knowledge, but it is a continuation of the same movement. It shows, in our power of knowing, an annex of our faculty of acting.

This raises a problem concerning the value of scientific knowledge. Is science able to grasp all the aspects of reality equally? If science is the work of intelligence, itself born of action, it must be able perfectly to grasp what is *solid* and *discontinuous* in reality. On the contrary, if there is in reality an element of fluidity and of continuity, intelligence is likely either to miss it entirely, or else to explain it away by turning it into something solid and discontinuous. This accounts for the very relationship of science to the various levels of reality. Science is perfectly at home in arithmetic and geometry (numbers and figures). There, its cognitive value is absolute. In physics, science exhibits a marked tendency to eliminate change and movement: of the continuity of motion, scien-

X. Maine de Biran's French Posterity 347

tific explanation only retains a succession of places occupied in space by the mobile; the continuous passage from one place to the other does not interest science as such. In biology, intelligence successfully deals with organisms, organs, tissues, cells, and the chemical elements of living beings, but of life itself it says nothing. In psychology, intelligence analyzes the continuous stream of consciousness into reasonings, judgments, concepts, images, sensations, feelings, volitions, and so on. There is no end to such a breaking up of the inner unity of the self. It is no wonder, then, that science considers inner life to be made up of distinct elements subjected to necessary laws, just as if the nature of soul were the same as that of physical reality. But the continuity of consciousness and the very possibility of liberty perish in the process.

To sum up, intelligence is characterized by a natural incomprehension of life. But it should not be impossible to reach reality itself in its intimate nature, without inflicting upon it this parceling out which is the proper work of intelligence. If it exists, such a knowledge of reality will be useless by definition, but it also will be a deeper and truer cognition than that of science. Art is a first example of such knowledge. It gives us a vision, one and global, of its objects. Of the landscape or of the man represented by a painter, countless sciences could know and say many things, but Rembrandt shows us the man and Ruysdael shows us the landscape to be grasped at once in their totality and their unity. This kind of knowledge, immediate, global, unrelated to action, and even essentially unemployable in view of action, is called "intuition." It is useless for action because, in its very origin, it is foreign to it.

Raised to the function of a method, intuition is philosophical knowledge itself. Philosophy can start from science, prolong scientific knowledge, and generalize its conclusions. This is the kind of philosophy naturally practiced by scientists when, at the term of their science, they undertake to philosophize. The evolutionism of Spencer is a good example of the kind of results such a method can yield. But philosophy can do the reverse, that is, instead of following the stream of science, go back upstream, remounting so to speak to the source, so as to rediscover what reality looked like prior to its parceling out by science. To do this is to break the conceptual crust imposed by science on the fluidity of motion and of life.[41] By an effort that runs counter to the natural movement of vulgar and of scientific knowledge, it restores the artificially broken continuity of reality. Instinct would give some idea of such knowledge, because cognition, life, and reality are one in instinct. But intuition is not properly life; rather, it is an immediate communing with life in the innermost depth of its fluid continuity.

Language goes along with action and with concepts. So it can be expected that philosophical intuition will be hard put to find adequate words to express itself. Naturally, all the preparatory and discursive part of philosophical inquiry will necessarily resort to common language, but reasoning can only pave the way to intuition, while intuition itself cannot be formulated in words. Because each word represents a distinct thing, spoken intuitions are broken intuitions; they become science, they cease to be philosophy. Only suggestion is possible for the philosopher at the very moment when, dialectics having reached its term, intuition must take the place of intelligence and of reason. Metaphor sometimes helps in suggesting what is ineffable of its own nature, but the true reward of philosophical speculation is not metaphor; it is, beyond metaphor, the cognitive equivalent of vital instinct which we call intuition.[42]

soul and liberty

Let us try to apply this method to the metaphysical problems of the human soul. What does intelligence, what does intuition say about it? As a center of perspective, let us choose the problem of liberty.

Taken in its simplest sense, the notion of liberty coincides with that of free will; it signifies the possibility, for one and the same subject acting under the same circumstances, either to act or not to act, to do a certain thing or to do something else.

From the point of view of intelligence, and therefore of science, such a notion does not make sense. The *ego* of every acting being is caught in a web of all sorts of external influences. First, that of the body, itself a part of the universe and, as such, submitted to the determinism of physical laws. Besides, the progress of science has reduced the order of physiological facts, that is, of life, to that of chemistry: how could the psychological be the only order of reality not subjected to laws? As a matter of fact it is. Limited from beneath by its body, the soul is dominated from above by the social order. The calculus of probabilities now applies to sociological facts (births, marriages, suicides, crimes, etc.). In short, direct observation shows that every decision of the will is caused by reasons, or motives, whose determining power ultimately accounts for our acts.

X. Maine de Biran's French Posterity

Deliberation is but the oscillation of a pair of scales; they seem to hesitate, but when they stop moving we know their position could have been foretold from the very beginning. In short, what we call free choice is our ignorance of the causes; science is ceaselessly restricting the area of this ignorance, and even though it should never be completely dissipated, the sensible hypothesis would be that causes unknown to us are at work. A fact without causes is a supposition unpalatable to reason.

Bergson never pretended that there was no determinism in the world. He did not even deny that there is determinism in psychological life. On the contrary, he was of the opinion that truly and completely free choices are scarce. His point was that not all choices are determined by pre-existing causes from which they follow as predictable effects. The applicability of statistics to human acts simply confirms that most men allow themselves to be swayed from without by social influences. During the course of a day, most of our actions are predictable. It can be foreseen that, given certain circumstances, practically everybody will behave in the same way. However, liberty can be somewhere without being everywhere; the question then is this: Is there, in certain human acts, an element of liberty?

The arguments against liberty drawn from physiology are all dominated by a general interpretation of the relationship of mind and body. When Bergson undertook to discuss the problem, the prevailing theory was that of so-called psycho-physiological parallelism. Considered as nearly as certain as a scientific law, this theory maintained that each and every psychological fact was attended by a corresponding physiological fact. Since physiological facts were subjected to strict determinism, psychological facts had likewise to be subjected to it.

The object of *Matière et mémoire* was to test this alleged scientific hypothesis. In it, Bergson established that, if the supposition were true, consciousness would be functionally useless, which is hard to believe. In fact, consciousness does perform a biological function, which is not vainly to duplicate physiological events, but rather to attend action and to enlighten it. Going further, Bergson established that psychological facts are indeed endowed with a reality of their own, other than that of the body.

His demonstration rested upon the distinction of habit and memory. Habits are made up of organized motions. They are rigged mechanisms stored up for use in given opportunities. Habits are dependent on body. But memories properly so-called are different. Each one of them is an image left in us by a past event and is as unique as the event itself is. If the hypothesis of psycho-physiological parallelism were true, the disappearing of a certain category of memories should be explainable by some physiological lesion affecting the very seat of our perceiving power. Now, precisely, such is not the case. In verbal surdity (inability to remember the meaning of words) the patient ought to be deaf; but he is not; he hears as well as we do, only he hears us speak as we hear a voice speaking a language unknown to us. In aphasia, there is loss of the aptitude to speak although the patient understands everything and knows full well what he would like to say, and although he suffers no paralysis of the organ of speech, still he cannot speak. What is lost is not the memory itself, it is the mechanism required in order to express it. I put in a phone call and get no answer. Am I to infer that the operator is dead? A simpler hypothesis is that the line is out of order. Such is the case with memory, and therefore with the soul. It needs a body to perform some functions and still more to communicate with other souls; it does not depend on a body for its existence nor for its own operations.[43]

The objections against liberty borrowed from the determination of psychological facts by other facts have been discussed by Bergson in his thesis on the immediate data of consciousness. The gist of his refutation is that psychological determinism rests upon a wrong assimilation of psychological facts to the material facts studied by sciences.

The determinists say that the stronger motives ultimately carry the decision, but strength is intensity, and there is no intensity, because there is no quantity, in psychological facts. The differences in intensity which some psychologists pretend to observe, and even to measure, are, in fact, purely qualitative differences. A source of light can be greater, stronger, and more powerful than another one. Its effect upon our sense organs can be more intense; it itself can only be qualitatively different. Several distinct whites are different whites. Psychological facts are qualitatively, not quantitatively different.[44]

For the same reason, psychological facts cannot be numbered. Number, a collection of units, implies the notion of space. Where there is no space, there is no number. Associationistic determinism then commits a twofold error. Because it conceives psychological facts as if they were material facts, it assimilates them to distinct, numberable and quantitatively calculable objects, and in consequence of this first error, it conceives of a deliberation of the will as if it were a mechanical process in which the stronger motives are bound to win.

Anybody observing himself in those cases when a decision of vital importance is at stake will realize that the maturation of the decision is a continuous process wherein the whole personality is engaged. The superficial psychological facts can be distinguished from one another, counted, and calculated. If I am deliberating with myself which way to follow to go to the airport, mechanism prevails and liberty is not at stake. There are indeed numerically distinct and calculable motives in such a discussion. But the choice of a vocation, the decision to risk one's own life for a cause, these are truly free choices flowing from the whole *ego* expressing itself in its acts.

The spirituality of the soul is implied in its immateriality. The human mind is obsessed by the world of action, which is that of space. By going beyond space, one sees intensity, multiplicity, and determination disappear. What is left, offered to intuition, are three immediate data of consciousness: quality, duration, liberty.

the world and creative evolution
All our arguments have tended to establish that determinism, perhaps true of the material world, is not true of the spiritual world, but is it absolutely true even of the world of matter? In discussing this new problem we must once more start from facts. In this case, the fact to start from is evolution. Let us suppose there is evolution, as science says there is; the problem for us will be to understand the nature of this evolutionary movement observable in material beings.

Two attitudes have been adopted by intelligence with regard to evolution. The first one is the mechanistic attitude. It supposes that the universe is reducible to certain laws, so that if, in a given moment, we knew the positions of all the elements of the world, along with all the forces of the universe in both their speed and direction, we could not only explain the totality of what is happening at that moment in the world, but even predict with certainty the condition of the universe at any moment in the future (Laplace, T. Huxley).

The second interpretation of evolution resorts to the notion of final causality. It sees evolution as the progressive fulfillment of a pre-established plan. We account for the acts of a man by his desire to attain a certain end. We conclude that he must have set up a course of action in order to reach it. Applied to the history of evolution, this explanation sees it as the progressive execution of a preconceived program.

Finalism and mechanism are traditionally at odds,[45] but, as a matter of fact, they both imply that time plays no part in evolution. If all events are foreseeable, or if all events have already been foreseen, the consequence is the same: the duration of the world does not affect its history. In both cases, there really is no duration. There only is time, which is the measurement of duration reduced to space. One hour at a good play and one hour at the dentist are the same time, but they are not the same duration. There still would be duration if there were no time, and duration is the stuff reality is made of. We perceive it in ourselves, as a one-way stream, a sort of vital impulse similar in itself to what in ourselves we call liberty.

Gathering together the scientifically known facts, and attempting a metaphysical interpretation of them on the basis of the notion of duration, Bergson describes the history of evolution conceived of as the work of the vital thrust in things. This history is that of a continuous effort of invention which, unique at its origin, scatters itself through the vegetable kingdom and the animal kingdom, where it branches off, on the one hand in the direction that leads to insects, especially to hymenopters, while, on the other hand, it follows the line of the vertebrates and culminates in man. The solution represented by the hymenopters is that of instinct. The solution represented by the vertebrates is that of intelligence, but, in both cases, the solution has been found by the same initial thrust, or impulse, which is the fundamental energy at work in the history of the world.

The view of the world proposed by this metaphysics certainly includes a sort of natural theology. Bergson seems intentionally to avoid the word, and not without having his reasons. The *Creative Evolution* embraces an immense problem, but its method remains the same as in the preceding works. It truly is a positivistic method, at least to the extent that its conclusions are not dialectically deduced from abstract notions. Bergson understood his conclusions as the most precise answers he could give to some scientifically established facts. He did not think his doctrine was science, he rather saw it as the ultimate explanation of the existence, nature, and structure of the world described by science. To him it was truly a philosophy.

This explains why his last conclusions have raised difficulties in the mind of many theologians. On the one hand, Bergson was a welcome ally. Having lift-

X. Maine de Biran's French Posterity

ed the Kantian ban on metaphysics, Bergson had dispelled, on the strength of arguments taken from science itself, the obsession of materialistic mechanism; man had recovered his soul along with his liberty; last but not least, metaphysics had once more assigned to the world one single creative cause. All this was highly satisfactory, but when some of Bergson's disciples hastened to substitute his own vital thrust for the God of classical theology, the theologians objected that the active power behind Bergson's creative evolution still had a long way to go before joining the God of Christian theology.[46]

What can be said in his favor is that Bergson himself had not undertaken to justify the existence of the God of Christian theology. Looking for a cause of the evolutionary world of modern science, Bergson had found it in a transcendent and creative spiritual energy whose efficacy leaves behind itself the world of matter, then the world of life, then the human world of knowledge and of free will, more or less as artists go through life leaving behind them their works. The artist is not any one of his works, nor the whole of them; he is himself and he is their cause. In a similar way, it can be said that the metaphysics of Bergson culminates in the affirmation of a transcendent spiritual energy, free and creative cause of the world.

morality and religion

Bergson himself was fully aware of the problems left unsolved by his metaphysical notion of the élan vital conceived as a substitute for the religious notion of God. He never ceased to think about these problems, but it took him many years to form conclusions he considered worth publishing. Twenty-five years separate the original publication of *Creative Evolution* (1907) from that of *The Two Sources of Morality and Religion* (1932). The reason for this delay is known. In approaching religious problems, Bergson could not possibly change his method. He still needed facts whereupon to rest his interpretation of religion. Now religious experience is the exclusive property of the mystics, and not being privileged with mystical experience, Bergson was for the first time in his life condemned to write about facts he only knew from hearsay. This also accounted for the peculiar characteristics of this last work of Bergson. A masterpiece of philosophical style just as the preceding ones had been, *The Two Sources* perhaps was applying a then ready-made method to the solving of a problem exceeding its possibilities.

By handling together the problems of morality and of religion, Bergson was implicitly affirming his intention once more to start from empirically given facts. His constant attitude is that of a spiritualistic empiricism vivified by a new notion of inner experience. In this case again Bergson could proceed very far without losing touch with experience. Moral codes and religious codes of human conduct are inseparable from constituted social bodies by which such codes are either promulgated or, at least, observed and enforced by sanctions. The influence of Durkheim's notion of "social fact" is perceptible in the part of Bergson's doctrine that deals with these ready-made moral or religious codes, of which conformism is the general effect. These societies and their codes constitute what can be called "closed societies." Their common end is to preserve and insure the cohesion and perpetuity of those social bodies. Such is the morality of "closed souls," or "closed societies" or "closed religions" and (the word had to come) of "static societies" or religions.

This new problem, however, is but one particular case of that of creative evolution. Just as in the preceding cases, so also in morality and religion there is an opposition between the two categories of "already made" and of "in the making." Every static system of relations between "things" is only the materialized, mechanized, and solidified residue left behind by some dynamic and creative energy. This second source of morality and religion is found in heroes and saints; each of us can share in it, in his own very modest way and at least from time to time, in those circumstances when, breaking through the solidified crust of moral and religious conformism, we succeed in producing moral or religious acts that truly are our own.

To do so is to join again the primary source of all reality, namely, the élan vital; the vital impetus whose creative evolution is the cause of all that which offers itself to observation as a being or a thing. This is the "open morality" of "open souls." It also is the origin of an open society which is that of a "dynamic religion." Bergson forcibly insists that there is no passing from the first kind of morality and religion to the second one. Just as one does not reach liberty through mechanism, but, rather, against it; or just as one does not attain intuition through intelligence, but, rather, by turning one's back upon it, so also, to overcome the static conformism of closed societies is the first requirement in order to join the dynamic and open ones. Assuredly, no man can exclusively live a life of total liberty. Intelligence, science, and moral codes are there to stay, along with intuition, metaphysics, and liberty; still, when all is said and done, since closed morality follows from an inversion of the creative effort of open morality, only a second inversion can free us from static conventionalism and open for us the way to moral heroism, to religious holiness.

Such has, in fact, always been the religion of the Prophets, of which the pagan religion of the "mysteries" was, so to speak, a sketch. Its true name is mysticism, whose ultimate effect is "a contact, and therefore a partial coincidence, with the creative effort manifested by life."[47] To which Bergson adds: "This effort is from God, if it is not God himself." And again: "The great mystic thus would be an individuality overcoming the limits assigned to the species by its materiality, thereby continuing and prolonging the divine action." Plotinus, and the wise men of the East, all bear witness to the reality of such experiences. But only Christian mysticism is complete mysticism, active, creative. As can be seen in the cases of Saint Paul or Saint Theresa of Avila, the end pursued by the Christian mystic is radically to transform humanity by first setting up an example; its ideal is that of a humanity that is divine. For this reason, "mysticism and Christianity condition one another, indefinitely. Still, there must have been a beginning. In point of fact, at the origin of Christianity, there is Christ."[48]

In a revealing statement, Bergson concludes that, if mysticism is what has just been said, it should provide us with a means to approach, "so to speak experimentally," the problem of the nature and existence of God.[49] One fails to see, Bergson adds, how philosophy could approach the problem otherwise. Since philosophy is about reality, it must be concerned with existing objects; now an existing object is an object that is being perceived or, at least, that could be perceived. It must be given in some experience, either actual or possible. The philosopher as such usually lacks this mystical experience; still, he is not totally foreign to it and if his own philosophy is such that its conclusions agree with mystical experience, how could he refuse to learn from the great mystics what religion and God truly are? Assuredly, to do so is, for the philosopher, to overstep the limits of philosophical demonstration. In *Creative Evolution*, the conclusions of biology were controlling and justifying those of metaphysical speculation. We now are in the order of verisimilitude only,[50] but truth is one, and if mysticism offers itself as the only efficacious remedy to the modern invasion of the world by unbounded mechanism, it would be senseless not to accept as true this indemonstrable but wholesome and extremely high probability.

The fecundity and the limits of the Bergsonian method are here apparent. Such as it is, the doctrine is the last word of the school of thought initiated by Maine de Biran. It has been a decisive vindication of the legitimacy of metaphysical speculation. Its incisive criticism of the kind of scientism that mistakes itself for a philosophy can be considered a definitive acquisition. Bergson has assigned to mechanism its proper place and set it in its exact limits. On the other hand, his obvious desire to push his demonstrations up to the point where metaphysics would coincide in its teaching with that of Christianity was bound to be frustrated because a metaphysical empiricism necessarily leaves out all that which, in Christianity, belongs in the supernatural order. The notion of the Church, to begin with, conceived of by Christianity as endowed with all the marks of a dogmatic, static, and closed society yet, at the same time, as an eminently open and dynamic society of saints, could not find a place in Bergsonism. The problem asked by Maine de Biran can be solved by faith only, and faith is beyond the borders of philosophy. Metaphysics can go as far as Plotinus, it stops short of Saint Paul.

It is no wonder then that those Christian philosophers who mistook the God of Bergson for that of Christian theology found themselves implicated in the difficulties of Modernism. Bergsonism, not Bergson himself, was responsible for these accidents, for despite his deep-seated desire to become a Christian, he never joined the Church. Nor did he ever intend to achieve a reformation of the theology of Thomas Aquinas, of which he knew next to nothing. Even there, however, his influence has been useful. There are such things as "closed" and "static" philosophies. Like the Church itself, Christian philosophy should be at one and the same time both closed and open, static and dynamic: closed upon the immutability of its unchangeable faith, but open by its dynamic effort ceaselessly to investigate the inexhaustible contents of given reality in the light of faith. There can be no such thing as a Bergsonian brand of Thomism, but Bergson has greatly helped some Christian philosophers to re-evaluate and revivify the dynamic elements included by Thomas Aquinas in his own doctrine. Bergson himself could not do this, because being was at stake, and not such as mere philosophy can determine its nature, but such as one can learn to know it in the metaphysics of *Exodus* alone.

XI. *In the Spirit of Criticism*

THE criticism of Kant began to filter into French philosophical circles first in an indirect way, through expositions and interpretations. The early translation of the *Critique of Pure Reason* by Tissot found an intelligent reader in Italy. Abbé Testa[1] put it to good use and ended his career as a declared follower of Kant. In France, the popularization of Kantianism did not take place before the translations provided by Jules Barni (1818–1878). From then onward the influence of Kant can be observed everywhere, but it would be difficult to find in France any real Kantian.

There is something final in the Kantian position of the philosophical problem; granting the initial assumptions of the doctrine, the conclusions cannot easily be rejected, but those initial assumptions themselves hang on a free decision of the mind, and since everybody feels free to modify them at will, the doctrine of Kant usually acts as an inspiration rather than as a model. The fact is obvious in the case of the great German successors of Kant—Fichte, Schelling, and Hegel. How to evade the agnostic conclusions of Kantianism was one of their main concerns. The problem was the same in France with Renouvier: if one accepts Kant's position of the philosophical problem, is there any way to justify the traditionally received metaphysical conclusions?

RENOUVIER'S NEOCRITICISM

The main representative of French neocriticism was Renouvier.[2] Like Auguste Comte, he was one of the many philosophers turned out by the École Polytechnique, by tradition a center of mathematical learning. With that exceptional mathematical formation, a mind fertile in abstractions and with a tendency, only too common among mathematicians, to handle concepts as if they were algebraic symbols, Renouvier has left us an enormous philosophical production (enough to fill about fifty volumes); but his position noticeably changed with time and a large part of his speculation was devoted to political problems, if not to say political action.

It has become usual to distinguish three main parts in his philosophical production: a first philosophy, usually called "the philosophy of the Manuals"; a second philosophy, which constitutes the center of his doctrine and is commonly called his "neocriticism"; a third philosophy which, on more than one point, marks a return to the spirit of the first period, but with a strong insistence on the notion of "personalism," the Kantian origin of which is evident.

Neocriticism is in fundamental agreement with Comte's positivism on two interrelated points: all knowledge is relative because things themselves are relative, and there is no metaphysical knowledge precisely because there is nothing absolute. As will be seen, his positivism will lead Renouvier to conclusions still more anti-metaphysical than those of Kant.

Our knowledge of things is submitted to the categories of understanding. So, by definition, it cannot reach beyond phenomena. The pursuit of any absolute is absurd, but the notion of "phenomenon" itself is not simple; it implies that of a representative and that of a represented. Now each one of these two elements possesses the characteristics of its very opposite. The knowing subject (the representative) is the object of its own reflection (the represented); as to the known object, it is in consciousness as a representation that does not distinguish itself from the representing subject. In this sense, object is subject and everything represented is representative at the same time. Renouvier sees himself halfway between materialism, which sees nothing beyond the represented, and idealism, which reduces reality to the representative element only. Truth lies in the union of these two opposite points of view; phenomenon, as given in and by the categories, will effect that unity.

Representation is possible only through the categories. Since all is relative, the first category is that of relation. Then come number, extension, time, and quality, which determine the appearances of all the relations. Renouvier's table eliminates the category of modality, because the notion is implied in the general conditions of the exercise of understanding in all the categorical orders. Over and above the preceding categories are the notions of cause and of end, which permit the ordering of all the categorical cognitions. At the summit is found personality, which implies both cause and end. Every representation involves

XI. *In the Spirit of Criticism*

all the categories and all the categories are comprised in that of personality, because it concerns the activity of the ego which forms all those representations.[3]

The main difference from Kant is that, on account of his strict phenomenalism, Renouvier denies the existence of any "thing in itself." The reason we know only phenomena in his doctrine is that there is no "noumenon."[4] To be a phenomenon and to be given in consciousness are one and the same thing. That which is in itself other than it is as a phenomenon (i.e., as appearing in cognition) simply is not.

Each being is a unit, but not a substance (substance is a thing in itself); it is only a relatively permanent pattern of associated phenomena. Every one of us communicates with other beings on account of the necessities of action. By "practical belief" we are led to posit the existence of a *non-ego*, then that of an *other-ego*.[5] The *ego* thus finds itself as a free agent in the middle of a chain of phenomena whose laws are the work of understanding. Since things are in themselves such as they are for us, that which is unthinkable does not exist. Such is, before anything else, actual infinity. An actually infinite number is unthinkable, since it always remains possible to add one more unit to any given number. Hence the universal "finitism" of Renouvier.

An important consequence of this feature of neocriticism is that it entails the elimination of the antinomies of pure reason. As Kant had understood them, the antithesis implied the notion of infinity, but if infinity is impossible, only the thesis of each antinomy remains possible. Consequently, the world is finite in both space and time; matter is composed of simple parts; human free will subsists even in the middle of determined phenomena; last but not the least of these consequences, the order of natural causes is a finite series of phenomena hanging on a first uncaused cause.

A general feature of the doctrine accounts for the passage from the second to the third philosophy of Renouvier. Unlike Kant, Renouvier does not consider evident the judgments of speculative reason. Will plays a part in every judgment and there is an element of "belief" at the basis of all certitude, even in the purely speculative order. In this sense, there is a primacy of practical reason. This entails a last difference from Kant: instead of speaking of several different critiques (of pure speculative reason, practical reason, and judgment) Renouvier recognizes only one single critique. The very title of the *Essais de critique générale* (1854) aptly expresses this feature of the neocriticism of Renouvier.

This third stage of the doctrine is characterized by an effort to reorganize around the notion of "person" the main conclusions of traditional metaphysics.[6] The universe is made up of monads (stable groups of phenomena); the human monad is a person on account of both knowledge and will. The moralism of Renouvier finds in the notion of "rational belief" a way to regain, by rational decisions of the will, a sort of substitute for the traditional conceptions of man and God. At one point in his life (about 1851), Renouvier severely blamed Kant for having restored, on the strength of practical reason, the metaphysical theses he first had ruined on the strength of pure reason. His own third philosophy has done pretty much the same thing.

In his *Philosophie analytique de l'histoire* (1898) Renouvier himself has stressed the analogies between his own conclusions and the traditional teaching of Christian theology. The verbal agreement is real, but there is no other one. One God (but a finite God: the permanent personality in the world); this finite God is powerful enough to have created *ex nihilo* our finite universe; the world was created good, but man has sinned against order and, being unable to recover lost justice, mankind shall have to be brought back to its original perfection. Renouvier has always been convinced that, under some form to be discovered, "a Christian philosophy will prevail."[7]

If one carefully scrutinizes the work of the French philosophers who undertook to criticize knowledge, he cannot fail to conclude that, in the last analysis, not one of them has kept faith with the formalism of Kant's *Critiques*. Now, formalism is the very essence of Kant's critical philosophy. His intention had been to determine the *a priori* conditions under which science and ethics are possible. Given what science and morality actually are, what must be the contribution of understanding to these disciplines to account for their being exactly such? The criticism of Kant never went beyond this problem; all the rest was carefully bracketed, including the "things in themselves," of which, by definition, we know nothing. Renouvier seems to have achieved a mixture of the criticism of Kant and of the relativism of Comte, two heterogeneous doctrines whose ultimate ends were not so irreconcilable after all.

Octave Hamelin

The influence of Renouvier was felt in the teaching of philosophy in French

XI. In the Spirit of Criticism

universities and colleges till the end of the nineteenth century. It was kept up by devoted disciples who, apart from writing books of their own, actively shared in the editing work connected with the publication of the two periodicals founded by Renouvier, *La critique philosophique* and *La critique religieuse*.[8] The most important of all the contributions to neocriticism, however, was to come later, with the work of Octave Hamelin[9] in the first years of the twentieth century.

Bergson had entitled his 1889 thesis *Essai stir les données immédiates de la conscience* (*Time and Freewill: An Essay on the Immediate Data of Consciousness*); it is certainly not unintentionally that Hamelin gave to his own 1907 thesis the title *Essai sur les éléments principaux de le représentation* (*Essay on the Principal Elements of Representation*). Bergson had interrogated immediate inner experience in order to find a way out of cut-and-dried rationalism; Hamelin was consciously going back to reason as to the only source of philosophical intelligibility. Starting from Renouvier, but handling the same problems in a spirit entirely his own, Hamelin devoted his reflection to what always remained, after Kant, a central problem of Kantianism, the notion of category. Great philosophies find in their essential weakness the source of their greatest fecundity. The doctrine of Locke intended to be a plain, objective description of the faculties and operations of the human mind: from Condillac to the last of the Italian ideologists, every one of his successors proposed a different analysis of man's understanding and will. There is simply no limits to that conceptual dismantling of the mind. The same can be said of Kant's doctrine of the categories, for they provide a marvelously simple answer to the problem of knowledge; category is an essentially *erkenntnistheoretisch* function, but how many categories there are, and which they are, and how they should be ordered, these and similar questions have provided an abundant material for discussion among the successors to Kant, including the French representatives of neocriticism. Renouvier alone has set up five tables of categories, all more or less different in contents and order. Hamelin observed that there still remained some empiricism in the way Renouvier had made his successive choices.[10] And the remark was well founded, but, at the same time as it stresses a weakness in Renouvier's doctrine, it points out what might well be a fundamental illusion in the mind of Hamelin himself. For it was his ambition to build up a system of the main elements of representation covering in totality the field of human knowledge. Hamelin was a personally modest man. He did not think he had faultlessly built up the all-embracing system of primary notions included in our cognitions, but he certainly believed in the possibility of successfully achieving the undertaking. The method had to to be reflexive, and its object was to discern the order following which all the fundamental notions at work in knowledge produce one another. In Hamelin's own words, his project was to "take each notion to its own place" (*l'amener à sa place*). Under a different name, the notion of category was thus becoming the very substance of philosophy. By the same token, philosophy was bound to become a pure rationalistic idealism. From this point of view, Hamelin's *Essay* marks an extreme limit which cannot be overstepped, even though it still can be reached in countless other ways.

The problem is to construct a system of notions which, although given *a priori*, will provide an adequate (i.e., necessary and exhaustive) expression of concrete reality. To reconstruct reality by means of concepts is necessarily to use a method similar to that of Hegel. It is *a priori* because it appeals to notions given to the mind; it is constructive, because it finds in the very way those notions beget one another a justification for uniting them by means of synthetic judgments. *A priori* synthetic judgments are the necessary tools of all idealism that does not want to condemn itself to a sterile repetition of some initial notion. To derive everything from the notion of pure being, if the attempt is carried out in an analytical way, is to go straight back to Parmenides: being is, not being is not, and there is nothing more to say. Some different method must be found.[11]

Hamelin finds it in what he considers a fundamental law of thought, to wit, the necessary correlation of opposite notions in the mind. This, of course, was to look to Hegel for an antidote to Eleaticism, but despite a striking external resemblance, the two dialectics differ in spirit. As Hamelin sees it, the inner dialectics of the mind consists in this, that every notion posited by the mind causes it to conceive another notion contrary to the first one. It is typical of Hamelin's dialectics that, in it, the two notions are conceivable only in their very opposition. Moreover, their opposition makes it necessary for the mind to conceive a third one which includes them both in its own unity. In order to include them, the third notion must be distinct from them, just as they are distinct from one another. The point Hamelin intends to make is that the three notions are not obtained by deduction from the first one; they all are given together as both distinct and necessarily connected by their very opposition, which is not one of contradiction but rather of complementarity.

XI. *In the Spirit of Criticism*

In conformity with the language of Hegel, Hamelin says that each and every thesis calls for an antithesis, which both excludes it and completes it; so there must be a synthesis to express this complementarity within the distinction. On the other hand, in the true spirit of Renouvier, Hamelin calls "relation" that threefold structure of thought and reality. Relation therefore is the simplest and most primitive law of reality, but at the same time it is also the primitive and simplest law of thought. Because every given object of knowledge is at once thesis, antithesis, and synthesis,[12] thinking itself is necessarily bound to pass from every notion to another one, and thereby not only to move, but to progress in multiplying its objects to infinity. Hamelin's dialectics thus proceeds from the more abstract to the more concrete. Had he heard of the fact and of its name, Hamelin would perhaps have admitted that concepts (i.e., the main elements of representation) release one another as in a sort of chain reaction.

The problem then is to constitute things by means of relations. The first element being *relation* itself, we begin by positing two terms each of which cannot be without the other one. One cannot conceive this without, at the same time, thinking of two terms each of which can be without the other one; this is *number*, that is to say, the relation whereby it is posited that one term is without another one. Each number has its own properties and it is enough to add one to any number in order to turn it into another number endowed with opposite properties; for instance, such is the case with the primary opposition of even and odd numbers. Number therefore is the antithesis of which relation is the thesis. This gives us a necessary correlation (thesis) of mutually exclusive terms (antithesis). Once more without any deduction, but in an immediate apprehension of their correlation, we perceive their synthesis. What is that which consists of elements that cannot exist together and, nevertheless, are impossible to disjoin and to separate? *Time* is such a synthesis of mutually exclusive moments given in the continuity of their succession.

The next notion is inseparable from that of time, for it is its opposite. It is the notion of a quantity (or number) whose parts are as mutually exclusive as those of time, and yet, from another point of view, given together and in an irreversible order of succession. Such is *space* which, unlike Renouvier, Hamelin puts after time and as its correlative. On the other hand, it is impossible to conceive time (thesis) and space (antithesis) without at once forming the notion of their synthesis. Such is *movement*, in which becoming is the unity of a series of terms succeeding one another in space as well as in time.

The preceding syntheses all imply variations in quantity: time is longer or shorter; space is greater or smaller; movement is faster or slower. The concept of such quantitatively determined composites calls for that of a different type of opposites in which the result of the composition is indifferent to quantity. Such is *quality*. One square inch of saturated blue is not more blue than a wide surface covered with the same color. There is more blue in a wider surface than in a smaller one, but the wider surface is not more blue, if the quality of the color is the same. But the position of movement (thesis) and that of quality (antithesis) call for their synthesis, and this is a very old one, since the notion of *motus ad qualitatem* already was in Aristotle the definition of *alteration*.

Following the same process, Hamelin opposes to the kind of change that ends in the suppression of its starting point (alteration, the act of becoming *other than* one was) a kind of change whose essence it is "to preserve the qualitative state taken as its origin." This is *specification*, which consists in uniting qualitative differences into genera, species, or generally speaking of classes, each of which gathers together, within one single notion, a plurality of univocal qualifications. Alteration (thesis) plus specification (antithesis) implicitly posit their synthesis, whose notion is among the subtlest developed by Hamelin's dialectics. The problem is to find a kind of relation (for relation is the very stuff things are made of) in which an alteration (the becoming of otherness) will be tied up with a specification (the preservation of sameness). Hamelin describes it as a relation by which "each and every part of things, in virtue of something outside of it, must be other than it would be if it were alone."[13] Such is *causality*, by which one being owes its specification to another being.

As can be seen, the principal elements of representation are wholly different, in Hamelin, from the categories of Kant and of Renouvier. They beget one another by a continuous process of complication. In this sense, they resemble much more the moments of which the logic of Hegel is made up, but here again there is a fundamental difference: instead of being a construction from being, they are a progressive construction of being in which reality is ceaselessly growing more complex and more rich by continuously adding to its own content.

This is particularly true of the notion of causality. Such as Hamelin conceives it, effect does not analytically follow from cause; it was not pre-con-

XI. *In the Spirit of Criticism*

tained within it; on the contrary, it adds itself to it, or, rather, the cause adds effect to itself as something it needed. Hamelin's is a creative dialectic. Far from including its future effect, the cause is lacking it and wanting it: "The cause calls for the effect: this is to say that, in a certain sense, the present state of things is not self-sufficient and that one never can conceive of it without anticipating the states still to come."[14] It is to be noted, however, that causality does not account for any particular goodness, perfection, or beauty of the effects. These are mere results; they are what they have to be, as can be seen in mechanical causality, where the essence of causal relation is clearly visible. Hence causality (thesis) calls for an antithesis, which is *purposiveness*, a principle of order and harmony necessary for the preservation of mechanical effects. Let us be careful not to conceive purposiveness as one particular case of causality, of which it is the very antithesis. Of itself, purposiveness does nothing; it produces nothing, but, rather, it is a sort of condition *sine qua non*: "it condemns to remain abstract, unreal, inexistent, the mechanisms that do not fulfill its requirements."[15]

The synthesis of causality and finality is *personality*. The key notion in the system of Renouvier thus retains its primacy in that of Hamelin. A free cause, aware of its own freedom and able to direct itself, man as a person remains on the same line as all the preceding terms in our progressive construction of reality. Like the views of the world exposed by Comte, by Lachelier, by Boutroux, and by Renouvier, reality exhibits a continuity of order along with a discontinuity in the degrees of perfection. There are lower and higher layers of reality, and the higher presuppose the lower, but they do not result from them. In the doctrine of Hamelin, the appearing of personality and of liberty as its typical attribute does not disrupt the balance of the system. Like the preceding notions, that of liberty arrives at its own place in the doctrine. As a privilege of personality, itself the synthesis of causality and finality, the existence of liberty is necessary, but the necessity that certain acts should be free establishes the presence, in the universal order of things, of a causality obeying a purposiveness.[16] There is then contingence in things, but contingence is not the ultimate in things; rather, in Hamelin's doctrine, everything is intelligible in its own right, and this is the reason philosophy can attempt to translate into a system of concepts the whole of reality; but since, in fact, there is in the world an element of contingence, our conceptual formulation of reality should take it into account. It does so by assigning to it its proper place in the universal system of relations where intelligibility finally coincides with reality.

Léon Brunschvicg

The doctorate thesis of Leon Brunschvicg[17] dealt with the problem of the modality of judgment. This was to start from the very part of the Kantian table of the categories with which Renouvier had first found fault, but Brunschvicg was interested in something more than a mere overhauling of the doctrine. To him philosophy is intellectual activity achieving the awareness of itself. Such a program had nothing new in itself. On the contrary, one could almost say that it had been the common program of all the French philosophers since Maine de Biran had initiated the practice of reflexive method, but whereas Maine de Biran, Ravaisson, Lachelier, and Bergson had all tended to use reflexive method as a means of overcoming the limitations of the ego, Brunschvicg expressly understood it as something not to be transcended. Intellectual activity achieving the awareness of itself contains the totality of the knowable as well as of the known.

Judgment is the proper act of intelligence, so such a philosophy had to start from judgment. Moreover, because modality presupposes in intelligence the right of judging, the problem of the modality of judgment had to come first. From this point of view, judgment manifests itself as the power inherent in the mind to apprehend two notions as one. This is the essential point to understand about the idealism of Brunschvicg, for all the rest will be nothing else than a thoroughly systematic interpretation of sciences, philosophies, arts, and religions in the light of his initial conception of judgment. Let us restate it: the spirit expresses itself in judgments; a judgment is the reduction to unity of two ideas simultaneously present to it. "If two ideas are simultaneously in one and the same spirit and united in that spirit, as being run through, so to speak, by one same stream of thought, it is because those two ideas are interior the one to the other and can constitute one single idea."[18]

In the philosophical language of Brunschvicg, the notion of "inferiority" plays an important part. It is, of course, a metaphor, since no attribute of space (inferiority or exteriority) correctly applies to the mind; but the meaning of the metaphor is fairly constant in the doctrine; that is interior to something which, being graspable along with it by a single act, is susceptible of becoming one

XI. *In the Spirit of Criticism*

with it in the unity of their common idea in the mind. Let it be added (although Brunschvicg himself does not expressly say so) that the notion of inferiority, being one with that of intelligence, or mind, or spirit, generally connotes the notion of good. All predicative judgments manifest that essential perfection of the mind—to be able to associate, to unify. The verb *is*, used as a copula, is the perfect manifestation of that unifying power; judgment is perfect when, being perfectly itself, it achieves complete inferiority at the same time as complete intelligibility and necessity.

The same verb *is* can also be used absolutely, and not as a copula. Instead of saying that a certain notion is identical with another one, we just say of something that *it is*. Since the actual existence of a thing can never be inferred from its notion, actual existence cannot possibly be conceived of as *interior to* the mind. On the contrary, that which actually exists is that which is outside the mind. Thus understood, existence is the very opposite of inferiority; so it is exteriority. And since inferiority is one with intelligibility, existence is bound to be the contrary of intelligibility. Inasmuch as, of its very essence, existence is the exclusion of inferiority, it is pure exteriority. Existence then signifies absolute exteriority to the spirit; consequently, it signifies being as impenetrable to the mind.

It is remarkable that, far from ridding philosophy from the problem of what to do with given reality, the absolute idealism of Brunschvicg obliges itself, from its very first step, to posit it as a foreign body unassimilable to thought *in virtue of its very definition*. In Brunschvicg's own words: "The duality of being and thought is decidedly primary and irreducible."[19] This leaves us with a philosophy in which being is bracketed at the very outset as the radical otherness, existence is destined to remain foreign to mind and to philosophy. It is no wonder that contemporary French existentialism singled out Brunschvicg's idealism as the prototype of the philosophy to be destroyed. It excludes from philosophical speculation the very subject matter of existentialism.

But even idealism cannot wholly ignore existence. Without otherness and plurality, the consideration of sameness and oneness would remain sterile. It is essential to the doctrine, being a dualism, to initiate and to keep up a dialogue between the mind and existence, that is, between sameness and otherness, between intelligibility and non-intelligibility. *Qua* pure and absolute givenness, being plays in the doctrine the part of an obstacle to which mind is bound to react. It is for mind the cause of a shock which sets it working. The unity of spirit and existence, of inferiority and exteriority, is consciousness, a fact mysterious in its nature as well as in its origin. Unlike Bergson, Brunschvicg refuses to probe into consciousness. On the contrary, he considers that, since it is thought itself, consciousness cannot have itself for its own object. The products of thought, not thought itself, are the objects of consciousness.

This determines the general plan of Brunschvicg's philosophy. Inferiority has always been trying to reduce the area of exteriority, to substitute sameness for otherness and unity for multiplicity. From this point of view, Brunschvicg himself would not have agreed that his doctrine should be called a pure idealism. There is enough reason in man to hold realism in check, but there is enough givenness and experience in the data of science to hold idealism in check. Still, the philosophical history of the human mind is that of a progressive elimination of exteriority by inferiority. In his short, but philosophy-packed *Introduction à la vie de l'esprit*, Brunschvicg determined the method and object of philosophical reflection, but the essential had already been said in his thesis on the modality of judgment. The aim and scope of such a philosophy is to interiorize knowledge, that is to say, to cause judgment to depend more and more upon itself and less and less upon exterior things. The doctrine is at least an invitation to absolute idealism. The spirit must finally find in itself the very reality it affirms, and because this is true in ethics as well as in science, it is the core and substance of philosophy.

Having to characterize his doctrine by traditional epithets, Brunschvicg has chosen to call it an "idealism," a "new idealism." In fact, an idealism without ideas. At the same time, he would call it a "critical idealism" because, beyond the deformations of Kantism by Fichte, Schelling, and Hegel, it goes back to the authentic spirit of the *Critique of Pure Reason*, which was that of a reflection of spirit upon itself as cause of science. Still, unlike the preceding idealisms, that of Brunschvicg did not want to "deduce the spirit"; nor did it want to determine the origin and filiation of the laws of understanding; rather, he wished to proceed to an analysis of the human mind, to discern the laws that guide its activity, and to discern the essential relations revealed by the progress of science and of morality.[20] At the same time, Brunschvicg claimed for his philosophy the title of "spiritualism." Indeed, his idealism was not of the type usually opposed to metaphysical realism, but, rather, it was a vindication of the rights of spirit con-

XI. *In the Spirit of Criticism*

ceived of as a living force. To Brunschvicg, the opposition idealism *vs.* realism was out of date; what was at stake in contemporary idealism was spirit itself.

Granting that there is matter and an external world subjected to necessary laws, there still remains a radical distinction between it and science itself: "Since it lays down the law for matter, science itself cannot be subjected to necessary laws; so it must be a reality distinct from matter."[21] This spiritualist affirmation of science does not overstep the borders of science; it is immediately implied in the understanding of science as science. A metaphysician may have to choose between materialism and spiritualism; a scientist has no choice. Spirit is that without which there would be no science. So a scientist may well profess materialism in words, he cannot be a materialist; not, at least, if he pays attention to what science actually is.

A last character of modern idealism permits us to distinguish it from mysticism, namely, its intellectualism. Here again misunderstandings should be avoided. Intellect is not a faculty among others; it is not something to be known, for instance as distinct from feeling or will; intellect is only knowable as that which produces science and morality. Intellect is known by its fruit.

This gives its philosophical meaning to the vast inquiry into the history of mathematics, physics, metaphysics, and religion undertaken by Brunschvicg and carried by him to completion. Taken as a whole, it constitutes a stimulating picture of the history of the human mind. But this history also is a last judgment. There are the good, whose patriarch is Plato, and the wicked, whose patriarch is Aristotle. There also is an angel of judgment, who knows by what signs the good can be told from the wicked. His judgments are hard, and there is no appeal. One would waste one's time reproaching Brunschvicg with misinterpreting many of the doctrines he has so severely judged.[22] He himself has been still more unjustly judged by the recent generation of the French existentialists in whose sight Brunschvicg represents the abstract and unreal philosophy of the professors, lost in a naïve optimism and with no feeling for reality. Brunschvicg himself was surely nothing like that. His last days, as a persecuted exile during the second World War, make it impossible to think he was not aware of the awful reality of evil. His final book, *L'esprit européen*, shows him unshaken in his spiritualistic faith and as confident as ever in the future of the spirit.[23]

XII. *In the Spirit of Scholasticism*

THE revival of Thomism that took place in nineteenth-century Italy was not initiated by any magisterial decisions of the Church. Contrary to what is commonly believed, the movement was born in the minds of Italian professors of philosophy in seminaries and convents, of their dissatisfaction with the philosophical tradition of the eighteenth century and its continuation in the early nineteenth-century Italian schools.[1] One of these professors, Sordi, specified that his own starting point had been, among other similar doctrines, the philosophy of Condillac, Wolff, and Soave.[2] In fact, very little else could be learned in schools. On the other hand, the traditionalist and ontologist reactions did not seem fit to meet the data of the problem. In order to react against sensism, these philosophers went to no less dangerous extremes, even to the extent of what appeared to Sordi as the pantheism of Rosmini and Gioberti. Whether or not Rosmini and Gioberti really were pantheists was another question. The point is that those Christian masters thought that the new Christian philosophies recently born in Italy were suspected of such errors.

Something else had to be found, and it was only natural to look for it in the writings of Thomas Aquinas, whose doctrine had always been more or less upheld in certain schools of theology, not indeed in its purity, but in something of its spirit. One of the main obstacles to the revival of Thomism in Catholic schools was precisely the introduction of non-Thomistic forms of scholasticism traditionally upheld in their own schools by certain religious orders. Thomas was not always welcome in such places. Writing about two Jesuit fathers, Sordi and Cornoldi, the Provincial Tedeschi said in 1865: "Those two members of the Society, well known as uncompromising Thomists, suddenly rose in defense of that commonly rejected doctrine.... Now their way of feeling and of thinking implies a condemnation of the whole body of the Society and, which is worse, of the Episcopate since, in their seminaries, the bishops have permitted freely

XII. *In the Spirit of Scholasticism*

the teaching of doctrines opposed to the notion of prime matter..."[3] It is therefore, at least in such cases, against the doctrinal preferences of their own superiors that the promoters of the movement advocated a return to the teaching of Saint Thomas Aquinas.

THE ORIGINS OF THE MOVEMENT

At first, there was no such thing as a movement. Vincenzo Buzzetti (1774–1824), a simple professor of philosophy at the seminary of Piacenza,[4] marks well the transition from the problematic of the eighteenth century to the revival of scholasticism. His unpublished works include *Refutation of John Locke*, *Refutation of the Idealism of Condillac* and, more typical still, *Solution of the Problem of Molyneux*. His *Institutiones philosophicae*, only the first half of which has been published, reveals the nature of the problem those early neo-Thomists had to solve. On the one hand, they had to rediscover the true doctrine of Thomas Aquinas hidden beneath the layers of alluvions deposited on it by the past five centuries. On the other hand, they could not content themselves with repeating the scholasticism of the thirteenth century. The reason for that impossibility is obvious: to go back to the doctrines of the middle ages, such as they were, would be to duplicate the situation which caused their destruction. The problem is hard to solve. By and large, its solution requires that two conditions should first be fulfilled: first, one must correctly understand the principles that dominate the doctrine of Saint Thomas; next, one must be able to distinguish, within the doctrine, the permanently valid principles from the changing data of the problems in which, during the course of history, they found themselves engaged.

Serafino Sordi, S.J. (1793–1865), a pupil of Buzzetti,[5] belongs to the first generation that found itself in a position to use the recently recovered scholasticism as a weapon against the philosophical errors of the time. And this is done by Sordi with as much precision as elegance. In opposing the doctrine of Rosmini's *New Essay on the Origin of Ideas*, Sordi goes straight to the central point: Are there innate universal ideas, or are they all formed by means of abstraction? The choice was important because one could not oppose innatism without siding with Locke against his Christian adversaries. The empirical element common to Aristotle and Locke was one of the disturbing features of neo-scholasticism in the eyes of both traditionalists and ontologists.

According to Rosmini, generalization was effected by the mind in adding to any particular notion the naturally universal idea of being, which is innate. The part played by the notion of being in the formation of universal ideas had already been stressed by Malebranche. Sordi rightly objects that, in fact, particular ideas themselves can be directly universalized. One cannot therefore distinguish between two elements in the notion, the one particular, the other universal by itself; all our concepts, including that of being, result from one and the same process of generalization and abstraction. Abstraction does not find the universal ready-made, it has to produce it. As to the other aspect of the doctrine, which considers generalization as resulting from a judgment, Sordi objects that judgments presuppose the existence of concepts, so it cannot be their cause. An idea is not general or common because I judge it to be such, but, rather, I judge it to be such because it is such.

Sordi applies the same criticism to the Rosminian position that "the common has no existence outside the intellect." Incidentally, let us note that many an Aristotelian would subscribe to that position, but Sordi simply follows the "moderate realism" traditionally attributed to Saint Thomas. Since intellect cannot perceive that which does not exist, all its notions must have some foundation in reality. The reason the common idea is found in the intellect is that it has a foundation outside the intellect. The difference is that, outside the intellect, being is found particularized by individuating characters, whereas, in the intellect, having been stripped of those characters, it is found in its universality.[6]

In his dialogue against Gioberti, Sordi maintains the same noetics. Gioberti upheld that knowledge is intuition and that in intuition there is an immediate apprehension of object by the subject, without any operation on the part of either. In short, the object of intuition is the idea, and the idea is nothing else than the object itself present to the mind.

Sordi observes that there are no such things as ideas in human knowledge; ideas exist only in the divine mind. Moreover, it cannot be denied that intuition is an act. If it is, it has to be an act of the intuited object or of the intuiting subject. That there is no change in the known object arising from the fact that it is being known, is true, but it is equally certain that, for the knowing subject, to achieve cognition is a change. In fact it must pass from potency to act with respect to knowledge. Moreover, since to know is an immanent operation, whose

XII. *In the Spirit of Scholasticism*

term is in the subject, intuition itself necessarily implies the presence of an image, or form, in the intuiting mind. Here again, the Aristotelian notion of abstraction is integrally maintained. Sordi is well aware that Gioberti was trying to avoid the very notion of interposed "ideas" which he himself was opposing. Gioberti had tried to justify intuitive knowledge as a sure means to cut the very root of idealism; but Sordi answers that, in traditional Aristotelianism, there is no "object" interposed between thing and intellect; the species, or phantasms, are not known objects, they simply are means of knowing.[7] From object to subject, there is no bridge to cross; the object is *in* the subject according to subject's proper mode of being.

From the fragments at our disposal, it is not easy to form a notion of Sordi's philosophy as a whole,[8] but there is no reason to doubt the authenticity of his Aristotelianism, at least under the form it had received from the medieval Thomist tradition. It seems to be less interested in the supreme principles of metaphysics than in the intermediate notions permitting an application of those principles to what we now call the philosophy of nature. Act and potency, substantial form conceived as principle of both being and operation, in short, all the notions that could serve as an antidote to the then obtaining materialistic and mechanistic interpretations of nature, seem to have detained the attention of Sordi. But our knowledge of his doctrine is too fragmentary to justify a global interpretation of it.

The situation becomes different with the Neapolitan Jesuit Matteo Liberatore, whose abundant philosophical writings authorize a general appreciation of his personal positions.[9] In an easy and conventionally elegant style, Liberatore attempted to introduce his contemporaries to what he himself considered the authentic doctrine of Saint Thomas or, rather, of scholasticism in general. The last edition of his *Institutiones Philosophicae* shows him more confident of final success than he was in the first one. His personal interest was in noetics and his treatise *Della conoscenza intellettuale*, translated into German and French, has certainly set up a comparatively new style in the history of the Thomist revival. It marks the time when the much-abused scholasticism begins to show itself aggressive and to indulge in open attacks against modern philosophies in general. Liberatore does not only oppose Kant, he derides him. Fichte, Hegel, Rosmini, and Gioberti are handled no more gently, but it must be conceded that criticism is with him secondary, and subservient to the exposition of truth. To the modern notion of idea conceived as the immediate object of the mind, Liberatore substitutes the Thomist notion of *species* conceived of as that by which objects are known. So the subjectivity of the *species* does not affect the objectivity of the known notions. Thus understood, idea (*species*) is not that which is known, but rather it is that through which its object is known. Liberatore demonstrates his own mastery of the Thomist noetics in discussing the arguments of the "ontologists," themselves grounded in the Augustinian tradition, to the effect that the human intellect cannot account for the necessity, eternity, and absolute certitude of true propositions.[10] Without any marked personal originality, to which he does not even pretend, Liberatore shows himself able to carry on an intelligent dialogue with the tenants of modern idealism; his work has certainly contributed to the spread of the notion that, after all, scholasticism still had something intelligent to say.

The rapid expansion of scholasticism in Italian schools surprised Liberatore himself, and indeed history witnesses the publication of many works of similar inspiration. The attention devoted to the metaphysics of being grows more and more marked; the fundamental Thomistic thesis of the real composition of essence and existence is explicitly upheld by Gaetano Sanseverino (1811–1865), whose remarkable erudition combines with a sincere intention to restate authentic Thomism, although, like many of his contemporaries and successors down to our own time, he attempts to force Thomism into a Wolfian framework.[11] Just at the same time, Joseph Pecci (1807–1890), a professor at the Roman College, at the Seminary of Perugia, and at the University of the Sapienza (Rome), published a commentary on Aquinas' *De ente et essentia* in which he likewise upheld the real composition (or, as they say) distinction, of essence and existence.[12] Joseph Pecci was a brother of Joachim Pecci, the future Pope Leo XIII. In 1883, Pope Leo XIII, with the collaboration of his brother, Cardinal Joseph Pecci, and of Fr. Cornoldi, S.J.,[13] was to found the Roman Academy of St. Thomas Aquinas. The figure of Cornoldi deserves to be singled out for particular consideration.

From the early years of the Jesuit scholasticate at Laval, France, when, with the other Italian scholastics, he found himself at war with the French scholastics who favored ontologism, till his later years when he familiarized himself with Thomism, Cornoldi's life followed the same course as the revival of the Christian scholastic tradition. Relating the reason for his choice, Cornoldi was

XII. *In the Spirit of Scholasticism*

later to say that there then was for him no other alternative than either to create a new philosophy of his own more or less borrowed from older ones, or else take up traditional scholasticism and strive to promote it. He decided in favor of the second course, but this decision set him in opposition to other members of the Society, especially Tongiorgi.[14] The question then was whether physics should be taught according to the principles of mechanism and in accordance with the spirit of modern science (Tongiorgi) or, on the contrary, following the scholastico-Aristotelian tradition (Cornoldi).

The conclusions of Cornoldi's controversy with the mechanistic physics of Tongiorgi, S.J., as well as against physical dynamism, were published by Cornoldi under the title *I sistemi meccanico e dinamico rispetto alle scienze naturali* (Verona, 1864). His refutation of those two systems rested upon the principles of scholasticism. The Collegio Romano tried to prevent the diffusion of the opuscule; some of its members even considered that the RR. PP. Liberatore and Cornoldi were a disgrace to the Society of Jesus. There was a sort of feud between the Collegio Romano, supporters of a more modern philosophy, and the Civiltà Cattolica favoring the revival of the doctrine of Thomas by Sanseverino and Cornoldi. They were good friends, but they did not agree on the opportunity of a return to Saint Thomas.

There would be no point in going over the traditional positions upheld by Cornoldi, but it is interesting to see what he himself considers to be the nature of the scholastic philosophy that should be revived. One of the first motives behind the movement is the desire to restore ideological unity within the Society of Jesus then torn apart by conflicting philosophies. Once the motive was admitted, another force necessarily worked toward the same end, to wit, the rule set up as early as the sixteenth century, that bound the masters of the Society to follow the doctrine of Thomas Aquinas. A certain amount of freedom was allowed, but, by and large, Thomism had then been established as the standard doctrine of the Society. Owing to the influence of some eminent Jesuits, Thomism then became the standard doctrine of the Church.

The personal mentality of Cornoldi had little to do with those general influences, but it accounts for his personal place in the movement. To him, intellectual unity was equally required in philosophy and in theology; hence, since there could be no theological unity unless there was philosophical unity, he could not admit of the coexistence of several different philosophies in the

Catholic schools. Moreover, although he himself did not expressly enunciate it as a principle, Cornoldi never agreed to distinguish between "differences" and "oppositions" between philosophical doctrines. This resulted almost inevitably from his passion for absolute unity coupled with his unconditional respect for religious unity. Faith is one; as an understanding of faith theology must be one; as a handmaid to theology, philosophy too must be one. Consequently, there must be one single philosophy, one and immutable as Christian faith itself. After recalling the words addressed by Bossuet to the Protestants: "You change, hence you are error" (*Vous changez, donc vous êtes l'erreur*), Cornoldi significantly added: "The same can be said of all the so-called modern philosophies, which, from the very fact that they are multiple and contrary, must, logically speaking, all be false, or, at least, all but one, and since they are varying, if they ever possessed one parcel of truth, it was for one instant only."[15]

Since he is speaking "logically," Cornoldi cannot doubt the validity of his inference. Neither does he doubt that since they are different, other philosophies are contrary and opposed. As shall be seen, this exigency of unity chiefly applies to the order of the principles, but, in that order, it is absolute. From this uncompromising point of view, the whole history of philosophy since the beginning of modern times appears to Cornoldi as a long chain of errors. There is no such thing as an anti-scholastic philosophy. Nor is there such a thing as extra-scholastic philosophy. Outside of scholasticism, there is no philosophy worthy of the name. This view of the history of modern philosophy deserves to be known because it has dominated many recent philosophico-theological controversies.

Its first tenet is that Descartes simply applied to philosophy the method Luther had applied to faith. This statement is responsible for the widely spread illusion that there is a deep analogy between the religious reformation achieved by Luther, who detested philosophy, and the philosophical reformation achieved by Descartes who, because he expressly kept out of theological problems, devoted himself to the quest of truth in the light of reason alone. However, "the philosophy of Descartes, which wanted to apply to reason the method applied by Luther to faith; then the philosophies of Locke, of Malebranche, of Spinoza, of Kant, of Fichte, of Hegel, of Schelling, and of so many others have shown how weak the most powerful intelligences are when they attack truth." In saying this, Cornoldi was simply reviving the time-honored argument used by the theologians against the weakness of human reason: the argument "by the contra-

XII. *In the Spirit of Scholasticism* 377

dictions of the philosophers," but there was a big difference because, this time, instead of opposing to the contradictions of the human reason the unchanging unity of faith, Cornoldi was pitting the truth of one single philosophy against the falsity of all the other ones. This raised two difficulties: Admitting that it was wrong for Luther to appeal to private judgment in matters of faith, does it follow that Descartes was wrong in appealing to the sole natural light of reason in philosophical matters? Whatever the answer, the question should at least have been asked.

Another question was waiting for an answer: If there is one single philosophy worthy of the title, which is it, or, more exactly, what is it? Cornoldi had an answer to this second question, and that probably explains why he did not find it necessary to ask the first one. The evident truth of scholasticism, as the only satisfactory answer to the problems raised by modern science as well as by the philosophies of all times, was in itself a decisive proof that Descartes had been wrong in giving up its principles. Still, there remained to define, or to describe with some precision, that unique body of philosophical truth.

Here again the position of Cornoldi has become so influential that it deserves to be carefully observed.

In a first approximation, scholasticism is identified by Cornoldi with that of Thomas Aquinas and Dante, for there is a touch of national feeling even in Cornoldi and, besides, he knew his Dante very well. In a broader approximation, the philosophy which alone can procure a reasonable explanation of all philosophical and scientific discoveries was the one that had been taught, for twenty centuries, with full authority and certitude by the most sublime geniuses; for it began under Socrates, "and in the following centuries, especially since the Christian era, it made admirable progress until it attained its point of perfection." So Thomas Aquinas and Dante are presented as embodying scholasticism at its best; in itself, however, that wonderful philosophy was "a body of doctrine that had satisfied the high intelligences of Plato, Aristotle, Cicero, Saint Augustine, Albert the Great, Saint Thomas, Saint Bonaventure, Dante, Bellarmine, Suarez, and such like."[16] Cornoldi was thus providing a notion of scholasticism wide enough to accommodate many different philosophies within its loose unity.

In order to reach a more precise determination of the notion, Cornoldi undertook to disengage from its history what he himself called the essentials of the scholastic philosophy, considered apart from the contingent elements that are due to the shifting nature of natural science. Considered as an interpretation of given reality, which is our starting point towards a knowledge of the ideal order, the "substance of the scholastic philosophy" is as follows: (1) all changeable things are made up of a determinable part and of a determined part, that is of potency and act; (2) corporal substances are really different and mutable in their substantial being; so we must distinguish within themselves a substantial potency (prime matter) and a substantial act (substantial form); besides substantial changes and diversities, there also are accidental changes and diversities, so that we should also posit accidental potencies and accidental acts.[17] Cornoldi's notion of natural philosophy thus was preparing the historical notion of scholasticism conceived of as a kind of common property jointly owned by all the doctors and masters included in the list of its representatives. It was becoming a sort of philosophical "common good." More important still, it was substituting for the metaphysical notion of being (in act or in potency) the bare notions of act and potency which, instead of remaining two intrinsic determinations of being, were becoming its determinant.

Cornoldi was not a man to stress the differences between his own positions and those of Thomas Aquinas. Perhaps he did not even perceive them, for the simple reason that what differences there might be, for instance, between the metaphysics of Thomas and of Suarez, remained for him enclosed within the unity of scholasticism as such. It is therefore difficult to attribute to Cornoldi any particular brand of scholasticism. One cannot easily find in his writings any clear-cut statement in favor of the composition of essence and existence in the Thomist sense of these terms; nor does he say anything definite against it. To him being is a particular case in the general problem of the nature of the universals; its concept is the most universal of all and includes possible being as well as actual being; essence is that on account of which being is that which it is; it is the "metaphysical form" of the thing; actual being is that which is posited in its own physical being; as such, it is said to be an *ex-sistent*. The very meaning of the word implies the notion of origin (*ex*); an ex-sistent is a being that has been brought from potency to act. "That is the reason the greatest philosophers of Antiquity, who wrote about God, did not demonstrate that He *exists*, but, rather, that He *is*. From this it can be seen that existence is the actualization of the thing posited out of its cause, or, in Saint Thomas' own words, existence is the

XII. *In the Spirit of Scholasticism*

act of essence, *actus essentiae.*"[18] A more passionate zeal for philosophical unity will never combine, in one and the same mind, with a more complete indifference to the authentic meaning of the philosophy of Saint Thomas Aquinas. This remark must be made because the deepest implications of the pontifical intervention are tied up with the fact that, just as there was no unity outside scholasticism, scholasticism itself was lacking unity.

It would not be fair to judge Cornoldi in the light of a situation which his own merits contributed to bring about and in which, for that very reason, he never found himself. More gifted for the philosophy of nature than for metaphysics, he concentrated his efforts on the restoration of hylomorphism, whose consequences in the philosophy of science and in anthropology are of decisive importance. There is absolutely no doubt that Cornoldi was a useful and a powerful influence at the service of a Thomistic restoration. He himself relates that, being at the Vatican, in the presence of Pius IX, along with other members of the recently founded Philosophico-Medical Academy, he heard the Pope declare absurd the proposition that "did he live in our own days, Thomas Aquinas would change the principles of his doctrine." There are no useless servants of truth, but one of the lessons we can learn from history is that the careful study of Thomas Aquinas himself is a strict necessity for anybody calling himself a Thomist.

Leo XIII

Pope Leo XIII[19] occupies a central place in the history of the late-nineteenth- and early-twentieth-century history of Christian philosophy. In reading him on the subject, however, one must keep in mind that, speaking as a pope, he was not expressing any personal ideas. On the contrary, speaking as a pope, he could only intend to express the thought of the Catholic Church. And that is what confers upon his testimony a unique importance. Whether or not the reader be a Catholic, or simply a Christian, or an agnostic, the historical and philosophical significance of the Pope's teaching remains the same. The point is that, in order to grasp their true meaning, the encyclicals of Leo XIII should be read as expressing the permanent, traditional, and authentic certitudes of the Catholic Church. It goes without saying that, for Catholic philosophers, their importance is much more than a merely historical one. In both cases, however, they should be read as expressing, in its very essence, the thought of a twenty-centuries-old religious body.

This would be true of the encyclicals of any pope. At the same time, because an encyclical purports to be, not an exposition of Christian faith, but a partial restatement of that faith on the occasion of various events and controversies, it always bears the mark of the time when it was written. This is easy to observe in the case of Leo XIII. His teaching concerning Christian philosophy obviously answers the complex problems raised, and incompletely solved, by the traditionalists, the ontologists, and the fideists of the nineteenth century. The Pope's encyclicals concerning social, political, and economic problems still more obviously reflect the thoughts of a pontiff who had witnessed the breakdown of the temporal authority of the popes in the pontifical states. As a bishop of Perugia, he himself had wielded political power, and having followed year after year the dramatic events that marked the reign of Pius IX, he found himself confronted with the task of reconstructing as much as possible of what had just been destroyed. His importance in this history is due to the fact that he deemed it necessary to associate philosophy with theology and with faith in his effort of religious restoration.

The encyclical *Aeterni Patris* (August 4, 1879) clearly shows that, in the Pope's mind, the restoration of intellectual and philosophical unity was a necessary prerequisite for the work to be done. The task of the Church is to teach the saving truth. Being religious in its essence, that truth is received by faith, but some philosophies are opposed to the teaching of religious truth, and this makes it necessary to philosophize against those false philosophies. For the same reason, it is still more necessary to philosophize in favor of religious truth. The object of *Aeterni Patris* was to show that, indeed, the Church has never ceased to put natural reason at the service of Christian faith, either in order to defend it, or in order to elucidate its meaning. Before recalling the past history of Christian speculation, Leo XIII observed that such is, indeed, the best possible way of philosophizing, namely, to combine the religious obedience to faith with the exercise of philosophical reason. That is what was done by the early Christian apologists, the Fathers of the Church, and, finally, the great masters of medieval scholasticism. The greatest among them was Thomas Aquinas. As a matter of fact, ever since the end of the thirteenth century, his authority has been recognized by popes and councils in many different solemn occasions.

XII. *In the Spirit of Scholasticism*

The Pope concluded that the safest way to restore philosophical and theological unity was to return to the traditionally approved doctrine of Saint Thomas. By a doctrinal act unique in the history of the Church, and which could not not meet with a measure of opposition, Leo XIII finally decided that as an answer to the ceaseless multiplication of philosophies incompatible with the teachings of Christianity, it was necessary to return to Thomas Aquinas as to the fountainhead of philosophic truth. Hence the title of the encyclical: "On the Restoration of Christian Philosophy in Schools." By the words "Christian philosophy" was meant the way of philosophizing described in the encyclical as that which unites obedience to Christian faith to the study of philosophy. Moreover, it was being stipulated that the only safe way to do so was to restore in all Catholic schools the doctrine of Saint Thomas Aquinas.[20]

Already in *Aeterni Patris* Leo XIII revealed his intention to resort to Thomism as the remedy against the political and social upheavals of the time: "Domestic and civil society even, which, as all see, is exposed to great danger from this plague of perverse opinions, would certainly enjoy a far more peaceful and secure existence if a more wholesome doctrine were taught in the universities and high schools—one more in conformity with the teaching of the Church, such as is contained in the works of Thomas Aquinas."[21]

The aim and scope of Leo XIII, then, was not to teach Thomism, but to invite all the Catholic philosophers to study it. As for himself, he intended to draw from the doctrine of Thomas Aquinas the remedy for the social and political evils of his time. For this reason, the main contribution of Leo XIII to Christian philosophy was in the fields of personal, social, and political ethics. At the same time, because practical philosophy derives its principles from speculative philosophy, the moral and social doctrine of the Pope presupposed a certain philosophical and religious conception of the world and to which it constantly refers, explicitly or implicitly.[22]

The world in which a Christian philosopher lives is a created world. In such a doctrine, even nature is God-ordained. True enough, there is no particular universe for the Christian apart from that in which all men have to live. Inasmuch as science is a truthful representation of the real world, the world of science is the world in which, like all other men, Christians have to live. Only, to those who wish to philosophize in the best possible way, the natural world of science is at the same time the work of God. Hence the twofold aspect presented by the doctrine of Leo XIII. In a sense, its worst adversary is naturalism, or rationalism, that is to say, atheistic naturalism and rationalism turned against faith. In another sense, Leo XIII never tires of reminding man that nature is sacred, necessary in itself and deserving of utmost respect, precisely because it is the work of God. This accounts for the complementary character of his conclusions on all problems: All that overlooks or denies the order of nature is wrong, because to go against nature is to go against the will of God. There is a sanction for that sort of fault, namely, the destruction of nature and of man. On the other hand, Leo XIII always reminds his readers that nature cannot subsist, even *qua* nature, if it separates itself from God. All the social evils, revolutions, wars, and disorders arise from the fact that by trying to do violence to nature men establish themselves in a state of organized rebellion against God.

The social unit is the family. Marriage is a natural institution willed by God in view of making possible the existence of societies; progressively corrupted by sin, it was restored, along with the whole order of nature, by the Incarnation of Christ. Marriage then became a sacrament by which the natural institution was restored and perfected. This is a perfect instance of what remains the constant position of Leo XIII in all his writings. The aim and scope of revelation, of redemption, and of grace is to constitute mankind in the supernatural order of grace, but, at the same time, it bears abundant fruit in the order of nature. In this case, by turning marriage into a sacrament, Christ made it indissoluble, excluded polygamy, and insured the respective rights of parents and children. *Because* Christian marriage is a sacrament, it forbids the licentiousness of the man, the slavery of the woman, the rebellion of children against their parents, and the exploitation of children by their parents. The aim and scope of the encyclical *Arcanum Divinae Sapientiae* (February 10, 1880) is to fight divorce as depriving marriage of its three main prerogatives, which stand and fall together: holiness, unity, and indissolubility. To legalize divorce is to shake the very foundations of the state by loosening the ties of its constitutive element. Above all, it is to oppose the natural order of things such as God has willed it to be. This takes us back to the key notion of the doctrine: "From the beginning of the world, it was divinely ordained that things instituted by God and by nature should be proved by us to be the more profitable and salutary the more they remain unchanged in their integrity."[23] To work for the salvation of souls and for the safety of the commonwealth are one and the same thing.

XII. *In the Spirit of Scholasticism*

The same principle applies to the solution of all the social problems. In that order, however, the notion of liberty is fundamental. Practically all revolutions are carried out in the name of liberty. What is then at stake is not the problem of natural liberty, which belongs to man by the very fact that he is endowed with a rational power of willing, but, rather, the problem of moral liberty, which is the power of choosing well in conformity with the prescriptions of reason. Man should be able himself to decide what he ought to do, but there again the depravation of the human will has made it necessary to provide external help. This help is law. In agreement with the doctrine of Thomas Aquinas, Leo XIII shows that law is necessary in order to protect the human will against its own weakness. Human law thus finds itself established between natural law (the natural order of things created by God) and the divine law (the ideal order defined by the knowledge and the will of God); there can be no such thing as a liberty to rebel against the divine and eternal law; on the contrary, obedience to the eternal law is the very standard and rule of the moral liberty of man.

The opposition of the Church against false liberalism has no other meaning. It is important to note that in refusing man certain so-called "modern liberties" Leo XIII merely takes stock of the fact that these are not genuine liberties. He does not refuse to grant them, his point is that, in point of fact, they do not exist. Since liberty is the power of choosing good rather than evil, there can be no liberty of worship (it is contradictory for us to say that we are "free" to worship false gods or not to worship the true one); this does not mean that the State should not tolerate a plurality of cults; on the contrary, toleration is justified if it is practiced in view of avoiding greater evils; the point is that what can be conceded as a civil right is not necessarily a religious right. And here again the gist of the problem is the same. Far from diminishing the liberty of man, his obedience to the law of God is that which makes him free. The authority of God over man "protects and perfects his liberty, for the real perfection of all creatures is found in the prosecution and attainment of their respective ends; but the supreme end to which human liberty must aspire is God."[24] And here again there is a sanction: in refusing to submit to God, man accepts by the same token to submit to man. The godless state is a human dictatorship, so to speak, by definition.

In such a doctrine, there is no true liberty without authority. Everywhere there is law, there is subordination of inferiors to superiors. This is already true of domestic law; modern moralists pretend that there should be no authority of parents over children and of husband over wife; Leo XIII does not deny that people can indeed live that way; in fact, many of them actually do so live, but they do not constitute a real family. They are just loose individuals who happen to live, part of the time, under the same roof. The same is true of political societies. Of itself, anarchism is a speculative possibility, but anarchy does not constitute a society at all. Men find themselves in a relationship of ruling and ruled, and that is the reason they constitute a definite order of social relations, that is, a society.

Once more, the same recurring error must be avoided in interpreting the teaching of the Pope. He does not say that society is better off with authority than without, but, rather, that where there is no authority, society does not exist. Now, authority rests upon a relationship of inferiors and superiors and, in point of fact, such relationship exists everywhere. God created beings that way, and this is why all authority is from God. The question of the form to be given to society is irrelevant to the present problem. The state may be an empire, a kingdom, or a republic; so long as it rests upon the recognition of some authority, it is a society worthy of the name. In saying that, ultimately, all political power comes from God,[25] Christian philosophy once more strengthens and confirms the political order. Should they only know it, far from looking at the Church as at an enemy, the modern political societies would see in it their natural ally against the forces of dissolution that permanently threaten their existence. In saying that rulers derive their power neither from themselves, nor from their electors, but from God, Leo XIII means to say that even in a country where the sovereign is elected by the people, the people are duty bound to obey him during the time of his tenure, precisely because, although their vote designates the sovereign, his authority does not come to him from his electors, but from God. The people therefore cannot take back that which it has not given. The ambivalence of the doctrine is once more visible. In insuring the submission of the citizens to the authority of the State, it protects the citizens against the encroachments of the political power. The citizens must obey the sovereign because his power comes to him from God, but, at the same time, there is no other reason why a man should obey any other man: "No man has in himself or of himself the power of constraining the free will of others by fetters or authority of this kind. This power resides solely in God, the Creator and

XII. *In the Spirit of Scholasticism*

Legislator of all things; and it is necessary that those who exercise it should do so as having received it from God."[26] No other principle is required in order to solve the problems related to the social structure of the body politic. Social and economic inequalities are given facts. They are facts of nature and, of course, societies should do their utmost in order not to increase natural inequalities by adding to them social injustices. On the contrary, just laws should compensate for natural inequalities rather than making them harder to bear than they are. Still, there always will remain inequalities in physical strength, in health, in intelligence, in will power, and from those natural differences between individuals social inequalities will inevitably follow. Things are that way, and nature is such, because God's wisdom wanted it to be such. In his celebrated encyclical *Rerum Novarum*, on the rights and duties of capital and labor, Leo XIII consistently applied the same ideas to the solution of the problem, or rather, since the problem essentially is a practical one, to the determination of the rules of conduct that permit its solution.

The unequal distribution of wealth is the most apparent of all the social inequalities; in the last analysis, it synthesizes the others as either their source or their consequence. The remedy proposed by socialism (i.e., communism) is to suppress private ownership and to transfer the right of property to the State. This is an old notion. It was familiar to the members of the primitive church and it is still applied in most of the modern religious orders, but religious communities essentially differ from natural political communities. Not all men are called upon to live in a state of perfection. Looking at the problem from the point of view of the natural conditions of social life, there is a big difference between admitting that, prompted by their desire of religious perfection, some men will willingly deprive themselves of some of their natural rights, and deciding that, in consequence of a political decision, all the citizens will be deprived of it by the State. A freely consented sacrifice is specifically different from a confiscation.

The objection of Leo XIII to communism is simple: the right to private property is a fact of nature; whatever we may say or do about it, there is no society whose members do not own something that is truly theirs and nobody else's. How much a man should be permitted to own is another question. Is it in the interest of all that no one should possess more than any one else, even if his productivity surpasses that of his fellow citizens? That, too, is a different problem, into which the encyclical does not pretend to enter. But it does deal with the principle, which is that, in fact, men work in order to acquire property. All solutions to the problem should take the fact into account.

For there is indeed a problem. Ever since the ancient guilds of workers have ceased to exist, the practice of usury and greed have reduced the mass of the workers to a condition resembling slavery. The question then is not how to deprive all citizens of their right to private property, but, rather, it is to see to it that all men be permitted effectively to enjoy that natural right. Man has a right to own part of the soil he cultivates; we say the soil, and not only the fruit. Within the family, parents must have the right to own at least what they need in order to provide for their children; the duty of the State is to help families fulfill this need, it is not to take away from them what little they do own. The only workable solution to the problem is to be found in harmonious co-operation between capital and labor. If it is not to remain a pious wish, this ideal will require another co-operation between State and Church.

The Church, while reminding all that poverty is no disgrace, since God himself chose to be a carpenter, will insistently remind the representatives of political power that the poor are entitled to special protection from the State. Private property should not, in fact cannot, be abolished, but good laws should prevent social troubles by abolishing their causes. This can best be achieved by insuring just wages for all workers, by facilitating access to private property for as many citizens as possible, by favoring the constitution of trade unions confining themselves to the economic betterment of the situation of wage earners. When all is said and done, it will always remain necessary to rely upon the Christian ideal of charity and brotherly love. Far from harming justice, charity will remain for us an invitation to achieve it.[27]

These notions were important in themselves, but still more important was the proof given by the Pope that the principles of Thomism could be applied to the solution of contemporary problems. Leo XIII initiated a new era in the history of Christian philosophy. With him the papacy assumed a teaching function that goes far beyond the limits of the doctrinal authority it had always exercised. The encyclical letters of the popes now give precise and detailed directives for the solution of many problems. From the encyclical *Rerum Novarum* of Leo XIII, through *Quadragesimo Anno* of Pius XII, to the recent *Mater et Magistra* (May 15, 1961) and *Pacem in Terris* (April 11, 1963) of John XXIII,

XII. In the Spirit of Scholasticism

a continuous doctrinal stream has never ceased to flow. As can be seen from the initial statement of *Mater et Magistra*, the avowed intention of the popes, in their capacity as bishops of Rome and teachers of the Church, is to show that the principles of Christian philosophy are perennial by a constant and necessary *aggiornamnento* of their practical applications.

Neo-Scholasticism

Although the first manifestations of the neo-scholastic movement took place in Italy, the Catholic world as a whole soon joined in. The revival of Thomism took all possible forms. A critical edition of the complete works of St. Thomas was initiated (the so-called Leonine Edition, which has not yet been completed). An immense movement of historical research devoted to the life, works, and doctrine of the saint soon followed; a complete bibliography of the studies devoted to those problems is hardly conceivable; necessarily incomplete as it is, the *Bulletin thomiste* gives at least a fair idea of the immensity of the work already done. Journals, reviews, and collections of all sorts, in America as well as in Europe, attempt to fulfill the program set up by Leo XIII: *Divus Thomas* (Piacenza); another *Divus Thomas* (Freiburg, Switzerland); *Ciencia tomista* (Spain); *La revue thomiste* (France); *The Thomist* (U.S.A.); these and many other similar publications sufficiently attest the vitality of the movement. As to its various orientations, we are still too near it to be in a position correctly to describe them. Still, in order not to leave in utter ignorance those who know nothing of the question, some relatively objective information can be gathered.

What Leo XIII had asked for was a revival of Thomism; what he was given instead seems to be something very much like Thomism, but not exactly it.[28] Let us call it neo-scholasticism. One of its main representatives, Fr. Agostino Gemelli, O.F.M., described it as follows: "By the name of neo-scholastic philosophy, one properly understands the restoration of medieval thought within the civilization of our own times, for indeed we consider medieval thought, not as the transitory expression of a civilization, but, in its substance at least, as a definitive conquest of human reason in the domain of metaphysics, a conquest that matured throughout Greek speculation and Christianity, and whose fundamental marks are realism and theism."[29] That program was put in execution at the newly founded University of the Sacred Heart, Milan, and the results were published in the collection *Vita e pensiero* and in the *Rivista di filosofia neo-scholastica*. Since a choice has to be made, no more representative name can be found than that of Francesco Olgiati and his book *L'anima di San Tommaso, saggio filosofico intorno alia concezione tomista* (Milan, Vita e pensiero, n.d.). The great merit of the book was to situate the "soul" of Thomism right where it is, in the notion of being.[30] Having to define his position at a time when there was an idealist revival in Italy (Gentile, Croce, etc.), Olgiati observes that "the metaphysics of today is not our own metaphysics." The metaphysics he intends to vindicate is the ancient metaphysics of being: "For us, being is the prime and formal object of reason. Human reason can know not only the phenomena given to us by the senses or by consciousness, but also being (τὸ ὄν) of which the phenomena are the sensible manifestation. We possess a faculty that does not stop at the phenomenal surface of reality, but reaches the constitutive element of things, being." For this reason, the primary notions flow from that of being: essence, unity, good, substance, purposiveness, and causality. In short, the first principles are laws for being and not merely laws for knowing. Such is the basis of that metaphysics. One could not imagine a more faithful interpretation of authentic Thomism; at the same time, Olgiati observed that Aristotle himself had begun his metaphysics with an historical survey of the philosophical speculation of his predecessors, and he rightly inferred that traditional metaphysics had to be preceded by a critical examination of the philosophical history of the human mind up to our own times. The dialogue with contemporary philosophy had therefore to be kept alive. In a deeply Thomistic spirit Olgiati observes that not all error is a pure error; there is a nucleus of truth in positivism; voluntarism is a useful invitation to scrutinize human activity, and even the "philosophy of the mind" can be partially justified when it is remembered that there is no "thinking" without a subject that thinks. Olgiati laid down what for Thomists is a golden rule: "We do not consider truth as a block of marble. A philosophical system is an organism, and its contacts with adverse streams of thought can help us to make more explicit that which is implicit in our own conceptions and thereby to manifest the vitality of our own philosophy."

By far the most important branch of the scholastic revival was the school of Louvain. Its origins are inseparable from the person and work of Cardinal Mercier.[31] Let us recall that the date of *Aeterni Patris* was 1879. As early as De-

XII. In the Spirit of Scholasticism

cember 25, 1880, Leo XIII invited Cardinal Dechamps to set up, in the University of Louvain, a distinct school whose function it would be to interpret for its students the doctrine of Saint Thomas Aquinas.[32] What was at stake was not a "chair," but a specialized school (*schola singularis*) devoted to the task of interpreting Saint Thomas Aquinas for students (*data opera... Thomae Aquinati interpretando*). That program was strictly Thomistic. In that school, the Pope then said, "teaching will be the more perfect as it will more closely adhere to the doctrine of Thomas Aquinas."

The intentions of Leo XIII were perfectly understood by Canon Aloïs Van Weddingen (1841–1890), author of a study on the encyclical *Aeterni Patris*, in which he stressed that what was required was a return to the very works of Thomas Aquinas, beyond those "inept abridgments which are held to be clear because they are superficial, and to be precise because they are trenchant." The first professor was the young abbé Désiré Mercier (1852–1926); the first title of the new chair announced an advanced course of lectures in the philosophy of Saint Thomas.[33] In 1889, answering the first intention of the Pope, Mercier succeeded in creating an Institute (and not just a simple chair of philosophy). The *Institut supérieur de philosophie* widely exceeded the initial program assigned by the Pope; included in the *Instituts supérieurs libres* of the university, it comprised a *Section de Philosophie* (*École S. Thomas d'Aquin*). Discussions could not but arise on the point of knowing if Désiré Mercier was not substituting a program of his own for the initial project of Leo XIII. The fact is beyond doubt, but another fact is no less certain: Désiré Mercier was never disavowed by Pope Leo XIII; on the contrary, whatever was done by him on his own initiative always met with the Pope's approval. Those who, rightly or wrongly, accused Mercier of betraying the intentions of Leo XIII (H. de Dorlodot), found the Pope siding with him against them. Unless one wants to be more of a Thomist than Leo XIII, this should suffice to settle the question.

Inseparable from the Institute was the foundation of the *Revue néoscholastique de philosophie* published by the Société Philosophique de Louvain, 1894; in 1936, it became the *Revue néo-scolastique de philosophie*; in 1946, the title was further modernized into *Revue philosophique de Louvain*. That significant evolution clearly shows that the whole undertaking was more in the nature of a neo-scholasticism than of a Thomism properly so called. In fact, its whole tendency, from the very beginning, had been to pit against modern positivism and scientism a doctrine just as strictly philosophical as that of its adversaries. Of course, it had to agree with the religious teaching of the Church and its principles should be those of Saint Thomas, but freely understood and never accepted for the sole reason that they were his principles. Authority is the weakest of all philosophical arguments.

This general tendency is visible in the "school of Louvain's" interpretation of the history of philosophy as well as of philosophy itself.

In the history of philosophy, Maurice de Wulf elaborated an interpretation of the Christian speculation of the middle ages which distinguished within it a common body of essentially philosophical truth. This he called "the scholastic synthesis"; aberrant specimens of medieval speculation (John Scotus Erigena) were considered apart under the title of anti-scholastics. This view raised considerable historical difficulties. On the occasion of its successive editions, de Wulf's *Histoire de la philosophie médiévale* underwent two main changes. First, it gave up the notion of a "scholastic synthesis" and substituted for it the less strict notion of a philosophical "common good"; secondly, this notion itself was toned down and the history tended to focus itself on the rise and growth of medieval Aristotelianism.[34] To the extent that it coincides with Aristotelianism, medieval philosophy cannot be suspected of being contaminated by Christian elements. In order to justify its attitude, the *History* of M. de Wulf progressively inclined to consider theological rather than philosophical the non-Aristotelian medieval schools, especially Augustinianisin. For the same reason and in the same spirit, greater importance was attributed to the so-called "Latin Averroists" and a new interpretation of their attitude was elaborated. The whole historical undertaking is dominated by the desire to establish the conclusion that, already in the middle ages, philosophy was a straight rational business essentially independent from theology, being, as it was, conducted in the sole light of natural reason.

The properly philosophical doctrine of the school derived its inspiration from the personal positions of D. Mercier, himself indebted, in addition to Thomas Aquinas, to Balmes[35] and to Kleutgen[36] for his initiation to philosophical research.[37] His main philosophical interest was in epistemology: how is intellectual certitude possible? In the several different redactions of his "criteriology," Mercier started from a distinction between the ideal order and the real order. The ideal order seems to have been for him the order of the essences or quiddities, abstracting from individuating circumstances, particularly from

XII. *In the Spirit of Scholasticism*

existence. This is the visible mark of Suarezianism left on his mind by the frequentation of Kleutgen. A reality prescinding from existence provides a fitting matter for judgments posited in the ideal order. Judgments of that sort achieve a synthesis of two ideal objects (essences or quiddities). In the real order, judgment bears upon actually existing essences. Hence its other name: judgment of experience. Experiential judgment establishes the relationships of essences to actual or possible things. As bearing upon the existential aspect of things, it affirms the same essence individualized by its haecceity: "What constitutes the essential difference between a judgment that is certain in the ideal order and a judgment that is certain in the experiential order? It is chiefly due to the diversity of the conditions under which the sensible substratum of the subject of the judgment offers itself to the mind." If the matter of the subject-concept is provided by imagination, the judgment belongs in the ideal order. If, on the contrary, the sensible substratum of the concept is provided by sensation, the judgment is experiential and belongs in the real order.

Like all the philosophies that describe reality in terms of essences and their essential determinations, that of D. Mercier finds it difficult to pass from the ideal order to the real order. Contingent and actually existing things mainly serve to lead us to the scientific knowledge of essences. How do we know that our judgments can apply to real objects? Because the object of concepts is essence, which, keeping faith with Suarez and Kleutgen, Mercier conceives "in its absolute condition, as an essence that neither includes nor excludes individuating marks, but simply neglects them." So ideal judgments *can* apply to actually existing objects, and we know that they do when the object of the concept is actually given in sense perception. True objective and real knowledge thus results from the coincidence in us of two irreducibly distinct cognitive acts, concept and sensation, the object of concept being given *in* that of sensation.

A necessary consequence of the doctrine is that the existence of the external order of reality needs to be justified. With keen insight, Mercier realized that, in his own doctrine, since essences are the object of scientific knowledge, their existence does not necessarily follow. There are cases when the objects of our judgments of reality do actually exist; in other cases, they do not, and in all cases it is up to reason itself to establish, by appropriate methods, the actual existence or nonexistence, of its object. Criteriology here assumes an extreme importance, and Mercier reaps the benefit attending all the metaphysics of essence, to find themselves naturally established, *qua* metaphysics, at the level of scientific demonstration. Now this was one of the main concerns of Mercier. In the opening lecture of his first course in the "Advanced Philosophy of Saint Thomas," whose echoes were not slow in reaching Rome, Mercier began by recalling that, according to Saint Thomas[38] "the proof from authority is the weakest form of proof." Whereupon, in a bold attempt to sum up the philosophy of Saint Thomas, he described it characterized by two features; first, the union of reason and faith; next, the union of observation and rational speculation, the combination of analysis and synthesis. The description was correct, but it was wide enough to authorize a large number of diverse Thomisms, including the personal Thomism of Désiré Mercier.[39] Now there is no objective yardstick wherewith to measure the Thomism of a Thomist, but this at least can be said that if there is a distinction of any sort between straight Thomism and neo-scholasticism, the doctrine of Mercier would better answer the notion of neo-scholasticism, so much so that his successors finally did away with the mention of "scholasticism" itself. As could be expected, the directives of Pope Leo XIII were differently understood in different places.

The French Catholic philosophers were no exception to this rule. A first interpretation of *Aeterni Patris*, on the French side, is represented by the disciples of Suarez. Whether or not Suarez can be considered a Thomist is not a question to be gone into here. The answer depends on the criterion adopted in the matter of Thomism. It is a fact, however, that some of the more important representatives of the Society of Jesus in France decided that they were both Thomists and Suarezians, because Suarez himself belonged in the Thomist school. In order to account for their decision, those Suarezians observed that one should distinguish between the doctrine of Thomas Aquinas and the proper way to understand and to develop it, which constitutes the common character of a school. Strictly speaking, that "Thomist" character must remain the apanage of the Dominican Order. Now, Suarez and the men of his generation owed their philosophical formation to Dominican masters. That, and his earnest intention to keep faith with the doctrine of the Master, is sufficient justification for connecting him with the Thomist school.[40] The same remark applies to his own disciples. Since they follow a Thomist, they themselves are Thomists. They profess what can be called "the Thomism of Suarez,"[41] which ultimately consists in turning Thomas into a Suarezian.[42]

XII. *In the Spirit of Scholasticism*   393

The typical representative of French Suarezianism in modern times was Pedro Descoqs, S.J. (1877–1946), author of a remarkable treatise of general metaphysics[43]; but various expressions of the same doctrinal tradition will be found in the collection *Archives de philosophie* initiated in 1923 and which represents perhaps the more original French contribution to neo-scholasticism. It would be easy to distinguish several different orientations among its contributors; Augustinianism is at work there along with idealistic tendencies of German origin. By and large, its intention was to share in the revival of scholasticism chiefly by showing that it still was capable of progress.[44]

Any attempt to classify the French contributions to neo-scholasticism would be at once nullified by quotable facts.[45] It is nevertheless permitted to say that one of the common tendencies was an effort to revive intellectualism. At a time when Bergson was despairing of intelligence as a means of metaphysical knowledge, this was an authentically Thomist move. To restore intelligence in its traditional dignity, recently usurped by intuition, action, and similar notions, was the primary philosophical preoccupation of Pierre Rousselot, S.J.[46]

Ever since the end of the eighteenth century, there seemed to be general agreement that reason was in favor of science and against metaphysics. Not only Kant, Comte, and its other adversaries, but even the supporters of metaphysics seemed to agree that, if traditional wisdom was to be restored, the undertaking should be carried out on the strength of something other than reason. Faith, tradition, common sense, feeling, morality, anything could be tried provided it was not reason. Pierre Rousselot made a decisive step toward the rediscovery of true Thomism when he stressed the fact that, for Thomas, reason is but another name for intellect. Reason is the discursive function of intellect, itself the power of forming by abstraction the principles of speculative and of practical knowledge. Having cleared up this point of history, and in such a way that his own doctrinal interpretation could not be contradicted, Pierre Rousselot developed a general view of the world of knowledge and of the world of things in which the medieval passion for impersonal rationality finds itself rooted in the medieval worship of personal intelligence. Both are one in the doctrine of Saint Thomas. Absolute life, infinite reason and subsisting truth do indeed exist—they are manifestations of God: "From this unique principle follow the three undeniable characters of the Thomist spirit: its religious dogmatism, its intellectual radicalism, and its 'mystical' scorn of discursiveness."

As faculty of the principles and an image of God in us, intelligence is in us "the faculty of the divine." This is manifested by the unifying power of intelligence which always aims at gathering together the dispersed conclusions of discursive reason. To do so intelligence must gather within itself the multiplicity born of its own unity.

In developing such views, Pierre Rousselot was offering an image of Thomism quite different from the one usually found in neo-scholastic textbooks. The substance was the same, the spirit was different, and it truly was the authentic spirit of Saint Thomas himself. All truth is excellent, every truth is divine. According to the maxim of Saint Justin, taken up by Saint Ambrose and not unknown to Saint Thomas: *Omne verum, a quocumque dicatur, a Spiritu Sancto est.* All truth therefore must be heartily welcomed, carefully preserved, and possessed with serenity. Let us consider justified all propositions rationally established; that is rational and logical radicalism. Let us confidently assent to the "yes" said by speculative reason to given reality; that is the objectivism of the intellect. Above all, let us assent to the intelligence that is its own act, because "all critique of knowledge finds its ultimate explanation in the theory of the divine intellection."[47] It was perhaps the boldest originality of Pierre Rousselot, although not the most visible one, that his whole interpretation of Thomism implied the intrinsic unity of its theology and of its philosophy. Not a neo-scholastic rationalism, only a Thomistic intellectualism could thus restore the doctrine to its integrity.

While some Thomists were thus attempting to stress neglected aspects of the doctrine, others were trying to renovate the traditional school scholasticism which sees in Thomism a modified version of the philosophy of Aristotle, plus, of course, the super-added Christian revelation. Two Dominicans represent that widely spread attitude of mind. By preaching, teaching, and writing, Father Sertillanges[48] largely contributed to making Thomas Aquinas better known in university circles. During many years of his long life, he was the interpreter of Thomism for the benefit of the non-Thomist French philosophical world. Well acquainted with positive sciences, Sertillanges always stressed the strictly rational aspect of Thomism as a philosophy, in both metaphysics and ethics. By the same token, he carefully determined the limits beyond which philosophical reason loses its competence. The unknowability of God (on account of His transcendency) assumed in his doctrine such an importance that he was

XII. *In the Spirit of Scholasticism* 395

charged with agnosticism, sometimes for having used expressions borrowed word for word from Saint Thomas Aquinas. He himself only professed an "agnosticism of definition," not of judgment nor of concept. In metaphysics, he considered the notion of creation to be a Christian "exclusive"; but he does not seem to have ever pushed beyond that notion up to the Thomist concept of being conceived as the pure act of *esse*. The composition of essence and existence plays practically no part in his own brand of Thomism. In fact, one may well wonder if he ever thought of it.

Father Garrigou-Lagrange, O.P., represents still another interpretation of the doctrine.[49] A respected master in the science of spirituality, he has taught with uncompromising authority a thoroughly rationalized Thomism in which metaphysics becomes an analytically deducible science. The doctrine admits such a thing as "the mystery of being," but then reason addresses itself to the first principles of the intellect and, applying them to the data of sense, it makes the affirmation of the existence of God appear as a strict logical necessity. These principles are the principle of contradiction, rooted in the objective identity of being with itself, then the "principle of *raison d'être*," which includes the principle of causality. The Leibnizian tendency to reduce the principle of causality to the principle of contradiction, through the principle of *raison d'être* (a variant of the principle of sufficient reason), makes itself felt in this peculiar variety of neo-Thomism whose tightly knit rational structure, it must be said, seems to answer the needs of many minds.

French neo-Thomism bore its most precious fruit in the work of Jacques Maritain.[50] A lay professor of philosophy, he first inherited the intellectual formation of the University of Paris, and after his conversion to Catholicism he resolutely embraced the doctrine of Saint Thomas Aquinas. Under the influence of Garrigou-Lagrange, he refused to distinguish, within the Thomist school, between the doctrinal positions proper to Thomas Aquinas himself and those of his traditionally followed interpreters, particularly Cajetan and John of Saint Thomas. Still, nothing resembles less the school work of a commentator than the personal, penetrating, and provocative contributions of Jacques Maritain.

Like the Thomism of Pierre Rousselot, from which however it is in other respects very different, the thought of Jacques Maritain is, indivisibly, a metaphysics of the intelligence and a metaphysics of being, but without Rousselot's marked tendency to reduce being to intelligence. In its general inspiration,

Maritain's philosophy was a vigorous protest against all the modern forms of anti-intellectualism, especially that of Henri Bergson. In opposition to the caricature of intellect criticized by Bergson under the name of "intelligence," and which was nothing more than the artificial clockwork of associationist psychology (Condillac-Spencer-Taine), intelligence is allowed to recover its Aristotelian and Thomist privilege of being a power of apprehending being as such, both in its depth and in its universality. An abstractive power, intelligence nevertheless remains an intuitive power, in the sense (as it seems) that it can reach in the data of abstract knowledge deeper layers of reality than those accessible to abstraction as such. This is particularly true of the intuitional element in our abstract notion of being.[51]

Armed with that purified and liberated notion of intellectual knowledge, Jacques Maritain has investigated three main fields of reality. First, knowledge itself. Equally opposed to the separation of that which is united and to the confusion of that which is distinct, his major work in the field of noetics, *The Degrees of Knowledge*, seeks "to distinguish in order to unite." It does so, first in regard to the fundamental distinction between the natural and the supernatural order (nature-grace, reason-faith, philosophy-theology, etc.). Always careful to keep nature and reason within the limits of their own order, Jacques Maritain is no less anxious to show them ordered toward the higher gifts freely conferred upon them by God. There is a continuity of order between the discrete decrees of knowledge. Let us note this typical feature of Maritain's effort to restore the doctrine of the Master to its all-comprehensive unity. Thus understood, Thomism includes within itself a philosophy and a philosophical wisdom, but itself is Wisdom to the highest degree and in the perfect acception of the term. In it, and without losing its distinct nature, the wisdom of Aristotle is absorbed in the Wisdom of the Holy Spirit.[52]

That all-comprehensive notion of intelligence and wisdom extends to man. Not without meeting stiff opposition, Jacques Maritain has undertaken to show that, for a being gifted by God with intellectual power, only an "integral humanism" provides a satisfactory notion of personal, social, and political ethics. What has sometimes been misread as a defense of naturalistic humanism is in fact an effort to establish that man is called upon to reach the perfection of his nature, including the higher degrees made accessible to him by the grace of God. Integral humanism includes within itself the order of divine grace. It is the

XII. In the Spirit of Scholasticism

humanism of man freely and gratuitously called by God to a more than human destiny. God himself has given man the very kind of nature that would be able to hear the call: intelligence which, granted the necessary help, can become capable of apprehending Being.[53]

From the same notion of intelligence as from a privileged center, one can attain the third preferred field of inquiry of Jacques Maritain. After metaphysics and ethics, esthetics. Completing the doctrine of Thomas Aquinas by a poetics and a philosophy of the fine arts which the Master never developed, our philosopher has found in his own notion of intelligence, completed by the doctrine of the divine ideas, the necessary elements required for a doctrine of "poetic knowledge." An idea is essentially the cognition of something to be made. As such, it is an object of intellectual intuition. Art itself is, according to its general definition by Thomas Aquinas, the right rule concerning the proper way of making things (*recta ratio factibilium*) as such, it stands entirely on the side of mind. The effect of art is the beauty of the thing made after its rule according to the intellectual intuition of the thing to be made. In its essence, and especially because its source is deeply hidden in intelligence, art communicates with being, the creative idea of all beings.[54]

A common feature observable in French neo-Thomism was the tendency to take Thomism back to its true origin, that is, not only to the authentic teaching of Thomas Aquinas, as Leo XIII has invited all Christian philosophers to do, but to theology, which was both its birthplace and its normal soil. In this respect, the two main Dominican schools of Le Saulchoir (*Revue des sciences philosophiques et théologiques*) and of Toulouse (*Revue thomiste*) exercised a decisive influence. The restoration of the Thomistic notion of theology in France was their work.[55] They taught philosophers how it is possible to philosophize *within* faith without betraying either faith or philosophy. Here, however, the history of philosophy merges in the history of theology. In all matters pertaining to the notion of Christian philosophy, philosophers can have their own say, but they cannot have the last word.[56]

XIII. *In the Spirit of Augustinianism*

THE traditionalist and ontologist orientations of Christian thought lost much of their vitality in France after Bautain, but this does not mean that all the Catholic philosophers rallied around Thomism. On the contrary, scholasticism has been violently opposed, even within the ranks of Christian philosophers, until this very day. The exhortations of the popes have failed to convince all the Catholics and, naturally enough, a still larger number of them felt free to philosophize in their own way before Rome had spoken in 1879. It would be difficult to synthetize those non-scholastic doctrines; not all of them were anti-scholastic; some of them borrowed elements from Thomism or did their best to avoid unnecessary oppositions. Generally speaking, they all felt inclined to follow the ways of inner experience opened by Saint Augustine, not however without taking with Augustinianism such liberties that it might be misleading to call them Augustinian.

ALPHONSE GRATRY

Alphonse Gratry[1] first received a solid mathematical formation; he even entered the École Polytechnique (1825) but he left it after two years of studies. Although born in a family where religious indifference prevailed (the father made his first communion several years after the son) young Gratry joined Bautain in Strasbourg and lived in the group of his disciples from 1828 to 1840. Still he was not exactly a disciple; ordained a priest in 1832, he became a chaplain to the École Normale Supérieure (Paris), engaged in an active controversy against Vacherot, with the consequence that he gave up his functions at the school. He then undertook to restore in France the Congregation of the Oratory (1852), all this without interrupting his literary activity. He wrote well. When he became a candidate for the French Academy, Thiers asked if he presented himself as a

XIII. *In the Spirit of Augustinianism*

philosopher or as a preacher, and indeed there is a little too much eloquence in his philosophy; but, for all that he is important, for, through Ollé-Laprune, a life line connects him with Maurice Blondel.

The titles of the two main works of Gratry, *De la connaissance de Dieu* and *De la connaissance de l'âme*, too closely recall the *noverim me, noverim te* of Saint Augustine to be a mere coincidence. Moreover, such a program fitted the French philosophical tradition which seeks in inner life the starting point of metaphysical speculation. Contrary to the Aristotelian order preferred by the scholastics, Gratry places metaphysics at the beginning of philosophy. In his Introduction to *De la connaissance de Dieu*, Gratry defines the philosophical order as follows: "The parts of philosophy are: (1) the knowledge of God (theodicy); (2) logic, which is a development of psychology and studies the soul in its intelligence, as well as the laws of intelligence; (3) ethics (*la morale*) which is another development of psychology, and which studies the soul in its will, along with the laws of will. We shall expound the different parts of philosophy successively. We shall begin with theodicy. That order is that of Descartes, of Fénelon, of Malebranche, of Saint Thomas Aquinas. Bossuet has followed the inverse order. But we prefer to begin with theodicy because, in our own opinion, theodicy implies the whole of philosophy. It presents it in its wholeness, in its unity; it contains all its roots."

This remarkable passage gives evidence that the Cartesian conception of the "tree of philosophy" was still alive in the mind of Gratry. But its characteristic feature is his pretension of following the order of Saint Thomas. In fact he does the very reverse, at least if what he calls philosophy is the philosophy of Aristotle upheld by the scholastics. But Gratry evidently has in mind the philosophy expounded by Saint Thomas in his *Summa theologiae* and in the *Summa contra gentiles*, two theological works in which he naturally follows the theological order, from God to things. Obviously, to Gratry, the philosophy of Thomas already was what Pope Leo XIII was to describe in 1879 as the Christian philosophy of Thomas Aquinas.

In agreement with Thomas Aquinas, Gratry admits that all knowledge begins with experience, but he widens the notion of experience. To him, experience is threefold in kind; external experience, whose object is the external world of sense; inner experience, whose object is the life of the soul; mystical experience, which relates us to the cause of our being. Two intellectual principles enable us to organize the data of sensibility; the principle of identity which insures the self-consistency of thought and the principle of transcendency, which is a natural disposition, or tendency, of reason to arise from any finite given thing to the infinite as to its cause. Infinitesimal calculus (remember Gratry's mathematical formation) and even plain induction bear witness to the existence in us of this principle.

The principle of infinity plays an important part in Gratry's theodicy. To him the proofs of the existence of God must be simple, accessible to all. They must therefore be prepared by the presence in the soul of some natural feeling, or confused desire, to which they bring satisfaction. Such is prayer, a universal fact in which intellect and will, mind and heart are equally involved. Now prayer need not necessarily assume the form of an explicitly religious act. Every time man feels himself related to something above himself, he is unconsciously praying. When Descartes says, for instance: "I feel that I am a limited being ceaselessly tending to, and aspiring toward, something better and greater than I," he is praying. Now, understood precisely thus, prayer is a movement of the soul from the finite to the infinite. In a sense, it is one with the basic intuition to which modern mathematics are indebted for the infinitesimal calculus. In another sense, it is akin to the dialectical process so well described by Plato. The "infinitesimal dialectical process" working on the data of experience (internal still more than external) progressively leads us to a valid knowledge of God.

The dialectic based upon the *sens de l'infini* does not rest upon the syllogism. With keen insight, Gratry observes that, far from resulting from syllogistic dialectics, that infinitesimal process is that whose conclusions provide syllogisms with the major premises they need in order to effect their own deductions. Different from syllogism, it is as strictly demonstrative as that classical principle of deduction. In fine, the more convincing proofs of the existence of God are reducible to it. What is remarkable in Gratry's metaphysical method is that it rests upon a fact which all natural theologies have to take into account, namely, the irresistible tendency of understanding to integrate any series the first terms of which are given to it. St. Thomas' proof of the existence of God by the degrees of being is a case in point, but even the protest raised by Kant against such a transcendent use of the ideas of reason, which he considers vain but unavoidable, bears witness to the reality of the fact. Gratry has clearly seen the decisive part played by that principle of induction in the history of the

XIII. *In the Spirit of Augustinianism*

proofs of the existence of God. He finds it in all the great metaphysicians from Plato through those of the middle ages and of modern times, up to his favorite, Fénelon.[2]

A philosophy of history completes Gratry's philosophy by showing that there is in the heart of man a feeling for things divine, which is the principle of mankind's slow progress toward morality and civilization. By and large, Gratry's philosophy continues the tradition of the philosophies of inner experience that originated with the doctrine of Saint Augustine. He himself felt at home in the doctrines of Pascal and even Malebranche (minus the vision in God), but the real importance of his doctrine consisted perhaps in that it paved the way to the religious philosophies of "immanence" and, first of all, to that of Maurice Blondel.

Léon Ollé-Laprune

Before Blondel, Léon Ollé-Laprune[3] was perceptibly influenced by Gratry, but his vast historical erudition exposed his mind to many different philosophical influences. Among these should be noted that of Renouvier who, with his insistence on the part played by will in judgment, provided him with a justification for a philosophy open to the possibility of religious faith.

The epigraph of Ollé-Laprune's main work, *De la certitude morale*, is borrowed from the words of Plato (*Rep.*, VII, 518c): It is with our whole soul that we must go to being, and to that which is the most evident in being, namely, good. By "moral certitude" we should not understand the low kind of certitude we say we have when we feel convinced without being able rationally to justify assent. The kind of certitude at stake is called moral because it depends on properly moral conclusions. It is at one and the same time both assent of reason and consent of the will; it is both knowledge and faith. The common clarity of the ordinary objects of knowledge hides from us the sight of the things of the soul, which are the objects of ethics and of religion.

Moral certitude has for its proper objects those of the moral order. The truths of the moral order are four in number: moral law, moral liberty, the existence of God and future life. To read those words is enough to show that what is at stake is the group of truths usually considered as the ultimate conclusions of philosophy. They also are those which criticism considers as indemonstrable, but the reason for this negation perhaps is that some error is made concerning the conditions of their demonstrability. The point Ollé-Laprune wants to make is an important one. The criterion of demonstrability applicable to scientific conclusions concerning nature may not apply to conclusions concerning different orders of reality. There may be conditions to the knowledge of moral truths and those conditions might well have something to do with the moral dispositions of the subject. This motive will often be recurring in the group of philosophers we now are studying. They all take into account the personal dispositions of the knowing subject.

Of course, there is a difficulty. If moral certitude is different because it implies personal conditions, how can it presuppose *subjective conditions* without itself becoming a *subjective certitude*? This is where reason has its part to play. Leaving aside supernatural faith, there is such a thing as a natural faith, a moral faith. Affirmations bear either upon abstractions or upon facts. There is therefore a certitude that can be called *real* and another one that can be called *abstract*. Abstract certitude attaches itself to *notions*, real certitude attaches itself to things. Now, since abstractions are for us only means of handling things, there can be no certitude for the mind that concerns itself with notions apart from things. When it is *real* (about things) certitude is immediate, experiential, and practical. Assent to it is "an immediate, complete, and vigorous assent to reality as present, acting, felt, or, at least, represented to the mind by some vivid image." Its very vividness is the reason it invites personal reaction to it and, in short, action.

In fact, abstract and formal knowledge is nowhere found in its purity except in mathematics; so the conditions of moral certitude should be neglected nowhere, but in the order of moral truths still less than anywhere else. Religious and moral truth is first established in conscience by education and personal experience; it then first assumes the form of an implicit certitude; the scholastics would call it an *habitual* certitude, for it is a state rather than an act. Second, from that habitual certitude, there arises an *actual* certitude, which is born as soon as reflection dwells on already possessed cognitions and declares them to be valid and rationally well founded. After being given in conscience, those certitudes then become objects of science. Both moments are necessary, but real knowledge, that is, knowledge of things apprehended as actually given, experiential and practical knowledge, is always given first; speculative knowledge

XIII. *In the Spirit of Augustinianism*

comes next; neither one is sufficient, for real knowledge is solid but obscure, whereas abstract knowledge is clear but flimsy and unable to provide motives for action.

One cannot follow the thought of Ollé-Laprune without realizing what a powerful incentive Maurice Blondel could find in it to develop a philosophy of moral and religious action. "To keep both distinct and united the elements of a natural whole, such is the law for true knowledge, and this is a great difficulty for an intelligence weak and distracted such as ours." Blondel could have written that sentence. It is equally remarkable that Ollé-Laprune already strove to consider the operations of the mind in their total complexity, yet without confusion of its powers. "Sometimes we distinguish to the point of separating, sometimes we unite to the point of confounding, and thus, by two contrary movements, our thought alters the nature of things and falsifies their idea." Hence the necessity of studying the role of will in knowledge in the different matters proposed to our assent. In all cases, the certitude never is that of intellect alone, but of man; complete certitude is *personal*; that which man knows, it is necessary for him that he himself should *be* it and even, in the admirable words of the Gospel, that he should *do* it (*qui facit veritatem*). "Certitude is the total act of the soul itself embracing, by a free choice no less than by a firm judgment, truth present to it as a light and a law, an object of contemplation and of love, of respect and of obedience."

In discussing the wrong ways of understanding moral faith and moral certitude in Kant, Fichte, and other philosophers, Ollé-Laprune gives evidence of his penetrating mind; he was no less familiar with Scripture and theology, and we see him going to great trouble in the hope of extracting from Saint Thomas some confirmation of his personal views. Among his contemporaries, he feels in sympathy with the Protestant philosopher Charles Secrétan,[4] but, on the whole, he goes his own way with a remarkable firmness of purpose in a matter where definite notions are so difficult to hold firm. His main point is that to acknowledge subjective elements in our recognition of truth does not cause truth itself to be subjective. There is there an inexhaustible field of exploration. Those who like Newman should read Ollé-Laprune; one can find no more discerning guides than those two in the exploration of the man within.

Maurice Blondel

The key notions of Ollé-Laprune's philosophy received an unexpected development in the doctrine of one of his students, Maurice Blondel.[5] Like his master, he was a Catholic layman whose uneventful life was that of a professor of philosophy in a French university. At the bottom of his doctrine churns the same problem whose presence is felt in the philosophical positions of D. Mercier and of Ollé-Laprune; how to be a philosopher, being a Christian, in a dechristianized society where the slightest trace of religion in a philosophical doctrine is enough to discredit it as guilty of irrationality? For Maurice Blondel, the problem was to elaborate a philosophy both purely rational and thoroughly Catholic. In order to construct it, he had to look for a small number of key notions, borrowed from inner experience, and capable of showing the supernatural order rooted in nature. The two notions of "action" and of "immanence" appeared to him to answer that need.

Blondel's epoch-making doctorate thesis, *L'action*, widely misunderstood on account of its novelty, but also because of a certain obscurity *sui generis*, has brought encouragement to the many minds in quest of a philosophy of inner life, both technical in its dialectic and religious in its aspirations. Although Blondel was squarely in the tradition of Bautain, Gratry, and Ollé-Laprune, he went his own solitary way, always in quest of a better formulation of his thought. The unusual character of his philosophical positions or, rather, of his personal way of asking classical questions, created around his doctrine an atmosphere of suspicion. Some people have a tendency to consider suspicious whatever they cannot understand. In the last analysis, the orthodoxy of his thought has been vindicated despite an often unnecessarily misleading language.[6]

Blondel has surely been right in his protest against the title of "philosophy of action" commonly given to his philosophy. The notion of "action" was the object of his thesis because of his desire to build up a philosophy of the "concrete." His initial "no" was directed against the notion of a philosophy of the "abstract." Only the concrete is real. Now, in man, action is precisely that through the mediation of which universal and singular, thought and being, meet in concrete reality.[7] Blondel himself has seen, in the peculiar nature of his posing of the philosophical question, the reason he spent his speculative life caught so to speak between two fires, the one directed against him by the philosophies of the singular and the other leveled at him by the philosophies of the universal. His own position always remained, in the concrete, beyond both singularity and universality.

Granting that Blondel was subjected to often superficial attacks, it is only fair to add that his favorite method of demonstration was to refute other people's positions. His pet target was what he himself used to call a "notional" conception of knowledge and reality. Being is not entirely contained in even the best defined notions of it; these notions are general, which reality is not. On the other hand, the immediate perception of a concrete individual also fails to reveal to us the wealth of its inexhaustible singularity; true reality is caught between these two insufficient modes of knowing. This does not mean that reality is not knowable, but, rather, that the known is not the whole of reality. Blondel was haunted by the feeling that this unknown side of reality is the more precious part of it. In order to see something of this *terra incognita*, he has steadily recommended not that the usual modes of knowledge should be rejected but rather that there should be adopted a conscious docility of intellect to the aspirations of will. For the will, which is love, is the ultimate reason for the exigencies of intellect. The will is always tending toward something else beyond what it wills; for the same reason, our intellect is always carried beyond its present object toward that which it does not know. The same remark applies to our own being. Only will can carry us beyond our present self. Understanding, mere intellectual observation of self, cannot guess anything beyond what it already knows, unless it yields to the desire of will. In short, consciousness is not the whole person; action is moving ceaselessly in the darkness that precedes and attends all subjective knowledge. This something still to be known that surrounds on all sides our awareness of action is not the least important part of action. But nothing else than action can enter it.

Though inseparable from the notion of action, that of "immanence" is not identical with it. As was said above, the proper function of that notion is to provide philosophy with a natural starting point from which to reach the supernatural. *A priori*, this looks like a contradiction in terms, unless, of course, one implicitly begins by supernaturalizing nature or by naturalizing the supernatural. Blondel was accused of doing both, and he complained bitterly about what appeared to him as willful misinterpretations of his authentic thought. He even assured his opponents that his notion of immanence had already been familiar to Thomas Aquinas. The *method* of immanence consisted in systematically applying the *principle* of immanence. In the form in which Blondel thinks he finds it enounced by Saint Thomas, the principle runs as follows: "Nihil potest ordinari in finem aliquem, nisi praeexistat in ipso quaedam proportio ad finem." What Thomas says is that nothing can be ordained to a certain end unless there be in the thing a certain proportion to that end. This is what Blondel translates as follows: "Nothing can enter man that does not somehow answer in him a need for expansion, whatever the origin or the nature of that appetite may happen to be."[8] There seems to be a fundamental ambiguity in the method of "immanence." First, nothing can be immanent in a being unless it be transcendent to it: unless it comes to it from above, it is not immanent in it, it is it. Second, Thomas Aquinas had simply said that no thing can be ordained to another without having in itself a certain aptitude to receive that thing; Blondel was making him say that there is, within such a being, a natural or supernatural need to transcend itself in order to reach its higher end. This he often called an "inefficacious natural desire." Despite this prudent clause, the theological difficulty remained. There can be no natural exigency of the supernatural. The order of the supernatural remains, by definition, the order of grace, that is to say, of a free and gratuitous gift of God.[9]

Blondel wanted to save an important aspect of truth, namely the description of the order of the created world that is found in *Summa Contra Gentiles*: "That all things are ordered to one end who is God" (III, 17). Now "all things tend to become like God as to their ultimate end" (19, 2). If this is true of beings devoid of knowledge, how much more true it must be of man! If the ultimate end of each creature is to attain God as closely as is possible for it, an intellectual substance must tend to the knowledge of God as to its ultimate end. That thesis, developed in *Contra Gentiles*, III, 25, embodies the truth of what Maurice Blondel strove to say. The world actually created by God makes sense and reveals an intelligible structure in the light of the end in view of which it was created; from no other point of view does it make sense; but it may be that the intelligibility of created nature is a secret held by Christian philosophy alone.[10] But Maurice Blondel had no patience with that notion, and he said so in no uncertain terms, although his own philosophy was a fine illustration of it.

XIV. *Early Twentieth-Century Philosophy in Italy*

It can be said of Italy,[1] just as correctly as of France, that although Kant found in it many readers, he really never had followers. It takes a veritable intellectual heroism to maintain a strictly critical attitude in practical as well as in speculative philosophy. Most of the philosophers who took their point of departure from Kant intended literally to depart from him and directed their investigations to the zones which Kant had expressly forbidden his successors to enter. Such was the case with Renouvier in France. Following other ways, but prompted by a similar spirit, some Italian readers of Kant, in the second half of the nineteenth century, attempted to use Kant as an antidote to materialism under all its forms.[2] The attempt was legitimate. To the reduction of everything to matter it is not arbitrary to oppose the Kantian reduction of the physical universe to the pure *a priori* laws of human understanding. The danger of the undertaking is that it works too well. There is an overwhelming temptation to overstep the frontiers of critical philosophy and to conceive the knowing subject, that is, the understanding itself, as a sort of spiritual force productive of knowledge and, by the same token, of the universe.

The Italian interpreters of Kant have done more than just spread the knowledge of his philosophy; several of them, at least, have shown a tendency to consider physical reality and morality as concrete manifestations of the spirit. The philosophy really at home in early twentieth-century Italy, and much more so than in France at the same date, is that of Hegel. Naples seems to have provided an early homestead for Italian Hegelianism. However, the main function of both Kant and Hegel seems to have been to provide Italian thinkers with a technical framework for their own spiritualistic idealism.

Benedetto Croce

The philosophy of Hegel has been interpreted by Benedetto Croce with extreme liberty.[3] He was less interested in the purely speculative aspect of the doctrine (although he did not neglect it) than in the light it throws on history as well as on the political problems of the state. Still, without Hegel, there would have been no Croce and, just as much as Hegel, Croce was out for a Unitarian interpretation of reality as a whole. According to him, a philosophy that is not able to account for the whole of reality is not a philosophy at all.

Croce distinguishes two general forms of knowledge. On the one hand, knowledge can be intuitive, obtained by imagination, having for its objects individuals taken in their singularity; on the other hand, knowledge can be logical, obtained by intellect, having for its object universals and relations between singular things. In short, knowledge is productive either of *images* or of *concepts*. Intuitive knowledge of singulars results in artistic or esthetic experience[4]; intellectual knowledge of the universal results in philosophy.

These two orders should not be isolated. On the contrary, speculative philosophy includes the two orders of esthetics and logic. As science of the pure concept, logic apprehends the universal in its unity with the singular.[5] The pure concept is the *a priori* synthesis of universality and of concreteness; hence the name given to its object: the concrete universal. On this point, Croce keeps faith with the authentic Hegelian spirit. What is it for a universal to be "concrete"? It is to be the reverse of an Aristotelian universal. According to the classical tradition, universals are obtained by *abstraction*, each and every one of them being set apart from all the others in virtue of the principle of contradiction. To be a certain object of intellection necessarily precludes the possibility of being any other. As Hegel said, there really are contraries but not all of them are mutually exclusive. Even when they are opposed among themselves, contraries are not opposed to unity and to being. One should rather say that concrete and true unity always is the synthesis of contraries. For this reason, the pure concept is correctly called a "concrete universal," since it is an *a priori* synthesis of contraries (i.e., a concretion of opposites) and of the universality proper to concepts.

The speculative part of philosophy (esthetics, logic) is matched by a practical one. Speculative philosophy belongs in the order of intuition and intellection, practical philosophy belongs in the order of will. At its lowest level of activity, will is concerned with procuring the goods necessary for life; the knowledge of how to achieve this end is economics. At a higher level, will aims to attain ends situated beyond this material one; economics deals with problems whose data is determined by particular circumstances of place and time; at this higher level, will is concerned with universally and permanently desirable ends; the determination of such ends is the business of ethics. Taken together, esthetics, logic, economics, and ethics make up the whole of the philosophy of spirit.[6]

These formal determinations of the object and parts of philosophy must be completed by a definition of the reality to which philosophical knowledge applies.

Although active in translating Hegel and diffusing the knowledge of his philosophy, Croce has nonetheless often said he was no Hegelian. And indeed a radical difference separates his philosophy from that of Hegel. In my philosophy, Croce said, reality is affirmed as being spirit, not, however, a spirit soaring above the world or circulating throughout the world; it is a spirit that coincides with the world. "The Spirit that is the World is the self-unfolding spirit, both one and diverse, an eternal solution and an eternal problem, and its self-awareness is philosophy, which is its history, or else it is its history, which is substantially identical with philosophy."[7] In this way, Croce intended to overcome what was left of abstraction in Hegelianism. Hegel himself would no doubt observe that he was being completely misunderstood; but the philosopher subscribing to the interpretation of his doctrine by his own successors has not yet been born.

This identification of philosophy with historiography offered Croce a great advantage. It enabled him to put to good use his remarkable erudition in the field of literary history and his no less remarkable talent for literary criticism. It also invited him to develop a notion of history permitting its integration with philosophy, and which can be considered the personal contribution of Croce to modern philosophy. He himself has dubbed it "absolute historicism" and defined it as a reduction of philosophy to the methodology of history.

The meaning of the doctrine is to be sought in Croce's personal experience of historical research work. However we may feel about the philosophical use he makes of it, the description itself is correct. To a true historian, Croce says, the history of the past arises out of life no less directly than that of the present. In other words, there is no difference between the history of the past and contemporary history, not because all history is of the past but, rather, because all history is contemporary history. Historical research turns past facts into present facts and true historians turn that which has once been interesting into a living interest experienced in present life.

In Croce's philosophy, history is the band binding and tying life and thought into a concrete unity, which is the very object of philosophy because it is the very substance of reality. This *nesso di vita e pensiero vella storia*, this history conceived as the thinking of an eternal present, was certainly not a solid foundation upon which to build a metaphysical interpretation of the world, but it symbolizes well enough the personal universe inhabited by Croce himself. It was a historian's paradise. At first, one says reality is history, but he soon gets used to saying that history is reality, which is after all not the same thing.

Giovanni Gentile

The career of Giovanni Gentile,[8] which was headed for a tragic end, has first been tied up with that of Croce. Gentile introduced Croce to the philosophy of Hegel, but they soon differed in their interpretation of the doctrine, including that of its political consequences. Gentile was a Hegelian rightist and a fascist. Croce was a Hegelian leftist and a democrat. At the speculative level, one of the most devastating criticisms of the "philosophy of the four words" is from the pen of Giovanni Gentile. Both were interested in Hegel, but they did not conceive of spirit in the same way.

There are metaphysics of the act of being; that of Gentile was a metaphysics of the act of thinking. The reason he always felt tempted to speak the language of traditional Christian theology is that, whatever else it may have been, his metaphysics was always a philosophy of "act." When Gentile says "thought" he does not mean "that which is being thought" (*il pensiero pensato*) but, rather, the thinking thought (*il pensiero pensante*).

This entails a modification of the classical conception of dialectic. "True dialectic is not that which presupposes concepts and describes them, it is that which produces them, looking out for them in the only place where they can be found, because it is the place where they are being produced, namely, in thought." According to the Hegelian tradition, to produce concepts is to unite opposites by an act of thought. Hence the consequence that the only true dialectical becoming is the becoming of thought in act, that is, of the very act whereby thought *is* the living unity of the opposites. Gentile used to call this thought in act, the self-awareness, "auto-consciousness." This is the act whereby the thinking subject becomes an object to itself or, in other words, a knowing wherein that which is being known is the same thing as that which knows. In a sense, this kind of knowledge is entirely different from all others, but, in another sense, it is implied in every other kind. There is no act of cognition that does not imply, over and above the knowledge of some particular object, that of the subject which knows it. So, inasmuch as it includes the knower, at one and the same time, as subject and as object, "auto-consciousness" includes, at one and the same time, the positing and the negation of a subject. This indivisible unity of thesis and antithesis, of being and non-being, constitutes the essential dialecticity of "auto-consciousness." Taken as a pure thesis (position) without antithesis (counterposition) the subject remains a mere abstraction. So also is the object a mere abstraction if it is reduced to the condition of an antithesis, without any thesis to oppose. The concrete lies in the unity of the synthesis, that is, in the last analysis, in the very act of thinking.[9]

This interpretation of the act of knowing entails a complete absorption of the object in the subject. In order to pass from psychology to metaphysics, the only thing to do is to extrapolate this observation. Or, rather, it is enough to take it such as it is. "Auto-consciousness" tells us what an act of thinking is in itself, unconditionally; by the same token, it tells us what a pure thinking subject is, when taken in itself and absolutely. This "I" is given to us empirically. So my own auto-consciousness is, first of all, the consciousness I have of myself as of a determined personality; none the less, at the very same time, I can signify by the same word, "I," the pure or formal subject, that is, myself as a pure abstract principle of cognition. Of course, this empirical "I" and this pure abstract "I" are one and the same reality. How many subjects of this sort can there be? Ultimately, only one. For indeed, since even the "I" exists as an object only inasmuch as it is posited by itself as a subject, one can infer that no known object pre-exists to the act of knowing; on the contrary, every time we know a certain thing, it is being created by an act of our mind. For instance, we can talk about love or hatred in the abstract, in which case they do not exist; for them to exist, our soul must either love or hate; it is only by loving or hating that we know what these passions really are. So knowledge is not an alteration of the subject by its object; it is a creation of objects by the knowing subject: *Pertanto la cono-*

scenza non e un alterazione, bensi una creazione della cosa.[10]

This invites us to posit one single subject with regard to which all the other subjects are mere objects. Such a pure thinking subject would be, by definition, the principle of all that which is, for the simple reason that, being the absolutely pure subject, he is positing all possible objects. In other words, every time anyone of us apprehends himself, beyond his own empirical "I," as a pure abstract "I," he is obscurely apprehending the absolute "auto-consciousness" that is the cause of the world.[11]

From this point of view, the universe is seen as the dialectical development of the spirit. This development is that of history itself,[12] and it takes place under three different forms, or dialectical moments: art, religion, and philosophy. Art is the moment of absolute subjectivity; religion is the moment of absolute objectivity, in which God is posited as absolute object. Philosophy absorbs within itself these two moments, because only the pure act of thinking reconciles, in positing them, subject and object.

It is a common feature of all the "philosophies of spirit" that they finally turn themselves into philosophies of religion and, as often as not, into religions.

The religion of the spirit professed by Giovanni Gentile betrays a refreshing candor and even perhaps a real desire to justify, in a way, the traditional positions of Christian philosophy. Unfortunately, this cannot be done. From the fact, admitted by all theologies, that there is something divine in truth, and something religious in the relationship of the human mind with truth, it cannot be concluded that truth is God and that this relationship itself is religion. Gentile was well aware of the problem. He has expressly refused to identify the personality of God, of which it is impossible to doubt, with the finite "I." Still, he himself could not find in his own philosophy of immanence any justification for the God of Christianity, personal, self-subsisting, both immanent in us and wholly distinct from us. Not having at his disposal the traditional notion of being Gentile hesitates between letting God dissolve into either the abstract generality of impersonal truth or else into the subjectivity of the thinking "I."[13] In the best of cases, the theology of the spirit is seen courting both disasters at once: "This personality of the true, which actuates itself logically in our thought, is endowed with absolute objectivity; in fact, it confers upon thinking that necessity and universality whereby, when thinking in conformity with truth, man overcomes his own finite particularity and dilates into the infinite and the eternal."[14]

One cannot have the conclusions of a philosophy without first subscribing to its principles. Many a modern philosophy seems to be haunted by the desire to remain Christian without preserving the God of Christianity.

Critical Idealism

The difficulties inherent in the philosophies of the spirit seem to have invited some Italian philosophers to keep closer to the critical position exemplified by Kant. On the other hand, none of them would content himself with merely abstaining from making suppositions about what reality is in itself. Thus situated between an absolute positivism refusing to transcend the data of experience, and the philosophies of the spirit absorbing objects into the knowing subjects, such philosophies have attempted to reach metaphysical conclusions starting from a frankly recognized dualism of subject and object.

Bernardino Varisco[15] soon realized that positivism, acceptable as a scientific attitude, cannot lead to properly philosophical conclusions (*Scienza e opinioni*, 1901). His distinction between the "known" and the "true" goes far beyond the mere assumption that demonstrative knowledge is not coextensive with the order of known facts. Besides scientifically known truths there still remains the immense order of perceived facts and of well-founded opinions that are not properly known and, nevertheless, are true. The supernatural, for instance, belongs in this order of "that which is not certain, but, nevertheless, is true" (*cio che non consta, ma che è vero*). It is noteworthy that, following his own way, Varisco arrived at an attitude analogous to that of Renouvier's last years: a sort of monadism, according to which "the universe is a plurality of monads, of active and conscious centers, the decrees of knowledge and of practical activity of which are gradual moments of the ordaining and unifying of reality."

Another philosopher whose doctrine has contributed to vindicating the necessity, or at least, the rational inevitability of, metaphysical speculation, was Piero Martinotti.[16] If to know is to achieve a logically unified body of propositions agreeing with experience, then to philosophize and to metaphysicize are one and the same thing. The Kantian dualism is thus preserved, but Martinetti also grants to Kant that "the reality with which we find ourselves confronted is not a material reality, foreign to spirit, but, rather, a complex of psychical processes, a spiritual reality, conditioned by the unity and activity of the subject."

The same necessities operative in the philosophies of Varisco and Renouvier are again seen at work in the doctrine of Martinetti. These philosophers set out with Kant, that is, they start from the subject; on the other hand, they do not want to be condemned to subjectivism nor, for that matter, to lose themselves in a hyper-subject such as the spirit of idealism; so they naturally go back to some modified version of the monadism of Leibniz. In such a doctrine, everything is a subject and, nevertheless, each and every subject, being a spiritual subject, is at one and the same time, the coincidence of itself and of the whole universe. Such an attitude not only leaves the door open to metaphysical speculation, it openly calls for it. In Piero Martinetti's own words, "the theory of knowledge can be characterized as a sort of critical introduction, of negative preparation for the positive work of metaphysics."

The vivid interest in religious problems displayed by Martinetti could not, however, enable him to go further in this domain than his principles would allow. To him, religion was not reducible to mere sentiment; neither could it be founded upon faith conceived as an assent to some supernaturally revealed truth or to some mystical intuition distinct from reason. Adopting, this time, a position similar to that of Léon Brunschvicg (not on account of any direct influence, but because such was the only way open to both) Martinetti finally posits truth (not being) as the very substance of the divinity: "The supreme religious value is therefore truth: each and every degree of our inner experience is a revelation; our whole activity is an elevation towards the unique truth that is the unique reality; all philosophy is a rationally lived faith." In short, "there is a mysticism of reason, which is the only true mysticism of enlightened spirits."[17]

The philosophy of Carabellese[18] is a "critique of the concrete." It also is an ontology, in the sense that it is a philosophy of being, but it is a concrete ontology because it refuses to separate thought from being. In reality, "thought is a thought that is; being is a being that thinks." A thus conceived ontology opposes idealism as well as realism, and it does so on the ground that, before anything else, knowledge is the knowledge of being (of something that is). For the same reason, philosophy is destined to remain an endless effort, because, from the very beginning of his reflexive life, man finds himself engaged in being without disposing of any means either to exhaust its content or to get out of it. Like Gentile, Carabellese favors a philosophy of immanence, but it is an immanence of being in thought and of thought in being.

Can that immanence be transcended? In a sense, yes, but the very effort to transcend it is the true meaning of transcendency. What is given is the concrete reality of being and thought wherein universality and singularity coincide, that is, vanish, as being mere abstractions. What has to be transcended, in this doctrine, is therefore not a notion, nor a couple of notions, but given being itself. This is to say that, whatever the result of the effort, we find ourselves, with Carabellese, completely outside of the limits of Kantian criticism. The notion of "thing in itself" is meaningless if it signifies a thing existing outside the mind but it can and must be preserved in the non-Kantian meaning of objective reality given in the mind. In order to transcend it, one should raise above the concrete and posit as a pure object, an idea, being in itself, that is, God.

It is therefore impossible to deny God by an act of thought, because, if God is the pure object of consciousness, to think God is to affirm God: "If you deny God, you don't think." It is interesting to observe, so to speak *in vivo*, the intrinsic necessity and perpetuity of the main metaphysical positions. Each particular doctrine modifies their data and, for that very reason, it differs from the other doctrines, but analogical transpositions always allow their observers to re-establish their fundamental correspondences. The metaphysical ontology of Carabellese is here joining the noetic ontologism of his predecessors. The essential characters of being as given in inner experience lead the mind to the essential attributes of the notion of being, which themselves lead the mind to God. Without thinking of God, one cannot think at all.

There is, however, a considerable difference between the being of Carabellese and that of Malebranche, of Gerdil, and of Rosmini. In his doctrine, God is immanent in thought as idea, or absolute object, not as a self-subsisting and, so to speak, external reality. Nothing can be given in mind as external to mind. In his penetrating discussion of the doctrine, M. F. Sciacca concludes that it is here a question of "a pure and simple pantheism and of an atheism, since the existence of God is denied" even when Carabellese seems to affirm it: "Carabellese calls God that which is not God and he ascribes to the concept of existence a very peculiar meaning."[19] The existence affirmed of God has nothing to do with empirical existence. Even granting this, however, it is not certain that Carabellese does not succeed, if not in reaching the God of religion, at least in attaining a god of philosophy who, because to him philosophy is metaphysics, ultimately coincides with a transcendent being, object of worship and of prayer.

The most disturbing of his assertions in this respect is his statement that, in the last analysis, it is in their effort to join God in his depth that the very being of religion and philosophy consists. Let us not forget the title of his master work: *The Theological Problem as Philosophy*. Finally Kant wins.

Italy is the seat of an intense philosophical production.[20] Perhaps on account of their sense of humor the Italian philosophers have seldom taken existentialism tragically.[21] On the other hand, the persistent vitality of the Christian tradition has prevented the rise of a philosophically significant Marxist school.[22] The influence of Croce seems to be on the wane, while that of Gentile remains active through the teaching of his many pupils.

Among the many names of Italian philosophers belonging to the present and to the recent past,[23] let us quote Annibale Pastore who, starting from a sort of scientism, progressively overcame the limits of his early logical positivism.[24] To the extent that it is a logicism, the doctrine is dominated by what he himself called a *logica del potenziamento* (abridged as *Ldp*). Its meaning seems to be that there is an active efficacy in the logical process itself, so that, owing to it, the logical entities of which discourse consists receive new meanings from the various systems of relations which the logical process obliges them to enter. For instance, in the traditional formula of the principle of identity, AA, the meaning of A cannot be twice the same, otherwise the proposition would be tautological, which it is not. It is the same as with numbers, a twice posited concept is two concepts. This leads Pastore to a universal relationism, since every thing and notion varies in consequence of any change in the things or notions to which it is related. This is the meaning of Pastore's notion of *potenziamento*; each and every being "potentiates" those to which it is related. The very nature of relation implies that this "potentiating" of the related beings should be reciprocal. After establishing the logical formulas required for a technical expression of his logicism, Pastore proceeded to the elimination of the notion of a prime, transcendent cause of the universe, in the interest of efficiency as well as of purposiveness. After the Second World War, however, he felt the need of a general reconstruction in metaphysics and ethics. This led him to a critique of Leninism and, finally, to a re-evaluation of the mystical meaning of Christianity.

Antonio Aliotta's[25] formation was influenced by the thought of De Sarlo.[26] According to Aliotta, realism and idealism are likewise overcome in the act of experiencing reality. In it, things exist only by virtue of their permanent rela-

XIV. Early Twentieth-Century Philosophy in Italy

tionship with consciousness while, in turn, consciousness exists only by virtue of its relationship with things.[27] Such was already the position of Aliotta in his early work, *The Idealist Reaction Against Science* (1912). The experience of the First World War killed his faith in idealism. The presence of evil in the world demanded an explanation which the natural optimism of idealism was unable to provide, but far from despairing of the future, Aliotta maintained that, despite all absurdities, moral invention and co-operation remain as possible in philosophy as they obviously are in science. Experience is a decisive criterion of truth and error in all domains. With deep insight Aliotta discerned the creative function of experience, and still more evidently of experiment. Instead of seeing it as a mere confirmation of an already conceived truth, he conceived it as the project of a synthesis still to be achieved. This agreed with his notion of life seen as a permanent conflict (*Eternal War and the Drama of Existence*, 1917). Life implies an ever-present necessity of making personal choices. Hence the title of Aliotta's major work, *Sacrifice as the Meaning of the World* (1940). There is a touch of pragmatism in the doctrine of Aliotta. One vainly looks in it for an objective criterion of good and evil set up by reason. On the other hand, Aliotta does not believe that, individually or collectively, man is the ultimate judge of moral values. Even though many men deny in words the existence of God, they all act as though they did believe in the subsistence of an objective order of morality, itself rooted in a subsisting divine being.[28]

Among many others whom one would like to be able to quote, let us mention the name of Arangio-Ruiz[29] who, feeling disappointed at the failure of Gentile's idealism to account for the objective requirements of morality, set up a "moralism" of his own. The reaction of Ugo Spirito[30] to the shortcomings of Gentile's immanentism as well as to those of Croce's historicism, was entirely different. He concluded that philosophy should not be identified with metaphysical conclusions, but rather with philosophical investigation itself, which thus became an end for itself. Ugo Spirito calls his doctrine a "problematicism," not because its conclusions are to him questionable (problematicism does not consider itself problematical) but because the very substance of that philosophy is problematicity itself.

In a different spirit, but also prompted by the wish to find a way out of idealism, Guido Calogero[31] is attempting a reduction of philosophical speculation to practical philosophy. Because cognition (the *logos*) is the activity of the very mind, it cannot become to itself an object of knowledge. Consequently the rules laid down by logic and noetics must find their field of application in the practical order. They are not laws for discourse, but for praxis.

An interesting feature of today's philosophical movement in Italy is the survival of the ambition to achieve all-embracing syntheses including the world of nature as well as that of man. There is certainly no trace of speculative shyness in the doctrine of Augustino Guzzo,[32] and still less in that of Carmelo Ottaviano[33] whose avowed intention it is to inaugurate a new philosophical era. His *Metaphysics of Partial Being* lays down the foundations for a metaphysical synthesis freed from the postulates that fettered the great philosophies of the past, Greek, Medieval and Modern. The undertaking is carried on on the strength of a new principle, that of "the non-constancy of the quantity of being." Since they are finite, particular beings are also partial; time and space are neither their receptacles nor their *a priori* forms, rather they are in them *negative properties* and *real deficiencies*. They betray the fundamental inability of things to exist "all together," or to be given all at once, which is typical of partial being. On account of their essential limitation, such beings must live a successive life, made up of moments that only are real one at a time. That metaphysical condition of man accounts for his desire of achieving a total simultaneity which, for him, would be beatitude. Metaphysics thus culminates in ethics, which Ottaviano conceives of as a rational systematization of the Christian view of life. He feels certain that the times are ripe for the opening of a new (and fourth) philosophical age. The metaphysics of partial being only marks its beginning.[34]

XV. *Existentialism and Phenomenology in France*

by THOMAS LANGAN

GABRIEL MARCEL

Contemporary existentialism was born in Germany and France at about the same time—the years just following World War I—but its fountainheads had no immediate connection with one another. That the same sort of vision of how to pose the questions of philosophy should come upon Heidegger and Jaspers without their knowing and reading each other, and upon Gabriel Marcel[1] without his reading either, might possibly be explained by their having had the same philosophical masters. But this common source must be searched for in quite a distant past—in the masters of *their* masters; one must go back at least to Hegel and Kant to find the roots of their common heritage. The immediate masters of Jaspers were Kierkegaard and Nietzsche; of Heidegger, Brentano and Husserl. Gabriel Marcel, perhaps the most independent creator of the three, owes the beginnings of his reflections to a revolt against the monism of German idealism, which makes him a kind of delayed-action Kierkegaard: his own human and religious sensitivities brought him to struggle with the descendants of Hegel, and through this struggle to invent what was, for France in the early twenties, a radically new vision of things. In several other important respects Gabriel Marcel resembles Kierkegaard: he could never fit into the established intellectual order (in this case, *l'université de France*); he is a religious thinker, and a religious *révolté* (a Protestant of Jewish background, he became an ardent convert to Catholicism in 1929, quite some time after he had established the basic horizons of his philosophy); he is, by conviction and inclination, an anti-systematic thinker.

philosophic method

Gabriel Marcel distinguishes three successive levels of intelligibility accessible to man: (1) *The level of existence*, which is that of *immediate consciousness* or of "pure empiricism," experience immediately lived, but neither explained nor understood. (2) *"First reflection"* explicitates elements of the primitively given experience by detaching them from the implicit texture of the empirical state, "objectivizing" them at the risk of forgetting the vital connection of the abstracted element with the rest of the real, especially the subject to whom it initially appears. *This is the realm of the particular sciences, of "objectivity," of "thought"*; the realm in which even the subject gets "objectivized," as it does in rationalistic philosophy; the realm that gives birth to "technology," which Marcel criticizes at length for its dehumanizing propensities. (3) The concrete philosophy that Marcel has sought to establish operates on a level of *second reflection*, which corrects the first reflection and, without losing any of the benefits of rationality, wins back the immediacy of existence, which here reveals for the first time its full sense, its *being*. Our most automatic movement is toward the objectivizations of "first reflection." What we must attempt is to create in ourselves a state of humble admiration for all of reality just as it is given to us; that is to say, we must work to dwell a moment in the first state, then we must seek to reflect on it in a way that will reintegrate all abstracted moments into the living whole.

Not that Gabriel Marcel wishes to suggest that reflection as such is desiccating; on the contrary, provided only that reflection seek to find in the depth of our experience the sense of life, it is not only acceptable, there is "no other recourse." (We shall see later that Marcel terms *recueillement* the attitude preparatory to this high-level reflection.) It is a lack of reflection, indeed a fear to reflect that keeps the technocratic world going. The dissolutions and objectivizations of first-analytic reflection are due to its being provisionary and incomplete.[2] To re-establish the immediacy suspended by them, philosophy tends toward the conquest of a *participation*, this time no longer existential, as in the brute empirical state, but ontological, a participation in being.[3] Thought must be pushed to reflect on itself until it is able to discover the living source of those contents it has, in first reflection, objectivized—sources at first only lived, but now consciously confronted. Reflecting on our ability to sense and on our state as incarnated beings, we will come to perceive that the "objective" world is undermined at its core, for technical thought can only be organized on the basis of givens, which basis is itself "impenetrable"; the category of the "it goes without saying" must be chased out of philosophy. Without ever becoming com-

XV. Existentialism and Phenomenology in France

pletely transparent to itself, reflection begins to feel out its own limits and to go beyond them by recognizing that it depends inevitably on the need for being from which it derives all its force.[4] Metaphysics consists then in a reflection on a reflection "by which thought tends towards the recuperation of an intuition which in some way loses itself to the extent it exercises itself."[5]

the ontological levels

The three levels of intelligibility correspond to three ontological levels: (1) that of immediate empirical *existence*; (2) that of a kind of objective possession of abstract objects, which we pile as a protectionist barrier against the rest of the world, and in which we erroneously and impoverishingly invest ourselves, which Marcel calls the level of "having," (*l'avoir*); and finally, (3) a level of participation in full, vital reality with the other, seized, not as my circumscribed possession, but in its own always transcending *being* (*l'être*). The practical exigencies of survival move us naturally and easily from *existence* to *having*—we want to possess things and hang on to them for our own sake. The movement from *existence* and *having* to *being* is never, however, automatic; it calls for a con-version, a free turning back from my natural egoism toward a devotion to a foreign reality in which I would participate for its sake. It may seem ironic, but this un-selfish movement is the necessary condition of my being as a *self*. Marcel terms this *free* act of thought divesting itself of its possessive abstractions in order to turn toward a participation in the fullness of a reality to which it must submit itself, an act of *faith*.[6] I must believe in the intelligibility of the world, if I am not to cede to the temptation to live it directly in an absurd empiricism, or if I am not to reduce it to my own practical, objectivizing schemes[7]; I must believe in myself, if I am not to turn in my resignation before the difficulties of living, or if I am not going to yield to determinism; I must believe in the person of the Other in order to love him genuinely, for himself, as he really is, and thereby discover the full reality of myself; I must believe in God in order to relate myself to Him, not as a construction of my fantasy, nor as an impersonal principle, but as He is in Himself, for Himself, in a genuine "I-Thou" relationship.

The new kind of intelligibility, the possibility of which is opened by our freely adopting that mode of being which is faith, Marcel terms *mystery*, which results from our refusing to reduce the being of what is Other to a mere problem, resolvable through an act of objectivization. For Marcel, the level of *avoir* and *problems*, the level of ego-centric possession, the level of science, of the chopping up and parceling out of reality, corresponds to the level which Heidegger terms "the inauthenticity of daily market-place existence." Marcel subjects the forms of inauthenticity to as rich and varied a description (a phenomenology of having, he terms it) as it has ever been subjected to by any philosopher, attempting, in the existentialist tradition of Kierkegaard and Nietzsche, to reveal the authentic goal of our lives, through description of the *negative* conditions of everyday existence. While space does not permit our reproducing any of these very rich concrete analyses here, we would point out a difference in accent that tends to distinguish Marcel's view of our everyday status from the accounts of Nietzsche, Kierkegaard, and Heidegger. Marcel tends to regard common man a bit more charitably, a bit less gnostically. He sees elements of authenticity in the common condition of us all; wisdom, indeed salvation is open to all, the first traces of it are to be found in the acts of devotion, fidelity, love, that touch every life. Salvation consists in bending our liberty to the fullest participation in these openings, which are there as a *call* to each one of us.

the mystery of being

In declaring that the authentic movement of philosophy, which is one with the movement toward salvation, opens us to participation in the mystery of being, Gabriel Marcel is doing the opposite of placing an opaque, an unknowable element at the center of his meditation. The reason we must speak of the mystery of being is not that being is obscure, but that it shines forth with too much light.[8] "Mystery" does not occur in the narrow and limiting objective order; what is not known in the order of facts or of scientific encounter can pose a *problem*, or it can be simply "unknown." For mystery to arise, I must face something that engages my whole being as subject: mystery and ontological participation are one. Some examples will illustrate this. There is a mystery of my relationship to my body. All the formulas that seek to express it are inadequate, yet each is in a sense true: I am not reducible to my body. They all betray a certain fundamental unity which is less "given" than *giving*, because it is the very root of my presence to the world, which the act of consciousness of self only inadequately symbolizes.[9] The central mystery is that of *presence*, whether of me to myself, of me to God, of me to other persons; all true presence transcends the problematic, although any presence can be viciously reduced to the level of problem.

XV. Existentialism and Phenomenology in France

Other mysteries of which Marcel treats again and again are the mystery of evil, the mystery of the world, the mystery of love, the mystery of knowledge—all realities we cannot objectively analyze and desiccate, as we are involved in them fundamentally, for they express our very insertion into being; such mysteries are to be illumined only by plunging deeper into the participations they invite, and are never to be solved, as they involve union with an other which by nature transcends us.

All of these mysteries are thus aspects of one central reality, the mystery of being,[10] that participation which founds my being as a subject. Irreducible and inviolable at the very heart of this way of viewing things, the apprehension of the mystery implies a personal act of meditation on my part, of interior gathering up (*recueillement*—the philosophic act *par excellence*), an act of concentration and deepening which transcends the distinction between "inside" and "outside" to achieve the "second reflection" at its best. There we shall discover that the "objectivized *moi*" of the realm of "having" gives way to the *je* (1) that is not centered on itself as something in isolation from the others but is by essence subject of a predicate. Marcel, on the tracks of Pascal's "*Le moi est haissable*" (The "me" is detestable), sees us born into the natural egoism of the baby's "That's mine" (*C'est à moi, ça*), "Not me" (*C'est pas moi!*), etc. Because as yet incapable of grasping the Other in his uniqueness and ineffable personality, he can not yet grasp himself as *je*, as the "I" of self-hood. "Mysteries are not truths which transcend us but truths which include us" (*nous comprement*). What the act of recollecting oneself seeks is (paradoxical as it may at first seem) an *experience of the transcendent*. My existence is intentional; if I withdraw sufficiently into the center of myself I shall discover that I am a being not transparent to itself, a being to whom his own being appears as a *mystery*, a being who should not, then, ultimately be centered on himself. In the mystery which includes me, which, indeed, I discover in the depths of my own being, I discover the traces of the transcendent.

"i love therefore i am"

Having discovered "being" in the depths of a subjectivity whose very reality is seen to transcend itself toward the other (and which without otherness could not be in the first place), and having discovered that it is only by a free act that we can turn away from our death-dealing ego-centricity and toward that Other which solicits us, Gabriel Marcel has certainly placed the mystery of love at the center of his philosophy. In turning toward the transcendence of an Other who is also free, in soliciting him to a mode of being-together, I must necessarily move beyond the divisions and conflicts of the realm of having, toward the discovery of the possibility of ultimate union of freedoms embracing the being for which they are made. Gabriel Marcel conceives of the act of participation through love as a kind of dialectic in which the subject first fully becomes subject, much as though he agreed with Fichte that only an adequate "objective opposition," namely the freedom of another person can reveal me to myself as person. Egoism is only a way of trying to assert myself without really loving myself; it ignores indeed the true self. Gabriel Marcel points to this fact of "experience honestly interrogated"; the more I manage to preserve an intimacy with my profound being the more I am able really to enter into deep contact with my neighbor. But we must remember that the converse is equally true. In other words, the development of free self-possession is essentially an affair of love, involving the other liberty as necessary means to self-discovery. *Je ne suis et tu n'es que si nous sommes*: I am and *you* are only if *we* are. There can only be dialogue when there are *two persons* present to one another.

What philosophical justification does Marcel offer for such assertions? Certainly no proof, for demonstration cannot be offered of fundamental experiences, which can only be directly lived. Some would argue that simply pointing to supposed realities is not enough to constitute a meditation, a philosophy. Such an accusation would not disturb Marcel. He might answer something like this: The only point is whether what I am saying is true. If, upon the most honest interrogation you are capable of, in the spirit of that *recueillement* indispensable for all second reflexion, you do not see these things, what can I, what can any philosopher do? The philosopher's only contribution, and what Marcel has achieved—this short presentation can scarcely give any measure of the *extent* of the endeavor—is to develop such fundamental insights through analyses which illumine the whole course and meaning of our lives; if this meditation is consistent—Marcel's is remarkably so—and if it succeeds in making us discover the force of these realities in our own lives, then the whole process is at least humanly justified. An incredible array of important phenomena comes to life when brought under the light of what critics might call the Marcelian "assumptions": among the more characteristic phenomena which no other philosopher of our time has been able to make so much of (in addition to those we have touched on already): fidelity, hope, vocation, family life, a kind of natural grace, the relationship of liberty to that grace; and, of course, the themes dear to all existentialists (in most instances independently of the others, and very often long before most of them): the limitations of technology as a philosophy of life, our incarnation, sensation is not perception, "concrete engagement," authenticity ("salvation"), ontological (existential) psychoanalysis.

We shall terminate by offering a thumbnail sketch of his treatment of just one of these themes, as some illustration of the possibilities for fresh analyses offered by the Marcelian horizons. The themes of vocation and hope are typically Marcelian, both in their unabashedly *interior* nature, and in the successful illumination they project on the time-dimension about which the other existentialists tend to be most vague: the future. Heidegger declared that futurity is *the* mode of authentic existence; if this is so, then the philosophy of Marcel can claim particular attention as the existentialism most capable of dealing with the concrete when it speaks of the future.

Marcel starts from the characteristic principle that "there is nothing in me, or outside of me, that should not be considered a gift," and that every gift is a call, by the very fact that I have been *entrusted* with it, to make it fructify. The task of determining what my calling is begins by reflecting on what I have been, on what I am. When, in deep *recueillement*, I come to see better what my "givens" are—my noblest possibilities; the deepest needs of the milieu in and for which I am, of those Others in co-presence with whom lies our salvation—then a vocation will begin to outline itself, not, certainly, as a predetermined course, but as a free call within a range of possibilities. Marcel insists that it would be a mistake to think that there is not something each of us can contribute to the "universal cause," something that is needed from me, that I can best contribute, and which will advance the reign of justice and charity among men.[11] *A tous tant que nous sommes*—for all, and everyone of us, to the extent that "we are"—that is the existential secret of our vocation and our liberty. Our vocation is not limited to something we produce—a great love can be part of a vocation; but there is no contesting the fact that "our calling" in the narrow sense is central. In this regard we must avoid two opposite extremes: a practical solipsism, which consists in thinking I can work out my destiny for myself, by myself, as though I alone counted. The other is a technocratic positivism, which would see each of us as nothing but a cog in the wheel of a great machine. To the extent that we abandon ourselves to the realm of "having" either error will tend to prevail; to enter the realm of "being" we must not forget the essential meaning of every man's vocation: "It is our task to personalize our rapports with Others to the maximum of our ability."[12]

The dedicated man is the freest man; he alone can escape the computable necessity that rules the realm of "having." This is the basis of Marcel's description of *free engagement*, the acceptance of a vocation founded in the fact that we owe our existence to what lies beyond us, and therefore in the doctrine that to be we must participate. The proof of a vocation is interior: it is to be experienced in the very living of such a participation. An act accomplished in the name of vocation may seem completely gratuitous to someone judging from the outside while the subject experiences it as so necessary that it transcends even the need for justification. This is a measure of the extent to which vocation is ontological, in Marcel's sense: it is lived interiorly in a spirit of receptiveness and self-recollection, it is carried out through engagement, and it finds its fruition in real intimate participation with others, all of which is necessarily impervious to criticism from idle bystanders.[13]

That every word Marcel has written invites one to look beyond natural grace to the supernatural, and beyond the plane of participation with other persons to the supreme origin of all the gifts which compose our existence, is obvious and intended. Marcel writes of our existence and our possibilities for being as he has lived them and understands them. The vast and fragmented corpus of his writings is amazingly consistent—I say, amazingly, for it is astonishing that such a huge and variegated, such a disorganized production, should preserve such unity. Only by comparing the whole of this complex vision with the whole of our individual lived experience can we measure the adequacy of this Christian existentialist mediation.

Jean-Paul Sartre

Chronology and nationality make us wonder, did Gabriel Marcel, the founder of French existentialism, have much influence on that *enfant terrible* of the next generation, the world-wide transmitter of the infection in its virulent form, the genial Jean-Paul Sartre?[14] That Husserl's influence on Sartre was greater there

XV. *Existentialism and Phenomenology in France*

can be little doubt. During a study year in Berlin in the early thirties Sartre plunged into the phenomenology of Husserl, to which he had been introduced by Raymond Aron, and all his major philosophical writings, including his important work, *Being and Nothingness*, are either expressly titled or subtitled "phenomenology," or are so presented in their introductions. By comparison, Marcel's relation to Husserl is much more indirect and even tenuous.

In truth, though, Sartre is no more easily classifiable a Husserlian than a Marcelian. At the time he first began reading Husserl, if we may take Simone de Beauvoir to witness, some of the major aspects of his independent convictions were already beginning to form. As a young student Sartre read *Le Journal métaphysique* and *L'Etre et l'Avoir*. But Sartre's convictions are really closer to Heidegger's than to anyone else's. Indeed, the least inadequate capsule classification is to make of him the extreme radicalization of a potentiality inherent in Heidegger's *Sein und Zeit*. The passion with which he has expressed his convictions has given his philosophy a hard-hitting tone and has tended to spill over into the most exciting literature written by any philosopher since *Zarathustra*.

In this regard the very opposite of Marcel, Sartre declares his starting point to be atheism. This "postulatory atheism" pronounciamento was no mere Madison Avenue blurb to attract attention to his position. No one since Nietzsche has been able to communicate so poignantly a sense of the paradox that man is at once utterly contingent and independent; unlike Nietzsche, who attenuates this through his doctrine of eternal return, Sartre never hesitates in pushing the consequences of these convictions to the bitter end. As he combines a Kierkegaardian gift for dramatizing his positions with an ability for Husserl-like sustained analysis, the result is some of the most engaging pages in contemporary philosophy. Had Sartre never written a line of pure philosophy he would be famous for his plays and novels; had he never written a line of fiction he would probably still have turned out to be one of the best-known philosophers, both because his philosophy is striking and because it is a serious effort to deal freshly with ancient and perennial problems.

being "in itself" and being "for itself"

Many have criticized Sartre for having made the fundamental distinction of his whole ontology (for Sartre proposes nothing less than a vision of Being as such; the subtitle of *Being and Nothingness* is "An Essay on Phenomenological

Ontology") too radical and too rigid. On the one side stands being *en soi*, "in itself," a monolithic mass of sheer reality, blind to itself, pitiless, inexorable in its absolute being-there; on the other stands the reality which we ourselves are, being *pour soi*, "for itself," able to gather itself up for a fleeting moment into an act of self-awareness, and, because aware, because of this capacity thus to separate itself off from the necessary course of things, able to direct its own future. One is easily shocked by the contrast between the unrelieved mass of the *en soi* and the nothingness of the *pour soi*.

But such assertions are really conclusions tightly drawn from the atheistic premise. If at the summit of reality there stands no infinite consciousness, self-penetrating and self-creating, responsible for the ordering of all that is, then being, in itself, is indeed a brute fact, going nowhere, come from nowhere, senseless, *ab-surd*[15]; and man who, alone of all things, knows, and knows himself, is nothing but a precarious epiphenomenon accidentally thrown up on the shores of the great ontological ocean, an accident that ex-sists (as Heidegger would say) by defying a dumb universe threatening to swallow him up again in death. What has man to oppose to nature? Nothing, really; just a certain in-gatheredness, a certain self-awareness, a tentative victory over the past, a modest command of the future, giving him the space to back up into in order to contemplate at least a part of Being as his *objectum*, permitting him to guide his own destiny—all of which adds up to...nothing.

Sartre is very explicit: All who do not believe in God must ultimately, if they are to be in good faith, come to grips with this stark reality of *la condition humaine*; recognizing the nothingness which permits the opening of historical horizons is the beginning of genuine human responsibility. Moreover, it is also the beginning of a sincere humanism, for it makes us realize that we have nothing in this world but our historic selves; if we abandon our solidarity, what is left?

But the first tenet such a doctrine must be certain it has secured is that such an existent, maintaining himself on the face of the ocean of being through the magic of nothingness, is really free. Sartre brilliantly musters all the weapons of phenomenology and all the hints of the earlier existentialists to battle the menace of determinism, which threatens every materialistic philosophy. He succeeds only too well, even to the extent, his critics maintain, of falling into a position hard to distinguish from idealism. Let us see the main outlines of his attack.

XV. Existentialism and Phenomenology in France

negativity as a way of pulling free of the "en soi"

The Sartrean "being-in-itself" is closer to Heidegger's notion of the totality of things-that-are (*das Seiende im Ganzen*) than to the Heideggerian conception of *Sein*, with this difference, that Sartre emphasizes how undifferentiated is the great bulk of being until negativity, conceived of as a defining delimiting influence, goes to work on it with its discriminating power. The Heideggerian *Sein* can "be" only by the human existent's bringing it to be from out of the abyss of nothingness; but Sartre's being-in-itself precedes, logically, the nothingness which goes to work on it.[16] Where does Nothingness come from? From a Being "such that in its Being, the Nothingness of its own Being is in question."[17] This cannot be any ordinary kind of *cause*, for to the extent that an effect is related to its cause it cannot involve even the tiniest germ of nothingness. But Sartre shows that when a human inquirer questions a thing, the cause-effect determinism is transcended, the questioner pulls free of that which is questioned, which, in order to be questioned, must possibly *not be*[18]; the questioner, by a double movement of nihilation, nihilates the thing questioned in relation to himself by placing it in a *neutral* state—and he nihilates himself in relation to the thing questioned by wrenching himself from being in order to be able to bring out of himself the possibility of a non-being. Man is the questioner, and because the questioner, the orderer. "In order for the totality of being to order itself around us as instruments, in order for it to parcel itself into differentiated complexes which refer one to another and which can be *used*, it is necessary that negation rise up not as a thing among other things but as the rubric of a category which presides over the arrangement and the redistribution of the great masses of being in things."[19]

Determinism is out of the question because the human order, the realm of the *pour soi*, is not ruled by causality, but instead dominates the order in which causality is found by its ordering negativity. Stated thus baldly, Sartre's thesis is very simple; much of the attractiveness of *Being and Nothingness* comes from the rich descriptions in which Sartre orchestrates the main thesis in a way that throws a fresh (and often disconcerting) light on many otherwise familiar phenomena. Imagination is shown to be an imagining of what is not there, perception is shown to be a deviation from a color or tonal norm, intellection is described in all its negative aspects, etc. Man is indeed finite, after all, and he is obliged to conquer the world with limited and limiting tools. Since Sartre's analysis it will be hard ever to lose sight of the full impact of this truth.

Sartre's object is to throw into relief the ultimacy of our responsibility and the grandeur of our liberty. If all the world's *sense* comes from us the orderers, then our acts alone legislate; everything we do introduces meaning into the world, a meaning that is, Sartre insists (without too well explaining why) *meaning for everybody*; hence, I should remind myself that every time I act, I structure the world *for everybody*.[20] But in a human world spun out of the gossamer stuff of negativity, our acts, instead of appearing to stand like so many pillars of Hercules, seem to take on a kind of weightlessness, and things in the world seem to lack reality. As two of the other important French phenomenologists will be most concerned to correct the orientation of existentialism in order to avoid this prime, idealist difficulty, it is essential that we see better why this problem arises.

the liberty in situation

Sartre not only recognizes that our liberty can act only in a situation, he is even careful to point out that liberty could have no meaning were there not the resistance of fact for it to overcome and mold in keeping with our ends. More than fifty pages in *Being and Nothingness* are devoted to describing all the kinds of Otherness with which our projects must be concerned, the brute factuality of things, the fact of my own past, the projects of other people. The problem is a real one, which existential philosophy has posed better than it ever was before in the history of philosophy. Sartre takes on the question a stand consistent with his whole outlook: There is indeed a brute factuality of things, people, my own past acts which has to be contended with; but which things, which acts, which other projects have to be significant *for me*, and what their significance is going to be, depends ultimately on my projects, which alone afford them a sense in my scheme of things. That mountain range on the horizon may be nothing to me; then one day, it may become a truculent obstacle; or a powerful tool, if my project should be to climb to where I can survey the valley.[21] Or take this engagement which I earlier undertook, and which now is part of that past which is there "pressing, urgent, imperious."[22] "Of course, the marriage I made earlier limits my possibilities and dictates my conduct; but precisely because my projects are what they are, I reassume the marriage contract. In

XV. Existentialism and Phenomenology in France

other words, precisely because I do not make of it a 'marriage contract which is passed, surpassed, dead' and because, on the contrary, my projects imply fidelity to the engagements undertaken...these projects necessarily come to illuminate the past marriage vow and to confer on it its always actual value. Thus the urgency of the past comes from the future."[23] My past consists of so many projects which when they were made were anticipations; it depends on my present projects to determine whether those anticipations have been fulfilled. If I have radically changed the fundamental projections underlying my life, then those past acts will be like the medieval walls of Carcassonne, a brute fact whose only significance is that of a *monument historique* reminding us of an epoch now definitively past. "It is the future which decides whether the past is living or dead."[24] Sartre does not ignore the weight of factuality; but he does reduce it absolutely to a minimum. As a result, he is reluctant to accord much determined independent reality to things, apparently for fear that it will then become difficult to keep open a place for the initiative of our freedom. (We shall review in the next chapter the original solution suggested by Sartre's friend, Maurice Merleau-Ponty, who, dissatisfied with Sartre's stand, will rethink the problem literally from the ground up, and reformulate the nature of man's insertion into the world.)

There is one kind of otherness, however, which is particularly resistant to a treatment that would reduce its originality almost to nothing—and that is the other person, who himself also enjoys freedom. Each man, when he finds himself in the world, discovers himself to be in the presence of meanings which have not come into the world through him; the world is given as already looked-at, furrowed, worked-over, its very contexture already defined by previous investigations.[25] He encounters the Other as brute fact. But he is free to regard the Other as Other-subject; by that very token he reaffirms his own freedom at the very moment he recognizes one of its limits, because only a free subject can recognize another subject, whose freedom however can come into conflict with mine. If he refuses to consider the Other, except as an Object, then he must see himself as a free unqualified transcendence.[26] Indeed, I never succeed in considering myself *really to be* what others see me "objectively" to be, an ugly Pole, lazy, generous, etc., just as I refuse to be reduced to my past: I may have done this or that disagreeable thing, but I am not really like that. If I do accept to consider myself ugly, or a Pole, these things can only take on in my life the sense my fundamental projects give them. I do not, of course, choose to be for the Other what I am—that is out of my control, but I can try to be for myself what I am for the Other, by choosing myself just as I appear to the Other. "I have at my disposal an infinity of ways of assuming my being-for-others, but what I cannot escape is the choosing of it, in one way or another."[27] To refuse in fury to be considered a Jew is a way of choosing myself-for-the-Other; so is passive resignation. The bourgeois can deny emphatically that there are any classes; in so doing, he is willing himself in a typically bourgeois manner. Here then are external limits to our freedom, but limits that are never really recognized as such, because they are internalizable, as Sartre says, only as *unrealizables*, in the sense of something one can get sufficiently beyond to recognize. The limits which freedom bumps up against are those which it imposes on itself.[28]

Freedom-in-situation is, then, neither simply subjective nor is it simply objective; as the meeting of the *en soi* and the *pour soi* it is both: Our projects here meet and envelop things from out of being-in-itself. Reciprocally, it is from these things that we borrow the permanence that we tend to give ourselves, as though the endurance of a certain unity to our personality were due to some objective factor, instead of, as is the case, stemming purely from our continually taking up again the same fundamental projections.[29] The permanence contributed by the *en soi* does serve continually to recall my projects to me, but it forces upon me no continuity of self. "When a man says, 'I am not easy to please,' he is entering into a free engagement with his ill-temper, and by the same token his words are a free interpretation of certain ambiguous details in his past. In this sense there is no character; there is only a project of oneself."[30] Of course, to the Other I am ill-tempered; this aspect is referred to me by the Other's look. My perseverance in maintaining this position depends not only on the Other, though, but on the position I take in regard to the Other.

The upshot of this doctrine of freedom, as Sartre would have it, is to affirm my absolute responsibility: this is my world, my past, my situation; I may not have willed to be born, that is, I am not the cause of my own being, but that being, once given me, is free; I have no choice but to live it in full responsibility; even the act of refusing this freedom, through suicide, is a free act.

Has Sartre succeeded in his attempt to elaborate a doctrine of freedom that will both explain the realities of our experience and establish our responsibility? The most famous of his contemporaries, Maurice Merleau-Ponty, Sartre's companion at the École Normale, will conclude from his own version of phenomenological analysis that he has not. Let us see what correctives he would suggest.

MAURICE MERLEAU-PONTY

the task of philosophy
"Philosophy," wrote Maurice Merleau-Ponty[31] in 1951, "must reflect on the mode of presence of the object to the subject—the conception of the object and the conception of the subject as they appear to phenomenological revelation—instead of substituting for this meditation the rapport of the object to the subject as it is conceived in an idealist philosophy of total perception."[32] Merleau-Ponty, the phenomenologist, objects that Sartre, the ontologist, has been guilty of a brand of such substitution. Sartre has preferred to argue the case for a Cartesian *cogito*—self-penetrating, utterly free, in some of his descriptions seeming only accidentally related to the material order—rather than meditate devotedly on the object's real mode of appearing to corporeal consciousness. Substituting an idea of absolute freedom as negation for the description of our actual incarnated insertion into the world, Sartre so opposes the being-in-itself and the being-for-itself that one hardly understands how the *en soi* and the *pour soi* can effectively interpenetrate. Yet the projects of the being-for-itself do in fact get incarnated in the being-in-itself: there admittedly exist cultural objects, institutions, languages, signs of all sorts which are intersubjective precisely because they manage somehow to be "out there" lodged in a materiality common to all the *cogitos*; conversely, being-in-itself in fact penetrates to the depths of the *cogito*, for our freedom is indeed that of a history engaged in a situation through the body, as Sartre admits, but what that must mean, explains Merleau-Ponty, is that the liberty is *motivated by the habits and dispositions of that body*. It is the role of phenomenology to describe the peculiarly human mode of this motivation, which is handled adequately neither in terms of mechanistic causality, which leaves no room for creative initiative, nor in terms of a Sartrean liberty, where the freedom-resisting weight of the *en soi* is insufficiently felt.

In *The Adventures of the Dialectic*, Merleau-Ponty sees Sartre and the overly materialist Marxists maintaining opposite extreme positions which both stem (like the "idealist"-"empiricist" controversy, as Kant construed it) from the same root inadequacy: their common failure to formulate our real presence to the world. The materialist conceives of the consequences of our acts as being indeed "out there," but so objectivized, so alienated as to constitute for the movement of material history a crushing weight, a necessity before which the poor individual is carried along like a rush-hour rider in the subway. Sartre, on the other hand, despite all his talk of engagement, keeps his existent so uninvolved, even in his own past acts, that history seems to have no effective weight at all; "engagement" is effective only for the present instant, and seems capable of becoming no-matter-what-no-matter-when.

The prime philosophical problem is to find a *middle way* between these extremes; the paradoxical reality of an incarnated liberty, of a cogito-in-situation—which is, after all, definitely something—has to be described in its position between determinism and the idealistic voluntarism of a freedom that would be indeed, in the final analysis, *nothing*.

In exploiting Kant's suggestion that the "mediating" role of the imagination reveals an "art hidden in the depths of the soul," which is neither mechanical nor purely spiritual. Merleau-Ponty's central notion—that of "*le corps propre*"— is an organizer of knowledge which can never be for itself self-transparent *cogito*. Let us see then what are the characteristic modes of an incarnated subject.

the structure of comportment

Merleau-Ponty carried out the phenomenological task of winning a place descriptively for the incarnated liberty basically in two stages. In a work of the late thirties (thus contemporaneous with Sartre's early phenomenological explorations and first hints of his ontology-to-be), Merleau-Ponty's is the existentialist's concern of saving the whole realm of human behavior (*comportement*) from the tendency of physiological psychology to absorb it into the mechanical. In *The Structure of Comportment*, this part of the program is carried out in two substages.

(1) Against the Pavlovians and against the subtler behavioristic efforts to construct a psychological scheme of explanation out of the materials of physiological analysis, Merleau-Ponty marshals all the help he can get from the Gestaltists to show that physiology itself can be guided in its explorations of the material structures of psychological functioning only by what we can get at directly of the whole phenomenal realm; that the rudimentary elements of phys-

XV. Existentialism and Phenomenology in France

iological psychology, like the notion of the "stimulus," already suppose in fact subject-object interpenetration and are therefore already taken from the phenomenal order which they are supposed to constitute; that the efforts to reduce psychological functions to a series of point-for-point contacts between receptor data and physiological structure fall down, except in artificial laboratory experiments of limited bearing and dealing with an altered organism in conditions unlike those of its natural life.

What the physiological psychologists have established, however (a point that will tell strongly against Sartre's self-transparent *cogito* later on), is that the material substructures in human behavior do count for something; the organism cannot be conceived, in the mode of the romantics, as a great self-transparent All-in-All. But if our psychic activities must be recognized as depending on material substructures and must, following phenomenal description, be grouped into certain levels about certain functions as centers, the effort at "atomization" (of seeking to understand psychic processes as paralleling physiological processes, themselves reconstructed element-by-element out of physical points to which it is supposed there corresponds in each case a univocal stimulus) can only be motivated by a prejudice in favor of mechanization, certainly not either by our common phenomenal experience, nor by the results obtained from trying to understand the real effects of genuine cases of lesion that have been observed for themselves rather than in the interest of "proving a point."

Merleau-Ponty's conclusion from the analyses of this first stage, then, is that comportment must be approached phenomenally, that is, on the level in which the particular stimulus appears integrated into a whole constellation of stimuli, receiving its sense among them according both to its place and to the kind of interrogation the organism carries out on an appropriate level characteristic of the kind of animal it is. In asserting this, he declares his independence of all the earlier philosophical and psychological divisions of our psychic activity. The advantage of the notion of "form" (*Gestalt*, the principle of organization of a psychic function or level) is that "it goes beyond the atomistic conception of nervous functioning without reducing it to a diffuse and un-differentiated function, it rejects psychological empiricism without going over to the intellectualist antithesis. An analysis of perception would lead to the re-establishment of a division (*coupure*)—no longer between sensation and perception, nor between the sensibility and the intelligence, nor more generally between a chaos of elements and a superior instance which supposedly organizes them, but between different types or levels of organization."[33]

A new phenomenal analysis of how we are in the world, that analysis of "perception" referred to in the text just cited, will obviously constitute, then, the second major stage in Merleau-Ponty's phenomenological program. Before proceeding directly to this immense undertaking, the task of that masterpiece of the early forties, *The Phenomenology of Perception*, Merleau-Ponty paves the way through a preliminary description, in the latter part of *The Structure of Comportment*, of the dialectic characteristic of human comportment in distinction from that of other organisms. Reduced to its schematic minimum, this detailed rich analysis of psychological data (including, prominently, Koehler's experiments with chimpanzees), along with Merleau-Ponty's own original description, comes to this: Man is able to master a more flexible and richer world because, in threading his way among the things that appear, he is able to structure them in his world, to give them a sense, through symbolization. The symbol is the instrument by which he gives himself a more flexible "distance" from things, as the word permits a varying of points of view of which other organisms are incapable. The preliminary analysis in the earlier work differs from the full descriptions in *The Phenomenology of Perception* in some not unimportant points of accent. In the interest of economy, however, let us pass at once to the later analysis, taking it in its own right, without pausing here to follow Merleau-Ponty's contrast of the human with lesser comportments.

the phenomenology of perception

Having rejected causal determinism as a way of explaining the presence of the object to the subject, Merleau-Ponty seeks some way of expressing the fact that nonetheless we are in some way fundamentally beholden to *givens*—the sensible thing; the other person; all the givens of the intersubjective world, e.g., language; even the givens of my own reality, those elements of a past which are sedimented in my body—our consciousness being intentional, i.e., always directed to knowledge *of*. Merleau-Ponty is convinced that the most fundamental perceptual encounter with an object involves a synthesis of data with the perceiver's appropriate stance, which stance, however, is elicited by the data; the resulting synthesis is the *perceptim*. The "Transcendental Analytic," declares *The Phenomenology of Perception*, lies in redescribing the matter-form relationship

XV. Existentialism and Phenomenology in France

of the "Transcendental Aesthetic." Indeed, what other philosophical problem has there been since the First Edition of the great *Kritik*?

Now, note well the ground rules for the fundamental perceptual encounter which we have just formulated. It must not be imagined that there is, on the one side, a "real" datum utterly *en soi* which is to be received into rigid mental molds standing ready, on the other, to absorb it into their form. Whatever "sense data" there may be is normally perceived within a perceptual field opened by the body to accommodate it, that is to say, the fundamental *perceptim* is lived already in a bodily founded context. The perceptual functions, or formal acts of the body, far from being rigid forms imposed on a received matter, are *for the sake of* accommodating the data, i.e., they are for the sake of knowing the thing (the data and the bodily knowing apparatus stand in a reciprocal relation to one another, a dialectic in which it is impossible to place the form on one side of the relationship and the "formed" on the other).

This dialectic of the fundamental perception combines to structure our world with all the other ways of "introducing a *sens*," levels of structuring-a-significance, of "objectivization," which, in function of a given culture, are introduced on the foundations of the basic perceptual forms. Merleau-Ponty can accept Hegel's invitation to introduce history into the "analytic" because the basic matter-form relationship has already been dialecticized, and the "ambiguity" of the original data affirmed.[34] The body can now be seen to add other structures than those rudimentary ones indispensable for the minimal organization of a perceptual object. The civilized man is distinguished from the primitive by the higher forms of signification with which he is armed in the encounter with experience. The habits and dispositions experientially (and perhaps hereditarily) accumulated in the body of civilized man permit him to perceive more than the primitive perceives, and make him better able to conquer out of an experience "that excess of the significative over the signifying" which makes possible a new act of expression, a new hold on the world.

The Structure of Comportment's exploitation of the notion of the *Gestalt* opened the way for *The Phenomenology of Perception*'s description of the mediating role of the body, through which Merleau-Ponty attempts to solve all the old epistemological *aporias*. We must think of the body as contributing *a priori* which are *lived*. This throws light on many problems: when consciousness becomes aware of itself, it finds itself already living, inhabiting a world that presents itself as having been the way it is prior to my becoming consciously aware of it; yet because the reality of this world is at least partly contributed by me, it does not have to be conceived as being "out there," unalterable, ahistoric; the *a prioris* can be changed, just as habits can be changed—for what is lived can develop and evolve. By placing part of *the weight of history* in the sedimentation of forms as habits in the body, Merleau-Ponty is able to account for its universality (same forms sedimented in many bodies); he is able to give the frames of history a kind of objective weight without risking giving them the mechanical necessity that would plague them if they were abandoned to an unliving world "out there"; at the same time, they are something I, as an individual center of initiative, can *get at*, to some extent anyway; my present will-acts can chip away at the sedimented weight of habits and predispositions deposited bodily in me, I can use parts of my experience against other parts, thus laboriously changing the historical course that is built into me. Finally, the greater the role accorded the body in structuring the world of our experience, the easier it becomes to explain the penetration of our projects, through its mediation, into the intersubjective world of things, where are deposited our words, our art creations, everything that incarnates our institutions.

Merleau-Ponty exploits these possibilities to the hilt in phenomenological descriptions of an incredible richness and variety. He likes to show how the *gesture* places an intention "out there" in the material world in which we all share; how the weight of an institution sediments not only in the tools and the objects which are its instruments, but in the habits and dispositions of those who have grown up participating in it. Above all, he handles brilliantly the problems of intersubjectivity: I can live with the other, I can have an idea of what he is thinking because my intentions too get expressed through the body, and are lived directly in an *intermonde*; he is neither an inaccessible, hostile stare, nor is he an "open book"; his inner thoughts remain hidden from me, but not entirely, just as I am not absolute master of my own consciousness—I do not lucidly grasp every facet of what I am, but neither is anything about me utterly hidden from me in a "sub-conscious," the things that well up from my past to affect my present are at least in principle subject to becoming better and better understood, just as I can come to know a person better and better the more I have seen him in action in varying situations.

Merleau-Ponty's theory concerning our incarnation was intended to pro-

XV. Existentialism and Phenomenology in France

vide what is needed to escape the dilemmas posed by the virtually unhampered Sartrean liberty. And such indeed is the crowning success of *The Phenomenology of Perception*: the same kind of dialectical relationship which characterizes my relationship to the "world" can be shown to explain naturally and inevitably the relationship of "motivation" that brings the otherness of my own past to influence my future projects. If the "sense" of a perception were unequivocally determined by data passively received according only to its own real structure, there would never be any room for the insertion of interpretation; but as the "sense" of the stimulus arises from its integration into a whole perceptual constellation by the functions of the organism, an integral reciprocal relationship is established in which there is clearly a place for the developing initiatives of the perceiver. The dialectic motivation-liberty echoes the same pattern on the level characteristic of the highest comportment, the one capable of the maximum initiative in developing the sense of its world. The past event, however sedimented in my body—as motor habit, as a vague general predisposition, as a vocabulary of signs ready for use, etc.—makes its demands on me now the way sense data do; its weight is felt, but integrated with my present projects. It solicits me to project in keeping with its vectors, and I cannot ignore them; but my projects are not necessitated by the weight of the past, following some rule of an ineluctable motivational calculus—for I can use some parts of that reality I already am against other parts of it. My liberty is not an ability to create anything out of nothing, but to build beyond my past by reordering it into new sense through the use of that initiative I possess. The formation of an idea is the noetic moment of the free act, an extension of sense beyond what has been previously rendered significant. The following text from *The Adventures of the Dialectic* compares the formation of the idea to the original perceptual act:

> Neither on the level of the perceived, nor on the level of the ideal, do we have anything to do with closed significations. A perceived thing is rather a deviation from a norm or a spatial, temporal or color level, it is a certain distortion, a certain "coherent deformation" of the permanent liens which unite us to sensorial fields and to a world. In the same way, an idea is a certain excess in our insight into the available and closed significations deposited in our language, their reordering about a virtual center toward which they tend but which they do not circumscribe.

the nature of our liberty

This careful formulation of the interplay between a givenness which is yet not absolutely determined and the acts by which we further determine and extend its sense provides the keynote for Merleau-Ponty's theory of our liberty as that of a being who must live in a "situation."

The situation in which the human existent discovers himself as he grows to self-awareness is indeed a determinate one—but *humanly* determined, that is to say, it is a moving and within limits moveable history; liberty is exercise of initiative within the limits of possible determination; this liberty is motivated, that is to say, it is solicited by the flexible givens of a situation, givens which in turn alter in function of the initiatives we take. That is why a course of action, given a personality and his situation, is neither predictable with certainty nor unpredictable; it is always *probable*. It is not fated that this young bourgeois will be incapable of associating himself with the revolutionary movement, but it is highly improbable that he will. And if he does decide to ally himself with the proletariat he will always be a "bourgeois intellectual Marxist," for the weight of the past cannot be wished away by a *fiat* of the liberty.

The sedimentations of history are deposited in the *intermonde* of structures that unite men intersubjectively, precipitated in the language available to think with, in the habits of thought and action accumulated in the body, in the institutions which call for my co-operation, in the material conditions of life at a given time and place. When I set out to think, the sense my thought will take is elicited by the conceptions that are most familiar—elicited, but not determined. For the thoughts I think will be *my* thoughts, ideas taken up into horizons that are uniquely mine, there to become personal expressions to which I am capable of adding "that excess of signification over and beyond what is signified," which is my very own experience.

The human order, then, is situated between the absolute determinism of simple mechanics and the chaotic weightlessness which must characterize a world created out of nothingness by the Sartrean liberty. In this order, the order of *sens*, of meaningful direction, of a dynamic signification in time, truth is never fixed and absolute, but then neither is it ever just nothing.

the problem of the objectivity of truth

We can understand from these last remarks why much of the focus of the last

XV. *Existentialism and Phenomenology in France*

essays is concentrated on the problem of the nature of truth. There is no greater challenge for a philosophy that would historialize everything than to explain the experienced fact of the necessity of universal truth. If the only *structure* in our knowledge is that of a provisional unity-in-becoming, so that all stabilities are only relative, in the sense that they represent elements moving slower than others, then "eternal truths" could hardly exist. If all "sense" is carved out creatively from the *inconcevable platitude de l'être*, as *Signes* declares, then it is hard to see what foundation there could be for those truths in the fullest sense which enjoy, as the *Phenomenology of Perception* puts it, "a signification applicable at all times." If all structure is but the result of a dialectical encounter between a dynamic "form" and an essentially indeterminate matter, then we should have to treat as the last word the unqualified statement in *The Phenomenology of Perception* which declares that every object is, always and in every respect, being imperceptibly made and unmade.

It is not surprising, then, that two of the most important recent essays are preoccupied with this problem: "Le Langage indirect et les voix du silence" (Indirect Language and the Voices of Silence) and "Sur la phénoménologie du langage" (On the Phenomenology of Language) (in *Signes*, pp. 49–104 and 105–122, the latter essay having been written in 1951). The rejection of the idealist's project of an absolute, i.e., a total truth, an objectivity formed by the perfect coincidence of a subject with itself, does not entail for Merleau-Ponty any lessening of the realization that intelligibility requires some endurance. For a thing to "signify" it must possess a sense beyond the moment of its apparition. If expression, as these last essays declare, is my way of "recuperating the world," then, for that possession to have a sense, it must, somehow, apply out ahead to what will be. And for there to be communication, there must be something won out of the flux of experience that can be expressed in a word available to another. Of course the truth can only *be* in the present, it can be made to be only by the here and now acts of a concrete subject; but our individual acts of expression are precisely equipped "to save, conserve, and take up again" preceding acts "to the extent they contain some Truth."[35]

The Heracleitan nature of this conception that truth is won temporarily and dynamically out of the flux of experience stands out starkly in another passage in the same recent essays.

> To say that there is a truth is to say that, when my *reprise* [my act of taking-up again] encounters a former or a foreign project and a successful expression delivers up what was before captive in being forever, then, in the thickness of a personal and interpersonal time is established an interior communication by which our present becomes the *truth of* all the other knowing events. It is like an edge [*coin*] that we force into the present, a kind of boundary which attests that at this moment something has taken place that Being awaited or "wished to say" from all time, and that will never cease, if not being true, at least signifying and exciting our thinking apparatus, if need be by drawing from it truths more comprehensive than that one. In that very moment something has been founded in signification, an experience has been transformed into its sense, has become truth.[36]

The kind of unity, the kind of *necessity* envisioned here is, then, purely historical; the only reality described is that of the *event*; an event occurs when something comes to expression; the enduring reality of an expression is dependent on its being freely taken up again, in a creative synthesis adequate enough to absorb it and prolong its existence in new horizons—that act of *Wiederholen* which Heidegger sees as the essence of thinking. Through this explanation, a kind of universality is indeed accounted for; what is not explained, however, is the possibility of *objectivity*—the experienced fact that some of our expressions say *things*, recuperating a world which reveals itself as existing independently of the knowledge act which gives us access to it. There is a phrase in the last quoted paragraph which says it perfectly: "at this moment something has taken place that Being awaited or 'wished to say' from all time," but unfortunately there is nothing in the rest of the essay to explain just how it can be, that something can be "*repris*" and "expressed," in Merleau-Ponty's sense of the term, with such necessity that it will then appear that it has always been. Having rejected all recourse to a notion of being-in-itself, indeed all "explanations,"[37] i.e., all unequivocal, once-and-for-all pronouncements about the way things are, having accepted the challenge of being a Hegelian without an Absolute Subject, the whole burden rests with the existential phenomenologist to make convincing the notion of a necessity which can only be the *reprise* of what is essentially a contingency—the fact that man happens to be the way he is. The existentialist-humanist view of man as "*cariatide du vide*" is ultimately a "skeptical" one, as Merleau-Ponty admits,[38] but skeptical in Montaigne's sense, of not accepting absolute explanations.

Merleau-Ponty has certainly himself worked unceasingly in this direction, but only to end with the "skeptical"[39] vision of the existentialist humanist as *cariatide du vide*. A severe idea and—if we may be permitted the term—almost vertiginous, that of man's expression as ultimate principle. "We must conceive of a labyrinth of spontaneous undertakings, which take each other up and sustain each other, sometimes crossing each other, sometimes confirming each other, but in the course of how many detours, what waves of disorder—and with the whole enterprise resting on itself. It is understandable that, confronted by that idea, which they glimpse as well as we do, our contemporaries retreat and turn aside to some idol."[40] The truth, declares the *Phenomenology of Perception*, is always "à faire."

Mikel Dufrenne

the notion of the a priori
Of all the phenomenologists, Mikel Dufrenne[41] has worked most consistently to break beyond the idealism of the Cartesian-Kantian heritage of "transcendental philosophy." He has carried on the endeavors of Scheler and Hartmann to restore to the object its commanding and "realistic" position. In his first major study—the most extensive application of phenomenology to the sphere of aesthetics, *La Phénoménologie de l'expérience esthétique*—while by no means neglecting the fact that an aesthetic experience is the act of a subject, he is mindful, as a phenomenologist should be, that acts cannot be understood without reference to the objects toward which they are intentionally directed. There is nothing surprising in this, nor in the fact that he devotes the entire first volume to the "aesthetic object." What is a bit different, however, is his unwavering persistence in treating this object as a thing, existing in itself, and known as it really is. The pivotal point of the analysis is always the question of how the thing itself presents its reality.

The very subject matter of Dufrenne's most recent book, *The Notion of the A Priori*, might seem at first glance to give the lie to this suggestion that we have to do here with a phenomenologist concerned to illumine and protect the "otherness" of the *noemata*, until we recall Scheler's efforts to mold a conception of the *a priori* to fit the exigencies of an experience of real things and of absolute "material" values. (See the chapter on Scheler earlier in this volume.) One of the problems that made it difficult to understand the exact ontological status of Scheler's *a prioris* was his hesitation about admitting that principle could be adequately found in perception, despite his explicit criticism of the Humeian-empiricist presumption that only atoms of sensation are given in empirical experience. Dufrenne, we shall see, is from the start free from the narrow presuppositions about sensation which have characterized most of the philosophers since the Renaissance; and his stand is still more forthright than Scheler's: He is convinced that our experience accords us access to the reality of objective things as they are in themselves; he admits that things have essences independent of any formative noetic act, that we possess a general human nature, and that we can enjoy certain knowledge of both.

But why then, one might wonder, does Dufrenne not simply dispense with the notion of the *a priori* altogether? Why take on the burden of the idealistic origin of the term, the obscurity surrounding Scheler's use of it, and the historical tendency, often so marked in Husserl, to think of the *a priori* as a constitutive function of consciousness?[42]

Dufrenne raises the question himself, and when he does, seizes the occasion "to give empiricism its due." He agrees that all knowledge begins in experience; in fact, he adds, our knowledge of the *a priori* itself is (and the paradox is only apparent) *a posteriori*, not just in the sense that we become aware of the subjective *a prioris* of our consciousness only in the actual acts of experiencing, but in the sense that many *a prioris* are actually objective, that is to say, they reveal something of the reality of things as they are independently of any constituting act of a consciousness. Such *a prioris* can be given *only* in empirical experience.[43] With their "empiricism" both Scheler and Hartmann would be in full accord.[44]

Yet, the passive receptivity of sense alone cannot explain my grasp of the objective structures. Dufrenne is convinced that perception itself is essentially concrete and dynamic, yielding only an unceasing flow of individual data, "always new, always refreshing, even when the contact with the sensible is mediated through knowledge [*savoir*] and habit."[45] He is not reverting to the empirical dust theory of sensation, only underscoring the concreteness, the dynamism, the "profiled" nature of the "given." This he contrasts with my ability from the first moment of an experience to grasp immediately, without having to go through the steps of an *apprentissage*, a certain basic sense of what it is to be an object—its spatiality, its thingly endurance in time, its substantiality. Evidently, I carry to the experience a subjective aptitude to grasp those aspects which present themselves immediately,[46] a primitive *savoir* which organizes the perception without proceeding from it. This is a fundamental objective *a priori*.

Not that I impose a form on experience. Dufrenne holds that whatever subjective aptitude the knower may have for grasping the major outlines of reality he possesses because his being is not foreign to that of the world; but what is grasped *a priori* is an aspect of the universe itself, an objective necessity, indeed a necessity of essence. "If the *a priori* is a form, it is of the universe and not of thought; it is not a rule *of* thought, but a rule *for* thought because it is imposed by the universe."[47] The formal *a priori* determines the object in general, and not just a region of objects; however, its "transcendental" character is not a determination of the knowing mind, but a reflection of the fact that it is proposed by all the objects, and is known *a priori* as a fundamental sense *of* these objects; it is thus really, as Scheler suggested, already "material"—part of the objective reality of the known thing.[48]

Dufrenne further agrees with Scheler that the difference between the "formal" and the "material" *a priori* is merely one of degree. The only justification for terming the most general *a priori* "formal" is its presence in all objects and the aptitude of all minds to make sense out of objects in this primordial way necessary if there are to be any objects in the first place. Actually, the formal *a priori* is itself really "material," in the sense that it is, just as much as the more determined (more particular) "material" *a prioris*, an expression of part of the real content of the things themselves. The distinction is a useful one to maintain, however, because, while all formal *a prioris* can claim materiality, the material *a priori* do not enjoy the transcendental universality necessary to be taken for "formal."

For the "material" *a prioris* are those essential aspects of regions of objects, or even, more restricted yet, species of objects within a region, which are grasped with the immediacy and certainty characteristic of *a priori* knowledge. The more specific the *a priori* (the more "material," therefore), the richer its content, or, as Dufrenne often puts it, the deeper it bites into the reality expressed.[49] Moreover, the more "material" the *a priori*, the more "historical" or "sociological" will be its realization; indeed some, as Scheler also suggested, are realized perhaps only by a single person. Conversely, even the most formal *a prioris* are not in every respect a-historical. Even as formal an *a priori* as causal connection is not realized so explicitly among the most primitive peoples as it is among all of the rest of the world.

Is all essential knowledge *a priori*? Dufrenne thinks not. Observation can yield an increasingly rich knowledge of the essence, for example, of a kind of virus. But the all-important empirical pursuit of the nature of things is guided by and depends upon our already being able to find our way about in a universe whose broad outlines are intelligible to us without their having to be painstakingly and uncertainly learned. If we think of the mind as a *tabula rasa* we should not for all that forget that while it as yet has no experience, it itself is not nothing. With our first experience of things begins a process of self-experience. We are prepared to grasp certain essential aspects of things by the fact that we realize the same characteristics in our very own being. The human consciousness comes to being at once from the inside and from the outside. The most general formal *a prioris* of material things are grasped by everyone immediately, certainly, all-pervasively because they express that aspect of things which we ourselves are. Because we are incarnate consciousness we know from *being it* what is substantiality, temporality, spatiality; we do not have to learn about these aspects of reality from the things outside us.

How then could there be an element of historicity in the realization of the *a priori*? There cannot be in the case of those most general formal *a prioris* that are read in every object and which form the very condition of there being any experience. If Dufrenne is right in asserting, as we just saw, that not all peoples experience the *a priori* of causality in the explicitly articulated way in which adult, civilized people do,[50] then this can only mean that that sort of causal connection does not stand at the very forefront of our experience the way time, space, and substantiality do. Just the same, when causality does come to be experienced *a priori*, there occurs an encounter between my lived reality and the object perceived. What I now grasp as belonging objectively to things, I also grasp as an essential possibility of many things, most of which I shall never individually experience; I do so in virtue of an immediate experience of it—the causality which I carry in my being. When only certain individuals or people in certain cultures are aware of an *a priori*, it must mean either that not all persons carry that particular reality within their very being, or that, if they do, it is sufficiently out of the main stream of their experience to have to await awakening through the right sort of objective encounter, and hence can lie dormant in a whole people. A very special musical sensitivity illustrates the first alternative, and the highly explicit experience of causality might serve for the second.

Let us pursue an example of the less general *a priori* in order to make this clearer. A given person may never have experienced the tragic, and for that matter, he could conceivably pass through life without experiencing it. He might read *Death of a Salesman* or contemplate a Rouault "Pierrot" and miss entirely the force of the tragic they embody. But if in the experience of one of these things another person grasps this element in them, he will be struck by the impression that he has always known what the *tragic* as such is, known it not as general idea but as a kind of sense many different things might have, and it will seem incredible to him that not everyone can experience the thing this way. What brings together the springtime, a child playing, and a Mozart *allegro con brio* as expressions of youth is not an *aliquod commune*, it is rather that the same sense inhabits them, *seipsis conveniunt*; that is why there can be more agreement (*convenance*) between objects of different species, for example between the music of Ravel and the poetry of Mallarmé, than between objects belonging to the same species, like the music of Ravel and the music of Cesar Franck.

From the basic perceptual experience of the *a priori* as objective constituent, whether "material" or "formal," of the thing, the activity of consciousness can move in either a formalizing or a generalizing direction, with the accent in the first case on the *a priori,* and in the second, on the *a posteriori*. In the first case, without perhaps ever ceasing to refer more or less remotely to sensible knowledge, the judgment turns in upon itself to make explicit its object, the consciousness taking fuller possession of that *a priori* which is in it, the idea of which was awakened by the perception; thus the geometer never ceases to experience in perception the originative consciousness of spatiality, but he does not look in the world for the means of making it explicit. In the case of generalization, reflection seeks to provoke new experiences with a view to reworking the concepts it has elaborated by discovering new determinations or new relations; the judgment in this case expresses an *a posteriori* synthesis.[51]

Dufrenne devotes the last section of the book to an explication of the Hartmann-like ontology implicit in his de-idealized conception of the *a priori*. The sort of familiarity between the subject and the world which it affirms requires that the subject be at once connatural with the world and independent of it. The world ceases to be an opaque *en soi*, a radically exterior and foreign given whose secret has to be forced, or rather which the subject makes intelligible by imposing on it the law of the understanding, or the law of the *praxis*; it has sense, which the subject need only bring out. When the object is thought about, it undergoes no metamorphosis, no "radical promotion," for it is its own possibility which comes to light in the consciousness; a possibility which seemed to appeal to the consciousness for realization. To know the world is to accede to its intention. Not that the consciousness is limited to a passive inscription of a sense, for this sense offers itself in a way that is always partial and precarious, and there is always work to do in bringing out the *a priori*. When the mind carries out its work of explicating, it is the world which is bringing itself to light.[52]

phenomenology of the aesthetic experience

The notion of the *a priori* already played a key role in the earlier *Phenomenology of Aesthetic Experience*. Now that we have had the advantage of seeing the notion more fully developed in the more recent book, we might turn to the two big volumes that constitute the *Aesthetic* and see at least something of the contribution Dufrenne's kind of ontology has made to this region of philosophy.

After affirming the strict reciprocity of the aesthetic experience and the aesthetic object, Dufrenne decides to break into the circle they form together on the side of the object. For the aesthetic object enjoys sufficient reality in itself to be normative. Volume I, then, is devoted to distinguishing the aesthetic object from other sorts of object, to an analysis of the relationship between the object and its execution (where those arts in which, like painting, the author himself is executant, are distinguished from those where, as in music and dance, he is not), and to a description of the kind of "world"—the sort of space and time—in which the different species of aesthetic objects are found. The temporal arts are distinguished from the spatial ones, and, as all art objects have both time and space, even though one or the other of these dominates, it has to be shown what in each instance the particular temporal-spatial relationship is.

XV. *Existentialism and Phenomenology in France*

Volume II, devoted to "The Aesthetic Perception," rethinks the relation between representation, imagination, and the affectivity in the aesthetic attitude. The interest of these analyses goes far beyond the particular question of our beholding the art object; for Dufrenne feels obliged in context to reformulate much of the basic epistemology of existentialism in terms of his own more realistic ontology. To cite but one example: Dufrenne meets head-on the challenge of Sartre's conception of the imagination as essentially negative. Characteristically, he emphasizes the validity of Sartre's suggestion that the imagination's legitimate task is opening up a space for our creativity, while almost imperceptibly dropping the elements in this position which he finds unsound. The following passage is typical:

> In reserving the word "imagination" uniquely for the power of denying the real in favor of the unreal, one risks not seeing that there is another way of denying the real, which is to go beyond it in order to return to it, just as there is a way of holding ourselves in the nothing [*néant*] in order to make being emerge. There is an unreal which is a pre-real: It is the constant anticipation of the real without which the real would indeed never be anything for us but a spectacle without thickness of space or duration.[53]

The second half of the volume is devoted to Dufrenne's analysis of the affective *a priori*. The sense in which the *a priori* is a part, or even the whole of our own reality, which we use "to preform the object in themselves"[54] is elaborately developed. The tragic and the grotesque, the joyous and the noble have to be lived in order to be seized in the object; and because they are first a part of me, my experience of them *in the object* always transcends the object toward a universality which the particular object by itself only partially authorizes. Even in its singularity, my own humanity prepares me to grasp in the uniqueness of the great work of art the humanity it encloses, "it is the human in me which encounters the human in the object. We rediscover in this fashion that reciprocity of two *profondeurs* [depths] which is the very definition of sentiment."[55]

The proof of the phenomenological movement's fertility lies in the ability of works like Dufrenne's *Aesthetics*, to which we have here little more than merely alluded, to bring significant new light to antique realms of philosophical consideration. That is why one work like *La Phénoménologie de l'expérience esthétique* is worth a dozen laudatory discussions of the method of phenomenology.

Paul Ricoeur

the misery and the grandeur of phenomenology

Paul Ricoeur[56] protests for good reason against the practice of applying to "the least analysis of experience or sentiment" the term "phenomenology."[57] *La porte étroite*, which alone leads to phenomenology, is the transcendental reduction.[58] Not only has the philosophy that fails to begin with a rupture of the natural "thesis" of a world of things, so that the constitution of the object in consciousness may be radically uncovered, no right to be called phenomenological, but what is graver than a mere abuse of terminology, such a philosophy runs a fatal risk of being truncated. Because it fails to bring out in the object the results of the subject's synthesis of *a priori* with *a posteriori* knowledge, such a philosophy is fated to miss the chance to render philosophical (i.e., accessible to reasoned analysis) what we live naïvely and directly as the "misery" of man: the disproportion between the finitude of our receptivity and the infinity implied in the knowledge of truth,[59] the limits of individual character and the limitlessness of the desire for happiness. The philosophy that misses the possibility for examining the "intermediary" position of man which the transcendental viewpoint opens up, will never help us understand the human situation as we live it, and will tend instead to oscillate between the extremes of "being and nothingness."

Not that merely adopting the transcendental viewpoint of reflexive analysis necessarily guarantees that the philosopher will never stray from the true path leading to the illumination of our central problem: the fragile human reality. In this regard, the examples of the two greatest exponents of transcendental reflection are instructive. Kant was so preoccupied with the problem of providing an explanation of the ground of Newtonian physics that his "phenomenology" (as he described in 1772 in a letter to Marcus Herz the proposal for what was to become the great *Kritik*) fails to describe carefully what is really important, and invents instead things like the dreadfully static conception of time in the "Transcendental Aesthetic." Husserl, on the other hand, does carry out a whole program of phenomenology; but having turned the simple meth-

XV. Existentialism and Phenomenology in France 451

odological conversion of the reduction into an idealistic metaphysical decision, he is bound to have trouble giving the receptivity—the finitude—of our reality its due place. The subtle and fatal transition from an abstention to a negation is clearly visible in the Second *Cartesian Meditation*. Having decided to abstain (*mich enthalten*) from posing the world as absolute, I gain a hold on it as world-perceived in the reflexive life, in short I get a hold of it as phenomenon; so Husserl can legitimately say, "the world is for me only that which exists and is worth something for my consciousness in such a Cogito." But witness him then dogmatically assert that the world "finds in me and draws from me its sense and validity.... Its total sense, both universal and special, and its ontologic validity are drawn by the world exclusively from these *Cogitationes*."[60]

Husserl thus leaps from the fact that the natural common sense attitude neglects to realize the importance of the rapport of things to consciousness, to the conclusion that the only reality of the phenomena lies in their having been constituted. This is why Husserl's phenomenology instead of serving an ontology becomes itself a metaphysics, or better "an implicit metaphysics of non-metaphysics," the notion of *évidence originaire* replacing the receptivity of an at least partially passive perception, and the "otherness" of the other becoming so critically reduced that this philosophy culminates in a transcendental solipsism. The great pioneer in the methodic application of transcendental analysis, Kant, had avoided this false course by sticking to his conviction that *existence* is irreducible, that the other person must be posed as an end in himself; in that sense his reality poses a limit to my consciousness, for here is an object that informs me most strikingly that it is not phenomenon *for* consciousness but a reality in itself which consciousness happens to know. The *Ding an sich*, as Ricoeur interprets the *Critique of Pure Reason*, is also just such a limit. The assertion that we cannot know being as it is in itself amounts to affirming that the phenomena which we constitute do not constitute being itself, "the *Denken* [in the sense of critique] poses being as that which *limits* the pretensions of the phenomenon to constitute the ultimate reality; thus the *Denken* confers on phenomenology its measure and its ontologic evaluation."[61]

Not that Ricoeur has forgotten the purely formal and postulatory way in which Kant brings in the limitative reality of the other person, nor is he espousing the phenomenon-noumenon distinction in just the way Kant formulated it. He is quite eloquent on the subject of the deficiencies of Kant's doctrine in these matters.⁶² But the point is that Kant did see in his own way that phenomenology cannot proceed directly along the royal road of a genetic analysis of the consciousness' constituting its objects and expect, after going back through reduction upon reduction, to come to the pure *Cogito* as ground of all being. Kant is a guide for correcting Husserl's idealism because he never lost the sense of the central dilemma of the human condition, the reality of which we feel directly in the *pathétique de la misère*, man's "intermediary" position, as a finite existent dependent on passivity for means which move toward essentially infinite ends. Two aspects of Kant's sensitivity to the intermediary nature of man stand out: (1) the central role he assigns the transcendental imagination as mediator between the finite sensible image and the unlimited idea; (2) the way in which he insists that the practical order transcends the theoretical, as though our consciousness were but part of a larger reality upon which it has indeed a hold, but always only a partial one.

"concerning the good use of husserlian phenomenology"

This is the title Ricoeur gives the last section of the 1953 article in *Esprit*, "Sur la phénoménologie." It is in the monumental *Philosophie de la volonté* (*Philosophy of the Will*), three volumes of which have already appeared, and especially in the first part of the second part, *Finitude et culpabilité*, I: *L'Homme faillible* (1960), that the "good use" of phenomenology is not only most amply sketched out, but actually put into practice.

There is a disproportion in man between his knowledge and his action, and between his action and his feeling. There is in man's immediate grasp of himself a richness of sense which reflection cannot equal. Yet the goal of reflection must be to achieve as comprehensive an elucidation of the human reality as it can. To start from anything less than a global view of his non-coincidence with himself and of the mediation which he realizes in existing would be to miss his essential reality from the outset. Philosophy must proceed by means of a secondary elucidation of a "nebula of sense" which is given first in a pre-reflexive existence but lends itself to reflection. Borne up by the non-philosophic, philosophy must live on the substance of what has been grasped without having been reflected on.⁶³ The ideal ground for a "philosophical anthropology" seeking to elucidate that immediately lived disproportion and intermediacy characteristic of man's ontic position, is some relatively accessible region or mode of our ex-

XV. Existentialism and Phenomenology in France

istence in which the disproportion and mediating-synthesizing role of man can be fairly clearly grasped, so that it can subsequently serve as guiding light (or, as Ricoeur says, *fil conducteur*—Ariadne's clue) to the other modalities of "intermediary man." The initial step then will be to separate (or "reduce") the region of a "transcendental reflection" from the pre-reflexive "matrix" of experience. Note the special accent Ricoeur places on the notion of "reduction." Taking up the transcendental viewpoint and inquiring into the subject's synthesizing act of making the object "stand there" in the horizons of consciousness is attending to only a single feature of the global totality of our directly lived experience. Transcendental analysis cannot then be the whole of philosophy; more properly it is a propaedeutic, intended to lead the way, to serve as an example for the subsequent investigation of those spheres of existence which lend themselves less well to reflective analysis than the sphere whose primary activity, after all, is *knowing*. The cognitive function is so thoroughly for the sake of the object, that we are able in this sphere to read the subject's synthesizing directly *in the object*. The synthesizing role of what Kant called "the third term," the "transcendental imagination," is discovered when transcendental analysis seeks to understand the rapport between the passively received date of perception and absolute truth, and to reconcile the finitude of receptivity with the infinity of the exigencies of truth.

The meditation on the disproportion between Reason and the Sensibility (or, more exactly, of the Word and the Perspective) having succeeded in bringing out, along with an insight into the nature of this disproportion lodged in man, some notion of his function as intermediary between the finite and the infinite, the philosopher can now proceed to fill in progressively the gap between the transcendentally reduced cognitive sphere and the englobing totality of the immediately lived sphere ("*la pathétique*"). Other forms of disproportion will then be found to characterize the non-coincidence of man with himself in the more opaque orders of *action* and *feeling*. At the term of this gradual enlargening of the sphere of reflection, what one would hope would happen would be that the sphere of pure reflection, become total comprehension, should equal the initial matrix of the *pathétique de la misère*. But the fact that we do live (*leben*) more than we consciously experience (*erleben*),[64] suggests that total comprehension is destined to remain an ideal, one always striven for but never totally attained. To affirm otherwise would be to forget our finitude. However, once armed with the kind of guide just described, one is in a position to go on enlarging the circle of comprehension indefinitely, and to make good use of any kind of light the pre-reflexive living of our situation may offer.

the philosophy of fallible man

We should not be astonished, then, to see Ricoeur, at a critical point in his own analysis, have recourse to a "hermeneutic"[65] consideration of the "symbolism of evil" in order to plumb the depths of Man's existence—an existent who is not only capable of error, but who has, as the myths tell us, actually fallen. To understand this fully, let us consider for a moment what Ricoeur is attempting to achieve in his monumental *Philosophy of the Will* and how the various parts thus far published contribute to the announced purpose.

Our task is complicated by the fact that Ricoeur has proceeded in anything but linear fashion. It is even too simple to say that the analysis unfolds in a series of enlarging concentric circles. When introducing the whole project of a philosophy of the will, Ricoeur announced that he would proceed first to a "pure description" of the relation of the voluntary and involuntary structures in a human nature considered in abstraction from "the fault." For this latter introduces concrete elements into the involuntary side of the dialectic which require difficult special elaboration, reserved for the volumes to come. What emerges in the volume published in 1950 under the title *The Voluntary and the Involuntary* is, as a later volume states it, a sketch "of the neutral sphere of the most fundamental possibilities of man, or, if you prefer, the undifferentiated keyboard [*clavier*] upon which could be played just as well the theme of the guilty man as the innocent,"[66] in short an *eidetic* analysis. *Finitude et culpabilité* has as its task to take away from these deliberately "abstract" analyses the parentheses in which they were enclosed, and so to deal with man as we actually have him, that is guilty man, thus achieving an *empirique de la volonté*.[67] Anyone contemplating the notions of the Fall, of Sin, of Evil in general is confronted with a mass of myths, a veritable *symbolique du mal*. *Finitude et culpabilité* intends to let those myths speak to us, as a prelude to attempting a properly philosophic reflection on whatever it is they will indicate to us.

Before attempting this hermeneutic listening to the symbols (which of course will have its own methodic rules; see below), the place (*lieu*) of the insertion of evil in the human complexus needed to be described; the "abstract"

XV. Existentialism and Phenomenology in France

analysis of the voluntary and involuntary failed to provide the complete philosophical anthropology necessary to the task. Hence Ricoeur devotes Part 1 of *Finitude et culpabilité* to the study of *L'Homme faillible* (Fallible Man) along the lines suggested above: using as his model the transcendental analysis of our synthesizing the object of knowledge, he proceeds to the study of man's mediating role in the modalities of action and sentiment. The hermeneutic unlocking of the myths of the fall, of chaos, of exile, takes us further than the philosophic anthropology's effort to render human fallibility comprehensible. But the anthropology's analyses of how through man evil "could come into the world" will help us find our way among the myths, which themselves speak an indirect and ciphered language. The earlier analyses of *The Voluntary and the Involuntary* were too narrowly centered on the structure of the will; the new elaboration of the concept of fallibility is the occasion for a much more extensive investigation of the structures of the human reality, of which the sphere of the will is only a part.[68] The duality of voluntary and involuntary finds its place "in a much vaster dialectic dominated by the ideas of disproportion, of the polarity of the finite and infinite and of the intermediary or of mediation."[69]

But how can one term *philosophy* a mediation that leads to a hermeneutic of myths, which hermeneutic is primarily concerned to follow the myths within their own horizons? The point is that the *Symbolique du mal* is to be followed by another volume which will seek *à penser à partir du symbole*, to think beyond symbol, using the symbol as a jumping-off point. There Ricoeur promises to encounter and debate with psychoanalysis, with modern criminology, and above all with political philosophy. "When one has taken part in the ghastly history which ended in the hecatombs of the concentration camps, in the terror of totalitarian regimes and in nuclear peril, one can no longer doubt that the problem of evil passes also by way of the problem of power and that the theme of *alienation* which runs from Rousseau to Marx by way of Hegel has something to do with the accusation of the old prophets of Israel."[70]

The central idea that will emerge in the promised Third Part is one that already loomed impressively in the "narrow" bounds of the problem of *The Voluntary and the Involuntary*, namely that of "the bond-will" (*serf-arbitre*), the free will (*libre arbitre*) which binds itself and discovers itself always already bound by its passions. *Finitude et culpabilité* ends its phenomenological analysis of the weakness in the human structure—its disproportion—by warning that it has clarified only a *possibility* of evil, while ethics traditionally begins with the alternative of good and evil presented as an already existent reality, "ethics conies on the scene too late."[71] Between the possibility and the reality lies the *fault*. The median area which it covers essentially involves an act of liberty. The only way to gain access to the intelligibility of an act of liberty is through another act of liberty—an *avowal*; only if we *avow* that the crucial transition from frailty as possibility of error, to the reality of evil, truly has something to do with us, can passion as the freedom-which-enslaves-itself be seriously considered.[72] The historical language of the avowal has been the symbols of evil; the avowal expresses itself in the intimate language of myth.[73]

ricoeur's phenomenological anthropology

There is no point in trying to condense into a few bald indications the rich phenomenology of *The Voluntary and the Involuntary* and *Finitude and Culpability*, nor in weakly parroting the hermeneutic of myths in *The Symbolism of Evil*. Our analysis of how it is constructed offers some idea of what *The Philosophy of the Will* is about and, what is more important, some clue to finding one's way about its sinewy corridors.

Ricoeur's originality should by now be fairly evident. Plato, Aristotle, Descartes, and Kant[74] are his teachers, as much as Husserl, Sartre, and Heidegger. His exploitation of classical texts often accord magnificent insights into some of their implications. Ricoeur has also evidently meditated deeply and sympathetically on many texts of St. Thomas. One of his important teachers that he will not let us overlook: Gabriel Marcel, whose work he contrasted in an early book with Jaspers, almost always to the advantage of Marcel, and to whom the monumental *Le Voluntaire et l'Involuntaire* is dedicated.

We have seen something already of how Ricoeur would go beyond Kant in the direction of a phenomenology uncommitted to Kant's Newtonian presuppositions and determined to flesh out what remains in Kant's analyses purely formalistic. And we have seen how he would avoid Husserl's error of transcendental idealism. To conclude, we shall content ourselves with underscoring a couple of points of contrast separating Ricoeur's "phenomenological anthropology" from the existentialism of his exact contemporaries.

For one thing, Ricoeur rejects the project of a "philosophy of perception," as he terms the effort to understand man uniquely in terms of the finitude of his

XV. Existentialism and Phenomenology in France

insertion into the world. Against this view, which tends to reduce intellection to a fixing of perspectives, and liberty to character, Ricoeur stresses that both the finite and the infinite must be involved in order to describe the tense composition of man, that Perspective and Truth, Character and the Good, Pleasure and Happiness are all manifested in him, and that their reconciliation constitutes the whole sense of the human drama. Attempts to achieve the unity of a philosophical wisdom at the relative expense of one member of the uneasy dyad pay the price of simply being wrong.

Another original feature—and in this Ricoeur corrects not only the Sartrean ontology, but its ancestor, the Cartesian as well—is a recasting of the being-nonbeing dichotomy in man. The finite side of the dyad is not nothing; the perspective is *a* partial truth, pleasure is *a* good, character is *a* necessary part of man's quest for happiness. Or, to put it another way, man is first of all something, a reality whose essential being is, as Spinoza said, *to posit* (*ponere*), not to take away (*tollere*). Man is first of all affirmation, indeed *joy*. The negation in man is not an effort to pull free from the *en soi* accumulated by his own dead past, rather it is a limitation that manifests itself interior to the affirmation: it is the manifestation of the Word in a perspective which "negates" it—in the sense that the Truth is only glimpsed partially; of the Totality of Ends in a character which can be only a partial realization of them; of Love in an attachment to the merely vital which negates it. "If we follow that existential negativity from the exterior toward the interior, it appears first of all as the difference between me and the other, then as the difference between me and myself, and is finally interiorized as the sadness of finitude."[75] Exploration of the whole range of this dialectic is the challenge Ricoeur's philosophical anthropology has set for itself. "Man is that plural and collegial unity in which the unity of destination and the difference of destinies are comprehensible in terms of one another."[76] But the comprehension of the unity of humanity which is here confidently affirmed as a possibility is still only that—a project—at least until the work of philosophical anthropology is completed. If I am to understand the profound sense in which truth is "transgressed" by the perspectivism in me—by my knowing the truth only from a point of view—then it is essential that I be able to oppose the perspectives of others to my own. Communication is here essential. The tension and strain of the multiplicity of human existences is a fact; but there is only tension because we are somehow meant to be parts of a whole—we are both *one* and *many*. Ricoeur's "hermeneutic" tries to reach through the many to the one. The *project* he has undertaken is an immense and exciting one.

NOTES

Preface

1. For comprehensive surveys of the whole field, see: (1) Friedrich Ueberweg, *Grundriss der Geschichte der Philosophie*, Part 5, "History of Foreign Countries," from the beginning of the nineteenth century up to our own times, ed. T. K. Oesterreich (12th ed.; Berlin, 1928). This history covers all the other European countries and adds information concerning Central and South American philosophers; even philosophy in Asia is represented in it. (2) Lucien Lévy-Bruhl, *History of Modern Philosophy in France* (Chicago: The Open Court Co., 1899). (3) D. Parodi, *La philosophie contemporaine en France* (Paris, 1920). (4) Émile Bréhier, *Histoire de la Philosophie*, Vol. II, "La philosophie moderne," Part 2, "XIXe et XXe siècles" (Paris, 1932). (5) M. F. Sciacca, "Il secolo XX," *Storia della filosofia italiana*, 2 vols. (Milan: Fratelli Bocca, 1947). (6) M. F. Sciacca, *La philosophie italienne contemporaine*, trans. Marie-Louise Roure (Paris and Lyon: E. Vitte, N.D.). (Sciacca's Foreword is dated Christmas, 1950.) (7) *Les grands courants de la pensée mondiale contemporaine,* published under the direction of M. F. Sciacca, Vol. I, Part 1, "Panoramas nationaux" (Paris: Librairie Fischbacher Marzorati, 1958).

PART ONE: GERMAN PHILOSOPHY

I. Post-Kantian Background

1. In addition to the work on each of the authors to be mentioned in this chapter, a list of which is included in each of the following sections, the following works tracing the post-Kantian movement as a unity are very helpful: Victor Delbos, *De Kant aux post-Kantiens* (Paris: Aubier, 1939); J. Maréchal, S.J., *Le point de départ de la métaphysique*, Vol. IV: *Le système idéaliste chez Kant et les postkantiens* (Paris: Desclée, 1947); Nicolai Hartmann, *Die Philosophie des deutschen Idealismus*, 2 vols. (Berlin and Leipzig: W. de Gruyter, 1923–1929); R. Kroner, *Von Kant bis Hegel*, 2 vols. (Tübingen: Mohr, 1921–1924).
2. Johann Gottlieb Fichte, b. Rammenau, 1762; d. Berlin, 1814. Born of peasant parents in Saxony, Fichte received his secondary education at Pforta, then studied in the 1780s at Jena and theology at Leipzig, where he was fascinated with Spinoza's thought. When

he lost his tutoring job in Warsaw, he went to Königsberg in the summer of 1791 to visit the master whose disciple he had become in his earlier Zurich tutoring days. As Kant could find no reason to be impressed with his self-invited visitor, Fichte set to work to give him one, applying Kantian philosophy to religious problems in an *Essay toward a Critique of All Revelation*, which was to make his reputation. Despite Fichte's ill-concealed sympathies for what was happening in France, the Duke of Saxony approved the thirty-two-year-old Fichte's appointment in 1794 to the important chair at Jena. Fichte rushed to complete a definitive statement of his developing thought that year, the *Basis of the Entire Theory of Science* (often referred to curtly as the *Wissenschaftslehre*), which achieves a genial systematization and unification of the Kantian critiques in a way that Kant eventually (after Fichte was in trouble in 1799 with the authorities) repudiated. The principal practical deductions following from this theory were made, first, in *Basis of Natural Right* (1796) and then in *System of Ethics* (1798). When Fichte was forced out of Jena on charges of atheism (not leveled directly against what he had written, but against an article published in the *Philosophical Journal* which he edited), he sought refuge in Berlin. After a flirtation with the romantics, Fichte broke forth in works of religious philosophy, *The Vocation of Man* (1800) and above all. *The Way to the Blessed Life or Doctrine of Religion* (1805–1806). Fichte also delivered more popular lectures and wrote on subjects such as *The Closed Commercial State* (1800) and *On the Characteristics of the Present Age* (1804–1805). During the Napoleonic invasions, Fichte went to Königsberg, returning in the summer of 1807 after the peace. With thoughts of these recent troubles, Fichte delivered his later famous *Addresses to the German Nation*. With the foundation of the University of Berlin in 1810, Fichte was named to the chair of philosophy, which he occupied (he was also for a while rector) until his death from typhus in 1814.

The *Sämmtliche Werke* were edited by Fichte's son, Hermann, in eight volumes (Berlin: Veit, 1845–1846); there are also three volumes of *Posthumous Works* (Bonn: Marcus, 1834–1835). There exists a more modern *Werke*, improved but not definitive, in six volumes (Leipzig: Meiner, 1911–1912). Fichte's *Life and Literary Correspondence* are also presented by Hermann Fichte, 2nd enlarged ed., in two vols. (Leipzig: Haessel, 1925). No adequate recent translation is available of any of Fichte's major works, although *The Popular Works of J. G. Fichte*, grouping most of the works after 1800, was prepared by W. Smith, in two volumes (4th ed. London: Trübner, 1889), and A. E. Kroeger translated *The Science of Knowledge* (Philadelphia: Lippincott, 1868), *New Exposition of the Science of Knowledge* (St. Louis: privately printed, 1869), and *The Science of Rights* (London: Trübner, 1889). James Collins, in his chapter on "Fichte and Schelling" in *A History of Modern European Philosophy* (Milwaukee: Bruce, 1954), has an excellent brief introduction. A longer study in English, R. Adamson, *Fichte* (Edinburgh: Blackwood, 1881), Xavier Léon's studies in French, *La philosophie de Fichte* (Paris: Alcan, 1902), and *Fichte et son temps* (2 vols. in 3; Paris: Colin, 1922–1927) are thorough, clear, and accurate. Fichte is placed in the whole movement of German idealism in two excellent works, Nicolai Hartmann, *Die Philosophie des deutschen Idealismus*, 2 vols. (Berlin and Leipzig, W. de Gruyter: 1923–1929), and R. Kroner, *Von Kant bis Hegel*, 2 vols. (Tübingen: Adohr, 1921–1924).

3. The three principles to be outlined here are developed in the *Wissenschaftslehre*, I, 1–3, which section is presented in translation in Rand's *Modern Classical Philosophers* (New York: Houghton-Mifflin, 1908), pp. 497–515.
4. G. W. F. Hegel, *Differenz des Fichte'schen und Schelling'schen Systems*, chap. 2.
5. See *The Way to the Blessed Life* (1805–1806).
6. *Grundlage der Gesamten Wissenschaftslehre*, Part II, "Grundlage des Theoretischen Wissens," para. B.
7. Ibid., p. 215.
8. The fundamental work is the *Grundlage des Naturrechts*, "The Foundations of Natural Right" (1796).
9. Cf. *Grundlage des Naturrechts*, "Deduction des Begriffes vom Rechte," chap. 1. Erster Lehrsatz, pp. 17–23.
10. *The Science of Rights*, trans. Kroeger, I, 4.
11. *Aufhebung* signifies in this context the uniting of a thesis and an antithesis in a synthesis that achieves a reconciliation and flowering of the essential contribution of the thesis and its corresponding opposition. The conception that law is not just an expression of a state of things but is actually society's major educative instrument, though first thought of by the Greeks, in its modern form grows out of the eighteenth-century notion of history's gradual education of mankind to its present high civilization. See Gilson and Langan, *Modern Philosophy*, pp. 395–402. Hegel enthusiastically adopts this notion of law.
12. In 1806, *Aphorism zur Einleitung in die Naturphilosophie, Sam. Werke*, I, 7:174.
13. Friedrich Wilhelm Joseph von Schelling, b. Leonberg, 1775; d. Ragaz, 1854. Schelling was a rabid and talented defender of Fichte's *Wissenschaftslehre* during his days as a co-student with Hegel and the poet Hölderlin in the Tübingen theology seminary. In the *Philosophical Letters on Dogmatism and Criticism* (1795) Schelling confronted Fichtean critical idealism with its emphasis on freedom and Spinozistic determinism as but representative of the highest development of what he there called "dogmatism." In *Ideas Toward a Philosophy of Nature* (1797) and *On the World Soul* (1798), Schelling worked to develop the implications of critical idealism for a doctrine of objective nature. Contact with the great romantics, above all the Schlegels at Jena, where he was named professor in 1798, pushed Schelling to develop the *System of Transcendental Idealism* (1800), *Exposition of My System of Philosophy* (1801), and *Bruno or On the Divine and Natural Principle of Things* (1802), which brought the first phase of his philosophy—what he was much later to term "negative philosophy"—to a climax. At the same time Schelling's bonds with romanticism continued to grow (he was now in the throes of a famous love for the extraordinary Caroline Schlegel, whom he married in 1803); Schelling was deeply moved by the writings of the early seventeenth-century theosophist, Jacob Boehme (see Alexandre Koyré, *La philosophie de Jacob Boehme* (Paris: Vrin, 1929), whose writings he felt could be organized in a rational way to build far beyond the "negative philosophy," whose inadequacies he began to feel acutely. At Würzburg (1803–1806) and Munich (1806–1820), in *Philosophy and Religion* (1804) and *Philosophical Inquiries into the Nature of Human Freedom* (1809), the problems of evil, of freedom, and of a practical encounter with the Absolute through action were

developed, in the beginnings of a whole new structure of rational inquiry. After Hegel published the *Phenomenology of the Spirit* in 1807, and began dismissing Schelling's Absolute, of whose "indifference" Hegel once said that it was "like the dark night in which all cows are black," Schelling had to take ungraciously to a back seat, becoming at Munich and at Erlangen (1821-1826) a center of anti-Hegelianisin. Schelling survived the days of Hegel's freshest impact, and once returned to Munich, after 1827, increasingly emphasizing existence, freedom, and creativity against the "negative conceptualizations" of Hegel, began to enjoy a newly increasing influence. The climax to this new popularity came in the form of a royal invitation in 1841 to present his positive philosophy as an antidote to Hegelianism in Berlin. Kierkegaard, Engels, and Bakunin heard him—and, with most of the rest of the learned public, were not impressed with the tired old fellow. So he went back to the more *gemütlich* Munich, where a long career of much-evolving thought came to an end as death caught up with him (1854) while he was preparing for publication an Introduction to the *Philosophy of Mythology*.

The *Sämmtliche Werke* were edited by Schelling's son, K. Schelling (14 vols.; Stuttgart and Augsburg: Cotta, 1856-1861). *Of Human Freedom*, translated by J. Guttmann (Chicago: Open Court, 1936) and *The Ages of the World*, a work begun in 1811 but reflecting mature views, translated by F. Bolman, Jr. (New York: Columbia University Press, 1942) are available in English. James Collins' chapter on Fichte and Schelling, in the book mentioned in our note on Fichte, provides an excellent summary introduction. Vladimir Jankelevitch, *L'Odyssée de la conscience dans la dernière philosophie de Schelling* (Paris: Alcan, 1933) Karl Jaspers' recent *Schelling* (Munich: Piper, 1955) are very illuminating studies. For a recent study of Schelling's theory of knowledge, see Rudolf Hahlützel, *Dialektik und Einbildungskraft, F. W. J. Schellings Lehre von der menschlichen Erkenntnis*.

14. The young Schelling's knowledge of the history of philosophy was still very limited. See Jankelevitch's Introduction to his translation of the *Letters on Dogmatism and Criticism* (Paris: Aubier, 1950).
15. Schelling, a year later, brings out these merits of Spinoza's conception in his *Ideas for a Philosophy of Nature* more strongly than in the *Letters* themselves.
16. In the *Seventh Letter*, Schelling condemns Spinoza for conceiving "Substance" with all of its emanations as given once and for all.
17. "No system can realize the passage from the infinite to the finite; for, though it is always possible to juggle with ideas, this game is always practically sterile. No system can fill up the abyss separating the two." *Seventh Letter*.
18. *Ninth Letter*.
19. Ibid.
20. Introduction to *Ideas for a Philosophy of Nature*.
21. Appendix to *Ideas for a Philosophy of Nature*.
22. *System of Transcendental Idealism*, III, para. 2, no. 3.
23. We shall show later in this study why transcendental philosophy tends to end in an aestheticism.
24. *System of Transcendental Idealism*, III, 4, 3.

25. Hegel characteristically makes of the aesthetic just one aspect, inferior to religion and philosophy, of Spirit's self-realization.
26. Reacting to criticism, Schelling published no major work after 1809. The best expression of the fruit of the lectures of this period are in the posthumous *Philosophy of Revelation* and *Introduction to the Philosophy of Mythology*.
27. Georg Wilhelm Friedrich Hegel, b. Stuttgart, 1770; d. Berlin, 1831. Hegel studied theology in Tübingen as a classmate of Schelling and the poet Hölderlin, neither of whom retained his pastoral vocation; Hegel, for his part, turned tutor, first at Bern and then, until 1800, at Frankfort. In 1801, the year he was named *Privatdozent* at Jena, Hegel published *The Difference Between the Philosophical Systems of Fichte and Schelling*, in which he leans toward Schelling. In the *Critical Journal of Philosophy*, which he founded with Schelling, he continued to attack Fichte, Jacobi, and Kant mainly because they placed faith above reason. In his important article, "To Believe and to Know," Hegel already defined philosophy as "absolute knowledge—a science of the Absolute—fulfilling what the faith is struggling toward only darkly." In 1807 appeared the monumental *Phenomenology of the Spirit*. From 1808 until 1816, Hegel directed the Melanchthon Gymnasium in Nürnberg, and published in three volumes (from 1812 until 1816) *The Science of Logic*. In 1817, at Heidelberg, he published an expose of the entire system, encompassing both the phenomenology and the logic, under the title *Encyclopedia of the Philosophical Sciences*. From 1818 until his death in 1831, Hegel enjoyed great success in Berlin. During this period he published the *Philosophy of Law* (1821) and an article on "The Proofs for the Existence of God" (1831). Most of his time in the later years was spent preparing the courses which were so eagerly followed. After his death these were edited as lessons on the philosophy of history, on the philosophy of nature, on aesthetics, on religion, on the history of philosophy.

The original *Werke* (19 vols.; Berlin: Duncker, and Humboldt, 1832–1845 and 1887) were rearranged in an edition by Glöckner (26 vols.; Stuttgart: Frommann, 1927–1939). A critical edition, started by Lesson and Hoffmeister, is almost complete (21 volumes projected; Leipzig: Meiner, 1905ff.). *Hegels Theologische Jugendschriften*, edited by Nohl (Tübingen: Mohr, 1907), contains some additional documents, and served as the basis for the translation by Knox and Kroner, *Early Theological Writings* (Chicago: University of Chicago Press, 1948). Also translated: *The Phenomenology of Mind*, trans. Baillie (2nd rev. ed.; New York: Macmillan, 1931); *Science of Logic*, trans. Johnston and Struthers (2 vols.; New York: Macmillan, 1929); *The Logic of Hegel*, a portion of *The Encyclopedia of the Philosophical Sciences*, trans. Wallace (rev. 2nd ed.; Oxford: Clarendon, 1892); *Hegel's Philosophy of Mind*, another section of the *Encyclopedia*, trans. Wallace (Oxford: Clarendon, 1894); *Philosophy of Right*, trans. Knox (Oxford: Clarendon, 1942); *Lectures on the Philosophy of History*, trans. Sibree (rev. ed.; New York: Dover Publications, 1956); *The Philosophy of Fine Art*, trans. Osmaston (4 vols.; London: Ball, 1920); *Lectures on the Philosophy of Religion, together with a Work on the Proofs for the Existence of God*, trans. Speirs and Sanderson (3 vols.; London: Kegan Paul, Trench, Trübner, 1895); *Lectures on the History of Philosophy*, trans. Haldane and Simpson (3 vols.; London: Kegan Paul, Trench, Trübner, 1892–1896).

The best introduction to Hegel in English is J. N. Findlay's *Hegel, a Re-examination*

(New York: Macmillan, 1958). The well-known commentaries—Stace's *Philosophy of Hegel*, McTaggart's *Commentary on Hegel's Logic* and *Studies in Hegelian Dialectic* and Mure's *Study of Hegel's Logic* are not too reliable. James Collins' chapter on Hegel in *Modern European Philosophy* (Milwaukee: Bruce, 1954) is brief and accurate. Jean Hyppolite's *Genèse et structure de la Phénoménologie de Hegel* (Paris: Aubier, 1946), is reliable.

28. Nicolai Hartmann commented on several occasions that Hegel is very successful as *Geistesphilosoph*, and much less so as *Naturphilosoph*; the dialectic, he adds, tends to be "real" when the phenomena described are themselves "restless" and moving, and less so when they enjoy in fact some objective stability. The remark does not quite hit the nail on the head, and indeed illustrates the difficulty even very great historians have in coming to grips with the problem of Hegel when they do not hang on firmly to their own deepest insights into the "intentional-transcendental" viewpoint. For, it so happens, Hartmann to the contrary notwithstanding, Hegel's descriptions are sometimes penetrating in the area of philosophy of nature, and sometimes very strained in "philosophy of spirit." Now, while other factors have also to be called into the account (including historical prejudices, *lacunae* in positive knowledge, and even the tendency once in a while to let the symmetry of the dialectical construction command instead of allowing the underlying intentional tension to appear), Hegel's descriptions fit best when the phenomenon described is in fact *essentially* existential-intentional, and tend to be strained when it is only *accidentally* so. When the phenomenon finds its sense essentially in the relationship between intentions, either between two subjects *qua* subject (e.g., the master-slave relationship), or between two concepts precisely in their *ideal* state (e.g., the ideal subject and predicate, analyzed in the *Logic*), or between a subject and the subject's *handling of* an object, considered precisely from the point of view of the subject's intention (*praxis*) (e.g., the transformation of natural objects through work), then the intentional dialectical analysis tends to illumine the phenomena as they really are. When, on the contrary, the thing analyzed finds its essential sense not in its *being known or handled* by an intentional existent, but, rather, precisely in its *otherness*, as a reality independent of our experience, in other words when it is an intention *per accidens*, the dialectical analysis tends to dissipate its objective sense, reducing it to the ideal negation which then enjoys only an obscure status in the final ideal synthesis. Thus, for instance, the dialectic of "here and now" in the opening pages of *The Phenomenology* perpetrates a terrible injustice against the concrete material thing's ability to present to experience the evidence of its own objective independence. And even in the case of the more existential-intentional phenomena which lend themselves best to dialectical description, those aspects of them which are most rooted in the objective world, which persist in fact and resist efforts to reduce them to ideal movement, are what get least well illumined; for instance, how that nature which is transformed in work actually mediates and bears the product, or how the historical sedimentations which structure class and individual personality are sedimented in the person and objectively structured in institutions.

29. *Phenomenology of the Spirit*, A, chap. ii.

30. What Hegel in the *Vorrede* to the *Phenomenology* terms *Erfahrung. Phänom. des*

Geistes, ed. Lasson, p. 14.
31. Ibid., chaps. ii and iii.
32. Ibid., chap. iv.
33. Ibid., chap. iv A.
34. "Der sich entfremdete Geist," ibid., p. 347ff. The notion of "world" should be understood here in the same sense it will have later for the twentieth-century existentialists; it is a fundamental notion in transcendental philosophy. Roughly, "world" designates the common intentional intersubjective horizons characterizing an era, or, for that matter, any intersubjective group.
35. The Engels-Leninist effort to make of a dialectic really installed in things the principle of explanation for all the dynamic structures in reality (there are for the Marxists only forces in motion) requires that the notion be rendered large enough to enclose any sort of objective opposition which may present itself in experience. Denatured of its "idealism," i.e., its intentionality, the dialectic becomes a mysterious law of forward-moving objective creativity in which material principles achieve the considerable feat of lifting themselves, through the resolution of opposites, to a qualitatively higher form of existence. When the authors of the official Soviet ideological *Handbook* are forced to explain this transition, they follow Lenin's example and cite Hegel's *Logic*. But if we reflect on the text in the light of what we have said here about intentional analysis, we are struck by the fact that the Hegelian text makes perfect sense when it is a question of *intentions* and becomes pure "mystification" when construed as a description of material processes. Hegel writes, "Thus in the inner, the properly self-movement, the general moving force...there is nothing else than this something-in-itself and its lack—the Negative of itself—grasped in one and the same view. The abstract self identity is not yet life, but only as the positive is in itself negativity, and thus goes out of itself and determines itself in change. Something is thus living only in so far as it contains contradiction in itself, and this power is to contain the contradiction in itself and to persevere in it." (*Logik*, II, Jubiläumausgabe, IV, p. 547) For the discussion in the Soviet *Handbook*, see *Grundlagen der Marxistischen Philosophie* (East Berlin: Dietz Verlag, 1960), pp. 270–284, and the commentary of Gustav Wetter, *Soviet Ideologie Heute: Dialektischer und Historischer Materialismus* (Frankfurt: Fischer Bücherei, 1962), p. 105. The materialist dialecticians always breathe visibly easier when they rejoin their preferred terrain of combat, that of social-economic-political relations. We see why: for there they rejoin the intentional—the relationship of subject to thing, and subject to subject, whether directly or mediated through humanized objects, the "abstractions" of "alienation," phenomena explicable only intentionally.
36. Each new *Gestalt* seems, when it is first discovered, to offer stability, it seems to have a reality in itself, a certain *Ruhigkeit*, as Hegel often terms it. But then the paradox, expressive of the dialectical nature of every subject-object relationship, begins to appear, as we are made to realize once again that the object depends on the subject and the subject on the object.
37. *Lectures in the Philosophy of History*, ed. Charles Hegel and trans. J. Sibree (New York: Dover, 1956), p. 31.
38. Hegel's own statement in the *Rechtsphilosophie* to the effect that philosophy can only

express what Spirit has already achieved could be misleading, were one to overlook the positive result for the advance of Spirit in such a *prise de conscience*. This theme is developed at length in the *Vorrede* of the *Phänomenologie*, pp. 16–19. The central role Hegel assigns language is proof that expression is itself the supreme *event*.

39. *Phänom. des Geistes*, p. 427.

40. The Hegelian ontology was accused by Marx of being overly *positivistic*, in the sense that it tends to consider *what is* to be the only possible reality, and therefore whatever has contributed to bringing it about must be "good." Marx would have us see that *what is* can enfold a large coefficient of non-being, or poorly realized possibility, provided we understand that human nature manifests in the present a noble potentiality which the actual situation is inadequately realizing or perhaps even temporarily frustrating. Ironically, because Hegel makes the *distinctions* into idea, i.e., into conceptual determinations interior to the *selbstentwicklung des Geistes*, in order to retain for the developed Spirit some content, he must be *conservative*, tending to consider all the distinctions which have been *aufgehoben* (i.e., which are steps in the long progressive process) as retaining an almost sacred, a virtually eternal, validity. While Marx, because he considers the distinctions material is revolutionary, i.e., he believes that against any material negation may be turned another material negation which will destroy the limits imposed by the first. He does not risk raising the problem of a *nirvana* because he begins with the givenness of real material distinctions, so that, although certain restrictions can be relieved, material limitation as such cannot. However the problem of conceiving of the form of alienations that will still endure in the classless society arises here. The contemporary Marxist attitude seems to be: Given that neither the distinctions, nor the instruments for combating the more painfully restrictive among them, are *ideal*, one has only to proceed against those that have already revealed themselves as painful and relievable, and then let the cure in its turn manifest its own limits and difficulties.

Here we see the inconvenience of eliminating completely everything which Hegel combined in the notion of *Idea*. For where is the assurance that, in throwing ourselves head-long into revolutionary negation-of-the-negation, we are not instituting material structures that may prove more restrictive than those they are intended to negate? Moreover, the very notion of *restriction*, of unhappiness, presupposes a vision beyond the materially given which makes the present restriction a *Leiden*. Has Marxism provided an epistemology that can account for this ideality?

41. See, for instance, *Philosophy of History*, trans. Sibree, rev. ed., pp. 29–30.

42. Ibid., p. 15.

43. Jean Hyppolite, *Genèse et Structure de la Phénoménologie de l'esprit de Hegel*, p. 512.

44. *Enzyklopädie*, ed. Lasson, V, p. 481.

45. In his youthful writing Hegel shows himself impressed by the early seventeenth-century mystics' intuitive position as pointing out the insufficiencies of Kantian formalism. But by the time of the *Phenomenology*, Hegel has become opposed to any form of intuitionisin which would render the concrete moments of historical positivity superfluous by suggesting some sort of immediate contact with an all-embracing All which supposedly exists without having to realize itself through the patient work of

the negative.
46. Feuerbach is discussed in the biographical note on Marx, see note 55, below.
47. As we shall see later, Husserl was more aware than anyone since Descartes of how difficult this is. Why does Hegel not speak of anything like the "phenomenological reduction," or at least the methodic Cartesian doubt, in which the transcendental viewpoint is overtly, for scientific reasons, adopted? It is not that he did not have hold of the implications of that transcendental viewpoint from which in fact he is operating. Hegel, instead of looking upon the full recognition of the implications of Spirit as something for the specialist in phenomenology to carry out professionally, considered this as something that has happened progressively, occurring, stage by stage, to the whole Western tradition, and, as each stage matures, having been taken explicitly possession of by the philosophy of each era. The transcendental intentional existence of men is always for Hegel first and foremost a complex interweaving of practical relationships, out of which grows the particular era's philosophical contemplation of what is implied in them. Thus "skepticism" is never more than a moment, albeit one that recurs in some form every time a false withdrawal from reality has to be combated. But, as Husserl himself knew, at least when he was old, the methodic doubt is never something so thoroughly in the hands of the philosophical expert that he need only wave the magic wand of the "reduction" to enjoy an absolute point of view free of all practical engagement and thus just contemplate *what is*. Hegel never falls into the trap of "presuppositionless philosophy." If we take Hegel's talk of *absolute Wissen* too literally we falsify his own best insights. We make him look too much like the Husserl of *Ideen I*, when in fact, overall, he is closer to the Husserl of *Krisis*. On the role of "skepticism" and "doubt" in the *Phenomenology* see the "Einleitung," pp. 67–68 (Baillie trans., pp. 135–137).
48. *Phenomenology*, "Einleitung."
49. *Wissenschaft der Logik*, ed. Lasson, I, p. 30.
50. *Enzyklopädie*, ed. Nicolin and Pöggler (Hamburg: Meiner Verlag, 1959), para. 25, Anmerkung.
51. Ibid., pp. 311–413.
52. First sketched out in the *Phenomenology of the Spirit*, Parts VII and VIII.
53. I would offer everything that has been said in this chapter as evidence to refute the claim of Eugen Fink, "Hegel's 'Phenomenology of the Spirit' has nothing to do with the term 'phenomenology' as it is used today." E. Fink, *Sein, Wahrheit, Welt* (The Hague: Nijhoff, 1958), p. 47. Herbert Spiegelberg, in *The Phenomenological Movement* (The Hague: Nijhoff, 1960), I, pp. 12–15, shows that Hegel exercised no direct influence on Husserl, which is certainly true, but then goes on to examine critically the French phenomenologists' tendency to consider Hegel's phenomenology a forerunner of their own. I would claim, however, that it is—in this sense: The same way of looking at things, that of the transcendental viewpoint, is operative in Hegel, Husserl, Heidegger, Sartre, Merleau-Ponty, et. al. Spiegelberg rejects the idea that Hegel's *Phenomenology* should be considered "phenomenological" in the post-Husserlian sense for the following reasons: (1) It is "not based on a specific method, but constituted merely a morphology of consciousness discovered without the application of a new

phenomenological method." *Respondeo dicendum quod*: Because Hegel did not spend most of his life (or any of it, for that matter) discoursing on the method one *ought* to apply, but simply went ahead and applied it, does not make the method any less methodical or any less new. That Hegel did indeed have a method to which he was faithful throughout the *Phenomenology* has been amply shown, I believe, in the present study. (1a) "There is not mention of any suspension of belief after the manner of Husserl's 'reduction.'" *Respondeo*: See our note 47 above. (2) "There is no explicit reference to anything like an intuitive method, even though Hegel wants his phenomenology to start from concrete experience. But there is considerable emphasis on the 'effort' of the 'concept' as opposed to the Romantic 'intellectual intuition' of Schelling." *Respondeo*: Once again, the question is Hegel's method, not what he says or does not say about it. We might say there is "intuition" in Hegel, but that it is a progressive intuition. (3) "There is no particular interest in insight into essential structures over and above what is implied in the use of the general dialectical method. Besides, it is exactly this dialectical method with its dubious claim to logical self-evidence that is phenomenologically questionable." *Respondeo*: The whole *Phenomenology* is devoted to disengaging a long suite of interdependent "essential structures," understanding this term in precisely the fundamental sense bestowed on it by Husserl in *Ideen I*. No one would claim that Hegel has made the evidence clear for every single transition from one moment of the dialectic to the other, just as no one can claim that any phenomenologist has ever displayed evidence perfectly adequate to render convincing every single descriptive claim he has ever made. But given that Spiegelberg never tells us what he thinks the "dialectical method" is, it is hard to know what he finds "dubious" about it. If our claims made in this chapter are correct concerning the aims and methods of the *Phenomenology*, then it is clear that the "dialectic" expresses what Husserl will term the *noesis-noema* structure of intentionality in a particularly dynamic and rich fashion.

54. Karl Marx, b. Trier, 1818; d. London, 1883. Son of a solid bourgeois lawyer, who converted to Protestantism while Karl was still a boy, Marx studied law, but above all philosophy and history, first in Bonn, then in Berlin. His dissertation in 1841, presented in Jena, was on the materialism of Epicurus. He returned to Bonn hoping for a university chair, but as he was already known as a member of the "Hegelian Left," the Prussian politicians, who reigned then in the Rhineland, would not have him, and indeed shortly thereafter denied Bruno Bauer, another of the group of young progressives, the right to teach. Marx was greatly influenced in Bonn by Ludwig Feuerbach's attacks on Christianity as man's creation of God as an escape from the hard realities of this world.

In 1842 Marx became editor-in-chief of a progressive newspaper founded in Cologne, *Rheinische Zeitung*. With the suppression of the newspaper in 1843, Marx, recently and very happily married, went into exile in Paris, where, with Arnold Ruge (1802–1880, "left Hegelian," later Bismarkian), he founded the *Deutsch-Französische Jahrbuch*, which came out only once. Eighteen forty-four was an important year: Marx wrote a series of extensive philosophical-economic fragments which reveal the origins of his thought in Hegel, but at the same time already bear the outlines of his mature position. It was the year too in which his close co-operation and friendship with Friedrich Engels began. In 1845, under Prussian pressure, Marx left Paris, tried settling in Brussels, but finally found that he could operate freely only from London. There, in absolute poverty, supported, beyond a pittance earned writing articles for the New York *Herald*, by regular help from Engels, who meantime had moved also to England and had begun working in the English branch of his family's textile business in order to help support Marx's work, in which he believed unflaggingly. In 1848, the two wrote together the outline of their political position, *The Communist Manifesto*. Marx, aware that he lacked the economic background necessary to support his vaster vision scientifically, had begun equipping himself from the early 1840s, and continued passionately for the next two decades, revolutionizing the economic science of his time. The fruits of these efforts appeared first in *Toward a Critique of Political Economy* (1859), and above all, *Capital*, the first volume of which appeared in 1867, the last two volumes being finished after Marx's death by Engels, working from almost finished drafts. Marx's extensive short essays and newspaper writings are grouped in the *Collected Works*. Most of this material has been translated into English and is available through the Four Continents Bookstore, a Communist outlet, in New York. A German edition, *Karl Marx, Friedrich Engels Werke*, to consist eventually of thirty-six volumes, is being issued in East Berlin (Dietz Verlag). Approximately twenty-two volumes have already appeared. The East German Communists have issued through the same channel the works of Lenin, in forty volumes. Both editions are based on the Russian edition issued earlier by the Institute for Marxism-Leninism of the U.S.S.R. in Moscow. The official doctrine of the Communist Party of the U.S.S.R. is contained in the *Lehrbücher* (see note below). A classical biography by a Marxist is Franz Mehring's *Karl Marx* (East Berlin: Dietz Verlag, 1960), originally written in 1917. Another biography is that of Isaiah Berlin, *Karl Marx, His Life and Environment* (2nd ed.; London, New York: Oxford University Press, 1956). On the relationship between Marx and Hegel, see Robert Tucker, *Philosophy and Myth in Karl Marx* (London: Cambridge University Press, 1961), Robert Heiss, *Die Grossen Dialektiker* (Cologne: Kiepenheurer u. Witsch, 1962), and by the same author, *Wesen und Formen der Dialektik* (Cologne: Kiepenheurer u. Witsch, 1959). Especially helpful for understanding the relations between Marx and the other "Hegelians" is Sidney Hook's *From Hegel to Marx* (Ann Arbor: University of Michigan Press, 1961). Herbert Marcuse's *Reason and Revolution* (New York: Beacon, 1960) and his recent *Soviet Marxism* are valuable.

55. That Marx took far more from Hegel than just the dialectic—the only debt he was wont to acknowledge (as for instance in the *Nachwort* of the second edition of *Das Kapital*, Bd. I, Ausgabe Kautsky [Kröner], 1929, p. 11) is an opinion of Robert Heiss to which we fully subscribe. "Marx took over from Hegel not just the dialectical method, but far more Hegel's description of bourgeois society, Hegel's sketch of the alienated world; in short he took over the dark description of the world which is always in Hegel's work cropping up in the background." R. Heiss, *Die Dialektik bei Hegel und Marx* (Bremen: Angelsachsen Verlag, 1961), p. 13.

56. "Not consciousness conditioning life but life consciousness," K. Marx, *Zur Kritik der politischen Ökonomie*, ed. Kautsky, 1930, p. lv.

57. W. I. Lenin, *Ausgewählte Werke* (E. Berlin: Dietz Verlag, 1961), I, p. 32.
58. An English translation of all but one of these manuscripts, with an introduction by Erich Fromm, is available. Cf. Erich Fromm, *Marx's Concept of Man* (New York: Ungar, 1961). These very revealing early fragments came to the attention of scholars only in the early 1930s. The first reaction to them was a tendency co think that the twenty-five-year-old Marx was still too strongly under the influence of Hegel, but that the fifty-five-year-old Marx, writing *Das Kapital*, had long since found his independent way. But this position was corrected thanks to a deeper penetration into the common underlying presuppositions of both Hegel and Marx by such historians as Koyré, Hyppolite, and Heiss among others (see note 54, above). Recently, this ground has been patiently and reliably worked over in the book by Robert Tucker.
59. "*Kritik der Hegelschen Dialektik und Philosophie Ueberhaiipt*," an 1844 fragment published with *Die Heilige Familie und andere philosophische Friihschriften* (East Berlin: Dietz Verlag, 1953), p. 85.
60. Ibid., p. 80.
61. *Osnovy Marksistskoj filosofii* (Moscow, 1958). All our references are to the German translation: *Grundlagen der Marxistischen Philosophie* (East Berlin: Dietz Verlag, 1960); *Osnovy Marksizma-Leninizma* (Moscow, 1959), German: *Grundlagen des Marxismus-Leninismus* (East Berlin: Dietz Verlag, 1960).
62. *Principles of Marxist Philosophy*, p. 169.
63. *Materialism and Empiriocriticism*, p. 80.
64. *Principles*, p. 172; Lenin, too, says as much, *Materialism*, etc., p. 257.
65. *Principles of Marxism-Leninism*, p. 113.
66. Engels' letter to Bloch, 21 September 1890, in Marx-Engels, *Ausgewählte Schriften*, Bd. 2, p. 458f.
67. I. P. Pavlov, *Polnoe sobranie sočinenij* (Collected Works), 2nd ed., Vol. III/2, p. 336.
68. *Principles of Marxist Philosophy*, p. 202.
69. *Principles of Marxist Philosophy*, pp. 668–690.
70. F. Engels, *Anti-Dühring* (Moscow, 1946), p. 351.
71. It accounts for the "intellectualism" in St. Thomas' theory of knowledge, so strongly underscored by many Neo-Thomists, e.g., Pierre Rousselot, *L'Intellectualisme de St. Thomas* (Paris: J. Vrin, 1913), J. B. Lotz, *Das Sein und das Urteil* (Pullach-bei-München: Berchonans-Kolbge-Verlag, 1957), and Karl Rahner, *Geist in Welt* (Munich: Kosel Verlag, 1938).
72. K. Marx, "Zur Kritik der Hegelschen Rechtsphilosophie," p. 27.
73. On the first origins and the positivist heritage of sociology see our chapter on A. Comte. For remarks on the later developments of sociology see also the chapters on W. Dilthey and on M. Scheler.
74. Cf. K. Jaspers' notion of *philosophisches Glauben*, Heidegger's analysis of *verstehen*, Husserl's notion of the *doxa*, Scheler's *Wertung*; cf. also, on his point, Kierkegaard, Nietzsche, G. Marcel, p. Ricoeur. The Neo-Thomist discussions of "faith and reason," while tending in fact to establish reason's reliance on faith for guidance in what to look for, and while underscoring effectively the potential nihilism of positions restricted to *natural* faith, nevertheless could be strengthened by a more explicit phenomenological

development of the fundamental ontological position of the existent, in order to bring out yet more compellingly why a faith is *ontologically* indispensable. This whole tradition's attack on scientism's pretended presuppositionlessness, and its careful cataloguing of the articles of positive science's *credo* is one of the great permanent, and perhaps eventually, civilization-saving accomplishments of the philosophical tradition described in this section.

75. Cf. for instance the two volumes *Soviet Ideologie Heute* mentioned above in note 34.
76. For these explorations of the non-Kantian *a priori* see especially the chapters on Scheler, Hartmann, and Dufrenne. In social psychology and sociology the problem threads throughout the works of Durkheim, Mauss, Thurstone, Parsons, Levy-Strauss, among others. For a bibliography, cf. Rene König, ed. *Soziologie* (Frankfurt: Fischer, 1958).
77. Max Scheler, *Die Wissensformen und die Gesellschaft* (2nd. ed., Bern: Francke, 1900), p. 144.
78. Ibid., p. 145.
79. See the chapters on Heidegger, Sartre, and Merleau-Ponty below.
80. On the romantics see, below, the introduction to the Phenomenological Movement. On Kant's Third Critique as anti-*Aufklärung* see Gilson and Langan, *Modern Philosophy*, pp. 440–448.
81. Arthur Schopenhauer, b. Danzig, 1788; d. Frankfurt am Main, 1800. Born into easy circumstances, he was raised in Danzig and Hamburg, bur always traveled widely so as to receive a very broad education. His father's suicide in 1805 freed him from the necessity of pursuing the commercial career that had been planned for him. Pursuing philosophy instead, he heard Fichte and Schleiermacher in Berlin c. 1812, contracting from their efforts a violent disgust for academicians. In 1813, Schopenhauer declared his philosophical independence as a thinker in his Jena thesis, *On the Fourfold Root of the Principle of Sufficient Reason*, and, the next year, declared his spiritual independence from his would-be novelist mother, from whom he contracted a hatred that extended to all women and practically to all of mankind put together. Schopenhauer had the good fortune to be able to afford financially such independence; and he used it well, writing in four years *The World as Will and Presentation* (1819), the labor connected with which he relieved by spells of reading Indian philosophy. Seeing that his masterpiece failed to buck the Hegelian tides, Schopenhauer had himself appointed *Privatdozent* in Berlin, and when his lectures failed to draw away Hegel's listeners (he scheduled them at the same hour), Schopenhauer, more persuaded of the stupidity of mankind than ever, withdrew to lavish his affection on his more intelligent poodles. From 1833 until his death in 1860, Schopenhauer played the misunderstood but still worldly-wise gentleman in Frankfurt, continuing to write. The year 1836 sees *On the Will in Nature;* 1841, two prize essays (one of which actually got the prize), later grouped as *The Two Fundamental Problems of Ethics*, one reducing free will to determinism, the other grounding morality in sympathy. In 1844, he issued a second edition of *The World as Will*, adding commentaries on the original text. He ended his life's work with a collection of essays, *Parerga and Paralipomena*, on every sort of topic, some of which have become very famous. The *Sämmtliche Werke* were edited by

Deussen and Hübscher (16 vols.; Munich: Piper, 1911–1942). *On the Fourfold Root of the Principle of Sufficient Reason* and *On the Will in Nature* have been translated and presented in a single tome by Hillebrand (rev. ed.; London: Bell, 1907). *The World as Will and Idea*, trans. Haldane and Kemp (5th ed.; 3 vols.; London: Kegan Paul, Trench, Trübner, 1906); *The Basis of Morality*, trans. Bullock (London: Swann, Sonnenschein, 1903); *Selected Essays*, chosen from *Parerga and Paralipomena* and trans. Bax (London: Bell, 1891) are also available in English. A new, more critical, translation of *The World as Will and Presentation*, by E. F. S. Payne, has just appeared (2 vols.; Indian Hills, CO: Falcon's Wing Press, 1958). An inexpensive edition of selections, *The Philosophy of Schopenhauer*, is available in the Modern Library.

F. Copleston, S.J., in his *Arthur Schopenhauer, Philosopher of Pessimism* (London: Burns, Oates, 1946), provides a good summary of this philosophy as well as a Thomistic evaluation. More biographical, but still valuable philosophically, is V. J. McGill, *Schopenhauer, Pessimist and Pagan* (New York: Brentano, 1931).

82. *The World as Will and Idea*, trans. Haldane and Kemp, II, pp. 364–389.
83. Ibid., II, pp. 388ff.
84. Ibid., I, pp. 168–175, pp. 219–221.
85. Ibid., p. 402.
86. Ibid., p. 147.
87. Ibid., III, 34, p. 146.
88. Ibid., p. 149.
89. See *World as Will and Idea*, Part IV, and the essay "On the Metaphysics of the Beautiful and On Aesthetics," in *Selected Essays of Arthur Schopenhauer*, ed. Bax (London: George Bell, 1900), pp. 274–317.
90. *The World as Will and Idea*, II, 42, pp. 178ff.
91. Ibid., 51, p. 187.
92. Ibid., IV, 55, p. 230.
93. Ibid., p. 237.
94. Ibid., p. 247.
95. Ibid., IV, 67, pp. 301–304.
96. *Essays*, pp. 265–66.
97. *The World as Will and Idea*, IV, 67, p. 307.
98. Ibid., IV, 71, pp. 332–333.
99. Ibid., 70, pp. 330–332.
100. Ibid. pp. 334–335.
101. Ibid., p. 329.
102. Ibid., p. 330.
103. Ibid., p. 335.

II. The Original Existentialist Revolt

1. K. Jaspers, *Nietzsche* (Berlin: DeGruyter, 1936), p. 21.
2. Søren Kierkegaard, b. Copenhagen, 1813; d. same, 1855. Born the seventh and last

child of his businessman father, in Copenhagen, May 5, 1813, and burdened with a hunched back and uneven legs, Søren made one forget these by a lively wit and brilliant personality. His powerful, moody father looked after Søren's formation with great care. They spent hours together on walks, exchanging imaginative inventions about everybody they met on the way. On the rainy days and cold winter afternoons, the promenade would take place purely imaginatively, as father and son sat playing their games in the study. In these exchanges, and in discussions with his intimate friends, the father unleashed the full force of his Lutheran conscience on the impressionable, imaginative boy. Though his interests were as literary and philosophical as religious, Søren, starting in 1830, followed the theological course at the university. His wit and his love for good conversation and a comradely dinner seemed destined to lead him more toward the romantic, aesthetic life than toward the life of a divine haunted by his father's "sin." But after 1835, as a series of deaths left him alone in the family with only his father and one brother, Søren began to wonder whether the material prosperity which had surrounded him was not a sign of God's displeasure. When at last his father confessed that as a young man he had once blasphemed, Kierkegaard returned to serious religion, a movement culminating in a moving experience, somewhat like Pascal's night of fire, in May, 1838. Shortly after his father's death in August, Kierkegaard wrote *From the Papers of One Still Living*, satirizing the aestheticism of Hans Christian Andersen, the principle that had, up to his conversion, governed his own young life. Kierkegaard finished his theological studies, publishing in 1841 his thesis, *On the Concept of Irony with Particular Reference to Socrates*.

In October of 1841, Kierkegaard broke off his engagement to Regina Olsen whom three years before he had worked so hard to win. The motivations of religious sacrifice that led to this act will never be adequately clear. Kierkegaard felt called to cry out as a prophet for the renewal of Christianity and against the bourgeois Established Church. Regina, whom he declared he truly loved, apparently was part of the old life he was to leave behind. In the "aesthetic works," attacks on the aesthetic and ethical ways of existing, Kierkegaard secretly addressed himself to Regina, trying throughout 1843 to explain in *Either/Or, Repetition*, and *Fear and Trembling* the deep sense of his action. In 1845, he summarized his insights into the three possible levels of existence in a collection of essays, *Stages on Life's Way*. About the same time he began publishing the works containing the bulk of his attack on the Hegelian philosophy that dominated Danish theological circles, *Philosophical Fragments* and *The Concept of Dread* (both in 1844), and *Concluding Unscientific Postscript to the Philosophic Fragments* (1846). Kierkegaard entertained the notion of retiring from this effort to a small rural parish. But by then he had become so embroiled in literary controversy that such an appointment was out of the question.

Kierkegaard had already begun his direct attack on smug Christendom in 1843 with a series of *Edifying Discourses*. These contrasted with his aesthetic works in presenting his own views directly, rather than obliquely through the personage of a pseudonymous author, as he had done in most of his earlier works. The hard reality of controversy only stiffened Kierkegaard in his conviction that he was called to fight the Established Church to the bitter end. He began to present his specific views of various phases of Christian existence in *Edifying Discourses in Various Spirits* (1847), *Works of Love* (1847), *Christian Discourses* (1848), and *The Lilies of the Fields and the Birds of the Air* (1849). The last great "existential" work, *The Sickness unto Death*, appeared in 1849, as did *Two Minor Ethico-Religious Treatises*. From then until his death in 1855, Kierkegaard turned out an unceasing stream of attacks on the Established Church, rising to a pitch in a series of articles in the *Fatherland* that went into every detail of Danish ecclesiastical life. The highlights of this last period are the three books, *Training in Christianity, For Self-Examination*, and *Judge for Yourselves!* At his death, Kierkegaard, turned entirely toward the grace of God, refused communion from the Church he viewed as counterfeit.

All of the works mentioned above, plus the *Journals* Kierkegaard kept throughout his life, have been translated into English. A complete list of these translations can be found in the bibliography James Collins has published in *The Mind of Kierkegaard* (Chicago: Regnery, 1953), an excellent introductory study of Kierkegaard's philosophical thought. Walter Lowrie has published both *A Short Life of Kierkegaard* (Princeton: Princeton University Press, 1942), and a much larger work, *Kierkegaard* (New York: Oxford University Press, 1938). For a good selection of primary sources, see Robert Bretall, *A Kierkegaard Anthology* (Princeton: Princeton University Press, 1940). Other important American studies include David Swenson's *Something about Kierkegaard*, ed. Lillian Swenson (2nd rev. ed.; Minneapolis: Augsburg Publishing House, 1945); Eduard Geismar, *Lectures on the Religious Thought of Sören Kierkegaard* (Minneapolis: Augsburg Publishing House, 1937); and Reidar Thomte, *Kierkegaard's Philosophy of Religion* (Princeton: Princeton University Press, 1948). Major European studies are: Eduard Geismar, *Søren Kierkegaard: Seine Lebensentwicklung und seine Wirksamkeit als Schriftsteller*, trans. E. Krüger and Madam Geismar (Göttingen: Vandenhoeck and Ruprecht, 1929), a major study of the origins and development of Kierkegaard's thought; Emmanuel Hirsch, *Kierkegaard-Studien* (2 vols.; Gütersloh: C. Bertelsmann, 1933); Jean Wahl, *Etudes Kierkegaardiennes* (2nd ed.; Paris: J. Vrin, 1949), brilliant flashes of insight amidst considerable disorganization.

3. *Fear and Trembling*, Prob. III, trans. Lowrie (New York: Anchor Books), p. 95.
4. "Diapsalmata," *Either/Or*, trans. Swenson (Princeton: Princeton University Press, 1944), p. 26.
5. *Either/Or*, p. 29.
6. Cited by Jean Wahl, *Etudes Kierkegaardiennes*, p. 67.
7. *Fear and Trembling*, p. 47.
8. Ibid., pp. 49–52.
9. Ibid., p. 97.
10. *Sickness unto Death*, trans. Lowrie (New York: Anchor Books), p. 146.
11. Ibid., p. 147.
12. Ibid., p. 236.
13. Ibid., p. 176. Such attention has been given to Kierkegaard's three spheres of existence that commentators have often neglected to point out that the vast majority of men so fail to realize themselves that their existence achieves neither of the three definite forms and hence their life is but what Kierkegaard has termed a subhuman

existence.
14. Ibid., p. 184.
15. Ibid., p. 194.
16. Ibid., p. 201.
17. Ibid.
18. Friedrich Wilhelm Nietzsche, b. Röcken, 1844; d. Weimar, 1900. Despite a strict religious upbringing in a household dominated by women, Nietzsche had, by the time he completed his university studies, lost his faith, eroded as it was by his admiration for the Greek civilization presented to him in his philological studies, and by Schopenhauer's philosophy. Brilliant philological essays at Leipzig helped him attain in 1869 the chair in that subject in Basel, where he remained for ten years, save for a stint in the Prussian army during the war of 1871 which must have compromised his health. *Die Geburt der Tragödie aus dem Geiste der Musik* (*The Birth of Tragedy from the Spirit of Music*) was written there in 1872, while Nietzsche was under the spell of Wagner, in whom he saw hopes of a German revival of the equivalent of Greek genius. But as the bourgeois 1870s unrolled, he became more and more convinced that German culture, Wagner included—especially Wagner!—was selling its soul to bogus nonsense of a very impure sort—Prussian bureaucratism, rule of the mediocre, anti-Semitism, indeed just about all those base idols which were to be erected on the altars of the Third Reich, alas in Nietzsche's name! Anyone who reads *Human-all-too-human, The Dawn, The Gay Science*, with the whole context in mind, will see that in the originative period 1878–1882 Nietzsche has laid the foundations for a philosophy that would countenance little that Hitler stood for, even though he cannot be absolved, being a destroyer of the old order, of being an indirect progenitor. In 1879, Nietzsche resigned from the university because of ill health; his life moved on toward increasing loneliness, toward increasing madness, and toward an increasingly brilliant production. *Also sprach Zarathustra* (*Thus Spoke Zarathustra*) (1883–1885) is virtually a poem, an extraordinary succession of aphoristic chapters written in flashing language, extolling the need for man to surpass his present state. *Jenseits von Gut und Böse* (*Beyond Good and Evil*) and *Zur Geneologie der Moral* (*Toward a Genealogy of Morals*) followed in successive years, both continuing the work of *Zarathustra* but in slightly less enigmatic form. As his mental powers broke down, Nietzsche turned more to polemic, anti-Wagnerian and anti-Christian, ever more violent and more disconcerting. After his death in 1900, his sister collected, arranged and even altered many of his notes to form an enormous tome, *Willen zur Macht* (*The Will to Power*), which appears, in its distorted form, to support many of the proto-fascist views she had evolved with her fanatic husband, William Forster. Frau Forster-Nietzsche's editorship was the worst turn in the sad destiny of Nietzsche.

A critical collected work, *Nietzsches Werke und Briefe, Historisch-kritisch Gesamtausgabe* (Munich: Beck, 1933ff.), is in the process of appearing, and should replace the two defective earlier editions, the so-called *Grossoktav Ausgabe* (2nd ed.; 19 vols.; Leipzig: Kroner, 1901–1913), and the so-called *Musarion-ausgabe* (23 vols.; Munich: Musarion, 1920–1929). *The Complete Works of Friedrich Nietzsche* have been translated into English, ed. O. Levy (New York: Macmillan, 1909–1913); and a handy collection of the major works is put out by the Modern Library as a "Giant." Several excellent studies of Nietzsche exist in English: on the biographical side, H. A. Reyburn, *Nietzsche: The Story of a Human Philosopher* (London: Macmillan, 1948); concerning his thought, W. H. Wright, *What Nietzsche Taught* (New York: Hucbsch, 1915); G. A. Morgan, Jr., *What Nietzsche Means* (Cambridge: Harvard University Press, 1941); W. A. Kaufmann, *Nietzsche* (Princeton: Princeton University Press, 1950), also available in an inexpensive edition (New York: Meridian Books, 1956). Karl Jaspers' *Nietzsche: Einführung in das Verständnis seines philosophierens* (Berlin: W. de Gruyter, 1936) provides an unsystematic but often enlightening existentialist evaluation. Heidegger's brilliant essays have just been collected in two volumes, *Nietzsche* (Pfüllingen: Neske, 1960).

19. *Thus Spake Zarathustra*, in *The Philosophy of Nietzsche* (New York: Modern Library, 1954), Prologue, #2.
20. *Beyond Good and Evil*, in *The Philosophy of Nietzsche* (New York: Modern Library, 1954), III, p. 438.
21. *Beyond Good and Evil*, III, #46, p. 432.
22. *Thus Spake Zarathustra*, chap. 66, p. 291.
23. *Beyond Good and Evil*, V, #188, pp. 476–77.
24. Jansenist congregation to which Pascal's sister belonged.
25. *Beyond Good and Evil*, V, #188, pp. 476–77.
26. Ibid., #194, p. 487.
27. Ibid., #201, p. 491.
28. Ibid., V, #202, p. 492, i.e., should it be confronted with an original force, emanating from a creative individual, which suggests that the community is not *all*.
29. Ibid., V, #202, pp. 493–95.
30. Ibid., #203, pp. 495–96.
31. Ibid., VI, #211, pp. 514–15.
32. Ibid., #206, p. 502.
33. Ibid., #204, pp. 498–99.
34. Ibid., #206, p. 503.
35. Ibid., #207, p. 506.
36. Subjectivism locks the individual ego in its own self-enclosed circle, making communication impossible, so that it seems condemned to dwell alone by itself—*solus ipsum*.
37. *Beyond Good and Evil*, VI, #207, p. 504.
38. Ibid., #208, p. 508.
39. Ibid., p. 509.
40. Ibid., #209, p. 511.
41. Ibid., #210, pp. 512–14.
42. Ibid., II, #44, pp. 428–29.
43. Ibid., pp. 429–30.
44. Ibid., VI, #213, p. 518.
45. *Thus Spake Zarathustra*, chap. 22, p. 79.
46. "Here I am like a cock in a strange farmyard, at which even the hens peck: but on that

account I am not unfriendly to the hens." *Thus Spake Zarathustra*, chap. 49, p. 185.
47. Ibid., chap. 13, p. 57.
48. Ibid., chap. 73, #18, p. 330.
49. Ibid., chap. 73, #17, pp. 329–30.
50. *Nietzsches Werke*, "Grossoktav Ausgabe" ed. Kroner, I, p. 367.
51. *Thus Spake Zarathustra*, chap. 42, p. 153.
52. *Ecce Homo*, in *Werke*, XV, p. 85. The place is easily found near Sils Maria; the pyramidal rock is still there. No historical marker mars the experience.
53. Unedited fragments, 1881–1886, in *Werke*, XII, p. 371. 54. Fragments, 1883–1888, *Werke*, XIV, p. 443.
55. Fragments, *Werke*, XII, p. 52.
56. Ibid., pp. 51, 53, 57.
57. *The Will to Power*, *Werke*, XVI, p. 356.
58. Ibid., p. 396.
59. *Thus Spake Zarathustra*, chap. 57, p. 246.
60. *Fröhliche Wissenschaft*, *Werke*, V, p. 265.
61. Fragments, *Werke*, XIII, p. 74.
62. *Thus Spake Zarathustra*, chap. 79, p. 364.
63. *The Will to Power*, *Werke*, XVI, p. 398.
64. *Thus Spake Zarathustra*, chap. 42, p. 155.
65. Fragments, *Werke*, XIV, p. 271.
66. Poems, *Werke*, VIII, p. 435.
67. Zarathustra had just explained that revenge is a function of justice, which is rooted in the former belief that the past was "an unrollable stone" crushing us with its fatalistic weight.
68. *Thus Spake Zarathustra*, chap. 42, p. 155.
69. Ibid., p. 156.
70. Fragments, *Werke*, XII, p. 57.

III. Beyond Positivism and Psychologism

1. Wilhelm Dilthey, b. Biebrich, near Mainz, 1833; d. Seis, near Posen, 1911. Like Fichte, Schelling, and Hegel before him, Dilthey became interested in philosophy through theological studies. He obtained his doctorate in Berlin, 1864, and lived successively in Basel, Kiel (1868), Breslau (1871), and finally, in 1882, moved to Berlin, where he remained until his death in 1911. Dilthey's thought developed slowly but in a way consistent with his early intuitions. What was to be his great work, a *Critique of Historical Reason*, was basically in preparation from about 1880 on, and was still far from finished when he died over forty years later. Dilthey's passion for the history of the human spirit led him to write biographical works and essays that today would be classified as "history of ideas." His *Life of Schleiermacher* and his *Early Life of Hegel*, the latter a work of his last period, are outstanding examples of the first; his *Conception and Analysis of Human Nature in the 15th and 16th Centuries*, of the latter.

Many of his works are concerned with what Dilthey termed *hermeneutics*, the effort to interpret works of poetry, music, art as well as great historic acts in terms of what they reveal psychologically about the developing human spirit. The essays collected into two volumes under the title *The Spiritual World* explain and practice this kind of historico-philosophical concrete analysis. Dilthey looked upon his life's work as preparatory, as laying the groundwork for the development of a method proper to the "sciences of the spirit," those *Geisteswissenschaften* capable of dealing with man as properly human. In the influence he has had on Husserl, Scheler, and Heidegger, his estimate of his contribution has been exact—it was indeed preparatory to great things. The *Gesammelte Schriften* is being reissued (all but two of the twelve original volumes; Stuttgart: Teubner). Not included in the *Gesammelte Schriften* are such important works as *The Life of Schleiermacher, Lived Experience and Poetry* (1905), and the *Correspondence with Graf Yorck*. Dilthey's *Essence of Philosophy*, trans. Stephan and William Emery (Chapel Hill: University of North Carolina Press, 1954), and his *Philosophy of Existence*, trans. Kluback and Weinhaum (New York: Bookman Associates, 1957), are available in English. H. A. Hodges has written an introduction to his thought, *Wilhelm Dilthey* (London: Kegan Paul, Trubner, 1944), which includes some short translated selections from his writings. Also see William Kluback, *Wilhelm Dilthey's Philosophy of History* (New York: Columbia University Press, 1956); O. F. Bollnow, *Dilthey, eine Einführung in seine Philosophie* (Leipzig and Berlin: Teubner, 1936); A. Degener, *Dilthey und das Problem der Metaphysik* (Bonn and Cologne: 1933); J. Meurers, *Wilhelm Dilthey's Gedankenwelt und die Naturwissenschaft* (Berlin: Junker and Dünnhaupt, 1933).

2. On the origins of positivism consult the Chapter on A. Comte in Part II, Chapter IX, of this book.
3. Cf. "The Essence of Philosophy," in *The Spiritual World*, Part I (*Gesammelte Schriften*, Bk. V), pp. 339–416.
4. Ibid., pp. 392ff.
5. Ibid., p. 390.
6. Ibid., p. 374.
7. Ibid., pp. 332–33.
8. "The Origin and Development of the Hermeneutic" in *The Spiritual World*, GS, V, p. 331.
9. "There can be nothing in any individual foreign manifestation which does not exist also in the living individuality which perceives it. One finds the same functions and the same constitutive elements in all men, only their importance being different." Ibid., p. 334.
10. Ibid., p. 330.
11. Ibid.
12. Ibid., pp. 327–28.
13. Ibid., p. 327.
14. "Ideas for a Descriptive and Analytic Psychology" in *GS*, V, p. 144.
15. Ibid.
16. Ibid., pp. 171–72.

17. Ibid.
18. Ibid., pp. 173–74.
19. Ibid., p. 175.
20. Ibid., p. 176.
21. Ibid.
22. Ibid., pp. 177–78.
23. Preface to *The Spiritual World*.
24. A thorough history of the origin and early applications of the terms is to be found in Herbert Spiegelberg's recent and definitive study, *The Phenomenological Movement* (The Hague: Martinus Nijhoff, 1960), I, pp. 8–11.
25. Franz Brentano, *Psychologie vom empirischen Standpunkt*, I, ed. O. Kraus, Buch II, p. 126.
26. See H. Spiegelberg, "Der Begriff der Intentionalität in der Scholastik, bei Brentano und bei Husserl," in *Philosophische Hefte*, ed. Maximilian Beck, V (1936), pp. 72–91.
27. *Psychologie*, I, p. 125.
28. See J. N. Findlay, "The Influence of Meinong in Anglo-American Countries," in *Meinong Gedenkschrift* (Graz: Steirische Verlaganstalt, 1952), pp. 9–20.
29. See Walter B. Pitkin, *On My Own* (New York: Scribner's, 1944), p. 319, cited by Spiegelberg, op. cit., p. 112—*q.v.* for a fuller account of the Husserl-James relationship.
30. Alexander Pfänder, a student of Theodore Lipps, was professor in Munich all his life. Husserl considered him one of the most devoted phenomenological workers, although naturally relations cooled later, as Pfänder failed to follow Husserl all the way to the radical critique. Pfänder's major works: *Phenomenology of Wishing* (1900); *Introduction to Psychology* (1904); *Toward a Psychology of Sentiment* (*Gesinnung*) (1913; 1916).
31. Both series are published by Nijhoff in The Hague.
32. Edmund Husserl, b. Prossnitz, 1859; d. Freiburg, 1938. His early formation in mathematics and, under Franz Brentano and Carl Stumpf, in psychology, left him haunted with the truly scientific character of mathematics and the lack of certainty and ultimacy of psychology. A central notion of Brentano also struck him very profoundly, the notion of intentionality—our knowledge is always knowledge *of* something, which Husserl takes to mean that the key to an explanation of knowledge lies in the constitution of the objectivity of the object. In 1913 Husserl's *Ideas for a Phenomenology* (critical ed. by W. Biemel; The Hague: Nijhoff, 1950) took the first overt steps in the quest for the foundations of objectivity in the constitutive activity of the transcendental ego. This work had been preceded by brilliant logical analysis, *Logische Untersuchungen* (2nd ed.; Halle, 1913) and a still earlier work on the nature of arithmetic in the course of which the need for a fundamental analysis of consciousness of a new sort became clear to Husserl. The implications for a "transcendental idealism" strongly suggested there are finally worked out in two works of 1927, *The Cartesian Meditations* (critical ed. by Strasser; The Hague: Nijhoff, 1950), and *Formal and Transcendental Logic* (Halle: Niemayer, 1930). The publication of these works marked the summit of Husserl's career at Freiburg-im-Breisgau, his brilliant disciple Heidegger succeeding him shortly afterward. In retirement Husserl completed one last major work, *Crisis*

of *European Sciences and Phenomenology* (ed. W. Biemel; The Hague: Nijhoff, 1954), which stresses the necessary critical contribution that phenomenology can make and thus become a foundation to the whole scientific edifice, and authorized the editing of *Experience and Judgment* (Prague: Akademia Verlag, 1939). Husserl left behind him in his papers, which Father Van Breda brought to Louvain to protect, many manuscripts, some very elaborated which he had never considered ready for publication. Posthumously these important works are gradually being published, notably the second and third parts of the *Ideas for a Phenomenology* and *The Idea of Phenomenology* (The Hague: Nijhoff, 1950). Critical editions of all the major works are also planned by the Husserl Archives. *Ideas for a Phenomenology* (*Ideen I*) has been translated into English by W. R. Boyce-Gibson (New York: Macmillan, 1931). *Cartesian Meditations*, trans. D. Cairns (The Hague: Nijhoff, 1900). Marvin Farber's *The Foundations of Phenomenology* (Cambridge: Harvard University Press, 1943) paraphrases part of the *Logische Untersuchungen*. *Vorlesungen zur Phänomenologie des inneren Zeitbewusstseins*, edited by Heidegger (1928), was translated by J. S. Churchill as *The Phenomenology of Internal Time Consciousness* (Bloomington: Ind. U. Press, 1904). The best general introduction to Husserl in English is Quentin Lauer's *The Triumph of Subjectivity: An Introduction to Transcendental Phenomenology* (New York: Fordham University Press, 1958), although Father Lauer tends to push Husserl into a more radical subjectivism than Husserl seems to intend. Also in English: E. Welch, *The Philosophy of Edmund Husserl* (New York: Columbia University Press, 1941). Suzanne Bachelard's *La Logique de Husserl* (Paris: Presses Universitaires de France, 1957) emphasizes more Husserl's faithfulness to certain empiricist themes. See also A. de Waelhens, *Phénoménologie et vérité* (Paris: Presses Universitaires de France, 1953), which traces the development from Husserl to Heidegger, and the important article, bearing Husserl's *imprimatur*, by Eugen Fink, "Die phänomenologische Philosophie Edmund Husserls in der gegenwärtigen Kritik," *Kantstudien*, XXXVIII (1933), pp. 319–83.

33. *Ideen*, Part I (1913).
34. *Formale und Transzendentale Logik*, in *Jahrbuch für Philosophie und phänomenologische Forschung*, Vol. X, p. 30.
35. *Krisis der europäischen Wissenschaften*, pp. 13–14.
36. Husserl means by "intention" more than is commonly included in the term "knowledge act." Sentiments, emotions, volitions can also "intend an object," for all of them "tend toward the thing."
37. *Formale und Transzendentale Logik*, p. 26.
38. Paragraphs 91–101.
39. Paragraphs 103ff.
40. Meaning mode of belief—for Husserl borrows Hume's term to express the act of consciousness posing the being of the object.
41. *Ideen I*, p. 243.
42. *Formale tend Transzendentale Logik*, pp. 30–31.
43. Ibid., p. 240.
44. Ibid., p. 245.
45. Ibid., p. 246.

46. Ibid.
47. Ibid.
48. From *solus ipsum*, the problem of being locked up within oneself once one retires reflectively to find within consciousness an ultimate criterion for truth.
49. *Cartesian Meditations*, trans. Peiffer and Levinas (Paris: Vrin, 1953), p. 75.
50. Ibid., pp. 77–78.
51. Ibid., p. 79.
52. Ibid., p. 79.
53. Ibid., p. 80.
54. Ibid., p. 81.
55. Ibid., pp. 81–82.
56. Ibid., p. 82.
57. Ibid., p. 88.
58. Ibid., p. 96.
59. Ibid., p. 92.
60. Ibid., p. 97.
61. Ibid., p. 118.
62. Despite his doctrine that time is the fundamental form of consciousness, Husserl, who after all had never been trained formally in the history of philosophy, was never very much interested in the historical aspect of Being's coming to be. To illustrate the extent to which the lack of historical consciousness was inveterate to Husserl's personality, Heidegger recounts how, when he was Husserl's assistant, he once inquired of the professor, as he returned from an important lecture, what he had said. When Husserl had finished summarizing his conference Heidegger asked him why he had said nothing about the historical implications of the discoveries he had been describing. "Oh, history, yes..." replied Husserl absent-mindedly, "I did forget all about that!"
63. Max Scheler, b. Munich, 1874; d. Frankfurt-am-Main, 1928. He studied sciences and philosophy first at Munich, then in Berlin, where he was influenced by Dilthey, Stumpf, and G. Simmel; then Jena, where he was influenced by the anti-Kantian, Bucken, and where also he began to teach in 1901. It was in that year that he encountered Husserl at a reunion sponsored by the *Kantstndien*. In 1907, he moved to Munich, becoming one of the centers of the Munich circle of phenomenologists and began work on his *Formalismus in der Ethik*. From 1910 to 1919 he was withdrawn from teaching, for personal reasons; fecund years—the *Formalismus* is completed, and the essays, *Vom Umsturz der Werte* (1915); the work on *Sympathie* (1918). He lived during this period in Göttingen (where he saw Husserl often) and in Berlin. Scheler had been converted to Catholicism at the age of 15, then tended to drift away. But the war brought about a second conversion in 1916. From then on, until about 1922, his works bear a strong imprint from that conversion, especially *On the Eternal in Man* (*Vom Ewigen im Menschen*) (1921). In 1919 he became professor in Cologne and Director of the Institute of Sociology. Never, by his own admission, a strictly believing Catholic, Scheler left the church after some marriage troubles; this crowned a long, gradual drifting away. In the works published after 1925, a pantheism manifests influences of Spinoza, Schelling, Schopenhauer, and Edward von Hart-mann; without

abandoning the theory of the irreducibility of Spirit, these works accord nevertheless a greater place to "the inferior and nonspiritual powers of being"; they are *The Forms of Knowledge and Society* (*Die Wissensformen und die Gesellschaft*) (1926) and *The Position of Man in the Cosmos* (*Die Stellung des Menschett im Kosmos*) (1928). A posthumous collection of five essays from the last period was published in 1929 as *Philosophical Worldview* (*Philosophische Weltanschauung*). The Works of Scheler (*Gesammelte Werke*), ed. Maria Scheler, are being brought out by Francke in Bern; starting in 1954, six volumes have already appeared. English translations: Scheler's work on *Sympathie* has been translated under the title *The Nature of Sympathy* by Peter Heath (London: Routledge and Kegan Paul, 1954); and a translation of *The Position of Man in the Universe* is to be brought out soon by the Beacon Press. The posthumous essays, *Philosophische W eltanschauung* have been translated by O. A. Haac under the title *Philosophical Perspectives* (Boston: Beacon Press, 1958). See H. Spiegelberg, *The Phenomenological Movement*, I, pp. 209–270 for a Scheler bibliography. Manfred Frings, *Max Scheler* (Pittsburgh: Duquesne University Press, 1965) is the first and only full-length study in English. A recent two volume French study provides an excellent introduction to his thought: Maurice Dupuy, *La Philosophie de Max Scheler* (Paris: Presses Universitaires de France, 1959); supplemented by a study of his philosophy of religion by the same author, *La Philosophie de la religion chez Max Scheler* (same publisher and date).

64. Scheler died just before the *Cartesian Meditations* were written; the criticism, however, is very much in the spirit of remarks he did make; we may make Paul Ricoeur directly responsible for it. Cf. "Kant et Husserl," *Kantstudien*, XLVI (1954), pp. 53ff.
65. Paul Ricoeur, "Sur la Phénoménologie," *Esprit*, XXI (1953), p. 838.
66. Title of the work reproduced in the *Gesammelte Werke*, Band 8.
67. In *Gesammelte Werke*, Band 8.
68. Op. cit., p. 204.
69. Scheler has been criticized for the impetuosity and the unevenness with which his descriptions are carried out. It is difficult to find in our time a corpus richer in insights and in descriptive fragments. Nor is the whole of a typical Scheler work lacking in significant architectonic symmetry. But rarely are his descriptions roundly developed; and rare is the work devoid of provocative assertions of speculations which are neither self-evident nor adequately supported by descriptive evidence proffered by Scheler. They are not for all that false—just unproved. Given the penetration and scope of Scheler's vision, many of these suggestions deserve to be taken up as hypotheses for which adequate descriptive evidence ought to be proffered.
70. *Die Stellung des Menschett im Kosmos* (Bern: Francke, 1962), p. 37.
71. This difficult theme, weaving through Scheler's writings, has been helpfully systematized and analyzed by Maurice Dupuy, *La Philosophie de la religion chez Max Scheler*. See Note 63 above.
72. Ibid., p. 258.
73. Ibid., p. 273.
74. "*Erkenntnis und Arbeit*," p. 273.
75. *Formalismus in der Ethik*, pp. 68–69.

76. Ibid., p. 72.
77. Ibid., pp. 46–47.
78. Ibid., p. 85.
79. Ibid., p. 59.
80. Ibid., p. 86.
81. Ibid., p. 64.
82. Ibid., pp. 104–108.
83. Ibid., p. 262.
84. Ibid., p. 267.
85. Ibid., p. 524 and Introduction, p. xii.
86. *Wesen und Formen der Sympathie*, p. 241.
87. *Das Ressentiment im Aufbau der Moralen*, in *Ges. Werke*, Band 3, pp. 35ff.
88. Nicolai Hartmann, b. Riga, 1882; d. Göttingen, 1950. He was a product of the Marburg School of Kantianism. However, his first major independent work, *Principles for a Metaphysics of Knowledge* (Berlin and Leipzig: DeGruyter, 1921) (2nd enl. ed.; Berlin: DeGruyter, 1925), showed that he intended to do more than rework traditional critical themes. For epistemology requires an ontology in whose broad compass it should occupy its place. The basic lines of that ontology are anticipated in the earlier work, and are developed fully in three subsequent studies, *On the Founding of Ontology* (Berlin: DeGruyter, 1935), *Possibility and Reality* (Berlin: DeGruyter, 1938) and *The Construction of the Real World* (Berlin: DeGruyter, 1930). This basic ontological effort has been supplemented by an immense work of "special categorial analyses," consisting of the *Ethics* (Berlin: DeGruyter, 1933), *The Problem of Spiritual Being* (Same, 1932), and a *Philosophy of Nature* (Same, 1949). To this list should be added a superb work of history in which we can trace Hartmann's personal efforts to go beyond criticism to ontology, namely the two volume study of *The Philosophy of German Idealist)!* (Vol. I: Fichte, Schelling and the Romantics [Berlin: DeGruyter, 1923]; and Vol. II: Hegel [Berlin: DeGruyter, 1929]). In addition to these major works, Hartmann wrote a great number of articles, some containing important statements of his thought, for example, "This Side of Idealism and Realism," in *Kantstudien*, Vol. XXIX; and "New Ways of Ontology," this latter being the length of a small book, and available in English, trans. Kuhn (Chicago: Roguery, 1953). The *Ethics* has also been trans. Stanley Coit (London: Allen and Unwin, 1932). Heinz Heimsoeth has edited a group of essays about Hartmann's thought under the title *Nicolai Hartmann; der Denker und sein Werk* (Gottingen: Vandenhoeck and Ruprecht, 1952).
89. *Principles of a Metaphysics of Knowledge* (1st ed.; Berlin: DeGruyter, 1921), pp. 48ff.
90. *Aufbau der realen Welt* (Berlin: DeGruyter, 1940), p. 210.
91. Ibid.
92. *Metaphysics of Knowledge*, pp. 51f.
93. Ibid., 2nd enl. ed., chap. 74.
94. *Aufbau der realen Welt*, chap. 73.
95. Ibid., pp. 52ff.
96. See Gilson and Langan, *Modern Philosophy*, pp. 415–416.
97. *Metaphysics of Knowledge*, 1st ed., pp. 54ff.

98. Ibid., p. 340.
99. Ibid., 2nd enl. ed., chap. 65.
100. Ibid.
101. Ibid.
102. Ibid., 1st ed., pp. 57ff.
103. *New Ways of Ontology*, trans. Reinhardt C. Kuhn (Chicago: Regnery, 1953), p. 13.
104. Ibid., pp. 13-14.
105. See the entire introduction to *Zur Grundlegung der Ontologie*, pp. 1-38, for an elaborate explanation of how ontology is indispensable to every basic department of thought.
106. *New Ways of Ontology*, pp 13-14.
107. Ibid., pp. 15-16.
108. Ibid., p. 19.
109. *Der Aufbau der realen Welt*, pp. 589-590. While paying lip-service to the phenomenologists for having pleaded for restoration of full description of what is given, Hartmann pays not the slightest attention to their criticisms of the whole status of natural science. Where he does make oblique reference to the phenomenologists' "hostility to science" he fails to account for it altogether (e.g., *Aufbau*, 590 and 590, n. 1). Max Scheler's penetrating criticism, *Erkenntnis und Arbeit*, left no impression. Moreover, when Hartmann speaks of "the phenomenologists" what he says usually will apply somewhat to aspects of the earlier Husserl and not at all to Scheler, to whose thought Hartmann obviously is singularly indebted.
110. Gilson and Langan, *Modern Philosophy*, pp. 199; 232f.
111. *Aufbau*, p. 392; also chaps. 12b and c.
112. *Aufbau*, p. 410.
113. *New Ways of Ontology*, p. 21.
114. Ibid., pp. 21-22.
115. Ibid., pp. 40-41.
116. *The Foundations of Ontology, Possibility and Reality* and *The Philosophy of Nature* also deal with the ontologic categories.
117. *New Ways of Ontology*, p. 52.
118. *Principles of a Metaphysics of Knowledge*, 2nd ed., chap. 62.
119. Ibid.
120. Ibid.
121. Ibid.
122. Ibid.
123. *Aufbau der realen Welt*, all of Part III, esp. sec. III, chaps. 50-54.
124. *Problem des geistigen Seins* (3rd ed.; Berlin: DeGruyter, 1960), pp. 158-161.
125. *Principles of a Metaphysics of Knowledge*, 2nd ed.; chap. 62.
126. Ibid.
127. *Einführung in die Philosophie* (Hannover: Hanckel, 1949), p. 167, diagram.
128. Ibid., p. 156.
129. *Principles of a Metaphysics of Knowledge*, 2nd ed., chap. 62.
130. Ibid.

IV. Two German Existentialists

1. Martin Heidegger, b. Messkirch, 1899. During his university days at Freiburg, Heidegger was already attracted by Husserl, whom he was to succeed in 1928 in the chair of philosophy at that university. It was while still a professor at Marburg, where he was named in 1923, that Heidegger wrote his fundamental work, *Sein und Zeit* (first published, 1927; 7th ed., Tübingen: Niemayer, 1953), which strikes out from phenomenology in an existentialist direction little approved of by Husserl. Heidegger also started his famous essay on Kant, *Kant und das Problem der Metaphysik* (Bonn: Verlag Cohen, 1929), while at Marburg, a great center of Kantian studies; it was published just after *Sein und Zeit*. The basic work did not complete the founding of the ontology promised in its introduction; but a series of pithy, profound, and enigmatic essays published since advance in that direction, notably: *On the Essence of Fundament* (Halle: Niemayer, 1929) and *Was ist Metaphysik?* (Bonn: Verlag Cohen, 1930), both written by 1930, and *On the Essence of Truth*, on which Heidegger worked progressively until its publication during the war (2nd ed.; Frankfurt: Klostermann, 1949). The line of this inquiry has led him to the conviction of the importance for Being of the poet's conceiving the Word in which Being is pronounced; this has led him to meditate on Hölderlin's poetry, seeking clues to the nature of originative thinking. *Hölderlin und das Wesen der Dichtung* (Munich: Albert Langen, 1937) incorporates much of the result of this endeavor, along with *Erläuterungen zu Hölderlins Dichtung* (Frankfurt: Klostermann, 1944) and essays in the two collections published postwar as *Holzwege* (Frankfurt: Klostermann, 1956) and *Vorträge tend Aufsätze* (Pfüllingen: Neske, 1954). Also included in these collections are important essays that carry out most of the program of "destruction of the history of ontology," i.e., an analysis of the history of philosophy as a revelation and dissimulation of Being, which was also announced in the Introduction to *Sein und Zeit* as part of the task of refounding philosophy. Six essays on language (including the charming "Dialogue with a Japanese") appeared recently as *Unterwegs zur Sprache* (Pfüllingen: Neske, 1959). The theme of "On the Essence of Fundament" is the subject of another recent 200-page book, *Der Satz vom Grund* (same editor and year). Heidegger's renowned courses have been edited in two volumes on *Nietzsche* (same editor, 1960). Heidegger's condensed style and original vocabulary make translation difficult. However, a translation of *Sein und Zeit* has at last been published, *Being and Time*, trans. McQuarrie and Robinson (New York: Harper and Row, 1962). A good translation of *Kant and the Problem of Metaphysics* (Bloomington: Indiana University Press, 1962) provides a good place to start reading Heidegger. *What Is Metaphysics?* (body of the essay only), *On the Essence of Truth*, and an *Essay on Hölderlin* are available in poor translation under the title, M. Heidegger, Existence and Being, ed., Werner Brock (Chicago: Regnery, 1949), together with a summary of main themes in *Sein und Zeit*. The important introduction to the fifth edition of *Was ist Metaphysik?* is translated by Walter Kaufmann in his book of readings, *Existentialism from Dostoevsky to Sartre* (New York: Meridian Books, 1956). Recently, *Introduction to Metaphysics* (New Haven: Yale University Press, 1959), *Question of Being* (New York: Twayne, 1959), *What Is Philosophy?* (New York: Twayne,

1958), and *Identität und Differenz* (*Essays in Metaphysics*) (New York: Philosophical Library, 1960) have also been translated. Two critical summaries of Heidegger's work are available in English, Thomas Langan, *The Meaning of Heidegger* (New York: Columbia University Press; and London: Routledge and Kegan Paul, 1959), and V. Vycinas, *Earth and Gods* (The Hague: Nijhoff, 1961); also a shorter summary by Marjorie Grene, *Martin Heidegger* (New York: Hillary House, 1957). A. DeWaelhens, *La philosophie de Martin Heidegger* (Louvain: Nauwelaerts, 1942), provides an excellent summary and critique of *Sein und Zeit*, and Werner Marx's *Heidegger und die Tradition* (Stuttgart: Kohlhammer, 1961), compares Heidegger's and Aristotle's ontologies. The latest account of Heidegger is by William J. Richardson, *Heidegger, Through Phenomenology to Thought*, Preface by Martin Heidegger (The Hague: Nijhoff, 1963).
2. *Sein und Zeit*, 7th ed., p. 34.
3. Ibid., pp. 180ff.
4. Ibid., pp. 2–3.
5. Ibid., pp. 372ff.
6. *Vorträge tend Aufsätze*, pp. 101ff.
7. "Die Frage Nach der Technik," in *Vorträge und Aufsätze*, pp. 13ff.
8. *Vorträge und Atifsätze*, pp. 71ff.
9. *Was ist Metaphysik?*, pp. 41ff.
10. *Sein und Zeit*, pp. 184ff.
11. *Was ist Metaphysik?*, 5th ed., *Nachwort*, pp. 48–49.
12. *Holzwege*, pp. 248ff.
13. *Vom Wesen der Wahrheit*, 2nd ed., pp. 14ff.
14. Ibid., pp. 23–24.
15. *Vorträge und Aufsätze*, 1st ed., pp. 145ff.
16. "Das Ding," in *Vorträge und Aufsätze*, pp. 163–186.
17. Cf. the letter to Jean Beaufret on Humanism.
18. *Was ist Metaphysik?*, 5th ed., p. 47.
19. *Holzwege* (Title page), "Forest people know the trails; they know what it means to be on the wrong trail."
20. Karl Jaspers, b. Oldenburg, 1883. Jaspers began his scientific career in pathology and psychology. His first major work, *General Psychopathology* (1913), grew out of his experience in psychiatry at the Heidelberg hospital. Already in his next published work, *The Psychology of Worldviews* (1922), an important shift of interest toward philosophical problems is evident. Soon Jaspers chose to change from the chair in psychology at Heidelberg to the chair in philosophy. In 1933, the extent and the vigor of his philosophy was revealed with the publication of the three-volume *Philosophie*. This expression of his own philosophy was preceded and succeeded by a series of historical studies, revealing Jaspers' concern for the history of philosophy. Jaspers published two works on Max Weber, one in 1921, the other in 1932, a far-sighted analysis of the *Spiritual Situation of the Times* (1931), and works on Nietzsche (1936 and 1946), Descartes (1937), and recently, Schelling, and most recently the first part of a unified history of philosophy, devoted to *The Great Philosophers*. This continued preoccupation with the history of philosophy stems from Jaspers' conviction that philosophizing

is not a purely private endeavor. Rather *Existenzphilosophie* is an expression, in our time, of the *philosophia perennis*. Despite an ever-tightening control from the Nazis, Jaspers was able during the time of the Third Reich to explore in two short series of lectures some of the problems that grew out of *Philosophie*, *Reason and Existenz* (1935) emphasized the bipolar relationship of those two principles in a way intended to stave off criticisms of "*Existenzphilosophie*" as irrational. The other lectures, entitled simply *Existenzphilosophie*, provided a succinct and somewhat popularized presentation of his basic positions. Since the War, Jaspers, who now occupies the chair in philosophy at Basel, has been working on a monumental four-volume *Philosophical Logic*, which will present the sum total of a life's effort, viewed from the standpoint of how every aspect of Being relates to Reason. The first volume, *Von der Wahrheit* (On Truth), over one thousand pages in length, appeared in 1947. Concurrently Jaspers has engaged in discussions of religious versus philosophical faith, *Der philosophische Glaube* (translated as *The Perennial Scope of Philosophy*, first appeared in 1947), and in discussions of problems confronting a rebuilding of Germany, *Vom europäischen Geist* (*The European Spirit*, 1947). In 1950, he published another lecture series offering a simplified introduction to his thought, *The Way to Wisdom*. English translations have been published of these works: *Man in the Modern Age*, translation of *Die geistige Situation der Zeit*, by E. Paul (New York: Anchor Books, 1957); *Reason and Existenz*, trans. William Earle (New York: Noonday Press, 1957); *The Perennial Scope of Philosophy*, translation of *Der philosophische Glaube*, by R. Manheim (New York: Philosophical Library, 1949); *The Way to Wisdom*, translation of *Einführung in die Philosophie*, by R. Manheim (New Haven: Yale University Press, 1951); *The Future of Mankind*, by E. B. Ashton (New Haven: Yale University Press, 1961). Introductions to Jaspers' thought in English are available in the chapter on Jaspers in James Collins' *The Existentialists* (Chicago: Henry Regnery Co., 1952), in the study of E. Allen, *The Self and Its Hazards: A Guide to the Thought of Karl Jaspers* (New York: Philosophical Library, 1951). Also recommended: M. Dufrenne and P. Ricoeur, *Karl Jaspers et la philosophie de l'existence* (Paris: Editions du Seuil, 1947), p. Ricoeur, *Gabriel Marcel et Karl Jaspers: Philosophie du mystère et philosophie du paradoxe* (Paris: Editions du Temps Present, 1947), and J. Pfeiffer, *Existenzphilosophie: Eine Einführung in Heidegger und Jaspers* (2nd ed. rev.; Hamburg: Felix Meiner, 1949).

21. *Man in the Modern Age*.
22. *Reason and Existenz*, p. 52.
23. Ibid., pp. 52–54.
24. Ibid., pp. 54–55.
25. Ibid., p. 57.
26. *Von der Wahrheit* (Munich: Piper Verlag, 1947), p. 662.
27. *Philosophie* (2nd ed.; Gottingen: Springer Verlang, 1948), pp. 342ff.
28. *Von der Wahrheit*, pp. 610–618; *Reason and Existenz*, p. 58.
29. *Reason and Existenz*, pp. 58–59; *Von der Wahrheit*, pp. 75ff.
30. *Von der Wahrheit*, p. 695.
31. *Philosophie*, pp. 467–512.
32. Ibid., p. 474.

33. *Reason and Existenz*, p. 59.
34. Ibid.
35. Ibid., p. 60.
36. Ibid.
37. Ibid., and *Von der Wahrheit*, p. 095.
38. *Von der Wahrheit*, p. 701.
39. Ibid., p. 709.
40. Ibid., pp. 683ff., 702.
41. Ibid., p. 698.
42. Ibid., p. 880.
43. Ibid., p. 881.
44. Ibid.
45. Ibid., p. 891.
46. Ibid.
47. Ibid., p. 328.
48. Ibid., p. 891.
49. Ibid., p. 967.
50. Ibid., p. 980.
51. Ibid., p. 992.
52. Ibid.
53. Ibid., p. 993.
54. Ibid., p. 994.
55. Ibid., p. 995.
56. Ibid., p. 996.
57. Ibid., p. 997.
58. Ibid., p. 996.
59. Ibid., p. 1001.
60. Ibid., p. 1003.
61. *Philosophie*, p. 786.
62. Ibid., p. 833.
63. James Collins, in the *The Existentialists*, pp. 99–110, discusses in detail Jaspers' criticism of metaphysics and offers a Thomistic criticism of the criticism. Compare our remarks in the Epilogue to the present history.
64. *Philosophie*, 2nd ed., p. 848.
65. Ibid., p. 850.
66. Ibid., p. 839.
67. See Jaspers, *Van Gogh and Strindberg: Philosophie*, pp. 840ff.; *Von der Wahrheit*, p. 917, on the role of art as *Chiffer*.
68. *Philosophie*, p. 842.
69. *Von der Wahrheit*, p. 1053.
70. Ibid.
71. Ibid., p. 1052.
72. *Philosophie*, pp. 875ff.
73. *Philosophie*, p. 876.

74. Ibid.

PART TWO: FRENCH AND ITALIAN PHILOSOPHY

Introduction

1. On the period: Jean Philibert Damiron, *Essai sur l'histoire de la philosophie en France au dix-neuvième siècle*, 3rd ed., enlarged (2 vols.; Paris: Hachette, 1834), which is a critical appreciation of the main philosophers of the period. Himself an eclectic of Cousin's school, Damiron published a *Cours de philosophie* (3 vols.; Paris: Hachette, 1831–1836). Marin Ferraz, *Histoire de la philosophie en France au dix-neuvième siècle. Traditionalisme et ultramontanisme* (Paris: Didier, 1880) includes J. de Maistre, de Bonald, Lamennais, Ballanche, Bûchez, Bautain, Gratry, etc. Also by Ferraz are *Etudes sur la philosophie en France au dix-neuvième siècle. Le socialisme, le naturalisme et le positivisme* (Paris: Didier, 1881; 2nd ed., 1882), which includes Saint-Simon, Charles Fourier, Pierre Leroux, Jean Reynaud, Gall, Broussais, Auguste Comte, Proudhon, etc.; and *Histoire de la philosophie en France au dix-neuvième siècle. Spiritualisme et libéralisme* (Paris: Didier, 1887), which includes Mme. de Staël, Laromiguière, Maine de Biran, Ampère, Royer-Collard, de Gérando, Victor Cousin, Théodore Jouffroy, Guizot, Charles de Rémusat, Adolphe Garnier, Emile Saisset and the development of spiritualism. For doctrinal expositions and critical interpretations see Félix Ravaisson, *La philosophie en France au XIXe siècle* (Paris: Imprimerie Impériale, 1868; several reprints, Paris: Hachette) and Charles Adam, *La philosophie en France (Première moitié du XIXe siècle)* (Paris: F. Alcan, 1894). Particularly recommended: the Italian *Enciclopedia filosofica* (4 vols.; Venezia-Roma: Istituto per la collaborazione culturale, Isola di San Giorgio Maggiore, 1957).

On the ideologist movement: Marin Ferraz, *Histoire de la philosophie pendant la Révolution (1788–1804)* (Paris: Didier, 1889) which includes Garat, Tracy, Cabanis, Rivarol, Condorcet, Volney, Mme. Condorcet, Villers, Sain-Martin, Chateaubriand, etc. François Picavet, *Les idéologues* (Paris: F. Alcan, 1891) is to be consulted on every member of the school. E. Joyau, *La philosophie en France pendant la Révolution* (Paris: Alcan, 1893). Gilbert Chinard, *Jefferson et les idéologues d'après sa correspondance inédite avec Destutt de Tracy, Cabanis, J.-B. Say et Auguste Comte* (Baltimore-Paris: The Johns Hopkins Studies in Romance Literatures and Languages, extra Vol. I, 1923) is an absolutely necessary source of information.

V. Ideology in France

1. Pierre Jean Georges Cabanis, b. Cosnac, 1757; d. Rueil, 1808. At first a poet (he translated Homer's *Iliad* into French verse), he turned to physiology and medicine; a friend of Mirabeau, he shared in the French revolution (the poison with which Condorcet committed suicide in his jail was given to him by Cabanis); after the death of Condorcet, he married his sister-in-law, Charlotte Grouchy; a fellow of the Institut de

France (1797), then a professor at the Paris School of Medicine, he was appointed a senator by Bonaparte (1799); displeased with Bonaparte's politics, he devoted the rest of his life to scientific research.

Main philosophical works: *Traité du physique et du moral de l'homme* (2 vols.; Paris, 1802), better known under the title it received in the second edition: *Rapports du physique et du moral de l'homme*, par P. J. G. Cabanis, membre du Sénat, de l'institut National, de l'École et Société de médecine de Paris, de la Société Philosophique de Philadelphie, etc. Later editions, 1815, 1824, 1830; 8th edition, 1844, includes a reprint of the following work: *Lettre posthume et inédite à M. F. (auriel) sur les causes premières*, ed. with notes by F. Bérard (Paris: Gabon, 1824).

Collective editions: *Oeuvres complètes* (5 vols.; Paris: Bossange, 1823–1825) and *Oeuvres philosophiques complètes*, ed. Claude Lehec and Jean Cazaneuve (2 vols.; Paris: Presses Universitaires de France, 1956).

Doctrinal: Damiron, *Essai…*, Vol. I, pp. 81–92. Picavet, *Les idéologues,* chaps. i, iii and iv. Gaetano Capone Braga, *La filosofia francese e italiana del settecento*, 3rd ed. (Padova: Cedam, 1942), Part I, chap. iv, pp. 170–171. A. Joussain, "Le spiritualisme de Cabanis," *Archives de Philosophie*, 21 (1958), pp. 386–409.

2. *Rapports du physique et du moral de l'homme*, 2nd ed., rev. and enlarged by the author (2 vols.; Paris: Crapelet, an-XIII-1805), Preface, Vol. I, pp. xiv-xix. It is divided into sections called "Mémoires."

3. Op. cit., "I Mémoire," Introduction, Vol. I, pp. 4–6.

4. Op. cit., I, pp. 6–7.

5. This is the gist of the message of Cabanis. Taking it for granted that, after Locke, Bonnet, Condillac, and Helvetius, nobody will refuse "to consider physical sensibility as the source of all the ideas and of all the habits that constitute the moral existence of man," he considers equally certain another conclusion obtained by the physiologists, to wit, "that all the vital motions are the product of the impressions undergone by the parts endowed with sensibility." The first conclusion is common to all the psychologists, the second one is common to all the physiologists, and if they are brought together, "these two fundamental results make up one and the same truth" (op. cit., "II Mémoire," Vol. I, 1, pp. 85–86). Instinct, in the language of Cabanis, precisely includes the whole of the physiological determinations whose source is to be found in organic sensibility, and which usually grow in it all by themselves. Contrariwise to what Condillac had thought, reasoning has nothing to do with instinct; even the will contents itself with directing its operations (op. cit., p. 86). This is why the disputes concerning the difference of sensibility and irritability are mainly about words (op. cit., pp. 90–91).

6. The substance of the treatise consists of observations and reflections concerning the relations between the psychological operations of man and his "physical organization." The work is divided into "Mémoires," among which are: II, Physiological history of sensations; IV, Influence of age on the ideas and on moral affections; V, Influence of the sexes on the character of the ideas and on moral affections; VI, Influence of temperaments…etc.; VII, Influence of the diseases…etc.; VIII, Influence of diet on dispositions and on moral habits; IX, Influence of climates on moral habits. The two

volumes of the *Rapports* clearly embody a physician's view of psychological life. Of the scientific works of Cabanis, two volumes should be known: *Du degré de certitude de la médecine*, 2nd ed., enlarged (Paris: Crapart, Caille et Ravier, an-XI-1803) and *Coup d'oeil sur les révolutions et sur la réforme de la médecine* (Paris: Crapart, Caille et Ravier, an-XII-1804).

7. Analysis and extracts are found in Damiron, *Essai...*, Vol. I, pp. 89-92.
8. Antoine Louis Claude Count de Destutt de Tracy, b. Paray-le-Frésil, 1754, d. Paris, 1836. Descendant of Walter Stutt who came from Scotland to France in the army of John Stuart (1420); an infantry colonel in 1789, joined the party of the Revolution; a deputy, but not enough of an extremist, he was arrested and only escaped death owing to the fall of Robespierre; after the return of civil peace, he devoted himself to philosophy and was made a fellow of the National Institute (section of the Analysis of Sensations, class of Moral and Political Sciences), 1795, then of the Académie française, 1808; after the deposition of Napoleon I, which he moved before the Senate, the government of the Restoration gave him a peerage and restored him to his title of count.

Main philosophical work: *Projet d'éléments d'idéologie* (Paris, 1801), republished as *Eléments d'idéologie* (*Elements of Ideology*) along with the other parts of the projected work, to be found in *Eléments d'idéologie* (3 parts in 4 vols.; Paris: Levi, 1825-1827); Vol. I, *Idéologie proprement dite*; Vol. II, *Grammaire*; Vol. III, *De la logique*; Vol. IV, *Supplements and Documents related to Public Instruction*.

Another part of the same work (*Eléments d'idéologie*, Part I, sec. 2), *De l'économie politique*, not included in the preceding edition, has been published under the title of *Traité de la volonté et de ses effets* (Paris: Courcier, 1815), and republished under the title of *Traité d'économie politique* (Paris: Lévi, 1822).

Another work, written in 1806-1807, the *Commentaire sur l'Esprit des Lois de Montesquieu* could not be printed in France under Napoléon I on account of its liberal tendency. Through Lafayette, the work was sent to Jefferson, translated and published at Philadelphia in 1811; it was retranslated into French and printed in 1817; this decided Tracy to publish his own original French text (Paris: Delaunay, 1819). See Gilbert Chinard, *Jefferson et les idéologues d'après sa correspondance inédite avec Destutt de Tracy, Cabanis, J.-B. Say et Auguste Comte* (Baltimore-Paris: The Johns Hopkins Studies in Romance Languages and Literatures, 1923) chap. ii, pp. 31-96. On the translation and publication of the *Traité d'économie politique* (or *Traité de la volonté*) (Paris, 1823), likewise procured by Jefferson, chap. iii, pp. 97-188. The titles of the two translations are: *A Commentary and Review of Montesquieu's Spirit of Laws*, prepared for the press from the original manuscript, in the hands of the publisher, to which are annexed, observations on the thirty-first book, by the late M. Condorcet, and two letters of Helvetius on the merits of the same work (Philadelphia, 1871). *A Treatise on Political Economy* (Georgetown, D.C.: Joseph Milligan, 1817).

Doctrinal and biographical: L. P. Conseil: *Mélanges politiques et philosophiques extraits des mémoires et de la correspondance de Thomas Jefferson, précédés d'un essai sur les principes de l'école américaine et d'une traduction de la Constitution des Etats Unis*, avec un commentaire tiré, pour la plus grande partie, de l'ouvrage publié, sur cette Constitution, par William Rawle (2 vols.; Paris: Paulin, 1833). F. Picavet, *Les idéologues*. Gaetano Capone Braga, *La filosofia francese e italiana del settencento* (rev. edition; Padova: Cedam, 1942), Vol. I, chap. v, pp. 212-248.

9. All those remarks are to be found in Tracy's *Elements of Ideology*, notes of the publisher and of the author, and prefaces for the editions of 1801 and 1804. Tracy will be quoted from the 1824 Paris edition in four volumes.

10. The *Elements of Ideology* is followed by a *Reasoned Abstract front the Ideology Doing for an Analytical Index*, Vol. I, pp. 285-337. All that which precedes is borrowed from that abstract as completed by means of the corresponding chapters of the *Elements*. See particularly the important chap. vii, "On Existence," *ed. cit.*, Vol. I, pp. 70-104; and chap. xi, "Reflections upon What Precedes and on the Way in which Condillac Has Analyzed Thought," pp. 154-167.

11. *Reasoned Abstract*, chap. xvi; cf. *Elements of Ideology*, chaps. xvi-xvii. Another short exposition of the whole doctrine is found, under the deceptive title of *Principes logiques* (i.e., Principles of logic, or collection of facts concerning human understanding) in *ed. cit.*, Vol. IV, pp. 190-259. As exposed in that early treatise, there is little difference between logic and ideology proper. Tracy says that logic needs to be thoroughly renovated. In the first place it must ascertain the first thing we are sure of. That first of all certitudes is our own existence, which consists in feeling. Being is feeling: "We only exist because we feel, we would not exist if we did not feel." And it presents this very curious formula: "Our existence consists in feeling it in the diverse modifications it receives, and, at the same time, we are quite sure that we feel that which we feel." This "I feel, hence I am," would have surprised Descartes; Tracy always maintained it, but with strange variations in formulas; for instance: "To think is to feel, and to feel is to apprehend one's own existence in some way or other; we have no other way to know that we exist..." etc., *Eléments d'idéologie*, chap. vii, *ed. cit.*, Vol. I, p. 79.

12. *Reasoned Abstract from the Grammar, ed. cit.*, Vol. II, Introduction.

13. *La logique*, Preliminary Discourse, *ed. cit.*, vol. III, pp. 11-12. Tracy has added to his treatise a *Reasoned Abstract from the Logic*, to serve as an analytical table: *ed. cit.*, Vol. III, pp. 433-470. It must not be forgotten that Tracy has always conceived his writings with the colleges and universities in view. Pedagogical preoccupations are everywhere perceptible in his works. See *ed. cit.*, Vol. IV, pp. 262-395: "Documents Concerning Public Instruction."

THE SAME SYSTEMATIC SPIRIT PREVAILED EVEN IN THE *TRAITÉ DE L'ÉCONOMIE POLITIQUE;* TRACY IS CAREFUL TO DEDUCE HIS RULES OF POLITICAL ECONOMY FROM THE PRINCIPLES LAID DOWN IN HIS *ELEMENTS OF IDEOLOGY*. Jefferson had his doubts about the necessity of that part of the work; see his revealing remark: "These investigations are very metaphysical, profound and demonstrative, and will give satisfaction to minds in the habit of abstract speculation. Readers, however, not disposed to enter into them, after reading the summary view, entitled 'On our actions,' will probably pass at once to the commencement of the main subject of the work, which is treated of under the following head..." Chinard, *Jefferson et les idéologues*, p. 143, and the pertinent remarks on p. 144.

14. Marie François Pierre Gonthier, Maine de Biran, b. Bergerac, 1766; d. Paris, 1824. Studied at the college of the Christian Doctrine (the "Doctrinaires"), Perigeux; entered

the Royal Guard (1784) and led a worldly life interrupted by the Revolution of 1789; retired in 1793 on the family estate of Grateloup (Dordogne); in 1795, appointed an "administrator" of his department, thus beginning a political career which, through many vicissitudes, lasted till the end of his life. Always in contact with philosophical circles, writing mainly for himself and publishing very little, he was nonetheless esteemed and admired by Cabanis, Tracy, Royer-Collard, Cousin and others. When he died, the complete published works of Biran consisted of three items: (1) *Influence de l'habitude sur la faculté de penser* (Paris: Henrichs, an-XI-1803) (anonymous); (2) *Examen des leçons de philosophie de M. Laromiguière* (Paris: Fournier, 1817) (anonymous); (3) "Exposition de la doctrine philosophique de Leibniz," in Michaud, *Biographie universelle*, XXII (1819), pp. 603–626. Practically the whole of his writings was posthumously published.

Main works: *Mémoire sur la décomposition de la pensée* (1805), in Tisserand, *Oeuvres de Maine de Piran* (14 vols.; Paris: Alcan, 1920), Vols. III and IV. *Mémoire sur les perceptions obscures* (1807), separate edition by Tisserand (Paris: A. Colin, 1920), and in Tisserand, *Oeuvres*, Vol. V, pp. 16–69. *Essais sur les fondements de la psychologie* (1812), in Tisserand, *Oeuvres*, Vols. VIII and IX. *Notes sur la philosophie de Kant* (1816), in Tisserand. *Oeuvres*, Vol. XI, pp. 271–294. *Défense de la philosophie, Origine du langage*, Définition de l'homme (3 essays directed against De Bonald, 1818), in Tisserand, *Oeuvres*, Vol. XII, pp. 45–223. *Nouvelles considérations sur les rapports du physique et du moral de l'homme* (1820), in Tisserand, *Oeuvres*, Vol. XIII. *Nouveaux essais d'anthropolgie* (1823–1824), in Tisserand, *Oeuvres*, Vol. XIV. *Journal intime*, ed. H. Gouhier (3 vols.; Neuchâtel: La Baconnière, 1955–1957).

Collected works: Pierre Tisserand, *Oeuvres de Maine de Biran*, accompagnées de notes et d'appendices (14 vols.; Paris: Alcan, 1920).

Anthology: Henri Gouhier, *Oeuvres choisies de Maine de Biran* (Paris: Aubier, 1942). An excellent selection, not of pages but of works, preceded by a most scholarly introduction.

Bibliographical: Henri Gouhier, *Oeuvres choisies de Maine de Biran*, pp. 45–62.

Doctrinal: Victor Delbos, *Maine de Biran et son oeuvre philosophique* (Paris: J. Vrin, 1931). Georges Le Roy, *L'expérience de l'effort et de la grâce chez Maine de Biran* (Paris: Boivin, 1937). Raymond Vancourt, *La théorie de la connaissance chez Maine de Biran. Le réalisme biranien et l'idéalisme* (Paris: Librairie philosophique J. Vrin, 1941). Henri Gouhier, *Les conversions de Maine de Biran* (Paris: Librairie philosophique J. Vrin, 1948). Jean Lassaigne, *Maine de Biran homme politique*, Préface de Henri Gouhier (Paris: La Colombe, 1958).

15. Let us recall that, in the language of Condillac, *analysis* is a twofold operation of decomposition and recomposition. It is opposed to *synthesis* in this sense that (always in Condillac's language) synthesis begins by arbitrarily composing without having first decomposed. On analysis in Condillac, see *De Part de penser*, chap. iv, in Condillac, *Oeuvres completes*, ed. Georges Le Roy (3 vols.; Paris: Presses Universitaires de France, 1947, 1948, 1951), Vol. I, pp. 769–770. On synthesis, see Condillac, *Essai sur l'origine des connaissances humaines*, Vol. II, chap. vii, pp. 24–25, 61–63.

16. The very notion of the "decomposition of thought," is the lifeline that, through Tracy,

connects Condillac with Maine de Biran. According to Condillac, to decompose a thought (for instance, a sensation) is simply "to represent to oneself successively the parts of which it is composed." On "l'art de decomposer la pensée," see Condillac, *Oeuvres complètes*, Vol. I, chap. iii, pp. 435–436. It is noteworthy that, according to Condillac, the order of analysis was the same as that of the generation of ideas: op. cit., Vol. I, chap. V, p. 437. Even the name "ideology," although coined by Tracy, betrays the influence of Condillac, in whose terminology every object of thought (i.e., every thought) is an "idea," including sensations. Ideas divide into sensible ideas (sensations) and intellectual ideas (representing objects after they cease to be perceived); "those ideas only differ as memory differs from sensation." Condillac, "Extrait raisonne du traité des sensations," Part IV, in G. Le Roy, ed., *Oeuvres complètes*, Vol. I, p. 334.

17. Pierre Laromiguière, b. Livinhac, 1756; d. Paris, 1837. Educated in a college of the Christian Doctrine; joined the congregation; was ordained a priest (1785) and began a teaching career. After the suppression of the religious orders (1790) he continued to teach and wrote a *Project of Elements of Metaphysics* (1794), strongly influenced by Condillac. His career as a professor followed the political vicissitudes of the country; on the whole, it was a successful one. In 1810, as a professor at the Faculty of Letters of Paris, he had young Victor Cousin among his pupils. In 1812, attacked by Royer-Collard, a younger colleague and enemy of Condillac, Laromiguière gave up his teaching activities but remained the head librarian of the University of Paris, and spent his remaining life in quiet retirement.

Main work: *Leçons de philosophie ou Essai sur les facultés de l'âme* (Paris: Bruno-Labbe), Vol. I, 1815; Vol. II, 1818; 3rd ed., 1823 (translated into English); 4th ed., revised, under the new title of *Leçons de philosophie sur les principes de l'intelligence, ou sur les causes et les origines des idées* (Paris, 1826), two simultaneous printings, one in two vols., 8°, the other, for students, in three vols., 12°; fifth edition, in collaboration with Francois de Chabrier de Peloubet (Paris, 1833), from which short passages had been deleted for reasons of opportunity. A sixth and posthumous edition was published in 1844; added, the *Discours sur l'identité dans le raisonnement*.

Laromiguière procured the first (posthumous) edition of Condillac's *La langue des calculs* (1798), followed by his own treatise *Les paradoxes de Condillac ou reflexions sur la langue des calculs* (1805), enlarged in a new edition (Paris: Bruno-Labbe, 1825) and still included in the 1844 edition of the *Leçons*. His thought always moved within the limits of Condillac's psychology. After opposing him, Cousin pretended to include him among the forerunners of his own eclecticism. In fact, Laromiguière was only one more witness to the tendency, observable among all the followers of Condillac, to restore to the mind some of its activity. Sensation is no longer considered a faculty of the soul. These are three in number: *attention* (the fundamental faculty); *comparison* (including judgment, memory); *reasoning*, which is but a twofold act of comparison (a comparison of comparisons). There is no comparison without attention, and no reasoning without comparison (reasoning is born of comparison as comparison is born of attention), so the whole human understanding is born of attention. A similar genealogy accounts for the faculties of the will: the elementary faculty in it is *desire*.

Just like attention, desire begets two more faculties; preference (or choice) and liberty. So much for the genealogy of the faculties. Now for the origin of our ideas.

The common origin of our ideas is "sensibility," which has four modes: (1) it undergoes the action of external objects: sensations; (2) it perceives the action of our faculties; (3) it perceives resemblances and differences, in short, relations, between ideas; (4) it perceives the difference between just and unjust, honest and dishonest. Those four modes of sensibility are as many different sources of ideas; hence four sorts of ideas: ideas of sensation, ideas of the faculties of the soul, ideas of relation and moral ideas. By restoring attention to its rank of primitive faculty of the soul, then by adding the principles of morality to the primitive objects of sensibility, Laromiguière contributed to a broadening of Condillac's absolute sensism then generally felt as a necessity.

Biographical: P. Alfaric, *Laromiguière et son école* (Paris: Les Belles Lettres, 1929). Doctrinal: Damiron, *Essai*, Vol. I, pp. 102–117.

18. "Essai sur les fondements de la psychologie," in Gouhier, *Oeuvres choisies de Maine de Biran*, p. 153.
19. Texts of Biran, with a remarkable commentary, in H. Gouhier, *Oeuvres choisies de Maine de Biran*, pp. 33–35.
20. "Notes sur Kant," *Oeuvres choisies de Maine de Biran*, pp. 211–212. On the sources of Biran's knowledge of Kant: Charles Villers, *Philosophie de Kant ou principes fondamentaux de la philosophie transcendentale* (Metz: Collignon, 1801), and J. Kinker, *Essai d'une exposition succincte de la Critique de la Raison Pure*, traduit du hollandais par J. Le F(èvre) (Amsterdam: Changuion et Den Hengst, 1801). See also *Oeuvres choisies de Maine de Biran*, p. 210. H. Gouhier refers to M. Vallois, *La formation de l'influence kantienne en France* (Paris: F. Alcan, 1924).
21. *Oeuvres choisies*, "Essai sur les fondements de la psychologie," pp. 78–80.
22. This is the justification for including Biran among the ideologists. His starting point is Condillac and, beyond him, Locke, who is the patriarch of the school. Biran himself, however, has been a point of departure rather than of arrival.
23. "Essai sur les fondements," p. 87.
24. Op. cit., p. 88.
25. Op. cit., p. 88. The "judicious philosopher" in question is Ancillon senior (see note h., p. 315). All this analysis follows the text of Biran himself (pp. 87–88).
26. "All that which a thinking or feeling being perceives or actually feels in itself or outside of itself by some external or internal sense, becomes for that being that which is called fact." Gouhier in *Oeuvres choisies*, "Rapports des sciences naturelles avec la psychologie," Introduction, Part I, p. 159. See also "Essai sur les fondements," chap. ii, p. 77: "All that which exists for us, all that which we can perceive outside, feel within ourselves, conceive in our own ideas, is only given to us as a fact."
27. "Essai sur les fondements," p. 87.
28. Gouhier, *Oeuvres choisies*, Introduction, p. 33.
29. "The vice in Kant's reasoning always consists in concluding from our invincible ignorance as to what a thing is in itself, to our ignorance of the absolute reality of that thing, such as we conceive it with our given faculties. It is possible that a thing be otherwise than we conceive it to be and it may have several attributes unknown to us;

it is likewise possible that the thing be not different from what we conceive it to be; it may well contain nothing more than the attributes, or even the only attribute under which it manifests itself to our mind: man is no judge of that question, because he only knows through his faculties, but he knows at least this, that the thing he conceives under an attribute essential to its nature, exists with that attribute.... The knowledge of ourselves as substances outside the act of thinking, that is to say outside of a determined thought and of a determined action, is not impossible, and it is included in the inner feeling of existence; it is outside that inner sense that there is no possible knowledge, because there is no subject." ("Notes sur Kant," in *Oeuvres choisies de Maine de Biran*, pp. 226–227.) The substitution of a metaphysics of cause for the traditional metaphysics of substance could not fail to meet with resistance in most minds. Man is a naturally substantialist philosopher. The main objection directed against his notion of cause was that, as Hume had already shown it, our mind has no idea of how the cause can produce its effect. We particularly do not know how the will can act upon the muscles that move the limbs. The answer of Biran naturally was that objections of that sort miss the whole point. The gist of his doctrine is that "the connexity of will and motion that constitutes the immediate inner apperception is not the object, but the very subject of all external perception." "Réponse à Stapfet" ("Answer to Stapfet") in *Oeuvres choisies*, p. 237. Note the expression: the connexity of will and motion *is* the very apperception of inner sense. This is possible only because the apperception of causality is not the awareness of a cognition, but of an act. The slightest departure from this point leads to either Hume or Kant.

30. Hence follows the fecund criticism directed by Biran against the naïveté of the physiologists who attempt to find in nerves, muscles, and even, in the ease of Gall, in the structure of the brain, the exact duplicate of the facts of consciousness which the reflexive method discovers in us by direct observation. The future criticism of psycho-physiological parallelism by Bergson was clearly anticipated by Biran. One should not commit the error of imagining Biran (or Bergson) as opposed to psycho-physiological research; he only stresses the fact that, however correlated, the two orders of facts are distinct in nature and that each obeys its own laws.

31. This section closely follows the remarkable text of Biran's "Answer to Stapfer," vii obj., in *Oeuvres choisies*, pp. 250–251. No effort was made to impart to the rugged philosophical style of Biran a smoothness it has not in French. All the ideologists were good writers; only Biran was more interested in what he wanted to say than in the way to say it.

32. "Essai sur les fondements," end of the General Introduction, in *Oeuvres choisies*, p. 148.

33. On this aspect of Biran's thought, see the admirable book by Henri Gouhier, *Les conversions de Maine de Biran* (Paris: Librarie Philosophique J. Vrin, 1948). Another revealing aspect of Biran's personality is his interest in the problems of education. The great metaphysicians of the seventeenth century left us no treatises on education. Renewing the sixteenth-century tradition of Montaigne and many others, Locke started a chain reaction of pedagogical treatises. Condillac, Rousseau, all the ideologists, have considered it a duty to explain how youth should be educated. Each particular

system of philosophy led to a particular system of education. Biran was fully aware of the pedagogical consequences of his own conception of human nature. In his own words, *speculative* philosophy is, at the same time, *practical*. If the apperception of the ego entirely rests upon the "primordial exercise of that hyper-sensible force or power of acting and moving we call *will*, it follows that the great division admitted by all schools between understanding and will is purely artificial, that it has no real foundation in our nature and, in fine, that the intelligence and the morality of man rest upon one and the same principle" ("Essai sur les fondements," in *Oeuvres choisies*, p. 135). There is therefore no point in cultivating the passive faculties of man (sensibility and imagination); these take good care of themselves. On the contrary, the active faculties greatly need to be cultivated. The principles upon which Pestalozzi has founded his pedagogy "happen to be absolutely conformable to those which the philosophy of the human mind could prescribe" (p. 139). Rousseau's *Emile* is not only an "immortal work on education," but it even could serve "as a sort of practical psychology for all that which concerns the successive order of the development of our intellectual and moral faculties" (ibid.). Biran goes as far as saying that "in order to judge of the truth or of the foundation of the psychological doctrines on the origin and generation of intellectual faculties, one should envisage them in their relations with the methods of education, which must be their applications only; it is chiefly here that practice confirms or destroys theory" (p. 140). What is wrong with Condillac is clearly seen by applying that principle, for indeed, if, in man, everything is reducible to *feeling*, then we just should let him feel as he well pleases; there would be no room left for any sort of education. Condillac, Tracy, and other ideologists have said many true and useful things, but when they are right, it always is despite their own system, and against it.

34. Rousseau also represents for Biran the inner moral instinct for "sympathy" without which society is impossible. "Fragments relatifs aux fondements de la morale et de la religion," in *Oeuvres choisies*, p. 258.

35. The substance of this section, "The Philosopher and His Philosophy," and all the preceding quotations, are borrowed from Biran's *Nouveaux essais d'anthropologie*, in *Oeuvres choisies*, pp. 287–311.

VI. Ideology in Italy

1. On philosophy in the early nineteenth century and its eighteenth-century origins, see Capone Braga, *La filosofia francese e italiana del settecento*, Vol. I, Part II (2nd ed., 1942, temporarily out of print); Vol. II (2nd ed.; Padova: Cedam, 1942-XX). M. F. Sciacca, *La filosofia nell'età del Risorgimento* (Milano: Vallardi, 1948), pp. 184–185, for bibliographical information concerning the history of philosophy in eighteenth- and nineteenth-century Italy; on the Italian ideologists, Sciacca, op. cit., Part I, chap. iv, pp. 115–170, bibliography, pp. 194–197; on the influence of Italian Jansenism (an aspect of the problem whose existence at least should be known), Sciacca, op. cit., Part I, chap. ii, §4, pp. 49–56, bibliography, pp. 187–188. See also the articles concerning each Italian philosopher in the *Enciclopedia italiana* (4 vols.; Venezia-Roma, 1957).

On Doria's *Difesa della metafisica degli antichi filosofi contro il Signor G. Locke* (Venezia-Napoli, 1732), see Sciacca, op. cit., pp. 82–83. Because of a possible connection with Gerdil, note the remark, p. 82, n. 2: "Doria stands, at the bottom, with Malebranche."

2. As a typical representative of the influence of Locke in Italy, Sciacca quotes and studies Antonio Genovesi (1712–1769). In the case of Genovesi, as in that of most Italian philosophers subjected to English and French influences, it should be remembered that there was a perceptible tendency to play down certain themes. For instance, there was little anti religious feeling at that time and in the works coming from that philosophical cycle (on the corrected Italian reprints of the *Encyclopédie*, see Sciacca, p. 88, n. 1). Genovesi wrote *Disiplinarum metaphysicarum elementa and Elementa artis logico-criticae* (Napoli, 1745), *Meditazioni filosofiehe sulla religione e sulla morale* (Napoli, 1758). On Genovesi see Capone Braga, article in *Enciclopedia filosofica*, Vol. II, pp. 625–627, with bibliography; on the limitations of his Lockianism, see Sciacca, pp. 88–98; on the school of Genovesi (including Melchiorre Delfico) (op. cit., p. 97). On the contrary, the more deeply Frenchified Italian circles also were the more radically minded in matters of philosophy, of religion, and of political doctrines. On the group of the newspaper *Il Caffe* (Brescia-Milano, 1764–1766), see Sciacca, pp. 98–109; the more important names of the group are P. Verri and Beccaria.

3. Expression of Sciacca, op. cit., p. 110. In n. 2, p. 110, Sciacca aptly answers the inevitable question: how was it that the doctrines of Locke and Condillac could be taught by priests and monks in so many convents and Catholic colleges? One reason was that Christian teachers educated in the scholastic tradition had nothing to object to in the doctrine that all knowledge comes from sense. The scholastics had all opposed the doctrine of the innate ideas in Descartes; they naturally sided with Locke against it. On the other hand, one must remember that Condillac himself was a spiritualist, that he believed in the existence of an immaterial soul and was in no sense an adversary of religious belief. A combination of Aristotle and Locke was far from impossible. In fact, it became a rather popular one in some neo-scholastic circles; philosophy prepared for school consumption usually admits a certain dose of syncretism. Besides, editions with critical notes were possible, such as that of T. V. Falletti, a canon regular of the Lateran, who translated Condillac "with notes and critical observations" (2 vols.; Rome, 1784).

4. Among the adversaries of Condillac, Sciacca mentions (p. 113) as "remembered and praised by Rosmini" (A. Rosmini, Preface to the *Nuovo Saggio*) the Milanese physician and philosopher Michele Araldi and the Barnabite architect, scientist, and philosopher Ermenegildo Pini (1739–1825), author of a *Protologia...* (Milan, 1803). For Pini, the protology "is the science that treats of the first principle, absolutely one and simple, as of a real and living entity, that has in itself the prime reason of the being and life of all other existent." See Sciacca, p. 114, n. 1, for other "anti-sensists" as well as for adversaries of irreligiosity. It is to be noted that the Italian Jansenists, while favoring the French religious reforms, were opposed to the sensism of Condillac, especially as justifying an ethical doctrine of pleasure (hedonism), of personal interest and self-love. For instance, the professor of moral philosophy at the University of Pavia, Pietro

Tamburini, author of lectures in moral philosophy, *Lezioni di filosofia morale* (7 vols.; Pavia: Galeazzi, 1803–1812) and Sciacca, p. 113. On Pini, whose protology should be further explored, see Capone Braga, *La filosofia francese e italiana*, Vol. II, p. 99. On Araldi, Braga, Vol. II, pp. 98–99. On Tamburini, Braga, Vol. II, pp. 11, 12, 98.

5. On the Italian translations of Condillac and of the first ideologists, see Sciacca, p. 112, n. 1.

6. Francesco Soave, b. Lugano, 1743; d. Pavia, 1806. Joined a religious order (the so-called *somaschi*) and dedicated his whole life to teaching; began to teach at Parma in 1765, two years before Condillac left the ducal court; for political reasons, he later went to Milan as a professor of philosophy; wrote a treatise against the French revolution in order to please the Austrian authorities (1795); on the arrival of French troops, left Milan for Lugano, where he continued to teach (Sant' Antonio College, where Manzoni was his pupil); from Lugano, Soave went to Naples, whence a local revolution chased him back to Milan; there the Austrian government restored him to his chair of philosophy, which he kept till the battle of Marengo (victory of Bonaparte over the Austrians, 1800); he then was called to the college of Modena as a professor of the analysis of ideas (or ideology), then to the University of Pavia, where he died.

Main philosophical works: *Istituzioni di logica, metafisica ed etica* (Milano: Marelli, 1791). *La filosofia di Kant esposta ed esaminata* (Modena: Eredi di B. Soliani, 1803). Two memoirs, both published in the *Atti dell' Istituto Nazionale Italiano* (Bologna, 1809); their respective titles are *Mentoria sopra il progetto di elementi d'ideologia del conte Destutt di Tracy* and *Esante dei principi metafisici di zoonomia di Erasino Darwin*.

Biographical and doctrinal: Capone Braga, *La filosofia francese e italiana*, Vol. I, Part II, pp. 124–159. Sciacca, *La filosofia nell' età del Risorgimento*, pp. 121–128, with bibliographical note, pp. 194–195. N. B.—Practically all the information on Soave included in this section is derived from Sciacca.

7. The twofold criticism of Kant and Erasmus Darwin is found in Soave's *Esame dei principi metafisici di zoonomia di Erasino Darwin*, pp. 47–48. The paper was read by Soave at the meeting of the National Institute (to which he had been appointed by Bonaparte) held on July 10, 1804: it is found in Vol. I of the *Atti*, pp. 47–48. Soave objects to the classification and description of man's faculties. After substituting his own views for those of E. Darwin, he concludes that where nothing has been proved, there is nothing to refute (p. 63). There is in the book nothing for the metaphysician. See Erasmus Darwin, *Zoonomia, or the Laws of Organic Life*, 3rd ed., corrected (4 vols.; London: J. Johnson, 1801), and Desmond King Hele, *Erasmus Darwin* (New York: Macmillan, 1963).

8. Soave's *Riflessioni sopra il progeno di elementi d'ideologia di Destutt-Tracy* was read at the National Institute's meeting, July 10, 1804, the same day, it seems, as the memoir on E. Darwin. It is found in the *Atti*, Vol. I, pp. 117–160; the remarks on Condillac are found pp. 110–112.

9. *Riflessioni*, pp. 120–122.

10. *Riflessioni*, pp. 126–129. Soave thinks Tracy had a duty to answer the question of Locke: can it be proved that matter is incapable of thought? (p. 130).

11. *Riflessioni*, pp. 139, 147–150. Soave deals with the problem of how we come to

knowing the existence of external objects. He does not object to the answer of Tracy (we learn the existence of bodies from the resistance they oppose to our movements and to our volitions); but he resents the suggestion made by Tracy, that, as yet, nobody ever thought of such an answer to the problem, for, he says, "I myself have already proposed it, as early as 1794, in my 'Conjectures concerning the way the existence of bodies makes itself known to soul,'" added to the fourth volume of the second edition of the *Istituzioni di logica, metafisica ed etica*. On the contrary, Soave does not agree with Condillac on the way man discovers his own ego. The first time a child experiences a sensation, he does not say *I*. Should that sensation endure for year after year, there still would be no *I*. There is no "I feel, hence I am." In order to perceive itself as a subject, the soul must first pay attention to sensations, compare, judge, reason, will, in short, it must perform the active operations in its power.

12. *Riflessioni*, pp. 152–153.
13. Melchiorre Gioia, b. Piacenza, 1767; d. Milan, 1829. Studied for nine years at the Albroni College and was ordained a priest (like Condillac, Laromiguière, and a few other ideologists) but the coming of Napoleon I stirred political passions in his heart. He became an active liberal politician and journalist whose career followed the vicissitudes of his party; at times he was in jail, at other times he was a high government official. Of all his functions the one he enjoyed most was that of director of statistics in the Home Ministry. At the end of his life, he was to write a *Philosophy of Statistics* (*Filosofia della statistical* (Milano: Pirotta, 1826). His really important philosophical works were all written during the last years of his life, after his retirement from active political life, between 1822 and 1829.

    Main philosophical writings: *Elementi di filosofia ad uso delle scuole* (Milano: Pirotta, 1818) (Gioia himself sometimes mentions the book under the title of *Elementi di filosofia ad uso dei giovanetti*. This work does not represent the final stage of his thought). *Ideologia* (2 vols.; Milano: Pirotta, 1822, 1823). *Esercizio logico sugli errori d'ideologia e zoologia, ossia Arte di trar profitto dai cattivi libri* (Milano: Pirotta, 1824).

    Biographical and doctrinal: Capone Braga, *La filosofia francese e italiana nel settecento*, Vol. I, Part II, pp. 160–217. Sciacca, *La filosofia nell' età del Risorgimento*, pp. 128–139; bibliography, p. 195.
14. M. Gioia, *Ideologia*, Vol. 1, pp. i–viii.
15. *Ideologia*, Vol. II, Part VIII, pp. 158–178.
16. *Ideologia*, Vol. I, p. 4. Gioia knows of the existence of a German philosopher by the name of Kant. To him, Kant simply is a philosopher who discarded all external origins of knowledge and recognized internal origins only. Gioia visibly sees the doctrine of Kant as one more brand of ideology. Still, he would like to look at it more closely: "Kant presented himself to Germany shrouded in a cloud of scientific words; at first, he caused surprise, then he became the object of a cult. In Italy, before kneeling down, we want to see the face of the idol. I therefore refuse to say in this book anything more about Kant. To repeat: *fiat lux!*"
17. *Ideologia*, Vol. I, p. 5.
18. *Ideologia*, p. 12; against Erasmus Darwin and Helvetius, pp. 25–26. On the all-importance of internal organization, *Ideologia*, Vol. I, Part I, chap. ii, §1, p. 27.

19. On intellectual instincts proper to man, *Ideologia*, Vol. I, Part I, chap. vi, §2, pp. 57-58; need of being esteemed, pp. 58-59; need of power, pp. 60-61; social instinct, pp. 62-64.
20. On the laws of intensity governing sensations, *Ideologia*, Vol. I, Part III, chap. ii, §§1-18, pp. 103-113. Here are, under abridged form, the laws established by Gioia: (1) the stimulation must last for some time in order to produce its effect; (2) diverse stimuli require diverse times in order to produce their respective effects; (3) the effect of a stimulus lasts for some time after its action has ceased; (4) the application of a stimulus to an organ, if it lasts long enough (even without harming it), finally exhausts its capacity; (5) an organ whose capacity is exhausted needs a certain time in order to recuperate; (6) that a degree of capacity exists for each organ, but it is not strictly invariable; (7) the gamut of the degrees of stimulation is not very wide (beyond its limits come disease and death); (8) the absence of accustomed stimulations is the source of animal desires; (9) after ceasing to function for some time, an organ gets very sensitive to the action of the various stimuli to which it was accustomed; (10) one diminishes sensibility by compressing the respective organs; (11) the continuous application of a stimulus diminishes its intensity (except in the cases when intellect is at stake: attention to ideas, to music, etc.); (12) the habit of using a certain stimulus creates such a need of it that its cessation is attended by pain; (13) the maximum sensibility of each sense is attained through the habitual, reflexive and delicate exercise of it (an exception to law 11); (14) an organ exhausted by the frequent repetition of a certain stimulus needs to be excited by the application of another stimulating substance.
21. Gioia deals with these problems in Vol. II of his *Ideologia*. For a general conspectus of the book, see Vol. II, Part VIII, chap. iv, pp. 190-194.
22. The *Esercizio logico* is an art of putting bad books to good use precisely because it teaches us to avoid their errors. The main faults to be avoided in writing are: *Style*: (1) lack of sense; (2) obscurity: (*a*) voluntary (*b*) involuntary; (3) ignorance of the question; (4) plurality of senses; (5) insufficiency of sense (insufficiently determined sense. It tells us to go neither right nor left, but not where to go). *Order*: (1) to place the difficult and complex before the easy and simple; (2) to place the less important before the necessary; (3) to separate things similar and to mix things different; (4) to repeat the same ideas (an ordinary consequence of disorder). *Ideas*: in a bad book there are four sorts of ideas: (1) false; (2) inaccurate; (3) omitted (absent when, given the aim and scope of the author, they ought to be there); (4) contradictory; in those cases, false ideas must be refuted, inaccurate ideas must be corrected, omitted ideas must be added, contradictory ideas must be harmonized. For false ideas, see *Ideologia*, Vol. II, pp. 1-266; inaccurate ideas, pp. 267-286; omitted ideas, pp. 287-304; contradictory ideas, pp. 305-320.
23. Julien Joseph Virey, who supplied Gioia with the complete stock of "contradictory" notions he needed in order to refute them, is the author of a history of the habits and instincts of animals: *Histoire des moeurs et de l'instinct des animaux* (2 vols.; Paris, 1822). See also his *Histoire naturelle du genre humain* (2 vols.; Paris, An IX-1800) and (3 vols.; Bruxelles, 1826), and *Philosophie de l'histoirie naturelle ou phénomènes de l'organisation des animaux et des végétaux* (Paris, 1835).

24. Giandomenico Romagnosi (or Gian Domenico), b. Salsomaggiore, 1761; d. Milan, 1835. Studied with the Jesuits (Borgo San Domnino, 1772–1775), then at the Alberoni College (Piacenza, 1775–1781); took his degree at Parma, 1786; by profession a lawyer till 1802; arrested for political activities, spent fifteen months in jail (Innsbrück), was found innocent and released; taught Law at Parma (1802), then at Milan (1806–1817); after the suppression of the Law School, taught law privately; arrested again by the Austrian government, was jailed again (Venice) and released a second time for want of proof to convict him; spent the remainder of his life in poverty but availed himself of his forced leisure to write his better-known philosophical works.

Main philosophical writings: *Che cosa è eguaglianza?* (*What is equality?*) (Trento, 1792); in *Opere* (Firenze: Piatti, 1832), pp. 189–196. *Che cosa è liberta?* (*What is liberty?*) (Trento, 1793), in *Opere*, pp. 197–215. *Ricerche sulla validité dei giudizi del pubblico a discernere il vero dal falso* (*On the value of public opinion as a judge of true and false*), written in 1795–1796, posthumously published (2 vols.; Milano: Fanfani, 1836). *Che cosa è la mente sana?* (*What is a sound mind?*) (Milano, 1827). Critical edition by G. Tarozzi (Lanciano: Carabba, 1936). *Vedute fondamentali sull' arte logica* (*Fundamental views on the art of logic*) (Milano, 1832), and ed. L. Caboara (Roma: Reale Accademia d'Italia, 1936).

Collective editions: Besides the Florence edition quoted above (Firenze: Piatti, 1833–1836), two other complete editions are: *Opere*, ed. C. Marzucchi (19 vols.; Firenze, 1832–1839; reprinted, Prato, 1833–1842). *Opere*, ed. A. de Giorgi (8 vols.; Milano, 1841–1848).

Biographical: A. Crespi, *Vita di G. D. Romagnosi* (Monza: Tip. Artigianelli, 1907). C. Cagli, *G. D. Romagnosi, la vita, i tempi, le opere* (Roma: Formiggini, 1935).

Doctrinal: A. Norsa, *11 pensiero filosofico de G. D. Romagnosi* (Milano: Lib. Editrice Lombarda, 1930) (bibliography). Capone Braga, *La filosofia francese e italiana del settecento*, Vol. I, Part II, pp. 218–307. Sciacca, *La filosofia nell'età del Risorgimento*, pp. 139–151; bibliography, pp. 195–196. A. Viviani, *Enciclopedia filosofica*, Vol. IV, pp. 182–185 (bibliography).

25. *Introduzione allo studio del diritto pubblico universale* (2 vols.; Parma: Scampa imperiale, 1805).
26. *Ricerche sulla validità dei giudizi del pubblico a discernere il vero dal falso*, in *Opere post biune* (2 vols.; Milano: Fanfani, 1836).
27. *Opere postume*, Vol. I, Part I, sec. 1, chap. iv, p. 52. The general conclusion stresses the essential fallibility of public opinion, but this does not mean that we cannot, and that we should not do all possible in order to cause truth to be known. See "Theorem on the perpetual fallibility of public judgments," in *Opere postume*, Vol. 1, Part I, sec. 4, p. 44, and Part II, sec. 2, chap. ii, pp. 164–166. Against Helvetius, Vol. I, Part I, chap. ii, p. 9. Sensations as *realità* rather than as *verità*, Vol. I, Part I, sec. 1, chap. i, p. 46. Active power of soul, Vol. I, Part I, sec. 1, chap. vii, pp. 61–63. Necessity of attention in view of abstraction and generalization, Vol. I, Part I, sec. 1, chap. viii, p. 64.
28. "Questo modo novello di riguardare l'ontologia," *Opere postume*, Vol. I, Part II, sec. 1, chap. xvii, p. 95.
29. *Opere postume*, pp. 94–95.

30. *Opere postume*, p. 95. Thus interpreted, the ontological notions listed and defined by Wolf are nothing else than the more abstract and universal of our notions. The Porphyry tree, with its key notion of being (*ens*) sums up the results of that analysis of the mind. Incidentally, there is an interesting object for philosophical reflection: in what sense was, or was not, the *ontology* of Wolf already an *ideology*?

It is necessary to posit real things as causes of the diversity and succession of ideas, *Opere postume*, Part III, sec. 1, chap. ii, pp. 266–269. Against pre-established harmony, chap. V, pp. 272–276. Feeling of the unity of ego, chap. vi, p. 277. Application to the existence of external things as cause of our ideas, chap. vii, pp. 282–284. Against the notion of an instinctive certitude of external world (d'Alembert), chap. xiv, pp. 310–312.

31. On the attitude of Romagnosi toward Kant, see the very precise discussion of Capone Braga, *La filosofia francese e italiana*, Vol. II, Part II, pp. 215–227. For the sophism at stake, p. 221.

32. Romagnosi speaks of it as of an "occult power," always at work in us. In sensations it makes us look at them well, so as to register them and to preserve them in our memory. In matters of ideas, it assents, dissents, doubts and constantly assists us in the task of ordering them in view of discovering good or of ascertaining it once found. The same power still is with us when we definitely decide in matters of scientific truth, of arts and of technical previsions. In its acts, "that power is simple, uniform, immutable, universal. Wishing to give it a name, we call it *rational sense* (senso razionale)." *Vedute fondamentali sull' arte logica*, quoted in Sciacca, *La filosofla nell' età del Risorgimento*, p. 145.

33. *Che cosa è la mente sana?* Part II, §45.

34. The ethical part of Romagnosi's doctrine cannot be separated from his philosophy of law, a widely cultivated specialty in Italy. On the properly philosophical principles from which ethics directly hangs, especially with respect to social ethics, see *Dell'Indole e dei fattori dell'incivilimento* (Milano, 1832), with an appendix (Milano: Silvestri, 1839).

35. Melchiorre Delfico, b. Leognano castle, in Valle Siciliana, 1744; d. Teramo, 1835. Studied at Naples; published a *Philosophical Essay on Marriage* (1774), followed by some essays on ethics whose printing was interrupted by censorship (the *Indizi di Morale*, 1775). His reputation as a radical was strengthened by his attack against the undeserved admiration generally bestowed on ancient Rome, its men and its laws: that inquiry into the true character of Roman jurisprudence was an appeal to legal, social and economic reforms, *Ricerche sill vero carattere della giurisprudenza romana e de' suoi cultori* (1791); for political reasons he sought refuge in San Marino and expressed his gratitude under the form of a history of that small but hospitable republic, *Memorie storiche della repubblica de S. Marino* (Milano: Sonzogno, 1804); thus personally acquainted with historical work, he expressed himself about its uncertainty and uselessness in his *Pensieri su la storia e su la incertezza ed inutilità della medesima* (Forli, 1806); went back to Naples and was made a minister of the Home Office at the time of the French occupation; at the end of the regime, devoted himself to philosophical research and published his "new inquiries into the beautiful," *Nuove ricerche sui bello* (Napoli: Agnello Nobile, 1818); spent his last years in his small city of Teramo,

undisturbed by political powers and respected by all.

Main philosophical works (besides the *Nuove ricerche sui bello*) are two memoirs: *ricerche su la sensibilità sensitiva considerata come il principio fisico delle specie e del civilizzamento de' popoli e delle nazioni*, in *Atti della Reale Accadentia delle scienze di Napoli*, Vol. I (Napoli, 1819), Part II, pp. 343–376 and *Memoria su la perfettibilità organica considerata come il principio fisico dell' educazione, con alsune vedute sulla medesima* (Napoli, 1819) in the same volume of the *Atti*, pp. 377–445. The *Ricerche* were read before the Academy, February 17, 1813; the two parts of the *Memoria* were read, 1814 and July 6, 1816, respectively.

Collective edition: *Opere complete di Melchiorre Delfico*, ed. G. Pannella and L. Savorini (2 vols.; Teramo: Fabri, 1901–1904).

Biographical and doctrinal: Capone Braga, *La filosofia francese e italiana*, Vol. II, Part II, pp. 1–33. Sciacca, *La filosofia nell' età del Risorgimento*, pp. 152–170. G. Semprini, *Il pensiero di Melchiorre Delfico* (Teramo: Casa editrice Teramana, 1935). G. Calo, *Dall'umanesimo alia scuola del lavoro* (Firenze, 1940).

36. See Delfico's *Memoria su la perfettibilità organica*, p. 434, where he contrasts two series of Italian words: *soave, dolce, ameno, molle, fluido*, and *acre, aspro, fiero, duro, terribile, feroce*.
37. *Memoria su la perfettibilità organica*, p. 439.
38. *Ricerche*, p. 346. On the various cases of imitation observed in children and animals, pp. 347–349. Turning from hearing to sight, Delfico assimilates writing to speech. Ideograms first were pictures representing objects, that is, imitating them; hieroglyphs "symbolize objects"; as in the case of onomatopoeia, that primitive mode of written expression was soon superseded by more abstract systems of signs.
39. On "physical sympathy" and "compassion," *Ricerche*, pp. 353–359.
40. *Ricerche*, pp. 362–363: "e la Città sacerdotale divenuta la scuola del bello e degli onesti piaceri..." etc.; on the notion of *civilizzamento*, p. 363; on the consequences of the doctrine in the field of education, pp. 363–371. A summary of the main theses maintained by the *Memoria* is provided by Delfico himself, *Ricerche*, pp. 372–375.
41. *Ricerche*, pp. 372–375. On the physical bases of education, p. 385. Against two authors who too narrowly restrict the field of human perfectibility through imitation and make it differ very little from that of animals, *Memoria*, p. 248. The two authors are Lamettrie and Gall. On the German physician Franz Joseph Gall (1758–1828), inventor of a pseudo science called phrenology, see Damiron, *Essai*, rev. ed., Vol. I, pp. 185–195. Gall held the view that all the so-called intellectual faculties derive from organism, but he considered the brain as containing a plurality of centers matched by a corresponding number of faculties. Damiron (p. 190) denies that Gall was a materialist, but this does not agree with the commonly received and more likely interpretation of the doctrine.
42. *Nuove ricerche sui bello* (Napoli, 1818). There is a sense of beauty; nature has generously dealt with our "sensation of beauty" (*la sensazione del bello*), p. 117; how nature teaches us by the senses of hearing and seeing what beauty is, pp. 173–174; how nature causes man to create arts by setting in motion its "imitative function," chap. iii, pp. 56–71, and Conclusion, p. 174; particularly in the arts of drawing, beauty should be

sought in a combination of qualities pleasing to sight and apt to arouse in the hearts a feeling of benevolence; exactly, that combination of visible qualities should cause in the will a movement of attraction and of assimilation to other human beings; in this sense, the beautiful provides a basis for social ethics by fostering in man the fundamental feeling of sociability. In the conclusion of his work Delfico specifies that he has shown "how, by means of the imitative faculty, nature invites us to sympathize with beauty, and how the Fine Arts, adding choice to imitation, extended the domain of beautiful beyond its natural frontiers" (that is, up to the order of morality), p. 177; given this subordination of the beautiful to the good, *expression* of feeling is of the essence of beauty in the arts; "some moral usefulness is the scope to which must tend all research in mental philosophy," pp. 178–179.

43. *Nuove ricerche sul bello*, p. 3.
44. *Nuove ricerche sui bello*, p. 5.
45. Pasquale Borrelli, b. Tornareccio, 1782; d. Naples, 1849. *Introduzione alia filosofia naturale del pensiero* (Lugano: Vanelli, 1824); *Principii della genealogia del pensiero* (Lugano: Vanelli, 1825); both published under the pseudonym (in fact, an anagram of his name) Pirro Lallebasque; second edition: *Opere filosofiche del Signor Lallebasque* (4 vols.; Lugano: Ruggia & Co., 1830). Converted to ideology by his discovery of the *Treatise of Sensations* of Condillac, he aimed to achieve the union of ideology and physiology, an idea decidedly in the air. On the life and doctrine: Capone Braga, *La filosofia francese e italiana*, Vol. II, Part II, chap. vi, pp. 34–69; on the *Genealogy of Thought*, pp. 49–54. Sciacca, *La filosofia nell' età del Risorgimento*, pp. 161–166; bibliography, p. 197. On minor representatives of the Italian ideology, Capone Braga, Vol. II, chap. vii, pp. 70–127; shorter account in Sciacca, *op. cit.*, pp. 151–153, note 3, and pp. 166–168, note 1, with the remark of that excellent historian: "Very numerous is the group of the minor Italian ideologists, whose works now are nearly all forgotten, objects of erudite research rather than of true history of thought," p. 151, note 3.

VII. THE CHRISTIAN REACTION

1. *Institutiones philosophicae auctoritate D.D. Archiepiscopi Lugdunensis ad usum scholarum suae diocaesis editae* (5 vols.; Lyons, 1792); many later editions, e.g., Bassano, 1831. Cf. Louis Foucher, *La philosophie catholique en France au XIXe siècle (1800–1880)* (Paris: J. Vrin, 1955), p. 13. Anonymously published, the *Philosophia Lugdunensis* was the work of an Oratorian, Fr. Joseph Valla.
2. On traditionalism as a whole: Marin Ferraz, *Histoire de la philosophie en France an dix-neuvième siècle. Traditionalisme et ultramontanisme* (Paris, 1880). Maurice de Wulf, *Histoire de la philosophie en Belgique* (Brussels, 1910), Part III. Walter Marshall Horton, *The Philosophy of Abbé Bautain* (New York: New York University Press, 1926), a very good introduction, not only to Bautain himself, but to the whole traditionalist movement in France. Foucher, *La philosophie catholique*, is fundamental.
3. Louis Gabriel Ambroise de Bonald, Viscount, b. near Milhau, 1754; d. Lyons, 1840. Studied at Juilly (Oratorians); served in the army during the reign of Louis XV; retired

in 1776 and began at Milhau a political career which was to take him through all the political regimes, with the exception of his years of voluntary exile in Germany during the French Revolution; served under Napoleon I, then under the Bourbon kings; given a peerage in 1823, he resigned it in 1830, and retired to Milhau, where he died.

Main philosophical works: *Théorie du pouvoir politique et religieux dans la société civile démontrée par le raisonnement et par l'histoire* (Constance, 1796), written at Heidelberg during his emigration. *Essai analytique sur les lois naturelles de l'ordre social, ou du pouvoir, du ministre et du sujet dans la société* (Paris, 1800). *Du divorce considéré au siècle relativement à l'état dotnestique et à l'état ptiblic de la société* (Paris: Le Clère, 1801). *La législation primitive considérée dans les derniers temps par les seules lumières de la raison* (2 vols.; Paris: Le Clère, an XI–1802). *Recherches philosophiques sur les premiers objets des connaissances morales* (Paris: Le Clère, 1818). *Démonstration philosophique du principe constitutif de la société* (1830).

Not to be listed among his works is the book written by his son Victor de Bonald, *Les vrais principes opposés aux erreurs du siècle* (Avignon: Seguin et Montpellier, A. Seguin, 1833).

Collective editions: *Oeuvres de M. de Bonald* (15 vols.; Paris: Le Clère, 1817; 3 vols.; Paris: Migne, 1859).

Biographical and doctrinal: V. de Bonald, *De la vie et des écrits de M. le Vicomte de Bonald* (Paris, 1853). R. Manduit, *La politique de Bonald* (Paris, 1813). Ferraz, *Histoire*, chap. ii, pp. 85–164. H. Mouline, *De Bonald* (Paris: Alcan, 1916). Victor Delbos, *La philosophie française*, chap. iv, "De Bonald et les traditionalistes," pp. 277–299. M. H. Quinlan, *The Historical Thought of the Vicomte de Bonald* (Washington, DC, 1953). Foucher, *La philosophie catholique*, chap. i, pp. 11–29.

4. De Bonald, *La législation primitive*, Book II, chap. xix. Wholly in agreement with the Christian inspiration of scholasticism, de Bonald shows no sign of any real intimacy with its thought. His own philosophical equipment owes nothing important to the medieval masters of Christian thought, but, rather, to the notion of reason and of nature developed by Malebranche and inherited from him by Montesquieu. His insistence on the notion of law as grounded in the nature of things has no other origin. His natural theology seems to be influenced by the "common sense" philosophy of Reid. By and large, de Bonald's philosophical universe is pretty much the same as that of the eighteenth century's philosophers; the fundamental difference is that he sees in Christianity the only possible justification for its existence. The two men he constantly has in mind are Rousseau and Montesquieu; following their example he has "dared to seek for the fundamental laws of societies," after which, having found them, "he interrogated nature about their motives, and time about their effects" (*Théorie du pouvoir*, Preface, Vol. I, p. 9). "I have often quoted Montesquieu and J.-J. Rousseau…," but he opposed both (*Théorie du pouvoir*, pp. 12–14). On the notion of law, "Montesquieu and J.-J. Rousseau agree between themselves, and I agree with them, because we all agree with truth" (*Théorie du pouvoir*, Vol. I, Book I, chap. i, p. 27). There are therefore necessary relations deriving from the respective natures of God and men. Like God, who created him in his image, man is intelligence and will (because will is in intelligence), love, and force or power. Since there is mutual love between God and

men, there are between them relations of will to will. Those relations are necessary (as grounded in the respective natures of God and man); thence those relations are laws; if there are laws between God and man, there is between them a society. Without that society of intelligence and love between God and man, man could not think of God. That society then is the natural religious society, the natural religion. "Society thus is the reunion of similar beings by laws or necessary relations, a reunion whose end is their production and their mutual conservation" (*Théorie du pouvoir*, Vol. I, p. 28). One and the same notion of law applies to religious and to physical societies (p. 31); both produce and preserve; at least, they ought to, but history shows that, in fact, although "natural religion and family still are societies of production, they no longer are societies of conservation" (p. 33); the cause for this disorder lies in the now unruly will of man. Only the supernatural religion of Christianity can remedy that disorder: Christianity in religion and monarchy in society are the two answers to the problem: "Thus the Christian religion and monarchy can be defined as *a gathering of similar beings, gathering whose end is their mutual conservation*, just as natural religion and family are defined, a gathering of similar beings, gathering whose end is their mutual production" (p. 38). This looks like a thoroughly Christianized *Esprit des Lois*.

5. De Bonald sees himself as a representative of "Catholic philosophy." He is not the only one, but he claims a place of his own in the group of the Catholic philosophers. A Catholic philosophy differs from eclecticism and similar doctrines in that it appeals to authority and revelation against personal reason and inspiration. "That revelation, *oral* for the first family, but later *written* for the benefit of the first public society, has been preserved by that very same nation miraculously subsisting among us." The Jewish revelation was crowned by the establishment of the Christian religion, which was the ultimate development of the primitive revelation, and whose external and political form is Christendom; "a gathering and a confederation of the more powerful and more enlightened nations which ever existed" (*Démonstration philosophique*, Introduction). This is where de Bonald defines his personal place in the group: "That revelation, which Messrs, de Maistre, de La Mennais, and d'Eckstein have understood and upheld as a truth of faith, a fact both religious and historical, it was my intention to give a philosophical or scientific proof of it; this is the reason I maintained the physical and moral necessity, nay, the physiological and psychological necessity, of a primitive transmission of language made to man by a being necessarily superior, and anterior to, the human kind" op. cit., *Oeuvres complètes*, Vol. XII, pp. 34–35. Hence the rationalistic trait typical of the traditionalism of de Bonald; no knowledge without a revelation, but the necessity of revelation must be rationally and scientifically demonstrated. His proofs of it are twofold in kind: (1) physical: the primitive gift of language to man is confirmed by daily experience, for if left to themselves, the deaf and dumb cannot think; besides, the fact that children learn language from their parents enables us to see, actually performed, the primitive operation of the transmission of language; (2) metaphysical: language cannot have been invented by men who, without language, could not even have thought of inventing it; it is necessary for man to think his language before speaking his thought ("la nécessité de penser sa parole avant de parler sa pensée," *Oeuvres complètes*, Vol. XII, p. 39) leaves primitive transmission as the only

conceivable origin of speech, and therefore of thought. De Bonald's is a traditionalism without scepticism.

6. At this point, de Bonald considers his inquiry as entering the field of "metaphysics or of transcendent philosophy, which is a knowledge of general truths." It is therefore very different from the sciences of nature properly so called. Each particular science considers and develops a particular kind of truth: historical, political, chronological, geometrical, astronomical, botanical, zoological, etc. (*Démonstration philosophique*, Introduction, p. 62).

7. From this point of view the theory of society is one with the theory of power. The social cell is the family (father, mother, *and* child); its structure can be extended to all types of society (power, minister, subject); being "an intelligence served by organs," man communicates with other men by means of language, an organic expression of his intelligence. Man transmits language to his children as it was transmitted to him by his parents, and so on, ascending from generation to generation up to the first family, which itself only can have received it from "a being exterior and anterior to man." Now animals are born perfect, whereas man is born perfectible; he must therefore learn to live, and since he can learn it only from other men, he must listen and *obey*; hence the power of the father (*Démonstration philosophique*, Vol. XII, chap. ii, pp. 94–98). This prototype of all power is (see chap. iii): perpetual, independent, and final in its decisions. Societies arise out of the *necessity* there is for families to form aggregates. The origin of societies therefore is neither the will of man (contract theory), nor coercion by the stronger (Hobbes), it is a natural necessity (chap. vi, pp. 108–117). Like domestic power, social power is one, perpetual, independent and final in its decisions. Some call it absolute, which is to give it a bad name, for indeed, although from its decisions there is no appeal, social and political power is not "arbitrary" (chap. vii, pp. 121–125). As de Bonald conceives him, man is born a part of domestic society, itself a part of political society, nor can he be conceived apart from those social groups. De Bonald is a complete anti-Rousseau: "Not only is it not up to man to constitute society, but it is up to society to constitute man, that is to say to form him by social education; so I dealt with social education. Man exists only for society, and society forms him for itself only; consequently man must place at the disposal of society all that which he has received from nature and all that which he has received from society, all that which he is and all that which he has" (*Théorie du pouvoir*, Preface, Vol. I, p. 3). Rousseau had complained that society was educating children for itself, not for themselves; this precisely is what de Bonald wants education to achieve, namely to educate children for society, both domestic, political and, of course, religious. Along with his theory of public administration, de Bonald's "Theory of Social Education" fills up Part III of his *Théorie du pouvoir*.

8. See *Recherches philosophiques sur les premiers objets des connaissances morales*, 2nd ed. (2 vols.; Paris: Le Clère, 1826), the best all-around exposition of his chief philosophical positions; on the distinction between the *native* and the *natural*, Vol. I, chap. ii, pp. 149–150. Particularly well-developed points in these *Recherches* are: "On the origin of language," Vol. I, chap. ii, pp. 119–259; "On the definition of man as an intelligence served by organs," Vol. I, chap. v, pp. 295–314; refutation of Condillac's sensism

as developed by ideology, Vol. I, chap. vii, pp. 333-364; "On the Prime Cause," Vol. II, chap. x, pp. 22-121; "On Man, or on the Secondary Cause," Vol. II, chap. xii, pp. 160-231: just as there is only one primary cause of the universe, namely God, so also, properly speaking, there is only one secondary cause, namely man, who acts by himself, intentionally and in full awareness of the means (p. 160).

9. The notion of divorce, which disunites father, mother and child, cannot be understood apart from that of society, which unites them. Marriage is one of the laws of *domestic* society; it is a *natural* law, because family is natural to man (just as the political state is natural to families and as religion is natural to individual men, to families and to States); the end of the law of marriage is the reproduction and, still more, the preservation of man; as all that which aims to preserve, it is good; so the law of marriage is a good law. But its structure should be correctly understood! "Composed of father, mother and children, family is an *actual* society made up of three persons: power, agent or minister, and subject, as in all societies." Considered as preceding family and producing it, marriage itself is a *virtual* society composed of three persons: father, mother and the child to come; in this sense, marriage is a contract between *three* persons, two present persons, and an absent one (the child). In it, the absent person is represented by the public power which guarantees its rights. That contract cannot be broken by the two stronger parties to the detriment of the weaker one; social power and religious powers forbid such an injustice. Hence, State legislation must forbid divorce. Although sanctioned by the law of religious society (the Church) the indissolubility of marriage is in itself a *natural* law. See *Du divorce*, particularly the summary of the doctrine in *Résumé sur la question du divorce*, 3rd ed. (Paris: Le Clère, 1818), pp. 291-334.

10. On God as creator of all societies, see *Théorie du pouvoir*, Book I, chap. i. The end of all society being to preserve, society is conservative by its very essence (chap. ii). The will of God tends to the same end; hence *omnis potestas a Deo* (Vol. I, p. 47). This religious notion of society presupposes that there is a God; now "all the peoples have acknowledged his existence; hence God exists, for indeed all the peoples can agree on a feeling only (*un sentiment*), not on an *opinion*; now, an existence of which all the people have a *feeling* is an existence real for all the peoples" (Vol. II, Part II, chap. i, p. 12); cf. chap. ii, p. 14: "men can have a *notion* of something that may exist; men can only have a *feeling* of that which does exist"; "that religion is feeling (*sentiment*) and not opinion, is a principle of the highest importance and the key to all the religious truths," p. 22 All men have the *sentiment de Dieu* (chap. iii, pp. 26-34). On spirituality and immortality of soul, chap. iv, pp. 34-39 (likewise attested by universal feeling). Existence of God, Spirituality and Immortality of soul, fundamental truths and basis of all religious societies (chap. v, pp. 40-45). All those developments tend to prove that all that which provides for the preservation of society is *necessary;* all that which is necessary is a truth; hence all the truths are useful to men or to society, and social laws are true, because "generally speaking, society is a reunion of similar beings, a reunion whose end is their production and their mutual conservation" (Vol. II, Part II, chap. vi, p. 46). On monotheism as the religious equivalent of political monarchism, p. 50. The general demonstration is summarized by de Bonald as follows (Book I,

Part II, chap. viii, pp. 63–64): "Men think of God; hence God can exist. Men have the feeling of God; hence God exists. If there exists a supreme intelligence of whom men have both the notion and the feeling, then there is a society of intelligence between that supreme intelligence and man: hence there is a *reunion* of intelligences; hence there is communication between intelligences, hence there is speech, hence there is writing, which only is fixed, or transmissible and transportable, speech; hence there is divine speech and divine *scripture* (writing)." Since Scripture contains the precepts given to societies, Scripture is necessary for the preservation of societies; hence it was not written by man, for man, a finite being, cannot do anything that is *necessary*; so the book of Scripture is made by God; it is the very language and writing of God; hence it is divine (p. 68). On the relationship of natural society and of religious society, see Book II, chaps. i–iii.

11. See de Bonald's critical remarks on Condorcet: *Observations on a posthumous work of Condorcet*, published as a supplement to the *Théorie du pouvoir*, Vol. II, pp. 452–488, especially the remarkable pages 486–488. Conservative as he is, de Bonald does not deny the possibility of a certain progress, within truth. "There will be no *new* belief; Christianity satisfies all the reasonable desires of the mind, all the needs of the heart; but there still can be new reasons to believe; in fact, the very sight of the way religion survives the most ferocious attacks of its enemies is one of them: "No, there will be no *new* belief, but ancient belief can assume new developments. These will cause it to be still more august and more lovable, *not to that world that sees the things of religion in a certain way*, that is to say, with indifference, ignorance, hatred or scorn; not to that world that seems to be big because it makes a big noise, but to that Christian world which, while finding enough lights in religion, remains nonetheless disposed to receive from it still greater ones, provided these be approved of by the high authority of the Church, which *probes all spirits and rejects none* ("qui éprouve tous les esprits et n'en repousse aucun"), *Démonstration philosophique*, Introduction, pp. 68–69.

12. Joseph Marie Comte de Maistre, b. Chambéry (Savoy), 1753; d. Turin, 1821. Studied law; a senator, had to flee his country when, in consequence of the revolution, Savoy was invaded by the French army (1792); became an envoy of Victor Emmanuel I, king of Sardinia, to the Russian court in St. Petersburg, where he spent fourteen years.

Main writings: *Considérations sur la France* (Basel, 1797; reprinted, Paris: Librairie philosophique J. Vrin, 1936). *Essai sur le principe générateur des constitutions politiques* (written 1809, published 1815). *Examen de la philosophie de Bacon* (1815); posthumously published (Paris and Lyon, 1836). *Du pape* (2 vols.; Lyon, 1819); (Paris: Garnier, several reprintings). *Les soirées de Saint Pétersbourg,* unfinished, published shortly after his death (Paris, 1821); (Paris: Garnier, several reprintings).

Collective edition: *Oeuvres complètes* (14 vols.; Lyon: E. Vitre, 1884–1893).

Doctrinal: Charles A. Sainte-Beuve, *Oeuvres* (Paris: La Pléiade, 1951), Vol. II, pp. 385–466. Damiron, *Essai sur l'histoire de la philosophie en France au XIXe siècle* (2 vols.; Paris: Hachette, 1828); 3rd ed., enlarged (1834), Vol. I, pp. 207–227. W. M. Horton, *The Philosophy of the Abbé Bautain* (New York: New York University Press, 1926), Introduction, pp. 3–16. G. Cogordan, *Joseph de Maistre* (Paris: Hachette, 1891). Michel Revon, *Joseph de Maistre* (Paris: Librairie de la Nouvelle Revue, 1892). Francois

Paulhan, *Joseph de Maistre et sa philosophie* (Paris: Alcan, 1893). Georges Goyau, *La pensée religieuse de Joseph de Maistre* (Paris: Perrin, 1921). René Johannet, *Joseph de Maistre* (Paris: Flammarion, 1932).
13. This can be seen from the problems discussed in his unfinished *Les soirées de Saint Pétersbourg*. The central difficulty is to justify the temporal government of the world by the Divine Providence. How can one justify the presence of suffering in it? De Maistre successively establishes that, in this world (1) both just and unjust suffer, but the just less than the unjust; (2) that the just do not suffer *qua* just, but *qua* man; (3) that man suffers in consequence of original sin; (4) that there are for man two ways to redeem himself from sin: prayer and reversibility (from Damiron's excellent digest of the doctrine, in *Essai*, Vol. I, p. 216). Reversibility here means the reversibility of merits, a doctrine according to which the merits of saints and souls in state of grace can be credited by God to sinners. *Du pape* is no less provocatively against current prejudice.
The starting point is that there can be no society without sovereignty; now, in principle sovereignty cannot hope to be obeyed unless subjects consider it as justified; this implies that it be considered infallible; for if subjects had a right to gainsay it, they would have no obligation to obey it. In point of fact, sovereignty does proclaim itself infallible or, at least, it everywhere acts as though it considered itself infallible. In no country does Law submit itself to challenge. This, which is true of all societies, is also true of the Church. Indeed, theological truths are general truths made manifest and divine in the religious order. Now. if one admits that there must be a truly universal and unique church, it must have a sovereign of its own. That sovereign is infallible as all sovereigns are, and for the same reason. Consequently pope and councils are as infallible as king and Parliament are in England, or as kings and Chambers are in France. There is, however, this difference—that the pope enjoys an infallibility more eminently divine than that of any king. Hence, an important consequence: in ease temporal sovereignty should degenerate into tyranny, and arbitration should become required, it would be only natural to resort to the more certainly infallible authority, that of the pope. Only the pope can authorize wronged subjects to subtract themselves from the jurisdiction of their natural sovereign. By way of commentary, let us note that there have been such eases in the Middle Ages, at any rate; and that is the only point we wanted to make, that the aptitude of de Maistre to run counter to popular opinion cannot be denied.
Essential passages: "*Infallibility* in the spiritual order and *sovereignty* in the temporal order are two perfectly synonymous words. Both express that High Power which dominates them all, from which all the others flow, which governs and is not governed, judges and is not judged," *Du pape*, Book I, chap. i; besides, infallibility is a fact: "Answering to the whole earth for eighteen centuries, how many times have the Popes been *incontrovertibly* wrong? Never." (Book I, chap. xv); infallibility defended against philosophical objections of unbelievers (Book I, chap. xvii); errors against pontifical infallibility exemplified by Locke and other opponents (Book I, chap. xviii). To conclude: "Everything then brings us back to the great established truths. There can be no human society without government, nor government without sovereignty, nor sovereignty without infallibility; and this latter privilege is so absolutely necessary, that one

is obliged to suppose infallibility even in the temporal sovereignties (where it does not exist) under pain to see the association dissolve. The Church asks for nothing more than the other societies, although it enjoys over them an immense superiority since, in other societies, infallibility is *humanly supposed* whereas, in the Church, it is *divinely promised*" (Book I, chap. xix).

14. De Maistre has written an anti-Bacon as his Savoyard predecessor Gerdil had written an anti-Locke and anti-Rousseau. His criticism is very severe; inspired of his own principles, it denounces him as the patriarch of the eighteenth-century philosophers. The main features of their doctrines are already visible in his own: conscious intention to eliminate metaphysics and to replace it with physics (letter of Bacon to a friend: "Do not worry about metaphysics; when true physics is found, there will be no metaphysics left"), "Examen de la philosophie de Bacon," chap. i, in *Oeuvres complètes*, Vol. VI; only one real science, physics, chap. xiii, p. 253; de Maistre denounces the *theomisia* of the eighteenth century ("to separate God from human reason is one of the main objectives of modern philosophy," chap. xiv, p. 277). Bacon's criticism of final causes has no other end; nothing displeased him more than the union of philosophy and theology; one already perceives in his language the incurable hatred of the eighteenth-century philosophers and scientists for religion and its ministers (chap. xix, pp. 450–451); the true order of sciences ought to be: (1) Theology, Ethics and Politics; (2) the sciences of nature. But the order was inverted under Bacon's influence, and yet: "Any nation in which that order is not observed, is in a state of degradation" (chap. xix, p. 455); "it is surprising to see the French nation, which God has blessed with such a metaphysician as Malebranche, prefer Locke to him (p. 452); this accounts for the superiority of the philosophy of the seventeenth century to that of the eighteenth: "The philosophy of the eighteenth century is therefore perfectly null (at least in so far as good is concerned), since it is purely negative…" (p. 455) (a point to be noted in view of Comte's philosophy); a river of mud carrying some diamonds covered Europe during the last century; the source was at Ferney (Voltaire's estate), but other influences were at work, particularly the *Social Contract* and the *Spirit of Laws*: Rousseau had corrupted the servants, Montesquieu corrupted the masters (pp. 458–459); from such principles the ruin of the State was bound to follow: "All nations begin by theology and are established by theology. The more religious the institution, the stronger it is" (p. 460); what is true of societies is also true of sciences: "The more prosperous theology is in a country, the more fecund in true sciences that country is"; in fact, "Copernicus, Kepler, Descartes, Newton, the Bernouilli brothers etc., are as many products of the Gospel" (p. 461) (note the omission of Galileo).

15. *Les soirées de Saint Pétersbourg*, VIᵉ Entretien, Vol. I (Paris: Classiques Garnier), pp. 341–342.

16. *Les soirees*…, Vᵉ Entretien, I, pp. 259–260.

17. *Les soirees*…, Iᵉʳ Entretien, p. 30. On public executioners (God punishes crime through *human* justice); on original sin repeating itself at every moment of time; on the true nature of savagery and the difference between savages and barbarians, pp. 58–81. This Second Conversation is typical of de Maistre's manner. From the point of view of philosophical content, the Fifth Conversation should be preferred for partial

reading.
18. On Malebranche, *Les soirees...*, Xe Entretien, Vol. II, p. 159; on Fénelon, p. 160.
19. *Les soirees...*, Ier Entretien, Vol. I, p. 69. On differences in positions and exchanges of thoughts between de Maistre and de Bonald on those points, see the excellent remarks in W. M. Horton, *The Philosophy of Abbé Bautain* (New York: New York University Press, 1926), pp. 15–16.
20. *Les soirées...*, Ier Entretien, Vol. I, pp. 95–121, particularly p. 97: "Thought necessarily pre-exists words which are but the physical signs of thought, and, in turn, the words pre-exist the bursting out of all new tongue which receives them already made and then modifies them as it pleases"; origin of ideas and origin of words (p. 103); the decision on the matter first rests with "authority" (pp. 103–104); on Thomas Aquinas' definition of truth (p. 110).
21. *Les soirées...*, Ier Entretien, pp. 112–114. In *Essai sur le principe générateur*, the problem of the origin of language is tightly bound with that of the origin of societies; see *Oeuvres completes*, Vol. I, §47: man has believed he had the power of creating, while he has not even that of naming; "he has believed that he has invented languages, while he can easily see that all human language is *learnt*, never invented" (p. 287); names are in no wise arbitrary (§50, p. 289); God names himself I AAI (p. 289); "only God has the right to give himself a name; indeed he has named everything because he has created everything" (p. 290). In the curious developments that follow those remarks, de Maistre stresses the fact that names are in essential relation to beings. Every time something important happens to a man, he assumes a proper name in order to mark the change in his being: baptism, confirmation, religious profession, election of a pope or crowning of a temporal sovereign, etc.; a writer will assume a pen name, and we will say of him that he made a name for himself (Vol. I, §§52–59, pp. 292–301). All those remarks suggest that the alleged arbitrariness in the imposition of names might well be an illusion.
22. As translated by AV. M. Horton in his *The Philosophy of Abbé Bautain*, p. 9. This is a favorite theme with de Maistre. See *Considérations sur la France*, chap. vi, where de Maistre lays down a series of axioms: (1) no constitution results from a deliberation; written constitutions only codify already existing rights, of which there is only one thing to say, namely "that they exist because they exist," (*Oeuvres complètes*, Vol. I, p. 68; (3) often enough the rights of the peoples have been conceded to them by sovereigns, but the rights of the sovereigns and of nobility, at least the radical and essential ones, have neither dates nor authors (p. 68); (8) in exceptional cases, when it has decreed the quick formation of a political constitution, Providence appoints a lawgiver (p. 70); (9) such lawgivers, however, only gather together elements pre-existing in received customs, and that bringing together "that rapid formation, which has something of a creation, is performed only on behalf of the Divinity. Politics and religion establish themselves together; the lawgiver is hardly distinguishable from the priest" (p. 71); (12) no assembly of men can constitute a nation; such an undertaking exceeds in madness all that the "bedlams" of the world could produce in the way of extravaganza (p. 72). The same points are taken up again in the Preface to the *Essai sur le principe générateur des constitutions politiques*, Vol. I, pp. 228–230. In the same *Essai*,

see §1; a constitution can be neither written nor created *a priori*, it is a divine work (Vol. I, §2, p. 237), an essential character of law is *not* to be the will of all (p. 237); the only exception to the rule, "that man can make no constitution and that no legitimate constitution should be written" (§26, p. 265), is that of Moses (§29, pp. 265–266), but God, not Moses, made the constitution, and its writing was more than human work; "since all constitution is divine in its principle, man can make nothing of the sort," except as an instrument of God (§30, p. 266). Some will say that this is theology, not philosophy; indeed, they ask why is there a school of philosophy in every university? Answer: "It is in order that the Universities continue to exist and that teaching be not corrupted" (§38, p. 275). See also *Etude sur la souveraineté* (written in Lausanne 1794–1796) published in *Oeuvres complètes*, Vol. I; on the origins of sovereignty: laws and sovereignty come from God and from man, but from God first (Part I, chap. i, p. 314); so society is not the work of man (chap. ii, p. 317); against Rousseau (chap. ii, pp. 317–322 and chaps. v and vi, pp. 333–341); Voltaire has dissolved society, and Rousseau wrote up the code of anarchy (chap. xii, p. 407).

23. *Les soirées de Saint Pétersbourg*, XIe Entretien, Vol. II, pp. 222–227. De Maistre has anticipated the French conservative historical myth of "the stupid nineteenth century," pp. 222–223. want to stipulate that this part of the discussion is led by the Senator, not by the Count, who is the qualified mouthpiece of the author. What de Maistre himself thinks of "illuminism" is found on pp. 232ff. On the so-called Unknown Philosopher, Saint-Martin (eighteenth-century French thinker, d. 1804, refusing the assistance of a priest), head of the sect of "theosophists," see the express reservations made by de Maistre (p. 234). What he objects to, in the sect, is its fundamental rejection of priesthood which, in de Maistre's mind, makes it a deadly enemy to Christianity (p. 237).

24. Félicité Robert de Lamennais (or la Mennais), b. Saint-Malo (Brittany), 1782; d. Paris, 1854. Educated in the country, largely by an uncle, but rather indocile, he was locked up, by way of punishment, in a library well stocked with the works of the Encyclopedists; he thus became acquainted with Rousseau, by whom he always remained influenced; for reasons not wholly clear, his first communion was deferred till he was twenty-two (1804); but then, urged by his elder brother Jean-Marie and by one of his directors at the seminary, he was ordained a priest (1816). The years 1816–1834 are those he lived in communion with the Church, writing for her defense, which he conceived in his own way; he then became the center of a small group of disciples on his family estate, La Chesnaie; in the group, among others, were Gerbet, Montalembert, and, for a time, Lacordaire: among the laymen, a master in the art of prose poem, Maurice de Guérin; from August 1830 to November 1831, he ran a paper with the motto *God and Liberty*; that venture made against him the unanimity of the two opposite Catholic parties, Gallican and Ultramontane (i.e., for the Pope against the State); he went to Rome with Montalembert and Lacordaire, received no definite answer from the Pope but, on their way back, the three friends learned of the condemnation of the doctrine of *L'Avenir* by Gregory XVI (encyclical *Mirari Vos*, August 15, 1832); after accepting the sentence, retired to La Chesnaie and progressively detached himself from the Church. After the publication of *Les paroles d'un croyant* (1834) he received new condemnation (encyclical *Singulari Nos*, July 1834); he gave

his own view of the events in *Les affaires de Rome* (Paris, 1836) and wrote a program of Christian socialism (*Le livre du peuple*, 1837). Elected a deputy to the National Assembly, he sat on the extreme left wing; he saw his political career broken by the rise of Napoleon III (beginning December 10, 1848). He ended his life in solitude and died unreconciled with the Church.

Main philosophical works: *Essai sur l'indifférence en matière de religion*, Vol. I (Paris: Tournachon, Molin et H. Seguin, 1817), Vol. II (1820), English translation by Lord Stanley of Alderley (London: Macqueen, 1895). *Esquisse d'une philosophie*, posthumously published (3 vols.; Paris: Pagnerre, 1840–1841); the third volume contains the treatise *De l'art et du beau*.

Collective edition: *Oeuvres complètes revîtes et mises en ordre par l'auteur* (12 tomes in 6 vols.; Paris: P. Daubrée et Cailliers).

Bibliographical: J. M. Guérard, *Notice bibliographique des ouvrages de M. de La Mennais, de leurs réfutations, de leurs apologies* (Paris, 1849). Paul Janet, *La philosophie de Lamennais* (Paris: Alcan, 1890). Ch. Boutard, *Lamennais, sa vie et ses doctrines* (3 vols.; Paris: Perrin, 1908). F. Duine, *F. Lamennais, sa vie et ses idées* (Paris: Garnier, 1922). Christian Maréchal, *Lamennais, la dispute de l'Essai sur l'indifférence d'après des documents nouveaux et inédits* (Paris: H. Champion, 1928). For a general conspectus, M. Ferraz, *Histoire…Traditionalisme et ultramontanisme*, chap. iii, pp. 165–268; good summary of the doctrine, pp. 223–224. For Lamennais and Italy, V. Gioberti, *Lettre d'un Italien à un Français sur les doctrines de M. Lamennais* (Louvain: Ansiau, 1841). Guido Zadei, *L'abate Lamennais e gli Italiani dei suo tempo* (Torino: Gobeta, 1925). L. Foucher, *La philosophie catholique*, chaps. ii and iii, pp. 31–70.

25. *Essai sur l'indifférence en matière de religion*, Vol. II, Preface and chaps. xiii-xiv. This second part of the *Essay*, published in 1820, constitutes the essential contribution of Lamennais to the development of traditionalism. It contains the germs of his future personal evolution. The same chapters extend to scientific knowledge the conclusions already obtained with respect to ordinary knowledge. A science is but an ensemble of ideas and facts on which men are agreed (chap. xiii). In short, they are conventionally accepted positions. Some of those conventions, whose terms are intelligible to all, are likewise accepted by all. They are absolute certitudes of common sense. Other conventions are restricted to a small group of men who agree on them as on principles for the interpretation of nature; "of this second sort are all the systems, all the theories, all the explanations of phenomena," but their certitude comes to an end. There is nothing more variable and less certain than science. Besides, mathematics rests upon postulates, which are universally accepted, indemonstrable conventions. Physics rests upon the postulate of universal order, itself expressed under two main forms: (1) the conviction that the same causes will bring about the same effects in the future as they did in the past; and (2) that among the infinity of possible explanations of given facts, the simpler laws are the truer ones. This cannot be proved; it is a generally accepted convention; common consensus makes us certain of them. The so called moral laws can be interpreted in the same way.

26. It is interesting to compare these early positions with those of his much later work, written at a time when he had already left the Church: *Esquisse d'une philosophie* (4

vols.; Paris: Pagnerre, 1840–1846); the work defines the philosophical constants of Lamennais' thought. According to the second volume of *Essai sur l'indifférence*, the traditionalism of Lamennais culminates in an ontologism (human reason *only* knows and is because it is a sharing in Reason or God). The doctrine of the *Esquisse* starts with the notion of being; without it there remains neither existence nor cognition (non-being is nothing, and what is not cannot be known). Being is necessary, one, infinite, eternal; in fact, being is God ("He Who Is," Part I, Book I, chap vi). This idea is found at the bottom of all philosophical systems: to theists, being is God; to atheists, being is creation. The existence of Being (God) and of the universe, are equally indemonstrable; "the object of philosophy is not to prove them, but to conceive them" (Preface, Vol. I, p. xii). God is neither an indeterminate being, nor a potential being; always in act, God eternally enjoys the fullness of existence. Absolute being has three main properties: (1) power (it is being because it owns the power of existing; it *can* be); (2) intelligence, because intelligence is a perfection, and since Being lacks nothing (otherwise it would be non-being) it has intelligence, or rather, it *is* intelligence; (3) love, which is the bond, the nexus of intelligence and power (being cannot know its own perfection without loving it). In fact, since, "considered in itself, infinite being is one and enjoys the most absolute unity, it follows that every one of its properties is the whole being itself in its substance" (I, i, 7). The God of Lamennais is the Christian Trinity, one God in three persons, living an eternally blessed life (Part I, Book I, chaps. ix-xi). Creation is not an emanation, but a free act; it takes place according to Divine Ideas. Now, outside of God, every being is a limited one; matter is his limit; so God creates matter (Part I, Book II, chap. v). Within its own limits every creature desires good and tends to achieve it; hence there is a universal law of perfectibility (heritage of Enlightenment), so that for creation there is a cosmic progress, a kind of continuous evolution (term not used by Lamennais) which consists of always more closely imitating its Creator. However, creation can never acquire the perfection of God, for if it did, it would no longer have limits; it would no longer be the Creation. Lamennais goes on to show that the vast organism called nature owes its progress to the co-operation of the three persons of the Trinity. True, there is evil in the world, but it is tied up with the essential limitation of beings (Part I, Book III, chap. iii). No evil, no creation—to create is a perfection; the creative act is not a diminution of divine being; so that perfection had to belong to God (Part II, Book I, chap. iv). He claims still to follow "the founder of Christian philosophy" (St. Paul), but to him, "grace is nature, and nature is grace" (chap. 8). Lamennais has naturalized Christianity.

27. *Essai sur l'indifférence*, Vol. II, chap. xv. On this ontological tendency of the doctrine, see note 26. Given the unbelievable influence of Lamennais in France and abroad, this aspect of his thought deserves to be kept in mind in dealing with ontologists properly so called.
28. *Against the invasion of the Seminaries by Descartes. On the philosophical doctrines concerning certitude in their relations with philosophy* (1826).
29. *Essai sur l'indifférence*, Vol. II, Part 3, chaps. viii–xi.
30. H. Denzinger, *Enchiridion symbolorum*, 31st ed., ed. by Carolus Rahner, S.J. (Freiburg im Breisgau: Herder, 1957). The doctrinal acts concerning Lamennais are found in

secs. mdcxiii–xvii (Gregory XVI). Thus the author of the fiercest attack ever launched against indifference in matters of religion was condemned for ultimately teaching "indifferentism" in such matters, because, having refused to accept any rational justification for the authority of the Church, he had made it impossible for himself to oppose any sect, doctrine, or opinion flatly rejecting that authority. Moreover, having begun by placing in authority the sole "criterion" of truth, and by identifying authority with that of the Pope, he ended by appealing to the authority of universal reason against that of the Church, universal reason being, of course, that private reason he had first denounced as radically unable to know truth.

31. *Esquisse*, uncompleted and posthumously published in 1841, contained a last part devoted to esthetics. That part of the third volume has been published separately under the title *De l'art et du beau* (Paris: Garnier, 1896). It is still well worth reading. Its metaphysics of the beautiful is entirely traditional (in its essence, the beautiful is a manifestation of truth, and since nothing can be manifested except by form, the beautiful is being itself as determined by form); but Lamennais has the merit of distinguishing between the metaphysics of the beautiful, a favorite hunting ground for philosophers, and the philosophy of art, to which they had given little attention. Artists are makers; at its very root the notion of art implies creation; "for indeed, to create is to manifest outwardly a pre-existing idea by conferring upon it a form perceptible to sense" (chap. ii). Perhaps under the influence of Germaine de Staël's book *De l'Allemagne* (London, 1913), and, at any rate, in accordance with the spirit of the times, Lamennais denies that the principle of art be imitation: "Of course, imitation is one of its elements, but it is not its principle. Art is only one face of the development of man, of its active powers." Its first appearance in the world marks a significant moment in the progress of man, and consequently, in the progress of being, which is its goal (chap. i). On the other hand, Lamennais opposes the theory of art for art's sake. Rooted in the active and productive powers of man, art "unites the laws of organism to those of intelligence and of love, thus directing them to one and the same term, the perfection of being in that which is highest in its nature." In short, "art is to man what creative power is to God: hence the word *poetry* (from *poema*, something made) taken in the fulness of its primitive acceptation" (chap. i). A good conspectus of the doctrine is found in chap. vii, "On music" and chap. xi, "Résumé and conclusions."

32. Lamennais himself has given a summary exposition of the doctrine developed in the *Essai sur l'indifférence* (see "Défense de l'essai" in Paris-Brussels edition of 1828, chap. X, pp. 134–146): (1) whoever breaks away from the Catholic religion necessarily is either a heretic, a deist, or an atheist; (2) diverse as they are, all the great error systems have in common the principle of the sovereignty of human reason, which is to say that (3) "every man, discounting all faith and all authority, must find truth by his reason alone, or, which comes to the same, by means of Scripture as interpreted by reason alone," (pp. 134–135; this contains almost the first half of the *Essai*); (4) if he thinks consistently, whoever starts from the principle of the sovereignty of reason ends in universal scepticism (p. 135); (5) nature does not permit man to live in that state of generalized uncertainty (p. 140); (6) but it is impossible "to find in reason the foundation of reason" (p. 143); (7) so it is necessary to believe (p. 143); (8) the first

belief is in the existence of God, guaranteed by the universal consent of all the peoples (p. 144); (9) he who does not believe in God, cannot reasonably believe anything (p. 144); (10) "all finite intelligences necessarily begin by faith, which is the foundation of their reason" (p. 145). This includes angels and also provides a possible definition of the position rejected by the Catholic Church under the name of "fideism."

Doctrinal condemnations in Denzinger, *Enchiridion symbolorum*, pp. 447–449.

33. The Lamennais experiment evidences the collective nature of traditionalism. In this his case anticipates that of Bautain. The main themes of Lamennais' *Essai sur l'indifférence*, Vol. II, are all borrowed from prior philosophies; there is no absolute rational evidence for, "strictly speaking, we cannot say *I think*; we cannot say *I am*; we cannot say hence" (*Essai*, "Du fondement de la certitude," Part III, Vol. II, chap. i, p. 115). Still it is vitally impossible for man to live in a state of complete doubt (Pascal); we are redeemed from it by "consentement commun, *sensus communis*; it is for us the seal of truth and there is no other" (Thomas Reid, p. 121); this assent to commonly received truth is submission to general *authority* (Maistre and Bonald, p. 134); if therefore there is a universally believed truth, it must be at once a truth of fact, a truth known by feeling, by self-evidence, but also by reason; since reason essentially is submission to the authority of *sensus communis*: "to deny it would be to destroy reason itself"; that factual truth is God (pp. 148–149). So God is known by submission to "common sense," itself the mouthpiece of God. There are many proofs of the existence of God (metaphysical, physical, mathematical), but they only explicitate a primitive and fundamental certitude (pp. 104–170). The same positions occur in Lamennais' "Defense de l'essai"; disastrous absurdity of Cartesianism "as giving man no other rule of truth than his own judgments" (Preface, p. 14); for reason, we substitute common sense (p. 15); philosophers, ancient and modern alike, have denied everything; this shows there is a radical vice in their philosophy; what is wrong in it is their "principle of the sovereignty of man," which came to them from the Greeks (chap. ii, p. 36). Conclusion (Tertullian): the method of the philosophers is the same as that of the heretics (chap. xv, pp. 207–213): "Principles, consequences, everything, then, is common between the philosopher and the heretic" (p. 213). These positions are practically common to all the members of the school, including Bonald and Bautain.

34. Louis Eugène Marie Bautain, b. Paris, 1796; d. Paris, 1867. Studied philosophy under Cousin at the École Normale (1813) with his young friends Jouffroy and Damiron, one of "the three inseparables"; ceased to be a Catholic, but without ceasing to believe in the possibility of metaphysical knowledge; taught philosophy at the Royal College, Strasbourg (1816), then at the University (1817); toured Germany with Cousin (visit to Hegel). In 1819, after a nervous breakdown, under the influence of a Catholic woman well versed in the knowledge of German philosophy (Mlle. Humann) he resumed his lectures at the University of Strasbourg, but with a changed mind: Kant's *Critique of Pure Reason* convinced him that metaphysical knowledge was impossible; Bautain then returned to the faith of his childhood and, in his course on metaphysics (1822) he began to extol religion at the expense of philosophy; suspended from his functions by the Government as endangering religion by his scepticism; he opened a private course at Strasbourg (1822) and lived surrounded by disciples (see

his *Philosophie du christianisme*) who formed with him "the Strasbourg School," while he became "le philosophe de Strasbourg"; entered the seminary of Molsheim (1828); ordained a deacon and a priest in the same year; taught with great success until opposition to his ideas began to make itself felt; was denounced for heresy by the bishop of Strasbourg (1834); published *La philosophie du christianisme* (1835). After a visit to Rome, Bautain signed a formula of retraction (1840); from then on his influence declined; moved from Strasbourg to the college of Juilly near Paris (1841); taught moral theology at the Sorbonne (1853–1863) and continued to express his ideas, under a much more moderate form in a long series of books, of which the last one (*Les choses de l'autre monde*) was completed in 1867, the year of his death.

Main philosophical works: *De l'enseignement de la philosophie en France au dix-neuvième siècle* (Paris: Derivaux, 1833). *Philosophie du christianisme. Correspondance religieuse de L. Bautain, publiée par l'Abbé H. de Bonnechose* (2 vols.; Paris: Derivaux, 1835). *Philosophie. Psychologie experimentale* (Strasbourg, Derivaux) and (2 vols.; Paris: Lagny, 1839). *Philosophie morale* (2 vols.; Paris: Ladrange et Dezobry, 1842). *Les choses de l'autre monde, journal d'un philosophe recueilli et publié par l'abbé Bautain*, posthumously (Paris: Hachette, 1868).

Biographical and doctrinal: Walter M. Horton, *The Philosophy of Abbé Bautain* (New York: New York University Press, 1926), extended bibliography, pp. 302–306; a mine of information on Bautain and his school (Ollé-Laprune, Maurice Blondel, Louis Laberthonnière, Edouard Le Roy, etc.). Louis Foucher, *La philosophie catholique en France au XIXe siècle*, "Le cas Bautain" (Paris: J. Vrin, 1955), chap. iv, pp. 71–98.

35. The essential document is the preface of Henri de Bonnechose to the *Philosophie du christianisme* (Paris-Strasbourg, 1835), Vol. I. On the circumstances of the publication, see W. M. Horton, *The Philosophy of Abbé Bautain* (pp. 80–82, 92–93). Bibliographical information about Adolf Carl, Theodore Ratisbonne, Isidore Goschler and Henri Cardinal de Bonnechose (p. 308). The historical and doctrinal background of Bautain's philosophy is found in the same book, "Louis Bautain: the Odyssey of an Ardent Soul" (chap. i).

36. Thirteenth Letter, to Adéodat (Theodore Ratisbonne) in *Philosophie du christianisme*, Vol. I, pp. 170–173. Bautain's perhaps is the more elaborate specimen of a traditionalist view of the history of philosophy. It is found in the Twenty-fifth Letter (end of Vol. I) and in Letters Twenty-six and Twenty-seven (beginning of Vol. II). The explosive part of the doctrine was its criticism of the scholastic method as applied in Catholic schools, Letter Twenty-eight (vol. II, pp. 44–96). Written several years before (1835), this letter was bound to raise opposition in most schools of theology.

Bautain maintains: (1) that scholasticism (Aristotle in theology) is not the only possible form of Christian speculation (in fact, it was a novelty in the twelfth century); (2) it is not even the best method: in sciences, syllogism is powerless; "as to metaphysic itself, which is the science of the principles, it stands to reason that one cannot found it on reason since, in order to operate, reason precisely presupposes the principles it should establish" (II, p. 51); (3) scholasticism has had its usefulness; it still remains a good training, but its method should not be applied to problems that do not belong in the sphere of rational knowledge; still, it is up to the authority of the Church to decide such questions (Vol. II, p. 54). In schools of theology, teaching is spoiled by pride: "There, too, man boasts of the power that was not given to him, of knowing God without God, of ascertaining by reason alone the truth of the revealed Word, of judging it, of sanctioning it before believing in it. But there again its work is sterility stricken...." Letter Twenty-eight (Vol. II, pp. 56–57); cf. pp. 57–58: "What they call philosophy in seminaries...only is logic applied to questions in metaphysics and ethics"; it remains foreign to the modern world (p. 58). This anti-scholasticism is still alive in minds formed in the traditionalist school of Christian thought. It is even common to all the forms of Christian anti-intellectualism.

37. It is typical of the "ardent soul" that the clear sight of a certain part of truth blinds him to the truth of the rest. The difference between the religious God of Christianity and the philosophical god of Greek philosophy is certain. The god of philosophical speculation is not the God of Christian salvation. On the strength of that certitude, Bautain infers that since philosophy cannot prove anything about the God of the Christian revelation, taken precisely as such, it can know absolutely nothing about God. This was the fundamental weakness of the position, namely, that it rendered *all* metaphysical science impossible for reason unaided by revelation. "It is the divine grace that attracts man; it is the divine word that announces to man the mystery of God and of eternity, which gives to man the keys of metaphysical knowledge; and it is the Church that teaches him how to use it" (*Philosophie du christianisme*, Letter Fourteen, p. 194). In these partly true and partly wrong sentences, the ambiguity of the doctrine becomes apparent.

38. *Philosophie du christianisme*, Letter Thirteen, Vol. I, p. 180.
39. Letter Fourteen, Vol. I, p. 185.
40. Letter Fourteen, pp. 189–191.
41. Letter Fourteen, pp. 189–191.
42. Letter Fourteen, p. 192.
43. "Before they tried to erect common sense as the supreme authority, individual reason had been credited with a power it never had had and which it never will have, that of raising itself by itself and by the natural light to the certitude of the existence of the true God, of the unique God." Bautain knows the objection: nature proclaims the power and the wisdom of its Author. Indeed, but what man wants to know is "his own Author, his own God, the God of man, and about that God, nature says nothing," Letter Fourteen (p. 194). Reason they say, can rise from effects to their causes, and indeed it can, but "between finite beings and an infinite cause, between contingent and temporary existences and absolute and eternal being, there is an abyss which reason will never bridge." Where did reason find the notion of a Prime Cause? Not in nature, not in itself. In letting us believe "that reason has the power of establishing by itself or of proving by means of arguments the truth of the existence of one unique God; prejudice tends to nothing less than to propagate among us the crime of idolatry" (Vol. I, p. 195). "The certitude of the existence of God presupposes the idea of God, and that idea is not obtained by speculation, by abstraction, but by faith born of hearing and of language, in God only" (p. 197, note *only*). Reason, nevertheless, has a part to play; it overthrows the obstacles. Its arguments have only a negative value: "When the

obstacles are destroyed, the battle is over" and man believes (p. 198).

44. The six theses subscribed to by Bautain on the order of his bishop are found in *Enchiridion Symbolorum*, 31st ed., nn. 1622-1627; French original, p. 452, note 1. Furthermore, on April 26, 1844, as he was thinking of founding a congregation, Bautain pledged himself never to teach: (1) that with the lights of right reason only, abstracting from revelation, one cannot give a veritable demonstration of the existence of God; (2) that by reason alone one cannot demonstrate the spirituality and the immortality of the soul or any other truth—natural, rational or moral; (3) that by reason alone one cannot have the scientific knowledge of the principles or of metaphysics, as well as of all the truths that hang on it, as constituting a science wholly distinct from the supernatural theology founded on revelation; (4) that reason cannot acquire a true and full certitude of the motives of credibility, those motives which render the divine revelation "evidently believable," especially the miracles and the prophecies, particularly the resurrection of Jesus Christ (p. 453, note).

45. Elements of an epistemology are contained in Letter Sixteen (Vol. I, pp. 213-229) which makes the distinctions between image, notion and idea: *linage* is the effect of a physical object acting upon sense through psychical light; *notion* is an abstract product of reason; *idea* is the effect of an object superior to the world of sense and acting upon our intelligence through the intelligible light; every idea answers an ideate and presupposes its action on us or its revelation to us; as we have the idea of Being, or God, it follows that God must have manifested himself to man; the Church is the trustee of His word). Without the dogma of the Trinity, no metaphysics is possible, Letter Nineteen (Vol. I, pp. 257-284). Philosophy is the science of man in his relationship to God, and vice versa; so it cannot be philosophy without being theology, and conversely; in the last analysis, there is only one philosophy, but it includes two philosophical doctrines, "traditional philosophy and rationalism," Letter Twenty-four (Vol. I, pp. 343-344). In his *Psychologie expérimentale* (2 vols.; Strasbourg: Derivaux 1839), published four years after his *Philosophie du christianisme*, Bautain avoided such burning issues. For a conspectus of his psychology (whose later influence we failed to detect) see W. H. Morton, *The Philosophy of Abbé Bautain*, chap. iii, secs. i and 2, pp. 142-208.

46. Gioacchino Ventura de Raulica, b. Palermo, 1792; d. Versailles, 1861. Joined the congregation of the Theatines (1817); was a successful preacher; was appointed by Leo XII a professor of Canon Law at the Sapienza, Rome (published *De jure ecclesiastico*, 1826); general minister of the Theatines (1830-1833); after the election of Pope Pius IX, favored liberal ideas in politics and (in agreement with Rosmini) advocated a Confederation of the Italian States under the presidency of the Pope; having recognized the Roman Republic, flew to Civita Vecchia under the protection of the French troops, then to Montpellier (1849), then to Paris where he began to preach with great success, although French was not his mother tongue; his conferences at the church of La Madeleine are among the best expositions of his philosophical doctrine.

Main philosophical works: *De methodo philosophandi* (Roma, 1828). *La raison philosophique et la raison catholique, Conférences prêchées à Paris dans l'année 1851* (4 vols.; Paris, 1852-1864). *De la vraie et de la fausse philosophie, En réponse à une lettre* de Monsieur le Vicomte Victor de Bonald (Paris: Gaume, 1852). *La tradition et les semi-pélagiens de la philosophie ou le semi-rationalisme dévoilé* (Paris, 1856). *La philosophie chrétienne* (3 vols.; Paris: Gaume, 1861), a sequel to the preceding work. *Essai sur l'origine des idées et sur le fondement de la certitude* (Paris, 1853).

Collective editions: *Opere complete,* 1852–1863 (31 vols.; Milano), 1856–1863 (11 vols.; Napoli); posthumous works (3 vols.; Venezia, 1863).

Biographical: P. Culterra, *Della vita e delle opere del Rev. P. D. Gioacchino Ventura* (Palermo, 1877).

Doctrinal: P. Séjourné, "Ventura," in *Dictionnaire de théologie catholique,* Vol. XV (1950), pp. 2635–2639 (includes an interesting doctrinal discussion). L. Foucher, *La philosophie catholique en France,* chap. ix, pp. 237–246.

47. Ventura de Raulica, *De la vraie et de la fausse philosophie,* §5: "The whole first volume of the *Recherches* (by de Bonald) is but a long and eloquent commentary of this proposition: For three thousand years there have been nothing else than false philosophies in the world; the only true philosophy is that which is now for the first time being offered to the world at the hands of M. de Bonald" (pp. 12–13).

48. *De la vraie et de la fausse philosophie,* §5, against the prejudice that it is not necessary to study scholasticism (pp. 12, 13–14). The whole §3 (pp. 6–10) is devoted to that point; particularly pp. 8–9 and 9–10, where Ventura rightly protests against Catholics' use of the famous words of Leibniz about the "gold still to be found in the dunghill of scholasticism." They speak of it from hearsay; had M. de Bonald known Thomas Aquinas at the time of his youth, he would have embraced his doctrine lovingly.

49. *De la vraie et de la fausse philosophie,* §9, pp. 25–27. Ventura stipulates that in fact, de Bonald did philosophize from faith, as a Christian should; only the revelation in which he wants us to believe is that of language made by God to society. His system boils down to this: "Begin by believing society because God has spoken to society" (§13, p. 39). On this point, Ventura was attempting to justify de Bonald against the rationalist interpretation of his thought by Viscount Victor de Bonald, son of the philosopher. Still, in the last analysis de Bonald was wrong in not knowing Christian philosophy; hence his illusion that, after Luther, Christian philosophy was waiting for a "new reformer" and that he himself, M. de Bonald, was the man (§18, p. 59).

50. The pamphlet is a lengthy answer to objections directed against Ventura by one of the sons of de Bonald, Victor de Bonald, himself a traditionalist (see preceding note). In it Ventura stipulates that his description of the evil effects of "inquisitive philosophy" is not directed against de Bonald, nor even against Descartes, but against pure and simple "rationalism," whose ultimate consequence is generalized scepticism and which has no other aim than to eliminate religious belief. According to tenets of this "rationalism" religion is not the last phase of the development of the human mind—philosophy will be the last one; consequently, "philosophy must judge, dominate and submit religion to itself" (§15, p. 45). However, Ventura holds the view that Descartes and Bonald did not go to such extremes only because they did not pursue inquisitive philosophy to its last consequences.

51. The Second Conference of 1851 is decisive on this point. In it, Ventura relates his own distinction of the two philosophies to an "important observation made by

Locke," to wit, that to want to discover a hidden truth is one thing, and that to want to acquire a proof of an already known truth is another thing. The whole history of philosophy is contained in this remark. Modern philosophy has been inquisitive only. "Inquisitive philosophy has rejected all truth that was not a conquest; demonstrative philosophy has eagerly grasped truth everywhere it found it.... Demonstrative philosophy, in the last analysis, is but the reason of man accepting the reign, acknowledging the laws, respecting the authority of religion and (*mark well this turning point in Ventura's argument*) of all that which Saint Thomas calls the conceptions common to all men. It is the reason that likes to submit to God, to depend on God and to use its freedom only within the limits assigned to it by God. So while inquisitive philosophy starts from doubt, demonstrative philosophy starts from faith. Inquisitive philosophy founds itself on the word of man and takes pride in doing so; demonstrative philosophy founds itself on the word of God, and it takes pride in doing so. Such, Brethren, is the philosophy which the Catholic reason (*la raison catholique*) has established in the early times of Christianity," *La raison philosophique et la raison catholique*, Second Conference, pp. 110-114. In opposing those lines to Viscount Victor de Bonald, Ventura triumphantly concludes: "Is not that clear, Monsieur le Vicomte? You asked for a precise definition of 'demonstrative philosophy' and I give you ten," *De la vraie* (§9, p. 23). That is the trouble—whichever definition we may choose among the ten offered by Ventura, they all include the ambiguous notion of a purely rational philosophy deriving its principles of some authority, including that of the Christian revelation.

52. Ventura, *La tradition et les semi-pélagiens*, Vol. III, §21, pp. 126-129; quoted almost in full by Séjourné in his article on Ventura, *Dictionnaire de théologie catholique*, col. 2638.

53. The bond between traditionalism and the notion of Christian philosophy (as well as between the danger of fideism that is naturally besetting it) finds its concrete expression in the collection of the *Annales de philosophie chrétienne*. That important publication ended at the time of modernism under the direction of Father Lucien Laberthonnière, still fighting scholasticism, Thomism, philosophism, intellectualism and rationalism in the name of faith, revelation and moral experience.

Augustin Bonnetty, b. Entrevaux, 1798; d. Paris, 1879, founded the *Annales de philosophie chrétienne* in 1830; subscribed the four propositions decreed by the Congregation of the Index, June 1855 (*Enchiridion symbolorum*, 31st ed.; pp. 462-463). Their import is: (1) there is no strife (*dissidium*) between faith and reason; (2) reason can prove with certainty the existence of God, the spirituality of the soul and the liberty of man; as faith is posterior to revelation, it is not fitting to allege faith in refuting unbelievers; (3) "the use of reason precedes faith and leads man to it through revelation and grace"; (4) knowledge of the method used by Thomas Aquinas, Bonaventure and other scholastics after them, is not the reason why naturalism and pantheism are today invading schools; doctors and masters, then, should not be blamed for having used it.

VIII. The Philosophical Reaction in France and Italy

1. Pierre-Paul Royer-Collard, b. Sompuis (Champagne), 1763; d. Châteauvieux (Loir-et-Cher), 1845. Between two periods of political activities he taught philosophy at the Sorbonne (1811); the opening lecture to his third year lecture course contains the essentials of his philosophical positions. In matters of philosophical opinions, Royer-Collard esteemed that "all that which is harmful is false, while all that which is wholesome is true." On that basis, he opposed the sensism of Condillac for "depriving the mind of its sublime origin, morals of its authority and man of his immortal destinies" (one instance among a thousand of his sententious style); persuaded that one cannot compromise with scepticism ("On ne fait pas au scepticisme sa part"), Royer-Collard adopted the general conclusions of the Scottish school of "common sense": the certitude of the fundamental notions, such as extension, substance, being, duration, etc., is guaranteed for us neither by passive sense experience, nor by empty and sterile reasoning, but by an active mental perception that carries with itself its own evidence and makes us perceive those realities. To affirm the objective value of human knowledge is not only to express a philosophical truth, but to perform a civic duty; for indeed, public and private morals, along with "the order of societies and the well-being of individuals are at stake in the debate between true and false philosophies on the reality of knowledge" (opening lecture for 1813). Royer-Collard's was sometimes called the "doctrinaire" system, and held responsible for the inspiration of the "doctrinaire" political regime (Guizot, etc.) All this was "bourgeois" *reduplicative tit sic.*

    Collective editions: André Schimberg, *Les fragments philosophiques de Royer-Collard, réunis et publiés pour la première fois à part, avec une Introduction sur la philosophie écossaise et spiritualiste au XIXe siècle* (Paris: Alcan, 1913).

2. Joseph Marie de Gerándo, b. Lyon, 1772; d. Paris, 1842. Began as exponent of traditional ideology with *Des signes et de Part de penser considérés dans leurs rapports mutuels* (4 vols.; Paris: Goujon fils, an VIII–1799). On a subject provided by the Berlin Academy of Sciences: *De la génération des conaissances humaines* (Berlin: Georg Decker, 1802), he shared first prize. *Histoire comparée des systèmes de philosophie relativement aux principes des connaissances humaines* (3 vols.; Paris: Henrichs, 1804), 2nd edition (4 vols.; Paris: A. Eymerv, 1822). *Histoire comparée des systèmes de philosophie,* Deuxième partie: *Histoire de la philosophie moderne,* 2nd edition published posthumously by the son of the philosopher, G. de Gérando (4 vols.; Paris: Ladrangc, 1847). In this same work, at the end of Vol. IV, is found a curious *Rapport historique sur les progrès de la philosophie depuis iqSp et sur son état actuel,* presented to the Emperor Napoleon I, February 20, 1808 (pp. 385–406). On de Gérando, Philibert Damiron, *Essai sur l'histoire,* 3rd edition. (Paris: Hachette, 1834), Vol. II, pp. 89–101.

3. Germany was far ahead of other countries in this respect; the ample history of J. Brücker dates from the eighteenth century. It was put on the Index as early as July 28, 1755, under the title: Brückerus, Iacobus: *Historia critica philosophiae a mundi incunabulis ad nostram usque aetatem deducta.*

4. Although still sensistic, the first memoir of Gérando for the Berlin Academy had already included a history of the problem (chap. v–xv). See the Introduction published by G. de Gerándo in *Histoire comparée,* Deuxieme partie (1847), Vol. I, p. vi: "How could one throw on the principles a brighter and a safer light than by presenting a

picture of the progress of the human mind? To witness the inquiries, the efforts and meditations of so many geniuses who devoted themselves to the pursuit of wisdom, to gather together the truths discovered by them, to observe their influence, but also to observe their errors, along with the causes and consequences of same—is there anything more worthy of our study and better calculated to impart safer directions to our mind?" Nothing can more efficaciously contribute to the restoration of philosophy (Vol. 1, p. vi). In the Memoir of 1808 to the Emperor, Gerándo successively examines the modern contributions to philosophy made in Scotland, in Germany and in France; extolling Reid's doctrine as "the code of good sense" (p. 410), he praises the Scottish school for having revived the pure doctrines of ancient wisdom (p. 409); Oswald, Beattie and Dugald Stewart receive their due share of praise (pp. 409, 411–412). Historical research is "as a treatise in experimental philosophy" (p. 434). The examples of the past prepare future progress. Eclecticism was to add precision to those views, but the historical discussion of past systems in the light of common sense, an essential feature of eclecticism, was already present in the writings of Gerándo.

5. Victor Cousin, b. Paris, 1792; d. Cannes, 1867. Studied philosophy at the École Normale under Laromiguière and Royer-Collard; the latter introduced him to Maine de Biran; began to teach at the same school in 1814; in 1817, having been informed of the doctrine of Reid by Royer-Collard, he devoted his lecture course to the philosophy of "common sense"; went to Germany to study Kant and devoted two years to an exposition of his philosophy (1819–1821); political events obliged him to abandon his chair at the Sorbonne (1821) and at the École Normale (1822); published the works of Proclus and translated Plato; went to Germany for the second time; was detained by the police on denunciations which came from France; was liberated after six months; recovered his chair at the Sorbonne (1827) and at the French Academy (1832); was a minister of public instruction (1840); became a sort of philosophical dictator and strove to impose the teaching of his own eclecticism; when Guizot became the prime minister, Cousin had no other choice than to give up his teaching activities. Cousin officially retired in 1852 and spent the last years of his life in peace.

Main works: Apart from his important contributions to the history of philosophy, Cousin has left significant contributions to philosophy itself. The best introductions to his personal doctrine are: M. Adolphe Garnier, *Cours de philosophie, professé à la Faculté des Lettres pendant l'année 1818 par M. Victor Cousin sur le fondement. des idées abstraites du Vrai, du Beau et du Bien, publié avec son autorisation et d'après les meilleures rédactions du cours par M. Adolphe Garnier* (Paris: Louis Hachette, ancien élève de l'École Normale, 1836). This is the redaction by Garnier, from notes of the famous lecture course of Cousin in 1818. *Fragments philosophiques*, 3rd ed. (2 vols.; Paris: Ladrange, 1838). Those fragments contain some parts of the 1818 lecture course written up by Cousin himself. The Preface to the second edition, very valuable for the autobiographical information it contains, has been preserved in this third edition.

Collective edition: *Oeuvres complètes* (10 vols.; Paris: Ladrange, 1851–1855).

Doctrinal: Ph. Damiron, *Essai sur l'histoire de la philosophie en France au XIXe siècle*, 3rd ed., Vol. II, pp. 152–196, for the works of Cousin till 1828; on later years, pp. 525–546. Marin Ferraz, *Histoire…Spiritualisme et libéralisme*, see above, note 1. Félix

Ravaisson, *La philosophie en France*, 4th ed., pp. 18–19, on the historical activities of Cousin; pp. 20–25, on the doctrine. L. Foucher, *La philosophie catholique en France*, chap. vi, pp. 145–166.
6. "Leçons de philosophie," in *Fragments philosophiques*, 3rd ed., p. 140.
7. *Fragments philosophiques*, Preface to the 1st ed., p. 49. It is noteworthy that, to Cousin, just as to Bonald and Maistre, "la philosophie du dix-huitième siècle" appears as a distinct historical entity. For instance, "The philosophy of the eighteenth century did not act that way; in fact, it could not" (p. 51). Cousin reduces its method to that of "observation." "We have faith only in it, we cannot do anything except by means of it, and nevertheless, in England as well as in France, it only has been able to destroy without founding anything" (p. 51).
8. Cousin was most explicit on this point. His edition of the commentary of Proclus on *Parmenides* of Plato was dedicated to his friends and masters, leaders of today's philosophy, Schelling and Hegel. Cf. "Hegel has much borrowed from Schelling; as to myself, much weaker than either one, I borrowed from both" (p. 29). Cousin then proceeds to show that fundamental differences separate him from these two masters, the main one is in the method his philosophy follows.
9. *Fragments philosophiques*, Preface to the 2nd ed., pp. 40–42. Cf. *Cours de philosophie*, ed. Garnier (Paris, 1836), p. 11: "I do not advocate the blind syncretism which was the undoing of the school of Alexandria and which wants by main force to bring together contrary systems; what I advocate is that enlightened Eclecticism which, judging all doctrines, borrows the true that is common to them and leaves out what they have of the conflicting and false; I mean that eclecticism which, being the true spirit of sciences, has created and promoted the physical sciences, is also the only one that can rescue the moral sciences from their immobility."
10. The lecture course in which Cousin exposed his philosophy lasted from 1815 to 1818; during this last year, he summed up his views; in 1826, after he had ceased teaching, he began to publish fragments of his lectures, especially of those given in 1818; in 1836, Adolphe Garnier reconstituted the 1818 lecture course and published it. This summary of the doctrine, along with the *Fragments* published by Cousin himself, constitutes our main source of information on his philosophy. In editing the 1818 *Cours de philosophie*, Adolphe Garnier added to it, by way of Introduction, an excellent abridgement of the work. For what precedes, see *Cours de philosophie*, pp. viii–xvi.
11. On the true, *Cours de philosophie*, pp. xvii–xviii. On the distinction of ideas and principles, p. xix.
12. On the beautiful, *Cours de philosophie*, lectures xix–xxi and xxvii. There must be something necessary and absolute in the idea of the beautiful, at least if the discussions of fine arts are not to degenerate into mere arbitrariness (lecture xix, p. 182); the pleasant is personal and arbitrary; the beautiful is common to all men (lecture xx, p. 197); art represents neither the individual nor the absolute, but the human life as a whole in its combination of visible and invisible, of infinite and of finite, of judgment and of sensation; art must then pursue a twofold goal: (1) to please physical sensibility and (2) to satisfy reason. The constitutive character of all art is expression; the beautiful in art is true and good, manifested to man in a form perceptible to sense;

Notes 527

had it no forms, the beautiful would be nothing but true and good; "the beautiful thus consists of two parts: a moral part and a sensible part. The moral part is good and true, of which the beautiful is the only manifestation; the sensible part is the form under which the true and the good manifest themselves to our organs. What has just been said of the beautiful exactly applies to art"; "the moral idea identifies the arts, the form of expression separates them" (lecture xxviii, pp. 283-284).

13. On that aspect of the doctrine of Cousin, Ravaisson has written most penetrating remarks: Instead of limiting observation to external facts, Cousin wanted to extend it to the inner phenomena. Consequently, "the true method in philosophy consisted, after describing and classifying the inner phenomena, in drawing from them the knowledge of that which soul must be, and then, from soul, to rise up to God by the way which Descartes had shown to us. Victor Cousin called this the psychological method. In other words, there are two orders of cognitions entirely distinct: the perceptions and the conceptions; the perceptions for the phenomena, sole objects of experience; the conceptions for the beings, and likewise for the true, the beautiful and the good, for space and time, etc. All the things that exceed the phenomena are taught to us, Cousin would say, by a sort of revelation, inexplicable, which is in us the work of reason." Ravaisson then goes on to show how that notion of a radical transcendency of rational truth over empirical reality was suggested to Cousin by the "abstract" aesthetics of Winckelman. F. Ravaisson, *La philosophie en France*, 4th ed. (1895), pp. 21-25-

14. Théodore Jouffroy, b. Pontets (near Pontarlier), 1796; d. Paris, 1842. Entered the École Normale (1813) where he came under the influence of Cousin; after a religious crisis (described in his *Nouveaux melanges philosophiques*), he became "an unbeliever detesting unbelief"; taught philosophy 1817-1822; deprived of his job in consequence of political troubles, lived by teaching privately; published a French translation of the complete works of Thomas Reid; in 1828 taught philosophy again at the École Normale and at the College de France. Main works: *Mélanges philosophiques* (Paris: Paulin, 1833), 7th ed. (1901). *Nouveaux mélanges philosophiques*, with notes by Ph. Damiron (Paris: Joubert, 1842), 4th ed. (1882). *Cours d'esthétique*, with the thesis of Jouffroy on the feeling of beautiful, Preface by Ph. Damiron (Paris: Hachette, 1843). Jouffroy professed eclecticism with particular stress on psychology; distinguished faculties as follows: (1) primitive inclinations (*a.* love of power, or ambition; *b.* love of knowledge, or curiosity; *c.* love of other men, or sympathy); (2) sensibility (aptitude to perceive pleasure or pain); (3) intelligence (perception, consciousness, reason); (4) expressive faculty (language, power of using signs); (5) motive faculty; (6) will. On the notion of "faculty"; "Des facultés de l'âme humaine," in *Mélanges philosophiques* (pp. 243-272). On eclecticism, "De l'eclectisme en morale" (pp. 273-279). On history of philosophy (common sense, spiritualism and materialism, scepticism) (pp. 105-188); on the philosophy of history (pp. 36-58); particularly Bossuet, Vico, Herder (pp. 59-63). A less systematic thinker than Cousin, but with a stronger grip on concrete reality, Jouffroy still found readers for some of his essays: "Comment les dogmes finissent" (pp. 1-19); "Du problème de la destinée humaine" (pp. 297-343); and "Méthode pour résoudre le problème" (pp. 344-375).

15. Two French attempts were made to restore metaphysics in its rights, and both were

of good quality, but their authors failed to catch the attention of the public; in a way, they are hardly beginning to be noticed by historians; the reason is that Bordas-Demoulin and Lequier tried to build up Christian philosophies completely unrelated to the medieval tradition—equally foreign to traditionalism and scholasticism, and opposed to eclecticism and the sensism of ideology, they escape classification. (1) Jean-Baptiste Bordas-Demoulin, b. La Bertinie (Dordogne), 1797; d. Paris, 1859. *Le cartésianisme on la veritable rénovation des sciences* (2 vols.; Paris: J. Hetzel, 1843). *Mélanges philosophiques et religieux* (Paris: Ladrange, 1846). Doctrinal: Ferraz, *Histoire de la philosophie en France au dix-neuvième siècle; Traditionalisme et ultramontanisme* (Paris, 1806), chap. viii, pp. 403–502 (Bordas-Demoulin is equally unrelated to traditionalism and to ultramontanism; Ferraz must be praised for having attracted attention to him). L. Foucher, *La philosophie catholique*, chap. v, B, pp. 116–130. By formation a mathematician, by vocation a metaphysician, by discipline a philosopher, and by perseverance an independent, he, moreover, picked the wrong title for his main work. Many mistake it for one more book on Descartes, but Bordas intended to show that, after a good start—the soul exists (I am a thinking thing) and God exists—Descartes had lost the right way. Had Descartes remained inside the soul instead of running out of it after the world of material things, he would have found in himself many other intelligible objects (ideas) such as quantity, life, etc., whose objective study constitutes true metaphysics. Soul is made up of these ideas, given to prior experience, which makes it possible to organize them intelligibly. Bordas does not conceive those ideas to be seen in God (Malebranche) but to be seen in the soul by the soul. The relation of our ideas to those of God is one of participation and of resemblance. The task of the philosopher is to start from ideas in us and to approach the ideas of God, which are their models and their causes, and thereby to order them all under the supreme idea of Good, or God. On the part played by Bordas in the dispute concerning the notion of mathematical infinite [Hoëné Wronski, *Introduction à la philosophie des mathématiques* (Paris, 1811), *Réputation de la théorie des fonctions analytiques de Lagrange* (Paris, 1812), *Contre-réflexions sur la métaphysique du calcul différentiel* (Paris, 1814), *Philosophie de l'infini* (Paris: Didot, 1814)] see the excellent exposition of L. Foucher, op. cit., pp. 120–124. (2) Jules g. Lequier, b. Quintin, 1814; d. Baie du Rosaire (Saint Brieuc), 1862. Mathematician by formation (Polytechnique School, where he studied along with Renouvier, 1834–1836), he led a solitary life in the quest of an inaccessible wisdom; he seems to have committed suicide, being of unsound mind. Posthumous work: *La recherche d'une première vérité. Fragments posthumes de Jules Lequier, ancien élève de l'École Polytechnique* (Saint Cloud: Berlin, 1865), new edition with biographical notes by Louis Dugas (Paris: A. Colin, 1924). An anthology, Jean Wahl, *Jules Lequier* (Paris-Genève: Les classiques de la liberté, Les trois collines, 1948). Doctrinal: L. Foucher, *La philosophie catholique*, chap. v, C (Paris: J. Vrin, 1955), pp. 130–144. The doctrine of Lequier is essentially a philosophy of liberty. Under the influence of Fichte, Lequier situates the starting point of philosophical reflection in a free option of the will, beyond the Cartesian intuition of the "I am a thinking and willing thing," in consequence of which both moral action and science become possible. This primary "I will" is an absolute beginning, independent of all knowledge since it is the condition of its possibility. Curiously enough, Lequier considers that only one philosopher has discerned well the essence of freedom—Aristotle: "An act is free when we can judge that, finding ourselves under identical circumstances, we could perform an exactly contrary act, a judgment that can be but a belief, not an evidence, since the experiment cannot be attempted because identical circumstances never occur twice in one and the same life" (Foucher, p. 130). To him, only Christianity (enlightened by faith) contains the secret of that truth. "That great truth of free will which all the philosophers, save only one, have missed, those that pretended to support it as well as those that opposed it, that truth *par excellence*, the alpha and, accordingly as you look at it, the omega of human knowledge, is the property of the Catholic church" (in Jean Grenier, p. 223, and Foucher, p. 137). So, around 1840, Lequier attempted to justify Catholicism by showing that liberty is its very core. "Catholicism is true because it is a religion of the liberty of man, because all its dogmas, as well as the ethics that follows from them, rest upon the presupposition that a free God has made man free." Thus understood, a Christian philosophy would be a *union* of reason in its power of producing science, arts and ethics, with the Catholic creed (Foucher, p. 137).

16. On that Italian period: bibliography by Michele Federico Sciacca, *Italienische Philosophie der Gegenwart* (Bibliographische Einführungen in das Studium der Philosophie, ed. I. M. Bochenski, 7) (Bern: A. Francke, 1948). Sciacca, *La filosofia nell'età del Risorgimento* (Milano: Vallardi, 1948); extended bibliographies pp. 184–198 and 451–465; besides doctrinal expositions, is extremely attentive to the historical and biographical setting of that philosophical movement. In studying the doctrines of the "risorgimento," it should be kept in mind that at that date the question of the Pontifical States created tension in the minds of Italian Catholics, priests and the religious. They had a divided allegiance as Italian patriots and as Catholics, equally anxious to be loyal to the Church and to the political aspirations of their country. Among the possible answers to the Roman Question (status quo, federation of Italian provinces under the leadership of the pope, Sicilian separatism, etc.) it was not easy to guess what would be later considered by the Church as the right one. Rosmini and Gioberti were priests, Rosmini with a vocation to sanctity, Gioberti (as it seems) with no vocation to lose; both were caught in that turmoil; some of their acts and sometimes their doctrinal positions must be appreciated in the light of that fact.

17. Pasquale Galluppi, b. Tropea (Calabria), 1770; d. Naples, 1846.

Main works: *Lettere filosofiche*, ed. with Introduction and notes by A. Guzzo (Firenze: Vallccchi, 1925). *Saggio filosofico sulla critica della conoscenza* (6 vols.); Vols. I and II (Napoli, 1819); Vols. III and IV (Messina, 1822); Vols. V and VI (Messina, 1832).

Doctrinal: M. A. Rocchi, *Pasquale Galluppi storico della filosofia*, with bibliography (Palermo: Trimarchi, 1934). Giovanni di Napoli, *La filosofia di P. Galluppi* (Padova: Cedam, 1947). M. F. Sciacca, *La filosofia voir età del Risorgimento*, pp. 171–183. G. D. Napoli, article in *Encyclopedia filosofica*, II, 576–589.

The starting point of Galluppi was the traditional view of the world: existence of God, of a universe distinct from thought and of the *Ego* as a spiritual substance. In that first period Galluppi derived his inspiration from Descartes and Malebranche,

Leibniz and Wolf. At the same time, since he favored a gnoseological approach to philosophical problems, he became acquainted with Locke and Condillac. The imbalance of his position was revealed to him by his reading of Kant. Without becoming a Kantian, he attempted to achieve a psychological critique of knowledge conceived as an analysis of human thought. "In the first book, I start from the composite fact of human knowledge. I rediscover two classes of cognitions: those of facts and those of reasoning. Both classes are twofold in kind: primitive and deducted. But at the moment I am to decide on the reality of knowledge, I find myself confronted with the difficulties of scepticism. I see that in order to solve them I must know the system of the faculties of the spirit and the simple products of those faculties. Accordingly, in Book II, I proceed to an analysis of the faculties, and to an analysis of the ideas in Book III, where, among other things, I set up a comparative exposition of the philosophy of Kant; in Book IV, I clear up from all points of view the problem of the value of our knowledge." Selections from the *Lettere filosofiche* by Mario Dal Pra, 2nd ed. (Padova: Cedam, 1948), p. 11. His critique of practical reason (theory of the will) is nearer to that of Kant than his notion of speculative reason, yet, on the whole, Galluppi keeps faith with the empiricism of the eighteenth century.

18. Antonio Serbati Rosmini, b. Rovereto (near Trent) 1797; d. Stresa, 1855. Studied theology at the Università di Padova; ordained a priest (1821); after two years of meditation in Milan, retired to the Holy Calvary Mount (Domodossola) where, living in poverty and prayer, he founded the Institute of Charity and gave it its Constitutions (*Constituzioni dell' Istituto della Carità*, 1828). Encouraged by Pope Pius VIII to follow his vocation as a writer, he began to publish his first important works; around 1831, composed his reformatory work on the five wounds of the Church (*Delle cinque piaghe della Santa Chiesa*), published later on (Lugano: Veladini, 1848); English translation by H. P. Liddon (London: Rivington 1883); did parish work in San Marco di Rovercto (1832); considered suspect by the Austrian government, left province of Trent for that of Piedmont (1836) and settled in Stresa where he engaged in intense literary activity; answered an attack by Gioberti; published his own *Vincenzo Gioberti e il panteismo* (1846); was envoy extraordinary of Charles Albert of Piedmont to Pope Pius IX, with the mission of establishing a concordate between Piedmont and the Pontifical States, to be followed by a Confederation (1848); having failed in his mission on account of the revolution and having fallen into disgrace with the Pope, left Rome for Stresa (1849); on his way there, learned that the *Cinque piaghe*, along with his book *La Constitution scion la justice sociale*, had been put on the Index (1849); spent the last five years of his life in the peace of Stresa, surrounded by friends (among whom the illustrious Manzoni) and secretly helping Gioberti (who was then a resourceless voluntary exile in France) with money, and conducting the affairs of his Congregation. No philosopher, whatever his philosophy, should leave Stresa without paying a visit to the tomb of Rosmini. Much of the opposition against him arose from political differences of opinion in a time when such differences were unavoidable. His philosophical doctrine was open to criticism, but even those who disagree with him on that score should not overlook, along with his philosophical importance, the nobility of his soul, the purity of his life and the ardent charity of a saintly priest wholly dedicated to the

service of Christ.

Main philosophical works: *Nuovo saggio suir origine delle idee* (4 vols.; Roma: Salviucci, 1830). *Principii della scienza morale* (Milano: Pogliani, 1831) (*Opere complete*, XXII–XXIII). *Il rimovamento della filosofia in Italia, proposto dal Conte Terenzio Mamiani ed esaminato da A. Rosmini Serbati* (Milano, 1836) (*Opere complete*, XIX). *La société e il suo fine* (Milano: Pogliani, 1839). *Trattato della coscienza morale* (Milano: Pogliani, 1839). *Filosofia del diritto* (2 vols.; Milano: Pogliani, 1841–1845). *Teosofia*, unfinished and posthumously published (5 vols.); (Vol. I; Torino: Societa editrice, 1859); (Vols. II and III; Torino: Sebastiano Franco, 1863–64); (Vol. IV; Intra: Bertolotti, 1869); (Vol. V; Intra: Bertolotti, 1875) (*Opere complete*, vols. VII-XIV). *Antropologia soprannaturale* in *Opere complete*, Vols. XXVII–XXVIII (1955).

Collective editions: *Opere complete, edizione nationale* (28 vols. to date; Milano: Fratelli Bocca, 1934–). Particularly helpful are the *Scritti autobiografici inediti*, ed. by Enrico Castelli; Vol. I and *Introduzione alia filosofia*, ed. by U. Redano; Vol. II (1934).

English translations: *Essay on the Origin of Ideas* (3 vols.; London: Kegan Paul, 1884). *Theodicy* (3 vols.; London: Kegan Paul, 1892). *The Five Wounds of the Church*, translated by H. P. Liddon (London: Rivington, 1883). *Psychology* (2 vols.; London: Kegan Paul, 1888).

Biographical: G. B. Pagani, *Life of Antonio Rosmini-Serbati* (London: Routledge, 1907). Claude Leetham, *Rosmini, Priest, Philosopher and Patriot*, Introduction by Giuseppe Bozzetti (Baltimore, Maryland: Helicon Press, 1958), contains an extended bibliography.

Doctrinal: as a general observation, practically all the books on Rosmini aim to show him and his doctrine such as their authors would have liked them to be; some indeterminate aspects of Rosmini's own thought may be responsible for such diversity in interpretations. As a first introduction: M. F. Sciacca, *La filosofia nell' età del Risorgimento*, pp. 262–300; bibliography, pp. 455–457. G. Calza and B. Perez, *Esposizione ragionata della filosofia di Antonio Rosmini*, Introduction by Bertolotti (3 vols.; 1878–79). T. Davidson, *The Philosophic System of Antonio Rosmini-Serbati* (London: Kegan Paul, 1882). Giovanni Gentile, *Rosmini e Gioberti* (Pisa: Nistri, 1888). G. Morando, *Esame critico delle XL proposizioni rosminiane condannate dalla S. R. Inquisizione* (Milano: Cogliati, 1905). F. Palhoriès, *Rosmini* (Paris: Alcan, 1908). G. Capone Braga, *Saggio su Rosmini* (Milano: Libreria éditrice milanese, 1914). G. Ceriani, *L'ideologia rosminiana nei rapporti con la gnoseologia agostiniano-tomistica* (Milano: Vita e Pensiero, 1938). M. F. Sciacca, *La filosofia morale di Antonio Rosmini* (Roma: Perrella, 1938). D. Morando, *La pedagogia di Antonio Rosmini* (Brescia: La Scuola, 1948). P. Piovani, *Rosmini e Vico* (Roma: 1954). D. Morando, article in *Enciclopedia filosofica*, Vol. IV, pp. 207–222.

Bibliographical: Carlo Caviglione, *Bibliografia delle Opere di Antonio Rosmini disposte in ordine cronologico* (Torino: Paravia, 1925). D. Morando, *Bibliografia degli scritti su A. Rosmini* (Milano: 1936), Vol. IX constitutes the first volume of the national edition of the *Opere complete*; ends with 1934.

19. French translation of the passage, F. Palhoriès, *Rosmini*, pp. viii–ix. A useful abridged exposition of his own doctrine by Rosmini is found in the *Breve sebizzo dei sistemi di*

filosofìa propria e del proprio, new edition by G. Bonafede (Padova: Cedam, 1941), p. xix.

20. We are following the *Nuovo saggio* in its English translation: *The Origin of Ideas*, new edition (London: Kegan Paul, 1886), Vol. II. Since the whole work is divided into continuously numbered paragraphs, only that number will be quoted in our references. On the nature of the idea of being in general (pars. 428–433). The notion of "something" in general is wholly indeterminate; its indeterminateness excludes subsistence and actual existence with all the individualizing determinations it includes; so the notion of being in general, on account of its very indeterminateness, is that of possible being only (pars. 434–436).
21. *The Origin of Ideas*, Vol. II, pars. 451–468.
22. *The Origin of Ideas*, Vol. II, par. 467.
23. *The Origin of Ideas*, pars. 480–482.
24. *The Origin of Ideas*, pars. 483–485.
25. *The Origin of Ideas*, par. 485, notes 2 and 3, where Rosmini manipulates Bonaventure (*Itinerarium*, Vol. V) (he himself adds *informs* to the text by way of commentary); Bonaventure uses "formetur" in the Augustinian sense: "ab ipsa formatur veritate" (*83 Quaest.*, 61), which cannot be construed as meaning that truth (being is not at stake there) constitutes intellect in the soul. There seems to be an equivocation in the position of Rosmini, but it may be a desired one. From the fact that without intelligible being, intellect would not *know*, he seems to infer that without it intellect would not *be*. When he lets himself go, Rosmini simply says: "the faculty of cognition *exists* in virtue of the union of the idea of being with our spirit" (par. 486).

Rosmini was careful to confront his own doctrine with those of modern philosophers as well as with the teaching of the Christian philosophers. The first volume of the *Origin of Ideas* is devoted to a critical assessment of the gnoseologics of Locke, Condillac, Reid, Dugald Stewart (including Adam Smith); he concludes that the Scottish School has not been able to overcome the difficulty arising from its reduction of the use to signs of our knowledge of Universals. All the preceding theories are sins by way of defect; they assign to ideas an inadequate cause. On the contrary, Plato, Aristotle, Leibniz and Kant erred by excess, in that they assigned to ideas a greater cause than is necessary. In fact, "in what he admits as innate in the Human Spirit, Kant errs at once by defect and by excess" (par. 364); the system of Kant is but a development of that of Reid (par. 365).

26. Rosmini's interpretation of Thomism on this point is found in the essay on the *Origin of Ideas*, Vol. II, par. 490, note 1; par. 495, note 2; par. 565, note 1. Rosmini is aware of the equivocation that there can be, in the mind of the reader (for he himself is clearly aware of what he is doing) between saying with Thomas Aquinas that all science is, *quodammodo*, innate in us in the light of the agent intellect (*in lumine intellectus agentis*) and saying, as he himself does, that all science is innate in us in the light of the idea of being "which constitutes us intelligent beings and rational animals" (par. 482). On the contrary, Rosmini really agrees with Thomas Aquinas, that our cognition of *all* objects presupposes sense perception. Being and its modes (the transcendentals) are innate; but being represents no actually existing objects; it is the *form* of intellectual

knowledge; the *material* must be provided by sense. This is the reason, far from attributing to man an intuition of God in this life, Rosmini refuses us the very possibility of forming a proper concept of God. There is as much empiricism in Rosmini's doctrine as in those of Aristotle and of Thomas Aquinas; his notion of intellect is not the same. See *The Origin of Ideas*, par. 475: "Since all acquired ideas are a compound of two elements, form and matter, a twofold cause is required for their explanation"; and par. 476: "The twofold cause is required for their explanation." The consequences concerning the notion of God will be explained in note 34.

27. *The Origin of Ideas*, par. 486.
28. *The Origin of Ideas*, par. 554.
29. *The Origin of Ideas*, pars. 555–557. Cf. par. 546. Rosmini then proceeds to unfold "the genesis of the supreme principles of reasoning." The first principle is the "principle of cognition," to wit: "The object of thought is *being*, either indeterminate or determinate"; the second principle, derived from the first, is the principle of contradiction: "That which is (being) cannot at the same time, not be" (pars. 561–565).
30. Genesis of the principles (pars. 558–569). Principles as applied ideas (pars. 570–573). Dealing with the origin of pure concepts, Rosmini naturally makes the most of the doctrine of Saint Augustine on the ideas of unity, number and such (pars. 579–582). Of course, he fails to find in Augustine his own reduction of all such ideas to that of "ideal being." Nor does he want too much his readers to forget that the said reduction precisely constitutes his own contribution to the problem: "Thus the consideration of each such concept has enabled some master mind (Augustine) to soar above the sphere of visible things, to transcend all nature and to fix its piercing gaze on the infinite. But, while noticing this fact, I am also bound to confess I have not found many who, by the contemplation I speak of, have been led so far as to discover that the seat of all those concepts is in ideal being, and who could, therefore, be in a position to express the great ideological problem in its completeness" (par. 579). *Not many* should probably be read as an understatement.
31. *The Origin of Ideas*, pars. 646–647. The notion of substance is inspired by an entirely different principle in that it brings in a certain notion of existential act. In Rosinianism, however, there is no act of the substance; on the contrary, substance is the very act, or energy, in virtue of which it exists: "Substance is 'That energy by which a being, and all that appertains to it, actually exists,' or, 'that energy in which the actual existence of the being is founded'" (par. 587).

The word "object" has been freely used in connection with the idea of "being." Rosmini has formed a completely definite notion of "object." It is defined by three characters: (1) object is not susceptible of being modified, and yet it is united with the knowing power in a way of its own; (2) in uniting itself with the knowing power, object does not cause that power to apprehend its own action, but rather to apprehend object itself (in other words, cognition is the apprehension of the known object, not of the knowing mind); (3) the perceiving power does not perceive itself along with object; because it apprehends object alone, object always remains separated from perceiving power; indeed, in the very act of apprehending it, the knowing power posits it in itself as the term of its cognitive act. It turns it into an *ob-jectum*, distinct from and opposite to the knowing power, *Logica* (par. 304).

32. Forty propositions extracted from Rosmini's writings were posthumously condemned. See *Enchiridion symbolorum*, 31st ed., arts. 1891–1930. The concluding censure stipulates that the propositions are condemned "in proprio auctoris sensu." On this doctrinal act, see the work of G. Morando quoted above, note 18.

33. This notion of "the divine in nature" is fundamental in the doctrine of Rosmini. It points out "the idea of being." Man has no intuition of God, but there is in the domain of created being something *divine* in itself that manifests itself to the human mind. That manifestation is immediate. It is divine in the sense that "by many characters, the notion of being is representative of God." God is the Absolute and we have no intuition of Him, but "the Absolute is inferred from intuited being."

    This seems to have largely contributed to the censure of the doctrine. It was a bit complicated for the censors. Intentionally or not, they missed the distinction between the notion of being (the divine in nature) which, as an idea, properly signifies something (possible being) divine in itself, and the actual essence of God. The gist of the position is that the idea of being does not point out the universe (a nondivine effect of God); nor does it point out the human mind (as something divine by participation); in thinking being, we are not thinking anything that God is not (the world or the soul); we are thinking something which God is, and which He is the only one really and fully to be—namely, being. Hence the formula of *the divine*. The *divine in nature*, that is to say the idea of being, does not signify a non-divine effect of a divine cause, such as the universe; nor does it point out something that is divine by participation, such as the human spirit; but it properly and truly *signifies* a something *divine in itself*, that is to say such as it belongs to divine nature," Antonio Rosmini, *Anthologie philosophique*, texts selected and ordered with a good biographical notice and with accurate bibliographical notes by G. Pusineri, D. Morando, G. Rossi, M. F. Sciacca; Introduction by Régis Joliver, translation by Dom Lucien David and Dom Lucien Chambat, of the Saint Wandrille Abbey (Lyon: Vitte, 1954), pp. 318–319. The whole sentence obviously bears upon the meaning of the abstract notion of possible being; it means that, in that idea, and in no other one, are included characters that properly belong to God. Here are the censured propositions: "(1) In ordine rerum creaturarum immediate manifestatur humano intellectui aliquid divini in se ipso, hujusmodi nempe quod ad divinam naturam pertineat; (2) Cum divinum dicimus in natura, vocabulum istum *divinium* non usurpamus ad significandum effectum non divinum causae divinae; neque mens nobis est loqui de *divino* quodam, quod tale sit per participationem."

34. There are few points on which Rosmini was more explicit. Besides, since the "material" of our concepts without exception is borrowed from sense, an intuition of God's being is impossible by definition, at least in this life and by natural means. On this point, see *Theodicy*, Book I, chaps. xiii–xvii, pars. 55–60: it is impossible for man to arrive at the perception of God in the present life. Four limitations of human reason make such a direct apprehension impossible: (1) "because none of the things that can be perceived by us has in it what is essential to God, namely, the identification of essence with perfection" (par. 75); (2) because "no finite intelligence can attain perfect knowledge of the absolute infinite" (para. 76); (3) because "the power of

understanding is given by God to each individual in a quantity so determined, that he who possesses it cannot ascertain in what relation his own faculty of understanding is to the difficulty of the questions that present themselves to him for solution" (par. 79); (4) because "the human intelligence cannot acquire any knowledge unless the materials for it be furnished by a cause extraneous to itself" (par. 86). Sense knowledge is the material furnished by nature (and, inasmuch as He is the author of nature, by God). Hence two consequences: (1) Rosmini agrees with Thomas Aquinas that we can know of God *that* he is, not *what* he is (par. 60); this Rosmini often expresses by saying that we have only a "negative" notion of God; (2) in Rosmini's authentic doctrine, the danger is not to attribute to man a natural sight of God, but rather, to account for the fact that, even starting from the notion of abstract being and its transcendental properties, we can form the notion that there is in reality such a Being, commonly called God. This difficulty accounts for the fact that Rosmini always resorted to a mild form of traditionalism in order to explain to the mind the presence of a confused notion of God (the God of nominal definition, likewise presupposed by the "five ways" of Thomas Aquinas). The problem of the origin of language is therefore solved by Rosmini in accordance with the doctrine of de Bonald. His own contribution to it is to show that, precisely because the mind, as we each receive it from God "is like a clean tablet, or an unwritten page," a *tabula rasa*, some being different from ourselves must write on that virgin page the teachings of wisdom. This is done by external objects and by our concepts of them designed by signs (par. 102); but another source must be invoked in order to explain how, from His vestiges in creation, mind can ascend to the Creator. For indeed, we could not know them as His vestiges unless we had some notion of God. Hence the teachings of Scripture, that God was the first to name the principal parts of creation, applying a special name to each, so that it might be fully knowable by man. By creating it, He had rendered it perceptible; by naming it, He rendered it knowable as the type of a species intended to serve as a light to the mind" (par. 106). "This naturally leads us to suppose that language would not be taught by the Supreme Instructor merely for its own sake, as the direct scope of the teaching, but only indirectly, as a vesture of, and an accessory to these great truths which revealed to man the end of his existence, and the loving care which Divine Wisdom took of him. Therefore, as I believe, the eternal truths were incorporated in language and conveyed together with it" (par. 108). Unlike sensism (Locke) and transcendental idealism (Kant), this doctrine does not lead to scepticism; on the contrary, it shows reason and faith complementary: "because reason is ignorant of some portion of truth, faith offers to lend its kindly aid in supplying the deficiency" (par. 133).

35. Hence the sixth condemned proposition: "In esse, quod praescindit in creaturis et a Deo, quod est esse indeterminatum, atque in Deo, esse non indeterminato, sed absoluto, eadem est essentia" (*Enchiridion*, art. 1896). The proposition must be read in its philosophical context, which is the Rosminian notion of essence. As has been seen above "Essence is what we think in the idea of a thing" (*The Origin of Ideas*, par. 646; cf. par. 1213). Thus understood, essence is no actual existing reality outside the mind: "Here some one may say: if such be the case, then the 'essence' is nothing but what we express in the definition of a thing. Exactly so" (par. 1214). As if to show that he was as

capable of misinterpreting others as they him, Rosmini presently adds: "and it was in this sense that the term *essence* was taken by the ancients. 'Essentia' (says St. Thomas) 'comprehendit in se illa tantum, quae eadunt in definitione speciei' *Summa theologiae* (I, iii, 3). The *species* is nothing but the idea." Of course, if "essence" in Rosmini is the same thing as "essence" in Thomas Aquinas, nothing is more condemnable than his proposition. In fact it is not, so his proposition is harmless. Unfortunately, Rosmini himself assures that the meaning of the term is the same in the two doctrines, so his censor must have felt thereby justified in condemning the proposition. For indeed, in authentic Thomism, to say that essence is the same in God as in things is a dreadful error.

Rosmini has several times described the genealogy of his own doctrine, that is, at least, how he himself saw it. For instance: "From this opinion (that ideas reside in God from all eternity) Malebranche deduced his own system, that man, like every other finite intellect, sees in God all that which he sees, a system ultimately vindicated by his Eminence Cardinal Gerdil from theological imputations against it. We ourselves do not entirely accept that system, of which it would be too long at this point to carry a criticism, but we do recognize in it a core of truth; and differences between the system of Malebranche and our own are seen in particulars only," *Breve schizzo*, ed. Bonafede, p. 35. Cf. pp. 76–77.

36. The more provoking statements of Rosmini on this point are found in his treatise *On the Divine,* posthumously published in the *Teosofia* and, later, as a distinct treatise. The main texts are found in French translation in the useful work: Antonio Rosmini, *Anthologie philosophique*. A very commendable starting point.

The controversial texts from *Il divino nella natura* are found in *Anthologie philosophique*, pp. 318–321.

37. *Anthologie philosophique*, par. 1457. A collection of other passages to the same effect is found in French translation (pp. 321–327); even the proofs *a posteriori* are, in a way, *a priori* (p. 327). The method of Rosmini on this point is sometimes described as a passage from ontology to theology. Moreover, the two moments likewise belong to both ontology and natural theology. The problem is: starting from the idea of *being in general*, to infer the real existence of *a Being*.

38. Rosmini alleges Aristotle *De anima* (III, lecture vii). In fact, this part of the doctrine comes to him from Malebranche, who established the reality of ideas by the invincible resistance they oppose to all efforts of the mind to change them.

39. Note the equivalence of the three terms: possible being is truth as the source of all other truths, and since its possibility is that of being, truth and being are identical.

40. Note this incidental assertion that the intellectual light of man is not his intellect, but rather, that his intellectual light is the very idea of being itself.

41. *The Origin of Ideas*, Vol. III, pars. 1458–1459.

42. Since it *subsists*, that eternally intelligent mind cannot be an accident; then it is a substance.

43. *The Origin of Ideas*, Vol. III, par. 1459.

44. After saying that being can "to use a Scholastic phrase, be predicated univocally of God and of creatures," Rosmini adds this footnote: "The reader can see this question

treated in the philosophical system expounded by Carlo Francesco da San Floriano, according to the mind of Duns Scotus. There the views of this acute genius of the Schools are compared with those of modern philosophers. The work was printed at Milan in 1771 (Vol. II, p. 103)"; *Origin of Ideas*, Vol. III, par. 1460, note. The univocity of being is common to many other theologians besides Duns Scotus; and his way of using it is very different from that of Rosmini.

45. In situating himself in the history of the metaphysics of being, Rosmini is very anxious to separate himself from Malebranche. As unjust to his great predecessor as his own successors were to be unjust to himself, Rosmini blamed Malebranche for having almost seen the truth, but not quite: "Instead of saying with St. Thomas that the idea of being is a created light, he will have it be God Himself: hence his error," *Origin of Ideas*, Vol. II, par. 1033. Malebranche never said that the idea of being was God, for the very simple reason that he always denied the very possibility of an idea of God. An Idea is a model, an archetype; there is no archetype of God. Rosmini mentions Thomassin as a predecessor of Malebranche; then a perhaps unjustly neglected Tyrolese Capuchin, Giovenale of Anaunia: "Solis intelligentiac cui non succedit nox, lumen indeficiens ac inextinguibile illuminans omnem hominem venientem in hunc mundum..., per P. Juvenalem Anaunienem, O. C." (Augsburg, 1680). Rosmini observes: "It is singular that Padre Giovenale died in the same year as Malebranche, 1713." On the two Fathers Ercolano and Filibert, of the Reformed Franciscans, authors of similar doctrines (par. 1034, note). On Gerdil (par. 1035, note). He freely acknowledges that the reasoning of Ficino, Thomassin, Malebranche, Descartes, and before them Saint Anselm (there even are traces of it in Augustine) contains elements of truth, but misses the fundamental distinction introduced by Thomas Aquinas between *being in potentia* and *being in act*. "It is by means of this distinction that St. Thomas demonstrates (I, ii, 1) that God is not among the things known through themselves." Right. But Saint Thomas did not prove the existence of God by means of that distinction. In identifying the distinction of *possible* and *actual* being with his own distinction of *ideal being* and *subsistent being*, Rosmini provided a Thomistic alibi for his own *a priori* proof of the existence of God.

46. Failing the original text of the *Principii della scienza morale*, its almost complete French translation will be found in Antonio Rosmini, *Anthologie philosophique*, pp. 385–499. Our own exposition of Rosmini's ethics follows the general lines of the treatise.

47. Vincenzio Gioberti, b. Turin, 1801; d. Paris, 1852. Studied theology; ordained a priest (1825); taught theology at the University of Turin; arrested and jailed for expressing liberal opinions (1833); exiled, went first to Paris where he declined a teaching position offered by Victor Cousin, then to Brussels where he taught in a private institution (1834–1843); the main part of his philosophical production dates from those years. Gioberti went back to Italy where he was given a hearty welcome by all, including Pope Pius IX; became a minister of state for a few days (1848), then a prime minister (1849); sent to Paris as an ambassador by King Victor Emmanuel II, Gioberti soon ceased to approve of the policy of his government; having resigned his charge, he retired to a private life of poverty until his death.

Main philosophical works: *Teorica del sovrannaturale* (1 vol.; Bruxelles: Hayez, 1838); (2 vols.; Capolago: Tipografia elvetica, 1850). *Introduzione allo studio della filosofia* (2 vols.; Bruxelles: Hayez, 1840); (4 vols.; Bruxelles: Meline, 1844). *Degli errori filosofici di Antonio Rosmini* (1 vol.; Bruxelles: Hayez, 1841: 3 vols.; 1843). *Del bello* (in *Encyclopedia e dizionario della conversazione* [Venezia: G. Tarso, 1841]), Vol. IV; 2nd ed. (Capolago: Tipografia elvetica, 1848). *Del buono* (Bruxelles: Méline, 1843), reprinted along with *Del bello*, under the title of *Del buono, del bello* (Firenze: Le Monnier, 1853). *Il gesuita moderno* (7 vols.; Losanna: S. Bonainici, 1846–1847). *Della filosofia della rivelazione*, posthumously published (Torino-Parigi: Botta e Chainerot, 1857). *Della protologia* (2 vols.; Torino e Parigi, 1857). *Cours de philosophie*, ed. by M. Battistini and Giovanni Calo (Milano: Fratelli Bocca, 1947), was taught at Brussels in 1841–1842.

Collective edition: *Opere complete di V. Gioberti*, edizione nazionale (Roma-Milano: Fratelli Bocca, 1938ff.). *Epistolaria*, ed. G. Gentile and G. Balsamo-Crivelli (11 vols.; 1927–1937).

Anthology, under the title of *L'educazione politica degli italiani*, by Stefano Mazilli (Firenze: Felice Le Monnier, 1941–xx).

Doctrinal: G. Saitta, *Il pensiero di Vincenzo Gioberti*, 2nd ed. (Firenze: Vallecchi, 1927). B. Spaventa, *La filosofia di Gioberti*, 2nd ed. (Napoli: Morano, 1886). G. Gentile, *Rosmini e Gioberti* (Pisa: Nistri, 1898). L. Stefanini, *V. Gioberti* (2 vols.; Torino: Bocca, 1947). M. F. Sciacca, *La filosofia nell'età del Risorgimento* (Milano: Vallardi, 1948), pp. 301–334; 457–458 (bibliographical). G. Mazzantini, article in *Encyclopedia filosofica*, Vol. II, pp. 735–740.

Several texts will be quoted from G. Saitta, *Gioberti*, an anthology with an Introduction (Milano: Garzanti, 1952), and from the edition of Gioberti's *Introduzione allo studio della filosofia*, with an Introduction and notes by Giulio Bonafede (Padova: Cedam, 1939–xvii).

48. "I am of such disposition that contradiction goads me into action and stimulates me…," etc., *Del buono*, Avvertenza, ed. Capolago (1848), p. 77. Besides this personal disposition, Gioberti shared with most of the other philosophers of the Risorgimento, and more than some, an intense nationalist feeling. According to him, the Italians had then lost, along with their independence as a nation, their intellectual independence. Hesitating between German, English and French systems, they contented themselves with a timid syncretism. Of those foreign influences, that of French philosophy is the worst. Wrapped up in their silly worship of Descartes, the French had nothing to offer beyond their own eclecticism and the pantheism born of Cartesianism. The one exception to Gioberti's detestation of French philosophers was Malebranche whom, naturally enough, the French have never been able to appreciate.

49. The following sentences of Rosmini are quoted by Gioberti from the *Nuovo Saggio* in his own Introduction to *Del buono* (pp. 34–35). According to Gioberti, the initial error of Rosmini was to think that "the psychological prime is not identical with the ontological prime. The erroneous consequences of that initial mistake are four in number: (1) all the ideas have their origin in the idea of being; (2) the initial idea of being represents possible being only; (3) the perception of the real existence of created

things is the effect of a judgment which associates sense perception with the idea of possible being; (4) the knowledge of the existence of Absolute Being, that is of God, is not obtained immediately and by intuition, but mediately and by way of demonstration only," *Introduzione allo studio della filosofia*, p. 67. So Gioberti reproached Rosmini for not being enough of an "ontologist."

50. See, in Gioberti's *Introduction to the Study of Philosophy*, the remarks on the "philosophical Prime" (*Il Primo filosofico*). There is only one single Prime; it is "psychological, ontological and philosophical" at one and the same time. The "philosophical Prime" includes the others. Indeed, the psychological Prime is the first Idea; the ontological Prime is the first thing. Since these two are identical, there is only one absolute Prime, which is the philosophical Prime, at once sufficient foundation for all the knowable and all the real (chap. iv).

51. The philosophical Prime implies a judgment, namely: Being is, in a necessary way, God himself who said so in saying I AM WHO AM. In this formula is expressed, along with the necessary existence of God, the fundamental law of being: that it is a duality reconciled in unity. In God, the judging is identical to the judged. On the contrary, in man, that first judgment is not intuitive; it is reflective. Man says, first to himself, then to others: *Being is*. In us this reflective judgment is a repetition of the prime intuitive judgment of God. This divine origin guarantees its necessity. Thus the authority of human reason is ultimate because it is a duplicate of the authority of the reason of God, which is its cause. From this precise point of view (that is, from the point of view of its necessity) the reason of man is the same as the reason of God: "La ragion dell' uomo, per questo rispetto, e veramente la ragion di Dio e quindi possiede un' autorità senza appello." The divine judgment of being, under the form of its human repetition, thus becomes the origin of philosophical knowledge. Assuredly we do not start from the divine judgment itself, but from its human repetition. Nevertheless, because "that link is conjoined with the divine judgment and derives from it all its strength, it follows that philosophy has its basis in revelation, that God is, strictly speaking, the prime philosopher and that human philosophy is the repetition and continuation of the divine philosophy," *Introduzione allo studio della filosofia*, chap. iv.

52. In a passage of his *Introduzione* (chap. iii) Gioberti complains that it is not possible to give of idea a definition both accurate and comprehensible. It is "the object itself of rational knowledge, with, however, a relation to our knowledge of it." So "the study of Idea is the substance of the whole philosophy" including the knowledge of metaphysics along with the main parts of the speculative sciences. Moreover, "Idea cannot be demonstrable because it is the source of all proof and of all demonstration." Inasmuch as God is Being, his existence cannot be demonstrated. Coming back to a notion familiar with Vico, Gioberti observes that "to prove is to create. So to prove God would be to create God. To prove man and the world would be to create both man and the world. Nevertheless, God is uncreated. Hence He is not provable. Man and the world are created, but not by man; hence they are demonstrable, but not by man. Man and world are demonstrable only by Him who creates them. The principle of their creation is also the principle of their demonstration. For man, proving it can consist only in repeating it reflectively. The divine proof of which we are the permanent spectators is

the ideal formula. By it God both affirms Himself and posits the world. The demonstrations of the existence of God are a reflective process which, as such, has its own value, but it presupposes the intuition of the truth it demonstrates," *Protologia*, as quoted by Bonafede, *Introduzione*, p. 29, note i. The point Gioberti wants to make is that, in seeing beings (that are not Beings) we intuit them as created. After that, our reasonings are but repetitions of that intuition whose content is wholly included in the formula: Being creates existents.

53. Texts in Saitta's anthology, pp. 65–71; or *Protologia*, extracts revised after the autograph manuscripts by Gustavo Balsamo-Crivelli, with Introduction and notes by Santino Caramella (Torino: Paravia, 1924), pp. 103–108.
54. *Del buono*, chap. viii, ed. Capo-Iago (1848), pp. 387–388.
55. *Del buono*, p. 390.
56. *Del buono*, pp. 401–404.
57. *Del buono*, pp. 405–417. Cf. *Del primate morale e civile degli Italiani*, edizione nazionale (1938–1939).
58. Giuseppe Romano, b. Termini (Sicilia), 1810; d. Constantinople, 1878. Despite the rabid hatred of Gioberti against the Jesuits, Romano never ceased to combine some of the main tenets of Gioberti with his own philosophical teaching. The fact is particularly visible in his *Theodicy* (1846). God is the prime intelligible, but we could not know Him if He Himself were not present to our minds. On the other hand, the confused presence of God to mind requires to be clarified by reflection. Without rejecting any method to prove the existence of God, not even the *a posteriori* demonstrations (this against Gioberti), Romano prefers the *a priori* method, especially following the great tradition followed by Plato, Plotinus, Sr. Augustine, St. Anselm, and, later by Thomassin, Malebranche, Bossuet, Fénelon, Gerdii and Gioberti (note the absence of Rosmini). Romano's preferred argument is as follows: Theorem I: "Absolute being, or God, truly is"; for indeed I have the idea of God; now I cannot have that idea unless God is actually present to my intellect; so God is present to me, and He is in act. Theorem II: "Infinite being is real"; for indeed my finite mind is unable to form the notion of infinite being; so infinite being is a reality present to my mind. Theorem III: "Supremely perfect being is real"; this is proved by the argument of St. Anselm in *Proslogion*. Theorem IV: "God necessarily is, or: the necessary being is real"; if being were merely possible, nothing would exist; so there must be something that always exists; if that is contingent, it is caused by God; if that is necessary, it is God. Such was the kind of philosophy taught at the Jesuit Collegio Massimo (Palermo) by Father Giuseppe Romano, colleague of the great Thomist Taparelli d'Azeglio. Romano simply implanted ontologism in Sicily.

Main philosophical works: *La scienza dell' uomo interiore e delle sue relazioni con la natura e con Dio* (4 vols.; Palermo: Francesco Lao, 1840–1846). *Elementi de filosofia* (Palermo: Vizzi, 1853). On the doctrine and influence of G. Romano: Salvatore Scime, *Il trionofo dell' ontologismo in Sicilia, Giuseppe Romano (1810–1878)* (Mazara: Società Editrice Siciliana, 1949); bibliography, pp. 263–265.

Less tightly bound to Gioberti, Orestes Brownson began by yielding to his influence; his critical interpretation of Gioberti is always instructive: O. A. Brownson, *Works*, collected and arranged by Henry F. Brownson, Vol. I, pp. 418–422; on his first contact with that author "in bad odor," Vol. I, p. 241, note 1. For his ulterior criticisms of the doctrine, consult the Index of Subjects under the word "Gioberti," same edition, Vol. XX, p. 527. In 1850 (*An a priori Autobiography*), after dissociating himself from many opinions and attitudes of Gioberti, Brownson concluded: "In a word, in those of his writings we have read, we find not a little extraneous matter that we do not like, and much, if not unsound, that is easily misapprehended, and not inapt to lead to dangerous errors; but we have, in what pertains exclusively to philosophy, found much that we most heartily approve, and which, in our age especially, needs to be profoundly meditated," Vol. I, p. 242, note.

59. A. M. Lepidi, O.P., b. Popoli, 1838; d. Rome, 1922. Master of the Sacred Palace, published his much discussed work in the journal *Divus Thomas* (Placentiae), founded in 1880 in order to support the program of action set up by Pope Leo XIII in favor of the restoration of Thomism and of its teaching in Christian schools. The objective was to restore "illud (institutum) Christianae Philosophiae, quod ab Ecclesiae Patribus in scriptis Doctorum, qui Scholastici nomen habuerunt, transmissum, maxima accuratione expositum et in formulam redactum est a viro post hominum memoriam praestantissimo, Thoma Aquinate." *Divus Thomas* (Placentiae), Vol. I (1880), p. 1. See *Examen philosophico-theologicum de ontologismo* (Lovanii, 1874); A. Lepidi, O. P., *Elementa philosophiae Christianae*, Vol. I, "Introductio ad universam philosophiam et Logica" (Lovanii, 1875); Vol. II "Continens Ontologiam in tres libros distributam, quorum primus agit de ente generalissimo, prout ab infinito et finito abstrahit; secundus de ente finito absolute spectato; tertius de ente finito cum relatione" (Lovanii, 1877). Lepidi resorted to the doctrine of the analogy of being in order to eliminate from ontology any danger of pantheism. In his recension of Vol. II, J. Vinati (p. 152, note 1) objected to the following sentence of Lepidi (*Elementa philosophiae Christianae*, p. 42): "The ideal properties of absolute general being, to wit necessity, immutability, eternity and exemplar or ideal universality, are not something merely subjective and logical, nor do they actually exist in nature, but they are something ideal, having in reality a foundation, which primarily is God" (p. 42). Lepidi wrote his opuscle by way of answer, and published it in *Divus Thomas*, Vol. I, pp. 172–176, 194–197, 213–216, 286–289. Conclusion of the doctrine: (1) every intelligible idea manifesting something as *being* is indissolubly tied up with an objective reality, either actually existing or possible; (2) every ideal cognition consists of a twofold element: a psychological element (since the known is in the knower) and a theological element, which is God; and indeed all the ideas represent a certain objective reality, which is necessary, immutable, eternal and whose ultimate foundation can be no other than Being Itself (*Ipsum Esse*); (3) the proper mark of finite being is its indifference with respect to existence and nonexistence (participated being), but the proper mark of infinite being is the absolute necessity of its actual existence (being by essence); (4) in short, the proper note, or mark, of finite being is to be dominated, while that of infinite being is to dominate (*Divus Thomas*, p. 289). A Second Part was devoted to the refutation of errors: "Materialism, subjective idealism, pantheistic idealism, ontologism, Sensism, in fine the system of the ideal form of the mind" (pp. 381–384, 434–439, 532–536, 606–611).

The published part of the treatise ends with the refutation of materialism. As often happens, the language of the *De ente generalissimo* disturbed its critics. Important works of Lepidi remained unpublished.

Doctrinal: G. Sestili, *Il padre Alberto Lepidi e la sua filosofia* (Torino-Roma, 1930).

60. Text published in *Divus Thomas* (Placentiae), Vol. IX (1889), pp. 571–575.
61. *Divus Thomas*, p. 575.
62. *Enchiridion symbolorum*, 31st ed.; articles 1059–1665.
63. On the group of ontologists active around Ubaghs, and on their doctrinal difficulties with Rome, see J. Henry, *Le traditionalisme et l'ontologisme à l'université de Louvain (1835–1865)*, an extensive study published in the *Annales de l'institut supérieur de philosophie*, Vol. V (Lovanii, 1924), pp. 39–150. Louis Foucher, *La philosophie catholique*, chap. iii, pp. 167–195.
64. On the names and main writings of the members of the group (Ubaghs, Tits, Lonay, Laforet, Claessens, etc.), see the article above by J. Henry, p. 44, note 1.
65. The beginning of the hostilities took place in 1836 (J. Henry, p. 114). In a curious note (p. 115, note 1) J. Henry specifies that, contrary to what was said, the Jesuits had no part in the denunciation of the doctrine: "At the beginning of 1843 five propositions were denounced by the Index. Mgr. Fornari, nunzio at Brussels, had taken the initiative of that move; the reaction of the propositions was due to Gioberti." Henry refers readers to the book of Daris, *Le diocèse de Liège sous l'épiscopat de Mgr. Théodore de Montpellier* (Liège, 1892). That incident throws a curious light on the reaction of Gioberti to doctrines whose origin is commonly traced back, partially at least, to his own influence. On the part played by Gioberti, see J. Henry, op. cit., pp. 98–99. Henry sees the origin of the Belgian movement in the publication of Gioberti's *Introduzione allo studio della filosofia*.
66. Henry, op. cit., p. 115, note 1.
67. Henry, op. cit., pp. 78–79, 80. The proof by the presence to the mind of the notion of infinite being: "The idea of infinity must be put in us by an infinite cause: God." The Cartesian origin of the argument seems evident.
68. J. Henry, op. cit., p. 148.
69. Louis Branchereau, b. S. Pierre-Montlimart, 1819; d. Issy, 1913. *Praelectiones philosophicae* (3 vols.; Clermont-Ferrand: Thibaud-Landriot, 1849), 2nd edition (9 vols.; Nantes: R. Mazeau, 1855). Doctrinal: A. Crosnier, *Louis Branchereau* (Paris: 1915). L. Foucher, *La philosophie catholique*, chap. vii, sec. ix, pp. 176–180. The text of the fifteen propositions summing up Branchereau's own brand of ontologism is given by Crosnier in the appendix to Foucher's book (p. 179, note 1).
70. As quoted from A. Crosnier by Louis Foucher, *La philosophie catholique*, p. 178.
71. Two other names deserve to be honorably remembered. (1) Flavien Hugonin, b. Thodure (Isère), 1823; d. Caen, 1898. Studied and taught at the "École des Carmes," Paris. Published his *Etudes philosophiques: Ontologie ou étude des lois de la pensée* (2 vols.; Paris: E. Belin, 1856–1857); was a professor at the Faculty of Theology, Sorbonne (1861); bishop of Bayeux (1867). After describing being in itself, then as known and under the form of truth, Hugonin attempted a comparison between ontologism and the doctrine of Thomas Aquinas. Refusing to assimilate Thomas in ontologism, he

observes that, in the doctrine of Thomas Aquinas, the natural light of reason in us is an effect of the uncreated light, caused in us by God but in no way identical with it. Then, going back to the classical position of the so-called Augustinian school, Hugonin objects that, in such a doctrine, our own truth is but a created truth; however, in itself, truth is uncreated; if, therefore, we only know truth in the created light of our own intellect, we do not know truth at all. The element of necessity included in all truth thus remains unexplained. In short, from Aristotle to Thomas Aquinas and Suarez, the error was made of looking at sensations for the characteristics of immutability and necessity, whose only conceivable foundation is God. See: Louis Foucher, *La philosophie catholiqtie*, chap. vii, §3, pp. 181–189; criticism of Rosmini by Hugonin, pp. 186–189. Orestes Brownson, *Works* (Detroit, 1882), Vol. I, pp. 408–437.

(2) Jules Fabvre D'Envieu, b. Labruguière, 1821; d. Saint-Martory, 1901. Introduced to Thomas Aquinas and Suarez, he attempted to reconcile the Thomist theory of knowledge with that of Saint Augustine: *Cours de philosophie ou nouvelle exposition des principes de cette science* (2 vols.; Paris: Durand, 1865–1866). *Defense de l'ontologisme contre les attaques récentes de quelques écrivains qui se disent disciples de Saint Thomas* (Paris: P. Lethielleux, 1862). *Réponse aux lettres d'un sensualiste contre l'ontologisme* (Paris: Durand, 1864). The "vision in God" is the ontologist dogma. It is the doctrine which relates the necessity of true knowledge to the intrinsic necessity of the Ideas in God. Augustine, Bonaventure and Thomas have held that doctrine. The position of Fabvre d'Envieu is particularly hard to justify with respect to Saint Thomas. See Foucher, §4, pp. 189–195.

IX. French Positivism

1. François Marie Charles Fourier, b. Besançon, 1772; d. Paris, 1837. Anonymously published his reformation scheme *Théorie des quatre mouvements* (2 vols.; Leipzig-Lyon: Pelzin, 1808). His great "scientific" discovery was the principle that there is a natural harmony between the passions of soul, so that, were they permitted to develop freely, personal and social happiness would prevail everywhere. The obstacles by society on the free gratification of desire is the main cause of man's misery. The ghost of Rousseau is haunting the doctrine. In common with other reformers of the same period, Fourier was putting great hopes on industry as a factor of human happiness; but agriculture remained for him the basis of society, *Traité de l'association agricole domestique* (2 vols.; Paris: Bossangc, 1822). The best exposition of his doctrine remains *Le nouveau monde industriel et sociétaire* (2 vols.; Paris: Bossange, 1829–1830). The only phalanstery built in France during his own lifetime was a failure. The plan met with better success in the United States where Fourier's doctrine was spread by Albert Brisbane (1809–1890). Between 1840 and 1850 there were at least forty-one American phalansteries. The better known phalanx was that of Brook Fann (West Roxbury, Massachussetts, 1841–1847) freely inspired by Fourier's ideas and spirit. Charles A. Dana and Nathaniel Hawthorne were among its founders. Father Isaac Thomas Hecker was a student there, and it attracted important visitors such as Ralph Waldo Emerson,

William Henry Channing, and Orestes Brownson. A fire destroyed it in 1849. *Oeuvres complètes*, 2nd ed. (6 vols.; Paris: La Phalange, 1841, 1845). Charles Gide, *Oeuvres choisies* (Paris: Guillaumin, 1890).

Doctrinal: Victor Considérant, *Exposition abrégée du système phalanstérien de Fourier*, P.-C.-E.-Mo...e, 3rd ed. (Paris: Librairie sociétaire, 1843). Hubert Bourgin, *Fourier, Contribution à l'étude du socialisme français* (Paris: G. Bellais, 1905). F. Armand, *Fourier* (2 vols.; Paris: Editions sociales internationales, 1937). Morris Hilquit, *History of Socialism in the United States* (New York-London: Funk & Wagnail's, 1903).

2. Victor Considérant, b. Salins, 1808; d. Paris, 1893. Disciple of Fourier, succeeded him as the head of the movement (1837); author of *La destinée sociale* (2 vols.; Paris: Bureau de la Phalange, 1838); a deputy after the revolution of 1848, he got involved in the riots of 1849, sought refuge in Brussels, visited the United States, where he founded the phalanstery of La Reunion at San Antonio, Texas.

Main works: *Principes du socialisme* (Paris: Librairie phalanstérienne, 1847); *Théorie du droit de propriété et du droit au travail*, 3rd ed. (Paris: Librairie phalanstérienne, 1848).

Biographical and doctrinal: P. Collard, *Victor Considérant, sa vie, ses idées* (Dijon, 1910). All studies on Fourier also deal with Considérant.

Besides the dominant influence of Fourier, Victor Considérant also underwent that of another utopian socialist reformer: Étienne Cabet (b. Dijon, 1788; d. St. Louis, Missouri, 1856); author of *Voyage en Icarie*, 2nd ed. (Paris: J. Mallet, 1842), written after reading Thomas More's *Utopia*. A disciple of Robert Owen, he sought to organize a community after his own doctrine. A group of about one thousand, five hundred Icarians sailed to America in 1848; they settled on the Red River, in Texas. In 1849 Cabet himself went to America and transferred the colony to Nauvoo, Illinois; in consequence of internal dissensions, he later moved to Saint Louis, Missouri, where he founded a new colony and died. Like Saint-Simon he considered his communitarian socialism the true expression of the Christian spirit: *Le vrai christianisme suivant Jésus Christ* (Paris: au bureau du "Populaire," 1846), 2nd ed. (1847). On his American foundations: J. Prudhommeaux, *Icarie et son fondateur Étienne Cabet, contribution à l'étude du socialisme expérimental* (Paris: E. Cornély, 1907).

3. Claude Henri De Rouvroy De Saint-Simon (count), b. Paris, 1760; d. Paris, 1825. Fought on the American side in the War of Independence; shared in the French Revolution; was imprisoned during the Terror; rapidly made a fortune after his release and spent his life loosing it, as he had made it, in land speculations and industrial ventures.

Main works: *Lettres d'un habitant de Genève* (no place or date, but probably published in 1802). *Du système industriel* (Paris: Renouard, 1821). *Le nouveau christianisme, dialogue entre un conservateur et un novateur. Premier dialogue* (Paris: Bossange, 1825).

Collective edition: *Oeuvres de Saint-Simon et d'Enfantin* (47 vols.; Paris: Dentu and Leroux; 1865–1878). This edition includes the works of Enfantin, who became head of the sect after the death of Saint-Simon; he wrote an *Exposition de la doctrine de Saint-Simon* (2 vols.; Paris: aux bureaux de l'Organisateur, 1828), 2nd ed. (1830).

Biographical and doctrinal: Georges Dumas, *Psychologie de deux messies du positivisme, Saint-Simon et Auguste Comte* (Paris: F. Alcan, 1905). Henri Gouhier, *La jeunesse d'Auguste Comte et la formation du positivisme. II. Auguste Comte et Saint-Simon* (Paris: J. Vrin, 1941) (fundamental).

4. Auguste Isidore François Marie Comte, b. Montpellier, 1798; d. Paris, 1857. After brilliant mathematical studies, entered the École Polytechnique, 1814 (end of Napoleon 1's empire); after the closing of the school (1810) lived by teaching mathematics; became acquainted with Saint-Simon; professed himself Saint-Simon's disciple and acted as his secretary; first publications, some of them signed by Saint-Simon, with whom he broke relations in 1824; resumed private teaching; wrote the first volume of his *Cours de philosophie positive* (1830); tutor at the École Polytechnique (1832); examiner at the same school (1837); from 1845 on, worked on the composition of his *Système de politique positive*, but, under the influence of a sentimental crisis, he also began to enlarge the part attributed to feeling and to teach the subordination of intellect to heart. He then progressively assumed the functions of a self-appointed high priest of a new universal religion—a strict atheism whose object of worship was man, that is to say the human kind itself, raised by Comte to the dignity of Great Being, or Great Fetiche. A conservative in politics, always hoping to win the Society of Jesus to his cause, he ended his life surrounded by a group of admiring and devoted disciples.

Main works: an extremely important early opuscule, *Plan des travaux scientifiques nécessaires pour réorganiser la société*, republished by Comte himself in the Appendix to Vol. IV of his *Système de politique positive. Cours de philosophie positive* (6 vols.; Paris-Rouen: Société Positiviste, 1830–1842, several reprints), 6th ed. (Paris: Alfred Costes, 1934). *Discours sur l'esprit positif*, a preface to Comte's *Traité philosophique d'astronomie populaire* (Paris: Carilian, 1844); several separate reprints, among which (Paris: Librairie Schleicher, 1909). *Discours sur l'ensemble du positivisme* (Paris: Mathias, Goeury et V. Dalmont, 1848), reprinted at the beginning of the *Systeme de politique positive ou traité de sociologie instituant la religion de l'humanité* (4 vols.; Paris: Mathias, 1851–1854). *Catéchisme positiviste ou Sommaire exposition de la religion universelle, en onze entretiens systématiques entre une femme et un prêtre de l'Humanité* (Paris, N.D.), reprints (Paris: Société Positiviste) and (Paris: Garnier, 1909). *Correspondance avec John Stuart Mill*, published by Lucien Lévy-Bruhl (Paris: Alcan, 1899).

English translations: *System of Positive Polity* (London, 1875–77). *The Catechism of Positive Religion*, translated by Richard Congreve (London, 1858); some modifications of the French original, introduced by Congreve and approved by Comte, were included in the later French editions of the treatise. *A General View of Positivism*, translated by J. H. Bridges (London, 1858). An excellent abridgment of the six volumes of the *Cours de philosophie positive* is due to Harriet Martineau, *The Positive Philosophy of Auguste Comte* (London, 1853 and 1896).

Anthology: ed. H. Gouhier, *Oeuvres choisies d'Auguste Comte* (Paris: Aubier, 1943).

Doctrinal: L. Lévy-Bruhl, *The Philosophy of Comte* (New York, 1903), excellent on the "philosophy," but leaves out the religion. To be completed by Edward Caird, *The Social Philosophy and Religion of Comte* (Glasgow, 1893). John Watson, *Comte, Mill, and Spencer* (Glasgow, 1895). Henri Gouhier, *La jeunesse d'Auguste Comte et la formation du positivisme* (3 vols.; Paris: Vrin, 1933, 1936, 1941). R. L. Hawkins, *Positivism in the United States* (Cambridge, 1938). Pierre Ducasse, *Essai sur les origines intuitives du positivisme* (Paris: Alcan, 1939). *Méthode et intuition chez Auguste Comte* (Paris: Alcan, 1939). *La méthode positive et l'intuition comtienne* (Paris: Alcan, 1939) includes a bibliography. A. Cresson, *Auguste Comte, sa vie, son oeuvre* (Paris: Presses Universitaires de France 1941).

5. Comte has several times described the nature of positive philosophy, but never more soberly and more clearly than in the *Cours de philosophie positive*, Vol. I, première leçon. The whole doctrine is actually or virtually included in that very remarkable text. There is food for thought in comparing the anti-metaphysicism of Comte with that of Kant (of whom Comte knew next to nothing) as well as in comparing Comte's philosophy of history with that of Hegel. The parallelism there was between wholly unrelated philosophical undertakings is a strong argument in favor of the notion that major systems of philosophy are spontaneous answers to collective questions obscurely but forcibly asked by contemporaries.

6. On the general hierarchy of the positive sciences, see *Cours de philosophie positive*, Vol. 1, deuxieme leçon. Comte insists that his classification of the sciences, though it looks historical, is in fact dogmatic. By and large, there is a correspondence between the philosophical order of the sciences in the classification and their order of appearance in history, but, "in considering the effective development of the human mind as a whole, it becomes more and more apparent that the different sciences were, in fact, perfected at one and the same time, and mutually so." Even the progress of certain arts has to be taken into account in order to explain the development of certain sciences. In calling his classification "dogmatic," Comte means to say that it expresses a rational interpretation of the order according to which the hierarchical layers of reality condition one another. This Comte calls a "natural and positive classification of the fundamental sciences."

7. Sociology divides into social statics and social dynamics. Social statics, a part of his doctrine too neglected by historians, is in reality full of interesting historical and sociological views. Its object is the study of the correlations between the diverse elements of a given civilization considered at a certain moment of its history. According to Comte (since all is relative, nothing absolute) there is always a correspondence between the respective states of religion, ethics, science, art and industry, within one and the same society at one and the same moment of its historical evolution. Instead of seeing industry as the determining factor, Comte sees the state of philosophy as the leading factor and determining element of each particular historical and social structure, in a certain civilization and at a given time. For instance, in the Middle Ages, the predominance of the "theological spirit" accounts for the condition of sciences and arts, as well as for the feudal structure of society in the various Christian countries. This explains why Comte himself came to feel more and more strongly that the advent of positivism should bring about new forms of arts and of poetry. Why should the new positivist type of society not find its Dante? Comte almost imagined that he himself was going to write the inevitably coming epic of the positive spirit. As to social dynamics, Comte felt he had completed it, at least in its substance, in formulating the

Law of the Three States. The whole development of the positive spirit through history, in all its phases and cases, was reducible to his law.
8. *Cours de philosophie positive*, Vol. I, sixième leçon, end of chapter.
9. Comte himself has summed up the main interventions of positive philosophy in the body of the fundamental sciences: *Cours de philosophie positive*, conclusions générales, lecture 58. In it he has proposed (as facultative) a dualist conception of chemistry, as a means of simplifying and systematizing that science; in physics, positivism has founded a sound general theory of scientific hypotheses; in astronomy, it has reduced to sensible limits the pretensions of the so-called "sidereal (stellar) astronomy" and insured the primacy of the research work concerning the human planet earth. Even in mathematics, positivism has effected a capital rectification of the essential bases of rational mechanics, of the whole of geometry and of the principles of analysis, either simple or transcendent. It is essential to understand that, in Comte's own mind, all these progresses were due to his considering sciences from the vantage point of the youngest of all sciences, sociology. The primacy of sociology is thereby objectively established. This establishes a positive connection between the speculative nature of positive philosophy and its practical destination. The "unity" of Comte's positivism is here at stake.
10. On the notion, object, method and content of sociology (or social physics, see *Cours de philosophie positive*, Vol. IV, leçons 50 (social statics, or general theory of the spontaneous order in human societies) and 51 (fundamental laws of social dynamics, or general theory of the natural progress of mankind).
11. On this (essential for an understanding of Comte's doctrinal evolution) see the excellent biography, by Henri Gouhier, *La vie d'Auguste Comte*, new ed. (Paris: J. Vrin, 1965). Also the chapter devoted to the psychological aspect of the problem in E. Gilson, *A Choir of Muses* (New York: Sheed & Ward, 1953).
12. For a well-balanced exposition of Comte's state of mind just before the sentimental crisis which, without changing the direction of the doctrine, altered its inspiration, see *Cours de philosophie positive*, Vol. VI, leçon 58, "Final appreciation of the positive method as a whole." The aim of the method is to achieve "philosophical unity, as constituting the first fundamental condition of the intellectual and moral reorganization of the more advanced populations." Its chief adversary is "the irrational dispersion of the scientific efforts." The danger is great. It should not be believed that even mathematics will indefinitely withstand the harmful influence of the "individual divagations" favored by the then predominating "philosophical anarchy." However, a true philosophical unity requires the preponderance of one of the sciences over the others. Of the six fundamental sciences, only two can be universalized—the first one and the last. Thus, we have to choose between admitting the primacy of the mathematical spirit or that of the sociological spirit. Mathematics had a "right" to prevail at the beginning of the evolution of man's knowledge; nevertheless, sociology now shows itself to be the only science qualified to direct, with real efficacy, the development of all the positive sciences and the organization of society. This is what Comte calls "the philosophical pre-eminence of the sociological spirit." Why is it "philosophical"? Because, as was said in note 9, sociology has given proof of its aptitude for reforming

and unifying the other positive sciences; it is therefore a true wisdom in comparison with them. The positive philosophy progresses from "a vain and sterile mathematical unity (of knowledge) to a true and fruitful sociological unity" (leçon 58). By the same token, the positive philosophy succeeds in reconciling speculation and action by founding sociology," "that final philosophy (which) tends directly to bring about the universal preponderance of ethics." The "admirable attempt of Catholicism" in the Middle Ages failed because it lacked the solid basis of positive philosophy. Thus, in justifying the passage from positive philosophy to positive politics, Comte was careful to observe that "henceforth, the entire normal preponderance of morals is no less required for the intellectual efficacy of the mental evolution than it is for its social destination" (Translated: my philosophy is one since, in it, even the final primacy of ethics, prepared by the initial primacy of science, is no less necessarily required for scientific progress than it is for moral and social progress. This is what Comte calls "the fundamental knot of positive philosophy").

13. Even this notion was to Comte a conclusion in positive philosophy. A mere glance at the classification of the fundamental sciences reveals that psychology is not one of them. It is not a science at all because as an individual man does not exist. In fact, there is no such being in the world as a lone individual. Moreover, what we call individuality is the particular combination resulting from two factors: the physiological structure of a certain body and the sociological situation assigned by history to a certain man (see the notion of social statics). Comte's man could be described as a body whose mentality is determined by its reaction to a given sociological moment. The last essential source of metaphysical illusions to be eliminated is the belief that man essentially is an individual. On the contrary, "from the static as well as from the dynamic point of view, man properly so called is fundamentally a pure abstraction; what is real in him is humanity only, especially in the intellectual and in the moral order" (leçon 58). In accordance with the early views expressed in the *Plan des travaux nécessaires pour reorganiser l'humanité*, Comte was announcing, toward the end of the last lecture of his *Cours de philosophie positive* (leçon 60) that his doctrine had provided the truth destined to be wielded by "a new spiritual power." He then stressed "the natural aptitude of the positive philosophy to make possible a spiritual association much wider than was permitted by previous philosophy." The "European case" is but a particular one.

14. The attitude of Mill was above reproach. After all, to follow Comte as a religious reformer (even if he was the High Priest of an atheistic religion) was implicitly to accept the teaching of his Positivist Catechism, to be married by him, to have one's own children baptized by him, etc. Mill, who had generously supported the undertaking of Comte, discreetly withdrew from the group. See the *Lettres inédites de John Stuart Mill*, ed. L. Lévy-Bruhl (Paris: Alcan, 1899); Emile Littré (1801–1881) collected the documents on the case and published them under the title of *Auguste Comte et la philosophie positive* (Paris: Bureaux de la Philosophie Positive, 1877). A. man of universal culture (a physician and the author of the monumental *Dictionnaire de la langue française*, never excelled since), Littré refused to follow Comte beyond the conclusions of the *Cours de philosophie positive*; with him, positivism became at once a straight scientism. He founded with G. Wyrouboff a journal entitled *La philosophie*

positive, an organ of the non-Comtian positivists; he was elected a member of the French Academy (1871). His wife had him baptized on his death bed (1881). Caro, *Littré et le positivisme* (Paris, 1883).

15. Letter to M. de Tholouze, April 22, 1851: A. Comte, *Correspondance*, Vol. III (Paris: Société Positiviste, 1903–1904), p. 101.

16. Hippolyte Adolphe Taine, b. Vouziers, 1828; d. Menthon-Saint-Bernard, 1893. Entered the École Normale Supérieure, Paris (1848) and prepared himself for a teaching career; read with predilection Aristotle and Spinoza; in 1851, failed to pass his Agrégation de Philosophie; the jury was presided over by Victor Cousin; after teaching philosophy and literature (his views in philosophy looked too radical), he resigned his position and came to Paris to study physiology, botany, zoology and psychopathology; successfully passed his doctorate (1853); began to write in diverse reviews; had a nervous breakdown (1856–1857); published his *Histoire de la littérature anglaise* (3 vols.; Paris: L. Hachette, 1864, 4 vols.; 1866); after a voyage in Italy, began to teach esthetics at the École des Beaux Arts, Paris (1865); deeply impressed by the French defeat in the 1870 war, but still more impressed by the Parisian rebellion (the "Commune"), which followed the war, Taine wrote his *Origines de la France contemporaine* (10 vols.; Paris: L. Hachette, 1876–1896), a history of the French Revolution still much discussed; a fellow of the French Academy (1878), he enjoyed his membership in that "club of intelligent people"; he spent the better part of his time in Menthon-Saint-Bernard (Annecy Lake) where he died in 1893; his tomb is there and attracts quite a few visitors.

Main writings (although all his writings are related to his philosophy, the following ones are of particular interest for doctrinal history): *Les philosophes français du XIXe siècle* (Paris: Hachette, 1857), 3rd ed. revised (1868), 8th ed. (Paris: Hachette, 1901 and often since). *La philosophie de l'art* (Paris: G. Baillière, 1865). *De l'idéal dans l'art* (Paris: G. Baillière, 1867), followed by diverse essays on art in the Netherlands (1868), in Greece (1869), and collectively published under the general title *La philosophie de l'art*, 3rd ed. (2 vols.; Paris: Hachette, 1881 and often reprinted since). *De l'intelligence* (2 vols.; Paris: Hachette, 1870 and often reprinted since).

Biographical: *H. Taine, sa vie et sa correspondance* (4 vols.; Paris: Hachette, 1902–1905). Victor Giraud, *Essai sur Taine, son oeuvre et son influence* (Paris: Hachette, 1902).

Doctrinal: Paul Nève, *La philosophie de Taine* (Paris-Louvain, 1908), bibliography, pp. 26–31.

17. Taine shows a great respect for Laromiguière, who inherited the method of Condillac: "As I believe, that method is one of the masterpieces of the human mind. We have forgotten it for thirty years and, today, we still are neglecting it"—*Les philosophes classiques du XIXe siècle* quoted from the 8th ed. (Paris: Hachette, 1901), p. 17. It should be noted that through Comte the eighteenth century taste for positive knowledge could reach Taine. Royer-Collard chanced upon Reid's *Inquiry* in the box of a secondhand book-dealer; he bought it for a few cents, and in doing so, "he had just bought and founded the new French philosophy" (pp. 21–48). On Maine de Biran (pp. 49–78), Taine does not seem to notice anything unusual about his philosophy. Cousin occupies the better part of the volume (pp. 79–288). Taine undertakes to account for

the success of Cousin's philosophy in *Pourquoi l'éclectisme a-t-il réussi?* (chap. vii, pp. 289–315). His answer is that at the time of Cousin there was a general rebellion in France against the cut-and-dried rationalism of the eighteenth century; the influence of Rousseau, Chateaubriand, Mme. de Staël, and other apologists of feeling and the heart then became predominant. Those excellent pages well deserve to be read; whether or not they account for the success of eclecticism is another question. At any rate, what they say sounds true. Moreover, Taine concludes that we are again reading the eighteenth-century authors; we want proofs: "A new philosophy will constitute itself" (p. 313).

18. Chapters xiii and xiv *On Method* are particularly significant (*Pourquoi l'éclectisme*, pp. 318–371). They consist of an imaginary dialogue between two philosophers—Mr. Peter and Mr. Paul. Mr. Peter will speak of analysis only; but analysis cannot work unless it applies to objectively given facts. For instance, if you are writing about the history of Rome, do not say: "The destiny of Rome was to conquer the earth," because you don't know if there are such facts as destiny, fate, etc. Rather you should write something like this: "On account of such and such factors, the Roman people first conquered the Mediterranean basin…etc." On the relation fact-cause: "What do I call a cause? It is a fact from which I can deduce the nature, the relations and the modifications of other facts" (chap. xiv, p. 351). "The progress of science consists in explaining an ensemble of facts, not by an alleged cause outside all experience, but rather by a higher fact (*par un fait supérieur*) that produces them. Thus, by rising up from a higher fact to a still higher one, one should arrive, for each genre of objects, at a unique fact, which is the universal cause." "The unity of the world thus progressively reveals itself; it does not come to it from any external cause: It arises from a general fact, similar to all the other ones; it is the generating law from which all the rest is deduced…" "The ultimate object of science is that supreme law; and he who, by one single leap, could transport himself into it, would see the eternal torrent of the events and the infinite ocean of beings flow from it by diverse and ramified channels, as from one source. That is the moment when one feels the notion of Nature form itself in the mind. Owing to that hierarchy of necessities, the world constitutes one single being, indivisible, of which all beings are members"; *Les philosophes classiques…*, chap. xiv, pp. 370–371. This is a typical example of what, around the middle of the nineteenth century, was considered a "scientific" way of philosophizing. A philosophical notion then became scientific by asserting itself without any justification. However, Taine is heard here as a weakened echo of Spinoza.

19. *De l'intelligence*, vol. II, Book IV, chap. i, par. 1, pp. 249–258. This, of course, was raising again the old problem of the "universals." Is there in nature such a thing as generality? Or does generality originate in the mind? It is typical of Taine that he considered it unscientific to discuss the question, much less ask it. He simply affirms what a scholastic would have called the "realist" answer to the problem, without bothering to justify it.

20. Taine thinks he is reviving the "language of calculus," guessed by Condillac and which has been allowed to lie neglected, dead and as good as buried for one hundred years. The reason for that neglect was that the view of Condillac was lacking proofs

(*De l'intelligence*, Preface, Vol. I, p. 3).
21. *De l'intelligence*, Vol. II, Book IV, chap. iii, pp. 462–464.
22. See *Essai sur Tite Live* (Paris: Hachette, 1856); *La Fontaine et ses fables* (Paris: Hachette, 1861); *Histoire de la littérature anglaiseiPhilosophie de l'art*; Johannes Schlaf, *Kritik der Taineschen Kunst theorie* (Wien and Leipzig: Akad. Verlag, 1906). Often severely judged from the point of view of philosophy, Taine's brilliant historical and cultural approach to art has been ceaselessly exploited after his death. This consists in accounting for works of art by everything else than the art of the artist. Countless brilliant lectures are still being given in the spirit of Taine; organized tours in art galleries usually follow the same method; and art is more and more tending to reduce itself to that which non-artists pretend to know about it.
23. The philosophically significant parts of the *Philosophie de l'art* are its First Book and its conclusion, *De l'idéal dans l'art*; but interesting remarks are scattered throughout the whole work. Besides, it should be remembered that, discounting the system itself, Taine's writings on esthetics abound in deep and brilliant observations that make them well worth reading. His sins are mostly of omission.
24. Theodule Armand Ribot, b. Guingamp, 1839; d. Paris, 1910. The dominant figure in French psychology for many years. Founded the *Revue philosophique* (1876); was succeeded by L. Lévy-Bruhl as its director; was generally a positivist (in the broad sense of the term); a professor of experimental psychology at the Sorbonne, then at the College de France (1888); Ribot was, with Espinas, the translator of Spencer's *Principles of Psychology*, a work whose influence is often perceptible in Ribot's writings. His works, all published in Paris, by Félix Alcan, include: *La psychologie anglaise contemporaine* (1870); *La psychologie allemande contemporaine* (1879); *Les maladies de la mémoire* (1881); *Les maladies de la volonté* (1883); *Les maladies de la personnalité* (1885); *La psychologie de l'attention* (1888); *La psychologie des sentiments* (1896); *L'évolution des idées générales* (1897); *Essai sur l'imagination créatrice* (1900); etc. Despite a general tendency to stress the element of activity in mental life (a trait which may have motivated the mention of his name by Lachelier), the place of Ribot in the history of French philosophy marks the moment when psychology separated itself from philosophy and turned itself into a separate science. From then onward the tendency was to have either a philosophy or a psychology. It is noteworthy, however, that the scientist's turn of mind, characteristic of modern psychology in France, never prevented philosophers from resorting to psychology in their metaphysical speculation. Ravaisson, Lachelier, Bergson and more recent ones have kept faith with the classical tradition of a metaphysical psychology.
25. These names belong to the history of psychology, understood as a distinct scientific discipline, rather than to the history of philosophy properly so called. The name of Gabriel de Tarde (1843–1904) should at least be mentioned as providing a transition from French psychology to French sociology. A magistrate, then a professor at the College de France, Tarde had elaborated, at the end of the nineteenth century, a sociology that was to provide an easy target for the coming school of Durkheim. Instead of resorting to the notion of "collective representations" or to that of "group mentality," Tarde accounted for social structures by means of simple laws well known

in individual psychology. Everything in the life of societies can be accounted for by the presence of exceptional individuals setting examples that are followed by the rank and file. Two words could characterize the doctrine: invention and imitation. It was a psychology of sociological facts. Tarde's psychosociology (*la sociologie de l'imitation*) was considered out of date by the pupils of Durkheim. His main works include: *Les lois de l'imitation* (Paris: F. Alcan, 1890). *La logique sociale* (Paris: F. Alcan, 1895). *Les lois sociales* (Paris: F. Alcan, 1898). Bibliography in M. M. Davis, *Psychological Interpretations of Society* (1902).

26. Émile Durkheim, b. Epinal, 1858; d. Paris, 1917. Studied philosophy at the École Normale Supérieure, 1879–1882; Ph.D. 1893; succeeded Buisson at the Sorbonne as professor of pedagogy, 1902; founder of the *Année Sociologique* (1897) and its director till his death.

Main writings (published by F. Alcan, Paris): *De la division du travail social* (1893); *Les règles de la méthode sociologique* (1894); *Le suicide, étude de sociologie* (1897); *Les formes élémentaires de la vie religieuse: le système totémique en Australie* (1912).

Biographical and doctrinal: C. E. Gehlke, *Durkheim's Contributions to Sociological Theory* (1915). R. Lacombe, *La méthode sociologique de Durkheim* (Paris, 1926).

27. Lucien Lévy-Bruhl, b. Paris, 1857; d. Paris, 1939. Professor of the History of Modern Philosophy, Sorbonne (1902); Academy of Moral and Political Sciences (1917). *La morale et la science des moeurs* (Paris: Alcan, 1903); trans. Elizabeth Lee, *Ethics and Moral Science* (London: A. Constable, 1905). *Les jonctions mentales dans les sociétés primitives* (Paris: Alcan, 1910); English translation (1926). *La mentalité primitive* (Paris: Alcan, 1922); English translation (1923). *L'âme primitive* (Paris: Alcan, 1927). *Les carnets* (Paris: Presses Universitaires, 1949) (indispensable). Among his contributions to the history of philosophy, note his excellent study, *Philosophy of Auguste Comte*; English translation (1903); Comte is one of the sources of Lévy-Bruhl's thought. But so was Hume. Chiefly interested in throwing light on the functioning of the human mind, and personally in favor of clear logical thinking, Lévy-Bruhl began by defining a "primitive mentality," or pre-logical way of thinking, which he conceived as dominated by the law of participation. Easy to observe in the reasonings of primitive men living in little evolved societies, it can also be detected in most of our own irrational ways of thinking, which are in all domains many. In the last years of his reflections, he regretted having spoken of a "primitive mentality" distinct from the logical mode of thinking typical of advanced societies. Still, the collection of facts analyzed in his books deserves to be consulted.

28. Frédéric Rauh, b. Saint-Martin-le-Vineux (Isère), 1801; d. Paris, 1909. Studied philosophy at the École Normale Supérieure; professor of philosophy at the University of Toulouse, then the École Normale Supérieure and the Sorbonne. Doctoral thesis: *Essai sur le fondement métaphysique de la morale* (Paris: Alcan, 1903). *L'expérience morale* (Paris: Alcan, 1890). In this second work, Rauh showed himself concerned with the problem of finding a place for a rational ethics halfway between sociology and metaphysics. Sociology can provide a science of man's ethical behavior, not a code of human conduct. By observing moral belief in action, such as it is seen in "liberated consciences," ethics can set up an ideal type of moral action that will serve as a moral

law for other human wills. These discussions were dominated by a practical problem. In a country where religious faith is no longer officially recognized as a matter for teaching, where positivism and scientism have killed metaphysics, and where the categoric imperative of Kant appears as arbitrary, what kind of ethics should one teach?

29. Durkheim, *De la division*, Preface, 2nd ed.; 4th ed. (Paris: F. Alcan, 1922), pp. 5–6.

30. *De la division*, p. 6. The conclusion of the book is interesting to read for what it says about a notion then very popular in France—solidarity. It seemed to be able to fulfill the twofold function of being a scientific fact and of providing a foundation for a deontology. The problem of finding in that which is, a justification for that which ought to be, or, in other words, to find a positive law capable of functioning as a normative law, perhaps an impossibility in itself, kept the representatives of the French lay system of public education busy during the first decade of the twentieth century. This is the reason solidarity was so popular with them around 1900.

For the personal views of Durkheim on educational problems, see *Education et sociologie*, with Introduction by Paul Fauconnet (Paris: Alcan, 1922).

On the ethics of solidarity, see the work of the statesman Léon Bourgeois (b. Paris, 1851; d. Epernay, 1925). *La solidarité* (Paris: A. Colin, 1896), 3rd ed., enlarged (Paris: A. Colin, 1902). No philosopher would take it seriously, but it constitutes a typical expression of the need of an objective foundation for moral prescriptions then generally felt in France. The "solidarism" of Leon Bourgeois was very popular in the moral teaching of elementary and secondary state schools. Solidarity is a fact: human beings *are* solidary; there is between them an interconnection and a community of feelings and interests—hence for all men the moral duty to recognize the fact and to act accordingly. Léon Bourgeois himself did not fail to realize that there is no necessary connection between solidarity as a physical fact (in an epidemic of typhus, for instance) and the moral resolve to order our whole activity to the common good of the community. In his own words: "There is a solidarity-fact, and there is a solidarity-duty; let us never confuse the one with the other." But he thought it necessary to observe the fact in order, to realize the moral necessity of the duty. The doctrine seemed to provide the much needed *morale laïque* for the French écoles laïques. Around 1900, countless college students had written essays on the question: How does physical solidarity provide a foundation for moral solidarity? The answer has never been found, but the question expresses under its crudest form the crucial philosophical problem raised by the constitution of a "social physics": Are we to consider that ethics, just as metaphysics, is an illusion dispelled by the rise of modern science? The tragic nature of the problem is only too visible; moral anarchy is for mankind a pretty dangerous condition under which to live.

31. Antoine Augustin Cournot, b. Grey, 1801; d. Paris, 1877. *Traité de l'enchaînement des idées fondamentales dans les sciences et dans l'histoire* (1801), 2nd ed. (Paris: Hachette, 1911). *Considérations sur la marche des idées et des événements dans les temps modernes* (Paris: Hachette, 1872). *Matérialisme, Vitalisme et Rationalisme. Etudes sur remploi des données de la science en philosophie* (Paris: Hachette, 1875). The starting point of Cournot's reflection is found in his early work, *Exposition de la théorie des chances et des probabilités* (Paris: Hachette, 1843). If one has time to read only one of Cournot's

books, the choice should be *Essai sur les fondements de la connaissance et sur les caractères de la critique philosophique* (2 vols.; Paris: Hachette, 1851), English translation with an introduction by Merritt H. More, *An Essay on the Foundation of Our Knowledge* (New York: Liberal Arts Press, 1950).

Doctrinal: F. Mentré, *Cournot et la renaissance du probabilisme au 19ᵉ siècle* (Paris: M. Rivière, 1908). A. Darbon, *Le concept de hasard dans la philosophie de Cournot* (Paris: F. Alcan, 1911). Bottinelli, *Cournot métaphysicien de la connaissance* (Paris: Hachette, 1913). R. Ruyer, *L'humanité de l'avenir d'après Cournot* (Paris: F. Alcan, 1931). A special issue of the *Revue de métaphysique et de morale* (May 1905) was devoted to the doctrine of Cournot.

32. Émile Meyerson, b. Lublin (Poland), 1859; d. Paris, 1933. A chemist by formation; after an unsuccessful industrial venture, he lived and wrote his works in France. *Identité et réalité* (Paris: F. Alcan, 1908), 2nd ed. (1912). *De l'explication dans les sciences* (Paris: Payot, 1921). *La déduction relativiste* (an attempt to extend his general interpretation of science to the physics of relativity). *Du cheminement de la pensée* (3 vols.; Paris: F. Alcan, 1931). *Essais* (Paris: J. Vrin, 1936), a posthumously published collection of essays. Few doctrines have been as commonly misunderstood as that of Meyerson. His point was that, in science, to explain is to assign the cause; but that, in fact, causality is understood as a relation of identity between cause and effect. The ready objection to this is that, were it so, nothing would ever happen; but that objection is precisely the point Meyerson was enforcing. Causal relations are not reducible to relations of identity, and since causal explanations are commonly reduced to such identities (i.e., perfect equalities) there is in nature something that escapes scientific explanation.

Doctrinal: André Metz, *Une nouvelle philosophie des sciences. Le causalisme de M. Emile Meyerson* (Paris: F. Alcan, 1923). Henri Sée, *Science et philosophie d'après la doctrine de M. Emile Meyerson* (Paris: F. Alcan, 1932).

X. MAINE DE BIRAN'S FRENCH POSTERITY

1. Jules Bachelier, *Lettres de Jules Lachelier (1856–1918)* (Paris: published by the family for private circulation only, 1933).
2. The distinction between the two types of philosophical formation was already known to Condillac—"We have four famous metaphysicians: Descartes, Malebranche, Leibniz, and Locke. Only the latter was not a geometer; and how far superior to the others he is!" Condillac, *Traité des sensations* in *Oeuvres*, ed. Georges Le Roy (Paris: Presses Universitaires de France, 1947), Vol. I, summary of Part I, p. 326.
3. Jean Gaspard Félix Lacher Ravaisson-Mollien, b. Namur (then a French city), 1813; d. Paris, 1900. Kept away from teaching obligations and preferred to fulfill administrative functions connected with the fine arts. Apart from his two volumes on the philosophy of Aristotle (in which he stressed the importance of his own notion of "act"), he wrote his short but packed thesis *De l'habitude* (Paris: Fournier & Co., 1938), republished in *Revue de métaphysique et de morale*, Vol. II (1894), No. 1; then, with introduction

by Jean Baruzi (Paris: F. Alcan, 1927). *La philosophie en France au dix-neuvième siècle* (Paris, 1868), 4th ed. (Paris: Hachette, 1895) exercised a deep influence; Bergson used to say that his own generation of students knew the book by heart. "Leonard de Vinci et renseignement du dessin," in *Revue Bleue* (November 12, 1887). *Testament philosophique et fragments*, ed. by Charles Devivaise (Paris: Boivin, 1838), includes the priceless notice of Bergson: "Notice sur la vie et les oeuvres de Ravaisson-Mollien," read in 1904 at the Académie des sciences morales et politiques.

Doctrinal: Joseph Dopp, *Félix Ravaisson. La formation de sa pensée d'après des documents inédits* (Louvain: Editions de l'institut supérieur de philosophie, 1933); an important study: bibliography of Ravaisson's writings (pp. 335–349)1 bibliography of studies concerning Ravaisson (pp. 353–301), stresses the influence of German romanticism, especially that of Schelling, under whom Ravaisson had studied in Munich. Incidentally, Dopp notes that Schelling had little esteem for Ravaisson's attempt to revive peripateticism, especially since, in his opinion, Ravaisson had misinterpreted Aristotle (pp. 127–128, notes).

4. Ravaisson's preference for Aristotle over Plato is deliberate. His objection to Plato is that Ideas are abstractions. As such, they are unable to account for the tendency of substances to attain determinate forms. Individuality, life, and life's dynamism oriented towards definite ends are not accounted for by Plato. However, operating individuals tending to definite ends are reality itself. Prior to Idea, a universal, there is an intellect, an actually existing subject. His criticism of Aristotle is noteworthy, because (although perhaps not fair to Aristotle himself) it correctly applies to some of his late successors. Ravaisson says that Aristotle has "thingified" act and potency and conceived them as two distinct entities which, of course, he could not reconcile after isolating them. See on this point, E. Boutroux, "La philosophie de Félix Ravaisson," *Nouvelles études d'histoire de la philosophie* (Paris: F. Alcan, 1927), pp. 196–198. This unfortunate dualism can be overcome by resorting to the notion of soul conceived as a living intelligence able to grasp within itself the spiritual activity which is its own being. A thus understood Aristotclianism would constitute an introduction to Christianity.

5. The continuity with Maine de Biran is perceptible in a passage of Biran's memoir on *The Influence of Habit on the Power of Thinking* (1803). In that memoir Biran has established, by an analysis of the effects of habit on our various faculties, that some faculties go on ceaselessly perfecting themselves while others are altered or degraded by the repetition of their exercise. "I found in the first ones (faculties) the action of an ever present will, directing the movements of the organs and helping to form habits by placing itself above these. As to the second class of faculties, I have shown how the absence of will, or of the first instruments upon which will exerts itself, leaves sensibility a prey to the causes of weakening or of alteration attached to sensations when they are continuous or frequently repeated," Maine de Biran, *Oeuvres choisies*, ed. Gouhier, p. 69.

6. Aristotle, *De memoria et reminiscentia*, ii, 452 A, 27–28.

7. Augustine, *Confessions*, III, 6, 11.

8. In *Philosophie en France*, Ravaisson notes that, in his last essays, even Théodore

Jouffroy had broken away from Cousin by revoking into doubt the proposition that "only the phenomena are an object of immediate cognition." This change of opinion was probably caused in Jouffroy by the growing influence of Maine de Biran. In his memoir *On the legitimacy of the distinction between psychology and physiology*, Biran had expressly stated that man is conscious of something else beyond mere phenomena, that "he reaches within himself the principles which produce them, his so-called Ego, so that soul feels itself to be the cause of its acts and apprehends itself as the subject of its modifications"; to which Biran added, "One must delete from psychology that consecrated proposition: soul is known to us by its acts and by its modifications only" (*La philosophie en France*, p. 26). For the sentence on the "specious parallelism," see p. 27.

9. Ravaisson, *Philosophie en France au dix-neuvième siècle*, pp. 242, 260, 281.
10. Jules Lachelier, b. Fontainebleau, 1832; d. same city, 1918. Professor of philosophy, École Normale Supérieure. General Inspector for philosophy in French colleges. *Du fondement de l'induction* (Paris: Ladrange, 1871). *De natura syllogismi* (Paris: Ladrange, 1871). His important essay, "Philosophie et métaphysique" (1885) was reprinted in all the editions of *Du fondement* since the second one. Complete works (2 vols.; Paris: Presses Universitaires), temporarily out of print. In our own text, all references giving the number of the page only (for instance, p. 44) refer to the original edition of *Du fondement*.

Doctrinal: Gabriel Séailles, *La philosophie de J. Lachelier* (Paris: F. Alcan, 1920). E. Boutroux, "Jules Lachelier," *Nouvelles études d'histoire de la philosophie* (Paris: F. Alcan, 1927), pp. 1–31.

11. As related by E. Boutroux, *Nouvelles études*, p. 2.
12. Lachelier, not a scholastic (although a practicing Catholic) and fully acquainted with the criticism of Kant, never hesitated to look to Aristotle for inspiration. His minor doctoral thesis, *De natura syllogismi*, bears as its epigraph: *ou pasa apodeixis syllogismos* (not all demonstration is a syllogism); his conclusion is that there are, indeed, fourteen valid modes of syllogism, just as Aristotle had said. Nobody was ever able to discover a fifteenth valid one—"After first describing twenty modes Euler has confessed that two of them, the fifteenth and the sixteenth ones, come to the same. In order to equalize their number in all the figures, Leibniz has simply taken into account the subalternations of the universal conclusions. As to those modes which a fertile genius has recently produced in Scotland (one hundred and eight, according to their author), if one observes that the same modes are repeated in the three figures, thirty-six are left, and if one suppresses the useless quantification of the predicates, all that are left are the very same fourteen modes of Aristotle himself. Since these contain in themselves even the meaning and nature of those that are attributed to Galen, one cannot marvel enough at the fact that the art of syllogizing has been both initiated and completed within one single little book by one and the same man" (p. 40). Concerning the saying of Parmenides, Lachelier knew full well it was open to different interpretations: "I believe we substantially agree, M. Zeller, yourself and I, on the meaning of my epigraph. Only, I wish to make Parmenides say that *in order to be thought, one must be*, and moreover, *that to be thought, adds nothing to being*. This, I concede, Parmenides

Notes   557

does not expressly say, but he must accept it, as I believe, in order to maintain the absolute unity of being." Letter to Boutroux, Paris, December 7, 1871, in *Lettres de Jules Lachelier*, p. 79.

13. Related by E. Boutroux, *Nouvelles études*, p. 19. Psychology *is* metaphysics if one subscribes to Lachelier's interpretation of the saying of Parmenides. Since "to be thought, adds nothing to being," the critical idealism of Kant can be directly read as a metaphysical realism. There is no "thing in itself" in a doctrine where "to be known" and "to be" are one and the same thing. It takes some reflection to get used to the position of Lachelier, but it is worth the effort. An amazing consequence of this position is that in it the Kantian category of causality expresses reality known in its intrinsic necessity, not the "subjective" (in the Kantian sense of the word) necessity of our knowledge of it only. See on this point the remarkable letter to Frédéric Rauh, Alençon, March 19, 1893, in *Lettres de Jules Lachelier*, pp. 153-156. Lachelier says that if the law of necessity ruling our thought is not merely an empirically given, psychological fact, if, rather, it appears to us with the character of internal necessity that makes it to be law in itself, and not only for us, I ask what difference there is between this law and the absolute (or the idea in itself of being), whose existence you do not concede to me? "For I do not in the least pretend that we find ourselves confronted with a being (*ens*) that is with us in the relation of object to subject; I am speaking only of being (*esse*). which I consider, not as an abstract notion, disengaged by our own intellect from concrete reality, but as the ideal substance of that which one calls reality is but the external manifestation" (pp. 154-155).

14. It is important to understand that, in the doctrine of Lachelier, the reflexive method reaches, at once, the inner essence of the mind and the external essence of reality. Such is the meaning of the epigraph borrowed from Parmenides. Nevertheless, Lachelier joins Kant in rejecting as self-contradictory all possibility to know "things-in-themselves." His reason is that he defines the thing-in-itself as that which reality is apart from our knowledge of it. Thus it becomes an absurdity to speak of a thing as known when it is not. The contrary evidence that to know a thing otherwise than as it is in itself, is not to know it at all, does not seem to have occurred to his mind. Still, if what Parmenides said is true, there is no problem. On Lachelier own position, see *Du fondement*, pp. 46-48. On his rejection of scepticism, absolute idealism and subjective idealism, pp. 54-61.

15. Lachelier does not deny that an idea always depends on prior ones in the order of logic. Ideas proceed from ideas, but they do so only within a mind. The mind itself is the cause of all its ideas; it causes them; they do not cause one another in the mind; and since matter is absent from the order of intelligibility, it can be said (in the sense suggested by Lachelier) that ideas are produced *ex nihilo materiae* "comme un monde."

16. One of the most famous philosophical statements attributed to Lachelier (who said many things he never wrote) is to be found in Ravaisson, *La philosophie en France*, 4th ed., pp. 95-96: "According to the expression used, in a public lecture (1864) on the proofs of the existence of God, by a young master now entrusted with part of the teaching of philosophy at the École Normale (M. Lachelier), one should say that

'nature is like unto a thought that does not think itself, hanging on a self-thinking thought (la nature est comme une pensée qui ne se pense pas, suspendue à une pensée qui se pense).'" This admirable formulation of the Aristotelian view of the world deserves attentive reflection, bike that of Ravaisson, the doctrine of Lachelier was a philosophy of act, in which, as in that of Aristotle, a self-thinking thought ultimately accounts for reality.

17. See Gabriel Séailles, *La philosophie de Lachelier*, pp. 124–125. The theological conclusions of Lachelier, as found in *Le fondement de l'induction*, are, if not vague in themselves, at least insufficiently demonstrated. It is hard to say if they could be fully justified on the basis of his own principles. The reason for his later silence lies perhaps in the feeling he had for a sort of gap between his religious beliefs (which he never gave up) and his natural theology. So he sought refuge in faith, better to Gabriel Séailles, Paris, March 7, 1883: "I acknowledge the justness of the criticisms with which you have concluded your article. Not only did I fail to explain how the imperfect proceeds from the perfect, but I am afraid I did nothing to establish the real existence of a perfect being, although my intention certainly was to do so. I do not feel more able to solve these questions today than I was fifteen years ago; only I believe that, today, I would be wise enough not to ask them. If I still have the strength to write something, I shall confine myself within the theory of knowledge, leaving the rest either to faith or to a philosophy of which I am not capable" (*Lettres de Jules Lachelier*, p. 125). Cf. "letter to Caro," Paris, February 11, 1876: "The origin of things does not alter their value...today we would not be less men than we are, even though we had begun by being apes. I would find no serious difficulty in following mechanical explanations the whole way, if I did not here run counter to Christian faith, which I refuse to give up at any price. The question arises, in the order of biblical facts, in the Old Testament as well as in the Gospel, between nature and miracle, history and legend: I acknowledge this, but I do not see, *a priori*, why legend would not be true against history" (p. 115). What he means by this is that "the conception of universal mechanism is but the beginning of philosophy and that, the farther from the beginning one proceeds, the more strongly one feels convinced of the belief in the absolute empire of liberty and of spirit" (p. 116). Lachelier was philosophically cut off from his own religious tradition. Hence his perhaps inextricable predicament, starting from Maine de Biran and Kant, of how to join the conclusions of Christian philosophy.

18. Emile Boutroux, b. Montrouge (then a suburb of Paris), 1845; d. Paris, 1921. Taught the history of philosophy at the Sorbonne; director of the Thiers Foundation, Paris.

Main philosophical works: *De la contingence des lois de la nature* (Paris: Germer-Baillère, 1874), 2nd ed. (Paris: Alcan, 1896); trans. Fred Rothwell, *The Contingency of the Laws of Nature* (Chicago: Open Court Publishing Co., 1920). *L'idée de loi naturelle* (Paris: Alcan, 1895). *Science et religion dans la philosophie contemporaine* (Paris: Flammarion, 1908). On the friendly relations between Boutroux and William James, R. B. Perry, *The Thought and Character of William James* (Boston: Little Brown & Co., 1935), Vol. II, chap. lxxxiii, pp. 560–569 (letters of Boutroux to James in Appendix XI, pp. 766–768). A. F. Baillot, *Emile Boutroux et la pensée religieuse* (Paris: La Nef de Paris, 1958).

19. *De veritatibus aeternis apud Cartesium* (Paris: Germer-Baillière, 1874), French translation by E. Canguilem (Paris: F. Alcan, 1927).
20. *La philosophie de Kant* (Paris: Librairie philosophique, J. Vrin, 1926).
21. *La philosophie de Kant*, pp. 267–268.
22. *La philosophie de Kant*, p. 269.
23. *De la contingence des lois de la nature*, p. 45.
24. *De la contingence*, p. 24.
25. *De la contingence*, chap. iv, pp. 66–67.
26. *De la contingence*, chap. v.
27. *De la contingence*, p. 84.
28. *De la contingence*, p. 97.
29. *De la contingence*, p. 118.
30. *De la contingence*, p. 126.
31. *De la contingence*, pp. 140–141.
32. Boutroux says, "a world," *De la contingence*, p. 153.
33. *De la contingence*, p. 153.
34. *De la contingence*, p. 155.
35. *De la contingence*, p. 158.
36. *De la contingence*, p. 161.
37. *De la contingence*, p. 164.
38. *De la contingence*, p. 165.
39. *De la contingence*, pp. 177–178. The reason for Boutroux's early interest in the Cartesian doctrine of the creation of the "eternal truths" here becomes evident. With respect to God, essences as well as existences are contingent.
40. Henri Bergson, b. Paris, 1859; d. Paris, 1941. Studied philosophy at the École Normale Supérieure; *agrégé* to the University; taught philosophy in various high schools and at the École Normale; professor at the College de France; ceased to teach after publishing *Creative Evolution* and devoted himself to the long preparation of his last great work on ethics and religion.

Main writings: *Essai sur les données immédiates de la conscience* (Paris: F. Alcan, 1889); *Time and Freewill: An Essay on the Immediate Data of Consciousness*, trans. F. L. Pogson (London: Swan Sonnenschein, 1910). *Matière et mémoire. Essai sur la relation du corps avec l'esprit* (Paris: F. Alcan, 1896); *Matter and Memory*, trans. N. M. Paul and W. S. Palmer (London: Swan Sonnenschein, 1911). *L'évolution créatrice* (Paris: F. Alcan, 1907); trans. Arthur Mitchell, *Creative Evolution* (London: Macmillan & Co., 1911). *Les deux sources de la morale et de la religion* (Paris: F. Alcan, 1932); *The Two Sources of Morality and Religion* (London: Macmillan & Co., 1935). "Introduction à la métaphysique," in *La pensée et le mouvant* (Paris: Presses Universitaires de France, 1934), pp. 177–288; *An Introduction to Metaphysics* (New York: The Liberal Arts Press, 1949).

Collected works: Henri Bergson, *Oeuvres*, Edition du centenaire, with notes by André Robinet and an introduction by H. Gouhier (Paris: Presses Universitaires, 1959).

Doctrinal: H. Wildon Carr, *Henri Bergson: The Philosophy of Change* (London: T. C. & E. C. Jack, 1911). Harald Hoffding, *La philosophie de Bergson* (Paris, F. Alcan, 1916).

Albert Thibaudet, *Le Bergsonisme* (2 vols.; Paris: Gallimard, 1924). Jacques Chevalier, *Bergson* (Paris: Plon, 1925). Wladimir Jankélévitch, *Bergson* (Paris: Alcan, 1931). Jacques Maritain, *La philosophie bergsonienne*, 2nd ed. (Paris: Rivière, 1930). Régis Jolivet, *Essai sur le bergsonisme* (Lyon-Paris: E. Vitte, 1931). H. Gouhier, *Bergson et le Christ des évangiles* (Paris: Arthême Fayard, 1961).

41. The essential text concerning method is *An Introduction to Metaphysics*. In a sense, all the works of Bergson are as many invitations to the effort as are required for the practice of the method. Its aim and scope is to rid the mind of its intellectual habits and to teach it to re-establish contact with the intuited continuity of becoming.

42. The central text on the relation of intelligence to intuition and of both to reality is found in *L'évolution créatrice*, pp. 147–190. The doctrine expressly opposes the Aristotelian notion that vegetative, instinctive and rational life are three successive degrees of one and the same self-developing tendency; Bergson sees them as three divergent directions of an activity which divided itself during its growth. Intelligence essentially is the faculty of fabricating artificial objects, particularly machine tools, which are tools for making tools; it deals chiefly with inorganic matter. On the contrary, instinct is the faculty, or power, of constructing organically structured instruments, namely, bodily organs; intuition is obtained at the end of an effort of the mind to contact instinct, and to coincide with it by a movement contrary to that of intelligence. Instinct and intelligence constitute two divergent but equally legitimate answers to the same problem. They are different in that intelligence is the knowledge of a form; instinct is that of a matter. This is the reason their competences are different: "There are things which only intelligence is capable of seeking, but which by itself it will never find. Only instinct could find them, but it will never seek them" (*Evolution créatrice*, chap. ii, p. 104). These considerations prepare the famous conclusion of Bergson; because intelligence has for its main object the inorganic solid, it does not perceive continuity clearly, but competently handles only discontinuity and immobility; "intelligence is characterized by a natural incomprehension of life" (p. 179). This statement has become a symbol for the so-called "anti-intellectualism" of Bergson. However, it should be noted that the "character" of intelligence stressed by Bergson is not its definition for him.

43. Concerning this notion of soul as a spiritual subject really distinct from its body, Bergson finds himself in deep agreement with Thomas Aquinas. In fact, they have a common Greek source—Plato, perfected by Plotinus. The personal contribution of Bergson was his discussion of the problem on the basis of the clinical and physiological facts known about aphasia. For this reason, *Matter and Memory* might well be the more perfect of all his works. It also is a more difficult one to read. Its conclusions are tied up with the refutation of the "psycho-physiological parallelism," at the time an undiscussed "scientific" hypothesis, but which today would receive few unqualified approvals.

44. The demonstration of psychological indeterminism rests upon a penetrating criticism of the famous Fechner Law, which established a calculable quantitative relation between the intensity of the stimulus and that of the corresponding sensation (sensation, according to the law of Fechner, increases as the logarithm of the stimulus). In

order to show the arbitrariness of the formula, Bergson demonstrated that the notion of "intensity" does not apply to sensations. Intensity is a quantitative notion, but there are no quantitative differences between sensations; they differ qualitatively only; a sound is neither high nor low—it is different; a light cannot be greater than another light—it is another sort of light. The analysis of the data of the problem (*Essai sur les données*, chap. i) shows Bergson at his best.

45. The doctrine of Bergson can be presented as a thrice-repeated demonstration of one and the same truth. The liberty of the human will is found in its aptitude to produce unpredictable acts, whose nature is such that its decisions are equally unaccountable for by mechanism and by the conventional notion of purposiveness (*Essai sur les données*); cosmic evolution is the effect of a creative power whose effects can be accounted for neither by mechanism nor by purposiveness, especially if the latter is understood as the execution of a pre-established plan; that creative evolution is change, becoming and a continual invention of new forms (évolution créatrice). Morals and religion are neither forms of behavior imposed from without; nor are they the fulfillment of a pre-existing moral and religious good proposed to man as his ultimate end, but rather they are invention and creation of new patterns of inner life by the moral hero and the saint. The unity of Bergson's philosophy is not that of a system, but of a method in applying one and the same leading notion for the solution of different problems.

46. Bergson had no objection to calling "god" the élan vital, which is the active factor of his creative evolution; see the two celebrated letters of Bergson on the question, in De Tonquédec, S.J., *Dieu dans dévolution créatrice* (Paris: Beauchesne, 1912). On the basis of that identification, the doctrine presents itself as follows: "The considerations exposed in my *Essai* throw light upon the very fact of liberty; those of *Matière et mémoire* permit tangibly to ascertain, as I hope, the reality of the spirit; those of *Evolution créatrice* present creation as a fact. From all this clearly follows the notion of a God both creating and free, who generates both matter and life, and whose creative effort prolongs itself, on the side of life by the evolution of the species and by the constitution of the human personalities. From all this, therefore, the refutation of monism and of pantheism in general follows." Granting all this, the "god" of the *Evolution créatrice* still remained very far from the God of Christian theology; but the same remark could be made about the notion of God obtained in the sole light of reason as the conclusion of an inquiry concerning the ultimate cause of physical reality. Moreover, at the time Fr. de Tonquedec published his book, Bergson was still preparing his masterwork on the two sources of religion and morality. When all is said and done, it seems fair to say that Bergson would have liked to have been able philosophically to justify the Christian notion of God; that he could do so on the basis of his own philosophy remains at least doubtful. From the point of view of religious orthodoxy, it is noteworthy that while the *Essai* and *Matière et mémoire* are on the Index, *Les deux sources* is not.

47. *Les deux sources*, chap. iii, p. 235.
48. *Les deux sources*, p. 250.
49. *Les deux sources*, p. 257.
50. *Les deux sources*, p. 274.

XI. In the Spirit of Criticism

1. On the beginnings of Kantism in Italy, see Michele Federico Sciacca, *La filosofia nell' età del Risorgimento* (Milano: Vallardi, 1948), Part II, chap. iv, §3, pp. 364–377; bibliography, pp. 460–461.
2. Charles Renouvier, b. Montpellier, 1815; d. Prados, 1903. A first group of works contains what is sometimes called "la philosophie des manuels": *Manuel de philosophie ancienne* (2 vols.; Paris: Paulin, 1844). *Manuel de philosophie moderne* (Paris: Paulin, 1842). *Manuel républicain de l'homme et du citoyen* (Paris: Pagnerre, 1848). A second group comprises the *Essais de critique générale*: Vol. I (Paris: Ladrange, 1859); vols. III and IV (Paris: Ladrange, 1864); enlarged editions of Vols. I and II (1875); of III, *Les principes de la nature* (1892); of IV, *Philosophie analytique de l'histoire. Les idées, les religions, les systèmes* (4 vols.; Paris: E. Leroux, 1896, 1897, 1898). *La nouvelle monadologie*, in collaboration with his disciple Louis Prat (Paris: A. Colin, 1899). *Histoire et solution des problèmes métaphysiques* (Paris: F. Alcan, 1901). *Le personnalisme, suivi d'une étude sur la perception externe et sur la force* (Paris: F. Alcan, 1903). From 1872 to 1889, published in a philosophical journal: *La critique philosophique*. From 1878 to 1885, published in another review, *La critique religieuse*.
    Doctrinal: Gabriel Séailles, *La philosophie de Charles Renouvier* (Paris: F. Alcan, 1905). O. Hamelin, *Le système de Renouvier* (Paris: F. Alcan, 1927). L. Foucher, *La jeunesse de Renouvier et sa première philosophie* (Paris: J. Vrin, 1927) (bibliography of Renouvier's works). G. Milhaud, *La philosophie de Charles Renouvier* (Paris: J. Vrin, 1927). Gallo Galli, *Prime linee d'un idealismo critico e Due studi su Renouvier* (Torino: Gheroni, 1944), pp. 101–230. R. Verneaux, *Renouvier disciple et critique de Kant* (Paris: J. Vrin, 1945). R. Verneaux, *L'idéalisme de Renouvier* (Paris: J. Vrin, 1945). Marcel Mery, *La Critique du christianisme chez Renouvier* (2 vols.; Paris: J. Vrin, 1952).
3. The singular (table of the categories) is here used in view of simplifying the exposition. Renouvier has successively offered five tables of the categories, the last one having been left incomplete. To conciliate them is not easy; it is not even easy to conciliate each one of the successive tables with itself. See R. Verneaux, *L'idéalisme*, pp. 144–146; four different tables are related and compared.
4. The neocriticism of Renouvier has one feature in common with the positivism of Auguste Comte. Renouvier himself has noted the fact. To him, as to Comte, "nothing is absolute, all is relative." In this sense the doctrine of Renouvier is a strict "relativism." Because nothing is absolute, there can be no "thing in itself," or noumenon. Consequently, things are just that which they are when known; this is the feature called the "phenomenism" of Renouvier. For that reason, the category of "relation" occupies a dominant place in the tables of the categories set up by Renouvier.
5. This is one of the more curious features of the doctrine. The relativism of Renouvier necessarily leads him to the conclusion that a certain number of vitally important certitudes (such as the existence of other beings) cannot be rationally justified. Hence his appeal to "natural faith," which does not seem very different in his doctrine from the "common sense," or the common consent of the Scottish philosophers. The position is acceptable in itself, but there is very little "criticism" in it.

6. On the very confused historical notion of "personalism," see Edgar S. Brightman, "Personalism" (including personal idealism) in *A History of Philosophical Systems* (New York: The Philosophical Library, 1950), chap. xxvii, pp. 340–352.
7. Renouvier, *Manuel de philosophie moderne*, p. 7; as quoted by Louis Foucher, *La jeunesse de Renouvier*, p. 217.
8. François Pillon, b. Fontaines (Yonne), 1830; d. Paris, 1914. Assumed responsibilities for *L'année philosophique*, founded 1867, which then became a monthly under the title *La critique philosophique* (1872–1889), and which then became *L'année philosophique* (1890), directed by Renouvier, Pillon and Dauriac.

Lionel Dauriac, b. Brest, 1847; d. Paris, 1923. École Normale Supérieure, 1867; Agrégé de Philosophie, 1872; doctorate in philosophy with a thesis on *Des notions de matière et de force dans les sciences de la nature* (Paris, 1878). *Les deux morales: La morale évolutioniste et la morale traditionnelle* (Saint-Denis: Charles Lambert, 1884). *Sens commun et raison pratique* (Paris: F. Alcan, 1887). *Croyance et réalité* (Paris: F. Alcan, 1889). A lover of music, Dauriac published, among other works in musical esthetics, *Essai sur l'esprit musical* (Paris: F. Alcan, 1904).
9. Octave Hamelin, b. Lion-d'Angers (Maine-et-Loire), 1856; d. Hucket (Landes), 1907. Professor of philosophy at the École Normale Supérieure and at the Sorbonne.

Main works: *Essai sur les éléments principaux de la représentation* (Paris: F. Alcan, 1907).

Doctrinal: see the attentive pages of Dominique Parodi, *La philosophie contemporaine en France*, 2nd ed. revised (Paris: Alcan, 1920), pp. 432–451. On Parodi's own philosophical positions, see his *Le Problème moral et la pensée contemporaine* (Paris: Alcan, 1909): Pure reason cannot hope to find in itself alone the very matter of morality; this is given to man by society or by instinct; but reason has to criticize such data; in doing so, reason introduces into it disinterested ends which are proper to it and constitute the very essence of morality itself.
10. In 1906–1907, Hamelin gave a lecture course on Renouvier at the Sorbonne. Unable to understand it, and even to take intelligible notes, the students begged him to let them have, after each lecture, the text of his own manuscript. Hamelin obliged. The lectures have been published under the title *Le système de Renouvier* (Paris: Librairie philosophique, J. Vrin, 1927). The same year Hamelin devoted his seminar to a commentary on Cicero's *De fato*; one sentence often recurred as a sort of refrain: "He who was born under a bad star, shall perish in the sea." He himself perished in the sea during the following summer recess, heroically trying to save a drowning person.
11. *Essai sur les éléments*, p. 5.
12. "We shall therefore admit, as a primitive fact that can be presented in several different ways, but which, as it seems, imposes itself with a singular force: that each and every *posed* entails an *opposed*, that each and every *thesis* leaves out of itself an *antithesis*, and that the two opposites only are meaningful inasmuch as they are reciprocally exclusive. But this primitive fact completes itself by another and equally primitive one. Since each one of the two opposites has sense only through the other one, they must needs be given together; they are parts of one and the same whole: thesis, antithesis, synthesis; here in three phases is the simplest law of things. We shall name it by one

single word—Relation" (*Essai sur les éléments*, p. 2). The insistence on eliminating all deduction from this primitive experience is striking—the three notions are given at once, even the passing from the one to the others is a fact. Incidentally, one may well wonder if even the pure idealism of Hamelin does not imply an empirical element. All is relation, but if relation is fact, all is fact. The triumphal conquest of all the fundamental notions by pure idealism should not make us overlook the element of arbitrariness introduced into it by its empirical starting point. Forgotten by even the philosopher, this remains in his doctrine as an ever-present original sin.

13. *Essai sur les éléments*, p. 206.
14. *Essai sur les éléments*, p. 251.
15. *Essai sur les éléments*, p. 321.
16. On personality, *Essai sur les éléments*, pp. 326–470.
17. Léon Brunschvicg, b. Paris, 1869; d. Paris, 1941. Taught philosophy at the Sorbonne. Main works (all Paris: Alcan unless specified otherwise): *La modalité du jugement* (1897). *Introduction à la vie de l'esprit* (1900). *L'idéalisme contemporain* (1905) (a collection of important essays). Les étapes de la philosophie mathématique *La causalité et l'explication physique* (1922). *Le progrès de la conscience dans la philosophie occidentale* (2 vols.; 1927). *De la connaissance de soi* (1931). *L'esprit européen* (Neuchâtel: Editions de la Baconnière, 1947) (a sort of philosophical testament written by Brunschvicg under tragic circumstances that were a challenge to his invincible idealism).
    Doctrinal: J. Messaut, O.P., *La philosophie de Léon Brunschvicg* (Paris: J. Vrin, 1938).
18. *La modalité du jugement*, p. 82.
19. *La modalité du jugement*, p. 98.
20. *L'idéalisme contemporain*, p. 170.
21. *L'idéalisme contemporain*, p. 7.
22. We would not let it be believed that Brunschvicg was narrow-minded, far from it. The modern studies of Pascal were initiated by Brunschvicg and, to a large extent, they were his personal work. Yet Pascal was not entirely a man after Brunschvicg's own heart. The uncompromising attitude of Brunschvicg in such matters was that of a philosopher entirely convinced that his philosophy was the right one. He therefore had a yardstick for measuring his judgments.
23. One should not forget the representatives of the typical French attitude called "rationalism." It does not aim at achieving philosophical views of the world, but it looks for the sensible thing to say in all matters to which reason can apply. Rational views of reality exclude explanations borrowed from unverifiable suppositions, especially from religious ones. Rationalism usually goes hand-in-hand with naturalism. Its immediate limits are all problems concerned with invention, production and, in short, "values." The notion of "normative science," if "science" is taken in its exact meaning, seems to be a contradiction in terms. Still, rationalism has always been very influential in France (remember Voltaire).
    André Lalande, b. Paris, 1807; d. Paris, 1903. The significance of his work, *La raison et les normes* (Paris: Hachette, 1948), lies in the fact that it courageously tackles this most difficult of all problems for a consistently rationalistic approach to reality (note that rationalism is the use of reason to the exclusion of, or prescinding from, all the

other powers of the mind). Lalande maintains the view that all the judgments of reason are "normative." From the level of logic and mathematics up to those of ethics and esthetics, our judgments never content themselves with saying: this is such; they all imply an affirmation of the type: this is better than that, which, incidentally, is true; but it has always been known that true is good. The stumbling block for rationalism is the reduction of good to true in the order of contingent being (remember Leibniz). At any rate, it is typical of Lalande to trust rationalism as the only attitude apt to bring about the agreement between human minds, not only in matters of philosophy but also in matters of morality as well. By the same philosopher, see also *La dissolution opposée à l'évolution dans les sciences physiques et morales* (Paris: F. Alcan, 1899), 2nd ed. under the new title of *Les illusions évolutionnistes*. His short *Précis raisonné de morale pratique* (Paris: F. Alcan, 1906), and, still more, his *Vocabulaire technique et critique de la philosophie*, 7th ed. (Paris, 1950), bear witness to A. Lalande's active desire to promote unity through reason. An entirely different type of rationalism, highly influential through the teaching activity of its author as a high school professor of philosophy and through his literary talent is that of Alain (pen name of Emile Chartier, 1808-1951). Collected works have been published in the "Bibliothèque de la Pléiade" (Paris: Gallimard), for instance, *Les arts et les dieux* (1958).

XII. In the Spirit of Scholasticism

1. On the origins of modern Thomism in Italy: A. Masnovo, *Il neotomismo in Italia* (Milano: Vita e Pensiero, 1923). Paolo Dezza, *Alle origini del neotomismo* (Milano: Bocca, 1940). Paolo Dezza, *I neotomisti italiani del XIX secolo* (2 vols.; Milano: Fratelli Bocca), Vol. I, *Filosofia Teoretica* (1942), Vol. II, *Filosofia Morale* (1944) (an anthology compiled from the writings of nineteenth-century Italian neo-Thomists).
2. On the testimony of Sordi, see P. Dezza, *Alle origini*, p. 40 and *I neotomisti*, Vol. I, p. 4.
3. P. Dezza, *Alle origini*, p. 94, and *I neotomisti*, Vol. I, pp. 4-5. For the opinion of Dezza himself, *I neotomisti*, Vol. I, p. 5, with the quotation from Sordi.
4. On Buzzetti, P. Dezza, *Alle origini*, pp. 14-27. *I neotomisti*, Vol. I, bibliography, and a fragment of his logic, Vol. I, p. 33-37. Published to date: *Institutiones philosophicae*, Tome I: *Logicam et Metaphysicam complectens* (Piacenza: Merlini, 1940).
5. Serafino Sordi, S.J., b. Piacenza, 1793; d. Verona, 1865. Bibliographical: P. Dezza, *Alle origini*, pp. 59-64. Particularly important: *Lettere intorno al Nuovo Saggio sull'origine delle idee dell' Abate Antonio Rosmini Serbati* (Modena: Vincenzo Rossi, 1843), 2nd ed. (Monza, 1851). *Saggio intorno alla dialettica ed alia religione di Vincenzo Gioberti* (Piacenza: Tipografia Vescovile Tedeschi, 1846) (a defense of the Society of Jesus against the rabid attacks of Gioberti, the treatise is sometimes attributed to G. Frassinetti). *I primi elementi del sistenia di V. Gioberti dialogizzati fra lui e un lettore dell'opera sua: scrittura che può valere d'Isagoge per l'introduzione allo studio della filosofia dello stesso signor Abate, con Prefazione* (Bergamo: Natali, 1849), in five parts: (1) "On Idea"; (2) "On Intuition"; (3) "On Psychologism"; (4) "On Ontologism"; (5) "On the Ideal Formula." *I misteri di Demofilo per S(erafino) S(ordi) Professore di filosofia* (Torino:

Castellazo and De Gaudenzi, 1850). *De studio theologiae in nostra societate* (Roma: Civiltà Cattolica, 1854) (opuscule of which only one copy remains; stresses the necessity, for the masters of the S.J., of keeping faith with the doctrines of Saint Thomas). Unpublished *Logica et Ontologia* and *Theologia Naturalis*, plus some Italian treatises to be found listed in P. Dezza, *Alle origini*, p. 64.

6. Fragment from Sordi's *Lettere*, in P. Dezza, *I neotomisti*, Vol. I, pp. 105–116.
7. Fragment from Sordi's *I primi elementi*, in *I neotomisti*, Vol. I, pp. 116–127.
8. Fragments from Sordi's unpublished dissertation *On Matter and Form*, in *I neotomisti*, pp. 157–175.
9. Matteo Liberatore, S.J., b. Salerno, 1810; d. Rome, 1892. An extremely prolific writer whose bibliography fills up over twenty-eight columns in C. Sommervogel, S.J., *Bibliothèque de la Compagnie de Jésus*, new ed., Vol. III (Bruxelles: O. Schepens; Paris: A. Picard, 1892), col. 1774–1803.

Main philosophical works: *Dialogo sopra l'origine delle idee* (Napoli, 1843). *Della conoscenza intellettuale*, 2nd ed., enlarged (2 vols.; Roma: Befani, 1873–1874). *Elementi di filosofia*, 5th edition (Napoli: Fibreno, 1852). *Institutiones philosophicae…ad triennium accommodatae* (3 vols.; Roma: Civiltà cattolica, 1860–1861). *Del composto umano*, 3rd ed., revised (Napoli: Giannini, 1880). *Degli universali. Confutazione della filosofia Rosniiniana…opuscoli sei* (Roma: Befani, 1883–1884); trans. Edward Hencage Dering, *On Universals: An Exposition of Thomistic Doctrine* (Leamington: Art and Book Co., 1889).

Other writings are listed in P. Dezza, *I neotomisti*, Vol. I, pp. 19–20. On Liberatore as successor to Sordi, see *Alle origini*, pp. 69–73; those pages are particularly important for their extracts from the prefaces of Liberatore to the 1860 and the 1881 editions of his *Institutiones*. From the first edition of the *Institutiones* (1840), to that of 1881, there is a constant progress toward scholasticism, both in public opinion and in Liberatore's own mind: "When I first published my *Philosophicae Institutiones*, forty years ago, nobody could have suspected the change in our own times which we are now witnessing by God's grace. At that time, the philosophy of Saint Thomas was so despised that quite a few, even among the best, would consider me insane for thinking it could be restored to its ancient place of pride." (*Alle origini*, p. 73). The feeling of relief expressed by the Provincial P. Ferrari to the General after the departure of Sordi and Taparelli: "Things are going more smoothly; they are teaching Thomism all right, but with prudence and moderation; 'fanaticism' has ceased to exist" (p. 69). Bibliographical: Sommervogel, *Bibliot. S.J.*, Vol. IV, pp. 1774–1803.

10. On this point, see *Della conoscenza intellettuale*, Vol. III, p. 5. Liberatore entertains sane views as to the true spirit of Thomism; he knows that scholasticism is an upshot of the "philosophy of the Fathers" much more than a continuation of Aristotle (IV, p. 2); to him Thomism essentially is a blending of pagan learning and of the Christian tradition of the Fathers (Vol. IV, p. 4). The crucial point in Rosminianism is well seen: the intellectual light is not (despite what Rosmini says) the innate notion of being, but, rather, it is the light of the agent intellect (Vol. VI, p. 4). After a pertinent discussion of Kant, Liberatore shows that the smaller the number of the *a priori* elements it includes, the better a noetics is (Vol. VII, p. 3). The keystone of the doctrine of Thomas

Aquinas is rightly seen in the notion that God is the cause of human knowledge as an "efficient" light, not as a "formal" light (Vol. VII, p. 7). On the debit side, it seems that noetics interested Liberatore more than metaphysics. In dealing with being he identifies essence with possibility either in itself or with regard to an exterior cause. No mention is made of the act of being conceived as a component element of finite and created being (Vol. VIII, p. 4). The influence of Leibniz's metaphysics on neo-scholasticism has been carefully studied in a highly instructive book: John Edwin Gurr, S. J., *The Principle of Sufficient Reason in Some Scholastic Systems, 1750–1900* (Milwaukee: The Marquette University Press, 1959); on Liberatore, pp. 132–142.

11. Gaetano Sanseverino, b. Naples, 1811; d. Naples, 1865. Main works: *I principali sistemi di filosofia discussi con le dottrine dei SS. Padri e dei Dottori del Medio Evo* (Napoli: Manfredi, 1853). *Elementa philosofiae christianae cum antiqua et nova comparata* (2 vols.; Napoli: Manfredi, 1862); Vol. III [*Philosofia Christiana*, 2nd ed., enlarged (Napoli: Manfredi, 1873)], has been supplied by Signorello. Ever since the seventeenth century, Catholic colleges felt the need to have textbooks written in view of classroom use and of covering the whole field of philosophy in two or three years. The scholastics used only the text of Aristotle in philosophy and only that of Peter Lombard in theology. The big *Summae* and Commentaries were theological works, and the questions in Aristotle (*Conimbricenses*, etc.) followed the order of the books of Aristotle, not that of the problems. Besides, these books were much too long. The first large-scale global exposition of philosophy distributed according to the order of problems was the encyclopedic work of Wolff. This largely accounts for the fact that the division of philosophy adopted by Wolff was adopted (with many modifications, but always recognizable) by modern scholasticism. Sanseverino's influence was considerable in this respect. The divisions of his *Elementa philosophiae christianae* (1873) are as follows: Vol. I, by way of introduction, an abridged history of philosophy which is followed by "Logic," "Dynamology" (theory of the faculties of soul); "Ideology" ("Idealogia," origin and nature of ideas understood as objects of the human mind: empiricism, innatism, Kantian transcendentalism, ontologism, etc.), "Criteriology" ("Criteriologia," on the criterion of truth); Vol. II, "Ontology" ("Ontologia," dealing with being as such and categories), "Cosmology" ("Cosmologia," nature of bodies, order and laws of natural beings, origin of the world with refutation of Leibnizian optimism); "Anthropology" (man, soul and body, origin of soul, its immortality), Part II, "Natural Theology" (existence and attributes of God, oneness of God, refutation of pantheism). The general position of Sanseverino is that which he calls "scholastic-Aristotelianism"; by and large, he shows a real understanding of Thomism; his own positions are as faithful as they can be in a work whose object is not to expound Thomism, but rather to use it as the backbone of a philosophy answering the intellectual needs of Christians, more particularly those of Catholics in the second half of the nineteenth century. A case in point is his upholding of the Thomistic real distinction of essence and existence, which he understands correctly and defends pertinently against misunderstandings: "Ontologia," art. V, "De entium essentia et existentia," pp. 47–60. It is noteworthy that Sanseverino uses the notion of "Christian Philosophy" without any misgivings; he probably is responsible for its adoption by Pope Leo XIII. At any rate, he makes that philosophy the subject

matter of his work: "Philosophiae christianae elementa tradituri," Vol. I, p. vii. Some features of the doctrine throw an interesting light on the origins of the revival of interest in the notion. First, the very origin of philosophy, which is "marveling" (Aristotle) but also the divinely made revelation of wisdom to man, as we know from the Sacred Books and from reason as well (Vol. I, p. viii). Sanseverino quotes Fr. Schlegel and Thomassinus on the subject. In short: "(1) the Greek philosophers borrowed from the wise peoples of the East, especially from the Jews, the main doctrines of which they composed their systems; (2) they themselves have discovered many truths by the natural light of the human mind and after bringing them into agreement with the teaching of tradition, they achieved a complete system of the sciences" (p. x). Striking a middle course between rationalism and traditionalism (Ventura, Bonnetty, p. x, note 2), Sanseverino retains revelation and tradition as a partial expression of the origin of philosophy (it is interesting to compare Sanseverino's *Introductio ad philosophiam... cum Historia philosophiae Christianae* (Sanfiori: A. Passenaud, 1880) with the historical section of Pope Leo XIII's encyclical *Aeterni Patris*). The scholastics considered and followed Aristotle as *the* philosopher, but they also opposed him fiercely on important points, so much so that the worst adversaries of scholasticism were the Aristotelians: "Ii, qui acerrimum, foedissimumque bellum philosophiae scholasticae indixerunt, Scholasticos, neglectis reliquis philosophis, uni Aristoteli, et, quod turpius est, perperam intellecto, veluti scopulo, fortiter adhaesisse praefracte asseruerunt, et inculcarunt" (p. xix, with the important note 1). On philosophy and theology, pp. xxi–xxiii. A less felicitous attitude of Sanseverino is his absence of scruples in interpreting the doctrines he criticizes and condemns. He calls Ockham a "disciple of Scotus" (Vol. I, p. xxiv, note 2), which is strange, since Ockham systematically opposed Scotus on the very notion of being. Naturally, Sanseverino spends little time in understanding the point of view of the philosophers he refutes. His discussion of Descartes' doctrine of the creation of eternal truths by God (*Ontologia*, art. 97) is a case in point. That the doctrine is false is one thing; that it is "absurd" and and "monstrous," is another thing. The conclusion of Sanseverino is right, but it misses the point.

The relationship of scholasticism and Aristotelianism, already discussed by Sanseverino, has been carefully examined by his disciple and continuator Salvatore Talamo, *L'aristotelismo dalla scolastica. Studi critici*, 3rd ed. enlarged (Siena: Editions San Bernardino, 1881). In this very intelligent and well-balanced book, Talamo maintains that: "If the Fathers cannot strictly be called Platonists because they made a larger use of Plato, neither can the Scholastics be called Aristotelians for having made a larger use of Aristotle; for indeed, in making their choice both the Fathers and the Scholastics resorted to a criterion higher than either Plato or Aristotle." That criterion was, of course, the doctrine of the Church (Preface to the 3rd ed., p. xii). The remarkable book of Talamo clearly shows the intimate bond there was, in both his mind and in Sanseverino's, between the two notions of "scholasticism" and of "Christian philosophy." They define the historical environment in which *Aeterni Patris* was born.

The Preface of Talamo to the third edition of his book answers objections raised by Count Terenzio Mamiani in the periodical *La filosofia delle scuole italiane*, 7 (12) (Roma, 1875), pp. 391ff. On Mamiani (1799–1885), see M. F. Sciacca, *La filosofia nell'età del Risorgimento*, chap. v, §2, pp. 400–405; bibliography, p. 462.

12. The main philosophical work of Joseph Pecci is his commentary on Thomas Aquinas' *De ente et essentia: Parafrasi e dichiarazione dell'opuscole di S. Tommaso: De ente et essentia* (Rome: Befani, 1882), followed by *Osservazioni sopra alcuni errori di Kant* (Rome: Befani, 1886). The commentary on *De ente et essentia* is not easy to find; fragments can be read in P. Dezza, *I neotomisti*, Vol. I, pp. 146–151. J. Pecci upholds the real distinction of essence and existence, but without the penetrating subtlety of Sanseverino. He considers essence and existence to be "due cose reali che si compongono insieme" (Vol. I, p. 148). Still, he does not admit of "two existences in one single subject, one for essence, and another one for being, which would amount to saying: Two things exist in me, for my essence exists and my being exists. That would be something absurd and ridiculous to say"; no, the being which essence receives is no other than that of the whole composite: "There is always one single existence, and never two, in any subject." In other words, "the composition of essence with being is not a composition of two existences, but, rather, of the possibility of existing with the act of existence" (p. 151). Existence is something that comes to man by creation, *ab extrinseco*. All that which J. Pecci says is true, but his language accounts for the often made objection that essence cannot compose with anything, because, taken apart from existence, it is nothing.

13. Giovanni Cornoldi, b. Venice, 1822; d. Rome, 1892. Entered the Society of Jesus in 1840; taught philosophy at Brixen (Bressanone) and Padua; one of the early contributors to the *Civiltà cattolica*.

    Main work: *Lezioni di filosofia ordinate allo studio di altre scienze* (Firenze: Luigi Manuelli, 1872), translated into Latin, German and French. See also: *Della pluralité delle forme secondo i principi filosofici di S. Tommaso* (Bologna: Tipografia arcivescoville, 1877); *Il Rosminianismo, sintesi dell'ontologismo e del panteismo* (Roma: A. Befani, 1881); *La filosofia scolastica di S. Tommaso e di Dante* (Roma: Befani, 1891); on Cornoldi's interpretation of *Aeterni Patris*, see *La riforma filosofica promossa dall' Enciclica "Aeterni Patris"* (Bologna: Mareggiani, 1880).

    Bio-bibliographical: Paolo Dezza, *Alle origini del neotomismo*, Part II, chap. ii, pp. 85–115; bibliography, pp. 118–123. Fragments in P. Dezza, *I neotomisti*, Vol. I, pp. 131, 139, 141, 151, 192, 275.

14. Salvatore Tongiorgi, b. Rome, 1820; d. Rome, 1865. Entered the Society of Jesus (1837); taught philosophy at the Collegio Romano (1853–1865). Author of well-known *Institutiones philosophicae* (3 vols.; Roma: Ex officina Soc. Aurelianae, 1801); we are quoting from the 4th ed. (Brussels: H. Goemaere, 1869). Philosophy is divided into: logic (including criteriology) (Vol. I), ontology and cosmology (Vol. II), psychology and theology (Vol. Ill). According to Tongiorgi, metaphysics used to divide into the science of immaterial being, *praecisive* (the science of the immaterial elements of beings) and the science of immaterial being *positive* (divine nature). Today, the distribution of sciences and studies has extended the limits of metaphysics. It now divides into *general* and *special*. General metaphysics is usually named *ontology*; its object is the ultimate principles and causes abstracted from things by the mind. Special metaphysics divides into three parts: *cosmology*, dealing with the more abstract

and general notions of physics (it is a kind of complement of physics); *psychology*, dealing with the human soul and its faculties; *theology*, dealing with God as object. "That division of metaphysics, first introduced by Wolff, has met with the approval of all his successors, and, as was said, it perfectly fits the present condition of sciences and studies. The Ancients, who included in metaphysics only our own ontology and theology, reserved for physics the questions we now discuss in psychology and cosmology" (Vol. II, p. 4). Being means either "that which exists" or "that which has some reality" (*res*); it is analogical by the analogy of attribution; a thing exists by virtue of its act of being (*actus essendi*), which judgment duplicates: *ens est; quod est, est* (Vol. II, p. 16); essence is that whereby a thing is that which it is; existence can be defined *praesentia in ordine physico, complementum possibilitatis, actualitas essentiae, ultima rei actualitas, id quo res constituitur extra causas suas* (Vol. II, p. 20). In any case, in created things, existence signifies "something by which they cease to be nothing, become other than mere possibles, are no longer contained in the ideal order and in the efficacy of their causes, but begin to acquire physical reality out of their causes; it is something not eternal but temporal, belonging to things not necessarily, but contingently, and which requires the efficacy of an appropriate cause" (Vol. II, p. 28). And here is the Wolfio-Suarez turning point: "Certainly, where all those conditions are fulfilled, everyone agrees that there is existence. Now all those marks belong to the entity of the real essence, as is evident. Ergo..." (Vol. II, pp. 28–29). Then existence is the very entity of essence posited in reality by its causes. Whence it follows that "essence is inseparable from the existence whereby itself actually is"; that nothing can exist by virtue of the existence of something else, nor without its own existence; in fine, that "the composition of the real essence and its existence is merely metaphysical, that is to say, it consists of parts distinguished by reason only": *compositionem ex essentia reali et existentia esse metaphysicam, nempe ex partibus ratione sola distinctis* (Vol. II, p. 29). Note the tendency to identify the real and the physical. Possible is not nothing, otherwise it could not acquire existence (Vol. II, p. 33). Possibility first arises from the essence (Vol. II, p. 38), and its intelligibility flows from the divine essence inasmuch as it is the object of the divine intellect (Vol. II, p. 40). For a criterion of real distinction (Vol. II, pp. 113–115). Tongiorgi introduces the Wolffian notions of "principle of sufficient reason" and of "principle of causality" (Vol. II, pp. 153–155); "principium rationis sufficientis ita enunciatur: *nihil est sine ratione sufficiente*. Huic subordinatur principium illud alterum, quod vocant causalitatis: *nihil fit sine causa*; quod etiam affirmative et clarius ita effertur: *quidquid existere incipit, efficientem sui causam habet*." Note the Wolffian subordination of the principle of causality to the principle of contradiction. Those elements, foreign to authentic Thomism, are now maintained as an integral part of Thomism by some of its modern exponents. In cosmology, also called *philosophia naturae* (note the appellation), Tongiorgi distinguishes three main systems: Aristotelianism (hylomorphic constitution of bodies); atomism (system of the simple elements); Kantian dynamism (there are, in matter, spiritual forces over and above the mechanical forces). Under the influence of modern chemistry, Tongiorgi concludes that the Moderns are right in rejecting the hylomorphism of the scholastics (theory according to which all bodies consist of matter and form) (Vol. II, p. 213);

after rejecting the other systems (including those of Leibniz and Kant) he himself concludes in favor of modern chemical atomism (Vol. II, pp. 232-233); "The ultimate elements of the bodies are the atoms—i.e., substances endowed with geometrical extension and with a power of resistance" (Vol. II, p. 251). Tongiorgi carries his own brand of mechanism to the point of rejecting the Newtonian hypothesis of "ether" as well as that of forces of attraction and repulsion between atoms (Vol. II, pp. 263-204). There is no real distinction between corporal substances and their accidents (Vol. II, p. 304); Suarez on the question (Vol. II, p. 310); on ensuing theological difficulties (Vol. II, pp. 311-316). Contingence of the laws of nature (despite their necessity *ex hypothesi*) (Vol. II, p. 393); on miracles (Vol. II, p. 401). The natural theology of Tongiorgi shows no such striking departures from scholastic tradition. Proofs of God's existence are reduced to three: metaphysical (it is contradictory that all that exists should be produced and contingent, so there is an uncaused necessary being); physical (the order of the universe can have no other cause than an Intelligence); moral (universal consensus of mankind). Note that Tongiorgi's atomism does not extend beyond the structure of corporal bodies; so it leaves intact the notion of form, and leaves man free to maintain the presence of purposiveness in the world; on the absurdities following from pure atomistic mechanism (Vol. HI, pp. 338-343). In modern doctrines, Tongiorgi particularly opposes pantheism (Vol. III, pp. 367-393), sensism (Locke, Condillac) (Vol. III, 176-184), ontologism (Malebranche, Gioberti) (Vol. III, pp. 215-243), Rosmini (Vol. III, 247), and traditionalism (Bonald, Bonnetty, Ventura) (Vol. III, 247-263). Tongiorgi himself finds in the Aristotelian doctrine of abstraction (as interpreted by the scholastics) nothing that is not possible; most is even likely (Vol. III, p. 197); so the explanation of human knowledge by the abstractive power of possible and agent intellect is acceptable: "Hypothesis ergo proposita possibilis est, ac verisimillima" (Vol. III, p. 198); "Si haec hypothesis recipiatur, explicatur optime quomodo intellectus noster objecta materialia percipiat" (Vol. III, p. 198). Tongiorgi is always clear, ordered and short.

15. We are quoting from the French translation of Cornoldi's main work, *Leçons de philosophie scolastique* (Paris: Lethielleux, 1878), Introduction, pp. 3-4. Even the French translation (1878) was older than the encyclical *Aeterni Patris* (1879) by one year. He went the whole way when he described the history of the modern philosophies as "the pathology of the human reason" (Introduction, p. 16).

16. Cornoldi, S.J., Introduction, p. 16. Same enumeration in *Leçons de philosophie scolastique*, Prolégomènes, p. 30. Cornoldi makes philosophical error responsible for social disorder; this was to be one of the key positions of Pope Leo XIII; moreover, he recalls that philosophy is essentially one, just as truth is one, so that one cannot profess "completely contradictory" doctrines without being in error (p. 31). Error is incoherent; and this is the reason that modern non-scholastic speculation cannot be called philosophy. Cornoldi's insistence on the value of scholasticism as the *only* philosophy able to justify the conclusions of modern sciences arises from his awareness of the major historical weakness of his position. In fact, at the very beginning of modern times, the inability of the scholastics to find a place for the new scientific notions aired by Descartes was one of the main causes of the downfall of scholasticism. Like

other metaphysics, scholasticism perished by its physics.
17. Cornoldi, op. cit., Introduction, p. 7.
18. Cornoldi, op. cit., lect. xvi, p. 120. If one wants to probe the nature of Cornoldi's own scholasticism, he can scrutinize the definition of "act" ("the determination produced by the active power in the passive power") (lect. xviii, p. 130); again (lect. vxxiv, p. 617), is given the description of how, in an existing being, essence is "really distinct" from being: here is a child; human essence does not change in him with years, but does being remain the same in him? No, since "the very being by which essence had been actuated has increased, etc." On the words of Pope Pius IX related at the end of this paragraph (lect. xxi, pp. 149–158).
19. Pope Leo XIII (Vincent Joachim Pecci), b. Carpineto, 1810; d. Rome, 1903. Studied at the Jesuit college of Viterbo and at the Collegio Romano; doctorate in theology (1832); ordained a priest (1837); governor of Perugia (1841); bishop of Perugia (1846–1877); elected Pope (1878); died after a reign of twenty-five years, having first been a bishop of Perugia for thirty-one years.

Main philosophical writings: *The Church Speaks to the Modern World. The Social Teachings of Leo XIII*, ed. with an introduction by Étienne Gilson (New York: Image Books, Doubleday & Company, 1954). For a complete study of his teachings: *Acta Leonis XIII (Acta Sanctae Sedis)* (16 vols.; Rome, 1878–1903).
20. The encyclical *Aeterni Patris* is included in *The Church Speaks to the Modern World*, pp. 31–51.
21. *Aeterni Patris*, ed. cit., p. 48. It is noteworthy that, in the very text of the encyclical, the Pope recalls the many approvals of Thomism by popes and councils ever since the fourteenth century (pp. 44–46, §§20 and 22). This was for him a way of making clear that his decision was not a personal one; as Pope Leo XIII, he was simply acknowledging what had already been, for over five centuries, the faith of the Church. Incidentally, this is what it means for the pope to be infallible. The pope is infallible when and because he is the mouthpiece of the Church. The decision of Pope Leo XIII was confirmed several times by his successors, so much so that the obligation for Catholic masters to teach the philosophy of Saint Thomas is now inscribed in the *Code of Canon Law*, Can. 1366, §2.
22. *Aeterni Patris*, ed. cit., Introduction, pp. 6–20.
23. *Arcanum Divinae Sapientiae*, ed. cit., pp. 88–109. Cf. the encyclical of Pope Pius XI on Christian marriage (*Casti Connubii*, December 31, 1930) in Terence P. McLaughlin, C.S.B., *The Church and the Reconstruction of the Modern World* (New York: Image Books, Doubleday & Company), pp. 118–165.
24. *Libertas Praestantissimum*, June 20, 1888, in *The Church Speaks*, §11, p. 64.
25. *Epistle to the Romans*, chap. 13, verses 1–2.
26. *Diuturnum*, June 29, 1881, in *The Church Speaks*, §11.
27. Ed. cit., pp. 205–240. To be completed by the encyclical of Pope Pius XI, *Quadragesimo Anno*, May 15, 1931, ed. Terence P. McLauglin, C.S.B., *The Church and the Reconstruction of the Modern World*, pp. 219–274. In the encyclicals of Pope Leo XIII and Pope Pius XI, the word "socialism" always means "communism," as it meant in the beginning and as it means still—certainly every time it is understood in the fullness of

its implications. Of course, it has nothing in common with social-mindedness.

28. Perhaps one should distinguish, within the consequences of the Leonine encyclicals, two movements of different inspiration: first, a revival of Thomism and of Thomistic studies; next, what we are here calling neo-scholasticism, which was an effort to apply the principles of Thomism (or similar ones) to the discussion of modern problems. It is remarkable that very few "neo-scholastics" doubted their ability to interpret Saint Thomas. Instead of proceeding to a reinterpretation of Thomism in its own terms, many neo-scholastics hastened to apply its supposed principles and conclusions to the discussion of modern problems.

   It is not easy to consider neo-Thomism as distinct from neo-scholasticism, properly said. As far as can be seen, those true Thomists did the only thing there was to do to restore the doctrine in its purity: they decided to teach nothing other than the very text of Thomas Aquinas himself. This was done by Salvatore Maria Roselli, *Summa philosophica ad mentem Angelici Doctoris S. Thomae Aquinatis* (Rome, 1777). See Amato Masnovo, "Gli albori del neo-tomismo in Italia," in *Rivista di filosofia neoscolastica*, Vol. XXIV (1922), pp. 32–38. The organ of this particular conception of the Thomistic revival was the journal *Divus Thomas* (Piacenza, 1880ff.); the subtitle presented it as a "commentary for the use of academics and colleges following the scholastics." Principally devoted to the study of Thomas Aquinas, it nevertheless published critical studies on modern philosophical works, especially those of Italian origin. The first volumes published in installments were the treatise of Lepidi, O.P. *De ente generalissimo*. Obviously, such a school of thought has little history. In 1884, *Divus Thomas* related the felicitous initiative of canon Désiré Mercier, in Louvain, who, instead of following the text of one treatise of Thomas Aquinas, gathered together in one single lecture course what Thomas had said concerning psychology in several different works. Another felicitous innovation was to teach Thomas Aquinas in French, which resulted in bringing fifty young laymen to attend the course. *Divus Thomas* published a summary of Mercier's French lectures, translated into, not Italian, but Latin.

29. A. Gemelli, "Neoscolastica," in *Enciclopedia Italiana*, Vol. XXIV, p. 581; as quoted by M. F. Sciacca, *La philosophie italienne contemporaine* (Lyon-Paris: E. Amitte, N.D.), p. 157. On the Milan neo-scholastic movement, Sciacca, pp. 157–159.

30. Francesco Olgiati's two essays: "Come si pone oggi il problema della metafisica" in *Rivista di filosofia neo-scolastica*, Vol. XIV (1922), pp. 14–28; and "Il misticismo e la metafisica dell'essere," op. cit., pp. 198–218 and 377–399. Bibliography concerning Olgiati, M. F. Sciacca, op. cit., p. 162.

31. On the history of the school of Louvain, including that of its founder and of its beginnings, see L. De Raeymaeker, *Le Cardinal Mercier et l'Institut Supérieur de philosophie de Louvain* (Louvain: Publications Universitaires, 1952), an indispensable source of information.

32. Text in L. De Raeymaeker, op. cit., Appendices, p. 231. The aim and scope of the planned foundation was to "continue the studies of the Thomistic wisdom" and to oppose modern errors, particularly those of "the naturalists and of the materialists." That Leo XIII thought genuine Thomism was to be taught is beyond doubt: "tanto meliorem disciplinarum fore rationem, quanto ad doctrinam Thomae Aquinatis propius

accesserit." The social function of "Christian philosophy" was recalled in the same document: "Neque eos posse melius tueri populorum salutem...quam si ad rem publicam accesserint (adolescentes) insidente penitusque in animis insculpta Christiana philosophia." In short, the problem was to prepare a social and political elite imbued with the sound philosophy of Thomas Aquinas. The same insistence on the function assigned "nascenti Scholae Thomisticae" (p. 241); the letter of Leo XIII to Cardinal Goossens, March 7, 1894, literally echoes *Humani generis*: "A recta enim et pleniore christianae philosophiae institutione quantum laudis praestantiacquc ad lycea et academias accedat, nemo sane non videt...sollers doctrinae sacrae adjutrix"; "At vero recte pleneque philosophari ii nimitum possunt qui in disciplina et ratione Scholasticorum diu sint multumque versati." In fact, the school rather played down its scholastic origins and the notion of "Christian philosophy" was not very favorably received among its masters. Prompted by their desire to distinguish sharply philosophy from theology, some of them insisted that the notion of "Christian philosophy" was just as meaningless as that of Christian physics or of Christian mathematics.

33. L. De Raeymaeker, op. cit., pp. 39–62; on Van Weddingen, pp. 44–46.
34. The concept of the history of medieval philosophy proper to Maurice de Wulf is found in the successive editions of his *Histoire de la philosophie médiévale* (Louvain: Institut supérieur de philosophie, 1900), 5th ed. (2 vols., 1924), 6th ed. (3 vols., 1934–37). English translation (2 vols.; London: Longmans Green, 1935); cf. L. De Raeymaeker, op. cit., pp. 198–199. *An Introduction to Scholastic Philosophy* (*Scholasticism, Old and New*) (New York: Dover Publications, 1950). Without entering the field of the history of history, it must be noted that the historical work of de Wulf was associated (quite legitimately) with the philosophical program of the incipient school of Louvain. It presupposes a definite notion of scholasticism (*Qu'est-ce que la philosophie scolastique?*) (Louvain: Institut supérieur de philosophie, 1899). It is a vast synthesis, a "system" endowed with a doctrinal unity of its own. Under its most perfect form, "it is the result of an intelligent eclecticism," independent and original; *Histoire de la philosophie médiévale,* 1st edition (1900), p. 147. It should not be identified with medieval philosophy, because at all times during the Middle Ages there had been an *anti-scholasticism* (p. 148). Pantheism is one of those anti-scholastic systems, cf. pp. 165–166. In the fifth French edition (1924), Vol. I, p. 14, de Wulf still maintained the existence of a "body of doctrines" patrimonial in nature: "Anselm of Canterbury, Alexander of Hales, Thomas Aquinas, Bonaventure, Duns Scotus, William Ockham, that is to say the greatest, and a hundred other ones with them, agreed on a large number of fundamental theories, and precisely those that determine the structure of a system..." And he proposed to call that "common synthesis" a "common possession," a *bien commun*. Answers to some objections (pp. 19–20). On the problem of the relation of scholasticism to theology (pp. 20–25). Bibliography (pp. 30–32).
35. Jaime Luciano Balmes, b. Vich (Catalonia), 1810; d. Vich, 1848. Studied at Vich and at the University of Corvera; licenciate, Corvera (1833); ordained a priest; taught mathematics at Vich (1834); wrote on social and political problems, but got our of politics after the failure of his most cherished project; died at the age of thirty-eight, universally esteemed and admired.

Main writings: *El protestantismo comparado con el catolicismo en sus relaciones con la civilizacion europea* (4 vols.; Barcelona: A. Brusi, 1842, 1844; Madrid, 1848), an answer to the similar work of Guizot and a refutation of it; English translation, *Protestantism and Catholicism Compared* (Baltimore, 1850). *El criteria*, new ed. (Paris: A. Bournet y Morel, 1849); English translation, *The Criterion* (New York, 1875). *The Art of Thinking* (Dublin, 1882). *Filosofia fundamental*, 2nd ed. (2 vols.; Barcelona: A. Brusi, 1846), new ed. (Paris: A. Bournet y Morel, 1847); English translation by Henry F. Brownson, with an introduction by Orestes Brownson (2 vols.; New York: D. & J. Sadlier, 1856). *Curso de filosofia elemental* (3 vols.; Madrid: E. Aguado, 1847).

Collective works: *Obras completas* (8 vols.; Madrid, 1948–1950).

Biographical and doctrinal: J. Raffin, *Balmes, sa vie et ses ouvrages* (Paris, 1849). *Pensamiento*, Numero extraordinario (Madrid, 1947).

As exposed in his *Filosofia fundamental* (quoted from H. F. Brownson's English translation), the doctrine of Balmes is a Catholic version of the philosophy of Reid (and, before Reid, Buffier), enriched with elements borrowed from Thomas Aquinas; but the general inspiration is not Thomist.

The center of philosophical interest is the problem of the criterion of truth and certitude, which will remain at the center of Mercier's philosophical reflection, along with the preoccupation, starting from Descartes, with overcoming the idealistic implications of the "I think." In fact, philosophy has yet to solve the problem. Certitude is a fact of nature. Common sense assures us of our own existence as well as that of the external world. Philosophy can do two things: demonstrate "the vanity of philosophical systems relating to the foundation of certainty" (Vol. I, §37); and investigate the source of certainty, not to justify it, but to say what it is. Certainty is a fact; but the basis of certainty is a philosophical question (Book 1, §6).

The expression "common sense" denotes "a law of our minds" or "a natural inclination of our mind to give its assent to some truths not attested by consciousness nor demonstrated by reason, necessary to all men in order to satisfy the wants of sensitive, intellectual and moral life" (Book 1, §316). In this sense (contrary to Descartes) *the principle of evidence is not evident* (Book 1, §221); its first foundation is "an irresistible instinct of nature" (Book 1, §224) plus the fact that, without it, thought becomes impossible; "from the combination of consciousness with intellectual instinct arise all the other criteria" (Book 1, §§23 and 238). There are therefore several criteria which "mutually aid and confirm each other," to wit: the *criterion of consciousness*, a primitive fact of nature; that of *evidence*, which reveals the existence of reason itself; that of the *intellectual instinct*, which causes us to objectivate our ideas; that of *common sense properly so called*, as defined above; that of *the senses*; and that of *human authority*, both of which are particular cases of common sense conceived of "as a means of satisfying the necessities of sensitive, intellectual and moral life" (Book 1, §337).

In the light of those combined criteria, the first idea is that of being; it is not innate (Book 4, §207) except inasmuch as intellectual activity itself is (as in Thomas Aquinas). Balmes calls it innate (Book 5, §74) in the sense that it cannot be formed by abstraction (Book 5, §77) because it is not representative (hence its indetermination); in the act by which we perceive being (i.e., existence) "is confounded with all other intellectual acts, as a condition *sine qua non* of them all, until reflection comes to separate it from them, purifying it and making it the object of our perception" (Book 5, §82). Being is not given to us as "possible being" (against Rosmini, Book 5, §§22–35); the notion of being minus existence is repellent to common sense (Book 5, §30); so the notion of a real distinction of essence and existence is meaningless (Book 5, §§90–94). General conspectus of the work in which he "proposed to examine the fundamental ideas of our minds, whether considered in themselves or in their relations to the world" (Book 10, 280–287). Note that to Balmes, "agent intellect," species and the whole process of abstraction "merit being called ingenious rather than extravagant, poetical rather than ridiculous" (Book 4, §§49–50): agent intellect is "a real magician."

36. Joseph Kleutgen, b. Dortmund, 1811; d. Caldaro, 1883. Entered the Society of Jesus in 1834. His main contribution to the scholastic revival was *Die Philosophie der Vorzeit, Verteidigt, 1860–1863* (3 vols.; Münster: Theissing, 1853, 1854, 1860), 2nd ed., revised (1867–1868); French translation by Constant Sierp, *La philosophie scolastique exposée et défendue* (4 vols.; Paris: Gaume, 1868–1870). By "Philosophie der Vorzeit," Kleutgen points out the philosophy taught in the Catholic schools from the early times of Christianity up to the end of the eighteenth century and placed by the theologians at the service of theology; his main targets are the representatives of more recent forms of philosophical teaching in Catholic schools: Lamennais and Bautain in France, Gioberti in Italy, Hermes and Günther in Germany. His own work is of very good philosophical quality and covers the main problems: (1) Intellectual knowledge; (2) Nominalism, realism, and formalism; (3 Certitude; (4) Principles; (5) Method; (6) Being; (7) Nature; (8) Man; (9) God. The substance of the doctrine is authentically scholastic and, to that extent, Thomist, but one could not learn to know Thomism from the book of Kleutgen, whose doctrine instead evokes Suarez to the mind. Being divides into actual (*wirklich, actu, énergeia*) and possible. The actual is known before the possible (Vol. II, Part 4, §3, art. 571, p. 54), and this is true of being as well as of knowledge; actuality precedes possibility (p. 56). The object of philosophy is all that which falls under the concept of being (art. 572, pp. 57–58). By *sein, ens*, is meant the abstract-universal (*das abstract-allgemeine*, p. 58). Philosophy considers essence as such, apart from actual existence. Whether or not Thomas Aquinas had taught the "real" distinction between essence and existence, is a point Kleutgen prefers to leave undecided (Vol. II, art. 574, pp. 62–63). He himself follows Suarez (Vol. II, art. 578, p. 69): there is between essence and existence a distinction of reason founded in reality. The foundation it has in reality is that creature has no existence of itself and is a mere possible (Suarez, *Metaphysicae disputationes*, disp. 31, sec. XI).

On this point, which is of decisive importance, it must be noted that the position of D. Mercier has been the very opposite of that of Kleutgen. Mercier deserves the praise of having rightly understood the Thomistic meaning of the composition of essence and existence. In agreement with Del Prado, O.P. (*De veritate fundamentali philosophiae Christianae*, Placentiae, 1899), Mercier vigorously upheld the reality of the distinction: *Ontologie ou métaphysique générale* in *Cours de Philosophie*, Vol. II, 3rd ed., revised and enlarged (Louvain-Paris, 1902), Part I, §6, pars. 47–53, pp. 109–136. Mercier even considered it possible (with Del Prado) to demonstrate the reality of the distinction; he also explained away the illusions which prevent its opponents from accepting the position of Saint Thomas (par. 59, pp. 129–132). On this central point, Mercier has faithfully observed the directives of Pope Leo XIII. Unlike Kleutgen, he sided with Thomas against Suarez; his metaphysics of being deserves a place of pride in the history of true neo-Thomism, not merely in that of neo-scholasticism. After him, the school of Louvain divided itself on the question.

On Kleutgen's positions: J. E. Gurr, S.J., *The Principle of Sufficient Reason*, pp. 126–131.

37. Georges Van Riet, "La critériologie de Mgr. Mercier," *Revue philosophique de Louvain*, XLIV (1946), 7–35; that excellent study provides a necessary starting point for the study of the doctrine. On the five different redactions of Mercier's epistemology (p. 10). The third, fourth, and fifth redactions only were printed, all under the title of *Critériologie générale ou théorie générale de la certitude* (Louvain, 1899, 1900, 1906). We are following (in an abridged way) the indications given by G. Van Riet on the early positions of Mercier. Despite its ulterior evolution, the foundations of the doctrine remained substantially the same. Our own indications concern the 1885 "Theory of Certain Knowledge" (pp. 13–23). On the 1889 "Theory of Certitude" (pp. 23–27). "By and large no significant changes are seen in the general part of critcriology" (p. 24); this time the distinction is made between physical and metaphysical certitude, both of which are cases of the certitude of evidence. On the doctrine contained in the published *Critériologie générale* (1899–1906), see Van Riet, op. cit., pp. 27–32. In assessing the work of Mercier, Van Riet observes that in it the certitude of the external world rests upon the certitude of internal reality (p. 34): "We think that his thought has undergone no evolution on this point; it affirmed itself as early as 1885 and was never withdrawn." Consequently, "the external reality is known through an inference; in this sense, the proof is of the *illationist* type." However, there is no illation from the idea of the thing to the existence of the thing, but "the intellectual certitude of the existence of extramental realities can be obtained only by resorting to the ideal principle of causality applied to sensations, themselves considered as internal realities, as acts of the subject" (p. 34). Putting more trust than Balmes in the power of reason, and neglecting less than Kleutgen the part of sense experience, it can be said of Mercier that, "by and large, he keeps very close to the German Jesuit." With Kleutgen, Mercier favors reason at the expense of experience (p. 35).

38. Thomas Aquinas, *Summa theologiae*, I, i, 8, 2m; quoted by D. Mercier, *Discours d'ouverture du Cours de Philosophie de S. Thomas* (Louvain: Charles Peeters, 1882), p. 5 (in L. De Raeymaeker, *Le Cardinal Mercier*, p. 49). In fact, Thomas himself was quoting from Boethius (*In Top. Ciceronis*, I, PL 64, 1166), and although he undoubtedly subscribed to the formula, he was quoting it in an objection and not in his own answer to it. In his answer to the objection, Thomas observes that, after all, "sacred doctrine makes use also of the authority of philosophers (weak as it is, compared with the authority of God) in those questions in which they were able to know the truth by natural reason" (*loc. cit.*, 2m). In turning that occasional remark into a sort of battle cry, Mercier certainly modified its Thomistic meaning. The opening lectures of the course were hailed with sympathy in Thomas Fontaine, *Divus Thomas*, 4 (Piacenza, 1884), pp. 178–181; the article was dated Louvain, December 22, 1883, under the title *Cursus*

philosophicus thomisticus in cath. Academia Lovaniensi. The tone is one of warm approval: "The new institution fully answers the wishes of the Pope; intimately imbued with Christian philosophy (*intimius imbuti et bene instructi Christiana philosophia*) its students are well qualified for entering public life" (p. 181).

39. In assessing the work of D. Mercier, one should remember that Louvain had been an active center of ontologism and of traditionalism; after the condemnation of the two movements, something new had to be found. At the Mechlen seminary, Mercier had heard one of his professors say that, as a believer and a philosopher, he rejected both traditionalism and ontologism, but that he had nothing with which to replace them. It is in that seminary, however, that he first read "the textbook of Tongiorgi, a professor at the Roman College: that work had been indicated to him by Richardson, a fellow student from England; that was his first contact with scholasticism" (L. De Raeymaeker, *Le cardinal Mercier*, p. 53 and note 20).

The history of the school of Louvain should include the comprehensive *Cours de philosophie,* particularly: *Logique et notions d'ontologie ou de métaphysique générale* (Louvain Museum and Paris, 1894). See also *Psychology* (Louvain, Bruxelles and Paris, 1892). Cf. L. De Raeymaeker, op. cit., pp. 96–97.

40. G. Picard, S.J., "Le thomisme de Suarez," in *Suarez. Modernité traditionelle de sa philosophie,* by several contributors (*Archives de philosophie,* vol. 18, Cahier I), pp. 108–109.

Joseph Maréchal, S.J., b. Charleroi, 1878; d. Louvain, 1944. Greatest name of the S.J. Faculties Saint-Albert de Louvain (organ: *Nouvelle revue théologique*), which was completely independent from the University of Louvain and represented still another brand of neo-scholasticism.

Main philosophical works: *Le point de départ de la métaphysique. Leçons sur le développement historique et théorique du problème de la connaissance.* Cahier I: "De l'antiquité à la fin du moyen-âge: La critique ancienne de la connaissance," 1st ed. (Museum Lessianum, philosophical section no. 4) (Bruges, Beyaert and Paris: Alcan, 1922). Cahier II: "Le conflit du rationalisme et de l'empiricisme dans la philosophie moderne avant Kant," 1st ed. (Museum Lessianum, no. 5) (Bruges and Paris: Alcan, 1923). Cahier III: "La critique de Kant," 1st ed. (Museum Lessianum, no. 6) (Bruges and Paris: Alcan, 1923). Cahier IV: "Le système idéaliste chez Kant et les postkantiens," 1st ed. (Museum Lessianum, no. 6) (Bruges and Paris: Alcan, 1947). Cahier V: "Le thomisme devant la philosophie critique," 1st ed. (Museum Lessianum, no. 8) (Bruges and Paris: Alcan, 1927). New editions, revised: Cahier I (1927, 1943); Cahier II (1942, 1944); Cahier III (1942, 1944); Cahier V (1949).

Biographical and doctrinal: *Mélanges Joseph Maréchal* (Museum Lessianum, no. 31) (2 vols.; Bruxelles: l'Edition Universelle and Paris: Desclée de Brouwer, 1950); bibliography of the writings of Maréchal, Vol. I, pp. 47–65; studies on his doctrine, pp. 65–71. The very title of the *Cahiers* is witness to the preponderance of epistemology used as a normal and inevitable approach to ontology. Whatever its intrinsic philosophical value, the method is difficult to reconcile with historical Thomism. Cahier V is of decisive importance. A shorter approach to Maréchal's position of the problem is his answer to the objections of Roland-Gosselin, O.P., in *Bulletin Thomiste* (January,

1927); see *Mélanges Maréchal*, Vol. I, pp. 75–101. Thomism wanted to explain how external objects can become internalized in the knowing subject; Maréchal wants to know "how formal determinations, emerging in the luminous zone of consciousness, can manifest straightway, not their own subjective reality, but that of "things in themselves which they specify" (p. 75). Is it possible, starting from the *species impressa* of Thomas Aquinas, to account for its "objectivation"? Stressing the "intentionality" of the species, Maréchal shows that, of itself, intelligence is tending to appropriate all the intelligibility of which it is capable. Intelligence is moved by an internal purposiveness towards an intelligible apprehension of being. Thus understood, the formal inherence of the object in the subject justifies the objective validity of intellectual knowledge, but our awareness of that relationship is due to the dynamism of intelligence of whose very essence it is to *tend toward* the totality of intelligible being (ultimately, God). Irrespective of its compatibility with Thomism (a problem external to its essence) the doctrine of Maréchal was of excellent quality; that it was an attempt to justify the conclusions of realism by a method not wholly free of idealistic implications is one more sign of the difference there is between neo-Thomism, neo-scholasticism and perhaps even plain Christian philosophy, for that is what the doctrine of Joseph Maréchal chiefly was.

41. Picard, op. cit., p. 113. See pages 112–113, an excellent conspectus of the Suarezian explanation of reality. It is dominated entirely by the notion of "essence." Only God is pure essence and therefore pure act; all the other essences are composed of act and potency; the form of the species actuates the possibilities of matter, and this is the first composition of act and potency, but there is a second one, because the creative action of God actuates the thus determined essence by giving it actual existence. The metaphysics of Suarez agrees with Saint Thomas' as far as it is possible without agreeing with its notion of being.

42. G. Picard expressly maintains that the arguments of Suarez (*Metaphysical disputations*, XXXL) against the real composition of essence and existence efficaciously justify the personal position of Suarez (distinction of reason founded in reality), p. 115.

43. P. Descoqs, S.J., *Institutiones metaphy sicae generalis. Eléments d'ontologie, I: Introductio et metaphysica de ente in communi* (Paris: Beauchesne, 1925). As a historical curiosity, see P. Descoqs, S.J., "Thomisme et scolastique," a long critical study of the book of Louis Rougier, *Ea scolastique et le thomisme* (Paris: Gauthier-Villars, 1925). Its discussion by P. Descoqs is found in *Archives de philosophie*, 5 (1927), 1–149. Full of mistakes and strangely indifferent to the use of quotation marks, the book of Louis Rougier was an enormous pamphlet. But Louis Rougier had identified Thomism with the distinction between essence and existence, and he had undertaken to prove that the "real" composition is a paralogism. This suited P. Descoqs so well that, after severely criticizing the book, he used it as a proof of the danger in identifying "the whole structure of the Christian philosophy with the distinction between essence and existence," an unsafe metaphysical position, to say the least (p. 148). The "rigidly Thomistic explanation" (p. 149) of the notion of being pleased Fr. Dcscoqs so little that even anti-Christian Louis Rougier was to him a welcome ally.

44. Introductory note of the review, *Archives de philosophie*, I, 1 (1923), p. 4.

45. Gonzague Truc, *Le retour à la scholastique* (Paris: La Renaissance du Livre, 1919). An important document concerning philosophical opinion is the work of John S. Szybura, *Present Day Thinkers and the New Scholasticism: An International Symposium*, with an introduction by the Very Rev. John Cavanaugh, C.S.C. (St. Louis: Herder, 1920); see particularly pp. 127–368. Particularly enlightening on the spirit of neo-scholasticism is M. de Wulf, *Scholastic Philosophy*, §23: "The new scholastic philosophy and religious dogma," pp. 190–199.

46. Jean Pierre Rousselot, b. Nantes, 1878; killed in action at Les Eparges, April 25, 1915. Main work: *L'intellectualisme de Saint Thomas*, 1st edition (Paris: Alcan, 1908); 2nd edition (Paris: Beauchesnc, 1924), with a biographical introduction by Léonce de Grandmaison and a bibliography of Rousselot's writings. English translation by Father James O'Mahony: *The Intellectualism of Saint Thomas* (London: Sheed & Ward, 1935).

47. P. Rousselot, op. cit., 2nd ed., p. 228.

48. Sertillanges (A. G.), b. Clermont-Ferrand, 1863; d. Sallanches, 1948. Entered the Dominican Order (1883). Main works: *Saint Thomas d'Aquin* (2 vols.; Paris: Alcan, 1910). *Les grandes theses de la philosophie thomiste* (Paris: Bloud et Gay, 1928); trans. Godfrey Anstruther, O.P., *Foundations of Thomistic Philosophy* (St. Louis: Herder, 1931). *Le Christianisme et les philosophies* (2 vols.; Paris: Aubier, 1939–1941). *Lumières et périls du bergsonisme* (Paris: Flammarion, 1943). *L'idée de création et ses retentisement en philosophie* (Paris: Aubier, 1945).

The first sentence of *Foundations of Thomistic Philosophy* is to observe that "those who know St. Thomas Aquinas well are at times tempted to ask whether, in spite of his world wide reputation, he is really understood by many." The remark applies even to many men who have devoted their lives to the study and teaching of Thomas Aquinas. One can read *Foundations of Thomistic Philosophy* from beginning to end without meeting the Thomistic notion of being (*ens* = *habens esse*), nor the composition of essence and existence, nor, consequently, the notion of God as the purity of *esse* understood in the Thomistic sense of the word. To Sertillanges the meaning of the "famous" composition of essence and existence simply was that, outside God, no being has of itself its existence.

49. Reginald Garrigou-Lagrange, O.P., b. 1877; d. Rome, 1964. Main philosophical writings: *Le sens commun; la philosophie de l'être et les formules dogmatiques* (Paris: Beauchesne, 1909). *Dieu, son existence, sa nature* (Paris: Beauchesne, 1915), 5th ed. (1928), English translation by Dom Bede Rose (St. Louis: Herder, 1934). *Le réalisme du principe de finalité* (Paris: Desclée de Brouwer, 1932). *La synthèse thomiste* (Paris: Desclée de Brouwer, 1946).

The thought of Garrigou-Lagrange is passionately engaged in controversy against modernism as well as against the doctrines of his contemporaries whom he considered were reviving modernism (Le Roy, Laberthonnière, Blondel). His own interpretation of Thomism attributes a primary importance to the possibility of concluding the existence of God from the first principles of understanding applied to sense experience. First notions and principles are endowed with an ontological value (to deny this leads to absurdity); the primary notion is being; the supreme principle (of contradiction or of identity) is the remote foundation of all demonstration of the existence of God.

The first determination of the *principle of identity* is the *principle of substance*; next comes the *principle of raison d'être*: "a more immediate foundation of the proofs of the existence of God, *the principle of raison d'être*; the principle is related to the principle of identity by a reduction to absurdity; in this sense, it is analytical" (p. 170); cf. *Le sens commun*, p. 208. The formula of that principle (unknown to Thomas Aquinas and Leibnizian in origin) is as follows: "All that which is, has its reason for being" (p. 171). It comes to Garrigou-Lagrange from Leibniz and Wolf through the immediate source of the empirio-criticism of African Spir, *Pensée et réalité*, trans. Penjon (Paris: Alcan, 1896), pp. 146, 203; (Garrigou-Lagrange, *Dieu*, p. 173, note 1). From the general principle of "raison suffisante" derives the *principle of efficient causality* properly so-called, the *principle of finality* and the *principle of induction*. The formula of the latter principle is: "All natural cause, under the same circumstances, produces the same effects" (*Dieu*, p. 189, note 2). Having established (against Kant) the transcendent value of the primary notions and having attributed to them an analytical necessity by derivation from the principle of identity, the five ways can be included within one single way of proving the existence of God; this all inclusive way "best represents the essential procedure of common sense rising up to God." The principle of this general proof is that *the plus does not come from the minus*; only the superior can account for the inferior (p. 232). Hence the general conclusion: God, and the true God, or radical absurdity (p. 750). Cf. Appendix I, pp. 703–773, particularly p. 772, where, from the fact that the principle of causality cannot be denied without contradiction (in the order of contingent beings) it is concluded that human reason cannot deny the existence of God without "sinking into absurdity." The formalism of the doctrine is explained by the tendency of Garrigou-Lagrange to reduce the notions of essence and *esse* to those of potency and act. The real distinction between essence and *esse* not only becomes a particular case of the distinction between act and potency, but becomes reducible to it. The same tendency is visible in the classical work of G. Mattiussi, *Le XXIV tesi della filosofia di S. Tommaso approbate dalla Congregazione degli Studi* (Roma, 1917); see Garrigou-Lagrange, *La synthèse thomiste*, chap. ii, pp. 69–89. The whole argument implies that for essence to be *really* distinct from existence it has to be potency only. Though this is made necessary by the identification of the notion of being with that of act, the consequence does not seem to follow in the doctrine of Saint Thomas. The distinction is real if, of itself, essence is pure potency *with respect to existence*. Let the remark be done in order to illustrate the true nature of the relation between the notions of being and act in Saint Thomas. One must interpret act in terms of being rather than interpret being in terms of act; so there is in being, owing to its *esse*, something that is in potency to it.

50. Jacques Maritain, b. Paris, 1882–. Mention of him had to be made here, although he is one of our contemporaries, because without him modern French neo-Thomism makes little sense. His main works will be quoted as we proceed in the description of his personal positions. Introductions to his philosophy are many and in many languages; among them: Charles A. Fecher, *The Philosophy of Jacques Maritain* (Westminster, MD: The Newman Press, 1953), with biographical, doctrinal and bibliographical note. Norah Willis Michener, *Maritain on the Nature of Man in a Christian*

Democracy, Editions "L'Eclair" (Canada: Hull, P.Q., 1955). Of exceptional quality from all points of view, Henry Bars, *Maritain en notre temps* (Paris: Grasset, 1959) contains an appendix on the chronology of the life and works of Jacques and Raissa Maritain, pp. 368–394. H. Bars, *La politique selon Jacques Maritain*, with a preface by J. Maritain (Paris: Editions ouvrières, 1961). Y. R. Simon, "Maritain's Philosophy of the Sciences," in *St. John's University Studies*, philosophical selections, 2 (1961) 25–30. D. A. Gallagher and I. Gallagher, *The Achievement of Jacques and Raissa Maritain: A Bibliography, 1906–1961* (New York: Doubleday, 1962).

51. In the spring of 1919 the "Intelligence Party" (*Le parti de l'intelligence*), a group with literary, cultural and political implications, was founded: *Réflexions sur l'intelligence et sur sa vie propre* (Paris: Nouvelle Librairie Nationale, 1924). *Distinguer pour unir, ou Les degrés du savoir* (Paris: Desclée de Brouwer, 1932); 4th ed. (1946); trans. B. Wall and M. Adamson, *The Degrees of Knowledge* (New York: Charles Scribner's Sons, 1938); better translation, from the fourth French edition under the supervision of Gerald B. Phelan (New York: Charles Scribner's Sons, 1959). The "degrees of knowledge" include those of rational knowledge (experimental science and philosophy) and those of supra-rational knowledge (theological wisdom, grace and mystical experience). This "summa" of Maritain's noetics is the necessary introduction to his metaphysics. The predominant importance of the problem of knowledge is one of the more clearly recognizable marks of the times on the doctrine. It is a noetic approach to metaphysics; see particularly "The Metaphysical Intelligible," *Degrees of Knowledge* (1959), pp. 210–220; being is the object of metaphysics; by being, we should here understand being as the ultimate object of formal abstraction, inclusive of its transcendental properties (good, true, beautiful) as well as of the "cleavages it presents throughout the whole extent of things" (one and many, potency and act) (p. 217); the doctrine is very discreet on the relationship essenceexistence (§11, pp. 216–217); the reason for that discretion probably is that in the last analysis the problem goes beyond the limits of noetics. On the relation of knowledge to reality (perinoetic, dianoetic, ananoctic) (p. 220). Knowledge, *by analogy*, of transcendent objects imperfectly seen in our concept of being (including its transcendental properties) is called *ananoetic intellection*. As knowledge of that object, metaphysics requires an art of "deciphering the invisible in the visible"; that which is invisible to us in the visible is so on account of its superior intelligibility; let us call it the *transintelligible*. That precisely is the object of metaphysical knowledge; as an ananoctic intellection of the transintelligible seen in the visible as in a mirror, metaphysics is essentially "specular" ("This is specular knowledge, or knowledge by analogy" §13, p. 218) and this feature suffices to define Maritainism by opposition to the philosophy of Kierkegaard, wherein real knowledge is defined as a non-specular mode of apprehending objects. The intellectualism of the doctrine (a genuinely Thomistic feature) is preserved even in what it says of our knowledge of God in this life. Fully aware that "whatever form our intellect may conceive, God escapes this intellect on account of His eminence" (p. 229), Jacques Maritain (along with R. Garrigou-Lagrange, *Dieu*, 5th ed., p. 512) carefully avoids the "agnosticism of definition" upheld by Sertillanges: "Thanks to ananoetic intellection (the Divine Nature) is constituted the object of an absolutely stable knowledge of a

science which contemplates and delineates in it determinations which imply negation only in our mode of conceiving" (p. 231). On negative theology, pp. 236–241. Cf. Appendix III, "What God is" (pp. 422–429) with the assimilation of the quidditative knowledge to that of the *raison d'etre* (p. 422) and the thesis that "we know the essence of God in a certain way (by analogy) without knowing *de Deo quid, est* (pp. 422–423). The influence of Cajetan is clearly felt (p. 423), although the doctrine of analogy in Cajetan differs from that of Saint Thomas. What is here called "some of St. Thomas' expressions, which might at first be misinterpreted" (p. 423, note 1) were precisely the forte of Fr. Sertillanges. For a discussion of Scrtillanges' position (pp. 425–429). On a personal feature of Maritain's Thomism: Laura Fraga de Almeida Sampaio, *L'intuition dans la philosophie de Jacques Maritain* (Paris: J. Vrin, 1963).

52. Maritain's metaphysics of being is best approached from his *Sept leçons sur l'être et les premiers principes de la raison spéculative* (Paris: Téqui, 1934); English translation, *A Preface to Metaphysics* (New York: Sheed & Ward, 1939), reprinted (1948). *Court traité de l'existence et de l'existant* (Paris: Paul Hartmann, 1947), English translation by Lewis Galantière and G. B. Phelan (New York: Panthéon Books, 1948). Maritain wishes to rescue from oblivion "the primacy which genuine Thomism attributes to existence and to the intuition of existential being" (*Court traité*, p. 11). Thomas has nothing in common with modern existentialism (Kierkegaard, Jaspers, Sartre, etc.); his own brand of existential philosophy does not suppress essences; it does not favor the notion of "a divine existence without a *nature*" (p. 14). At the origin of metaphysics is the "intellectual intuition" of being (p. 37); the "intuition of being, *secundum quod est ens*" (p. 38). On this intuition, see *Sept leçons sur l'être*, pp. 35–50, and *Court traité*, p. 39. Being is thus attained, "or perceived, at the summit of an abstractive intellection, of an eidetic or intensive visualization, which is so illuminative and so pure only because one day intelligence was awakened in its depth and transilluminated by the shock of the act of existing grasped in things and because it has elevated itself to receiving it or to listening to it within itself in the intelligible and superintelligible integrity of the tone peculiar to it" (p. 39). The fact that the intuition at stake was first experienced *un jour*, one day, clearly shows that it had little to do with the metaphysical recognition of the act of being of finite things. What is here at stake is an intellectual intuition of being under the impact of the experienced act of being. As far as can be seen, the intellectual intuition of being bears upon the abstract notion of being, inasmuch as it includes an apprehension of the *actus essendi*. This would be the summit of natural knowledge. It is not a common experience; it is not enough to teach philosophy, "be it even Thomistic philosophy," in order to have that intuition. "Let us say it is a matter of chance, or of a gift, or perhaps of docility to light" (p. 41). Comparison between the concept of existence (*esse*) and of that which is (*ens*) (pp. 42–48), and the important note 1 (p. 49). Whether or not there is a place in Thomism for an intellectual intuition of being is a problem; at any rate, the doctrine is in keeping with Maritain's intention to set the highest value on intelligence; the doctrine also permits legitimation of the importance attributed to the positive side of analogy in our knowledge of God; in this sense it fulfills the role performed by negative theology in the doctrine of Thomas himself. Obviously this metaphysics of being is existential, but it is not an

existentialism. Maritain once said that the equivalent of the philosophy of existence in Thomas Aquinas is to be found in the *Secunda Secundae*. Thomist existentialism remains an intellectualism; it is intellectual in its mode, though practical in its object. Its object no longer is the actual existence given in things, but the very act which the liberty of the subject will cause to exist (p. 80). Perhaps the more real point of contact between this doctrine and modern existentialism is the recognition of the fact, so ably opposed to Hegel by Kierkegaard, that in its effort to achieve knowledge of the subject, philosophy must turn it into an object. This is a limit for philosophy: philosophy is entirely circumscribed within the relation of intelligence to object; whereas religion is concerned with a relation of subject to subject (p. 119).

53. Although he does not like the word, Maritain's philosophy has always been "engaged" in the social and political problems of his country and of his time. This simply means that, as a true philosopher, he has always philosophized within reality (and within faith, which is supernatural reality). His general intention can be summed up as that of achieving a Christian humanism in opposition to the atheistic humanism of Karl Marx. With unerring insight, Maritain has perceived the "religious" significance of Communism in *True Humanism* (New York: Charles Scribner's Sons, 1938), chap. ii, §1: "The roots of the Atheism of the Soviets" (p. 27). All socialism is not necessarily atheistic (p. 80); but even socialist humanism is encumbered with wrong notions about labor, man and society. Only "integral humanism" can bring an answer to those difficulties. As an ideal, it involves a criticism of "the bourgeois type of humanity" (p. 85). "My new humanism certainly wishes to change the bourgeois man" (p. 86). This undertaking is one with that of bringing about a new Christendom; for indeed, in order to change the bourgeois man, it is necessary to change man himself, that is, to achieve a "transfiguration" by which, knowing himself to be changed by grace, man will want to become and to be the image of God. Another name for that undertaking would be, "the socio-temporal realization of the Gospels" (p. 86). Hence the need of a "new form of sanctity chiefly characterized by a "sanctification of *secular* life" (p. 116). Thus we reach a "prospective" view of the social order (it has to be prospective in order to answer Marxism) which is "the *concrete historical ideal* of a new Christendom" (p. 121). A new Christendom would be a type of civilization animated from within by Christianity and answering the needs of the epoch we are about to enter (p. 126). Seen in the abstract, the new temporal regime would be both *communal* (common good is other than and higher than the mere sum of individual goods) and *personalist* (i.e., it is essential to common good that it should serve the supernatural and supertemporal ends of man as a person (p. 127). We should here mention, as one of the points of the doctrine that brought about controversy, that the mediaeval idea of a Holy Roman Empire is rendered obsolete by this conception of a new Christendom (pp. 137–139). The future society described by Maritain presupposes the "liquidation of capitalism" (p. 184) by transferring capital from private ownership to the service of work. Note that private "capital" (wealth as a productive force) is not the same as private property. In planning for the future, one should keep in mind that politics is of the order of "existences," not of essences; concrete situations to be ordered, not logical necessities to be unfolded, are at stake (p. 213). The crowning piece of the doctrine is

a philosophy of political action. Nowhere better than in the latest expressions of his political thought can one see how deeply unified Maritain's philosophy is, and up to what point its unity is that of his own powerful personality.

Apart from *Humanisme intégral* (Paris: Aubier, 1936), English translation, *True Humanism* (New York: Charles Scribner's Sons, 1938), see *Religion et culture* (Paris: Desclée de Brouwer, 1930), English translation included in *Essays in Order*, eds. Charles Dawson and J. F. Burns (New York: Macmillan, 1931) [new ed., *The Persistence of Order*, 3 vols. (Providence: Cluny, 2018)]; new edition of the French text, with an added preface (Paris: Desclée, 1940).

54. *Art et scolastique* (Paris: Art catholique, 1927), new ed., enlarged (1930); English translation, *Art and Scholasticism* (New York: Charles Scribner's Sons, 1930). *Frontières de la poésie*, same publisher (1935); *Art and Poetry* (New York: Philosophical Library, 1943). *Creative Intuition in Art and Poetry* (The A. W. Mellon Lectures in the Fine Arts), Bollingen Series (New York: Pantheon Books Inc., 1953).

Art and Scholasticism applies to the notion of the "fine arts" the scholastic notion of *ars* understood (in contradistinction to that of doing) as the right rule of making things. The intellectualism of Maritain's esthetics springs from the same source as that of the whole doctrine. The crucial point of *Creative Intuition* is the relationship it introduces between poetic intuition, conceived as transcendent, and the artistic activity of reason dictating to the artists the necessary moves for the actual production of their works. As reason prescribing the right rule for making, "art" never fulfills the aspirations of the creative intuition, of which it is never more than a partial expression. One cannot stress too strongly the "contemplative" nature of creative intuition; despite the fact that it has making as its end, its knowledge remains and keeps it aloof from the contingencies of its actual realization in matter. The personal nature of the doctrine is the more evident as there is in Thomism a metaphysics of the beautiful (as a transcendental), though no mention is made of any one of the fine arts. To compare with Thomas Aquinas, Umberto Eco, *Il problema estetico in San Tommaso*, Edizioni di "Filosofia" (Torino, 1950). V. L. Simonsen, *L'esthétique de Jacques Maritain*, with a preface by J. M. Copenhague (Munksgaard, 1956).

55. General position of the problem: Charles Journet, *Introduction à la théologie* (Paris: Desclée de Brouwer, 1947). Introduction to the problem in the doctrine of Thomas Aquinas, and recent controversies on the subject: Gerald F. Van Ackeren, S.J., *Sacra doctrina: The object of the first question of the Summa theologica of St. Thomas Aquinas* (Roma: Catholic Book Agency, 1952).

On the history of the revival of the notion of Thomist theology, especially in France: see the writings of M. D. Chenu, O.P., *Une école de théologie, Le Saulchoir* (Le Saulchoir, 1937). *Toward Understanding Saint Thomas*, trans. A. M. Landry, O.P., and D. Hughes, O.P. (Chicago: Regnery, 1964). *Saint Thomas d'Aquin et la théologie* (Paris: Editions du Seuil, 1959). *Is Theology a Science?*, trans. A. H. N. Green-Armytage (New York: Hawthorn Books, 1959).

56. The quarrel about the notion of "Christian philosophy" arose largely out of a misunderstanding. The question was: Is not the notion contradictory since, in it, the adjective destroys the noun? The notion found supporters and adversaries among

laymen and priests, Thomists and non-Thomists. Its adversaries maintained that the formula *philosophia ancilla theologiae* was not intended as a definition of philosophy but rather of its theoogical usage. And they were right. Its upholders maintained that such was precisely the reason the notion of "Christian philosophy" was a necessity, for if *philosophia ancilla theologiae* does not describe philosophy correctly, it correctly describes it in its symbiosis with theology. See M. de Wulf, *Scholastic Philosophy*, p. 198. "La notion de philosophie chrétienne," in *Bulletin de la société française de philosophie*, meeting of March 1931, pp. 37–93. There is considerable literature on the subject. It is being mentioned here because it is ultimately tied up with the recent vindication of the rights and dignity of theology as a science. If theology is perfect wisdom, it is difficult for a Christian to maintain that philosophy can escape its influence. Whether or not the notion of Christian philosophy is self-contradictory has been discussed in E. Gilson, "La possibilité philosophique de la philosophie chrétienne," in *Revue des sciences religieuses* (1959), 168–196.

XIII. In the Spirit of Augustinianism

1. Auguste Joseph Alphonse Gratry, b. Lille, 1805; d. Montreux, 1872. Main philosophical works (all published Paris: C. Douniol): *De la connaissance de Dieu* (2 vols.; 1853); *De la connaissance de l'*âme (2 vols.; 1858); *La logique* (2 vols.; 1855); *La philosophie du Credo* (1801). *Les sources, conseils pour la direction de l'esprit* (2 vols.; 1861), a reprint of *La logique*, Book VI; *Les sophistes et la critique* (1864).

   Biographical and doctrinal: Albert Aubin, *Le P. Gratry. Essai de biographie psychologique*, with a preface by Henry Cochin (Paris, 1912). B. Pointud-Guillemot, *Essai sur la philosophie de Gratry* (Paris, 1917). A. D. Sertillanges, O.P., *Le christianisme et les philosophies*, Vol. II (Paris: Aubier, N.D.).

2. See the excellent pages devoted to Gratry by Louis Foucher, *La philosophie catholique* (Paris: J. Vrin, 1955), chap. viii, pp. 197–236.

3. Léon Ollé-Laprune, b. Paris, 1839; d. Paris, 1898. Studied and taught philosophy at the École Normale Supérieure, where Maurice Blondel was his pupil. Main writings (all published Paris: E. Belin): *De la certitude morale* (1880); *La philosophie et le temps présent* (1890); *Les sources de la paix intellectuelle* (1892); *Le prix de la vie* (1894). *Eloge du P. Gratry* (1896); *La raison et le rationalisme*, with a preface by Victor Delbos (Paris: Perrin, 1906).

   Biographical and doctrinal: G. Fonsegrive, *L. Ollé-Laprune, L'homme et le penseur* (Paris: Bloud, 1912); M. Blondel, *Léon Ollé-Laprune* (Paris: Blond, 1932).

4. Charles Secrétan, b. Lausanne, 1815; d. 1895. *La philosophie de la liberté* (2 vols.; Paris: Hachette, 1849). *La raison et le christianisme* (Lausanne, 1863). *La philosophie de Victor Cousin* (Paris: Grassart, 1868). *Théologie et religion* (Lausanne, 1883). *Le principe de la morale* (Paris, 1884). *Le civilization et la croyance* (Paris, 1887). *Correspondance inédite de Ch. Renouvier et de Secrétait* (Paris: A. Colin, 1911).

   Doctrinal: Louise Secrétan, *Charles Secrétan, sa vie et son oeuvre*, 4th ed. (Paris: Payot, 1912). Fr. Abauzit, *L'énigme du monde et sa solution selon Charles Secrétan* (Lausanne,

1922). Edmond Grin, *Les origines et l'évolution de Charles Secrétan* (Lausanne, 1930). André Burnier, *La pensée de Charles Secrétan et le problème du fondement métaphysique des jugements de valeur moraux* (Neuchâtel, 1934), bibliography, pp. 241–244). Thought affirms God by necessity of its own structure (quoted from Burnier, *Précis élémentaire de philosophie*, p. 13); the object of philosophy is to understand the first principle, or cause, of all things, namely God. Christianity is the only satisfactory expression of this principle. It likewise accounts for world history, a drama in three acts: creation, fall and redemption. The personal feature of Secrétan's own theology is that God should not be posited as a necessary being; otherwise, being necessary, all the rest would necessarily follow from him. So the essence of God is liberty.

5. Maurice Blondel, b. Dijon, 1861; d. Aix-en-Provence, 1949. Taught philosophy at the University of Aix-en-Provence (1896–1927). Main works: *L'Action. Essai d'une critique de la vie et d'une science de la pratique* (Paris: F. Alcan, 1893), anastatic reproduction (Paris: Presses Universitaires, 1950). Unless otherwise indicated, all the following works were published (Paris: F. Alcan): *La pensée*: I. *La genèse de la pensée et les paliers de son ascension spontanée* (1934); II. *Les responsabilités de la pensée et la possibilité de son achèvement* (1934). *L'être et les êtres. Essai d'ontologie concrète et intégrale* (1935). A new redaction of his first work: *L'Action*: I. *Le problème des causes secondes et le pur agir* (1936); II. *L'action humaine et les conditions de son aboutissement* (1937). On the problem philosophy-religion (all published Paris: Presses Universitaires de France): *La philosophie et l'esprit chrétien*: I. *Autonomie essentielle et connexion indéclinable, La philosophie et l'esprit chrétien* (1944); II. *Conditions de la synthèse seule normale et salutaire* (1946). *Exigences philosophiques du christianisme* (1950). Important early essays reprinted in *Les premiers écrits de Maurice Blondel* (1956), including the epoch-making "Letter on the exigencies of contemporary thought in matters of apologetics" (1896). *Lettres philosophiques de Maurice Blondel* (Paris: Aubier, 1961).

Doctrinal: F. Lefevre, *L'itinéraire philosophique de Maurice Blondel* (Paris: Spes, 1928). Paul Archambault, *Vers un réalisme intégral* (Paris: Bloud, 1928). A. Cartier, *Existence et vérité* (Paris: Presses Universitaires de France, 1955). Henry Duméry, *La philosophie de l'action* (Paris: Aubier, 1948). André Hayen, S.J., *Bibliographie blondélienne* (Museum Lessianum) (Paris: Desclée de Brouwer, 1953). Henri Brouillard, *Blondel et le christianisme* (Paris: Editions du Seuil, 1961).

6. For a searching criticism of the doctrine, see Joseph de Tonquédec, S.J., *Immanence. Essai critique mr la doctrine de M. Maurice Blondel* (Paris: G. Beauchesne, 1913). Incidentally, let us note that de Tonquédec, S.J., excusable as he was for sometimes losing his patience, was perhaps not well inspired in singling out the notion of "immanence" as the center of his own exposition and refutation of the doctrine. The choice was theologically justified, but the philosophical keystone of the doctrine is the notion of "action."

7. The doctrine should be studied in the first edition of *L'action* (1893), rather than in its second and revised edition, in which, having to face attacks from opposite sides, he tried (as he so often did) to deny the consequences of what he had said and, to that effect, to change his formulas without changing his meaning. Action is conceived by Blondel, in deep agreement with Ollé-Laprune (*qui facit veritatem*), as the necessary

condition for "real" knowledge. Blondel is no idealist; man's action does not cause things to be, but it enables him to distinguish, within the diversity of appearance, that which is reality: "For science (abstract and speculative), what difference is there between that which seems ever to be and that which is? And how is reality itself distinguished from an invincible and permanent illusion, or, so to speak, from an eternal appearance? For practice on the contrary, things are different; by doing as though it did exist, only practice possesses that which is, if it truly is." *L'action*, p. 403. Action then is the true answer to the problem of finding a criterion of knowledge. To content oneself with looking at things, is to be left without any valid criterion for discerning reality from illusion. Action is here taken in its broadest meaning, as including all its particular modes. Blondel particularly refuses to oppose it to intelligence, as though it were exterior to it and impervious to it. In this complete sense of the verb, to act is to strive to achieve an agreement among knowing, willing and being. This applies to our knowledge of God; pure speculative and abstract consideration fails to reach Him. The question is not to know if the *unum necessarium* can be attained as the abstract term of some reasoning, but if it can be included as a living truth in the development of concerted action (p. 340). The only absolutely irrefutable proof of Being is found in action—that is, in using it and in practicing it. This result is obtained by man's effort to scrutinize his inner life. In examining himself in order to know what he is, what he wills and what he does, man perceives himself as a perpetual effort to overcome himself: "There is at the bottom of my conscience an *I* that is no longer me…" (p. 347); "… in my action there is something I have not yet been able to understand or to equal" (p. 339). That which we know of God is that excedent of inner life that demands to be employed; "we cannot know God without wanting to become Him somehow" (p. 354). God's *raison d'être* for us is that He is "that which we cannot be by ourselves nor do by our own forces" (p. 354). Among the differences between Blondel and Ollé-Laprune is the former's initial ignorance of scholasticism (both philosophical and theological) which, however, he never ceased to attack, deride and charge with all sorts of philosophical and religious sins.

8. *Bulletin de la société française de philosophie* (August 1908), p. 326.
9. The notion of immanence plays an important part in the doctrine, but it remains very vague, and it is perhaps best approached from the point of view of its function in the general economy of the system. The starting point should be Blondel's own experience when he passed from the "peacefully spiritualist" teaching received in a French province to the milieu of the École Normale Supérieure, where every doctrine submitting to some external authority was disqualified by that very fact; *Le problème de la philosophie catholique* (Paris: Bloud et Gay, 1932), p. 11. In order to meet that challenge, Blondel had to maintain that, in a sense, everything comes to the soul from within. That was the meaning of "immanence," largely interchangeable with "inferiority." The better to justify the notion, Blondel imagined an opposite error, which he called "extrinsecism" (everything comes to the soul from without); extrinsecism is also a "monophorism" (it is a one way relation, everything coming to the soul, which gives nothing of its own); in short, scholasticism is supposed to represent more or less completely such a position, according to which "the supernatural only is such if it is a

wholly external contribution, an addition superadded to a motionless nature already constituted in itself, a mere appendage extrinsically imposed by an authoritarian dictate upon an amorphous passivity, upon a mere *non repugnantia*; a dictate introduced and acknowledged by the sole way of sense and of reasoning, and without any inner disposition having prepared any expectation of it, without leaving for us any possibility of conceiving that this contribution implies, along with an external empirical and historical promulgation, an inner transcendency, an immanent exteriority and superiority" (p. 28). The notion of "immanent transcendency" was perhaps for Blondel an invincible obstacle. He cannot be blamed for having found it hard to define. Perhaps what he could have done was not to undertake a general reformation of the "ancient doctrinal apologetics" and not to denounce its "philosophical inconsistency" on the strength of that notion (p. 27).

10. *Le problème de la philosophie catholique*, Part III: "Etat actuel du problème de la philosophie catholique et conditions préalables de la solution," pp. 127–177. The object of the book is to establish the possibility of a "Catholic philosophy" that is not a "Christian philosophy." On the impossibility there is to establish, by history, the factual existence of Christian philosophy (pp. 127–135); on the refutation of Bréhier (pp. 136–155); on how one can conceive a philosophy spontaneously and implicitly reserving the eventual place of a supernatural "indeterminate, yet such as only Catholicism can fill" (pp. 160–166); on how one can try to realize at least in the mind, the normal spontaneity and the formal autonomy of a philosophy called "Catholic" (pp. 166–169). In fine, "even for the truths that Revelation can confirm, more precise or more clear in the rational order as well as in the psychological and the moral orders, the epithet *Catholic*, applied to the word *philosophy*, remains in many ways ambiguous and should be used with discretion and prudence, *secundum quid* and not *simpliciter*" (p. 109).

XIV. Early Twentieth Century Philosophy in Italy

1. An absolutely necessary book is Michele Federico Sciacca, *Il secolo XX, Storia della filosofia italiana* (2 vols.; Milano: Fratelli Bocca, 1947); abundant bibliography, Vol. II, pp. 705–900. Also to be consulted on the philosophy of religion in contemporary Italy (and elsewhere): Sciacca, *Il problema di Dio e della religione vella filosofia attuale*, 2nd ed. (Brescia: Morecelliana, 1946).

   Bibliographical: *Bibliografia filosofica italiana dal 1900 al 1950* (4 vols.; Roma: Edizioni Delfino, 1950).

2. On the development of neo-Kantianism in modern Italy, see Sciacca, *Il secolo XX*, Vol. I, chap. v, pp. 143–203. Without this excellent work, as well as without *Il problema di Dio*, I would not have dared to write the present chapter; I want expressly to acknowledge my indebtedness to their author.

3. Benedetto Croce, b. Pescasseroli, 1800; d. Naples, 1952. Among his many writings, the more important remain the four volumes of his *Filosofia dello spirito*: (1) *L'estetica come scienza dell'espressione e linguistica generale* (1902); trans. Douglas Ainslie,

Aesthetics as Science of Expression and General Linguistic, 2nd ed. (London: Vision Press, 1959); (2) *Logica come scienza del concetto puro* (1905); trans. Douglas Ainslie, *Logic as the Science of the Pure Concept* (London: Macmillan, 1917); (3) *Filosofia della pratica; Economie ed etica* (1908); trans. Douglas Ainslie (London: Macmillan, 1913); (4) *Teoria e storia della storiografia* (1917).

To this fundamental work, the following ones should be added: *Materialismo storico ed economia marxista* (1900); trans. C. M. Meridith, *Historical Materialism and the Economics of Karl Marx* (London: Latimer, N.D.); *Nuovi saggi di estetica* (1920) contains *The Breviary of Aesthetics*, the English text in the book of *The Opening of the Rice Institute* (Houston, Texas, 1912), Vol. II, p. 430. *Etica e politica* (1931); English translation, *Politics and Morals* (New York: Philosophical Library, 1945).

Essays to be found in English translation: *The Essence of Aesthetics*, trans. Douglas Ainslie (London: Heinemann, 1921); *The Defence of Poetry: Variations on the Theme of Shelley*, translated by E. F. Carritt (Oxford: Clarendon Press, 1933). *European Literature in the Nineteenth Century*, trans. Douglas Ainslie (London: Chapman, 1924); *History as the Story of Liberty*, trans. Sylvia Sprigge (New York: Norton, 1941); *History of Europe in the Nineteenth Century*, trans. Henry Furst (London: Allen & Unwin, 1953).

Anthology: *My Philosophy and Other Essays on the Moral and Political Problems of Our Time*, selected by R. Klibanski, trans. R. G. Collingwood (London: Latimer, 1913).

Biographical: *An Autobiography*, trans. R. G. Collingwood, preface by J. A. Smith (Oxford: Clarendon Press, 1927).

Bibliographical and doctrinal: general survey in M. F. Sciacca, *Il secolo XX*, pp. 311–364; bibliography, pp. 783–796, contains enlightening remarks of the doctrine itself. As a comprehensive doctrinal and bibliographical study of the doctrine: G. Castellano, *Introduzione allo studio delle opere di Benedetto Croce* (Bari: Laterza, 1920). Castellano, *Benedetto Croce, il filosofo, il critico, lo storico*, 2nd ed. (Bari: Laterza, 1936). Castellano, *L'opera filosofica, storica e letteraria di Benedetto Croce* (Bari: Laterza, 1942). H. Wildon-Carr, *The Philosophy of Benedetto Croce: The Problem of Art and History* (London: Macmillan, 1917). R. Piccoli, *Benedetto Croce: An Introduction to His Philosophy* (New York: Harcourt Brace, 1923). A. Caracciolo, *L'estetica e la religione di Benedetto Croce* (Arona: Paideia, 1958). V. Mathieu, *Enciclopedia filosofica*, Vol. 1, pp. 1356–1364; with bibliography.

4. Knowledge is either *intuitive* or *logical*. Intuitive knowledge is obtained through imagination; it bears upon individuality and is knowledge of individual things. Logical knowledge is obtained through intellect; it bears upon the universal and upon the relations between individuals. In short, knowledge is productive of *images* or of *concepts*. Intuitive knowledge is self sufficient (against Kant): the impression of a landscape, a musical motive (soft or violent) and the words of a lyric can be perceived as intuitive facts without admixture of intellectual and logical relations. Even when it contains concepts, which is the more common case, a work of art remains an object of intuition and what it contains of logical elements is included in it as art. This specificity of intuition as the power productive of art is the more personal contribution of Croce to esthetics. Its consequences go to infinity. It is noteworthy that, in such a doctrine, art remains fundamentally knowledge; its root is intuition. On the other

hand, *intuition* is identical with *expression*: "intuitive knowledge is expressive knowledge...intuition or representation is distinguished as *form* from what is felt and suffered, from the flux or wave of sensation, or from psychic matter; and this form, this taking possession, is expression. To intuit is to express; and nothing other (nothing more, but nothing less) than to express; *Aesthetic*, trans. Douglas Ainslie (New York: The Noonday Press, 1960), chap. i, p. 11. The same conclusion applies to art; those who say that art is intuition plus something else, have never been able to say what that something else actually is. Above all, art is *not* an expression of intuition; it is "an expression of impressions, not an expression of expressions" (chap. ii). All men have intuitions, so all men are artists, more or less; between the common man and the so-called *genius*, the difference is quantitative. Despite their distinction, esthetic and intellectual knowledge are not separate; for esthetic knowledge can stand by itself, but intellectual knowledge cannot suffice to itself with the support of esthetic knowledge (chap. iii). There can be intuition without concept; there can be no concept without intuition. There was poetry before there was prose, but there was never prose without poetry. In short, expression and concept make up the whole of human cognition, and the speculative life of the mind consists in passing from one to the other and back. An abridged exposition of Croce's esthetics is his *Brevario di estetica. Quattro lezioni* (Bari: Laterza, 1913), 3rd ed. with added essays (1925) (the book was written in answer to an invitation extended to Croce by the University of Houston, Texas): art as vision or intuition (p. 15); distinction between intellectual knowledge (p. 23); distinction between religion—"the artist neither believes nor disbelieves his image, he produces it" (p. 25). It is in this general framework that Croce deals with the particular problems of esthetics, among which: the beautiful in nature and in art (chap. xiii); art and techniques (chap. xv); historical criticism of literature and of art (chap. xvii). By a necessary consecution of ideas, linguistics is finally identified with esthetics (chap. xviii). Indeed, since esthetics is the "science of expression," it truly constitutes a "general linguistic." To study general linguistics (that is, the philosophical problems of linguistics) is to study problems of expression, hence, it is to study esthetics problems. In short: "Philosophy of language and philosophy of art are the same thing" (*Aesthetic*, Conclusion, translated by D. Ainslie, p. 112).

5. Logic is a distinct science endowed with a distinct object. That object is not to facilitate sciences nor to provide them with appropriate methods. In itself, logic is a branch of speculation entirely devoted "to the task of inquiring into the nature of thought, as exemplified by science as a whole and by the particular sciences." B. Croce, "The Task of Logic" in *Encyclopedia of the Philosophical Sciences*, Vol. I, *Logic* (London: Macmillan, 1913), p. 200. Not only is logic a science, it is the only science in the exact sense of the word. Empirical sciences are not so. In dealing with the nature of thought, logic is at grips with thought itself as an unanalyzable act. This does not prevent philosophers from dividing thought into concept, judgment and conclusion. The reason for this is that names have been substituted for thought as it wells up from the mind. *Logical grammar* has invaded the field of *formal logic*, which in turn invaded the field of *psychological logic*. Now those various logics are other than *philosophical logic*. Just as with the other philosophical sciences (esthetics, ethics) when we try to expound

logic for itself, it becomes the whole of philosophy. Practically all the confusions recently introduced into esthetics, ethics, and logic arose from the fact that those parts of philosophy were handled as separate sciences. Philosophical specialism, an error of the last ten years, has played havoc with philosophy. Here Croce is waging war against the *separatists*, an error whose climax was reached when the problem of the classification of the sciences themselves became a separate problem. As understood by Croce (under a freely interpreted Hegelian influence), logic excludes from its proper sphere the concepts of the sciences of nature and of mathematics; abstract concepts of that sort are inadequate for reality. Through reality, Croce points out the true universal (which is not the abstract one) so that, in the last analysis, logic is at one and the same time the science of the pure concept and of absolute reality. In Croce's own words: logic is the only science that "really gives us the universal, that is, the philosophical concept or Idea, or, in other words, Philosophy itself, which is the fundamental faculty of the universals" (*The Task of Logic*, p. 209). Thus understood, logic is far from being a science of words: "It is the science of the true science or of the philosophical concept; in other words, it is the philosophy of philosophy" (ibid.). The aptitude of Croce to handle abstractions (of which his treatment of logic is a good example) should not make us forget what perhaps is one of the more precious features of his philosophy, namely that intentionally and consciously it remains one with thought in its simplest uses. Common knowledge, scientific knowledge and philosophical knowledge, however they may differ by distinctive features, remain one knowledge; and, within knowledge itself, there is nothing superior or inferior, more or less noble, because everything is necessary, being one. Croce sometimes speaks of a natural "democracy" within the life of the mind. Where the higher is impossible without the lower, it is rather vain to speak of ranks.

6. History is intentionally left out as a distinct branch of philosophy. The notion of history is present everywhere in the philosophy of Croce, but it does not denote a third kind of knowledge besides intuition and concept. In its form, history is a particular case of esthetics. And indeed it does not consist in connecting abstract concepts; on the contrary, it deals with particular facts which it sees and makes us see. Consisting of expressed intuitions, history belongs in the order of art. Objections to that conclusion arise from the false notion that to consider history as art is to deprive it of its dignity or, at least, of its character of seriousness. But this is to forget the essentially theoretic function of intuition. History *represents* Napoleon, the Reformation, the Unification of Italy, etc. as nothing else can. It represents persons and events as individual facts. The point Croce wants to make is that, because history deals with individuals, of which philosophers agree that there are no concepts, it imparts knowledge by means of "representations." The difference with the poietic arts is that historical intuition is that of the *real*, non-historical intuition is that of the *unreal*. How do we know the distinction? History itself does not invent it. Historicity appears as distinct from mere imagination "as any one intuition is distinguished from any other: in memory" (*Aesthetic*, chap. iii, p. 28). In other words, history itself is not concerned with the question of what the theory of history is. History just builds up its representations to make them as convincing as possible. History and the theory of history are altogether

different things. So history is not science, yet it is as certain as intuition is. To the sceptical question: "How are you sure that on November 1, 1517, the theses of Luther were nailed to the door of the church in Wittemberg?" we should not try to answer by any "scientific" demonstration. Mankind answers: "I remember it" (*op. cit.*, p. 30).

7. As always with Croce, the definition of an order of knowledge is not to be confused with that of its object. As a definite type of cognition, history is expressed intuition, that is, art. But historicity itself is a character of the real and inseparable from it. Inasmuch as it is intuition of reality and representation of it, or its conceptualization, history enjoys the privilege of achieving the coincidence of thought (as intuitive knowledge) and reality (as historicity of the real). History thus intuits (and makes us intuit) the unfolding of the spirit immanent in reality. To anyone convinced that the notion of' God necessarily points out a transcendent being, the philosophy of Croce is a straight atheism, just as those of Comte, of Hegel and of many others after them. In Professor Sciacca's own words: "The whole philosophy of Croce tends to realize one single end—concreteness as absolute identity of the Spirit and the Real; and, in consequence, the elimination of all residue of transcendency, whether this be the Idea of transcendental idealism, or the 'fact' of the positivists, or the God of religion, or the matter of the materialists and the nature of the naturalists. In short, he tends to eliminate all forms of dualism" (*Il secolo XX*, p. 348). Croce pursues that work of elimination through the systematic reduction of everything to historical becoming. So Croce cannot be refuted from the point of view of any philosophy he would subscribe to outside his own, nor can Croceism be overcome from within. One can only oppose his philosophy with another philosophy. For a criticism of Croce from the point of view of Christianity, see A. Lombardi, *La filosofia di Benedetto Croce* (Roma: Bardi, 1940) and M. F. Sciacca, *Il secolo XX*, pp. 350–351 and note 83 bis.

8. Giovanni Gentile, b. Castelvetrano (Trapani), 1875; d. Florence, victim of a political murder, 1944. The more important of his writings remains the *Teoria generale dello Spirito come atto puro*, in the *Opere complete di Giovanni Gentile* (Florence: Sansoni, 1938). I am following the fourth edition of this work (Bari: Laterza, 1924), particularly the general conspectus of the doctrine given by Gentile himself in chap. xvii, "Epilogue and Corollaries." English translation of this work, *The Theory of Mind as Pure Act*, trans. H. Wildon-Carr (London: Macmillan, 1922). Also published in the *Opere complete*: *La riforma dell'educazione* (1928); *The Reform of Education*, trans. Dino Bigongiari, with an introduction by Benedetto Croce (New York: Harcourt, Brace & Co., 1922). *Introduzione alla filosofia* (1933). *Sistema di logica come teoria del conoscere*, Vol. I (1940). *La filosofia dell'arte* (1931).

Bibliographical and doctrinal: M. F. Sciacca, *Il secolo XX*, pp. 796–805; general survey of the doctrine (pp. 364–402); on the influence of Croce and Gentile (pp. 402–467). E. Chiocchetti, *La filosofia di Giovanni Gentile* (Milano: Vita c Pensiero, 1922) (with critical appreciation). V. La Via, *L'idealismo attuale di Giovanni Gentile* (Trani: Vecchi, 1925). From a Thomist point of view: P. Bartolomei, *L'idealismo italiano contemporaneo esaminato alla luce della dottrina di San Tommaso d'Aquino* (Torino: Marietti, N.D.); English translation by P. Romanelli Gentile, *The Philosophy of Giovanni Gentile. An Inquiry into Gentile's Conception of Experience*, Paterno Library of Italian Studies

(New York: Vanni, 1938). Domenico d'Orbi, *Lo spirito come atto puro in G. Gentile* (Padova: Cedam, 1957). V. A. Bellezza, *Encyclopedia filosofica*, Vol. II, pp. 631–643, with bibliography.

9. This is why the doctrine is often called an "actualism" or a "philosophy of act." Gentile himself has called his doctrine an "absolute idealism" (*idealismo assoluto*). An idealism because, from Plato to our own times, the word *idea* has always pointed out the object of a cognition, of an intuition. "Absolute" because a non-absolute idealism leaves out of its interpretation of reality something for which it cannot account; it is, by definition, incoherent. His actualism follows from this premise, for indeed, in order to be absolute, an idealism must posit the idea as being identical with the very act whereby it is known.

10. This follows with necessity from Gentile's decision to achieve an "absolute" idealism. The notion of subsistent Ideas comes from Plato's failure to grasp the identity of the knowing act with its known object. Similarly, the Hegelian attempt to deduce the concrete from the abstract was bound to fail; instead of attempting to deduce thought from nature and spirit, absolute idealism deduces from spirit both nature and thought. In order to achieve this result, it starts from the thought that is absolutely ours, the I, or ego, conceived as a concrete act.

11. Understood in the sense of "to "think" (*pensare*), thought is activity; that which is being thought (*il pensato*), is the product of this activity; it is the thing (*cosa*). As active, thinking is the cause of itself (*causa sui*), therefore it is liberty. That which is being thought, the "thing," merely is an effect "whose principle is external to itself and, therefore is mechanism." The notions of "being" and "becoming" are deduced in the same way: activity becomes, the thing is; activity realizes itself in itself as other; it is "relation to itself": a *unity* that is absolute, infinite and without *multiplicity*.

12. A philosophy of history finds its natural place in Gentile's idealism, or, rather, since in it reality flows from the self-developing activity of the ego, nature is history by definition. The world can indifferently be called "either nature or history." Both nature and history, in opposition with Spirit as pure act and as produced by it, belong in the common class of the non-ego. Gentile explains this point by an example. The movement of the earth is a natural fact; the theory of Copernicus is considered an historical fact, but both are facts. When it was discovered by Copernicus, the theory of the motion of the earth was a spiritual act, but now that it offers itself to minds as an already accepted truth, it presents the character of *autonomy* and of the objectivity typical of facts of nature. In short, from the spiritual act it was at first, the theory of Copernicus "has become an historical fact." Confronted with a nature from which the notion of purposiveness has been expelled, science sees it as "foreign to the spirit." As to history, it is drowned in "the bottomless sea of the past" wherein lie hidden the origins of civilization. So "both naturalists and historians shall stop at the *that*, without seeking after the *why*." Moreover, nature displays itself in space, while history displays itself "at least in time, which itself is, as we know, a sort of space"; so, in a sense, "nature and history communicate in the character of spatiality." Only Spirit is free from the multiplicity of space and time; it is the absolute Ego, creator of both nature and history.

13. Gentile considers his doctrine as "the more mature form of modern Christian

philosophy." Compared with it, both mysticism and intellectualism are one in turning spirit into an object, a thing doomed to remain external to us forever. According to Gentile, Spirit is not an intellect; as the Self-thinking Thought of Aristotle, it is love and will. For us God no longer is an ideal and external model. On the contrary, God becomes the very effort of the soul, or rather, man himself transcending his own nature and becoming God. In Gentile's own words, what is at stake is no longer the God "who already is, but the God who generates himself in our very selves inasmuch as by our whole being we are raising ourselves up to him." It is no wonder that the complete works of Gentile were put on the *Index librorum prohibitorum* on June 20, 1934. Still, it is interesting to understand in what sense Gentile could consider himself a Christian. To him his doctrine may ultimately have been a moralism, being the philosophical gospel of a free and redeeming spirit in a liberated and redeemed world.

14. On Gentile's philosophy of religion, see the chapter devoted to the question in M. F. Sciacca, *Il problema di Dio e della religione nella filosofia attuale* (Brescia: Morcelliana, 1946).

15. Bernardino Varisco, b. Chiari, 1850; d. Chiari, 1933. First a professor of mathematics, then of philosophy at the University of Rome. Among his many works: *Scienza ed opinioni* (Roma: S. A. Dante Alighieri, 1901). *Le mie opinioni* (Pavia: Bizzoni, 1903). *La conoscenza* (Pavia: Bizzoni, 1905). *I massimi problemi* (Milano: Libreria éditrice Milanese, 1910), school edition by G. Alliney (Firenze: La Nuova Italia, 1925). *Linee di filosofia critica* (Roma: Signorelli, 1925), 2nd ed. (1931). *Sommario di filosofia* (Roma: Signorelli, 1928). Posthumous: *D all'uomo a Dio* (Padova, 1939). For extensive bibliographical information, M. F. Sciacca, *Il secolo XX*, p. 763, refers to G. Alliney, *Varisco*, Milano, 1943; for studies on the doctrine, Sciacca, op. cit., pp. 762–765; doctrinal study and appreciation, pp. 206–226. G. Alliney, *Enciclopedia filosofica*, Vol. IV, pp. 1522–1525, with bibliography.

16. Piero Martinetti, b. Pont Canavese (Aosta), 1871; d. Turin, 1943. *Introduzione alla metafisica: I. Teoria della conoscenza* (Torino: Clausen, 1904), reprinted (Milano: Libreria editrice Lombarda, 1929). *Saggi e discorsi* (Milano: Libreria editrice Lombarda, 1926). *Ragione e fede* (Milano: Edizione della Rivista di Filosofia, 1934), enlarged edition (Torino: Einaudi, 1942). Bibliography in *Il secolo XX*, pp. 765–767; on the doctrine, pp. 205–253. Cf. Francesco Romano, Il *pensiero filosofico di P. Martinetti* (Padova: Cedam, 1959).

17. On the religious thought of Martinetti, see M. F. Sciacca, Il *problema di Dio* and *La philosophie italienne contemporaine*, French trans. Marie-Louise Roure, with a preface by R. Jolivet (Paris-Lyon: Vitte, 1951), pp. 117–120. On the school of Martinetti, ibid., pp. 181–183.

18. Pantaleo Carabellese, b. Molfetta, 1877; d. Genova, 1948.

Main works: *L'essere e il problema religioso* (Bari: Latcrza, 1914). *La coscienza morale* (La Spezia: Tipografia moderna, 1915). Il *problema teologico come filosofia* (Firenze: Sansoni, 1931) (considered his main work). *Critica del concreto* (Pistoia: Pagnini, 1921), 2nd ed., enlarged (Roma: Signorelli, 1940). *Che cosa è la filosofia* (Roma: Signorelli, 1942).

Doctrinal: Carabellese's self-presentation: "La coscienza," in M. F. Sciacca, *Filosofi*

italiani contemporanei, 2nd ed. (Milano: Marzoratti), pp. 205–223. G. Mattai, *Il pensiero filosofico di P. Carabellese* (Chieri: 1944), with bibliography. M. Manno, *Enciclopedia filosofica*, Vol. I, pp. 890–894, with bibliography.
19. *La philosophie italienne contemporaine*, p. 195.
20. On Italian philosophy today: M. F. Sciacca, "Storia della filosofia italiana," *Il Secolo XX*, with ample bibliographical information. *La philosophie italienne contemporaine*, abridged version of the preceding book (Paris: Emmanuel Vitte, 1950).

Self-presentations: Sciacca, *Filosofi italiani contemporanei*, 2nd ed. (Milano: Bocca, 1947); N. Abbagnano, A. Aliotta, V. Arangio Ruiz, A. Banfi, A. Baratono, F. Battaglia, C. Bontadini, C. Bozzetti, p. Carabellese, S. Caramelia, A. Carlini, E. Castelli, G. Galli, C. Giacon, A. Guzzo, V. La Via, M. Maresca, C. Mazzantini, F. Olgiati, U. A. Padovani, A. Pastore, A. Renda, M. F. Sciacca, U. Spirito, L. Stefanini. Each notice is attended by a bibliography. Other volumes of self-presentations: *Filosofi che si confessano*, ed. Giuseppe Michele Sciacca (Messina: G. d'Anna, 1948). *La mia prospettiva filosofica* (Padova: Editoria Liviana, 1950).

21. C. Michelstaedter, b. Gorizia, 1887; d. Gorizia, 1910. A notable exception. Posthumous works: *La persuasione e la rettorica*, 2nd ed. with appendices (Firenze: Sansoni, 1922). *Dialogo della salute. Poesie* (Genova, 1912). *Opere* (Firenze: Sansoni, 1958). Doctrinal: G. Chiavacci, *Il pensiero di C. Michelstaedter*, in *Giornale critico della filosofia italiana*, 1–2 (1924). Chiavacci, article in *Enciclopedia filosofica*, Vol. III, pp. 588–591, with bibliography.

The essence of his message was an opposition between "persuasion," which is the real possession of actual life and reality, "rhetoric," or mock persuasion, which lives in the expectation of some inaccessible good to be attained in the future. Man is naturally misled by the illusion that the future can be turned into the present, so he runs away from "persuasion," the possessed realities of life, and seeks refuge in an unreal future. Thereby, man deprives himself of himself; for what he desires is in himself, only he does not know it; so he does not know what he wants; neither does he know what he does nor why he does it. The cause of that inner rift is that we are trying to compensate for a primitive privation without realizing that if we were to succeed in doing so, life would come to an end. The drama is that, in us, the reality of life is swayed by the unreality of persuasion. M. F. Sciacca sees in F. M. Michelstaedter "a spiritual brother of Nietzsche and a forerunner, almost unknown outside of Italy, of Heidegger" (*La philosophie italienne contemporaine*, pp. 95–96); Michelstaedter's suicide at the age of twenty-three marks the beginning of a road littered with corpses (p. 97). Sciacca also relates the philosophy of Abbagnano to existentialism.

Nicola Abbagnano, b. Salerno, 1901–. Main works: *Le sorgenti irrazionali del pensiero* (Napoli: Perrella, 1923). *Il problema dell'arte* (Napoli: Perrella, 1925). *La fisica nuova* (Napoli: Guida, 1934). *Il principio della metafisica* (Napoli: Morano, 1936). *La struttura dell' esistenza* (Torino: Paravia, 1939). *Introduzione all'esistenzialismo* (Milano: Paravia, 1942), 2nd ed. (1947). *Filosofia, religione, acienza* (Torino: Paravia, 1947). Doctrinal: V. Mathieu, *Enciclopedia filosofica*, Vol. I, pp. 4–6. For an Italian interpretation of existentialism, Luigi Pareyson, *La filosofia dell'esistenza e C. Jaspers* (Napoli, 1940). Pareyson, *Studi sull'esistentialismo* (Firenze, 1943).

22. Antonio Banfi, b. Vimercate, 1886–. Main works: *La filosofia e la vita spirituale* (Milano: Isis, 1922). *Principi di una teoria della razione* (Firenze: Nuova Italia, 1926). "Verità ed umanità nella filosofia contemporanea," in *Studi filosofici* (1948), the whole first number; in this work Banfi completed the evolution that led him from critical rationalism to Marxism. Doctrinal: Self-presentation, *Filosofi italiani contemporanei*, pp. 55–103. G. M. Bertini, *Antonio Banfi* (Padova: Cedam, 1943). J. Chaix-Ruy, *Revue thomiste*, XLVII (1947), 394–398.

23. As a tentative classification of today's Italian philosophical orientation, Chaix-Ruy proposes: ontolo-gism, problematicism and a new spiritualism of Platonist and of Augustinian inspiration—"Philosophes italiens d'aujourd'hui," in *Revue thomiste*, XLVII (1947), 383.

24. Annibale Pastore, b. Orbessano, 1808; d. Torino, 1956. Professor of philosophy at the University of Turin. Main works: *Logica formale dedotta dalla considerazione dei modelli meccanici* (Torino: Bocca, 1906). *Del nuovo spirito della scienza e della filosofia* (Torino: Bocca, 1907). *Dell'essere e del conoscere* (Torino: Mem. Acc. Scienza, 1911). *Il pensiero puro* (Torino: Bocca, 1913). *Il problema della causalità, con particolare riguardo alla teoria del metodo sperimentale* (2 vols.; Torino: Bocca, 1921). *Il solipsismo* (Torino: Bocca, 1923). *La logica del potenziamento* (Napoli: Rondinella, 1936). *Logica sperimentale* (Napoli: Rondinella, 1939) (Pastore founded a Laboratory of Experimental Logic at the University of Turin). *La volonté dell'assurdo. Storia e crisi dell' esistenzialismo* (Milano, 1948).

   On the doctrine: F. Selvaggi, *Dalla filosofia alla tecnica. La logica del potenziamento* (Roma, 1947). Selvaggi, article in *Enciclopedia filosofica*, Vol. III, pp. 1206–1208, with bibliography. Pastore himself exposed his own thought in *Filosofi italiani contemporanei*, pp. 401–423.

25. Antonio Aliotta, b. Palermo, 1881–. Main writings: *La reazione idealistic a contro la scienza* (Palermo: Optima, 1912); English translation (London, 1914). *La guerra eterna e il dramma dell' esistenza* (Napoli: Pcrella, 1917); French translation: *Eternité des esprits* (Paris: Aubier, 1921). *L'esperienza nelle scienze, nella filosofia e nella religione* (Napoli: Perrella, 1935). *Il sacrificio come significato del niondo* (Roma: Perrella, 1946); 2nd ed. (Roma: Cremonese, 1959). *Realismo e idealismo* (Roma: Cremonese 1948). Aliotta is the present editor of the journal *Logos*. On the doctrine: *La philosophie italienne contemporaine*, pp. 2 14–2 17. *Revue thomiste* (1947), pp. 384–387.

26. Francesco de Sarlo, b. San Chirico Raparo, 1864; d. Florence, 1937. Professor of philosophy at the Institute of Higher Studies (Florence). Among his pupils were: A. Aliotta, G. De La Valle, Ed. Levi, G. Capone Braga, G. Garin, etc. Main writings: *Metafisica, scienza e moralité* (Roma: Balbi, 1898). *Psicologia e filosofia. Studi e ricerche* (2 vols.; Firenze: Sandron, 1918). *Gentile e Croce. Lettere filosofiche di un superato* (Firenze: Le Monnier, 1925). *Esante di coscienza (Quarant'anni dopo la laurea)* (Firenze: Bandettini, 1928). *Introduzione alla filosofia* (Roma, 1928). *L'uomo nella vita sociale* (Bari: Laterza, 1931). *Vita e psiche* (Firenze: Le Monnier, 1935). Doctrinal: homage volume dedicated to De Sarlo, *Logos*, fasc. 3 (1933). G. Ponzano, *L'opera filosofica di F. De Sarlo* (Napoli: Rondinella, 1940). *Revue thomiste* (1947), pp. 384–387. *La philosophie italienne contemporaine*, pp. 75–81. A. Aliotta, *Enciclopcdia filosofica*, Vol. I, pp.

1487–1489. The general tendency of De Sarlo relates to the metaphysical psychologism so common in France in which psychology is not the empirical science that goes by that name, but rather a philosophical discipline that deals with the various structures of the mind in its effort to know the orders of reality. But as it pertains to our knowledge of reality, the latter is also a science. The intentional character of knowledge is a marked feature of the doctrine.

27. *La guerra eterna e il drama del'esistenza*, p. 111; as quoted in *La philosophie italienne contemporaine*, p. 215.
28. The natural theology of Aliotta has undergone a final change. He seems to have started from a more or less Bergsonian view of God, conceived "not as an accomplished reality existing outside of its own work, but as the limit towards which all the spiritual activities are tending." "True religiosity is not a mystical surrendering, but consists in the strenuous effort that creates higher harmonies through the experiencing of opposites. To him who laments over the miseries of this world, one single piece of advice should be given: do work, fight, in order to make it a better world. Expect no help from another man, put thy trust in thyself only. Nothing is determined; no fate forbids thee from transforming reality." This same relativism applies to art (there is no absolute beauty, only art evolving its works through centuries); in logic (affirmation of a living and concrete logic of identification through love and sacrifice, over and above the abstract logic of concepts); in ethics: position of a freely creating God, to whom the act of creating is "an act of sacrifice, a free determination, a gift of his own being made by God": *Revue thomiste* (1947), p. 386. Summing up that aspect of the doctrine, Chaix-Ruy writes that "creation is a sacrifice, and, by the same token, it is the model of all the sacrifices we are called upon to make."
29. Vladimiro Arangio-Ruiz, b. Naples, 1887; d. Florence, 1952. Main works: *Conoscenza e moralité* (Città di Castello: 1922). *Arte e filosofia* (Genova: 1935). *Umanità dell' arte* (Firenze: Sansoni, 1951). Self-presentation, "Il mio moralismo," in *Filosofi italiani contemporanei*, pp. 41–53. Doctrinal: Dario Faucci, "L'umanesimo di Arangio-Ruiz," in *Filosofia*, II (1960), 297–315. D. Faucci, G. Chiavacci, V. E. Alfieri, *Vladimiro Arangio-Ruiz* (Torino: Edizioni di filosofia, 1960).
30. Ugo Spirito, b. Arezzo, 1896–. Main works (all published at Firenze, Sansoni, unless indicated otherwise): *La vita come ricerca* (1937), 3rd ed. (1948). *La vita come arte* (1941), 3rd ed. (1948). *Il problematicismo* (1948). *La vita come amore* (1953). Self-presentation "Finito e Infinito," in *Filosofi italiani contemporanei*, pp. 459–482. Doctrinal: Ginepro Zoppetti, "Ugo Spirito e il problematicismo," in *Studia Patavina*, 6 (1959) 48–72; "Il problematicismo di Ugo Spirito," 6 (1959), 325–361. "Il problematicismo di Ugo Spirito e la critica," 6 (1959), 414–440. Salvatore Porrino, "Ugo Spirito: Scienza e pace," in *Rivista di filosofia neo-scolastica*, 52 (1900), 85–92.
31. Guido Calogero, b. Rome, 1904–. Main works: *La conclusione della filosofia del conoscere* (Firenze: Le Monnier, 1938). *La scuola dell' uomo* (Firenze: Sansoni, 1939). Written while in jail for political reasons (1942), *Lezioni di filosofia*: I. "Logica, gnoseologia, metafisica"; II. "Etica, giuridica e politica"; III. "Estetica, semantica, istorica" (3 vols.; Torino: Einaudi, 1948). Doctrinal: *La filosofia oggi*, II, 3rd ed., pp. 42–43. Elvira Pera Genzone, *Guido Calogero* (Torino: ed. Filosofia, 1961). Genzone, *Nous e dianoia nel*

pensiero di Guido Calogero (Torino: ed. Filosofia, 1960).
32. Augusto Guzzo, b. Naples, 1894–. Main works: *Idéalisme e cristianesimo* (2 vols.; Napoli: Loffredo, 1936). *Sic vos non vobis* (Napoli: Loffredo, 1939–1940). *L'esperienza e la filosofia* (Roma: Perrella, 1942). *La filosofia domani* (Milano: Bocca, 1945). *L'io e la ragione* (Brescia: Morcelliana, 1947). *La moralita* (Torino: Cuneo, 1950), *La scienza* (Torino. Cuneo, 1950). Self-presentation in *Filosofi italiani contemporanei*, pp. 299–309. A. Di Lascia, "L'antropologia filosofica di Augusto Guzzo," in *Rivista Rosminiana*, LIV (1960), 124–137, 178–195.

Luigi Pareyson, b. Piasco, 1918–. Represents a quite personal expression of Christian personalism. Apart from his excellent studies on existentialism (*Studi sull'esistenzialismo* [Firenze, 1943]), L. Pareyson has published *Esistenza e persona* (1955), as well as a philosophy of art: *Estetica. Teoria della formatività* (Torino, 1964). According to his view of art, all human operation is "formative"; it necessarily has to be, at once, invention and production, since, in order to make, man has to invent ways of making. The essence of art therefore is not contemplation, but rather production. The poetic activity of the artist is not a knowing, but a making. In order to make, art brings into play the "formativity," or informing power of the form. Its effect is to achieve a reciprocal harmony of parts and whole which is, in matter, a reflection of its own unity.

33. Carmelo Ottaviano, b. Modica, 1906–. Main philosophical works: *Critica dell' idéalisme* (Napoli: Rondinella, 1936). *Il pensiero di Fr. Orestano* (Palermo: Industrie riunite siciliane, 1938). *Metafisica dell' essere parziale* (2 vols.; Roma, 1942), 2nd ed. (Roma, 1946), 3rd ed. (2 vols.; Napoli: Rondinella, 1954). The work is divided into ten parts: (1) philosophy and its method; (2) logic; (3) gnosiology; (4) metaphysics; (5) physics; (6) esthetics; (7) religion; (8) ethics; (9) sociology and politics; (10) pedagogy. The author sees his work as an introduction to the Fourth Age of Philosophy (*verso la Quarta Età*).The notion of *sinetericità*, which runs through that immense doctrinal synthesis, points out the fact that beings that are different, and even opposed, are nevertheless tied together by necessary ontological relations. Difference itself always implies a certain togetherness. On the part played by that notion in the various departments of Ottaviano's doctrinal synthesis, see *Metafisica*, Vol. II, 3rd ed., pp. 680–682.

34. Spain is developing a new school of philosophers. Its philosophical situation resembles that of Italy at the time of the *Risorgimento*. The political conjuncture dominates the speculative problems. The notion of *Hispanidad* answers in Spain that of *Italianità* in Italy. Cervantes haunts the minds of the Spanish philosophers as Dante haunted those of the early modern Italian thinkers. The first notable philosophical writers are deep essayists and moralists rather than technicians in the field of speculative philosophy (Miguel de Unamuno, 1804–1930; José Ortega y Gasset, 1883–1955). A more recent generation is joining the main stream of Western thought, and without losing its Spanish character, sharing in the common work. For a general survey: Alain Guy, *Les philosophes espagnols d'hier et d'aujourd'hui. Epoques et auteurs* (Toulouse-Paris: Editions Privat, 1956). As a companion volume, see the anthology published by same: *Les philosophes espagnols d'hier et aujourd'hui. Textes choisis* (Toulouse: Privat, 1956).

XV. Existentialism and Phenomenology

1. Gabriel Marcel, b. Paris, 1889–. Educated at the Lycée Carnot, *agrégé* in philosophy, never followed the teaching career one might have thought him destined for. Playwright, literary critic, lecturer, no more than he could ever agree to conform his thought to the rigors of a system could this independent spirit ever himself follow the narrow road of a *lycée* professor. All of his activities were nevertheless consistently directed to the same goal: that of advancing his very personal, very searching quest to understand as concretely as possible the sense of human existence. Begun in the years preceding World War I, Marcel's *Journal métaphysique* records the day-to-day struggle to break clear of University philosophy toward a personalism, first suggested to Marcel by the philosophy of the great American thinker, Josiah Royce; then to break free of Royce's categories, still too idealistic for Marcel. The experiences of the war brought on a great evolution, and considerable pause in the *Journal*. Gabriel Marcel's official duty of searching for missing persons deepened his conviction that there is something abiding in every individual person, and that the whole sense of existence is somehow involved in whatever that enduring element may be. Although the *Journal* was not originally intended for publication, Marcel eventually despaired of being able to systematize its great maze of insights, and so published it in 1927 (Paris: Gallimard). In 1928, he took up the *Journal* again, publishing the entries from then until 1933, along with four essays, as *L'Etre et l'Avoir* (*Being and Having*) (Paris: Aubier). A very important statement of his philosophical aims and methods was appended to the 1933 edition of one of his best-known plays, *The Broken World*. This essay, significantly entitled "Position of and Concrete Approaches to the Ontological Mystery," was published separately (Paris: Vrin, 1949). Four important collections of essays have appeared, *Du Refus à l'invocation* (*From Refusal to Invocation*) (Paris: Gallimard, 1940); *Homo Viator* (Paris: Aubier, 1945); *Les Hommes contre l'Humain* (*Men Versus the Human*) (Paris: La Colombe, 1951); *L'Homme problématique* (*Problematic Man*) (Paris: Aubier, 1955). Invited in 1949 to give the Gifford Lectures (Gabriel Marcel is a gifted linguist), the philosopher delivered himself of a heroic (although only partially successful) effort to disengage methodically the main outlines of his life's meditation. The two-volume work that resulted is entitled *Le Mystère de l'Etre* (*The Mystery of Being*) (Paris: Aubier, 1951). English translations of many of Marcel's works are available. *Positions et approches, etc.*, along with two essays translated by M. Harari, are grouped under the title *The Philosophy of Existence* (New York: Philosophical Library, 1949). *Being and Having*, trans. K. Farrer (Boston: The Beacon Press, 1951); *A Metaphysical Journal*, trans. B. Wall (Chicago: Regnery, 1952); *Homo Viator: Introduction to a Metaphysics of Hope*, trans. Emma Craufurd (Chicago: Regnery, 1951); and *The Mystery of Being*, Vol. I: *Reflection and Mystery*, trans. G. Fraser, and Vol. II: *Faith and Reality*, trans. R. Hague (Chicago: Regnery, 1951) are likewise available. The best general introduction to Marcel's thought is the two-volume work undertaken by a Belgian Jesuit friend at Marcel's request that someone help codify his discoveries: Roger Troisfontaines, *De l'Existence à l'Etre* (Louvain: Nauwelaerts; and Paris: Vrin, 1953). Paul Ricoeur has confronted, point by point, the existential philosophies of

Marcel and Jaspers, in a work entitled *Gabriel Marcel et Karl Jaspers* (Paris: Editions du Temps Present, 1947). Four valuable critical essays along with an autobiographical sketch have been edited in a dedicatory volume by Étienne Gilson, *Existentialisme chrétien: Gabriel Marcel* (Paris: Plon, 1947). The philosophies of Sartre and Marcel are contrasted in the dissertation of Sister Mary Aloysius Schaldenbrand, recently published as *Phenomenologies of Freedom* (Washington: Catholic University Press, 1960). See also J. P. Bagot, *Connaissance et amour; essai sur la philosophie de G. Marcel* (Paris: Beauchesne, 1958); M. M. Davy, *Un philosophe itinéant: G. Marcel* (Paris: Flammarion, 1959).
2. *Mystère de l'Etre*, I, p. 46.
3. Ibid., pp. 130–131, and *L'Homme contre l'Humain*, p. 198.
4. *Positions et approches concrètes du mystère ontologique*, pp. 275–276.
5. *L'Etre et l'Avoir*, pp. 170–171.
6. *Journal métaphysique*, p. 70.
7. This need to will to move beyond the confines of my natural empirical milieu (the bodily *Umwelt*, as Scheler calls it) is an important theme with many existentialists (Scheler and Merleau-Ponty).
8. *L'Etre et l'Avoir*, pp. 162, 165, 170.
9. *Journal métaphysique*, pp. 20–21, *L'Etre et l'Avoir*, p. 161.
10. *Mystère de l'Etre*, I, pp. 144–148.
11. *L'Homme contre l'Humain*, pp. 203–204.
12. From a speech on Radio Cologne, November 1951.
13. *Du Refus à l'Invocation*, pp. 72–73; *Mystère de l'Etre*, II, pp. 114–115.
14. Jean-Paul Sartre, b. Paris, 1905. Like his classmate Maurice Merleau-Ponty, he is a product of academic French philosophy training—École Normale Supérieure, the *agrégation*, followed by years of teaching philosophy in the provinces (Le Havre for Sartre) before being called to a Paris *lycée*. When fame finally came to Sartre, it came rapidly, but not at first for his purely philosophical writings. Rather it was the partly autobiographical novel, *La Nausée*, published in 1938, that first attracted wide attention to him. Earlier he had published *L'imagination* (Paris: Presses Universitaires de France, 1930), an historical survey of descriptions of the imagination culminating in Husserl's phenomenology. Later came Sartre's own original descriptions, interpreted in a fashion which permits a ready glimpse of his developing ontology: *L'Imaginaire: Psychologie phénoménologique de l'imagination* (Paris: Gallimard, 1940). A brief treatise on the emotions, *Esquisse d'une théorie des émotions* (Paris: Hermann, 1939) and an important article, Husserlian but again with glimpses of the Sartre to come, "The Transcendence of the Ego" (1936, see note on English translation below), were published before the monumental *L'Etre et le néant: Essai d'ontologie phénoménologique* (Paris: Gallimard, 1943). About this same time Sartre established himself as a playwright of genius.

After the war, he attempted a brief, rather superficial and more optimistic restatement of the main philosophic theses in the article, *L'Existentialisme est un humanisme* (Paris: Nagel, 1940), and launched a leftwing review, *Les Temps Modernes*, in which he has become a commentator on political events. There has been talk for years of a monumental treatise on man, but instead of it, Sartre has just published a huge *Critique de la raison dialectique*, Vol. I: *Théorie des ensembles pratiques* (Paris: Gallimard, 1900), which is preceded by a reprint of a long article from his review, entitled "Question de methode." The first volume is an effort to rework the ground of *Being and Nothingness* dialectically; ostensibly it is directed at showing better the interpenetration of what in the earlier work seemed to be two separate principles, the being-in-itself and the being-for-itself. Whether the attempt has succeeded or not cannot be determined until the second volume is published. It can be safely declared in any event that the work establishes a powerful new chapter in the contemporary development of dialectical philosophy.

English translations: *Existentialism*, translation of *L'Existentialisme est un humanisme* by B. Frechtman (New York: Philosophical Library, 1947). *The Psychology of the Imagination*, anonymous translation of *L'Imaginaire* (New York: Philosophical Library, 1948). *The Emotions: Outlines of a Theory*, trans. B. Frechtman (New York: Philosophical Library, 1956).

Secondary studies: Wilfred Desan, *The Tragic Finale* (Boston: The Beacon Press, 1959). P. Dempsey, *The Psychology of Sartre* (Westminster, MD: The Newman Press, 1950). Maurice Natanson, *A Critique of Jean-Paul Sartre's Ontology* (Lincoln: University of Nebraska Press, 1951). Iris Murdoch, *Sartre, Romantic Rationalist* (New Haven: Yale University Press, 1953); based largely on Sartre's novels. Two studies important in the development of a Sartrean ethics: F. Jeanson, *Le Problème moral et la pensée de Sartre* (Paris: Editions du Myrte, 1947) and Simone de Beauvoir, *For a Morality of Ambiguity*, trans. B. Frechtman (New York: Philosophical Library, 1948).

15. In an effort to get across how radically devoid of built-in explanation the ultimate brute factum really is, Sartre asserts of the *en soi* that it is *de trop*, which we might translate, with Helen Barnes, *superfluous*. There is no *need* for being, no reason for it; at best it is "contingent," to apply a category that rightly only belongs to the order of the *pour soi*, p. lxvi, but which Sartre will employ for the *en soi* to express its being "from the senseless," (ab-surd), for it has in itself no intelligible necessity (*Being and Nothingness*, p. lxvi).

16. "Thus even though being cannot be the support of any differentiated quality, nothingness is logically subsequent to it since it supposes being in order to deny it, since the irreducible quality of the *not* comes to add itself to the undifferentiated mass of being in order to release it... We must be careful never to posit nothingness as an original abyss from which being arose" (*Being and Nothingness*, p. 15).

17. Ibid., p. 23.
18. Ibid., pp. 3–6, 23.
19. Ibid., p. 24.
20. *L'Existentialisme est un humanisme*, p. 70.
21. *Being and Nothingness*, pp. 482–483.
22. Ibid., p. 498.
23. Ibid., p. 499.
24. Ibid., p. 500.
25. Ibid., p. 520.

26. Ibid., pp. 526–527.
27. Ibid., p. 529.
28. Ibid., p. 531.
29. Ibid., p. 552.
30. Ibid., p. 552.
31. Maurice Merleau-Ponty, b. Paris, 1907; d. Paris, 1961. He was a classmate of Sartre at the École Normale Supérieure, *lycée* professor of philosophy, professor at the Sorbonne, then in 1952 named at an unusually young age professor of philosophy at the Collège de France. That an "existentialist" should thus be honored by being named to this distinctive academy (intended to provide ideal conditions of liberty and research facilities for the outstanding professor in each major field) is to be explained as much by what we might call the scientific respectability as by the incontestable originality of Merleau-Ponty's two major works. As a serious coming-to-grips with the limits of the philosophy underlying physiological psychology, and as a learned exploitation of the break-throughs offered by Gestaltist psychology, *The Structure of Comportment* (Paris: Presses Universitaires de France, 1942) quickly attracted the attention of continental thinkers in all the human sciences. *The Phenomenology of Perception* (Paris: Gallimard, 1947) established the breadth and depth of the original position that had been stated much more summarily in the earlier work, and at the same time, achieved a post-Husserlian high point, unrivaled until then except by Sartre's *L'Imaginaire*, in the application of phenomenological description as a way of philosophizing. The postwar years brought two collections of essays, the bulk of which tend to develop the central theme of this philosophy: that truth, for the temporal being who is man, must be understood as *setts*, and that man organizes the *sens* of the world in symbols; hence the titles of the two collections, *Sens et nonsens* (Paris: Nagel, 1948), and *Signes* (Paris: Gallimard, 1960). The most important new development in those years, however, was Merleau-Ponty's entry into a high-level debate with Marxism. This effort appeared in two stages, *Humanism and terror* (Paris: Gallimard, 1947); and *The Adventures of the Dialectic* (Paris: Gallimard, 1955), between which there occurred an evolution in the direction of increasingly independent rethinking of what is most challenging in the Marxist perspective. Merleau-Ponty's inaugural lecture at the Collège de France, "Eloge de la Philosophie," has been published (Paris: Gallimard, 1953). At the time of his early death, Merleau-Ponty was finishing a new major philosophical pronouncement on the intelligibility of what is not said explicitly in every expression, foreshadows of which are to be found in the first essay in *Signes*. Present plans call for publication of this work, as well as some recent lecture courses on Marx and Hegel given at the Collège de France. English translations: *The Primacy of Perception and Other Essays*, ed. J. Edie (Evanston, IL: Northwestern University Press, 1964); *The Structure of Comportment*, trans. A. Fisher (Boston: Beacon Press, 1963); *The Phenomenology of Perception*, trans. Colin Smith (New York: Humanities Press, 1962); *Signs* (Evanston, IL: Northwestern University Press, 1904); *Sense and Non-Sense* (Evanston, IL: Northwestern University Press, 1964). Secondary studies: Thomas Langan, *Merleau-Ponty's Critique of Reason* (New Haven: Yale University

Press, 1966); Alphonse de Waelhens' work, *Une Philosophie de l'ambiguité* (Louvain: Publications Universitaires, 1951), although excellent, appeared before either *The Adventures of the Dialectic* or *Signes*. *The Problem of Embodiment* (The Hague: Nijhoff, 1964) contains sections on Marcel, Sartre, and Merleau-Pontv. See Spiegelberg.

32. *Signes*, p. 116.
33. *La Structure du comportement*, p. 100.
34. "Ambiguity" suggests that the *en soi* "means nothing" in itself. This does not wish to suggest that a given datum can be integrated into just any pattern of *sens*; if the signification giving act pays no attention to the data's solicitations, the result will be the *non-sens* of fantasy. Until taken up into the dialectic of *sens*, however, the datum is more like an open possibility than a fixed entity.
35. *Signes*, p. 119.
36. Ibid., p. 120.
37. Ibid., pp. 307–308.
38. Ibid., p. 248.
39. Ibid., p. 250.
40. Ibid., p. 306.
41. Mikel Dufrenne, b. 1910–. A close friend of Paul Ricoeur, with whom he collaborated in writing a critical summary of Jaspers' philosophy, Dufrenne made his début as an independent thinker in 1953 with the publication of the two volume *Phénoménologie de l'expérience esthétique* (*Phenomenology of the Aesthetic Experience*) (Paris: Presses Universitaires de France, 1953). Although not the first work on the subject in the phenomenological tradition (Moritz Geiger and Roman Ingarden were the pioneers), nothing on this scale has ever appeared, nor is there any work in the phenomenological literature of such clarity, and few achieve more sustained description. In the same year appeared as well *La Personnalité de base* (*The Fundamental Personality*) (Paris: Presses Universitaires de France, 1953). The ontology underlying the large work on aesthetics is developed in *La Notion de l'a priori* (Paris: Presses Universitaires de France, 1959). Dufrenne has several times taught for a term in the United States, and has shown more familiarity with contemporary Anglo-Saxon philosophy than most of the phenomenologists. This is evident in the Powell lectures he delivered recently at Indiana University, and published under the title *The Problem of Language* (Bloomington: Indiana University Press, 1963). At the University of Poitiers he is professor of sociology as well as philosophy.
42. Husserl did distinguish, it is true, the contingent from the absolute *a priori*, the former being approximately the real structures in things themselves; but the notion gets largely pushed out of sight as Husserl goes about his critical business.
43. *The Notion of the A Priori*, pp. 56–57.
44. M. Scheler, *Formalismus in der Ethik*, p. 72; N. Hartmann, *Der Aufbau der realen Welt*, p. 8.
45. *Notion of the A Priori*, p. 63.
46. Ibid., p. 63.
47. Ibid., p. 75.
48. Ibid., p. 86.

49. Ibid., p. 86.
50. Whether this is true is a question for anthropology, where here, as often, it serves as philosophy's handmaiden.
51. Ibid., p. 121.
52. Ibid., p. 257.
53. *La Phénoménologie de l'expérience esthétique*, II, 443.
54. Ibid., p. 592.
55. Ibid.
56. Paul Ricoeur, b. Valence, 1913-. The leading Protestant voice in French phenomenology, Ricoeur is the outstanding historian of the phenomenological movement, the translator of Husserl's *Ideen*, and a critical commentator of Husserl's works without equal. His introduction to and notes accompanying the *Ideen I* translation are very helpful (*Ideés directrices pour une phénoménologie* [Paris: Gallimard. 1950]). His analysis of *Ideen II* and of the *Cartesian Meditations* appeared as articles: "Analyses et problèmes dans *Ideen II* de Husserl," *Revue de Métaphysique et de Morale*, LVI (1951), 357-394, LVII (1952), 1-16; "Etudes sur les *Méditations Cartésiennes* de Husserl," *Revue philosophique de Louvain*, LII (1954), 75-109. Analyses of the overall significance of Husserl's philosophy and of the phenomenological method as such are to be found in several articles: "Husserl et le sens de l'histoire," *Revue de Métaphysique et de Morale*, LIV (1949), 280-316; "Sur la phénoménologie," *Esprit*, XXI (1953), 821-838; "Kant et Husserl," *Kantstudien*, XLVI (1954), 44-67; "Phénoménologie existentielle," *Encyclopédie française*, XIX (1957), 19, 10, 6-12. Ricoeur offers a splendid capsule view of the development of German philosophy in this century in the appendix he added to the third edition of E. Bréhier's little *Histoire de la philosophie allemande* (Paris: Vrin, 1954). In several other important articles, Ricoeur discusses the problems of method and analysis that face him in his great task of carrying out *The Philosophy of the Will*. "Méthodes et tâches d'une phénoménologie de la volonté," *Problèmes actuels de la phénoménologie* (Paris: Desclée de Brouwer, 1952), 113-140; "L'Unité du volontaire et de (l'involontaire) comme idée-limite," *Bulletin de la Société Française de la Philosophie* (1951), 1-29; "Sympathie et respect: phénoménologie et éthique de la deuxième personne," *Revue de Métaphysique et de Morale*, LIX (1954), 380-397; "Le Symbole donne à penser," *Esprit*, XXVII (1959), 60-76. Three volumes of *La Philosophie de la volonté* (*Philosophy of the Will*) have appeared thus far: *Le volontaire et l'involontaire* (Paris: Aubier, 1950); *Finitude et culpabilité*, I: *L'homme faillible* (*Finitude and Culpability*, I: *Fallible Man*), and II: *La symbolique du mal* (*Symbolism of Evil*) (Paris: Aubier (1960). A fourth volume, in which the results of the symbolic analysis (or "hermeneutic") of evil will be analyzed philosophically, is expected soon. Ricoeur has just finished a study of Freud's "Analytic hermeneutic," *De l'interprétation* (Paris: Le Seuil, 1965). Two early works deserve mention: Ricoeur's collaboration with Dufrenne in an analysis of *Karl Jaspers et la Philosophie de L'Existence* (Paris: Editions du Seuil, 1947), and Ricoeur's critical comparison of *Gabriel Marcel et Karl Jaspers* (Paris: Editions du Temps Présent, 1948). Ricoeur is currently professor at the Sorbonne.
57. "Sur la phénoménologie," *Esprit*, XXI (1953), 821.
58. "Kant et Husserl," *Kantstudien*, XLVI (1954), 45.

59. *Finitude et culpabilité*, I, 36.
60. Ricoeur cites Husserl, *Cartesianische Meditationen*, Husserliana I, 60; and again, p. 65; Ricoeur's analysis is in the *Kantstudien* article cited above, "Kant et Husserl."
61. Ibid., p. 54.
62. See for example, *Finitude et culpabilité*, I, 56; and "Kant et Husserl," p. 67.
63. *Finitude et culpabilité*, I, 24–25.
64. As Merleau-Ponty, following Husserl, puts it.
65. A term, which we first encountered in Dilthey's philosophy, for the special way of reading a text full of symbolic meanings. The symbols must be interrogated as message-bringers, for theirs is the role of the god Hermes.
66. *Finitude et culpabilité*, I, 9.
67. "The empirical consideration of the will" includes the concrete factor of the actual event of man's fault, while the *eidetic* analysis in *The Voluntary and the Involuntary* abstracts from this whole consideration. "Empirical" is used here to suggest that only a concrete grasp of man as he now actually is can open this dimension to our consideration.
68. *Finitude et culpabilité*, pp. 10–12.
69. Ibid., p. 12.
70. Ibid., p. 13.
71. *Finitude et culpabilité*, I, 159.
72. "The space where evil manifests itself appears only if it is recognized and it is recognized only if it is adopted by deliberate choice; that decision to understand evil through the liberty is itself a movement of the liberty which takes evil upon itself; the choice of a center of perspective is already the declaration of a liberty which recognizes itself responsible, which swears to hold evil as evil committed and to avow that it depended on the liberty that it should not have been" (*Finitude et culpabilité*, I, p. 15).
73. Ibid.
74. *The Voluntary and the Involuntary* appropriates very heavily the insights of *The Treatise on the Passions of the Soul*.
75. *Finitude et culpabilité*, I, 154.
76. Ibid.

Designed by Fiona Cecile Clarke, the Cluny *logo
depicts a monk at work in the scriptorium,
with a cat sitting at his feet.*

*The monk represents our mission to emulate
the invaluable contributions of the monks
of Cluny in preserving the libraries of the West,
our strivings to know and love the truth.*

*The cat at the monk's feet is Pangur Bán, from the
eponymous Irish poem of the 9th century.
The anonymous poet compares his scholarly
pursuit of truth with the cat's happy hunting of mice.
The depiction of Pangur Bán is an homage to the work
of the monks of Irish monasteries and a sign
of the joy we at Cluny take in our trade.*

"Messe ocus Pangur Bán,
cechtar nathar fria saindan:
bíth a menmasam fri seilgg,
mu memna céin im saincheirdd."